Black Bride of Christ

Black Bride of Christ

Chicaba, An African Nun

in Eighteenth-Century Spain

Edited, Translated, and with an Introduction by

SUE E. HOUCHINS
AND
BALTASAR FRA-MOLINERO

VANDERBILT UNIVERSITY PRESS

NASHVILLE

© 2018 by Vanderbilt University Press
Nashville, Tennessee 37235
All rights reserved
First printing 2018

Design and composition: Dariel Mayer

Library of Congress Cataloging-in-Publication Data on file
LC control number 2015044913
LC classification number BX4705.T457 P3613 2016
Dewey class number 271/.97202 B
LC record available at *lccn.loc.gov/2015044913*

ISBN 978-0-8265-2103-3 (hardcover)
ISBN 978-0-8265-2104-0 (paperback)
ISBN 978-0-8265-2105-7 (ebook)

According to family lore, my maternal great-grandparents, Logan and Mary Lea, absconded from slavery shortly before Emancipation. They must have envisioned the hardscrabble life ahead of them, so, as the story goes, they did not leave empty-handed. These two skilled workers—a carpenter and a dressmaker—appropriated the tools essential to the trades they had plied in bondage and would continue to practice in freedom. My mother, whom they reared, told me that they believed the mark of true maturity was producing offspring whom they nurtured, sheltered, and educated. They built houses for each of their children and sent each to school at least through the secondary level; some made it through college and beyond. But my great-grandparents never learned to read and write. This was a great disappointment for them both, and in the light of this "failure," they deemed themselves in some sense "unsuccessful." They were convinced that the narratives of their endurance and resistance through slavery, Reconstruction, and Jim Crow were worthy subjects for books that had gone unwritten.

   This book is for them.

—Sue E. Houchins

I dedicate this book, and all the work I put into its production, to my husband Charles I. Nero, the love of my life and my companion in the adventure that is the recovery of our histories. We have discussed Teresa Chicaba at the dinner table, in the kitchen, and while traveling with Carlos and Bernardo, our two beautiful sons. They are the daily blessing of our union. Together my family is the inspiration in my study of the African diaspora.

   I also dedicate the book to the memory of my parents. Baltasar Fra was an intelligent boy whose teacher told my grandmother, la señora Farruca, that he should get an education if she could afford it. He had to leave for a Jesuit vocational school in Madrid, because back at home the public high school was not meant for the son of an illiterate peasant widow. Many evenings I used to go to the church of the Black Madonna of La Encina with my mother and carry her rosary and her veil. Pilar Molinero was an attentive reader of St. Teresa of Ávila, and she was one of those quietly brave Catholic women who stopped using the veil to go to church.

—Baltasar Fra-Molinero

Contents

Acknowledgments	ix
Preface: This English Translation and Its Introduction	xv
Introduction	
SECTION 1: Context and Exposition of the *Vida*	1
SECTION 2: Discussion of the *Vida* by Chapters	55
Gallery of Figures	119
Translation of the *Vida*	127
Appendixes	
APPENDIX 1: Carta de Pago (Letter of Payment)	267
APPENDIX 2: Act of Profession	271
APPENDIX 3: Obituary of Sor Teresa Chicaba contained in the Acts of the Chapter of Toro	275
APPENDIX 4: Last Will and Testament of Juliana Teresa Portocarrero, Marchioness of Mancera	277
Bibliography	281
Index	295

Acknowledgments

We each encountered Sor Teresa Chicaba before we met one another. Back in 1994, a colleague who knew of Baltasar's work on texts produced by and representing members of the African diaspora wrote to tell him about a Black nun who had lived in Spain during the eighteenth century. Enclosed in this letter was a prayer card, a booklet that depicted the saint, briefly related her biography, and recorded a short invocation to her. Around the same time, while attending a party to celebrate her entering the Baltimore Carmelite Monastery, Sue came across a postcard of a Black nun in prayer that was affixed to a hostess's refrigerator. The caption printed on the back simply read, "Sor Teresa Chikaba, Salamanca." This became her party favor and eventually found its way into her breviary. Both of us wish to thank these benefactors and to apologize for no longer remembering their names, for they launched us on the researches that years later have culminated in this volume.

The note prompted Baltasar to embark upon a traditional course of scholarly investigation. Early in his project, he met John Hope Franklin; in a conversation at the Bates College Multicultural Center, the late historian encouraged him to translate and publish Sor Teresa Chicaba's *Vida*, the biography extolling her holiness. From that time on, the then-director of that center, Czerny Brasuell, became a constant source of inspiration and encouragement in furthering the production of this book about the saint toward the goal of creating a study appropriate for scholars and students. Baltasar visited the convent of Las Dueñas in Salamanca where Chicaba's body is interred, and he combed through censuses and wills in various Spanish archives.

In the meantime, from her workroom in Carmel, Sue made informal inquiries of two sources: First, she contacted Sister Luisa Santa Cruz, OCD, a Spanish Carmelite, who asked the Dominicans in Salamanca to send information about Sor Teresa to Baltimore. The bundle from Spain contained a note requesting suggestions for how to put Chicaba's name before Catholics in America and a stack of the same prayer cards that had inspired her coeditor. Second, she made inquiries about Chicaba of her friends, the nuns of Saint Dominic's monastery, then in Washington, DC. At that time, Sister Mary Paul, OP, knew little about the African nun, but she answered questions about Dominican traditions and their contemplative Third Orders in the United States. Sue's first speaking engagement after she left the monastery was at the invitation of Olga Barrios, a professor at the University of Salamanca, to deliver a paper at her institution. During that conference, fellow presenter

María Frías Rudolphi, Lecturer in English Philology at the University of A Coruña, introduced a small group of African American scholars—Frances Smith Foster, an emerita professor from Emory University, who writes about nineteenth-century Black American women; Richard Yarborough, professor of African American literature at UCLA, and Sue, who researches and teaches about literatures and religions of the African diaspora—to the nuns at the convent of Las Dueñas. Sue's friends encouraged her to do further research on Chicaba.

Sue and Baltasar met on a cold evening in 2003 at a restaurant in Lewiston, Maine. An interdisciplinary search committee was interviewing Sue for a position in the African American Studies and Women and Gender Studies programs at Bates. When the atmosphere shifted from interrogation to conversation, the group began to discuss their current projects. Baltasar spoke about his recent interest in a Black nun who lived in Spain in the eighteenth century. "You are speaking about Chicaba, perhaps?" was the response from Sue. By the end of that dinner, we had sealed an agreement to translate Sor Teresa's hagiography and to pool the results of our research.

The Dominican nuns of Las Dueñas in Salamanca not only provided us with a photocopy of Chicaba's saint's life, *Compendio de la vida exemplar*, but they also shared and granted permissions for our use of other documents from their archives that shone light on her time as a religious. When we began our relationship with the community, Sor María Eugenia Maeso, OP, the author of the prayer booklet (ca. 1990) that originally captured our attentions, was in the process of publishing a modern hagiography, *Sor Teresa Chikaba. Princesa, esclava y monja*. This nun became our informant. She was the quintessential example of intellectual integrity and openness, if ever there was one, so that ideological differences expressed during our visits were never an obstacle to a cordial two-way exchange of information and viewpoints. Indeed, the inordinate amounts of sweet *amargillos* and *almendrados* that she pressed upon us at the end of each visit betokened the pleasantness and generosity of our colloquy. She has maintained contact with us through the entire project, by letter until email recently replaced her elegant cursive.

Two other Spanish archives deserve our recognition. The director of the Archivo Histórico Provincial de Salamanca, Luis Miguel Rodríguez Alfajeme, promptly helped us locate and copy the important *carta de pago* (letter of payment) that contracted Teresa Chicaba's relationship to the convent of La Penitencia in Salamanca. Equally, the staff at the Archivo Histórico de Protocolos Notariales in Madrid, located near the Prado Museum, graciously allowed us to reproduce the last will and testament of the Marchioness of Mancera, who, upon her death, emancipated Chicaba. They also alerted us to other useful documents related to the lives of women slaves in Madrid in the late seventeenth century as well as to the Manceras' purchases of slaves—Christian and Muslim—some of whom, no doubt, lived with Teresa Chicaba during her sojourn in Madrid.

We also wish to thank the New York Public Library's (NYPL) Schomburg Center for Research in Black Culture—particularly Steve Fulwood for his assistance in securing a copy of the manuscript poem on Sor Teresa Chicaba that is housed in their collection. There is no record of how this manuscript reached the NYPL; however, we conjecture that the founder of the collection acquired it while abroad. Arturo Schomburg, an Afro-Puerto Rican bibliophile, travelled extensively in the early part of the twentieth century. During that time he delved into the history of Blacks in early modern Spain. He and other scholar-artists of the early diasporic movement, the Harlem Renaissance, were among the first to investigate and write about the accomplishments of African-descended peoples who lived in the very heart of the empires of slavers.

By the time we agreed to work together, Baltasar had already produced a rough first draft English translation of the *Vida* with the assistance of historian Nishani Frazier, then a graduate student and now a professor at Miami University of Ohio. However, Sue's addition to the project offered a second opportunity to confront the hagiographer Paniagua's archaic, florid Spanish. Using the preceding version as reference, we completed a more polished rendition of the work, where we endeavored to keep a sense of the linguistic style of its era while making it accessible to a modern reader. We then enlisted the aid of professor of languages Jerome M. Williams of West Chester University, PA, who works with Spanish texts written during the sixteenth, seventeenth, and eighteenth centuries, to edit our translation. He compared our interpretation with the original text, suggested a few changes, and recommended some emendations to the notes of the translated text. His encyclopedic knowledge of early modern Spanish and Spanish American religious and intellectual literature is second only to his rigorous approach to scholarship about Blacks in colonial Spanish America.

Since the *Vida* opens in Africa, it behooved us to reconstruct the seventeenth-century history of Chicaba's birthplace, *La Mina Baja del Oro*, and the ethnic group to which she most likely belonged. African scholars André Teko and Moses Panford, the first a Guin-Mina from Togo and the second an Akan from Ghana, confirmed that Chicaba was probably of the Ewe people and that her name meant something akin to "The golden child is here," or "This is the golden child." This indication of her identity, when taken with what we knew of the history of the West African region *La Mina Baja del Oro* during the seventeenth and eighteenth centuries—group migrations and inter-ethnic warring prompted and exacerbated by the trade in slaves—enabled us to provide a sketch of her African background and to explore the developing politics of race in the early modern era.

From the beginning stages of our work, scholars such as Kathleen Myers, Electa Arenal, and Stacey Schlau, who have been pioneers in research and publishing about early modern Spanish and Spanish American women writers, generously became invaluable sounding boards for our ideas. However, while feminist scholars have made great advances in excavating the history and writings of women and in analyzing gender in the hispanophone world, the discussion of what Kimberlé Crenshaw has termed "intersectionality"—the reciprocal impact of race and gender—seems to get scant attention in the academic literature on Spain and Spanish America of this period. The violence and invective to which fellow servants and nuns subjected Teresa Chicaba in her masters' house and in the convent not only exemplified racial slurs, but were also inflected by Chicaba's gender. We are grateful, therefore, to Kimberlé Crenshaw and the organizers of the Fourth Annual UCLA Critical Race Studies Symposium: Intersectionality, Challenging Theory, Reframing Politics, Transforming Movements (2010) who provided a forum for Sue to discuss these comingling discourses. In addition, we are grateful to Jaqui Goldsby, professor of African American Studies and English at Yale, who alerted us to the history of Pauline de Villeneuve in Nantes, and to Cyprian Davis, OSB, a historian who pioneered the study of Black Catholics.

We took a cue from Paniagua's prefatory essay to the *Vida*, which reports that he disseminated information about Teresa Chicaba's life of virtue by sending her funeral oration throughout the Spanish-speaking world. So, in the spirit of diasporic studies, we decided to accept as many invitations as possible to share information and to welcome feedback about the African nun of Salamanca. Baltasar was the first to deliver papers about his preliminary work on Sor Teresa, attending the First Conference on Spanish Slavery held in Habana, Cuba (1998); Congreso Internacional: Mujeres Escritoras, Edad Media, Moderna Temprana e Hispanoamérica in Mexico City (2000); the International Colloquium Genre(s): Formes et identités génériques held in Montpelier, France (2001); the Twelfth Symposium on Afro-Hispanic Literature in Alcalá de Henares, Spain (2001) to which Wilfrid Miampika invited him; the Asociación Internacional de Hispanistas in Paris (2010); and at Spelman College at the invitation of Julio González (2012). Recently Omer Oke of Africforum, an NGO in Bilbao, invited Baltasar to participate in a morning radio show about Chicaba and to speak to an audience that included quite a few young African Basques, who were particularly interested in the African past in Spain (2015).

Sue's presentations, which began later, were usually delivered before a different type of audience: she was an invited lecturer at the annual meetings of the Black Catholic Theologians Symposium in Houston, Texas (2005); the Academy of Hispanic Catholic Theologians in the United States in San Antonio, Texas (2006); the Augustus Tolton Center for Black Catholic Ministry, Catholic Theological Union, Chicago, hosted by C. Vanessa White (2006); the Ralph Bunche Center for African American Studies and the Center for the Study of Women, UCLA, hosted by Richard Yarborough (2006); the University of California Department of American Studies and Ethnicity hosted by Ruth Wilson Gilmore (2007); and at Writing about Slavery after *Beloved*: A Conference on Literature, Historiography, Criticism, Nantes, France, hosted by Michel Feith, who teaches African American literature (2012).

Together we spoke at the Annual Meeting of the Multi-Ethnic Studies Association: Europe and the Americas in Pamplona, Spain (2006), invited by Joycelyn Moody, a scholar of African American women's spiritual literature; at a symposium at the International Slavery Museum in Liverpool entitled Iberian Atlantic, Beyond Slavery (2007); and at the Fourteenth Berks Conference on the History of Women, Minneapolis (2008). We have made a number of presentations before the College Language Association, an organization founded by professors in Historically Black Colleges and Universities; the members of this organization have been particularly supportive of our work.

When Margaret Musgrove, a professor of English and the director of the Women's Center, invited us to give a lecture at Loyola University, Maryland (2012), we took the opportunity also to give a seminar at the Baltimore Carmelite Monastery. These nuns helped us understand that Chicaba was never a professed nun, no matter if Paniagua, abetted undoubtedly by Teresa Chicaba and her Dominican sisters, reported that the bishop's change of heart had enabled some kind of elevation in the African woman's monastic status. Despite the two earthly ceremonies—one before the diocesan prelate and another private one in the hands of a Dominican brother—and the celestial affirmations by the saints of her order, the precise status of Teresa Chicaba in the monastic hierarchy remained, at best, marginal canonically and, at least, ambiguous in the *Vida*'s representations.

As word of our project became known, we received an invitation to write the entry for Sor Teresa Chicaba in the *Dictionary of African Biography*, edited by Emmanuel K. Akyeampong and Henry Louis Gates Jr. (2012). In addition, we submitted a sample selection of an early version of the translation to the anthology *Afro-Latino Voices*, edited by Kathryn Joy McKnight and Leo J. Garofalo (2009).

Sue is profoundly grateful for the subvention of her work provided by a Woodrow Wilson Foundation Career Enhancement Fellowship and by positions as Chancellor's Fellow in the Rhetoric Department, University of California, Berkeley, under the mentorship of Judith Butler, and twice as Research Associate at the Women's Studies in Religion Program at Harvard Divinity School, mentored by Director Ann Braude and Acting Director Joan R. Branham as well as Karen L. King, Hollis Professor of Divinity. Also, she wishes to thank the members of her writing group in Cambridge for their support: Bernadette Brooten, Florence Ladd, Faith Smith, Susan Lanser, and Thandeka.

Our home institution, Bates College, deserves a special place in our list of acknowledgments, for it has generously funded our project through several Faculty Development Grants, which defrayed expenses for travel, researching and reproducing documents and illustrations, and copyediting both the translation and the introductions.

— Baltasar Fra-Molinero and Sue E. Houchins
Bates College, Lewiston, ME, Summer 2015

Preface
This English Translation and Its Introduction

This is a translation of the 1764 edition of the *Compendio de la vida ejemplar de la Venerable Madre Sor Teresa Juliana de Santo Domingo*, the life-story of the African Sor (Sister) Teresa Chicaba, a nun who belonged to the Order of Saint Dominic, the Dominicans. We prefer this edition for two reasons. The first is that modern translators and editors of eighteenth-century texts usually work from the final version of the book that has been vetted (examined) by the author. The second reason is that the 1764 edition (a reprint of the 1752 edition) mentions in its preface the circulation of the *Vida* throughout Spanish America, which establishes this text as African diasporic.

Translating into English an eighteenth-century Spanish work is a task that presents unique challenges. For instance, the original text attempts to imitate models from the previous century; it is verbose, grandiloquent, and elaborate. Rendering the flavor of this style without putting modern English readers to sleep or causing them to procrastinate is a balancing act. We have modernized some expressions while remaining attentive to certain linguistic practices common to religious literature among English-speaking Catholics. For this reason, we have decided to spell and capitalize religious names following the extensive—154—rules enumerated in the *Writing Handbook* edited by Michael P. Kammer, SJ, and Charles W. Mulligan, SJ (Chicago: Loyola University Press, 1958). Prior to the Second Vatican Council (1962–1965), students in Catholic educational institutions used this manual as a guide to English usage and grammar. The rules for capitalization from this text reflect the theology of its day—a system of beliefs similar to those espoused by Paniagua and Chicaba. Using this handbook has helped us reflect the religious context of the hagiography and to maintain a consistency throughout our translation.

The translation of racially charged terms has proven difficult. Today's Spanish and English readers generally consider pejorative some racial markers customarily used in the eighteenth century. Therefore we were attentive to words such as *negra* or *negrita* when they appear in the original Spanish, and they received different translations depending on their context.

We have kept Spanish place names in their original form when they denote a particular location, so we preserved names like *La Penitencia*, *Las Dueñas*, and *San Cayetano*—that is, names of monasteries and convents. However, we translated the initial mention of titles like "the convent of Saint Mary Magdalene of La Penitencia" in order to preserve the sense of the institution.

When we embarked on this translation, we believed that Sor Teresa Chicaba's *Vida* would be interesting and helpful to an audience of students and researchers in a variety of fields, such as Spanish and hispanophone, African diasporic, women and gender, and Black Catholic religious studies. In fact, it was the multifaceted aspect of the project that attracted us, for we are each housed in interdisciplinary programs at Bates College in Maine—African American, Latin American, and women and gender studies. However, as we began to share our work at conferences and in seminars in the United States, Europe, and Latin America, we discovered that the historical contexts and theoretical methods we had assumed were common in allied disciplines were not necessarily part of the scholarly repertoire of our colleagues elsewhere.

Our conversations on these occasions were instrumental in changing some of our approaches to the text, and these meetings also gave us a sense of what background information, theoretical principles, and technical practices we would have to explain thoroughly to those not trained in literary, critical race, or gender studies. For this reason, we have augmented our introductory material on the *Vida* with information about some hagiographies that are in intertextual relation with Chicaba's life story, and we have included discussions of African American spiritual and slave narratives.

Given the diverse readership of this edition, our notes may appear too simplistic to some part of the audience. Summarizing Saint Teresa of Ávila's life in a note will appear presumptuous to a scholar in the Hispanic world. The same will be true of the description of Phillis Wheatley to a specialist in African American culture. However, as different communities of researchers have developed their fields in relatively total isolation from each other, we thought it important not to take knowledge for granted. Not many who work in the Spanish and Spanish American past acknowledge the African diaspora, in spite of the ten million enslaved people who ended up in the former territories of the Spanish and Portuguese empires during the Atlantic slave trade. Conversely, some scholars in the English-speaking world write about the African diaspora with considerable disregard for the fact that the fulcrum of the experience happens south of U.S. shores on the Gulf of Mexico.

We also realize that those in other disciplines use different methodologies that stem from a variety of theories about how to analyze documentary sources. So we have detailed how we inferred that the subject of the narrative may have a "voice" in the text and from where in the document she speaks. We use a combination of initial endnotes with subsequent parenthetical citations in the text of our introduction for material we consulted to give context to and to interpret the saint's life. In addition, we have included extensive explanatory endnotes. We are aware that the prefatory sections in this volume are lengthy, but we anticipate that they will assist our projected audience with understanding and enjoying this exemplary life of an African nun in eighteenth-century Spain.

Introduction: Section 1
Context and Exposition of the Vida

The saint's life entitled *Compendio de la vida ejemplar de la Venerable Madre Sor Teresa Juliana de Santo Domingo* (Salamanca, 1752) is the foundational documentary evidence in the case for beatification of the eighteenth-century African religious, a nun, Sor Teresa Juliana de Santo Domingo (c. 1676–1748), who was named "Chicaba" at birth.[1] As such, it is the most significant and comprehensive source of information about her. The *Vida* (Life) is one of the elements prescribed by the directives of the Council of Trent for the process of canonization. In the eighteenth century, these items included (1) the preaching and distribution of a funeral oration, (2) the publication of a longer narrative of the venerable candidate's life and a detailed account of her spirituality (i.e., a hagiography), and (3) the pictorial representation of the holy person.[2]

Juan Carlos Miguel de Paniagua, a Theatine priest, delivered the eulogy at Sor Teresa Chicaba's funeral mass, which he then expanded and published as *Oración fúnebre en las exequias de la Madre Sor Teresa Juliana de Santo Domingo* (Salamanca, 1749).[3] Three years later, he sent to press a comprehensive account of her virtuous life. What he had heard of the African sister from devoted visitors to her convent, his fellow priests, and members of her religious community must have captured his imagination and prompted him to establish a relationship with Chicaba during the last months of her life. This familiarity with her story qualified him to become her official hagiographer, though he had been neither her confessor nor spiritual director, as was common for most biographers. As the full title indicates, the *Vida* is a compendium or compilation of texts, which Paniagua said he had culled from her poems, her autobiographical writings, and their extended conversations, which he used to expand the *Oración fúnebre*.

According to the narratives of both the eulogy and the hagiography, Sor Teresa de Santo Domingo was born in the West African territory known to seventeenth- and eighteenth-century Spanish and Portuguese navigators and slave traffickers as La Mina Baja del Oro.[4] The text of the *Vida* opens with a lament about how few facts the author can muster concerning Chicaba's childhood given how young she was—about nine years old—when abducted into slavery, but it also reports the names of her mother and brothers, which suggest that her people were Ewe.[5] She was initially sent to the island of São Tomé, where she was baptized and given the name "Teresa"; from there, she was shipped to Spain, surviving illness during the arduous first leg of the Middle Passage. Perhaps her youth or her enslavers' belief that the *manillas* (gold bangles) she wore were the signs of her exalted social status among her ethnic group convinced them that she might bring a special profit in the Spanish market. In Spain, Juliana Teresa Portocarrero y Meneses, then the Duchess of Arcos, purchased Teresa Chicaba. When she married Antonio Sebastián de Toledo, the second Marquis of Mancera, she brought Chicaba to her new household in Madrid.

As a member of the Manceras' retinue, Teresa Chicaba must have habituated herself to the piousness of her mistress and developed an intense spiritual life that in time became her key to freedom. Though the *Vida* is at pains to depict her status in the religious, aristocratic household as almost that of a privileged foster child, the narrative relates several accounts of her mistreatment by others who were in service to the Manceras, particularly by a cruel and abusive governess.

At the behest of the marchioness, who died in 1703, Teresa Chicaba was freed to enter a convent.[6] The Dominicans of La Penitencia in Salamanca accepted her after she had been rejected by several other monasteries because of her skin color. Race put her at a disadvantage within the highly stratified social hierarchy of monastic houses of the era, even within her own religious community. The sisters first received her as an aspirant. Then, at the command of the local bishop, they granted her some vaguely defined status, probably as a secular member of their order. Later, the local bishop presided over what the *Vida* describes as an irregular profession of some kind: the ceremony was performed earlier than church canons prescribed, and her contract with the convent does not clearly specify her status in the order. Sometime later, a Dominican friar regularized her vows and designated her as a "white-veiled" member of the order.[7] Her duties were to perform menial labor in the convent.

Despite her initial marginality in the community, Teresa Chicaba eventually gained recognition as a healer and a sister with prodigious religious gifts. The annuity bequeathed to her in the marchioness's will, as well as donations from people who sought her prayers, allowed her to establish ascendancy in the monastery among nuns who could make their professions only thanks to her financial help with their dowries. Sor Teresa Chicaba died on December 6, 1748. Notwithstanding her inferior status in the order, her piety, her acts of charity, her mystical experiences, and her fame as a healer or miracle worker moved her order soon after her death to begin the process for her beatification.

As a biography of a saintly African woman, the hagiography exhibits the two cultural backgrounds of its subject—African and European—by occasionally reflecting a syncretization of Catholic piety with religious practices retained among some peoples of the African diaspora. The *Vida* also combines the attributes of two types of texts that trace part of their origins in the oral accounts of their protagonists and associates: the hagiography and the as-told-to slave narrative later found in the Americas. As a consequence, these genres produce questions concerning the relationship between authorial and informant voices.

Paniagua did not publish his life of Sor Teresa Chicaba in a vacuum. The *Vida* and the earlier *Oración fúnebre* were probably part of a two-pronged mutual effort by the nuns of La Penitencia and the Theatine priests to promote the canonizations of both Teresa Chicaba and her Theatine confessor and spiritual director, Jerónimo Abarrategui. First, it is possible that the Dominicans in her community had sensed the presence of an unusually saintly person among them—an occurrence they had occasionally detected since the Middle Ages—and had therefore requested that a priest interview their African sister. Second, by the time Paniagua took on the task of writing Teresa Chicaba's hagiography, he was the rector of San Cayetano, the college of his order in Salamanca, and as such, he was invested in the canonization of Abarrategui, the founder of that institution. In addition, his friend Diego Torres Villarroel, a secular priest and one of the most popular writers in Spain during the period, was working on the hagiography of Abarrategui. Also, Paniagua must have been aware of another association between Chicaba and his order: the Marquis of Mancera was a protector and patron of the Theatines and, according to the *Vida*, several priests of this order became Teresa Chicaba's spiritual directors during her enslavement in Madrid.[8] Therefore, by promoting Chicaba's cause, Paniagua advanced both the case of Abarrategui and the prestige of his own order, which had benefited from the patronage of a grandee of Spain. This might explain why the Dominicans did not commission a member of their own order to write Chicaba's life, or why a Theatine chose to take on the task.

The *Oración fúnebre* was a text that circulated among Paniagua, Torres Villarroel, and others. Torres Villarroel refers to Sor Teresa Chicaba twice and at great length in his hagiographic *vida* of Abarrategui.[9] This saint's life appeared in the same year (1749) that Paniagua published Chicaba's *Oración fúnebre*. In addition, Torres Villarroel mentions the *Oración fúnebre* as he summarizes Teresa Chicaba's life in Abarrategui's life story. His purpose in writing about Chicaba was to demonstrate the extent of his priestly subject's spiritual influence; thus, she becomes an example of a saintly nun who followed Abarrategui's spiritual direction (Torres Villarroel 57–58). A similar summary of her life appeared the same year in the *Acta Capituli Provincialis provinciae Hispaniae Ordinis Praedicatorum* (Acts of the Chapter of Toro).[10] Paniagua was therefore involved in a typical effort to promote a member of his order by contributing to a corpus of literature that included Abarrategui's spiritual entourage. By documenting the holiness of Teresa Chicaba, a woman whose soul was his spiritual responsibility, he enhanced Abarrategui's saintly reputation. As a sign of their close association and mutual holiness, Torres Villarroel mentions Sor Teresa Chicaba as one of the people who had a vision of Abarrategui's death and ascent to heaven (107–9).

The *Oración fúnebre* in honor of Sor Teresa Chicaba must have been quite a success, for Paniagua records in his dedication of the *Vida* that the text circulated throughout Spain and went as far as the Spanish American colonies. Besides the *Oración fúnebre* and the *Vida*, there is extant at least one other document written in the decade or so after Sor Teresa Chicaba's death in an effort to promote her beatification. In 1757, a priest from Zaragoza, Luis Soler y las Balsas, wrote a poem entitled *Vida de la Venerable Negra, la Madre Sor Theresa Juliana de Santo Domingo*, based on the *Oración fúnebre*.[11] He composed this work in *seguidillas*, a popular stanza form that became a favorite mode for conveying other hagiographic material.[12]

Also, her community commissioned two portraits of Teresa Chicaba. One picture, probably now lost, depicted her standing next to Abarrategui. This painting was clearly part of the joint effort to promote their causes. The other portrait is still on display in the convent of Las Dueñas in Salamanca (Figure 1). It represents Sor Teresa Chicaba in the habit of the Dominican order, kneeling in adoration before a monstrance that contained a Communion host or wafer. In this picture, one of her favorite saints, Vincent Ferrer, to whom the *Oración fúnebre* and the *Vida* are dedicated, watches over her.[13] The legend at the bottom of the portrait explains Teresa Chicaba's African origin and name. The text of this caption reiterates the same details of her life that appear in Torres Villarroel's book and in the minutes of the Dominican chapter (assembly) of 1749, as well as at the end of the document of her profession.[14] Along the bottom of the extant portrait is the following obituary, serving as a kind of abbreviated biography or hagiography:

> True portrait of Mother Sor Theresa Juliana de Santo Domingo, daughter of the King of the Lower Gold Mine, Professed Tertiary in the Convent of Saint Mary Magdalen, popularly known as La Penitencia, of Dominican nuns in Salamanca. A woman in whom grace performed repeated miracles, and through them took her away from Guinea, her homeland, and directed her to this Convent where she lived, according to general opinion, in evident sanctity for many years. After a full life in high esteem she rested in peace on the sixth day of December in the year 1748 at the age of 73.[15]

A similar short text was appended in a different hand under Sor Teresa's signature at the bottom of her official so-called act of profession (Appendix 2),[16] and it is preserved to this day in the museum of Las Dueñas, the monastery of the second order Dominicans in Salamanca, where Sor Teresa Chicaba is now buried.[17]

The signature on this act of profession is a small but crucial piece of evidence of Chicaba's literacy. The name she signs is "Soror Teresa de Sto. Domingo," which she separated and divided between two lines of text. This same signature appears on a letter written to a Father Figueroa in 1730, twenty-six years later, and in this case, the same hand produces the entire text of the document (see Figure 2). This is the only extant autograph example of her writing.[18] Had Chicaba been unable to sign for herself, her act of profession would most likely have recorded it. She would have signed her vows with a cross, and a notary would have indicated that she could not write, which was customary with legal documents. Also, it is highly unlikely that the same person would have signed for her in the same manner on two different occasions separated from each other by two decades. The only difference between the two signatures is a *rúbrica* (flourish), which is present in the act of profession but not in the more private, informal autograph letter. The presence of the *rúbrica*, a frequent addition to official documents, indicates quite clearly that Teresa Chicaba was skilled and experienced in the use of the ink pen, for a person merely able to sign her name would not have attempted this embellishment. Clearly she was aware of the protocols of signing official documents.

The autograph letter further substantiates our contention that Chicaba was literate because it contains certain spellings that are consistent with a person who spoke with an Andalusian accent, the dialect typical of the region where she spent her first years in Spain, before she moved with her mistress to Madrid.[19] It is doubtful that a nun from the area around Salamanca (as were most members of La Penitencia) would have written like a southerner or tried orthographically to reproduce Chicaba's pronunciation.[20] Importantly, the text of the *Vida* itself further asserts her full literacy—the ability both to read and write—when it relates her capacity to set up and sing from the Roman and the Dominican versions of the Divine Office.

Also, among the important papers pertaining to Chicaba is the record of the transportation of her body during the Napoleonic occupation of the city in 1810 from La Penitencia, which was scheduled for demolition, to the convent of Las Dueñas, the second order Dominican nuns cloistered in the same city.[21] This document and her bodily remains are still in Las Dueñas. That her community decided to remove Chicaba's body to the security of the consecrated ground of another Dominican house attests to the high regard in which her sisters in both communities held her.

The effort to have Chicaba canonized continues today. Not long ago, the Dominican convent of Las Dueñas in Salamanca created a small museum for the edification of the laity as well as the veneration and promotion of Chicaba's cause for sainthood. The exhibit, situated on the second floor of the spectacular Renaissance cloister of the convent, houses two personal relics of Chicaba's, a clay drinking cup with an inscription in Arabic, and a shoe reported to be hers. It also displays the extant portrait as well as some other documents related to her life, most of which we will discuss in this introduction. In addition, Sor María Eugenia Maeso, OP, has published both a transcription of the *Vida* into today's Spanish spelling, and a modern hagiography that is heavily dependent on Paniagua's book. *Sor Teresa Chikaba: Princesa, esclava y monja* (2004) is a document that, like the *Vida*, has as its ultimate goal Sor Teresa Chicaba's beatification. This modern hagiography, on the one hand, establishes Chicaba's historicity and, on the other, makes the case for her sanctity to a twenty-first-century Catholic audience. As a hagiographer 250 years after Teresa's death, Maeso has had to contend with the lack of material documentation related to her subject. This is also our problem as translators and annotators of this critical edition.

Because of this dearth of what one might call direct evidence of Teresa Chicaba's life—currently consisting of her act of profession, the autograph letter bearing her signature, and the record of the marchioness's bequest—we rely heavily on the third-person narratives of her life (the *Oración fúnebre* and the *Vida*), archival material (such as her profession, censuses, accounts of comparable monastic houses, and treatises by missionaries), and recent historical and literary studies (particularly research by Africanist and feminist scholars) to reconstruct a version of her story and to sketch the historical, social, and religious contexts in which she lived.

HAGIOGRAPHIES AND *VIDAS* IN GENERAL

This volume contains the first English translation of the *Compendio de la vida ejemplar de la Venerable Madre Sor Teresa Juliana de Santo Domingo*. As a hagiography, this work is an example of a biographical genre that recounts the lives and describes the spiritual practices of holy people—saints officially canonized by the Church, individuals informally recognized by local devotees, or respected ecclesiastical leaders. André Vauchez expands this explanation of the subjects of the genre by "includ[ing] accounts of persons regarded as holy or exemplary in their own time, even if they were not formally canonized."[22] As a type of biography or an example of life-writing, a hagiography is often called a *vida* in Spanish. However, the term *vida*, particularly during the Counter-Reformation in Spain and its colonies, referred not only to formal hagiographies but also to autobiographical texts written by a devout person as an examination of conscience in preparation for confession or spiritual direction as well as to a compilation of such self-writing by a cleric. This volume employs these terms—hagiography and *vida*—to refer to the official text compiled by Juan Carlos Miguel de Paniagua for the purposes both of edifying and inspiring a faithful audience as well as providing evidence for Sor Teresa Chicaba's canonization.

According to Antonio Rubial, since the Counter-Reformation these spiritual narratives have traditionally contained three essential elements that indicate saintliness in Catholic women's lives: virtue, visions, and illness.[23] Even though contemporary readers most often associate hagiographies and *vidas* with medieval legends, these life-writings proliferated with the encouragement of the Council of Trent after 1545 and with the increased use of the printing press, which facilitated their dissemination. They continued in popularity through the eighteenth century, when there was a shift in religious life—particularly the vocations of women—from contemplative (enclosed) nuns to active apostolates working outside the convent walls. This inspired Catholics to consider different models of saintly behavior and thereby transformed the writings that recorded and reproduced sanctity.[24] Still, the hagiography is one of the most long-lived genres, "beginning with St. Luke's rendering of St. Stephen's martyrdom in Acts and having no *de facto* end."[25]

Derived from a conflation of oral and textual sources, hagiographies were often compiled from the spiritual writings of their subjects, spoken and written testimonies of members of their extended religious community, and autobiographical data told to or written for a confessor, spiritual director, or priest-friend, sometimes in obedience to a request from a prioress.[26] On occasion, when a religious order believed it had in its midst a particularly exemplary person who might become a candidate for canonization, its members might invite a cleric to interview the person during the months preceding the subject's death. Such was the case with Dorothea of Montau (d. 1394).[27] It might have been what happened with Teresa Chicaba as well, since Paniagua steadfastly maintained that he was neither her confessor nor her spiritual director. However, as explained above, he took a strong interest in the beatification of her confessor Jerónimo Abarrategui and even wrote the "censure" (official theological opinion) appended to that hagiography.

Caroline Walker Bynum states that saints are, "as the current jargon has it, 'socially constructed,'" and their legends are "fashioned and authenticated in a complex relationship between clerical authorities and the adherents who spread the holy person's reputation for virtue and miracles." Hagiographies, therefore, are profoundly political. Yet this has not disqualified works in this genre as sources for historical research. In fact, historians, anthropologists, and literary critics from the last half of the twentieth century until the present have used these saints' tales to examine "popular mentalities" and to produce demographic data about an era. With the rise of women's studies, researchers have begun to look seriously at these documents as reflections of women's "domestic and urban life."[28]

For instance, some contemporary social and literary historians contend that sacred autobiographical and biographical literature by and about religious women of colonial Spanish America offers one of the richest sources for ascertaining historical and social contexts of the era, especially from the seventeenth through eighteenth centuries. Because the writing and dissemination of sacred life-stories flourished during the colonial period, when religious institutions and narratives served to establish and consolidate people's identities as Christian Spanish subjects and citizens of particular localities in the empire, researchers have come to appreciate the role of *vidas* (e.g., autobiographies, hagiographies, and confessional accounts) not simply for how they elucidate the life of a particular individual but also for how they illuminate the values, mores, and traditions of the culture. Thus, writing about and by religious women in Spain and Spanish America has become a particular focus of scholarly attention. Literary critic Kathleen Ann Myers, concurring with Mexican philosopher Edmundo O'Gorman, maintains that no matter "how exhaustive and well documented" historians' narratives may be, these same historians "will never penetrate the secret interior of the most significant events" if they do not consider the stories of holy women's spiritual journeys (4–5).

The proliferation of all the genres of spiritual life-stories in Spain and Spanish America reflects the centrality of Catholicism to readers in those regions, and the importance of the narratives of its exemplary women and their ways of perfection. Women, especially women religious (nuns), examined their consciences, made notes on that process of self-discovery, and sometimes wrote autobiographical accounts of their conduct in preparation for confession.[29] Sometimes spiritual directors and confessors told nuns to keep written records of their spiritual activities or, as was the case with the Counter-Reformation mystic Teresa of Ávila, to write complete autobiographies.[30] These documents were examined for their orthodoxy, and often edited by the nuns themselves and/or their more theologically savvy male allies. The results were sometimes published and disseminated among their sisters in the same religious order, and then distributed more widely—across Spain and throughout the colonies. Upon the death of a holy subject, members of her religious community and her benefactors sometimes chose someone, usually a priest who had known the woman and was familiar with her life and writings, to compile her official hagiography.

Even though Paniagua asserts several times in Chicaba's *Vida* that in preparing the hagiography, he relied heavily not only on his conversations with his subject but also on her own writings, modern scholars contend that with the paucity of material proof of her literacy and in the absence of archival examples of her autobiographical manuscripts, all references to her written production must be fabrications, for it was rare for a Black woman and former slave to read and write.[31] However, we maintain that it was likely that Chicaba's membership in the Mancera household, where literacy for women was valued, exposed her to the custom of writing examinations of conscience and the reading of the Divine Office.[32] Further, by recording Chicaba's literacy as a matter of fact, Paniagua was probably not simply repeating a trope common to the *vidas* of some nuns (especially Discalced Carmelites), but rather indicating her difference from most Africans, even the very few who had been singled out for their piety, for the most common sign of holiness among Blacks was their simple, steadfast religious devotion in the absence of education or the reading of religious books and tracts.[33]

The issue of literacy vs. illiteracy occasionally figures in the spiritual biographies of European women as well. For example, fourteenth-century Catherine of Siena claimed that God miraculously enabled her to write so that her *Dialogue* with Him would not have to depend on scribal fidelity to her dictation, and seventeenth-century Ana de San Bartolomé, the illiterate or semiliterate secretary of Teresa of Ávila, supposedly also received the gift of literacy through divine intervention.[34] The eighteenth-century Afro-Brazilian woman religious leader Rosa Egipcíaca da Vera Cruz claimed that God bestowed literacy on her one day after Communion.[35] The nineteenth-century Protestant African American Shaker visionary Rebecca Cox Jackson also asserted that God had conferred on her the abilities to read and write, thereby ensuring her unmediated access to His Word and accurate transmission of His messages to others through her.[36] Clearly this is a convention in women's spiritual narratives—written against a social background that discourages the education of women and finds mystical experiences suspicious—that *author*izes women to express and record their spiritual journeys, especially their encounters with the Divine (Ibsen 22).[37]

Another aspect of literacy was surprisingly a problematic issue even for women who produced an extensive oeuvre. For instance, while the correspondence Teresa of Ávila left behind testified to her literacy, the Congregation of Rites responsible for deciding her worthiness for canonization determined that the doctrine in her books was, in the words of Bishop Lorenzo Otaduy, "elevated beyond the resources of any woman, particularly one without study of theology."[38] Therefore, as it says in article 56 of the documents on canonization, the content of her work was "not acquired or taught by human industry, but infused by God through the medium of prayer" (Slade 129). In other words, her great work *Las Moradas* (*The Interior Castle*) and even her autobiography, *El libro de la vida* (*The Book of Her Life*), which served as a model for most Spanish-speaking women's *vidas*, could not have been products strictly of her own intellect. As scholar Carole Slade declared, "In giving Teresa sainthood, the Church deprived her of authorship" (129).[39]

Thus, no matter how successfully a woman's autobiography had weathered inquisitional scrutiny during her lifetime, how exemplary it was of her saintly behavior, or how influential it was for her Catholic audience, a hagiography written by a cleric—therefore, a male—was necessary for the canonization process prescribed by the Council of Trent. Such was the case even with Teresa of Ávila, for whom the famous Renaissance poet Fray Luis de León began a hagiography. His hagiography conforms to many of the same arguments and literary formulae with which Paniagua would later comply in writing Chicaba's *Vida*. For example, faced with the necessity to prove the *limpieza de sangre* (purity of blood) of Teresa of Ávila's ancestry in the face of her *converso* background, Luis de León ascribes a noble origin to her parents.[40] Also, he describes her as precociously saintly, especially in her search for solitude during her childhood. The text of the biography of her namesake Teresa Chicaba also employs both of these topoi. However, Luis de León's work differs from others in this genre in that it is a forthright apologia of the many mystical experiences Teresa of Ávila describes in her writings. These reports of direct communication with God form the center of concern in the canonization process. There were those who believed they were a manifestation of a diabolic intervention (Slade 129). Many hagiographies, Chicaba's included, present the saint's life as a struggle against evil personified by the devil. In Fray Luis's depiction of Saint Teresa's struggles, the Inquisition and inept confessors constitute the presence of evil in her life. The former doubted the authenticity of her encounters with the Divine, and the latter counseled her to avoid solitary prayer. It is they who must be vanquished.[41] While unusually tenacious and intelligent women such as Teresa of Ávila might, during their lifetimes, convince the male authorities of their holiness, the task of pleading their cases before the councils that certify sanctity was in the hands of males, their advocates and hagiographer-interpreters.

Aware that the protocols of saintly humility dictated that men acted as recorders, mediators, in the production of spiritual autobiographies, scholars have become concerned "whether hagiographical and mystical treatises by and about women . . . might be too opaque, too constructed by high-status male authors to give any window on women's lives" (Bynum ix). Evidence of *true* "sainthood is derived from the third person narrative in exemplary lives . . . where the narrator must have been close enough to the subject to vouch for her sanctity. Third person was the mark of authenticity" for the religious audience of saints' lives, for it was unseemly to write about one's own holiness. But for today's scholars who seek "historical or verifiable certitude," the question of authenticity, which is usually vested in the protagonist-subject of the book and textual evidence by and about her preserved in archives, this genre—especially in the instance of a text written by a man about a woman's life—poses some evidential difficulty (Bynum ix). *Vidas* are not the kind of documents that provide a transparent lens or direct insight on the historical realities of the experiences of holy women—especially those of holy African women whose social location is at the intersection of race (Black) and gender (woman).[42] So feminist scholars investigating saints' legends not only from the Middle Ages but also from the modern period up to and including the eighteenth century are developing methodologies for finding the aperture in these texts through which to "illuminate the past with a fierce and probing light [as well as] to raise, with nuance and power the fundamental issues of *interpretation*" (Bynum ix; italics added). Teresa Chicaba's hagiography exemplifies all of these aforementioned issues modern critics raise about authenticity, historicity, authorship, and the scholarly usefulness of saints' lives. Yet it is by thoroughly analyzing these impediments to a straightforward understanding of this document that the reader begins to grasp the complexity of eighteenth-century Spanish society's discursive construction of the Catholic African female.

The spiritual biographies written in the languages spoken by the common people—the vernacular—create a particular difficulty for the modern reader, for this genre does not distinguish between historicity and a religious reality that a present-day secular audience would characterize as highly fictionalized. These works are profoundly metaphorical and symbolic. Thus, this kind of story's verifiability is often in question. These narratives were intended not simply to record events in the life of saints or would-be saints from the early Christian period through the Middle Ages into early Modernity, periods when a belief in miracles was common. But, through accounts of extraordinary phenomena, these stories also provided evidence of the sanctity of the subject, and they served the confessors and directors who requested their production as valuable models for audiences of homilies and devotional reading. Especially during the Middle Ages, when the primary purpose of "saints' legends"—as they were sometimes called—was to glorify the holy protagonist and to exemplify the material and spiritual benefits of following the way to Christian perfection, their narratives paid scant attention to what modern scholars would now call "historical truth."[43] However, when Paniagua compiled the *Vida*, he and his contemporaries had greatly reduced the number of marvels in these texts—though some were still present—under the pressure of the Protestant Reformation and eighteenth-century Enlightenment rationality.

The Narrative of Mary of Egypt, a Model Hagiography

One means of exploring the evolution of the hagiographical genre and its recording of miracles is through excavating the archeology of a saint's story that was told and retold during the preceding centuries. The many hagiographies of Mary of Egypt serve here as an example of the relationship between works of the genre of women's spiritual narratives, from the sixth-century legend through several medieval versions of the same fable and by its intertextual connections with other more modern *vidas*.[44] At first glance, Mary of Egypt's story of a repentant harlot who spent forty-seven years as a hermit in the desert near the River Jordan to compensate for her sins bears little resemblance to the biography of chaste Teresa Chicaba related in this volume.[45] Yet the life of Mary of Egypt conspicuously conforms to two different hagiographic structures—one transformative and the other transcendent—each of which usually defines only a single narrative. The transformative structure recounts the story of radical *metanoia*.[46] On the one hand, in the medieval hagiography, Mary of Egypt desires sexual pleasure that can never satisfy her, so she is thereby doomed to a restless search for fulfillment until grace intervenes to inaugurate a change of heart and provide the opportunity for finding peace. On the other hand, the transformation of Chicaba entails her conversion from religious ignorance, a fruitless search for the object of worship in African belief systems, to Christian knowledge through the mediation of the Virgin Mary (Chapters 3 and 4). The spiritual transformations of both women are allegorized and secured by their removal to new isolated and isolating locations: Mary across the Jordan into the desert and Teresa to enslavement in Spain.

The second hagiographic structure is the more narratively "static" transcendent portion of the text. Medievalist Evelyn Vitz explains: "The desire of [some] saints is different not only in content but in structure.... [They] are extremely resistant to having a 'story' at all, to desiring, or being part of, any significant narrative 'transformation.'" She elucidates further: hagiographic subjects who focus single-mindedly on God "can provide no transformation." Their legends disappoint the reader who expects narrative movement or progression. These plots—if one can call them that—are "less about a modification, from something to something else, than of an increase, through degrees, from partial to complete, not yet perfect to perfected" (Vitz 395–97). The transcendent portions of each legend ensue when Mary of Egypt and Teresa Chicaba, through "perfect" contemplation and purgative suffering, "submit" themselves to serving God. In fact, the period of transcendence in the Mary of Egypt tale is almost a textual silence, marked by her years of eremitical absence. For Teresa Chicaba, this is the period when she is occupied with the drudgery of the kitchen and the infirmary at La Penitencia, when she longs to trade her metaphorical role as the biblical housekeeper Martha for the more contemplative character of Mary of Bethany (see the discussion below of Chicaba's poem in Chapter 35 of the *Vida*).

However, a reader familiar with hagiographies recognizes Teresa Chicaba as the textual kin of one of the earliest hagiographic contemplatives, a saintly woman of a fourth-century legend, who wandered "through the kitchen render[ing] any service. She was, as they say, the sponge of the monastery." According to historian-philosopher Michel de Certeau, she was "the excluded one," a hermit in the midst of a community.[47]

The fourth-century tale of the unnamed kitchen servant, the legend of Mary of Egypt, and the story of Teresa Chicaba are interrelated texts. In his article on the fourteenth-century Spanish prose version of this tale, the *Estoria de Santa Maria Egipcíaca*, John Maier identifies slavery as an important motif in an intertextual relationship between the medieval hagiographic transformational narrative and the *Vida* of Teresa Chicaba.[48] The story opens with Mary in Egypt carrying on a profligate life when she decides to go away:

> She moves away from her home and away from her past as she leaves Alexandria and goes to Jerusalem where she has visions which lead to her spiritual reformation. The passage from Egypt to Israel in light of the change which will come about has a fairly obvious analogue in the exodus of the Hebrews. Just as they left slavery in Egypt for the freedom of the Promised Land, so too, retrospectively, does Mary's journey represent a passage out of the slavery of sin into the freedom of divine grace and spiritual wholeness. The power of the image as an encompassing structure is too powerful to overlook. (Maier 426)

"Slavery" is a code shared in this series of religious texts. The fourteenth-century legend of Mary of Egypt harkens back to the biblical narrative of the Israelites, and it reaches forward four hundred years into the future hagiography of Sor Teresa, where spiritual thralldom intersects with literal bondage. Paradoxically, in eighteenth-century Spanish theology and ideology, enslavement is an instrument of religious freedom. That is, eighteenth-century Christian (Catholic and Protestant) thinkers rationalized the horrors of the slave trade and the transportation of captives as the means to save Africans from paganism, to liberate Blacks spiritually through their subjugation.

Maier goes on to observe that it is only when spiritual forces block Mary's entrance to the temple in Jerusalem that she sees the "error of her ways," receiving and accepting the grace to repent. Thus, her remorse opens the "passage to freedom." He then expands his reading of her debarment beyond its "pietistic Christian" context and argues that the denial of entrance to the place of "collective worship" represents her exclusion from "the symbolic center of the community" whose beliefs and worldview she has until now repudiated. Consequently, her compunction and submission to the will of God—her obedience—gains her admission to the church in Jerusalem and Christian society. This act prepares her to embark for the desert, the site of transcendence. And it signals a change in the hagiographic narrative structure (Maier 426).

Exclusion from religious communities constitutes an intertextual relationship between the stories of Mary of Egypt and Teresa Chicaba, as well as the tale of the fourth-century kitchen drudge. In this light, Chicaba's rejection by several monasteries is a later stage of her transformation, as is her "pilgrimage," the long journey across Spain to Salamanca. For some religious authorities—such as voting members of second order convents—her color betokened her spiritual inappropriateness for a religious vocation, but her visit to a monastery during the journey to La Penitencia dispelled the misgivings of nuns who had previously refused her admittance. When both a financial inducement and a sincere endorsement by her sponsor to the bishop of Salamanca subsequently gain Chicaba provisional entry to the Dominican third order convent, the narrative of her transcendence begins. Once Teresa Chicaba enters La Penitencia, the text of the *Vida* slows down to a narrative halt. The absence of progression in the *Vida* is similar to Mary of Egypt's years in the desert across the Jordan River.

The theory of intertextuality enables critics and historians to understand the relationship between texts as something different than literary influence or the association between a model/template to its copy/reproduction. *Influence* and *reproduction* are authorial acts. Intertextuality focuses instead on the ability of signs—that is, language itself—to transform texts through their relationship over time in changing ideological, cultural, and social contexts. The notion of "authorship" is a relatively modern one—developing roughly two hundred years before the publication of the *Vida*. Furthermore, the genre of hagiography during its heyday, unlike the later associated forms of autobiography or biography, places very little emphasis on the specific writer, originator, or creator of the text, so attribution of all or parts of Sor Teresa's exemplary life to a single contributor or source becomes problematic. In the compendium that Chicaba's *Vida* constitutes, there are several sources of information that correspond to different voices. Among modern readers, there may be not only a scholarly curiosity—indeed, a sense of intellectual responsibility—that drives readers toward teasing out the voices in the text, but also a political obligation to restore verbal agency to the subject of the *Vida*. However, establishing a clear separation between Chicaba's "voice" and that of Paniagua in *her* story is not completely possible.[49]

This introduction does not ascribe unreservedly to the school of thought that understands written works as intertextually determined or, in the words of theorist Roland

Barthes, "always already written," where the author is merely an instrument of the text. In other words, the purpose here is not to reiterate, alongside others, that "the author is dead."[50] Instead the attention to intertextuality in this hagiography is intended to problematize and emphasize what scholars have long noted: many hagiographies are produced as a kind of collaboration among the saintly subject, the assumed author or compiler when known, the "cult" that venerates the saint, her monastic community, the audience, *and* textuality itself.[51]

The title page of the *Vida* bears the name of Juan Carlos Miguel de Paniagua as the *compiler* of the work (the compendium). The licenses to print and publish the work, the ecclesiastical assurances that the text contains nothing theologically objectionable, and the prologues all attest to Paniagua's responsibility for the document. This is as it should be, for it was customary for clerics to serve as mediators between religious women and the public.

Because Sor Teresa Chicaba was alleged to be the recipient of religious favors—spiritual visitations and prescient dreams—a religious authority with pristine credentials had to vouch for her sanctity and the religious orthodoxy of these gifts. This mystical path was the usual mode Catholic women chose to explain their religious insights since the academic world and the formal study of theology were out of bounds to them. However, this strategy was fraught with danger; for women, especially African women, risked censure, imprisonment, and even death if their ideas were perceived to challenge theological orthodoxy.[52] For this reason, clerics directed women experiencing extraordinary graces and religious gifts to seek the guidance of a confessor or spiritual director and to keep a written record of their devotional life. For example, in seventeenth-century Lima, while the white upper-class mystic Saint Rose achieved sainthood, some of her sisters of a lower social status faced the Inquisition instead of beatification.[53] The convent, however, was always a safer place for a Black woman to record her spiritual life. This was the case of Úrsula de Jesús, a Black *donada* of the convent of Santa Clara in Lima and a contemporary of both Saint Rose and Saint Martin de Porres, the first Black person to be canonized in the modern era.[54] The first woman of African descent to have been credited with writing, or dictating, her spiritual autobiography, Úrsula de Jesús exercised extreme care in what others directed her to produce, thereby establishing her bona fides with the ecclesiastical authorities.

Sor Teresa Chicaba was equally monitored in her spiritual activities inside La Penitencia. Paniagua's close associate, his fellow Theatine Jerónimo Abarrategui, was Chicaba's most influential spiritual director. It is entirely possible that he instructed her to keep a record of her life just as other clerics instructed the women under their supervision to document their experiences in conjunction with the spiritual practice called an "examination of conscience." These records were not just random notes or diary entries, but narratives that reflected on the women's pasts and recorded their efforts to overcome their spiritual shortcomings. Sisters used their written observations as mnemonic devices in preparation for their general confessions. In turn, some of these priests used their confessants' and directees' writings to produce religious biographies and devotional literature (Ibsen 24).

Without written sources for these *vidas*, there is no way of knowing whether or how much the clerical authors and editors enhanced, elaborated on, or subtracted from their informants' reports, so it is impossible for a twenty-first-century reader to rely on these hagiographies as faithful, accurate representations of their subjects' lives. Yet the saints do exist in and through texts—their self-authored *vidas*, hagiographies, and the few documents recording major events in conventual archives and legal records—as well in some portraits and engravings. Even if Roland Barthes is correct about the function and the *almost* autonomous power of texts, some shadow of the nuns' subjectivity still shines through the interstices of their "telling" of their own lives, the priestly biography, and the facts the reader-audience of their cults (sisters in their communities and associates who met them in the *locutorio* or speak room) can remember or believe, as well as within the dictates of textuality itself.[55] All have some hand in the making of the legend. The hagiography, despite its ascription to a single author, is a collaboration of sorts, in which a sister finesses some small control over the recounting of her story through her notes, her *selective* memory, and her analysis of particular events that she makes available to the priest for the book. In this regard, Paniagua's *Vida* of Sor Teresa Chicaba may not reveal an exact image of its subject, but it allows readers and researchers to construct an idea or notion of what must have been a very impressive African woman. And it reveals something about European notions of Africa and about the institution of slavery, as well as the structure and politics of women's religious orders. Sor Teresa Chicaba's *Vida* is a window into the construction of gender as well as the historical-discursive formation of race, and the intersection of these two social structures in Spain during the eighteenth century.

How the *Vida* negotiates the issue of Chicaba's African origins as an obstacle to her sainthood is a case in point. Africans were not considered appropriate subjects for Catholic hagiographies or the sainthood they promoted. An assertion of royal descent expedited the path to canonization. The rules for sainthood required that the candidate be the legitimate issue of a blessed marriage. Black slaves, lacking evidence of both, were not fitting candidates for sainthood. Thus, the theology and the associated racial ideology of the era precluded such subjects from hagiographies. The *Vida* needed to represent Chicaba's race positively against the discourses of its time, which were decidedly anti-Black. A close reading of the *Vida* reveals a tension between the dominant ideology of the day and the textual space that resists these beliefs—a site in the narrative that the reader could argue Chicaba and Paniagua constructed together. The description of her parents and family as members of her country's royalty stands in tension with their Blackness and their African origins, but it serves to mitigate Chicaba's abject status as a slave by asserting her exceptional pedigree. However, Teresa's rejection by several convents that would not accept a Black nun was testimony to the impossibility of her claims of legitimacy and high lineage to displace completely the negative aspects of the doctrine of *limpieza de sangre* that prevailed in her time.[56] Occasionally the narrative transforms her Blackness into a mark of divine choosing; for instance, during her journey to enter the convent in Salamanca, a blind man recognizes her skin color and thereby her specialness by simply touching her (Chapter 21).

Of course, a modern reader might conjecture that Chicaba's royal origins were probably a fiction created by Paniagua, the Manceras, and/or the convent. Her official portrait seems to corroborate this by inserting a European crown and scepter on the ground at the bottom, on the right hand side. However, more likely, this portion of her story may have been the combination of two other sources: First, it was customary to attribute nobility to Africans who assimilated well to European cultures, and this nine-year-old captive seemed to do that.[57] Second, Sor Teresa's faint memories of her happy childhood in Africa probably coalesced with what both she and Paniagua had heard about the gold bangles she wore when she arrived at Cadiz. The traffickers must have thought they had captured a "treasure" when they saw her jewelry.

Names suggest more of her family history. In Ewe, *Chicaba* refers to gold, and the name of her brother Juachipiter may be a composite of *Watchi* (an ethnic group in Northern Togo), and *pitê* (a jeweler's file). These two names seem to indicate the rough geographic area from which she came, the African ethnic group to which she belonged, and the importance of her father. If he was a smith, as these names suggest, he would have been revered among his people for his power to transform ore—iron or gold—into useful and beautiful objects. Among some West African peoples, men who do this work have extraordinary spiritual properties, such as a kind of second sight and sometimes the power to heal, so perhaps Chicaba's father possessed an ability also attributed to his daughter.[58]

The dictates of the hagiographic genre in the eighteenth century—especially in Spain—also required that the saint's narrative tell of her early and sustained membership in the Catholic Church. A sign of Chicaba's status as one of God's elect is the account of the visitations of the White Lady and her Child to the precociously religious Chicaba in Africa, and her first baptism and renaming as "Teresa" there (Chapter 4). Later in the *Vida*, the report of her parents' conversion and death frees her from the obligation to marry her putative uncle and return to her people to govern them (Chapter 17).[59] The story of her choice to remain in Spain confirms her religious vocation, foreshadowed in her childhood betrothal to the White Child whom the reader identifies as Christ, to become his chaste bride, a nun.

The *Vida* struggles under the influence of the Enlightenment to moderate the amount of visitations and miracles in the narrative. In fact, this concern is expressed by Bernardo de Rivera, the author of the Opinion that precedes the text of the hagiography.[60] Nonetheless, a saint's life still had to present some remarkable experiences as signs of the subject's holiness. One example was Chicaba's rescue from drowning in the pool at Madrid's Buen Retiro Park by an unidentified stranger, who was later recognized as an angel (Chapters 10 and 11). Another is her capacity to subdue the devil possessing her charge María Francisca (Chapter 31). However, the final miracle in the text, the transformation of Teresa's pigmentation from Black to white, indicates the lingering tension between race and saintliness and faintly echoes the intertextual relation with Mary of Egypt.

The thirteenth-century Spanish version of the life of Mary of Egypt declares that "no one else so beautiful was born" (123). It adds, "Her arms, her body, all of her / Was white as crystal" (124) until her penitential sojourn in the trans-Jordanian desert transformed her: "Her face was Black and beaten / By the cold wind and the frost" (138).[61] When the monk Zosimas ventures into the wilderness to give her the Eucharist, he cannot immediately find her at their appointed meeting place. Intuiting that she is dead, he prays for help in locating her body: "He turned his eyes to the right. / And saw a brightness; / Toward the light he moved. / He saw the body; he was very glad" (156).

Mary's journey to holiness is the reverse of Teresa Chicaba's. The Egyptian saint moves from the city, with its connotation of civilization in dominant Western ideology, to the "savage" wilderness of the desert; Chicaba, from the problematic "savage" space of Africa to Europe, which was synonymous with civilization in the eighteenth-century worldview. Mary turns Black, and Teresa, white. However, the closing scenes of each hagiography create a complexity around the motif of skin color. For medieval audiences and writers of hagiographies, "light and "brightness" also constitute synonyms for "white" and antonyms not just for "darkness" but also for "Black." In his article on Black-skinned otherness in monastic literature, David Brakke discusses the association of Ethiopians with Blackness and that pigmentation with the devil. He cites 1 Thessalonians: "You are all children of light, children of the day; we are not of the night or darkness"; and then he argues that light clearly continues to be associated with godliness and eventually "white" people and the darkness of the devil became linked to Blackness and Black people.[62]

Of course, in both the legends of Mary of Egypt and Teresa Chicaba, the significance associated with these skin colors is transvaluated. For instance, Mary's beauty, as epitomized by her white complexion, facilitates her attraction and consequent illicit congress. Ironically, Blackness usually is a sign of lasciviousness or hypersexuality (Brakke 509; Scheil 141–42) but in this case, it is her whiteness that makes her an occasion of sin; her Blackness makes her undesirable and un-desiring. Only at her death does "lightness" return to signify newly achieved purity. And in the chapter of Sor Teresa's *Vida* that relates the story of the beautiful Turkish girl who has been seduced and abandoned, the text maintains that Chicaba's "ugly" Blackness protects her from the sexual attentions of others and keeps her chaste (Chapters 11 and 12). Light marks Mary's resting place for the holy monk Zosimas and for the lion (a traditional symbol of Christ and the resurrection) that digs her grave; if this light indicates through its brightness a lifting of the pall of penitence and expiation, then how does the lightening/whitening of Teresa Chicaba's body at the end of her life function in her narrative?

As the association between skin color and moral state develops over centuries into a racial discourse, the metaphors of light and dark become those of white and Black. Under the pressures of the hagiographic necessity to offer "proof" of holiness in tension with the difficulty of imagining and writing about an African or Black saint, the influence of textuality and the authority of ideology hold sway. Evidence of Teresa Chicaba's sanctity requires a fundamental somatic change, the transformation of her phenotypic racial identification. This is a miracle that the members of her religious community, those who sought her advice and spiritual assistance, and the reader-audience of the *Vida* can believe, want to believe. So powerful was this conviction about the altered appearance of Chicaba's body that it remained an unproblematized matter of fact in the leaflets and prayer booklets distributed at the monastery where she is buried until the mid- to late 1990s.

The function of this conclusion to Teresa Chicaba's life is at least threefold: First, it endorses the reluctant decision of the third order Dominicans, the "Magdalenas," of La Penitencia in Salamanca to accept this African woman in their community. Second, it "resolves" the contradiction that the subject's racialized gender creates by means of an account structured through intertextuality and by genre to represent the dominant ideology of the Catholic Church. And, third, by so doing, it endorses a casuistic and profoundly ephemeral process of Black subjectivization—a reluctant recognition of the possibility of personhood for Chicaba and, by extension, other Black Catholics—albeit in terms that ultimately reinscribe and recuperate the hierarchical structure of color and the superiority of whiteness over Blackness. Thus, the *Vida* shores up the Spanish discursive edifice of differences (racial and gendered).

Through its representation of Teresa as finally so saintly as to be white, the hagiography enables the reconstruction or recirculation of a Western sense of its own subjectivity by defining Sor Teresa's sanctity in terms that affirm the value system that sustains the domination of Blacks, women, and Black women. So when, as Paniagua claims, he circulated Chicaba's story (in the *Oración fúnebre* and possibly in the *Vida*) throughout Spain and its colonies and thereby across the hispanophone Black diaspora, it is as an example of the rewards of religious and social conformity. Whether African-descended peoples read the work that way is another question.

If, as theorist Homi K. Bhabha contends, subjectivization through stereotypical representations of the Other is a process shared by both the oppressor and the oppressed, then the report of Chicaba's posthumously transformed body not only reproduces whiteness, but it also constructs Black female subjectivity.[63] Thus, one must assume that the dissemination of the *Vida* accomplishes its purpose by reproducing in its slave and emancipated Black audiences the abject humility and obedience—the virtues portrayed in the "loyal" hagiographic text—prescribed for Africans.

However, the analysis in this edition of the *Vida* contends that there must be a Brechtian "disloyal" text present behind or interwoven in the obvious orthodox, "loyal" hagiography.[64] That is, even in this most traditional and conformist work, there are scenes of counterdiscourse and subversion: for example, the representation of the passage aboard the ship to Spain and into enslavement as so horrific that Chicaba contemplates jumping overboard (Chapter 6); her vindication against the vengeful accusations of members of the Mancera household (Chapters 9, 10, and 11); her ability to convert the Turkish girl when wise priests and theologians had failed (Chapter 12); her defiant appropriation of a holy picture of Christ as the Ecce Homo, which had been distributed to everyone in the household except her (Chapter 13); the cruelty of fully professed nuns (Chapter 25); and, most importantly, the poetic plaint based on the story of Mary and Martha (Chapter 35). Yet these scenes probably would not transform the racial politics of their Spanish and *criollo* readers—people not of indigenous descent born on the American continent—for these depictions rely on and do not displace the structures of power that underpin both the eighteenth-century Church and Spanish society. But some portion of the Black audience might have detected the resistance in the text.

Adapting Chicaba's Spiritual Biographies for Hispanophone Audiences

The *Oración fúnebre* and the *Vida* refer to Chicaba's fame throughout Spanish America, but without giving any specifics. Paniagua's dissemination of her spiritual biographies would not have been unusual. Through this practice, the author inserts her story into two dispersions or cultural diffusions: the formation of Spanish and Spanish American female identities, and the creation of a Black Atlantic and an African diasporic consciousness. An earlier section of this introduction asserted the popularity of *vidas* in their many forms. Sacred biographies regularly circulated throughout the Spanish world, where an individual reader studied and reflected on the faithfulness of holy women and men who emulated the life of Christ, and where collective audiences listened intently to the legends of saints. *Vidas* were regular fare in convent refectories and were diversions during the nuns' recreation periods, when a designated lector declaimed the lives of martyrs, hermits, virgins, mystics, and founders of religious orders. Lay audiences, too, appreciated these stories for their felicitous blend of romance and edification. Families, sometimes with their slaves and servants, listened to the stories in the evening after supper, and lay ecclesial groups—sodalities and confraternities—included such readings at their gatherings (Myers 5).[65]

These legends chronicled exemplary lives. Readers attempted to conform their way of living to the model provided by the central figure of a *vida* and the shape of her quest. They also attempted to apply this model to the narratives—autobiographical and hagiographical—that represented their spiritual path. But this does not mean that the dictates of the genres were too rigid to allow for variations in plot and tropes that permitted individuals from different cultural, temporal, and social locations to invest in and generate their particular stories.

The *Oración fúnebre* and the *Vida* are cases in point. For example, the texts had to make an argument in favor of what Spaniards believed impossible—an African woman saint. So both the funeral oration and the life-story had to reenvision Chicaba's place of origin and the people among whom she was born. Africa, in the minds of eighteenth-century Spaniards, was the site of savagery and paganism from which its inhabitants had to be saved by either missionary conversion in situ or transportation, transmigration, and enslavement into some other environment where Christian masters and priests could "civilize" and transform them into Christians.[66]

Each of the two biographical works used a different model for her homeland. In Chicaba's time, there were two tropes of Africa that corresponded to geographic divisions of the continent and that constituted different yet overlapping ideological identifications. The Roman names of "Africa" (today's Northern Africa) and "Ethiopia" were related to the Bible and a biblical understanding of the Black inhabitants of the area. The relatively new term "Guinea" was associated with the development of modern slavery and the region south of the Sahara. The earlier work, the *Oración fúnebre*, compared Chicaba to the figure of the Queen of Sheba. Some believed Sheba was located in present-day Ethiopia or Eritrea. For others, she was akin to the "Black but comely" spouse of the Song of Songs, the biblical book that spiritual theologians had since the Middle Ages read as an allegory of mystical union of the soul (always female) with Christ.[67] Significantly, this figure of African-ness as an Ethiopian monarch becomes a way to suggest Sor Teresa's royal origins.[68]

However, the Africa of the *Vida* is Guinea, which does not benefit from even the slightest amelioration through biblical associations. Therefore, the hagiography has to assure its readers that Teresa Chicaba was uncontaminated by her African origins. The text organizes the defense of its subject on a number of fronts. It reframes the place of her birth, La Mina Baja del Oro, as a country organized in a social hierarchy that mirrored Europe. It describes her people as members of a civilized kingdom beset by the savagery of surrounding cannibals. As evidence of this, the *Vida* asserts Chicaba's royal lineage, the precious daughter of the king. This account of her noble lineage constitutes her *probanza*, the certification of *limpieza de sangre* necessary for canonization in the eighteenth century. Then, to further distance her from the taint of paganism, the *Vida* depicts her miraculous baptism and betrothal to the Child Jesus while still in Africa prior to her capture. The hagiography repeatedly presents Africa as a spectral temptation calling Teresa back to barbarity, an enticement she eschews in favor of Christian redemption in Spain. So when her putative uncle presents himself to the Mancera household, she, like the many virgins in saints' lives, refuses to marry and return home with him to Africa.

Just as the genre of spiritual biography had to adapt to Chicaba's Blackness, it also adjusted the traditional discourse on suffering to conflate it with her status as a slave. Great Catholic saints have lamented their sinfulness and acknowledged the need to purify their souls through suffering. Thus, traditional depictions of heroines in *vidas* require that they embrace affliction—physical and psychological—to indicate their spiritual identification with the crucified Christ. This same cleansing and redemptive power of anguish and wretchedness was the rationale for subjecting heathen Africans to slavery; afflictions were instruments of salvation for their alleged innate errantry. In Sor Teresa's hagiography, these two theologies of suffering merge. The text attributes many of the slights, injustices, and violent attacks she endures because of her color as the means to imitate Christ. In this way, the Christian Spaniards in the Mancera household and her sister nuns who mistreat her, an innocent victim, are absolved from blame, and the society that circulates and supports these prejudicial ideologies goes unexamined.

The variations on the hagiographic conventions of social identity (what might be termed "race") and agony (sometimes called "mortification of the flesh and the spirit") do not constitute departures from the prescriptions of the genre. In fact, they are dependent on the values and forms that *vidas* have always represented—that is, the superiority of Catholicism and European identity as well as the humility and enduring patience of the subject of the narrative. These afflictions are especially appropriate when the subject is African and female. An audience in the Catholic world would recognize these as customary premises for a traditional story of a spiritual quest, but this account was different enough to pique the curiosity not only of Spaniards and white *criollos* but also people of African descent in the Spanish-speaking parts of their diaspora.

The extent to which Chicaba's *Vida* could be considered resistant to normative ideology lies less in how it subverts its genre than in its invitation to imagine an African woman worthy of a hagiography with the sanctity that the commissioning of its writing implies. Women of Spanish descent may have read this as just one more story valorizing their own aspirations and way of life, but perhaps they would also have glimpsed a challenge to their convictions about African inferiority—that is, amorality and ignorance.

Priests and civil authorities may have circulated the spiritual biographies among Blacks as salutary examples of orthodox Catholic belief and saintly comportment in contemporary times. There is ample evidence of an audience of Catholics of African descent in the baptismal and marriage records throughout Latin America.[69] In addition, Blacks, both free and enslaved, formed numerous *cofradías* (religious confraternities) with written constitutions that contained an obligatory phrase expressing gratitude for the acquisition of Catholicism from their ancestors through enslavement by the Spanish.[70] These religious organizations were an integral part of Black civil society in urban locations, and they generated the need for spiritual instruction to which these saints' legends could have contributed. Some Catholics of African descent might have interpreted the stories in a slightly different way from Spanish readers. They might have discovered in the biographies a subtext where their humanity and potential for piety was extolled and the suffering because of their color was acknowledged. That would indeed have been empowering.

Spiritual Narratives in the African American Diaspora

While this volume focuses on an eighteenth-century spiritual narrative by and about an African woman living in Spain, and while there is no evidence that Teresa Chicaba's story reached an Anglophone audience, we translator-editors believe that a short discussion of African American spiritual narratives in conjunction with the *Vida* situates this hagiography in an African diasporic context. Some Black American Protestant spiritual narratives have much in common with the life-story of Chicaba, the Catholic. Obviously, the Black protagonist/subject of this Spanish saint's legend and the originators—authors and oral chroniclers—of the many narratives of Blacks in North America share a history of violent relocation and slavery as well as the harsh legacy of discrimination. Both the *Vida* and Black spiritual writings employ religion as the idiom through which they straightforwardly or subtly make a case for the human dignity of their central figure in particular and Black people in general.

Students of late-eighteenth- and nineteenth-century American literature are familiar with both self-written and as-told-to autobiographical slave narratives of manumitted and fugitive peoples of African descent in North America.[71] This genre evolved from the spiritual autobiographies/narratives of the Protestant religious tradition, which African Americans adapted to their own religious and political purposes. As a powerful instrument of antislavery propaganda that argued for giving "political and economic freedom to Afro-Americans," The secular slave narrative owed its success to the Black spiritual autobiography that had laid "the necessary intellectual groundwork by proving that [Blacks] . . . were as much chosen by God for eternal salvation as whites."[72] Protestants promulgated a spectrum of rationalizations and justifications for enslaving Blacks that ranged from the assertion that the Creator had not endowed Blacks with souls—that is, that Africans were not human—to the hypothesis that, as descendants of the Canaanites or of Noah's transgressive son, Ham, Africans were cut off from all access to The Word (Logos)—understood as both the Gospel and Christ. Therefore, their souls were in some way inherently defective or guilty of an inherited sin for which enslavement was the price of restitution.[73] So early African American writers reasoned that if the impediment to emancipation—freedom—centered on Europeans' equating "pagan," "African," "Black," and "slave" as synonymous terms, then one strategy for breaking this association was conversion, the altering of one's religious status from heathen to Christian.

These writers had at their disposal two already popular autobiographical genres upon which to model their apologias for freedom: captivity stories and Puritan conversion narratives. These literary forms chronicled the individual's personal journey from ignorance to knowledge, from captivity to freedom, and/or from heathen benightedness to Christian enlightenment and deliverance.[74] Fully fifty years before the first fugitive slave narrative, Briton Hammon (1760), James Gronniosaw (1770), John Marrant (1785), and George White (1810) wrote variants of the spiritual autobiography. Hammon's fourteen-page narrative at first glance appears to be a secular treatise, but as critic Joycelyn Moody observes, the tract begins and ends with extended invocations of God and God's providence.[75] But Gronniosaw's autobiography is a self-conscious intervention into the American Protestant literary tradition, for he models his text on the works he had studied during his service as a slave and later a freedman servant in the household of a Dutch Reformed minister. "Moreover, Gronniosaw clearly sought not only to emulate the literary form used by his Puritan predecessors but also to demonstrate that, though he was Black . . . he too could develop a personal relationship with God. Gronniosaw's deployment of the conventions of the spiritual autobiography affirms his sagacity and humanity as well as his piety; his literary descendants perceived the advantage and followed suit" (Moody 5).

The first autobiographical act of a Black woman in North America, the as-told-to or transcribed "Petition of an African Slave to the Legislature of Massachusetts" (1783) by Belinda, argued that she shared the same desire for freedom that motivated colonists to declare their independence from the despotic rule of the English monarch and that "the Almighty Father intended [the same liberty] for all the human race."[76] Belinda's short document shares with Paniagua's *Vida* of Chicaba the representation of the life of a pre-adolescent girl in Africa—in the former case, one who lived along the banks of the River Volta (Belinda 253) and who was wrenched from the hands of her parents while they were praying in the sacred groves consecrated to "the great Orisa, who made all things" (Belinda 254). Both texts depict a quasi- or proto-Christian community in what was heretofore considered a heathen locale, and they portray a preternaturally pious child removed from the care of a loving family. Further, the biographers or the women themselves through their transcribers suggest that captivity in a Christian land and conversion to—adoption of—the religion of their enslavers establishes them as "free moral agent[s] accountable for [their] own actions" (Belinda 254). Conversion bestows both salvation and agency.

Belinda's petition to the Massachusetts General Court (1783) for an allowance from the estate of her former owner, Colonel Isaac Royal, a Tory long fled to England, as a "reward for virtue and just returns for honest industry," is ostensibly a secular document, yet it draws on Protestant rhetoric and theology to make its case (55). It thereby demonstrates that no rigid division between sacred and secular texts obtained in the eighteenth and nineteenth centuries. In fact, early autobiographical texts authored by Black women in North America were, like those written by their male counterparts, spiritual narratives that also expressed strong political arguments in favor of freedom for captured Africans.[77]

For example, Maria Stewart's 1831 essay, entitled "Religion and Pure Principles of Morality," introduced her first volume of exhortations, prayers, and meditations, *Productions* (1835). It contains autobiographical material: "I was born in Hartford, Connecticut, in 1803: was left an orphan at five years of age; was bound out in a clergyman's family; had the seeds of piety and virtue early sown in my mind; but was deprived of the advantages of education though my soul thirsted for knowledge."[78] She continues in the same paragraph to tell of her marriage to James Stewart in 1826 and her widowhood in 1829, and she ends this short narration of her life by reporting that she came "to the knowledge of the truth, as it is in Jesus, in 1830, [and] in 1831, made a public confession of [her] faith in Christ" (4). This latter experience constituted a *metanoia*—the act of transformation that is central to saints' legends, as in the case of Mary of Egypt—whereby she was changed into an independent spirit who was willing to suffer martyrdom for God and for the sake of her "brethren . . . Afric's sons [and daughters]" (4–6). She implies that such was the case with her friend, the radical Black abolitionist author David Walker, who died mysteriously in 1830 after the publication of his *Appeal*.

Stewart's speeches and David Walker's *Appeal to the Colored Citizens of the World* (1829) espouse "employing evangelical religion not only for individual regeneration but also for radical social transformation."[79] Both writers believed that religious conversion, biblical study, and righteous living would confirm the humanity of slaves, bestow religious meaning on their suffering, enable them to endure oppression, and to transcend it; most of all, it would engender "the religious impulse to destroy social structures upholding their degradation and submission and replace them with institutions based on Christian love and justice" (Hinks 232).

While Maria Stewart clearly targets Blacks in general as the audience of her speeches and meditations in *Productions* and later in *Meditations* (1879), she directs much of her work to African American women in particular: "O, ye daughters of Africa! awake! awake! arise! no longer sleep nor slumber, but distinguish yourselves. Show forth to the world that ye are endowed with noble and exalted faculties. O, ye daughters of Africa! what have you done to distinguish yourselves beyond the grave?" (Stewart 6–7). Further, she explains to her Black sisters who struggle against the oppressive yoke of slavery that only virtue, racial unity, tireless industry, frugality, the thirst for knowledge, and education will free Black people.

Joycelyn Moody situates Stewart's oratory within the genre of the jeremiad, prophetic lament and warning (29–31). Stewart argues that historical precedent—"her spiritual legacy from . . . women long ago"—gives her the authority to exhort, write, and advise not only her own people but also all heads of religious and governing bodies:[80]

> In the 15th century, the general spirit of this period is worthy of observation. We might then have seen women preaching and mixing themselves in controversies. Women occupying the chairs of Philosophy and Justice; women harangueing [sic] in Latin before the Pope; women writing in Greek, and studying Hebrew; Nuns were Poetesses, and women of quality Divines; and young girls who had studied Eloquence, would with sweetest countenances, and the most plaintive voices, pathetically exhort the Pope and the Christian Princes. . . . Women in those days devoted their leisure hours to contemplation and study. (Stewart 77)

Despite protestations of ignorance, Stewart was clearly acquainted with histories or some early holy women's autobiographies and spiritual narratives; she establishes her genealogy through these literary forebears and endows a future lineage of Black women self-writers through the works of these same visionary foremothers, "autobiographers who wrote during the Middle Ages and Counter-Reformation—e.g., Christina of Markyate (twelfth century), Julian of Norwich (1342–c. 1420), Margery Kempe (c. 1373–1438), and Teresa of Ávila (1515–1582)" (Houchins xxxi).

The writers enumerated above satisfy Antonio Rubial's definition of saintly Catholic women, as do most of the Black women authors of spiritual narratives—Maria Stewart, Jarena Lee, Zilpha Elaw, and Julia Foote, among others—most of whom, as Joycelyn Moody asserts, exhibit virtue, experience illness and suffering, and see visions (Moody 24). Two contemporaries of Stewart, Jarena Lee and Zilpha Elaw, recount bouts with sickness as they moved along the mystical path to holiness or what Methodists called "sanctification"[81] Prior to her conversion, Lee experiences the "weight of her sins" as a profound depression and a lingering physical illness until she was "converted to God . . . under preaching" by Reverend Richard Allen, founder of the African Methodist Episcopal Church.[82] During the intervening years, before she asked God for the gift of sanctification, she was buffeted by Satan and became "sick through the violence of [her] feelings"—so sick, in fact, that she had to spend time under the care of a "colored physician" (3–9). When Elaw ignores her call to "ministry . . . the Lord used other means to move [her]. . . . God lay her upon a bed of affliction, with a sickness which, to all appearance, was unto death," and she found no relief until she renounced all attachments to earthly things and beings, rededicated herself to God, and began to preach to people who had attended a revival.[83] Later, writer-orator Julia Foote experiences periods when she doubts her vocation as a preacher; on those occasions, she is shrouded in a dark depression, her appetite leaves her, and she is sleepless. Her "husband and her friends said [she] would die or go crazy. . . . [She] expected to die and be lost, knowing that [she] had been enlightened and had tasted the heavenly gift" but had not shared the gospel through ministry. So it was not until an angelic messenger reaffirmed her call and she acquiesced to God's will that the sickness left her.[84]

A similar illness afflicts Teresa Chicaba while she is still a slave in the Mancera household. Shortly after she affected the conversion of the Turkish girl, she falls so gravely ill that it would take a miracle to cure her. A holy Franciscan produces plums "out of season . . .

in the worst of winter," which she eats to regain her health. These heavenly fruits signify to the Mancera household that she is both gifted by God and a gift to them from God. And in gratitude for the celestial favor, she redoubles her spiritual exercises in preparation for her vocation as a nun (Chapter 12).

Visions of and visitations from heavenly beings are common to some of these Black women writers of sacred narratives, whether Catholic or Protestant. The most striking example of such an experience and the case most resembling Chicaba's is that of Julia Foote, who seeks a license to preach over the objections of Methodist clergy, just as the former slave Teresa de Santo Domingo desired to profess solemn vows and wear the veil of a Dominican nun over the opposition of the bishop.

Foote describes a Sabbath evening when she was praying to discern the true source of her impression that God had called her to the ministry. She became lost in ecstasy, during which an angel appeared and led her before the Holy Trinity. The Father asked her to make a choice: to obey His command to preach or to be eternally damned. In fear, she submitted to His will and followed Him to a body of water where she was handed over to Christ, who purified her in spiritual baptism and affirmed her pledge to travel across the country evangelizing. Still, she feared that no one would believe she had the authority to preach, so "Christ then appeared to write something with a gold pen and golden ink, upon golden paper. Then he rolled it up, and said to [her]: 'Put this in your bosom, and, wherever you go, show it, and they will know that I have sent you to proclaim salvation to all.' He then put it into my bosom." Upon awaking, she looked for the letter, and when she could not find it, friends explained that the license was "written on [her] heart, and was to be shown in [her] life" (69–71).[85]

When confronted with her self-doubt as well as the sexism of her Black pastor and the conference of her church, Julia Foote envisioned her ordination by Christ Himself in the presence of the communion of saints. Similarly, Teresa Chicaba received spiritual baptism at a fountain in her native land—not at the hands of a European priest but from a spiritual presence—and later, when her Blackness was considered an obstacle to her profession as a nun, she visualized making her solemn vows in the hands of none other than Saint Dominic, the founder of her religious order, before an assembly of the souls of past nuns. For Julia Foote and Teresa Chicaba, true Christianity was no respecter of hierarchical social categories of difference, so they sought and received authorization of their self-understanding from Heaven.

Maria Stewart, Zilpha Elaw, and Julia Foote looked to the scriptures for valorization. In response to a "spiritual interrogation—'Who shall go forward and take off the reproach that is cast upon the people of color? Shall it be a woman?'" (Stewart 51), Stewart makes bold to answer that she will take on this burden because she follows in the steps of the biblical Deborah, "mother and judge of Israel," and "Esther, the queen and advocate for the Jews" (75). Lee, too, finds a precedent for women preaching in the figure of "Esther, the queen, who fasted and prayed, commanded the men of Jerusalem and the women of Zion to pray" (44). Elaw and Foote argue that early Christian women preached the gospel: "That women as well as men were" filled with the Holy Ghost on the day of Pentecost, "Women and men are classed together, and if the power to preach is short-lived and spasmodic in the case of women, it must be equally so in that of men; and if women have lost the gift of prophecy, so have men" (Foote 78). Observing a contradiction in the Pauline epistles that advise women to be silent in church, Foote argues that Paul says, "'There is neither male nor female in

Christ Jesus.' Philip had four daughters that prophesied and preached. Paul called Priscilla, as well as Aquila, 'helper' or as in the Greek, his 'fellow laborer'" (79). Both Elaw and Foote cite the instance of Phoebe, the deaconess of the Church at Cenchrea, as another example of a woman minister in the scriptures. Some of these spiritual narrators contend that, since Mary Magdalene was the first to see the risen Christ and preach his resurrection to the apostles, she was the foremother of all Christian women preachers (e.g., Stewart 75; Lee 10).

All of these African American women make the case, not only by scriptural references to the early Pauline assertion of the equality of slave and master but also by the sheer act of writing about their conversions and sanctification, that slavery was sinful. The poem attributed to Sor Teresa in Chapter 35 of the *Vida* is also an example of a unique interpretation of a Bible passage. Chicaba's poetic exegesis of the biblical story of Mary and Martha is a similar intervention into the racial politics of convents in particular and the Church in general. In this unusual expression of what the text describes as "jealousy" of Christ's love for others, Sor Teresa Chicaba makes bold to question the traditional distinction between the sisters who do menial labor (presumably "white-veiled" nuns or religious seculars) and the choir nuns, whose work it is to pray and contemplate.

The similarities between Teresa's *Vida* and the spiritual autobiographies of African American women reflect the development of the "intercultural and transnational formation" that Paul Gilroy describes, identifies, and names as the Black Atlantic. This is a complex association that speaks of (1) the African cultural relationships (religious, musical, and/or linguistic retentions, for example) among people from different ethnic groups scattered by the slave trade and emigration to several destinations—European and American—as well as (2) comparable political and social strategies for attaining respect and freedom, and also (3) the different ways these people of African descent recreate their identities through interactions with the very societies that enslave and colonize them. Diaspora does not imply that the various communities from which Europeans and others extracted slaves were homogeneous; it does not mean that Black people globally blended or coalesced their cultures into a uniform manifestation of Africanity; nor is the trajectory of Black influences unidirectional from the Continent to Europe and the Americas. The transnational/international diaspora does not necessarily create lines of direct geographical contact or traceable literary and historical influences, for the diaspora is a network. It is a tangle of rhizomatic strands through which African-descended travelers in texts and across the seas learn and transmit intelligence—knowledge and strategies—throughout the territories of the Black Atlantic. Belief in an international multiethnic and diverse community of Blacks emboldens such public intellectuals as David Walker to address his *Appeal* "to the Coloured Citizens of the World" and the nineteenth-century politician author Martin Delaney literally to explore the expanse of the Black Atlantic—the Americas, Europe, and Africa—and to write his fourth novel, *Blake*, about an Afro-Cuban sailor who roams the diaspora. Also orator Maria Stewart, who both reminds her African American audiences of the oppression they endure in common with Africans and harkens back to European feminist intellectual progenitors, exhibits the double consciousness Gilroy says is a hallmark of Black Atlantic thought.[86]

The *Vida* records in microcosm a story of African diffusion through the episodes of Chicaba's transportation to Spain and her memories of her natal home, as well as through the story of the "uncle" who has been living in France and who traveled to Spain in order to return with his "niece" to Africa. Her participation in the diaspora continues through the initiative of her Spanish hagiographer who sends her life-story abroad. Thus launched, her spiritual narrative enters the transnational, international, and multicultural dispersion not as a point of direct contact or intersection with Black women spiritual writers elsewhere but as a history of a distant colleague in the common struggle to assert an imagined community of Black women's humanity, whether those women were slaves, ex-slaves, or free-born. The discussion here that places these Catholic and Protestant works side-by-side is not an assertion of the uniformity or seamlessness of the cultural productions of African and African-descended people or the impact of the early work on those texts that follow, for the diaspora is fragmented and discontinuous.[87] In fact, the decision to express a similarity of concerns through different religious metaphors attests to the centrality of the belief that differing Christian theological tenets could and would make the case—deliberately or inadvertently—for freedom and human dignity, even for those occupying the intersectional social locations of Blackness and femaleness, through seemingly unrelated/unconnected texts across geographically disparate locations.

Voice in Women's and Slaves' Narratives

Some literary historians may question how the editors of this English translation of the *Vida* can claim to detect Chicaba's voice in her "life narrative," which was recorded by a European cleric.[88] Indeed, this disjunction between the perspective of the subject and that of the amanuensis/author is not only a concern in this particular text, but it was also and is to some extent still an obstacle to establishing a definite provenance and clear lines of attribution for other hagiographies, spiritual, captivity, and/or proto-slave narratives about and/or by women, Blacks, and especially Black women.[89] In other words, present-day readers traditionally ascribe the authorship of the several autobiographical and biographical genres listed above to the person named on the title page, most often a male—with the exception of captivity narratives where a man masquerades as a woman. However, recently some scholars have striven to identify and distinguish between the contributions of the individual members of collaborative teams, to disentangle their textual presences.[90]

Historian Allan Greer observes that saints' lives were "sites where notions of gender difference and racial hierarchy were enunciated, qualified, challenged, and inverted" (324). Hagiographies subtly contested, interrogated, and expanded their contemporaneous discourses, yet "followed conventional patterns, dividing along gender lines and displaying cultural ideals about male and female religiosity" (327). For instance, men heroically renounced "wealth, power and sex," whereas "women saints were more likely to pursue private and inward spirituality" (328).[91] Paraphrasing Caroline Walker Bynum's description of "archetypal" women saints' lives, Greer observes that "female texts trace the subject's life from early childhood, recounting dozens of anecdotes along the way, some of them seemingly trivial" (338). These are stories of "consistent lifelong virtue" (339), where few women encounter dramatic crises or turning points in their saintly trajectories (324, 326, 338, 339).[92] The *Vida* conforms to this model. But while Greer focuses on the re-presentation of women and the colonial Other, another school of historians and critics are more concerned with discovering what hand women subjects might have had in their own representations/re-presentations, even in those written by men that conformed strictly to the formulae of the genre.

Catherine M. Mooney edited a collection of essays by medievalists who have developed methodologies for discerning variations between the voices and perspectives of saintly subjects and their transcribers (1). All but one of these articles analyzes hagiographies composed by men about holy women; however, the technologies they propose are heavily dependent on the availability of a substantial selection of documents authored separately by all parties involved in the production of the saint's textual life, her *vida*. Such is not the case with Teresa Chicaba, for what writings she may have left behind either in her own monastery or with Paniagua have disappeared. Nevertheless, Mooney maintains that while the analyses in her book "are not specifically about women who left no writings of their own or for whom no vestiges of their *voices* or personal agency can be clearly discerned in *other texts*, [these articles'] insights about relationships between male writers and holy women represent an important contribution to the scholarly quest to develop strategies for reading with a sharper eye male-authored portrayals of such women" (4; emphasis added). The quest to discern Chicaba's "voice" in the *Vida* entails several strategies: starting with interpreting the *Oración fúnebre* in order to make a comparison between it and the hagiography. The primary purpose of the formal eulogy is to extol the virtue of the deceased nun and to tell her life-story as an elaborate, extended metaphor—a reworking of a traditional motif (that is, a topos). As a genre, this requiem positions its speaker, Paniagua, metaphorically beside her bier to gesture toward his absent subject; thus, her "voice" is essentially missing from the text except for a few direct quotations sparsely dispersed throughout the presentation. By placing this first iteration of Chicaba's biography next to the hagiography, a critic might be able to become familiar with the author's voice, as it speaks uninterrupted by the protagonist's narrative interventions.

The other reading strategies focus on the *Vida*: beginning with a short discussion of the poem in Chapter 35, attributed directly to Chicaba, about the biblical Martha and Mary; followed by a longer analysis that employs a combination of materialist criticism and structural analysis. This method unites gendered and racial readings appropriate to the historical and geographical contexts of the hagiography with a structural search for places of narrative contradiction and ambiguity that mark sites where Chicaba's *implied* or marginal "voice" influences the trajectory of the plot toward its logical conclusion. Her whispered textual utterances work like those of a prompter from the wings of a stage; they are muted interventions that impact the performance and articulation of ideology in the work.

The final strategy is a semiotic reading of coded language that examines occasions in the *Vida* that seem emblematic of its origins in conversations. That is, they display features of orality and thereby disclose the voice of a Chicaba speaking, not necessarily through quotations but in depictions of subtle resistance to her oppressive situation.[93] Often these are passages illustrative of what feminist critics Joan Newton Radner and Susan Lanser call "implicit codes," which they admit are sometimes "acts whose very codedness is arguable" (6). To assert the presence of such coding in this hagiography is to confront difficulties in establishing where there are inconspicuous interventions by the teller (in this case, the story's subject), in the author's discourse (i.e., what the nun conveys through subterfuge that the priest then probably relays unintentionally). Further, one must theorize about "the interpretations that may be constructed by the original receiving community [*loyal* Spaniards and *disloyal* Blacks] and by outside observer-analysts like ourselves" (Radner and Lanser 6). African American feminist poet and critic Harryette Mullen describes similar textual acts as examples of "runaway tongues": the rhetorical skill exhibited by "slaves who individually and collectively refuse to know their place."[94]

CHICABA'S SILENCE IN THE *Oración fúnebre*

The *Oración fúnebre* in honor of Chicaba consists of a synopsis of her biography elucidated through two topoi: Chicaba as a new Queen of Sheba and as an embodiment of the three gifts of the Magi. These two expanded motifs are paeans to her royal mien and virtuous life, and therefore could not have originated from her or represent her voice. Rather, they are the products of Paniagua's grandiloquence. This extravagant prose constitutes the first serious foray in the campaign for her canonization.

For instance, the eulogy draws on several elements in the account of the Queen of Sheba's visit to the court of King Solomon (1 Kings 10:1–10; 2 Chronicles 9:1–9) to establish Chicaba's eligibility for sainthood through biblical precedents. Paniagua must have been aware of the genealogical tradition that reckoned the queen's descent back to Noah's cursed son Ham and thereby identified her as Ethiopian or Black.[95] According to various interpreters of the story, the Queen of Sheba had heard reports about the king's great wisdom and the lavishness of his court, and her expedition was to ascertain the veracity of this information and to compare her status and intelligence to his. If the stories about him were true, then she hoped to discover the source of his good fortune and wisdom. She tested his acumen with riddles, and she observed the opulence of his household, which included wives, courtiers, and servants. His magnificence was beyond all imagining. Solomon's achievements, she concluded, were due to the power of his God: "Blessed be the Lord your God who delighted in you and has set you on the throne of Israel; because He loves Israel unendingly, he has made you king to maintain law and justice" (1 Kings 10:10).[96] When she departed, she presented him with gifts of gold, jewels, spices, frankincense, and myrrh. This is a variation on a conversion narrative.

The queen's journey from curiosity to conviction is allegorically parallel to Chicaba's transportation to Spain for catechesis. The *Oración fúnebre* draws a parallel between Chicaba, the young princess from the gold mining area of West Africa, and the Queen of Sheba, whose aristocratic station and bearing, intelligence, great wealth, and power mitigated her inauspicious lineage. Not only is the captive purported to be royalty, it justifies her removal from her home and her pursuit of the God to whom she has pledged her troth. But also in the course of his eulogy, Paniagua transforms the metaphors representing Chicaba from her personification of the noble gift-bearer to the gift itself. That is, by a kind of synecdochic sleight of hand, he reenacts the transmogrification of enslavement, the turning a human into a thing. Thus, when in the eulogy Paniagua depicts Chicaba as the "golden gift," he silences her by objectifying her as a commodity.[97]

The literary convention of the Magi worked in much the same way—through metaphors of precious gifts and a long pilgrimage. Thus, the topoi of the Queen of Sheba and the Three Kings complement each other in Paniagua's depiction of Sor Teresa as an asset to La Penitencia, Salamanca, and indeed Spain itself.[98] Wise Men, Kings, and Magi—these are the titles by which Christianity knows the visitor-astrologers who follow a star to the Holy Family (Matthew 2:1–12) The eulogy drew analogies between their pursuit of a star to find the Christ Child and Chicaba's search for the First Cause. She sought the Creator in her people's god, the Morning Star, before she discovered the Madonna and Child through a mystical encounter. However, this was but the beginning of her quest that necessarily led her to Spain and the convent by way of enslavement. In a sense, the prescient and sagacious African child was much like the Magi, who "as wise men, seers and dreamers . . .

come from a remote land in quest of knowledge. . . . Intellectual zeal, the willingness to adventure for the sake of finding truth is manifest in the progress of these travelers."[99] So it was with Chicaba, explains the funeral oration. However, the text did not dwell on the analogy between its subject and the kings. Rather, it focused on her as the personification of the gifts: gold, frankincense, and myrrh. She was a treasure who enlarged the coffers of the national and monastic spiritual economies in the several meanings of the term: first, as a slave in the household of aristocrats; second, through her prayers and sacrifice; and third, through her dispersal of resources bequeathed to her by the marchioness and the largesse donated by her admirers.

The rhetorical structure of the encomium left little space for the "voice" of Chicaba to interject her version of the narrative through diverting the plot from an unambiguous, triumphal conclusion that confirmed dominant ideology of the era. There is no inkling of her defiance of social norms or resistance to oppression, nor is there a sense of her determination for self-liberation—all present in the *Vida*. The *Oración fúnebre* and the *Vida* share the same narrative matter, but their tropeic foundations and written performances are completely different.

IDENTIFYING CHICABA'S GENDERED AND RACED "VOICE" IN THE HAGIOGRAPHIC STRUCTURE

Catherine Mooney's call (quoted above) for a strategy to guide the historian or literary scholar toward identifying and disentangling the contributions of the principals of a hagiography betrays a common slippage among the terms "voice," "agency," and "writer/author." Discerning the differences between the teller or tellers of/in the story supposedly indicates the relationship of the informant to the scribe in/of a given text. In the case of the polyvocal *Vida*, this task is complex because it requires developing a method for teasing out occasional distinctions in perspective between Paniagua and Chicaba. Determining what constitutes whose "voice" includes performing historically appropriate gendered and racial readings of the text, and then searching for places of contradiction and ambiguity in the narrative that mark a site where Chicaba's implied "voice" critiques, either obviously or subtly, the dominant ideology of the era.

The poetic plaint in Chapter 35 that retells and reinterprets the biblical story of the two sisters of Lazarus is the most obvious place to listen for Chicaba's voice because the text identifies these stanzas as her composition.[100] These lines constitute a daring interpretation of the passages in the tenth chapter of the Gospel of Luke. Here the poem's persona makes so bold as to ask Christ to reconsider His pronouncement that Mary, who has not helped to serve Him, "has chosen the better part"—that is, to sit in conversation with the Master. And He adds emphatically that this privilege shall not be taken from her. The verses seem to question the justice of a conventual hierarchy that rewards those who enjoy a life of prayer at the expense of others who must perform the menial labor that maintains the household. A religious woman such as Chicaba, who understood herself as a contemplative, as a choir nun, might question her assigned role as convent drudge, for clearly this was not her choice. Instead of resorting to orthodox Catholic theology to explain this disparity, the speaker understands her place among so many brides of Christ because she has "seen it before" in polygynous marriages. It stands to reason that this gesture toward an early Ewe marital structure most likely reflects a textual intervention by the hagiographic subject, Chicaba. In spite of the efforts of the first chapters of the *Vida* to depict Chicaba's people in a European mold, this slippage in the poem quoted late in the text briefly turns the arc of the narrative back toward its beginnings. The "teller's" voice reminds the readers of her origin.

Feminist-narratologist Susan Lanser specifies two schools of critics for whom "voice" has significance: One such group consists of those who study the history and representations of "silenced communities—peoples of color, people struggling against colonial rule, gay men and lesbians," and women.[101] They use the lenses or refracting prisms of gender, race, class, and/or sexuality as mechanisms of analyses. Detecting "voice" is essential to their study of categories of difference that, in Joan W. Scott's words, "signify relationships of unequal social and political power" and, as such, is fundamental to scrutinizing ideologies embedded in texts.[102] The second group comprises structuralists, particularly narrative theorists, who use the term differently. In the formalist field of narrative poetics, "voice" is a property of the *teller* of the tale—even in written works—and is discrete from the author or other characters in the story. In this sense, it is a technical term connected to "specific forms of textual practice" (Lanser 5).

However, Lanser holds that these seemingly oppositional interpretations of "voice"— one that concentrates on the representation of social discourses and their ramifications, the other on narrative technique and structure—"converge in what Mikhail Bakhtin has called a 'sociological poetics'" (Lanser 5). In other words, the various forms of "materialist poetics"—theories and analyses of race, gender, and class—and narratology provide technologies that are combined to detect, examine, and critique ideologies expressed openly and/or embedded in oral and written communications.

According to the critical theorist Catherine Belsey, literature is an ideological apparatus, for literary works represent the human relationships (e.g., interpersonal, political, and religious) that are necessary for the "existence and perpetuation" of hegemonic social and economic systems. Understood as a comprehensive set of normative principles espoused and promulgated by the dominant class, ideology continues and propagates itself through "a range of representations (discourses, images, myths)" that purport to reflect simply and directly "the real relations" (i.e., social, economic, and political) that people inhabit.[103] However, it is more accurate to describe ideology as constituting, in the words of Louis Althusser, "the imaginary relationship of individuals to their real conditions of existence."[104] That is, it is "both a real and an imaginary relation to the world," and it unobtrusively directs and shapes how people negotiate their lived social relations while it obscures the consequences of conforming to its tacit directives (Belsey 57). Because dominant ideology functions to "naturalize" social reality, it supports structures of unequal power in the society that represents itself in discourses. This feigned "naturalness" enables dominant constructs of sociality—for instance, slavery and gender relations in seventeenth- and eighteenth-century Spain—to take on the status of "commonsense" or unquestionable creed. The purpose of a hagiography is to represent a life-story that exemplifies conformity to the dominant ideology that its loyal audience understands as reasonable and foundational. In doing so, it attempts to elide any internal contradictions, ambiguities, and silences that are constitutive of ideology. Thus, it suppresses and/or co-opts or recuperates alternate discourses or "voices."

The "voice" of the *teller*, as an articulation from a stifled or subordinate social position, is what Radner and Lanser identify as an *implied* presence in the margins of the text.[105] It inhabits and emanates from incongruities and absences in ideological representations. In this context, the *Vida* has two "tellers": first, the obvious voice of the author/narrator Paniagua, who is a spokesperson for normativity and who relays what he has learned about Teresa Chicaba, the subject, in conversations with her and from her autobiographical musings and, second, the subject's voice sometimes quoted directly but more often filtered through the author at a remove of time and place. She is an *implied* narrator, the original story*teller*.

On its face, the *Vida* appears to be a representation of eighteenth-century dominant ideology authored by Paniagua; and, as such, it is riddled with inconsistencies and stifled speech. As the life story of a Black woman (ex-)slave, it is the ideal text for cultural/political analysis of race and gender, where a critic-theorist can discover the "voice" of the *teller* at sites of ideological contradiction or ambiguity around the issues of slavery. For instance, while the story is at pains to depict the abduction of Chicaba as an idyllic encounter with a gallant escort, the ensuing voyage aboard the ship gives lie to this portrayal: ominous black birds hector the slaver, and the captive child is tormented by a desperate thirst. In a similar equivocation about her status in the Mancera household, the *Vida* describes the affections of the marquis and the marchioness as almost parental. But to keep order among the other servants, they had to "hide their love for her" (Chapter 9), which is the reason she ate and lived with the servants and another slave, the Turkish girl. There she became vulnerable to attack not only from her unconverted roommate but also from the free Christian servants in the residence. Her isolation facilitated this violence and abuse, which was emblematic of the culture of slavery. Direct references to "slavery" are sparse in the first half of the text; however, there are more forthright descriptions of her status as a bondswoman after she enters La Penitencia. From that point on, the *Vida* represents the menial tasks assigned her in the community as simply aiding her development of the virtue of humility—e.g., Chapter 23. It is through these and other situations that the marginal teller implies the conditions of her oppression.

Isolation in both her secular and monastic habitations signaled Chicaba's profound social difference as a racial Other. Only the inducement of an exorbitant dowry paid from the marchioness's bequest secured her acceptance in any convent, and once she arrived at La Penitencia, it appears that she was never allowed to reside in canonical enclosure with the rest of the community. At first, the hagiography presents her segregation as either a practice associated with her status as a postulant—a neophyte—or as a spiritual trial. Gradually the issue of her marginalization diminishes as the chronicle progresses so that only a savvy reader who traces the location of Teresa Chicaba's lodging throughout the remaining text is aware that she continues to occupy the liminal space of the infirmary. However, the incident that recounts the displeasure of her Spouse for permitting priests to visit her "cell" reveals that her lodgings are not in the cloister. Those familiar with conventual architecture know that nuns' quarters in enclosure do not open into secular space—that is, "outside." Had her cell really been inside the cloister, it would not have been accessible to the clerics.

There are at least two ways to understand this episode that appears in Chapter 29, in the last third of the *Vida*. Either it is erroneous to assert that the community allotted her a proper "cell," whose location complied with the regulations of canon law for enclosure; in which case, this is an instance of ideology functioning to naturalize her liminality by obscuring her status as permanent "outsider."[106] Or this is an attempt on the part of the implicit teller to emphasize the extent of Teresa's (or her own) exclusion from the community. Analyzed through this political poetics, Christ's reprimand of her for violating the seclusion expected of His spouse makes clear to her and to the audience of the hagiography, through the implied narrator, that He is the true arbiter of consecrated space. Thus, by mandating her claustration, He situates her room "virtually" inside the enclosure and signals that she is a true member of the community of His spouses. She is a "sister," no matter the lived reality. This is also an implied rebuke to the community that excludes her.[107]

Therefore, the location of her cell architecturally and textually provides an opportunity for political and structural analysts to examine two kinds of intersectionality: discursive (race and gender) and theoretical (structuralist). For instance, occasionally the convergence of the social formations of race and gender has the tendency to elide one or the other discourse; but the anxiety attendant to the placement of Chicaba's quarters is where discursive confluence is so conspicuous as to stimulate an examination of the *Vida* through this compound lens of materialist poetics. That is to say, her Africanity was not the only obstacle to Chicaba's wholehearted acceptance to La Penitencia, but it also was the commonly held conviction that her gender, transmogrified by its connection to her race, produced an inclination toward profligacy. Her Blackness always put her claims to being and remaining a virgin in doubt. Thus, the apparition of her censuring Spouse in Chapter 29 is of utmost importance because it constitutes an acknowledgment of the precariousness of her reputation; an assurance that Christ and His mother supervise and guard her virtue; an authentication of her sacred espousal; and finally her re-positioning, relocation, into the symbolic heart of the convent community.[108]

The narrativization of ecclesiastical anxiety about the assignment of a cell to Teresa Chicaba exposes a tension between the marginal "voice's" own understanding of her relation to Christ as well as to the Dominican order versus the hagiographic apparatus that represents a contrasting and exclusionary religious orthodoxy. These instances of contestation comprise a series of a second type of "intersectionality," which is the combination of two strategies of analysis—materialist (social and political) and structural—that is, sociological poetics. Each theoretical system enables analysis of different modes of ideological production: Materialist poetics directly probes depictions of political, social, economic, gender, and racial discourses. The function of structuralist poetics, the narratological project, is multiple. One aspect examines discrete elements of a story—for example, episodes such as Chicaba's first lonely nights in the infirmary and the vision discussed above—while another component follows the way a plot unfolds and its trajectory toward "conclusion." This method of analysis allows the critic to see that "narrative technique not simply as a product of ideology but as ideology itself" (Lanser 5). Put another way, it allows us to see narrative practice not simply as a vehicle for ideology but as ideology itself.

The course of the narrative comprises the story's attempts to replicate dominant ideology, sometimes in tension with forces of resistance—contradictions internal to ideology (i.e., counterdiscourses)—and thereby to reinforce or to transform normative beliefs. By plot—in two of its meanings, by cabal and by structure—narrative organizes or orders episodes, parts of the story, to conform to ideological (theological, sexual, and social) assumptions and early-modern economic values. Thus, by design, it produces the impression of logical progression and aesthetic resolution. In this way, narrative both produces and is integral to ideology. To describe narrative as "a way of reasoning about a situation" suggests that the plot that structures the story is a mechanism of its logic, an engine that generates "meanings through temporal succession."[109] So movement from the beginning through the middle to the end corresponds to "problem, complication, and resolution."[110] Namely, the story seems to represent cause-and-effect relationships through the chronological sequence of events—as in the *Vida*. No matter whether the ordering is arranged temporally or causally, the narrative is teleologically determined.[111] Not only does each structural element of narrative govern the outcome of the story, but also, in a sense, the literary argument is often tautological, for it is but a reiteration, a repetition of dominant ideology. The results are rigged—they are structured and ultimately predictable. Such is the case in the *Vida* in the accounts of the assignment of lodging and the stories of "the cell."

This hagiography shares narrative conventions with some other genres that conform to their own versions of narrative teleology. For example, one can perform a gender-reading of the story as a spiritual variation of the romantic-marriage plot, whose trajectory moves from first encounter through betrothal to formal nuptials. Or one can execute a racial study of the *Vida* as an early version of the slave narrative, which passes from capture and enslavement through transportation, bondage, perhaps to the acquisition of literacy, concluding in freedom.[112]

While the rationale of a nun's story is to extol virginity and to portray the struggles requisite to preserving celibacy, it is also an account of the fulfillment of a great love between Christ and His intended that culminates in permanent vows and enclosure. Early in the *Vida*, the young Chicaba is drawn to an empyreal presence who is incarnated as the White Child; and after a series of assignations between them in an Edenic glade, she pledges herself to Him forever. From this point on, the momentum of each episode is single-mindedly directed toward meriting and achieving vowed union with Him, to becoming a bride of Christ.

The degree to which the *Vida* achieves the objective of this marriage is a measure of the relative power of competing ideologies: the drive of the marriage plot toward marital union versus the insistence of the racial narrative for separation or segregation. The tug of racial division distorts the arc of the plot trajectory causing the story to miss its target by a few degrees, an amount so small as nearly to conceal its failure. Though there is a description of some kind of profession ceremony in Chapter 24, the text represents the teller bemoaning her status as just that of a third order *secular* and not a fully professed *religious*.[113] Only by resorting to the realm of the supernatural through a vision of the assembled community of all deceased Dominicans gathered before the founders of the order can the plot resolve itself. (Later, in Chapter 35, the narrative records a poetic lament attributed to Chicaba; this poem describes the inequitable treatment of her by Christ's "other wives." A longer discussion of this piece is in the synopses of chapters that follow.) Thus, the transformative capacity of plot structure is never fully achieved through Chicaba's mystical "marriage," her profession—the necessary condition for her residing in the cloister—in the material ("real") world; so the narrative must resort to the spiritual domain to suggest a possible modification of ideology. This is the same solution the story performs to overcome the obstacle to her living in enclosure.

Desire for enclosure must seem incongruous to those who read the *Vida* as a slave narrative, a genre that moves from bondage and subjugation to manumission. In this sense, the plot trajectory appears to have achieved its target halfway through the story, when the hagiography creates the impression that Teresa Chicaba achieves manumission to enter the convent *during* the marchioness's life—an assertion contradicted by historical evidence. For the aristocrat's behest insists that *after* her death, the young slave should receive her freedom. Whatever the circumstances of Chicaba's emancipation, the next episode constructs what will become an important feature of liberation narratives: the journey away from the site of confinement toward freedom. Thus, the description of her elaborate expedition to La Penitencia emphasizes her turning her back on the place of her enslavement. But in one sense, she never accomplishes her objective; for the episcopal authority first nullifies her acceptance to the monastery and then demands the payment of an extortionate dowry to the convent. Every stage of the process to full admittance is thwarted so that she never achieves solemn profession as a nun, acceptance to the choir—that group of sisters who constitute the communal governing body and who participate in the most important liturgies—and residence in the cloister. The paradox that enclosure represents in the discourse of freedom rests in the conviction that the deeper a nun goes into seclusion, the more she curtails her mobility in and contact with the secular world, the freer she becomes. For when one considers the relative privacy of a cell, the jurisdiction monastic communities had over their finances and close associations, and their arrangements for communal governance, then nuns were some of the "freest" women in Europe during that time. Therefore, had the narrative been able to record Chicaba's attainment of a place in the architectural and social core of La Penitencia, the plot would have reached the resolution one expects in slave narratives—especially the prevailing model based on the stories by and about men—complete escape. The conclusion of Sor Teresa's story prefigures that of an African American woman more than a hundred years in the future, when Harriet Jacobs contrasts gaining legal emancipation with achieving the material circumstances that free women of her station expected. At the end of *Incidents in the Life of a Slave Girl*, Jacobs laments: "Reader, my story ends with freedom; not in the usual way, with marriage. I and my children are now free! We are as free from the power of slaveholders as are the white people of the north; and though that, according to my ideas, is not saying a great deal, it is a vast improvement in *my* condition. The dream of my life is not yet realized. I do not sit with my children in a home of my own. I still long for a hearthstone of my own, however humble."[114] This foregoing address to the audience is a metafictional, self-conscious confession of the structural incompleteness of the narrative, but the *Vida* makes no such admission. Instead, the text attempts to recover from its inadequacy through ambiguity or recourse to subterfuge. Like Harriet Jacobs, Chicaba never achieves a "room of her own."

Episodes that ambiguously represent Sor Teresa's virtual religious professions and conventual inclusion not only mark sites of gender and racial intersectionality, but they also simultaneously indicate "the juncture of 'social position and literary practice'"—that is, the confluence of materialist and structural analyses—that "embodies the social, economic, and literary conditions under which [voice] has been produced" (Lanser 5). These are some of the locations where the implied teller emerges through the interstices of the narrative to express herself subtly, sometimes only as the presence who tugs the ideological arc out of alignment (Lanser 4–5). So not only do readers encounter a representation of the subordinate subject through the direct quotations that the dominant author repeats in the text; but they can also recognize Chicaba in the limens of this polyvocal narrative through her impact on its plot structure.

Clearly the Sor Teresa encountered through this method is not completely congruent with the historical person who is the model for this hagiography, because this life-story is like other biographical texts—even those with ample archival evidence—an act of representation/re-presentation. Consequently none of their subjects can ever be fully accessible. This is especially so when the researcher's instrument for discerning the subject's "voice" or her intervention in the work is heavily dependent upon textual interpretation through materialist poetics, structural analysis, and semiotics (deciphering codes).

CHICABA'S "CODED" RESISTANCE

At first glance, interpretation seems unstable ground on which to found the contention that Teresa Chicaba's perspective is sometimes observable in the *Vida*. However, Radner and Lanser contend that there are "texts that may be implicitly coded." The African "nun" occasionally communicates through this kind of covert "set of signals"—whether it is by what she says, the dissimulative language she uses, the behavior she exhibits, or the literary structures and conventions she disrupts. This kind of encryption becomes necessary "when there is a situation of oppression, dominance, or risk for an individual or identifiable group." Members of these subordinated groups form the disloyal minority of a complex audience that is composed of themselves—those competent in deciphering or interpreting messages of opposition, defiance, resistance, or revision—and of the privileged—those occupying positions of power that allow them the luxury of being culturally monolingual. The textual performance that everyone witnesses is *supposed* to appear uncoded. Or put another way, the presentation is meaningful on its face, independent of any secreted message, because the best concealment of these instances of alterity is their apparent integrality to the dominant discourse professed in or by the text. But for a few, there are two legible stories available for their interpretation (Radner and Lanser 3–10).

These secondary accounts or messages are not necessarily deliberate, intentionally or consciously executed. Rather, they arise out of the lived context of its subaltern subjects. These subordinate narratives "infect"—so to speak—the body of the text unbeknownst to the document's primary producer/author and often even to the infiltrating agent/teller as well. As a consequence of the illusiveness of these shadow stories, even their "very codedness is arguable" (Radner and Lanser 5–7).

Yet there are strategies for extracting and interpreting "plausible, if provisional, meanings" from texts embedded with implied codes, and for discerning the perspective of subordinate subjects/tellers. First, the encoder must belong to a class of people who by their relative powerlessness or the nonconformity of their subject are at risk of censorship, discipline, or punishment. Membership in such a group often necessitates the use of some form of subterfuge, which one might call a "code." The initiator of such acts of symbolic resistance need not employ an agreed-upon set of signals, nor should she have a particular target audience in mind, nor should she intend, consciously or subconsciously, to transmit hidden messages. The primary audience and the "intentionality" that an act of coding seems to suggest derives from the relative jeopardy of the teller's life-situation and the social position of most of those like her; it is a condition of the context in which she lives or they live. One might metaphorize coding as an "instinct" or a complex reflexive behavior triggered in particular situations; thus, it is unintentionally launched and "targeted"—what Radner and Lanser might term "operationally intentional." "Careful and respectful scholarship grounded in the *specific cultural context*" from which the text or performance emerges and that it represents should enable the proficient researcher "to posit whether an act of coding has occurred" (Radner and Lanser 9; emphasis in the original). Familiarity with conventions and conditions of production (i.e., cultural and historical contexts) assists or authorizes the reader to infer not only the presence of cultural encryptions but also the "meaning" of their concealed messages. In this regard, "interpretation" is always an act of inference through which the critic-researcher, perhaps more than the historian, approximates a plausible understanding, explanation, of a text and approaches—but cannot fully capture—the voice and perceptions of the subject/teller of the narrative.

It seems reasonable to infer, therefore, that as a slave—albeit a "privileged" one—and a religious "sister" with an inferior, anomalous monastic status, Chicaba probably instigated small acts of "day-to-day resistance" to the socioreligious system and its executors that oppressed her.[115] And undoubtedly, through insistent repetitions of her version of events, she must have interfered with some preconceived notions of saintliness and thereby promoted, even retrospectively, "manipulations" of the hagiographic narrative. That is, a reader can detect through sociological poetics and semiotic analysis at least two types of defiance in the *Vida*: structural/textual "revisions"—for lack of a better name—and instances of "coded" resistance and personal assertion. All categories constitute sites where Teresa Chicaba's "voice" emerges.

The *Vida* is an amalgam of two genres, a hagiography and a proto-ex-slave narrative. Though both these forms are present in the *Vida*, they are in tension. Materialist and structural poetics seem well suited for disentangling these genres. The former endeavors to depict its protagonist as compliant with the principles of the Church, the State, and the family/household, when it acts as an agent of or in accord with the preceding two institutions. Although Chicaba's perspective often synchronizes with the ideology of the saint's legend, one must consider that even her cooperation in the compilation of her life-story is a small act of resistance, for she is insisting on her place in the canon of the Church's elect—an assembly from which she traditionally would be excluded. However, the raison d'être for ex-slave narratives is the depiction and instigation of resistance to the status quo; therefore, scrutiny focused on this genre benefits from attentiveness to coded counternarratives.

In this regard, the *Vida*'s audience might better distinguish her voice contesting the hagiographic representations through the medium of its embedded ex-slave narrative. For example, both literary forms examine the issue of suffering. On the one hand, the hagiography sees anguish or mortification as a means of attaining identification with Christ's passion; therefore, devout spiritual practice encourages those striving for holiness to embrace and endure pain without complaint. This is the advice to Chicaba of her confessor whom the household servants tormented for his association with her. The *Vida* is faithful to the same ethos; therefore, the text resorts to spiritual explanations for some of the violent attacks she sustains: The devil is the cause of her near-drowning in the pool at Buen Retiro Park and for the dangerous malice of the Turkish girl. Chicaba's humility prevents her seeking the protection of her masters and exacting revenge from those who were instruments of evil. Instead, through her prophetic gifts, she learns that Providence has assessed the appropriate reparations for her pain. Reports in the *Vida* that she knows of the sad fates of her persecutors are one kind of implied code.

On the other hand, narratives of ex-slaves, with their focus on violence as the engine of bondage, depict gratuitous physical brutality. Historian Nell Irvin Painter contends that the sadism of slavery has the potential to "soul-murder."[116] This is a far cry from the redemptive picture that Christian theology draws of the benefits of suffering. Though Painter's typology of maltreatments applies to the system of U.S. slavery, one may infer that those held in subjugation in Spain suffered comparable physical cruelties. Similar to various harrowing incidents in the *Vida*, chronicles of the lives of ex-bondswomen in the Americas involve, indeed emphasize, matters of the body—sexual abuse, ruthless beatings, and heavy manual labor.

The incident of the Turkish girl is an example of how the *Vida* negotiates a balance between the hagiographical necessity to preclude stories that impugn Chicaba's chastity and the narrative's obligation to lay bare the sexual exploitation of slave women. Spaniards were undoubtedly aware of improprieties that occurred with the enslaved. Like their Euro-American counterparts, they blamed the women for instigating the carnal activity. But by making a priest culpable for the seduction and abandonment of the non-Christian slave, Chapter 11 undertakes to reverse received notions about bondswomen's willing availability to sexual advances. By displacing this breach of virtue onto the deceived Turkish girl, the narrative maintains Chicaba's innocence, even as she inhabits a site fraught with danger and eros. The nocturnal attacks of the devil using the guilt-ridden roommate as his agent may be a credible explanation of the protagonist's jeopardy for the eighteenth-century reader. But the description of these assaults may also be Chicaba's implied code for male intrusions into their private spaces and her defiance of their abuse. Also, the story of the African woman's escape from sexual peril entails further ideological resistance to the situation through the reverse logic of the narrative. Her Blackness is a sign of her paradoxical association with evil and lasciviousness; but it is also a mark of her physical unattractiveness; thus, her dark complexion paradoxically is said to protect her from sexual advances and thereby ensure her purity.[117]

If her skin color guarded her virtue, it did not protect her from the taunts and blows delivered by the other retainers. They mocked her by calling her *infanta* (the little princess), a sarcastic reference to the rumors circulating about her royal origins, her treatment as the masters' favorite, or perhaps her bearing—how she carried herself. Whatever motivated their derision, the label both affirmed and denied her aristocratic claims to nobility. The worst offender among the staff was the very *aya* (governess) appointed to teach Teresa Chicaba the "exercises and accomplishments required" of a woman of a certain station (Chapter 9): presumably etiquette and deportment, perhaps some forms of needlework, and most assuredly, in the devout Mancera household, all the skills necessary to participate fully in religious devotions—e.g., reading prayer books and saints' lives and writing her examination of conscience. Performing these tasks placed the teacher in an untenable situation. She was to instruct a slave, a member of the underclass, in the skills appropriate to those in the strata above them both. This must have enraged the *aya* beyond her capacity for self-control.[118]

After a statement at the beginning of the text that Paniagua used writings by and conversations with Sor Teresa to compile the *Vida*, the episode with the *aya* is the first intimation of how the slave may have become literate. The subject of literacy has been central to the study of American ex-slave narratives from their emergence at the end of the eighteenth century through the twentieth century. The early audience believed that if the author of the autobiography could write, it evidenced the "reliability of the text"—that is, its authenticity.[119] Some recent scholars share this view. Also, when these works were published, Euro-Americans generally believed that the capacity for literacy evinced Black writers' aptitude for rational thinking. These works thus verified that their authors "understood and participated appreciably in the life of the mind" (Barrett 118) and that they grasped the meaning of their subjugation.[120] Though the intellectual ability their narratives demonstrate established their personhood as well as their right to emancipation, it did not distance them completely from the commonly held association of Blackness with bodiliness, for graphic descriptions of arduous physical labor and brutal physical abuse are an obligatory component of these stories.

Ex-slave life-stories authored by men, especially the 1845 life of Frederick Douglass, established the prototype for the components of the narrative; they moved from capture or birth, through the violence and miseries of enslavement, the representation of the acquisition of literacy, to escape. But according to Harryette Mullen, the few extant autobiographical accounts of ex-slave women do not emphasize literacy—even the works manifestly authored by the protagonists (244).

African American women's narratives, like Chicaba's *Vida*, are a composite of two genres, one literary and the other principally oral. In the case of the American texts, the former is the sentimental novel, which advocates submission, and the latter is the resistant slave narrative, whose substratum betrays its origins in orality (Mullen 245). Sor Teresa's hagiography is a similar splicing of literary and oral, submission and resistance, saint's life and slave's chronicle. African American women and Afro-Spanish Sor Teresa write from their bodies and record their experiences as females entrapped by slavery, marked by beatings, and enclosed in constricted domestic spaces. For example, the governess inscribed Chicaba's body with lifelong scars as payment exacted for the humiliation of having to instruct a slave; these stripes were the price the child paid for the literacy she erroneously hoped would attain her membership among the choir nuns of a religious community—a group for whom literacy was a prerequisite. In spite of the divine retribution the teacher supposedly suffered, she was ironically doubly successful: She probably taught Chicaba to read and write, an act that should have given the slave access to the life of the mind, as the West understood it. And she branded the child physically thereby substantiating that a Black woman would always be primarily identified by and associated with corporeality. In other words, it is implied in the account of the *aya*'s "merciless blow," which caused its victim to suffer for the rest of her life, that emancipation could not completely free a slave from the effects of that violent institution. No amount of patronage, education, or careful rearing would be sufficient to relieve one of the stigma, the imprint of cruel domination.[121]

While the *Vida* portrays the anguish Chicaba endures at the hands of fellow servants in the Mancera household, the story to this point does not describe the labor she actually performs there. This is part of the loyal narrative's project: to gloss over or obscure her position as a slave in the household. But shortly after she enters La Penitencia, as she begins to have doubts about her vocation there, she starts to compare the tasks expected of her in the monastery with those in her former situation. Chapter 23 catalogs the communal decisions that marginalized her during her novitiate and caused her to suffer: The nuns "did not allow her to attend liturgy"; they "treated her like a *slave*" (emphasis added). This offhanded reference to her previous status lies in sharp contrast to the oft-repeated description of her as happy with and grateful to the Manceras; but it is congruent with the paean in Chapter 25 that lists humility as the first among all her virtues. The text implies that her "humble resignation" prior to entering La Penitencia prepared her for religious life, where she served God by "serving each of the nuns" as infirmarian and scullery servant. However, twelve chapters later the *Vida* records the poem attributed to her, where she becomes an exegete of the biblical story of the sisters Mary and Martha.[122] The hagiography describes the verse as an expression of jealous passion for Christ, her Spouse. However, a closer reading of the work invites another interpretation. This poem is a complaint about the drudgery of the work she performs; and as such, it is an instance of her coded resistance specifically to her misuse in the monastery and by implication, insinuation, to her previous labor in the household of the grandee.[123]

Finally, Radner and Lanser identify another form of implied coding: *appropriation*. This involves adapting the strategies of the dominant culture to the uses of those who are oppressed and disenfranchised (10). For example, though Chicaba's status at La Penitencia gave her no voice in convent governance, she used her access to funds from either the Mancera behest or personal benefactors she cultivated in her office as an extern (someone not cloistered from the public) to pay the dowries of novices who were short of funds: "How many sisters are now happily nuns who when they entered did not have any dowry other than what they obtained through the agency of Teresa" (Chapter 34)? This story of her largesse is a subtle boast uttered *sotto voce*, and it suggests that she must have eventually developed influence among the sisters of the chapter (choir nuns who governed and held offices). Thus, when someone sympathetic to Sor Teresa was elected prioress, an adversary complained "in the shrillest of tones: 'It is a tough thing that we must be ruled by a negress, and because the prioress is totally under her influence, we must live subjected to her will'" (Chapter 27). One can infer from this disgruntled sister's rant that Chicaba eventually found an alternate strategy to opposing her persecution as an outsider or liminal agitator; instead, she wrought change incrementally from within the system, through the strategy of appropriation.

Obviously these readings of Chicaba's voice are subject to interpretation, and admittedly interpretation is a political act. The authors of this introduction believe that ferreting out and analyzing the coded communication in a work such as the *Vida*, when performed rigorously—as the writers hope they exemplify here—can provide a medium through which the "subaltern can speak."[124] When in the name of scholarly "objectivity" one is blind to Chicaba's presence in the margins of the hagiography and deaf to her voice speaking from the subtext, one has embraced another form of political action. To ignore the plausibility of Sor Teresa's covert interventions, revisions, and strategies of resistance in the narrative is to misrepresent this attentive and perceptive woman—who must have benefited from her rearing in the court of an aristocrat—as naïve about the importance of Paniagua's proposed endeavor and as passive or submissive in his process of recording her life. The interpretations in this introduction to the English edition of the *Vida* characterize an alternate politics of reading inspired by what scholar Marcus Rediker calls "history from below."[125]

Rediker explains that his grandfather, a Kentucky coal miner, was the inspiration for the kind of research he does: writing the history of slaves chained in the crowded holds of ships, common seamen, pirates, and members of America's working class—those who have been "left out of elite, historical narratives." These are people who "did not speak through documents of their own making," yet he manages to encounter them by "reading until [he] hears their voices" (n.p.). Conscientious close reading is what he is describing here. It is also how historian Nell Irvin Painter describes her research process: her multiple readings of the same archival documents enable her to excavate the secrets buried within these records—"to hear subaltern voices and recognize phenomena that had not previously been investigated seriously" (127). In part, this introduction is an attempt to listen for Sor Teresa Chicaba's voice, and it is also an invitation from two literary researchers and theorists to others—especially those trained as historians—to continue work on this subaltern subject and on the African diasporic sisters still hidden in monastic annals.

NOTES TO THE INTRODUCTION: SECTION I

Where not otherwise noted, the translations provided are our own. We use a combination of notes and parenthetical citations to credit sources. With multiple references to a single work, we use an endnote the first time and parenthetical citations thereafter.

1. The cover of the 1764 edition (Figure 3) contains the following details:

    Compendio de la vida exemplar de la Venerable Madre Sor Teresa Juliana de Sto. Domingo, tercera professa en el Convento de Santa Maria Magdalena, vulgo de la Penitencia, Orden de Santo Domingo de la Ciudad de Salamanca. Su author el R. P. Don Juan Carlos Pan y Agua, Lector de Sagrada Theologia, y Rector de el Colegio de Clerigos Regulares Theatinos, vulgo de San Cayetano: Quien reverente lo dedica, y consagra A. S. Vicente Ferrer. Segunda impression: En Salamanca, por Eugenio Garcia de Honorato y San Miguel, Impressor de dicha Ciudad, y Real Universidad.

    Compendium of the exemplary life of the Venerable Mother Sister Teresa Juliana de Santo Domingo, professed tertiary in the Convent of Saint Mary Magdalene, better known as La Penitencia, of the Order of Saint Dominic, in the City of Salamanca. Its author is the Reverend Father Don Juan Carlos Paniagua, Lecturer in Sacred Theology and Rector of the Theatine College of Regular Clerics, better known as San Cayetano. He dedicates it reverently, and consecrates it to Saint Vincent Ferrer. Second printing: In Salamanca, printed by Eugenio García de Honorato y San Miguel, printer for this City and Royal University.

    Although the front page does not specify a year, the license to print is dated early 1752. The 1764 reprint has fewer pages than the 1752 edition but bears no difference in the text. The convent of Las Dueñas in Salamanca owns a copy of the 1764 reprint; we used their copy to create this edition. Sor María Eugenia Maeso published a limited edition of the 1764 reprint with modernized spelling and punctuation. See *Compendio de la Vida Ejemplar de la Venerable Madre Sor Teresa Juliana de Sto. Domingo, Tercera profesa en el convento de Santa María Magdalena, vulgo de la Penitencia, Orden de Santo Domingo de la ciudad de Salamanca. Su autor el R. Don Juan Carlos Pan y Agua. . . .*, transcribed by María Eugenia Maeso, OP (Salamanca: Imprenta Calatrava, 1999).

2. The Council of Trent (1545–1563) was convened by the Catholic Church in response to the Protestant Reformation. Its primary purpose was to make a definitive determination of the doctrines of the Church. In her book *Neither Saints nor Sinners*, Kathleen Ann Meyers discusses the spiritual biographies and autobiographies of women in Spanish America. She summarizes those councillor actions that are important to understanding the function of hagiographies thusly: "In general, the post-Tridentine church (the Catholic Church after the Council of Trent) created a more centralized role for itself in the supervision of individual spirituality through the use of three specific processes: confession, canonization, and inquisition" (Oxford: Oxford University Press, 2003), 8.

3. Juan Carlos Miguel de Paniagua, *Oracion funebre en las exequias de la Madre Sor Teresa Juliana de Santo Domingo, de feliz memoria, celebradas en el dia nueve de enero en el Convento de Religiosas Dominicas, vulgo de la Penitencia* [Funeral oration in tribute to the Mother Sister Teresa Juliana de Santo Domingo, of happy memory, celebrated on the ninth day of January in the Convent of Dominican Religious Women, better known as La Penitencia] (Salamanca, 1749).

4. La Mina Baja was a generic name given to the coastal area east of Elmina, which was sometimes called the Gold Coast of Western Africa. This area, also known as the Slave Coast, extended through present-day eastern Ghana, Togo, Benin, and the western coastal states of Nigeria.

5. The people known today as Ewe are an ethnic group formed after successive migrations sometime before and during the seventeenth century to what is present-day southeastern

Ghana (the Volta Region), southern Togo, and western Benin from either a Yoruba area in Benin, western Nigeria, or lands east of the Niger. Many Ewe were known in Spanish America as Mina. The name Ewe became used in the nineteenth century through extensive contact with Christian missionaries (Meera Venkatachalam, "Between the Devil and the Cross: Religion, Slavery, and the Making of the Anlo-Ewe," *Journal of African History* 53.1 [March 2012]: 49). Given the descriptions in the *Vida*, it is arguable that Chicaba lived somewhere near the Keta Lagoon and near the sea. This area saw an increasing interaction with the Atlantic slave trade after the Spanish *asiento*—monopoly of the slave trade—was acquired by the Dutch. See Emmanuel Kwaku Akyeampong, *Between the Sea and the Lagoon: An Eco-social History of the Anlo of Southeastern Ghana, c. 1850 to Recent Times* (Athens: Ohio University Press, 2001), 44. Our informants identified the origins of the names of Chicaba and most of her family as belonging to the group of Ewe languages. See Section 2 of the Introduction.

6. We know the subject of this book by several names: Teresa Juliana del Espíritu Santo (her name in the Marchioness of Mancera's last will); Sor Teresa Juliana de Santo Domingo; Sor Teresa de Santo Domingo (she seems to have dropped Juliana, the name of the marchioness, soon after she entered the convent); Sor Teresa; Chicaba; and Sor Teresa Chikaba (the name one finds on the prayer cards distributed by the Dominicans in Salamanca and on the stained glass window at Providence College, a Dominican institution in Rhode Island [Figure 4]). We will use Sor Teresa, Sor Teresa Chicaba, Teresa Chicaba, and Chicaba in this edition.
7. See Section 2 for a fuller explanation of this category of nun.
8. In his last will, signed in 1715, the Marquis of Mancera gave five hundred ducats for the construction of the Theatine college of San Cayetano in Madrid. In a previous will, signed in 1704, he declared that he had fulfilled all the terms of the will of Doña Juliana Portocarrero, his second wife (Archivo Histórico de Protocolos Notariales de Madrid, protocolo 13993, fol. 24r–48v, February 11, 1715).
9. Diego Torres Villarroel, *Vida exemplar y virtudes heroicas de el Venerable Padre Don Geronymo Abarrategui y Figueroa, clerigo reglar Theatino de San Cayetano y fundador de el colegio de Salamanca de San Cayetano y S. Andrès Avelino de la misma religion* [Exemplary life and heroic virtues of the Venerable Father Don Jerónimo Abarrategui y Figueroa, Theatine regular cleric who lived in the College of San Cayetano and San Andrés Avelino of the same order, and founder of this college] (Salamanca, 1752).
10. The obituary in this text covered three pages (29–31). It summarizes the details contained in the *Oración fúnebre*. The male members of the Dominican order read this account of Chicaba's life before the assembled chapter (voting members) and thereby signaled their intention to contribute to the effort of expanding her fame in order to start the process of canonization (*Acta Capituli Provincialis provinciae Hispaniae Ordinis Praedicatorum, celebrati in conventu Sancti Ildephonsi Regali Taurensi Die 27 Aprilis, anni Domini 1749*. Madrid, 1749). See Appendix 3.
11. The title page of the manuscript (Figure 5) contains the following details:

> Vida de la Venerable Negra, la Madre Sor Theresa Juliana de Santo Domingo de feliz memoria, Religiosa Profesa de la Tercera Orden de N. P. Sto. Domingo en el Religiosissimo Convento de Dominicas, vulgo de la Penitencia, de la Ciudad de Salamanca. Compuesta por un Devoto de Sn. Vicente Ferrer, Quien la dedica al mismo Santo. Con todas las licencias poeticas necesarias. En Zaragoza, año M.DCCLVII. (Por el D. D. Luis Soler y las Balsas)

> Life of the Venerable Black Woman, Mother Sister Teresa Juliana de Santo Domingo of happy memory, Professed Religious of the Third Order of Our Father Saint Dominic, in the Most Religious Convent of Dominican Nuns, better known as La Penitencia, in the City of Salamanca. Written by a Devotee of Saint Vincent Ferrer, and consecrated to the same Saint. With all the necessary poetic licenses. In Zaragoza, year 1757. (By Doctor Don Luis Soler y las Balsas)

The poem exists in a manuscript form, with the only known copy located in the New York Public Library's Schomburg Center for Black Research.

12. The use of *seguidillas* in hagiographic poems was fairly common at this time; see, for example, a contemporary poem by José Joaquín Benegasi y Luján, *Vida del portentoso negro San Benito de Palermo descripta en seis cantos jocoserios, del reducidissimo metro de seguidillas, con los argumentos en octavas* (Madrid, 1750).

13. Saint Vincent Ferrer (1350–1419), to whom Paniagua dedicates the *Vida*, is one of the most famous saints in the Dominican order. More than eight hundred miracles were attributed to him. Sor Teresa would become devoted to him to the end of her life. He participated in the forced conversion of many Jews in Spain before and during the pogroms of 1391. In 1412, during his stay in Salamanca, he preached a series of sermons on the end of the world, which gained him the title of Apostle of the Apocalypse (Vicente Galduf Blasco, OP, *Vida de San Vicente Ferrer* [Barcelona: Juan Flors, 1961], 189). During these sermons, he launched virulent attacks against the Jews of Castile and his anti-Jewish activities provoked the forced conversion of many in the kingdom of Aragón (Joseph Pérez, *Los judíos en España* [Madrid: Marcial Pons Historia, 2005], 134).

    The cult of Saint Vincent Ferrer was heavily promoted in Spanish America during the eighteenth century. They emphasized his capacity to cure the plague and also his association with the Last Judgment, when the angel brings the gospel to every nation. This was a message directed to the different indigenous populations. Sor Teresa Chicaba may have felt an affinity for this concept of preaching to "every nation, and tribe, and tongue, and people" (Revelation 14:16). Laura Ackerman Smoller, *The Saint and the Chopped-Up Baby: The Cult of Vincent Ferrer in Medieval and Early Modern Europe* (Ithaca, NY: Cornell University Press, 2014), 287.

14. Another summary of Chicaba's life appeared in Bernardo Dorado's *Compendio histórico de la ciudad de Salamanca, su antigüedad, la de su santa iglesia, fundación y grandezas que la ilustran* (Salamanca, 1776). In this work, the author quotes an epitaph that was said to be on Sor Teresa Chicaba's gravestone, which no longer exists.

15. "Vº Rº de la Mª Sor Theresa Juliana de Sto. Domingo, hija de el Rei de la Mina Baxa de el Oro, Tercera Profesa en el Convento de Sª Mª. Magdalª. vulgo dela Penitencia de Religiosas Dominicas de Salamcª mujer en quien la gracia hizo repetidas maravillas y sacandola acosta de ellas de la Guinea su Patria la dirigio a este Convento en donde vivio con opinion de notoria Santidad muchos años y llena de ellos y buena fama descanso en paz el dia 6 de Diciembre de el aº de 1748 a los 73 años de su edad."

16. Text and translation:

    > Fue esta Sra hija lexitima de el Rei de la Mina Baja de el oro y de su Muger llamada Abar. Llamaban en su tierra a la Me. Theresa la Chicaba. Sacola la Divina Providencia a costa de Maravillas de su tierra y protejida de la Divina Gracia, hizo en este Convento una vida tan ejemplar como ajustada. Fallecio el dia 6 de Diciembre de el año de 1748 con la misma virtud y comun edificacion que havia vivido: sus virtudes estan epilogadas en la oracion funebre que se dijo el dia 9 de enero en las exequias q a expensas de Devotos se hicieron a su memoria en la Iglesia de este Convento.

    > This lady was the legitimate daughter of the king of the Lower Gold Mine and his wife, called Abar. In her land, they called Mother Teresa, Chicaba. Divine Providence took her out of her land through a miraculous intervention. Protected by divine grace, she led a life in this convent as exemplary as it was observant of the rules. She passed away on December 6, 1748, with the same virtue and usual fortitude she had lived. Her virtues are eulogized in the funeral oration delivered on January 9, 1749, during the tributes paid by her devotees and celebrated in her memory in the church of this convent.

17. In a regular act of profession, a nun recites her vows in chapel before her prioress and community. Then she signs a document listing the promises she has just made to be chaste, humble, poor, and obedient. Strictly speaking, the signed document is the act of profession. The translators of this *Vida* have never seen this document, if it exists, for Sor Teresa Chicaba. The so-called act of profession in Appendix 2 does not contain her vows, so it looks like an act of profession after the fact without being a real act of profession. It retroactively includes her

in the community by making it look like she professed, when in fact there is no documented evidence that she did. This is important, because convents lived by written documents.

18. An autograph is a document written entirely in the hand of its author, who signs the document, as opposed to a printed text or one written by an amanuensis. This is a transcription of Sor Teresa Chicaba's only extant autographed letter (Figure 2):

> JMJ. Recibi su carta de Vd con mucho gusto y selebro su buena salud de Vd y ciento el no poder el ynbiar a su conocido de Vd el algua [sic] de nuestro padre pues en santo tomas la tienen para los enfermos. Discuro me tendra Vd en memoria para encomendarme a Su Majestad me aga la que debo cer y a Vd me le guarde muchos años Salamanca y enero 30. / Su menor cierba / Sor Teresa de Santo Domingo / Mi padre fray bisente figeroa.
>
> JMJ [Jesus, Mary and Joseph] / I received your letter with great pleasure. I celebrate your good health, and I am sorry I could not send your acquaintance the water of our Father, because they have it for the sick in [the church of] Santo Tomás. I hope you will keep me in your memory and commend me to His Majesty [God] so He makes me what I should be, and may He keep you in his care for many years. Salamanca, January 30. / The least of your servants / Sor Teresa de Santo Domingo / To my father Fr. Vicente Figueroa.

19. The idiosyncratic spellings in the letter denote the dialectal form of Andalusian Spanish spoken around the town of Marchena, where Chicaba lived with the Marchioness of Mancera before moving with her to Madrid. These spellings show the substitution of the letter *s* for *c* (*selebro* for *celebro*) and *c* for *s* (*ciento* for *siento*, *cer* for *ser*, *cierba* for *sierva*). This was typical of someone whose pronunciation did not make a distinction between the phonemes /θ/ and /s/, as many Andalusian speakers did not and still do not. Castilian Spanish, however, does make this distinction. The nuns of *La Penitencia* would have reflected this phonemic difference in their spelling by the middle of the eighteenth century, since most of them were from the region around Salamanca, where Castilian Spanish was the norm. None of them would have written this autograph letter for her. Another idiosyncratic spelling appears in the word *discuro*, for *discurro*. Apparently Sor Teresa Chicaba did not distinguish between the simple trill *r* and the multiple trill spelled in Spanish with *rr* between vowels. This spelling pattern can be observed today among some speakers of Spanish from the coastal areas of the Gulf of Biafra. See Amado Alonso, "Historia del ceceo y del seseo españoles," *Thesaurus* 7 (1951): 111–200.

20. According to Concha Torres Sánchez, in *La clausura femenina en la Salamanca del Siglo XVII: Dominicas y Carmelitas Descalzas* (Salamanca: Ediciones Universidad de Salamanca, 1991), almost 90 percent of female postulants to the Carmelite and Dominican convents in Salamanca were from that city itself (61–78).

21. Traditionally, Catholic religious orders have had a first order, of men, and a second order, of women, who live enclosed lives. A third order was constituted of nuns or sisters who in general came from less aristocratic origins and followed a different rule, sometimes with more lax obligations of claustration than those of second order nuns. This is the case in Salamanca, where Las Dueñas was a second order convent and La Penitencia was a third order Dominican convent. See "Life in La Penitencia—Chapter 19 to the Conclusion" in Section 2, "Discussion of the *Vida* by Chapters" for more information on religious life.

22. André Vauchez, *Sainthood in the Later Middle Ages*, translated by Jean Birrell (Cambridge: Cambridge University Press, 1997), chapters 9 and 10 (145–247).

23. Antonio Rubial García, "Las santitas del barrio: 'Beatas' laicas y religiosidad cotidiana en la ciudad de México del siglo XVII," *Anuario de Estudios Americanos* 59.1 (2002): 23.

24. Jodi Bilinkoff, *Related Lives: Confessors and Their Female Penitents, 1450–1750* (Ithaca, NY: Cornell University Press, 2005), 116.

25. Thomas J. Heffernan, *Sacred Biography: Saints and Their Biographers in the Middle Ages* (New York: Oxford University Press, 1988), 18.

26. Bilinkoff, 1–46. For example, Anne of Saint Bartholomew wrote an autobiography "in obedience to the orders" of her prioress, Teresa of Ávila, during 1607–1624. See Ana de San

Bartolomé, *Autobiography and Other Writings*, edited and translated by Darcy Donahue (Chicago: University of Chicago Press, 2008), 37. In the 1890s, Thérèse of Lisieux wrote *Story of a Soul*, her autobiography, under the orders of two prioresses: one was her sister Pauline, known as Mother Agnes, and the other was Mother Marie de Gonzague.

27. Catherine M. Mooney, "Voice, Gender, and the Portrayal of Sanctity," in *Gendered Voices: Medieval Saints and Their Interpreters*, edited by Catherine M. Mooney (Philadelphia: University of Pennsylvania Press, 1999), 8. This collection of eight essays uses various methodologies to extricate female voices from male-written hagiographies. See also Bilinkoff, "Whose *Life* Is It Anyway?" in *Related Lives*, 46–79.

28. Caroline Walker Bynum, "Foreword," in Mooney, *Gendered Voices*, ix–x.

29. Kristine Ibsen, *Women's Spiritual Autobiography in Colonial America* (Gainesville: University Press of Florida, 1999), 11–13, and all of chapter 2, "Body and Soul: Self-Representation as Confessional Discourse," 19–47.

30. Saint Teresa of Ávila, known also as Saint Teresa de Jesús, was born in Ávila, Spain, on March 28, 1515. She died in Alba de Tormes, on October 4, 1582. According to her hagiographers, who followed her own testimony in the *Libro de la vida* (*The Book of Her Life*), as a child she was adventuresome and courageous. When she was seven, she and her brother Rodrigo decided to venture into *tierras de moros* (territory under Muslim control) so that they could be martyred for the Church. But their plans were thwarted when their uncle found them outside the city walls and returned them to their family. At twelve she began to develop an appetite for books of chivalry, and in her adolescence she considered marriage. However, during a spiritual and psychological crisis probably precipitated by her mother's death, she was placed by her father into the care of Augustinian nuns at Santa María de Gracia, where Teresa attended the convent school. On November 2, 1535, she entered the Carmelite Monastery of the Incarnation in Ávila. Shortly after receiving the habit a year later, she fell seriously ill. For roughly twenty years she struggled to be more devout and prayerful. She is noted for her reform of the Carmelite Order, an eremitical community inspired by an earlier tradition. In 1562 she founded the first monastery of Discalced Carmelite nuns in Ávila, dedicated to Saint Joseph. Other foundations followed, paid for in part with money sent to her by her brother Lorenzo, who was living in Quito (Homero Serís, "Nueva genealogía de santa Teresa [Artículo-reseña]," *Nueva revista de filología hispánica* 10 [1956]: 374). Under the instruction of her directors, she became a prolific author of works on the spiritual life. Among the most famous are her autobiographic *Libro de la vida*, *Camino de perfección* (*The Way of Perfection*), and *Las moradas del castillo interior* (*The Interior Castle*).

31. A few girls who were favored slaves of educated women received an education from their sympathetic mistresses. Such was the case of the African American poet Phillis Wheatley. However, when her mistress, Susanna Wheatley, published Phillis's work, the community of male scholars and ministers doubted that she, or indeed any Black, had the intellectual skills to write such poetry, so a group of them convened to examine her. It was common to doubt whether Blacks had the capacity for literacy and learning. Readers, scholars, and historians often challenged Black authorship of narratives, poems, and essays; hence, it became customary to feature pictures of the Black authors reading or writing as the frontispieces of their books. These engravings were to certify the slaves' literacy. Well into the twentieth century, some scholars called into question the authorship of African-descended writers such as Harriet Jacobs. Henry Louis Gates Jr., *The Trials of Phillis Wheatley: America's First Black Poet and Her Encounters with the Founding Fathers* (New York: Basic Books, 2003), 1–29.

32. Regarding the Manceras' support of literacy for women, see our discussion of their sponsorship of the scholar-poet Sor Juana. The Divine Office or the Liturgy of the Hours is discussed in Section 2, in relation to Chicaba's literacy and as part of her religious vocation.

33. In the funeral oration for another Black woman, the 1735 *Sermón fúnebre* in honor of Magdalena de la Cruz, the preacher indicates that the Black woman he is eulogizing was a *bozal* from Cape Verde (Pedro Contreras, *Sermon funebre en las honras de la venerable Magdalena de la Cruz, negra de nacion* [Seville, 1735]). The word *bozal* means someone who could not master or

had not yet mastered speaking standard Spanish, and who certainly could not read or write. It also refers to a slave newly arrived from Africa.

34. Born Ana García Manzanas (c. 1549–1626), Ana de San Bartolomé entered the first monastery of the Discalced Carmelites, San Jose in Ávila, eight years after it was founded by Teresa of Ávila. During Saint Teresa's life, Ana acted as her assistant and traveled with her as she founded other monasteries. Upon Teresa's death, Ana testified at Saint Teresa's beatification process and later created foundations in France and the Low Countries. After years as a "white-veiled" nun, she professed as a choir nun in 1605 and became the prioress of the foundation in Paris. She died in Antwerp in 1625, where she had acquired fame as a liberator, through her prayers, of the Catholic city against the troops of William of Nassau. She was beatified in 1917. See Ana de San Bartolomé 6–15.

35. Rosa Egipcíaca da Vera Cruz was an African woman born in the same geographic area as Sor Teresa Chicaba. She lived in Brazil, where she gained her freedom after a series of visions. She moved to Rio de Janeiro and founded a religious convent for wayward women. Rosa Egipcíaca was unable to read and write until one morning after taking Communion, when a voice told her that the Holy Spirit would give her a blooming pen with which to write a book entitled "Theology of the Love of God." Her signature is attached to several documents before the Portuguese Inquisition in Lisbon, where she was imprisoned. Luiz Mott, *Rosa Egipcíaca: Uma santa africana no Brasil* (Rio de Janeiro: Editora Bertrand Brasil, 1993), 248–49.

36. Saint Catherine of Siena (1347–1380) corresponded with important ecclesiastical and political leaders of her time. She enjoined the pope to return to Rome from Avignon. She is credited with having written her *Dialogue* in five days in the midst of an ecstasy. The Catholic Church declared her a doctor of the Church, as it did with Saint Teresa of Ávila and Saint Thérèse of Liseux. Rebecca Cox Jackson, founder of a Black Shaker community, claimed that when she discovered that her brother did not record her spiritual reflections honestly, she asked God for the gift of literacy, and her prayers were answered.

37. Ibsen suggests that these disclaimers are part of the "rhetoric of humility": it is a way for authors to excuse their weaknesses in writing and to allay anxieties—both their own and those of clerical authorities—about women *writing* about theological topics (chapter 2). In "Wondrous Words: Miraculous Literacy and Real Literacy in the Convents of Early Modern Spain" (in *Women's Literacy in Early Modern Spain and the New World*, edited by Anne J. Cruz and Rosilie Hernández [Burlington, VT: Ashgate, 2011]), Darcy R. Donahue observes that literate nuns, those who could read or write, were not as rare in early modern religious communities as one might suspect—especially in monasteries of the Discalced Carmelites, where the works of founder Teresa of Ávila became models for spiritual narratives. (Even today, the sisters of the Baltimore Carmelite Monastery describe the writing of life-stories, lengthy obituaries, poems, songs, skits, and plays as a part of their order's culture—the charism that sets it apart from some other orders.) Donahue claims that "some degree of literacy was required for entrance into most religious orders" and that "this often varied tremendously according to social background. . . . These differences in social background were reflected in the internal division within convents between choir nuns or nuns of the black veil and house nuns [lay sisters] white-veiled nuns" (106). Some nuns could only sound out words phonetically; others could read for comprehension. However, Donahue observes that writing was the "more dangerous of the literacy skills in the eyes of the outside world" (108).

38. Quoted in Carole Slade, "The Role of Teresa's Books in Canonization Proceedings," in *Teresa of Ávila: Author of a Heroic Life* (Berkeley: University of California Press, 1995), 129.

39. Slade cites Silverio de Santa Teresa, *Procesos de beatificación y canonización de Santa Teresa de Jesús* (Burgos, Spain: Monte Carmelo, 1934–1935), 1:451, 484; 2:151; 1:273, in her *Teresa of Ávila: Author of a Heroic Life* (129–32). Saint Teresa of Ávila's official iconography represents her in the act of writing a book while looking up to heaven as if receiving inspiration.

40. *Converso* (and its feminine form, *conversa*) is a term used in Spain for Jews or Muslims (and their descendants) who converted to Catholicism in Spain and Portugal, especially during the fourteenth or fifteenth centuries. For further discussion, see Antonio Dominguez Ortiz, *Los*

judeoconversos en España y America (Madrid: Ediciones ISTMO, 1971), and Albert A. Sicroff, *Los estatutos de limpieza de sangre: Controversias entre los siglos XV y XVII* (Madrid: Taurus, 1979).

41. Fray Luis de León, *De la vida, muerte y milagros de la Santa Madre Teresa de Jesús*, in *Obras completas castellanas*, prólogo y notas del Padre Félix García, OSA (Madrid: Biblioteca de Autores Cristianos, 1957), 921–41. Known in the Spanish-speaking world as Fray Luis, he was one of the most famous poets of the Spanish Renaissance, and the first editor of *Libro de la vida*. Himself of Jewish descent, he was the victim of Inquisitorial persecution because of his translations of the Hebrew Bible into Spanish. Luis M. Girón-Negrón, "'Your Dove-Eyes among Your Hairlocks': Language and Authority in Fray Luis de León's 'Respuesta que Desde su Prisión da a sus Émulos,'" *Renaissance Quarterly* 54.4 (2001): 1197–250.

42. "Intersectionality" is a term common to American women's studies that refers to the theory and methodology of analyzing the connections and interrelations between several social locations (positionalities)—such as gender, race, social class, or sexuality—and how they interact on several dimensions, thereby mirroring social inequalities. See, for example, Kimberlé Crenshaw, "Mapping the Margins: Intersectionality, Identity Politics, and Violence against Women of Color," *Stanford Law Review* 43.6 (July 1991): 1241–99. Literary theorist and critic Valerie Smith simply defines "intersectionality" as "the interactions of race and gender as they shape lives and social practices," in *Not Just Race, Not Just Gender: Black Feminist Readings* (New York: Routledge, 1998), xiv.

43. Hippolyte Delehaye, "Hagiography," *The Catholic Encyclopedia*, vol. 7 (New York: Robert Appleton Company, 1910), www.newadvent.org/cathen/07106b.htm.

44. Ronald Pepin and Hugh Feiss, OSB, trans., *Saint Mary of Egypt: Three Medieval Lives in Verse* (Kalamazoo, MI: Cistercian Publications, 2005). This anthology of medieval editions contains three versions of the Mary of Egypt hagiography: one originally written in Latin by Flodoard of Reims in 966 CE; another by Hildebert of Lavardin written in Latin; and a thirteenth-century life of Mary (to which we will refer) written by an anonymous Spanish poet. The historical introduction to these hagiographies contends that "the earliest mention of Saint Mary of Egypt may occur in the *Life of Kyriakos* written by Cyril of Scythopolis near the middle of the sixth century" (8). Later, the introduction relates that "the story of Mary of Egypt was destined to be retold many times in many languages, beginning with the *Old English Life of Saint Mary of Egypt*" (21). One of the editors of this translation of the *Vida* of Teresa Chicaba became acquainted with the hagiographies of Saint Mary of Egypt over thirty years ago through the work of and conversations with two professional colleagues and friends, Phyllis Johnson and Brigitte Cazelles (both now deceased), who wrote *Le Vain Siecle Guerpir: A Literary Approach to Sainthood through Old French Hagiography of the Twelfth Century*, North Carolina Studies in the Romance Languages and Literatures (Chapel Hill: University of North Carolina Department of Romance Languages, 1979). Hugh Magennis, an editor and translator of the Old English text, dates the oldest version of this work to the very early eleventh century (*The Old English Life of Mary of Egypt* [Exeter, UK: University of Exeter, 2010], 14). Jane Stevenson traces the history of the legend in an anthology of historical criticism on narratives of Mary of Egypt in medieval insular literatures (works from the British Isles, including Wales, and Iceland) written in Latin and the vernacular. She follows the "peculiar success of the story," which "flourished throughout Europe" from the mid-sixth century until the late twentieth century, when Mary "provided the theme for two novels, a poem, and two operas" (Jane Stevenson, "The Holy Sinner: The Life of Mary of Egypt," in *The Legend of Mary of Egypt in Medieval Insular Literature*, edited by Eric Proppe and Bianca Ross [Dublin: Four Courts Press, 1996], 19–50). While the commemoration of Mary of Egypt's feast was dropped from the Roman Catholic Church calendar in the twentieth century, it is still celebrated in some eastern Orthodox churches. The best edition of the Spanish medieval version is still Manuel Alvar's *La vida de Santa María Egipcíaca* (Madrid: Consejo Superior de Investigaciones Científicas, 1970). See Jerry R. Craddock, "Apuntes para el estudio de la leyenda de Santa Maria Egipcíaca en España," in *Homenaje a Rodríguez Moñino*, vol. 1, edited by J. Homer Herriott, et al. (Madrid: Castalia, 1966), 99–110. Proof of the popularity of the legend of St. Mary of Egypt in Spain is

the play *La gitana de Menfis, Santa María Egipcíaca* (The Gypsy [Egyptian] of Memphis), written by Juan Pérez de Montalbán (1601–1638) that saw its text reprinted during the eighteenth century. This play omits the change of skin color in the female protagonist that is present in the medieval versions of the legend. However, the title racializes her by using the polysemic term *gitana* (Egyptian and also Gypsy).

45. The trope of the desert is important in much of mystical literature. It is the place of solitude where the individual can encounter the Divine; thus, it can also be a place of serenity and happiness or of purgative suffering, as it is in the story of Mary of Egypt.
46. Evelyn Birge Vitz, "La Vie de Saint Alexis: Narrative Analysis and the Quest for the Sacred Subject," *PMLA* 93.3 (May 1978): 397. See also John R. Maier, "Sainthood, Heroism, and Sexuality in the *Estoria de Santa Maria Egipçiaca*," *Revista Canadiense de Estudios Hispánicos*, no. 3 (Spring 1984): 424–25. "Metanoia" refers to a radical repentance.
47. A cenobitic monastic life is one that is lived communally. The eremitic life is that of a hermit. There are reformed religious orders that describe themselves as hermits, such as the Discalced Carmelites founded by Teresa of Ávila. These nuns live together as a community but stress solitary prayer in each member's individual cell. The fourth-century story of the saintly kitchen drudge is related by Michel de Certeau in *The Mystic Fable*, vol. 1: *The Sixteenth and Seventeenth Centuries*, translated by Michael Smith (Chicago: University of Chicago Press, 1992), 32–35.
48. In *The Pursuit of Signs: Semiotics, Literature, Deconstruction* (Ithaca, NY: Cornell University Press, 1981), Jonathan Culler writes that intertextuality "calls our attention to the importance of prior texts, insisting that the autonomy of texts is a misleading notion and that a work has the meaning it does only because certain things have been previously written. . . . The study of intertextuality is thus not an investigation of sources and influences as traditionally conceived" (103). It is more than delineating the genealogy of a text; but rather identifying codes (some of "whose origins are lost" [102]) and cultural presuppositions or conventions that make the meaning of discourses (loosely, written or spoken communication) possible.
49. See a longer discussion of this question of voice and orality in the sections on voice and slave narratives.
50. Roland Barthes, *S/Z* (London: Cape, 1974), 21; Roland Barthes, *Image-Music-Text* (London: Fontana, 1977), 143.
51. Catherine Mooney, in "Voice, Gender, and the Portrayal of Sanctity," uses the term "collaborator" both for, in the strictest sense, multiple writers conferring closely to produce a document and for an individual compiler of a saint's life who uses some of his or her conversations with and writings by the subject of a narrative, usually with the saint's knowledge of and/or the permission of his or her community for the production of a life-story (1).
52. The Afro-Brazilian Rosa Maria Egipcíaca da Vera Cruz clearly modeled her life in the legend of Saint Mary of Egypt. Her claim to transcendence, unlike that of Sor Teresa Chicaba, ended disastrously. She was born in the same area of the coast of West Africa, near Ouidah (Mott 13), and was enslaved at the age of six. Brought to Brazil, she was raped by her first owner during puberty. She lived in the Minas Gerais region, where she was forced into prostitution. Her period as a sex worker might account for her adoption of the name Egipcíaca, after Mary of Egypt, the saintly "harlot." Having experienced repentance, she became famous for a series of public episodes of demonic possession. After she gained her freedom, and following the orders of a priest, she moved to Rio de Janeiro. There she founded a confraternity of former prostitutes, many of them Black and mulatto, called Recolhimento de Nossa Senhora do Parto (Mott 259). She was greatly acclaimed and supported by civil and religious authorities. However, once she started denouncing the corruption of certain priests and claimed that her visions of God gave her authority over men and even the angels, Rosa Maria Egipcíaca was abandoned by the clergy who had formerly supported her, and they denounced her to the Inquisition. She was imprisoned and sent to Portugal to be tried by the Holy Office on accusations of heresy and witchcraft. Rosa Maria Egipcíaca da Vera Cruz, as her complex name indicated, chose to see herself as a new Mary of Egypt; and like her namesake, she changed her life from that of a harlot to a hermit of sorts. She chose to add the surname "Vera Cruz" (True Cross, or Holy

Cross) to commemorate the Egyptian woman's search for truth. She also traveled, in this case from the distant district of Minas Gerais to Rio de Janeiro, and she showed her repentance. Unlike Mary of Egypt, whose story was taken seriously by the priest Zosimas, Rosa was, because of her race and former slave status, unable to convince the church authorities of her spiritual superiority. Her claim to mystical authority in criticizing her contemporaries was unacceptable to the clergy of Rio de Janeiro, who were comfortable with only her first aspect, that of the repentant prostitute.

53. The number of hagiographies of nuns seemed to multiply by the eighteenth century in Spain and Spanish America. The social extraction of many of these nuns was humbler. Perhaps this fact attracted the attention of the Holy Office. Even their confessors and spiritual directors were under suspicion. See Isabelle Poutrin, *Le voile et la plume: Autobiographie et sainteté feminine dans l'Espagne moderne* (Madrid: Casa de Velázquez, 1995), 195.

54. A *donada* (literally "given") was a religious woman in a convent who occupied the lower ranks in its hierarchy. She would be above slaves and other servants because she had entered an official relation with the convent for the rest of her life. The category also applied to men, known as *donados*. For example, this is how earlier hagiographies describe Saint Martin de Porres's (1579–1639) affiliation with the Dominican monastery of Lima. *Donadas* and *donados* were less prevalent in Spain than in Spanish America, where a large proportion of *donadas* were women of African descent. Nancy E. van Deusen, *The Souls of Purgatory: The Spiritual Diary of a Seventeenth-Century Afro-Peruvian Mystic, Úrsula de Jesús* (Albuquerque: University of New Mexico, 2004).

55. The *locutorio* (sometimes translated as "locutory," "speak room," or "visiting parlor") is a room in a cloister where nuns could speak to visitors, albeit through a grille or grate.

56. Saint Dominic (1170–1221), the founder of Chicaba's religious order, was the object of a true investigation as to his nobility centuries after the saint had been canonized (1234), particularly during Chicaba's time. This controversy took a virulent turn in Salamanca during the last years of Chicaba's life. The intellectual atmosphere between the university (which pushed for historical accuracy) and the different religious orders (which saw the move as an attempt to attack the reputation of a religious order) became so poisoned by the acrimony of the debate that the Inquisition ended it and decreed silence over the matter. Juan Luis Cortina Iceta, *El siglo XVIII en la pre-ilustración salmantina: Vida y pensamiento de Luis de Losada, 1681–1748* (Madrid: Consejo Superior de Investigaciones Científicas, 1981), 460.

57. George Boulukos, "Olaudah Equiano and the Eighteenth-Century Debate on Africa," *Eighteenth-Century Studies* 40.2 (Winter 2007): 241–55.

58. See a longer discussion of this in Section 2, in the analysis of Chapters 1 through 6.

59. In *The Negro in France* (Lexington: University Press of Kentucky, 1961), Shelby T. McCloy states that "in seventeenth-century France some Negro princes, actual or alleged, began to appear" (15), and recounts the stories of two such men—Zaga-Christ, "supposed son of the Negus of Ethiopia" (15), and Aniaba, reportedly the son of an Ivory Coast chieftain. Aniaba received a commission as captain in the French cavalry and in 1700 failed to assume rule of his purported kingdom (16–18), a story reminiscent of the episode with Chicaba's uncle in Chapter 17.

60. Father Bernardo Rivera praises Paniagua for having found a middle ground between the "humble fears and superstitious tales of heroism" in his hagiography. Rivera cites Paniagua's "method for using critical rigor," which allows an author to tell stories of ecstasies and miracles as part of "well-ordered devotion" (*Vida* 5–6). The author of the Judgment, Sebastián Flores Pavón, repeats the same fears about writing a history that includes supernatural events by warning against "the two extremes of thoughtless acquiescence and overconfident incredulity" (*Vida* 10). Paniagua himself partakes of this intellectual discussion in his prologue when he protests that he has used only "the most authentic sources" (*Vida* 16). The page numbers in this note refer to the 1764 Spanish edition.

61. Anonymous Spanish poet, "The Life of St. Mary the Egyptian" in Feiss and Pepin, *Saint Mary of Egypt*. "Her arms . . .": "Braços et cuerpo et todo lo al blanco es como cristal" (67). "Her face . . .": La faz muy negra et arrugada de frio viento et elada" (74). "He turned": "Torno los

ojos a diestra parte houo A ojo huna clarjdat / aquella lumbre sse allego vio el cuerpo muchno [sic] se pago" (P. Sánchez-Prieto Borja, Rocío Díaz Moreno, and Elena Trujillo Belso, "Santa María Egipcíaca," in *Edición de textos alfonsíes en Real Academia Española: Banco de datos* (CORDE). Corpus diacrónico del español, 82. *dspace.uah.es/dspace/bitstream/handle/10017/7297/Vida%20de%20Santa%20Mar%C3%ADa%20Egipc%C3%ADaca.pdf*.

62. David Brakke, "Ethiopian Demons: Male Sexuality, the Black-Skinned Other, and the Monastic Self," *Journal of the History of Sexuality* 10.3/4 (July/October 2001): 507. See also the following: Heather Knorr, "The Struggle between Reason and Will in the *Vida de Santa María Egipcíaca*" (MA thesis, University of North Carolina at Chapel Hill, 2006), 17–21; Andrew Scheil, "Bodies and Boundaries in the Old English *Life of St. Mary of Egypt*," *Neophilologus* 84 (2000): 137–41; and Pearl Suson Ratunil, "Medieval Blackness: Blackness and Medieval Hagiography" (PhD diss., University of Illinois at Chicago, 2008), 1–25.

    In Spanish and Spanish American hagiographic literature the devil appears to nuns in the figure of a Black or mulatto man. In *Libro de la vida*, Saint Teresa of Ávila describes the devil as *un negrillo* (a little Black boy) who made her laugh (Santa Teresa de Jesús, *Libro de la Vida*, edited by Otger Steggink [Madrid: Clásicos Castalia, 1986], chap. 31, para. 4, p. 402 [Note: the Works of St. Teresa are traditionally quoted through chapter and paragraph]). However, other nuns later on would have visions that were less humorous, in which the racialization of the devil was mixed with an element of eroticism, such as Mother María de San José (1656–1719), a Mexican nun of Oaxaca who saw the devil appear to her at the age of eleven in the form of a naked mulatto man. See Kathleen A. Myers, "El discurso religioso en la fundación del Convento de la Soledad: La Crónica de la Madre María de San José (1656–1719)," in *Mujer y cultura en la colonia hispanoamericana*, edited by Mabel Moraña (Pittsburgh: University of Pittsburgh Press, 1996), 126.

63. Brakke uses Homi K. Bhabha as a lens through which to understand the role of Ethiopian demons in the works of the desert fathers. This introduction expands on that use of Bhabha's "The Other Question: Stereotype, Discrimination and the Postcolonial Prerogative" and "Of Mimicry and Man: The Ambivalence of Colonial Discourse," in *The Location of Culture* (London: Routledge, 1994), 67–77.

64. Teresa de Lauretis, "Sexual Indifference and Lesbian Representation," in *Performing Feminisms: Feminist Critical Theory and Theater*, edited by Sue-Ellen Case (Baltimore: Johns Hopkins University Press, 1990), 33–35. De Lauretis discusses Brecht's use of the terms "loyal" and "disloyal." Audiences and players who are "loyal" to maintaining the ideologies of ruling classes occupy the foreground of the stage; they are the focus of the bourgeois audience in attendance. The stagehands and workers in the wings and background enact another ideology and perform for the disenfranchised. That is, there are potentially at least two audiences to every text: one that reads the orthodox narrative, and another that sees a story resisting dominant ideology or orthodoxy.

65. Similar practices probably occurred in Spanish, Portuguese, and Spanish and Portuguese American Black confraternities, which were devoted to the cults of Black saints such as Saint Benedict of Palermo, Saint Elesbaan, and Saint Ephigenia. For the history of Black religious confraternities in different Spanish cities, see Aurelia Martín Casares and Christine Delaigue, "The Evangelization of Freed and Slave Black Africans in Renaissance Spain: Baptism, Marriage and Ethnic Brotherhoods," *History of Religions* 52.3 (2013): 214–35; Hipólito Sancho de Sopranis, *Las cofradías de Morenos en Cádiz* (Madrid: Instituto de Estudios Africanos, 1958); Isidoro Moreno Navarro, *La antigua hermandad de los negros de Sevilla: Etnicidad, poder y sociedad en 600 años de historia* (Seville: Universidad de Sevilla, 1997); A. J. R. Russell-Wood, "Black and Mulatto Brotherhoods in Colonial Brazil: A Study in Collective Behaviour," *Hispanic American Historical Review* 54 (1974): 567–602; Nicole von Germeten, *Black Blood Brothers: Confraternities and Social Mobility for Afro-Mexicans* (Gainesville: University Press of Florida, 2005); E. Valerie Smith, "The Sisterhood of Nossa Senhora Do Rosario: African-Brazilian Cultural Adaptations to Antebellum Restrictions," *Afro-Hispanic Review* 42:1/2 (2002): 121–33. See also Cyprian Davis, *The History of Black Catholics in the United States* (New York: Cross Roads, 1990). Black Catholics in the United States also organized in confraternities

during slavery. See Cyprian Davis, OSB, and Jamie Phelps, OP (eds.), *Stamped with the Image of God: Africans as God's Image in Black* (New York: Orbis Books, 2003), 16–18.
66. A. J. Saraiva, "Le Père Antonio Vieira S.J. et l'esclavage des noirs au XVIIe siècle," *Annales: Economies, Societés, Civilisations* 22.6 (1967): 1294.
67. The "Black bride of Christ" theme was popular among Blacks, as demonstrated by the Mexican case of Juana Esperanza de San Alberto, a Black convent slave who was considered one of the official founders of her convent in the city of Puebla, once the other nuns renounced selling her. She claimed to be "the Spouse to the King, although I am Black, I am beautiful" (José Gómez de la Parra, *Fundación y Primero Siglo. Crónica del primer convento de carmelitas descalzas en Puebla: 1604–1704*, Introducción de Manuel Ramos Medina [Mexico: Universidad Iberoamericana, 1992]. Quoted in van Deusen, 30).
68. It is important to note that the existence of a population of free and enslaved Blacks in Spain was never associated with the cult of the Black Madonna in Spain. The cults of Our Lady of Montserrat, Our Lady of Guadalupe (in Extremadura, in Spain, and in Mexico), and Our Lady of Atocha (a favorite Dominican advocation in Madrid) were never associated with real people of African descent in Spain or Spanish America. The cult of the Black Virgin goes at least back to the Crusades, although its origins could be found earlier, in the case of the Christian kingdoms of the Iberian Peninsula. See Ean Begg, *The Cult of the Black Virgin* (London: Arkana, 1996), 21ff. It is also worth mentioning that the Marquis of Mancera, during his tenure as viceroy of Mexico, was active in the propagation of the veneration of Our Lady of Guadalupe, the first and most important nonwhite apparition of the Virgin Mary in Spanish America whose devotion was sanctioned by the Catholic Church. See Manuele Rivera Cambas, *Los gobernantes de México desde don Hernando Cortés hasta el c. Benito Juárez* (Mexico City, 1872), 1:230.
69. Jane Landers, "Cimarrón Ethnicity and Cultural Adaptation in the Spanish Domains of the Circum-Caribbean, 1503–1763," in *Identity in the Shadow of Slavery*, edited by Paul E. Lovejoy (London: Bloomsbury Academic, 2009), 32.
70. Carmen Mena García, "Religión, Etnia y Sociedad: Cofradías de Negros en el Panamá Colonial," *Anuario de Estudios Americanos* 57.1 (2000): 149. Black confraternities functioned as social organizations, in many cases along ethnic lines, for the mutual protection of Blacks in Spanish America. See Nicole von Germeten, "Juan Roque's Donation of a House to the Zape Confraternity, Mexico City, 1623," in *Afro-Latino Voices: Narratives from the Early Modern Ibero-Atlantic World, 1550–1812*, edited by Kathryn Joy McKnight and Leo J. Garofalo (Indianapolis: Hackett, 2009), 83–103.
71. In the words of Philip Gould, "The slave narrative first emerged during the 1770s and 1780s in the context of transatlantic political and religious movements which shaped the genre's publication history, as well as its major themes and narrative designs. These late eighteenth-century works reveal what Paul Gilroy calls the 'transcultural international formation' of the 'Black Atlantic'" ("The Rise, Development, and Circulation of the Slave Narrative," in *The Cambridge Companion to the African American Slave Narrative*, edited by Audrey Fisch [Cambridge: Cambridge University Press, 2007], 11. *dx.doi.org/10.1017/CCOL0521850193.002*).

Drawing on the work of Henry Louis Gates Jr., Deborah Jenson sketches a definition of the slave narrative in North America: "In the Anglophone context, the slave narrative is generally marked by testimony about 'becoming the legal property of another human being,' as Gates says—about capture and captivity, or birth and youth in slavery" (*Beyond the Slave Narrative: Politics, Sex, and Manuscripts in the Haitian Revolution* [Liverpool: Liverpool University Press, 2011], 3). In other words, the genre is defined by both its subject matter and the trajectory of its narrative from birth or capture through enslavement to freedom. Gates further notes that "there is an inextricable link in the African American tradition between literacy and freedom. . . . Sometimes the [narratives] were dictated, as in the case of Mary Prince, but more often than not they were 'written by themselves,' a crucial argument in the discourse of race and reason" (Henry Louis Gates Jr., *The Classic Slave Narratives* [New York: Signet Classics, 2002], xiii). As-told-to slave narratives, therefore, are works dictated to and recorded by another person acting as a scribe. Some of these were published before the Civil War, and others later as part of a WPA project that recorded the stories of freed slaves still alive in the twentieth century.

Our associating the *Vida* with the slave narrative is not an attempt to collapse the oral and written narratives by enslaved people into one genre or to ascribe to what critic Robert Reid-Pharr calls "a 'Big Bang' conception" of Black Atlantic culture ("The Slave Narrative and Early Black American Literature," in Fisch 137–38). Rather, we contend that Chicaba's story conforms to the definition sketched above, that it was published around the same time (or a few years earlier) that works of this genre appear in America and Britain, and that, like slave narratives, it is a hybrid of other literary forms. Our assertion is not an Anglo-centric co-optation of literatures in other languages, but it is a declaration of the similarity of some historical stresses that many Black diasporic peoples have experienced.

72. William L. Andrews, *To Tell a Free Story: The First Century of Afro-American Autobiography, 1760–1865* (Chicago: University of Illinois Press, 1986), 7.
73. Charles T. Davis, "The Slave Narrative: First Major Art Form in an Emerging Black Tradition" (1979), in *Black Is the Color of the Cosmos: Essays in Afro-American Literature and Culture, 1942–1981*, edited by Henry Louis Gates Jr. (Washington, DC: Howard University Press, 1989), 90.
74. William L. Andrews, editor, *Sisters of the Spirit: Three Black Women's Autobiographies of the Nineteenth Century* (Bloomington: Indiana University Press, 1986), 1. In "Redeeming Bondage: The Captivity Narrative and the Spiritual Autobiography in the African American Slave Narrative Tradition" (in Fisch 83–98), Yolanda Pierce maintains:

> If the central message of Christianity is the redemptive work of Christ on the cross, in which the sacrifice of one redeems the sins of all, it is no wonder that enslaved men and women take this message to heart both for their spiritual and earthly needs. The rhetorical message of the Christian faith promises freedom, liberation, and deliverance from bondage, particularly for those wrongly punished. The signs, symbols, and stories of this belief system reinforce the notion that the very least, the most humble, and the most abject are the ones who eventually inherit the kingdom. What other message could provide such hope and offer so many scriptural parallels to the situation of the enslaved African population? (93)

75. Joycelyn Moody, *Sentimental Confessions: Spiritual Narratives of Nineteenth-Century African American Women* (Athens: University of Georgia Press, 2001), 3–5.
76. Belinda, "Petition of an African Slave, to the Legislature of Massachusetts," c. 1782, in *American Women Writers to 1800*, edited by Sharon M. Harris (New York: Oxford University Press, 1996), 253.
77. One of the earliest and most famous slave narratives embeds a spiritual biography as well. For example, the engraving at the front of *The Interesting Narrative of the Life of Olaudah Equiano or Gustavus Vassa, the African, Written by Himself* (Middlesex, England, 1789) depicts the protagonist of the autobiography holding a Bible open in his lap. Included among his many experiences depicted in the text is the story of his conversion during the First Great Awakening when he was inspired by the preaching of George Whitefield.
78. Maria W. Stewart, *Productions of Mrs. Maria W. Stewart* (1835), in *Spiritual Narratives*, introduction by Sue E. Houchins (New York: Oxford University Press, 1988), 3.
79. Peter P. Hinks, *To Awaken My Afflicted Brethren: David Walker and the Problem of Antebellum Slave Resistance* (University Park: Pennsylvania State University Press, 1997), 232.
80. Sue E. Houchins, "Introduction," in Houchins, *Spiritual Narratives*, xxxi.
81. Catholic mystics (such as Julian of Norwich, William of St. Theirry, and Teresa of Ávila) describe their spiritual union with God as so intimate that it conformed their will to that of the Deity. Methodist spiritual doctrine promulgated during the Second Great Awakening held that "the soul 'pilgrimaged' toward 'Christian perfection' or evolved in accordance with a prescribed 'order of salvation.' After a prolonged period of self-doubt, each person was 'graced' with knowledge that her sins were forgiven and she was 'justified' before God. Finally, through the interaction of faith, hope, and most importantly, love, the soul was gifted with 'a

new birth' . . . and she received 'sanctification'—the sharing in the divine nature, dwelling in God" (Houchins xxxiv).
82. Jarena Lee, *Religious Experience and Journal of Mrs. Jarena Lee* (1849), in Houchins, *Spiritual Narratives*.
83. Zilpha Elaw, "Memoirs of the Life, Religious Experience, Ministerial Travels, and Labors," in Andrews, *Sisters of the Spirit*, 76–82.
84. Julia Foote, *A Brand Plucked from the Fire. An Autobiographical Sketch* (1886), in Houchins, *Spiritual Narratives*, 66–68.
85. This passage is faintly reminiscent of a passage in Teresa of Ávila's *Book of Her Life* that we discussed in connection with Sor Teresa Chicaba in Section 2, "Life in La Penitencia— Chapter 19 to the Conclusion."
86. Paul Gilroy, *The Black Atlantic: Modernity and Double Consciousness* (London: Verso, 1996), 1–71.
87. Allen Greer, "Colonial Saints: Gender, Race and Hagiography in New France," *William and Mary Quarterly*, Third Series, 57.2 (April 2000): 323–48. This article begins by comparing Catholic hagiographies with Puritan spiritual narratives, the model for African American spiritual narratives and the slave narratives that follow (324–27).
88. Greer uses the term "life narrative" for hagiography throughout his article.
89. Gould, "Rise, Development, and Circulation." Slave narratives emerged in the English-speaking world in the late eighteenth century. "Evangelical Christian groups often sponsored and oversaw their publication. By the 1780s, new political organizations, like the English Society for Effecting the Abolition of the Slave Trade (1787) and the Pennsylvania Abolition Society (1775/1784), dedicated to the abolition of the slave trade, also played a role in encouraging and publishing these narratives" (Gould 11). By using the term "proto-slave narrative," we are suggesting that this hagiography, which precedes the first anglophone slave narratives by less than fifty years, bears many of the features of the genre that had already begun to develop in the Americas and England. Frances Smith Foster notes that before the 1770s "African Americans were writing and publishing sermons and minutes of meetings, poems, essays, and autobiographies," in *Love and Marriage in Early African America* (Lebanon, NH: Northeastern University Press, 2008), xv. As mentioned above, critic Robert Reid-Pharr cautions scholars not to ascribe to a "Big Bang Theory" of African diasporic literature ("Slave Narrative," 137). That is, captives from a multitude of African ethnic groups dispersed throughout the world by the trade in slaves desired to be free and produced oral and written literary genres to argue for emancipation. Writings that make a case for the end of slavery appear in other European and creole literatures. See, for example, Deborah Jenson, *Beyond the Slave Narrative: Sex, Politics, and Manuscripts in the Haitian Revolution* (Liverpool: University of Liverpool Press, 2010).
90. Spanish scholar Beatriz Ferrús Antón is a worthy exception to the tradition of ascribing authorship to Paniagua, as her essay on Chicaba and the text of the *Vida* tries to establish the presence of the sister's voice, resisting the dominance of Paniagua's text. Ferrús Antón gives credit to the *Vida*'s assertion that there was a sort of ur-text written by Sor Teresa Chicaba herself from which Paniagua would have censored and suppressed parts of her voice. Ferrús Antón maintains that Chicaba's own *vida* would probably have been hyperbolic or boastful of the presence of her own Black body against Paniagua's attempts to erase it. See Beatriz Ferrús Antón, "Sor Teresa Juliana de Santo Domingo, Chicaba o escribir en la piel de otro," *Cuadernos dieciochescos* 9 (2008): 181–92. Ferrús Antón describes Chicaba as a slave-nun who defied the barrier between Blacks and whites in Catholic monasteries (185). The author is clearly not aware that the Marchioness of Mancera had freed her slave Teresa del Espíritu Santo on her deathbed. Chicaba entered the convent of La Penitencia as a free woman, as the dates of the marchioness's death and Chicaba's act of profession indicate, as does the bequest of money in the marchioness's will. Ferrús Antón also calls Paniagua Chicaba's confessor, something he was not.
91. Greer also discusses hagiographies of loyal "good Indians" who converted to Catholicism

and later sacrificed their lives in battles against the Iroquois in New France. He describes a few narratives produced in the Americas that recounted the stories of people of color.

92. Greer asserts that the title "saint" is not reserved for those who have been canonized but includes those about whom narratives were written "in the hope that their accounts would be accepted as evidence in a future canonization trial, but just as often with a more immediate motive of providing inspiration to readers" (325–26).

93. For extended discussions of orality in slave narratives see Doveanna S. Fulton, *Speaking Power: Black Feminist Orality in Women's Narratives of Slavery* (Albany, NY: SUNY Press, 2006).

94. Harryette Mullen, "Runaway Tongue: Resistant Orality in *Uncle Tom's Cabin, Our Nig, Incidents in the Live of a Slave Girl*, and *Beloved*," in *The Culture of Sentiment: Race, Gender, and Sentimentality in 19th Century America*, edited by Shirley Samuels (New York: Oxford University Press, 1992), 246.

95. John L. McKenzie, "Sheba," in *Dictionary of the Bible* (New York: Macmillan, 1965), 79, 697. Today's biblical scholars locate Sheba in modern-day Yemen (St. John Simpson, "Queen of Sheba: Treasures from Ancient Yemen," *Journal of the Royal Asiatic Society of Great Britain and Ireland*, Third Series, 15.1 [April 2005]: 102–4). David M. Goldenburg thoroughly analyzes the so-called Curse of Ham, in *The Curse of Ham: Race and Slavery in Early Judaism, Christianity, and Islam* (Princeton, NJ: Princeton University Press, 2003); see especially the first twenty-three pages. Goldenberg explains that the association of Noah's banishment of his son Ham with the "curse" of racial Blackness and slavery is not supported by the biblical verses in Genesis 9:18–25, but it developed over time. Toward the end of his monograph, he maintains that the link between Black skin color and slavery occurred in seventh-century Arabia, after the Islamic conquest of Africa (170). However, the text from Genesis continued to be cited as justification for enslavement, segregation, and apartheid through the twentieth century.

96. All biblical quotations used by us and not quoted in other sources are from *The Holy Bible: Revised Standard Version*, Catholic edition (Camden, NJ: Thomas Nelson, 1966).

97. See a longer discussion of the motif of the gift in Section 2.

98. The story of the Queen of Sheba's visit to Solomon's court becomes closely associated with the Epiphany—the journey of the Magi to the newborn Christ and the presentation of gifts—from the twelfth century through the Baroque era. For example, the Queen of Sheba and Solomon are represented in stained glass windows across from the Adoration of the Kings in Canterbury Cathedral, which was designed in the late twelfth century. The following explanation is inscribed on these scenes: "The queen gives these presents to the house of Solomon; in such wise the Kings give to the threefold Lord three gifts" (quoted in Paul F. Watson, "The Queen of Sheba in Christian Tradition," in *Solomon and Sheba*, edited by James B. Pritchard [London: Phaidon Press, 1974], 118–19). Watson tracks the popularity of these two themes in paintings, stained glass, and friezes. He observes that the theme reaches a high point in popularity during the seventeenth and eighteenth centuries—especially for devotional purposes in Catholic churches (132). In seventeenth-century Spain, the theme of the Queen of Sheba was the source of two plays by Pedro Calderón de la Barca (1600–1681), *La sibila de Oriente y gran reina de Sabá* and his religious allegorical play (*auto sacramental*) *El árbol del major fruto*. An *auto sacramental* was a religious play that flourished in Spain during the Counter-Reformation period. The goal of these plays was to celebrate the Eucharist by making the end of the performance become a veritable adoration of the consecrated Host, transforming drama into theological mystery. In her official portrait, Sor Teresa Chicaba appears kneeling down in adoration of the Eucharist as well, as a Christianized Queen of Sheba. In both plays, the Queen of Sheba is depicted as a pagan ruler in search of the true wisdom from King Solomon. See Françoise Gilbert, "Las varias formas de saber y su transmisión en el auto de Calderón *El árbol del major fruto* (1677)," in *La transmission de savoirs licites ou illicites dans le monde hispanique (XIIe–XVIIe siècles)*, partie 1-1/3, Colloque international organisé par l'équipe "Littérature espagnole médiévale et du siècle d'or" (LEMSO), rattachée au laboratoire FRAMESPA, sous la direction scientifique de Amaia Arizaleta, Françoise Cazal et Luis González Fernández (Toulouse, France: Université Toulouse II-Le Mirail, 2008), 267–90.

99. Mary Hale Shackford, "The Magi in Florence: An Aspect of the Renaissance," *Studies in Philology* 20.4 (October 1923): 379.
100. A longer explication of this poem appears in Section 2.
101. Susan Snaider Lanser, *Fictions of Authority: Women Writers and Narrative Voice* (Ithaca, NY: Cornell University Press, 1992), 3.
102. Joan W. Scott, "Gender: A Useful Category of Historical Analysis," *American Historical Review* 91.5 (December 1986): 1054, 1067. In this article, Scott analogizes gender, race, class, and sexuality as constitutive elements of social relations of power and oppression. In this context, women, Blacks, and slaves are Lanser's "silenced ones," clamoring to be heard from below.
103. Catherine Belsey, *Critical Practice* (New York: Methuen, 1980), 56–57. We have substituted the more general term "economic and social" for "capitalism" in the original quotation, for we have observed that ideologies accustom themselves to the societies and economies and the historical moments that produce and reflect them. We (and others) maintain that they conform to the contexts that produce them; so contrary to some philosophers' beliefs, they are not, as Althusser claims, transhistorical in their specificity. Because Belsey is drawing upon Marxist thinker Louis Althusser, her discussion of ideology is understood to be a critique of capitalism.
104. Louis Althusser, "Ideology and Ideological State Apparatuses," in *Lenin and Philosophy and Other Essays*, translated by Ben Brewster (New York: Monthly Review Press, 1971), 162.
105. Joan N. Radner and Susan S. Lanser, "Strategies of Coding in Women's Cultures," in *Feminist Messages: Coding in Women's Folk Culture*, edited by Joan Newlon Radner (Urbana: University of Illinois Press, 1993), 6. Radner and Lanser use the term "implicit coding" to refer to the strategies a woman narrator (and by extension, Blacks and Others) registers her alternate realities, inserts voice. This act of encryption is not necessarily an indication of purposeful or unconscious intentionality. See the discussion of this later in this section.
106. This same difficulty is apparent in the modern hagiography of Saint Martin de Porres (1579–1639), the first Black canonized by the Catholic Church in modern times (1962). In his Dominican convent of Lima he was a *donado* (literally "gift"), and someone who did not profess regular vows like the white friars. His place was in the kitchen and in the infirmary—there were two, one for friars and one for people of color who served in the convent—as well as out running errands for the monastery. Like Sor Teresa Chicaba, his death occurs in "his cell," the historicity of which is rather doubtful. See Salvador Velasco, OP, *San Martín de Porres: La vida de "Fray Escoba"* (Madrid: EDIBESA, 1992), 56, 277.
107. The authors of this introduction are aware that in an earlier era Hispano-Arab women and *conversas* were excluded from living in enclosure. By the time Chicaba enters La Penitencia, these groups of women were no longer a visible part of monastic communities because of the proofs of *limpieza de sangre* required. However, this is not the point of the argument that this introduction endeavors to make. Rather, we read the issue of her exclusion from the enclosure in the context of a narrative that never describes explicitly Chicaba's status as a member of the monastery. In fact, the narrative elides the nature of her final profession. "Exclusion" in this context emphasizes her canonical ambiguity, liminality as well as how race makes her marginal in convent society. In fact, it is by her exclusion that we infer her canonical status—if indeed she has any affiliation other than contractual with the convent—as a third order *secular* Dominican. We have not seen for ourselves any official unequivocal, unambiguous source in the *Vida* or in the only monastic archival material available to us about her official status. This conventual exclusion is prefigured by Chicaba's liminality in the Mancera household before she enters La Penitencia. See, for instance, the discussion of the distribution of the picture of *Christ of Medinaceli* in Section 2.
108. The reader of the *Vida* will note that the presence of clerical guests is no insurance of appropriate behavior since it was a priest in the Mancera household who seduced the Turkish girl.
109. Peter Brooks, *Reading for the Plot: Design and Intention in Narrative* (New York: Knopf, 1984), 9–12.
110. Marilyn R. Farwell, *Heterosexual Plots and Lesbian Narratives* (New York: New York University Press, 1996), 29.

111. Jonathan Culler, *Structuralist Poetics: Structuralism, Linguistics, and the Study of Literature* (Ithaca, NY: Cornell University Press, 1975), 209.
112. In this regard, we will discuss the genre of the Byzantine romance, which also uses pilgrimage as a trope. See Section 2.
113. See a more complete discussion of Chicaba's ambiguous position in Section 2.
114. Harriet A. Jacobs, *Incidents in the Life of a Slave Girl: Written by Herself*, edited and introduced by Jean Fagan Yellin (Cambridge, MA: Harvard University Press, 1987), 201.
115. This term is from an article by Raymond A. Bauer and Alice H. Bauer, "Day to Day Resistance to Slavery," *Journal of Negro History* 27.4 (1942): 388–419. A more recent article by Phillip D. Morgan maintains that "in work and in play, in public and in private, violently and quietly, slaves struggled against masters. Wherever and whenever masters, whether implicitly or explicitly, recognized the independent will or volition of their slaves, they acknowledged the humanity of their bondpeople. Extracting this admission was, in fact, a form of slave resistance, because slaves thereby opposed the dehumanization inherent in their status" (*Slave Counterpoint: Black Culture in the Eighteenth-Century Chesapeake and Low Country* [Chapel Hill: University of North Carolina Press, 1998], xxii). However, we are aware that there is disagreement among historians as to whether small, personal acts of defiance constitute "resistance." There are some who contend that only larger acts that impact the community of enslaved people make for "resistance," but even these scholars agree that the model that they are supporting is male-centered. Ben Schiller is of the school that limits the use of the term "resistance." He gives a summary of issues on this side of the disagreement in "Selling Themselves: Slavery, Survival, and the Path of Least Resistance," *49th Parallel* 23 (Summer 2009): 1–23; www.49thparallel.bham.ac.uk/back/issue23. We, literary critics and perhaps literary historians, are looking at the work of scholars such as Radner and Lanser, who have developed a typology of women's coded resistance to uneven power relations that favor (white) men. Also, we are grateful to Harryette Mullen's discussion of Black female resistance—resistance at the intersection of race and gender—much of which is gestured or oral. (See citations of these works in the discussion to follow.) We hold that what Mullen describes in her article as well as some of the instances of the "implied voice" we describe in this introduction are analogous to an incident depicted in Toni Morrison's novel *A Mercy* (New York: Knopf, 2008): when Vaark, a white moneylender and rum trader, tours the plantation of a Portuguese plantation owner, he sees in the corner of his eye that slaves are exchanging furtive glances, "judging the men who judged them" (22). Here, we are endeavoring to describe and analyze Chicaba's "furtive" communication in the margins of the text.
116. Nell Irvin Painter, "Soul Murder and Slavery: Toward a Fully Loaded Cost Accounting," in *U.S. History as Women's History: New Feminist Essays*, edited by Linda K. Kerber, Alice Kessler-Harris, and Kathyrn Kish Sklar (Chapel Hill: University of North Carolina Press, 1995), 125–46. Painter asserts, "We all know on a certain, almost intuitive level that violence is inseparable from slavery, but historians rarely trace the descent of that conjunction" (126).
117. See a longer discussion of this topic in Section 2.
118. The behavior of the servants and slaves below stairs as described in the *Vida* makes the Mancera household appear to be something of a madhouse. This representation is something of an implied code as well. See our later discussion on Byzantine romance.
119. Lindon Barrett, "African American Slave Narratives: Literacy, the Body, Authority," *American Literary History* 7.3 (Autumn 1995): 417.
120. Valerie Smith, *Self-Discovery and Authority in Afro-American Narrative* (Cambridge, MA: Harvard University Press, 1987), 3.
121. In the words of J. Michael Dash, "Even if the mind chooses to forget, the body bears the signs of the past violation" ("Writing the Body: Edouard Glissant's Poetics of Re-membering," *World Literature Today* 63.4 [Autumn 1989]: 610).
122. Historian Gerda Lerner discusses the feminist hermeneutics of deeply religious Black women mystics in eighteenth-century America. They employed a rich repertoire of biblical interpretations in their preaching; these constituted interventions in the racial and gender politics of the

time (*The Creation of Feminist Consciousness from the Middle Ages to 1870* [New York: Oxford University Press, 1993], 105–10).
123. See a longer discussion of this poem in the Section 2.
124. Gayatri Chakravorty Spivak, "Can the Subaltern Speak?" in *Marxism and the Interpretation of Culture*, edited by Cary Nelson and Lawrence Grossberg (Urbana: University of Illinois Press, 1988), 271–313. See this canonical essay on the silencing of brown women and those in the underclasses for a discussion of the subaltern.
125. Marcus Rediker, "The Poetics of History from Below," *Perspectives on History: A Newsmagazine of the American Historical Association* 48.6 (September 2010): 36–38; *www.historians.org*.

Introduction: Section 2
Discussion of the Vida *by Chapters*

LIFE IN GUINEA—CHAPTERS 1 THROUGH 6

When Chapter 1 of the *Vida* of Sor Teresa Juliana (née Chicaba) opens, its hagiographer-compiler Juan Carlos de Paniagua laments that, while biographers of European "heroes" have the advantage of knowing about their subjects' backgrounds—their place of origin and their people—this protagonist is from a "remote" region of the world and belongs to a nation about which Europeans know little. So he must depend primarily on the information Sor Teresa provided him to reconstruct her early years, her lineage, and the customs of her people.

Likewise, we, the editors of this English translation and authors of its introduction, confront a paucity of unequivocal data about Teresa Chicaba's life because there is so little archival evidence or textual corroboration (that is, primary source material) for events recorded in the *Vida*. Therefore, we try to exercise caution in speculating where Teresa Chicaba intervenes and/or collaborates in Paniagua's narration of her story. The protocols of historical and literary research require this careful distancing of our subject—no matter how the biography's representation of her intelligence, courage, and compassion evokes our empathy. For this reason, this section of the Introduction speaks more about the text than about the eighteenth-century collaborators, Chicaba and Paniagua, who produced it.

Because of our backgrounds in Africana and gender studies, we are aware of a tendency among some scholars to devalue biographies or autobiographies written during slavery through the mediation of a European male amanuensis or compiler-author. They also call into question the ability of eighteenth- and nineteenth-century Blacks and women, especially of Black women, to insert their voices and perspectives into texts by and/or about them. In fact, a few scholars also dispute any characterization of these protagonists as exercising even a small amount of influence over their representation.[1] However, given our academic training, we see a strong resemblance between Teresa Chicaba's eighteenth-century *Vida* and recorded oral narratives of African Americans in the late eighteenth through nineteenth and early twentieth centuries, which displayed acts of resistance to oppression. Sor Teresa's story is both a hagiography and a kind of early slave narrative that embeds within its text a genealogy containing other genres, including the spiritual autobiographies and biographies discussed in the summary above. In other words, this is a story of an African woman who escapes from slavery through the exhibition of her extraordinary holiness, attains a reputation for sanctity and healing, exercises some small power within the religious community that never accepted her in the upper ranks of its social hierarchy, and manages to have her autobiographical writings and oral history recorded. The movement from slavery to freedom is the defining trajectory of the slave narrative. The *Vida* meets this key expectation of the genre and another as well—the assertion of Chicaba's literacy, if not the depiction of the exact process by which she learns to read and write. However, unlike the canonical African American slave stories, with which many are already familiar, this biography is not in the first person, nor does it claim Teresa's authorship of or authority over the text. Therefore, not being conventionally autobiographical, the *Vida* falls within that less respected category—for some of today's readers—of as-told-to slave narratives. And like many of these documents, it engenders misgivings in modern audience members who seek assurance as to the veracity of the text— a guarantee of historical accuracy, realism, and verisimilitude no life-representation could ever really deliver.

In lieu of Teresa Chicaba's missing autobiographical notes and Juan Carlos de Paniagua's interview records, there exist the marchioness's will, the nun's official contract with the third order of Saint Dominic at La Penitencia, an autograph letter, accounting data from women's monasteries, documents concerning the slave trade and slavery, historical studies of Spain and Africa during the late seventeenth and early eighteenth centuries, and other secondary and tertiary sources. These provide contexts for comprehending this narrative, which sometimes seems oddly outdated and unapproachable, and for reconstructing its elusive protagonist—at least in part.

That said, the first paragraph of the *Vida* makes one of the few references to Chicaba's role in the production of her narrative. Here the hagiographer differentiates immediately and forthrightly between himself and his subject, for he acknowledges his debt to her for information about her place of origin and her people. And in doing so, he introduces the first two contextualizing discourses through which to begin reading the book: Africa (its history, society, culture, religions, and representations) and Chicaba's color (what today's reader might identify as an early stage in the development of racial ideologies).

One can assume, given how little her collaborator must have known about Guinea in general and her place of birth in particular, that the few details about her early years in Western Africa are largely her contribution, albeit filtered through years of acculturation in Spain. Therefore, the depiction of Africa in this and the following five chapters mingles Europeans' prevailing notions about that large swath of the continent from which they captured slaves and the specifics about the region of Chicaba's origin.

In eighteenth-century Spain, *Guinea* referred to present-day West Africa, and the audience of the *Vida* would have known or deduced from the discourse of the first six chapters that this name designated the geographical area that was the source of slaves.[2] The representation of Africa/Guinea depicted in this text is a composite of ideas that existed in the European imagination at the time. What became known as the Dark Continent in the nineteenth century, in part because it was still unmapped by European explorers and missionaries, was in earlier times a continent supposedly darkened by its ignorance of the Christian God, as is apparent in the sonnet at the beginning of the hagiography, which describes Chicaba as having emerged from a dark mist. This is most likely a reference to the "pagan" origins of her people, who supposedly had not yet been exposed to the light of the Christian faith; it is also an allusion to her skin color, with its symbolic meaning as a physical mark of paganism. A rationale for enslaving Blacks was a religious one: to remove them from Guinea, the site of heathenism. To establish the legitimacy of the trade in Blacks from this benighted region, the king of Portugal had obtained a papal bull that justified their enslavement.[3] Thus, geography, the discourse of race, the practice of slavery, and religious conversion became inextricable.

By identifying a specific region in Guinea as Chicaba's homeland, the *Vida* is able to begin constructing a narrative of exceptionalism that will eventually serve to exempt her and her people from the taint of heathenism. Teresa Chicaba was born in the territory known to Spanish and Portuguese navigators of the seventeenth and eighteenth century as La Mina Baja del Oro, on the west coast of Elmina (today's Ghana, Togo, Benin, and western Nigeria), part of what was called the "Slave Coast."[4] This area was inhabited at the end of the seventeenth century, as it is today, by Ewe-speaking people.[5]

The names of her mother and brothers, though changed and misspelled in the text, are traceable to Ewe, a language with several different dialects, spoken from Accra, Ghana, to the western coastal states of Nigeria. These linguistic variations, taken with the aforementioned large geographical area associated with Teresa, evidence the complexities of the society in which she was reared. The word *Chicaba* (also spelled *Chicava*), Sor Teresa's African name, is a direct reference to gold. In spite of phonological changes since the late seventeenth century, *Chicaba/Chicava* is still recognizable as a compound of two words, *shika* or *sika* (gold) and *va* (to arrive), meaning "the gold has arrived" or "the golden child is here."[6] The *Vida* records Sor Teresa's memory of her siblings' names, one of which was *Juachipiter*. As we mentioned earlier, *Juachipiter* (or *Joachipiter*, as it is spelled in Chapter 5) was probably a compound word, joining *Watchi* to *pitê*.[7] In the cultures of the Ewe and of the Akan, another ethnic group of the area, there was a strong relationship between gold, spiritual power, and chieftaincy. Given both Chicaba's and her brothers' names, one can hypothesize that her people may have been connected in some way to goldsmithing and jewelry production.[8]

The *Oración fúnebre* composed in 1749 gives Chicaba's mother's name as *Abar*, which is not from the same linguistic group. Probably this indicates that Chicaba's mother did not belong to the same clan as her father or did not originate from the same area, but rather from a neighboring territory.[9] This would be in keeping with the complex migratory history of the Ewe (sometimes called Krepi or Peki), whose oral tradition recounts a number of resettlements over several centuries. They first traveled west from present-day Nigeria and Benin to make way for a growing Yoruba population and their territorial expansion (Law, *Slave Coast* 14). Afterward they settled in the walled city of Notsie in central Togo until the repressive regime of King Agokoli necessitated a second relocation. Then they broke into three groups, traveled farther west, and by the mid-seventeenth century inhabited the areas where they are now, in southeast Ghana and Togo.

As a means of promoting their separate identities, each group of Ewe has fostered its own legends of their exodus. Migration stories and travel narratives have been integral to Ewe tradition.[10] Given the estimated birth date of Teresa Chicaba in 1676, the memories of this trek must have been vivid for her elders, who would often have narrated their history at gatherings. The motifs of transportation and removal that repeat themselves throughout the *Vida* may have begun to infiltrate her personal narrative even here in its beginning.

Certainly the conflicts and skirmishes described in the early chapters of the hagiography may reflect the competition for land in the new territories the Ewe occupied. Small autochthonous groups were already in residence when the refugees arrived. Oral tradition has it that these people first "lived alongside the immigrants for some time" and then disappeared.[11] Probably some of these indigenous people married into the families of the new arrivals. However, given the strong patrilineal-patrilocal organization of Ewe society, most of these unions probably consisted of women from the original population joining the households of newcomers. This might account for the atypical name of Chicaba's mother. Those who did not assimilate into the new communities began their own treks away from Ewe-dominated territories.[12]

Also, in some locations where arable land was scarce, Ewes began to form "new social organizational units," clans, related through the father's line. Historians and anthropologists usually date clan formation from the 1670s to the early 1700s. Additional migrations of incoming Ewe fleeing from what they had previously hoped would be their safe new settlements to escape the expansion of Akwamu, an Akan empire, put greater pressure on the land and precipitated interclan disputes and battles. The Akwamu were active participants in the slave trade. Sometimes their raids spilled across the Volta River into Ewe territories (Greene, *Gender*, 21–59). This atmosphere of conflict forms a background for the early chapters of the *Vida* and facilitates an analysis of several narratives about Chicaba's family and her people. In this context, the *Vida* depicts her father as a courageous military leader and a king of a civilized people beset by marauding "cannibal" invaders. Further, the story portrays him as a head of a monogamous family unit similar to what Spanish readers found acceptable, given their own social structures.

In truth, the Ewe of the seventeenth and early eighteenth centuries organized themselves into towns (*du*) composed of several clans with a chief (*fia*), "and several towns would have made up a state (*duk*☐)" governed by a "head chief" (*fiagã*). These federations "did not form one united kingdom, but rather separate autonomous states allying themselves with others whenever the political need arose" (Meyer 1–15). However, Chicaba's homeland, as represented in the first six chapters, is an imagined kingdom fashioned after European royal courts, complete with palaces, courtiers, and servants. That is to say, the *Vida* renders the society of the Mina Baja del Oro as a nation governed by a strong monarch and organized to meet the expectations of an eighteenth-century Spanish intellectual. Further, the representation of a monogamous, patriarchal nuclear family, which Chicaba's unnamed father oversaw, supposedly mirrored that state in microcosm. Yet, the Ewe were not monogamous, nor did they establish a polity that was so vertically ordered or unified.

The mechanisms by which the image of Eweland becomes transformed may be too complex for the modern scholar to decipher: Were they a result of the subject's aging memory or do they reflect an impulse to describe her past in dignified terms that the hagiographer would understand? Did the demands of the genre require this sanitized reimagining, or was it the hagiographer's desire to translate her exceptional chosen status into terms his audience, and indeed he himself, could comprehend? More important than motives for the depiction is what the modern reader gleans from the necessity to conform Chicaba's natal land to Spanish expectations. Clearly the alterations in the depiction of her early background are the text's attempts to negotiate for its readers the tension between their notions of the pagan and savage people who inhabit Guinea and their impressions of the pious person, Chicaba, with whom they interacted in Spain. To do so, they had not only to construct her society to resemble their own, but they also had to contrast her people with those barbarous inhabitants of the territories that surrounded them.

The story in Chapter 3 of the attack on the young Chicaba by "cannibals" went beyond any paganism a reader might have expected and instead dwelled on the ultimate foreignness and horror provided by such a comparison. The logic of the narrative is that, although she was the daughter of a civilized albeit non-Christian ruler, Chicaba lived surrounded by cannibals and savages. Such was the hazard of dwelling in Guinea, where she had to exist in proximity to absolute evil, from which she was precariously insulated and protected only by a last-minute rescue. Her father arrived in the nick of time at the head of his army, thereby emphasizing how close she was to peril.

Because Chicaba's people were not cannibals, she could be eligible for sainthood. Yet it is this proximity to ultimate savagery that made imperative her extraction from Africa and her enslavement—events to be understood as acts of physical and spiritual rescue. The image of Africa in the *Vida* contains an embedded narrative of conquest, for the presence of man-eaters would justify future interventions in Africa; thus, the practice of enslavement would become an act of salvation. In a sense, her geographic location highlights her liminality, for she is both of Africa and apart from it. This representation of Guinea creates a further tension in the hagiography, for it cannot reconcile Teresa Chicaba's place of origin as the homeland of a would-be saint with its characterization as a land of savages and would-be slaves. This duality is untenable.

One means of resolving this tension between pervasive notions about Chicaba's native land and her moral rectitude was to describe her social origins in the terms of foundational theories of European social hierarchy of the period. The epitaph on her tomb, recounted in the *Oración fúnebre* and quoted by an eighteenth-century historian of Salamanca, repeats the duality of identifying her as a princess-slave, in which the first term leads to the second (Figure 6).[13] The Spanish believed in a direct relation between blood nobility and moral worth. Thus, the assertion of Chicaba's royal lineage—that is, her *nobility*, in all the valences of the word—saves the hagiographic text and the cause it promotes. Her birth into a ruling class is the guarantee of her saintliness. Even today an essential designation used by the Dominican community in Salamanca to identify her is "Princess." For example, the title of the recent Spanish biography edited by Sor Maria Eugenia Maeso is *Sor Teresa Chikaba: Princesa, esclava y monja* ("*princess*, slave, and nun"; our emphasis).[14] The first line of the prayer booklet distributed to visitors at the convent of Las Dueñas (a community of second order Dominicans) begins, "Oh God, who did not prevent a princess from suffering. . . ." The title ascribed to her in these two current texts and on the few websites dedicated to her appears to affirm that she was truly her father's daughter, the offspring of a "king." These present-day descriptions show how the cultural revisions wrought by the *Vida* persist in impacting the representation of Chicaba and her Ewe kinspeople despite research in African studies during the intervening centuries.

However, by an eighteenth-century European calculus, the father in the narrative is a "king" because he leads "troops" into battle; he consolidates far-flung territories of his domain, as his trip to secure distant lands in Chapter 5 affirms; and, perhaps most importantly, he seems to be a spiritual leader. These responsibilities probably only signify the duties of a mature, trustworthy, active male member of Ewe society during the period barely a generation after a mass migration to new lands. Indeed, he might have been a member of a clan council or even a chief in a *duk*☐. Nevertheless, there is no strong indication that he was a paramount chief, a status closest to what Europeans would consider a monarch. For until the third decade of the nineteenth century, the Ewe were a cluster of independent small states, and they did not establish strong *fiagãs* until they extricated themselves from the century-long suzerainty to the Akan (Meyer 1–5).

But more important than establishing the historical and anthropological accuracy of the *Vida*'s textual representation of Chicaba's background is determining the mechanisms and logic of the hagiography's cultural accommodations for its Catholic Spanish readers. Earlier, we explained the significance of upholding Teresa Chicaba's noble lineage to determine the necessary "purity of her blood," and of demarcating the boundaries of her country to establish her as civilized in contrast to the barbarous others in Guinea. The hagiography must adopt complex strategies to confront its subject's obvious difference from other would-be saints and simultaneously to demonstrate her commonality with them. Despite the genuine disparity between the Ewe and European worldviews and customs, the *Vida*'s intuition about the important relationship between religious practice and polity during the period is ironically correct and in some ways comparable.

When the opening chapter recounts how the putative king and queen (supposedly Chicaba's parents) led their people in prayer on feast days, it is reflecting the European conviction that a head of state governs by divine right and therefore models appropriate reverence for and devotion to the deity. In a sense, this representation of the protagonist's father as a worshipful king of the Morning Star contains a small grain of truth. For among the Ewe, the status of a deity as primary depended on and reflected "the influence of changing power relations within the upper and middle Slave Coast"; that is, the conceptualization of a supreme being—envisioned very differently from an omnipotent, omniscient, and transcendent deity—was "intimately intertwined with the realities of daily political and religious life" and shifted as the character of those relations changed.[15]

Whether the deity these people in the Mina Baja del Oro worshipped was the Morning Star and whether they were monotheistic (as the *Vida* depicts them) are other matters entirely, but their representation lies at the heart of the *Vida*'s attempt to negotiate the issue of Chicaba's religious background. The text observes that her dark complexion, like that of all the inhabitants of the region, indicates blindness to the Christian God and an inclination to participate in barbarous ceremonies. So the hagiography must mitigate the threat of spiritual contamination that her people's religious error poses to her sanctity. It protects her in a number of ways—sometimes by elevating her clansmen above neighboring ethnic groups, and at other times by denigrating them to emphasize their inherent simplicity and innocence. For instance, by characterizing them as practitioners in a pagan cult that lacked buildings (temples) dedicated to worship, the text primitivizes her people, but by asserting that they perform no sacrifices, it exculpates them of the most barbarous practices the reader might imagine. The alleged worship of the Morning Star must have conjured associations with the diabolic, for "Lucifer" means "morning star." But Teresa Chicaba's people seem to have only one god, so readers might have assumed that they were more culturally and religiously advanced than their neighbors (Chapter 2). Furthermore, the wisdom that prompts the child's misgivings about whether the star is the First Cause indicates that she is especially sensitive to what Thomas Aquinas defined as "actual grace." In keeping with this teaching, Chicaba's intrinsic reason was enough to make her search for the true God, since He endows all humans with grace, which allows them to know Him through the exercise of reason, independent of their circumstance.[16]

The portrayal of some African peoples as worshipping a supreme being and extrapolating from that practice a latent monotheism was a fairly typical act of cultural translation during the late seventeenth and early eighteenth centuries. In fact, the debate about the concept of a supreme being in West African religions has continued into the twenty-first century.[17] According to Olabiyi B. Yai, explorers like William Bosman could not understand spiritual beings that existed on a horizontal level with humans. They introduced the concept of a vertical spiritual hierarchy to explain in European terms the complex religious system of divinities in the Bight of Benin.[18] The *Vida*, written about the same time as Bosman's travel narrative, introduces what seems to be the fiction of the Morning Star as the supreme deity of Chicaba's people. This assertion may just indicate confusion on the part of the compiler of the hagiography and his informant about how to identify a sky-god, Mawu, for the European reader. According to Sandra E. Greene, the residence of this Ewe and Fon god is the heavens, "the expanse which is on high, the celestial vault" ("Supreme Being" 127). The hagiography is silent about Mawu's coexistence with *trowu* or *voduwo* (other deities).[19] Instead, it offers an account of the Ewe as worshiping one god, and by doing so, the narrative constructs Chicaba as a member of a superior people prepared to accept the true monotheistic religion, Christianity. This description of Chicaba's African religion explains the Black nun's difference from other Africans and, therefore, her supposed suitability for conversion.

The *Vida* is less concerned with an extended discussion of the Morning Star, which even a child—albeit a special one—realizes cannot be the Creator God; rather, the text emphasizes Chicaba's encounters with the White Lady and Child (Chapter 4). The story echoes John of the Cross's description of a mystical encounter in solitude and thereby identifies the child's vision as the Madonna for its devout readers.[20] The initial meeting with the Virgin takes place near a fountain and perhaps is an indication of a syncretism that blended an Ewe *tro*, a water deity, with the Catholic figure of Mary.[21] There are at least two easily identifiable entities in the lore of the region. The first is Mama Bate, who is associated with the Anlo region in the southwest corner of present-day Ghana. Tradition has it that she was one of the original deities, who lived in human form on the land before it was occupied by several clans in the mass migration of the seventeenth century (probably a god of a people who inhabited the area before the Ewe) (Greene, *Gender* 107).[22] A clan founder encountered her while he was hunting, and she showed him where to get water in an estuary of the Volta. In an interview recorded by Greene, attesting to the deity's association with water, a votary said: "People from this clan are strong-willed and physically strong. It's the *leopard* spirit that is the ruling spirit of the god. . . . When [the *trouna*, priest] recites prayers over a calabash of water and pours it on the ground, one can see fish and shrimp jumping out of the water, no matter how small the pool" (54; emphasis added). So powerful is Mama Bate that there is no need to wash clothes used in her rituals. Instead the priest lays them out on a flat tray and an immediate downpour cleans them. In a second related legend from Dahomey, a princess encounters a *panther* by a fountain; her servants flee in fear, leaving her alone with the beast. When they return with warriors to rescue her, they find her alive and well. The panther has disappeared. Nine months later, the princess gave birth to a male child—the founder of the clan.[23]

The stories of deities connected with bodies of water in this littoral homeland of Ewe abound. The account of the White Lady, seemingly an example of syncretism between West African religious symbol systems and Catholicism—the first of several miraculous occurrences associated with water in the *Vida*—indicates a textual strategy of cultural translation as well as a reflection of the possible enculturation of the hagiographic informant. It may also indicate an intervention in the era's politics of canonization to assure church officials and faithful readers that Guinea was not necessarily a site inimical to the production of Christians.

This first encounter with the White Lady is a crucial case in point, for the *Vida* transforms Chicaba's birthplace into a cradle of proto-Christian virtue. Peru is similarly portrayed in the narrative of the Inca Garcilaso, which predated the *Vida*, and Africa in the autobiography of Olaudah Equiano, published almost forty years after Chicaba's narrative.[24] The episode at the fountain attests to her baptism and renaming as Teresa as a supernatural or angelic intervention in her spiritual life while still in Guinea prior to her encountering any Europeans. The hagiography supplies corroboration of this miracle in the form of an assurance by her confessor.

The depiction of her christening in Chapter 4 is one in a series of proofs from these early chapters that Teresa Chicaba was chosen for sainthood despite her birth and childhood in allegedly unenlightened and unconverted Guinea. Such was also the purpose of the reports of her healing powers in Chapter 3.[25] This divine approbation is further evidenced in the preservation and insurance of her chastity by occasioning her capture by slavers prior to her entrance into the seclusion prescribed for adolescent girls. This time of isolation (gbelelew☐w☐) for an Ewe girl occurred shortly after the onset of menses. At the conclusion of her retreat, the young woman became a candidate for marriage (Meyer 71). Since the encounter at the fountain also marks Chicaba for marriage to Christ, participation in this Ewe rite of passage was textually impossible. The text of the *Vida* cancels Chicaba's initiation into her people's religious system by inserting her mystical baptism and betrothal to the Child Jesus.[26]

The last of these initial incidents that support the *Vida*'s claim for Chicaba's sanctity is the awarding of a kind of retroactive grace or spiritual credit for her parents' and their subjects' conversions in the future, years after these opening episodes. That is, their spiritual preparedness and their eventual acceptance of Christianity through the efforts of the Capuchins, who supposedly proselytized years after her enslavement, become a means to reconfigure Sor Teresa's genealogy as the offspring of Christian parents and to "redeem" La Mina Baja del Oro by reconstructing it as an appropriate birthplace for a would-be saint (Chapters 1 and later 17). Both revisions were necessary to plead the case for canonization in the eighteenth century.

When the *Vida* gives credit to Capuchins for converting Chicaba's parents, it might be referring anachronistically to religious expeditions the Vatican Society for the Propagation of the Faith and Spain sent in the 1650s to the kingdom of Arada, in Western Africa.[27] A purpose of these exploratory journeys was to ascertain whether the inhabitants of Guinea were amenable to genuine Christian conversion. In fact, this mission ended in failure in spite of King Phillip IV's initial diplomatic support.[28] However, one of this project's by-products was the composition of the first bilingual Spanish-Ewe catechism, the *Doctrina christiana* (Madrid, 1658).[29] Also, a priest in this group of emissaries, José de Nájera, wrote a kind of memoir, *Espejo mystico* (Madrid, 1672), where he describes aspects of the religious and legal systems of Arada—such as the practice of divination using cowrie shells—that reflected the influence of the Yoruba, in whose territory the Ewe had lived prior to their migration.[30]

Nájera came to the conclusion that, even though he found examples of natural goodness in the inhabitants of Arada, true Christianization was impossible without the help of

European monarchs. For instance, he recounted the case of a Black woman who was the only person to offer the missionaries shelter and food after they had been mistreated by the king and his officers. The Europeans were afraid that the food she offered them might be poisoned. But the translator explained that the old woman had offered it first to her god to be blessed before presenting it to them, for she considered the missionaries *bodunos*—that is, friends of God (36). Nájera presented this example in order to contrast African generosity with the selfishness of Christian Europeans. He was confounded by what he articulated as a discourse of color difference: Why was Christianity natural to white people of Europe? Because if religions were based on personal merit, Blacks, Caribs, and Moors would take precedence over Catholics (37).

In addition, Nájera recounted that the king of Arada wished to establish some sort of syncretic religious practice that would accommodate European Christianity, the religion of the powerful slave traders. So at one point, the king, after seeing an altar in the missionaries' quarters, expressed his wish to have one in his palace. However, though he claimed that he wanted to become a Christian, he would not renounce his many wives (95). The missionaries and he compromised: an altar with a crucifix was installed, but the Capuchins would not say Mass on it. The episode ended badly for the missionaries, because the king complained, in Portuguese, that their god had not spoken or answered his requests during the whole time he had been in the palace. Furthermore, the king seriously doubted the power of this god because his hands and feet were nailed down (95–96). A representative of the Catholic missionaries responded bluntly. He called into question the king's capacity to communicate with his own gods (*bodos*) as he claimed. Thus, the debate encountered an impasse, as did this particular missionary venture. The Christian failed to understand that Ewe and Fon religions do not require permanent loyalty or fidelity to a god. Rather, the degree of devotion is contingent on the efficacy of the entity propitiated.

The foregoing episode highlighted for Nájera the differences between a European missionary without effective power and an African ruler with the power to decide whether it was necessary for his people to accommodate a new god. In other words, the missionary realized that Christianization was as much a political enterprise as a religious one. And, given the importance of trade in people and goods, economics and catechesis were also inextricably connected. The issue was one of authority and influence. For instance, the territories and nations were active in an intense trade of materials and mores: Gold, textiles, slaves, and religious beliefs were among the commodities and customs that, when exchanged, advanced the production of social mixture and hybridity.[31] Reports by diplomatic and commercial agents from the Netherlands, Portugal, France, England, Spain, Denmark, and Brandenburg acknowledged that African leaders understood that showing interest in European religion—its different forms of Christianity—was an instrument to attract commerce. Therefore, the rulers of Arada and Ouidah (Whydah) frequently asked the bishop of São Tomé to send priests to their lands.[32] They did not primarily intend to open the area for conversion to Christianity; rather, they were attempting to establish diplomatic ties through missionaries, whom these rulers knew enjoyed prestige among European Catholics.[33]

Therefore, once African kingdoms became Christian, as in Kongo, the rulers demanded the creation of a local, indigenous priesthood. But there was European opposition to the funding of a seminary in Angola for Blacks. Instead, Black seminarians were to be sent to Lisbon, where they could learn proper customs; they did not have enough examples in their homeland, where whites were so scarce. Christianity was identified with the white race (Brasio, vol. 13, doc. 206), so Capuchin priests and Portuguese colonists in Angola saw this attempt to train Africans as a dangerous move, for it could result in the expulsion of European missionaries (Brasio, vol. 13, doc. 165). In addition, Europeans began to realize that the kind of cultural assimilation that encouraged African participation in institutions of power had a negative effect: Black clergy "believed they had not been born in Africa, but in Europe."[34] For instance, a Jesuit visiting Mina, Arada, and Werri complained of another problem with training Africans as priests. He claimed to have observed an inappropriately presumptuous attitude among local Black priests, who "after they dressed like whites, acted like whites" (Brasio, vol. 13, doc. 463). In other words, they believed they were entitled to the privileges associated with whiteness. Some of the Europeans writing about the area during the late seventeenth and early eighteenth centuries displayed their antipathy toward this behavior by acculturated Guineans by claiming that Africa was not and could never be Christian.

The opening chapters of the *Vida* reflect this profound ambivalence in European attitudes toward Chicaba's birthplace, for if Guinea could never be a locus of salvation, then her worthiness to be a subject of a hagiography and the eligibility of her candidacy for sainthood were questionable. In this light, true Christian conversion only becomes possible by literally removing the chosen bride of Christ from the site of Blackness, benightedness, to the heart of whiteness and the true faith. Developing notions of "race" combined moral attitudes about skin color with the religious categories of pagans and nonbelievers. Thus, Black skin metaphorized moral debility across the bodies of Guineans. Likewise, early modern Spanish texts used the word *raza* as a derogatory term to indicate religious dissidents, such as Jews, Muslims, heretics, witches, and people condemned by the Inquisition. Adding Blacks to the category was easy enough.[35] This rationale formed the theological basis for modern slavery, especially among Iberian nations that asserted they had the right, and indeed the duty, to enslave "pagan" (non-Christian) peoples in sub-Saharan Africa and thereby to remove them from the moral contamination of their native lands to either Europe or other territories under Catholic political, economic, and religious control—that is, the Spanish and Portuguese empires in the Americas. Therefore, the hagiography represents Chicaba's kidnapping or capture not as the tragedy it will become when the young Teresa looks back toward the shore and her home in Chapter 6. Rather, her enslavement was a means of expunging the spiritual taint of race.

The *Vida* gives an account of Chicaba's capture that is almost blissful. The child is resting under a tree after a long walk in the meadow in search of the White Lady and her Child. A ship appears on the horizon, and a gallant Spanish youth, invisible to all but the child, comes ashore and gently conducts her aboard the vessel—what the reader recognizes immediately as a slave ship. But this is not the traditional swain familiar to the Spanish readers of ballads and romances. Though his benignity signals that he represents a divine intervention into the little girl's life, he is after all separating her from all that is familiar and dear, and this foreignness bodes ill for her (Chapter 6).

Her peril is the result of an act of disobedience; she has left the family compound or "palace" against her father's orders. This transgression seems to go counter to earlier descriptions of her character as obedient, mature, and too serious to engage in childish play. Yet a devout reader might recognize in her actions the reflection of two episodes from the Christian Bible: the first, the story of the Christ Child who wandered away and was lost in the Temple (Luke 2:41–50). His excuse to his parents was that He had to be about His

Father's business; in other words, He had a religious calling—a vocation, so to speak—that surpassed His obligations to Mary and Joseph. The other instance is of Christ's requiring his true followers to forsake their parents and their homes to follow Him (Matthew 10:37–40). Given the text's report of Chicaba's betrothal to the White Child, understood as Christ, at the very fountain that she was seeking when kidnapped, the audience might understand her disobedience and subsequent enslavement as the necessary means of ensuring that she will fulfill her destiny to become the bride of Christ.

There is another scriptural echo in this episode, for the thirsty and forlorn girl under the tree is reminiscent of Hagar, Sarah's slave, who escapes to the wilderness and then sits hopelessly in the shade of a tree to contemplate her fate (Genesis 16:15–24). There an angel appears and induces her back into servitude. When one reads this episode of the reenslavement of Hagar next to the story of the White Child's enticing and teasing of Chicaba with a ribbon, the depiction of the African child's calling takes on a sinister cast—especially in the light of moral arguments circulating in the Catholic world that decried the slave trade's use of trinkets and worthless objects as lures to capture Africans.[36] A combination of these readings produces a textual lapse, where the *Vida* implies that through His implication with slavery, Christ becomes the Master Enslaver—something that will echo through the chapters on Chicaba's religious life. It is an example of the *Vida*'s double discourse on slavery. On the one hand, it accepts the legitimacy of slavery without questioning, and on the other, it grows in its understanding of the horrors and degrading depths of slavery, which makes for a very uncomfortable text to read.

This final episode in these chapters that introduce Guinea begins a series of ambiguities that reverberate throughout the *Vida*, a religious text that must necessarily embrace a theology of suffering or mortification, which is represented in the tree of life (a prefiguration of the cross) standing in the mystical desert of this scene. The desert is traditionally understood as a site of spiritual purification. Chicaba's sojourn under the tree prefigures not just her spiritual life of contemplation in solitude, but also her travails yet to come, in Europe.

The scene of her kidnapping at the end of Chapter 6 shows the presence of two perspectives, as if competing narratives of the same event were colliding with each other. One, from the point of view of normative European ideology, represents the abduction as a miraculous translocation of the child Chicaba into the land of salvation, where she will rejoin the White Child to whom she is betrothed. The other tells a counterstory of terror and threat.[37]

The first story or "voice" shows the little girl Chicaba wandering alone, reaching the coast, resting under a tree, and toying with her gold bangles as a Spanish ship appears on the horizon. A "gallant young man" seizes her by the arm that is adorned with the jewels that will be the external mark of her royalty—her identity document, so to speak. The scene contains a mystical element, for the Spanish youth is an angelic figure that is visible only to Chicaba, not to the ship's crew. But once she is on board, the scene turns into a nightmare for her, and the alternate narrative takes over. The girl realizes that the ship is departing, and she tries to jump overboard to reach the shore. However, a hand holds her back; it is none other than that of the White Lady. Later, the girl is the victim of a terrible thirst and gestures frantically for help, but the sailors cannot interpret her needs. She sees a glass of water and grabs it frantically.

The presence of these two conflicting narratives, which describe the scene of the kidnapping into slavery as both a miraculous event and a terrifying experience, provokes a breakdown in the ideological unity of the narrative. For while it is at this juncture, the *Vida* gives a miraculous interpretation of the scene of enslavement as one ordained by Divine Providence with the intervention of the Virgin Mary at the critical moment of Chicaba's near-death, but it cannot erase the counternarrative of impending disaster. This is the meaning of Chicaba's attempt to throw herself overboard until she realizes that she cannot swim. The excruciating thirst and the later attack by a flock of black birds trying to tear her apart (Chapter 7) are typical motifs in narratives of the Middle Passage's horrors and deliria. It was common for captives aboard slave ships to suffer from hallucinations because of lack of water. Attempts to leap overboard are also amply documented in diaries and narratives about life on slave ships.[38] But one can even interpret the presence of the Virgin Mary as an integral element of a Middle Passage episode, for as the White Lady consoles Chicaba and dries her tears, she also makes her forget the family she is leaving behind. This is reminiscent of what Saidiya Hartman describes as the concerted efforts of African slavers to make captives "lose their mothers" and forget their kin and homeland through sorcery. The captors hoped thereby to stave off the future revenge of angry ancestral spirits.[39] But the experience of the African diaspora is one of remembering the moment of capture, and this conflicting set of details in the *Vida*—the marvelous together with the horrific—creates a narrative collapse in the text.

There are two other impulses that must be reconciled before the narrative of the Middle Passage can get under way. On the one hand, Chicaba longs to return to her people, her house, her mother, and her motherland, but attempting to do this would mean that she would die by drowning. On the other hand, another scene is occurring at the same time elsewhere: the *Vida* depicts the frantic efforts of her mother to find her daughter, and her anguish when she realizes that Chicaba is gone forever. This episode must have been imagined but never witnessed by Chicaba. Both episodes—the mother's and the daughter's—are characterized by anxiety. The two recollections—the scene lived and the scene imagined—correspond to the reflection of a slave who later in life confers appropriate meaning on the childhood memories of her kidnapping and realizes the enormous impact of slavery on the people left behind.

The narrative of Chicaba's abduction also bears striking similarities to the popular, highly spiritual genre of Spanish Byzantine romance, which developed after the Council of Trent and was suffused with allegorical themes reflective of the piety of the Counter-Reformation. In these stories the protagonist often endures periods of captivity and enslavement.[40] The *Vida* shares with this genre other themes, such as the defense of chastity, the motif of pilgrimage, and the arrival at a place of high spiritual significance where the narrative ends. For example, Chapters 5 and 6 develop the theme of abduction. They first tell us of the danger Chicaba faces at the hands of barbarous enemies who captured her when she was still with her family, and then of her subsequent seizure and miraculous transportation to the slave ship. This episode, which takes place on a beach, is similar to one in Heliodorus's *Ethiopian Story*, a popular book in Renaissance Spain. In this tale, pirates capture the young heroes near a sandy riverbank; this initiates their period of captivity and enslavement.[41] Like the narrative practice of Spanish Byzantine romance, which often shifts settings, the episode of Chicaba's kidnapping is briefly interrupted when the action moves back to the palace and the aforementioned frantic mother. Then the story returns once again to the slave ship, and its terrors and miraculous interventions. Abduction and captivity are the sites where the protagonists test and prove their moral fortitude. But the similarities between Byzantine romance and the *Vida* are more than narrative strategies. In many ways, they illustrate the concept of implied code discussed in the first section of this introduction. Teresa Chicaba probably was familiar with Byzantine romance from either her own reading or dramatic recitations before the Manceras. Paniagua would also have known the genre. So perhaps Chicaba and Paniagua collaborated in using elements of Byzantine romance and its moral imperatives for different purposes. From one perspective, Chicaba's story of transportation from her homeland to Spain is reminiscent of the theme of the journey from barbarity and paganism to the land of salvation. From another perspective, the displacement originates in a traumatic abduction, not a liberation, which includes many violent episodes that endanger Chicaba's life. This is an involuntary quest that constantly tests her moral fortitude.

ENSLAVEMENT—CHAPTERS 7 THROUGH 18

The *Vida* reports that Chicaba was kidnapped when she was nine years old. Since she arrived in Spain in 1685, the estimated date of her birth was 1676; therefore, her life in Africa must have spanned part of the prolonged period (1671–1720) of great political instability in the states along the Slave Coast. At this time, the principal regional paramountcy of Arada found its authority challenged by its dependencies—Ouidah, Great Popo, and Dahomey—as they sought greater shares of the slave trade. The proliferation of gangs of bandits that raided the area for human plunder further destabilized the territory. In addition, the refugees fleeing the expansion of the kingdom of Akwamu and its bid for inclusion in the transatlantic trade moved across the Volta and into the western Slave Coast, where they were paradoxically further subjected to invasions of those seeking human cargo. The expanding European market for slaves fueled, if not precipitated, these conflicts among these African polities (Law, *Slave Coast* 224–34). In 1673 the merchants of São Tomé had been authorized by the Portuguese crown to do trade with the Mina Coast.[42] In the year that the *Vida* approximates Chicaba's birth, the Portuguese crown established the Company of Cacheu and Cape Verde to control the exportation of slaves from the Mina Coast to São Tomé. This trade in captives from the Mina Coast received further stimulus when ship captains began to navigate to this area rather than journeying to Angola, where a smallpox epidemic had been declared (Verger 47).

In addition, there were Spanish ships sailing the route from Western Africa to other places in the Atlantic. Many of these vessels were dedicated to and named after religious figures: for example, *Nuestra Señora del Rosario*, *Santiago*, *Santo Domingo*, *San Juan Bautista*, and *San Vicente*. Some owners, especially those from Seville and the coastal area of Cádiz, christened their barques after patrons of their particular geographic region; such was the case of an owner from the Canary Islands who called his vessel *Nuestra Señora de la Candelaria*.[43] In general, between 1681 and the end of the century the export and transportation of slaves was so widespread that it is difficult to establish a reliable estimate of numbers shipped to the Spanish mainland (Vila Vilar 129).

During the voyage, Chicaba's diet most likely consisted of sardines, salt cod, and other preserved fish or meat, as well as *bizcocho* (hardtack). The combination of this salty fare, small water allotments, and the heat in the close quarters caused many bondspeople to perish from dehydration.[44] Therefore, the *Vida*'s description of Teresa tottering on the "brink of death" and crying from thirst seems a faithful representation of her plight aboard the slaver (Chapter 6).

The narrative reports that, during this leg of the Middle Passage, the crew observes the gold and jewels Chicaba was wearing. They take these as signs of her elevated social status and begin to identify her as an African princess, for her adornments distinguish her from the other captives on board—even her female cousin, whom the *Oración fúnebre* reports was captured with her but about whom there is no further record. The *Vida* erases Chicaba's companion from the scene and never mentions her again. Her cousin disappears into the anonymity of a modern slave society.

Spain was such a slave society. The straightforwardness with which everyone accepted the institution of slavery and the insignificance of Black humanity meant that their enslavement was of no moral consequence in either the Catholic or the Protestant world; thus, the issue was not the subject of extensive disputations until the late eighteenth century. This relative dearth of writing on the subject evidences that Blacks were not on the minds of most philosophers and social moralists of the seventeenth century. Even the British philosopher John Locke, writing about political tyranny as a form of slavery during his exile in Holland in the 1680s, was in favor of white people, Europeans, enslaving others.[45]

Most discussions of the enslavement of Blacks in Spain and Latin America in the sixteenth and seventeenth centuries did not address the issue in terms of the commodification of Africans. Rather, it was a question of early international law—whether the Atlantic slave trade itself was legitimate. The legality of enslaving Blacks was a separate issue from that of slavery, for Spaniards believed that the institution of slavery was a normal practice that had occurred since time immemorial. Therefore, moralists like Tomás de Mercado, Frías de Albornoz, and a few others cast doubt on the legitimacy of the slave trade, using arguments concerning the legal authority of the traffickers (García Añoveros 178ff.). An encyclical of Paul III in 1537 condemned the slave trade, but not slavery. However, popes had always made a distinction between the enslavement of Indians, as well as other "native" peoples, and that of Black Africans. In 1639 Urban VIII had condemned the enslavement of "native" populations, by which he referred basically to indigenous peoples of the American continent, specifically those of Brazil. Curiously, Spanish moralists hardly ever cited these papal documents.[46] None came to the conclusion that slavery itself was morally wrong—not even the Jesuit Alonso de Sandoval, author of *De instauranda aethiopum salute* (Seville 1627 and 1647), a treatise on the indoctrination of Black slaves as Christians, where he denounced the mistreatment of Black slaves at the hands of their owners.[47]

Two Capuchin friars, Francisco José de Jaca and Ephiphane de Moirans, were different from their contemporaries; in 1681, they preached against the institution of slavery in Havana, Cuba.[48] When Jaca and Moirans went to Rome with a petition to abolish slavery in the Spanish and Portuguese empires, the diplomatic channels of the Vatican and Spain were forced to take notice. By the time Chicaba arrived in Spain in 1685, the Spanish Council of the Indies—the governmental body that advised the king on issues related to the overseas empire—had become aware of theologians' movements against slavery and the slave trade in which the king of Spain held the monopoly. The Council of the Indies issued a recommendation to the king that is a model of casuistic duplicity. The councillors rejected all the testimonies concerning the atrocities committed against Blacks in the New World. As politicians, they observed that the Spanish American empire would not survive without slaves.[49] Therefore, they concluded that the king could keep his slaves and continue the slave trade, but they entreated slaveholders to provide for the proper religious care of their slaves and to desist from the mistreatment of Blacks.[50] Spanish politicians were more concerned that the slave trade was in the hands of foreigners—many of them Protestant—and that this was detrimental to the economy of the Spanish empire.[51]

Also, religious communities and individual nuns and priests as well as ecclesiastic authorities themselves composed an important contingent of slave owners throughout the Spanish-speaking world.[52] For example, Diego Torres Villarroel, the author of Father Abarrategui's hagiography, owned slaves who lived as part of his household.[53]

Antislavery opinion in the Catholic world did not benefit from access to the press. Jaca and Moirans wrote their allegations only to the pope and other church authorities. The manuscripts of their condemnations were not meant for public debate or publication in the press, which was heavily regulated; furthermore, if their arguments had been printed, they would not have passed the scrutiny of church or royal censors. By contrast, opposition to slavery in Protestant lands on both sides of the Atlantic—such as the Quaker declaration of 1688—was helped and developed through the existence of an emerging public opinion and its medium, the press. In countries like Holland and England, the Crown found itself less and less able to clamp down on everything that was published.

Although slavery remained legal in the absence of a large public outcry against the institution, scholars agree that after the middle of the seventeenth century, the population of slaves in Spain had declined rapidly from its peak fifty years earlier.[54] While no general statistics exist on the number of slaves in Spain during the seventeenth and eighteenth centuries, studies of other geographic areas also indicate declining numbers, in Extremadura, southeastern Andalusia, and the main urban centers.[55] The chief cause for this demographic decline in the slave population of Spain was the growth of trade directed to the American colonies, which was in the hands of non-Spaniards. There were other reasons for the waning numbers, among them the royal policy of confiscating male slaves to serve as rowers in the navy, as laborers in the mercury mines of Almadén, or in other public works, which discouraged the risky investment in human property.[56]

However, the archival records do give a sense of the makeup of the Black population in Spain and of the social networks they developed. For example, the baptismal records of three populous parishes of Madrid indicate a total of 347 slaves of all races and nationalities for the period from 1650 to 1700 (Larquié 52). Those transported to Spain by various routes constituted two groups: One consisted of Muslims who were either part of the trans-Saharan traffic or victims of the war between Spain and the Ottoman Empire. The other was made up of Black non-Muslims. The latter was the case for most of the 137 slaves sold in Valencia during the second half of the seventeenth century.[57] Some arrived from sub-Saharan Africa through Atlantic routes, and still others arrived in Spain from the American colonies as part of their owners' entourage, as was the case in the city of Granada.[58] The most complete studies of slave populations are those of the Canary Islands, where there was more slavery because of its sugar plantation economy. Even there, the number of baptisms of slave children decreased from a maximum of 13 percent (256 baptisms) in the first decade of the seventeenth century to only 3 percent (87 baptisms) in the first decade of the eighteenth century.[59]

Race in Spain and Spanish America was a category dependent on the association of religious difference to phenotype and ethnic background, and it had become the defining factor for enslavement by the second half of the seventeenth century.[60] While there was a general prohibition against bringing Muslim slaves to the American colonies, no such impediment existed for the peninsular part of the Spanish monarchy.[61] A significant number of *moros* (men presumed to be of North African descent) were enslaved by the authorities and sold in Valencia between 1670 and 1690 in spite of their protestations of being free people. No document was necessary to detain them; their ethnicity was sufficient (Kamen 227–31). Phenotype and cultural traits relegated them to the group of people who were appropriate targets for enslavement. Persons suspected of being of Muslim descent were always in danger of being sold into bondage by the authorities unless they could either prove their free status through written documents or present witnesses as to their social connection to a former master.

Slaves in the main cities of Spain formed family and social networks that still require further in-depth study. In some cases, the first thing they did when they were manumitted was to travel in search of relatives in distant cities. For example, an Algerian man in his fifties traveled from Oporto to Madrid to be reunited with his cousin, a slave of the Marquis of Monterrey (Kamen 233). The Muslim slaves in the household of the Marquis of Mancera probably belonged to this important social network, from which Chicaba would have been excluded, given her strong identification with Christianity.[62]

Black slaves from Guinea and Muslim slaves constituted separate groups in Spain. Proof of this is the presence of church activity among the former and its almost total absence in the latter, for rather obvious reasons. Blacks acted as godparents for the children of other Black people in Spanish cities. The children of Muslim women were obligatorily baptized, and in these cases the godparents were normally their owners, free people in the household, sextons, or even priests, as well as other people whose Christian names do not reveal their ethnicity. Priests, who were quite conscientious about indicating the racial and ethnic classification of parents and children, are silent in the cases of godparents.

Another social network for Blacks was available through religious confraternities, which had been a fixture of Spanish society since the fifteenth century. Every important city on the Iberian Peninsula had at least one.[63] In Madrid, in 1682, Lourenço Mendouça, a Black man from Brazil, was appointed procurator of the Confraternity of Our Lady Star of the Blacks.[64] This is also an indication of how close the relationship was between Blacks from both sides of the Atlantic, and how they shared the common goal of abolishing slavery on religious grounds. Lourenço Mendouça traveled to Rome to advocate for his fellow Blacks and mulattoes. He requested that the pope declare free all Christian Blacks and mulattoes from Brazil, thus abolishing Black slavery there for all practical purposes. His mission to Rome coincided with that of the two Capuchins, Jaca and Moirans, who personally pleaded in front of the Vatican authorities to condemn the slave traffic and slavery itself in the Americas as a sin punishable by excommunication.

Madrid's enslaved population was employed in a variety of ways. For example, many slaves worked in hospitals, which left them exposed to infectious diseases. Spanish hospitals understood their mission as a blend of medical care and the religious preparation for death; thus, all wards bore the names of patron saints, which supposedly provided spiritual protection for those interned. Records from the general hospital in Madrid indicate that a significant number of male and female slaves worked there. Most of these were Black, but there were also some of other races, who had been sold or donated to serve the sick. Many Black women tending patients fell ill themselves. Following common social practice, they left last wills and testaments. These documents were a hybrid of civil and religious declarations. As members of the Church, these slaves exercised their religious rights, and in their wills, they bequeathed all they had—most often just a few ducats they had been able to save during their lives—for Masses and other pious works. In death the slave behaved like the aristocrat. The difference between an aristocrat and a Black woman slave was the number of Masses that each could sponsor. Yet the slaves' attitudes were the same as those who occupied higher social positions. Both Spanish citizens and their slaves were persuaded that they possessed similar agency in this respect.

However, the ethics of slavery were tied to religious notions of obedience—to the relinquishing of one's agency at the command of another. José de Nájera, in his *Espejo mystico*, recounted the anecdote of his disciple, who felt like a slave when he had to show happiness while complying with orders he abhorred. In explaining his feelings to the priest, the disciple said that when he had to obey commands against his will, he did not feel like a son to God, but like a slave to his master (187). One can speculate that Chicaba, whose unquestioning obedience the *Vida* extols, must have also been an unhappy slave in the household of the Marquis and the Marchioness of Mancera, in spite of the benevolence of her owners, who, as the *Vida* maintained, treated her more as a daughter than as a slave.

The presence of the marquis and marchioness in Chicaba's life was an invaluable asset in her plans for obtaining freedom and entering the convent of La Penitencia. The Marquis of Mancera, who enjoyed a long political career, had to have been a man with a high sense of his own importance. When he arrived in Mexico he was greeted with a festival that hailed him as a new Aeneas.[65] During his tenure as viceroy (1664–1673), he witnessed the creation of triumphal arches in his honor that represented him as the Greek mythological figure Perseus defeating the Medusa.[66] A typical aristocrat of the period, the marquis Antonio Sebastián de Toledo was both a religious man and someone given to a variety of intellectual explorations that were not part of Catholic orthodoxy. For instance, astrology was popular in Mancera's viceregal court.[67] In addition, together with his first wife, Leonor de Carreto, he was a mentor and supporter of Sor Juana Inés de la Cruz, in a court that fostered an intellectual climate for women.[68]

Upon his return to Madrid in 1700, the Marquis of Mancera played a significant role in the tumultuous events that preceded the end of the Hapsburg dynasty and the arrival of the Bourbons. He occupied important positions in the court of King Carlos II of Spain, and he was a well-known member of the party of the Queen Mother, Mariana of Austria, to whom he owed his appointment as viceroy in Mexico.[69] In fact, the *Oración fúnebre* describes the "presentation" of Chicaba to him as a gift not from Carlos II but from Mariana. As a member of the Council of Italy and then the Council of State, Mancera intervened in favor of the Austrian candidate, Archduke Karl, in the intense disputes for the Spanish succession, and only at the end of the life of Carlos II—who died childless—did he switch his vote in favor of the future Philip V of Anjou, the grandson of Louis XIV.[70] The episode in the *Vida* where Juan Francisco announces that Chicaba is her parents' sole successor (Chapter 17) is almost a parody of the historical events taking place in Madrid at the time.

The *Vida* depicts the marquis as the recipient of a royal gift, Chicaba, on the basis of his tenure as viceroy of Mexico and his familiarity with people of other races and ethnicities, called "foreigners" in the text of the *Vida*: "The king heard that the marquis liked 'foreigners,' a natural result of the compassionate love with which he consoled and ministered to the Indians during his tenure as viceroy" (Chapter 8).[71] Chapter 11 repeats the same sentiment. This fictional ceremony of the bestowal makes Chicaba not an ordinary slave but a royal gift. The term used in the Spanish original is *esclava presentada*, a slave given as a present. In this regard, the *Vida* follows the extended motif of the golden gift of the *Oración fúnebre*.

The idea is the same, but with the specific reference to King Carlos II, whose donation of Chicaba to the marquis is said to have followed God's design. This is a key passage to understanding how the narrative disguises the dire situation of Chicaba's enslavement. A gift is not for future sale; the recipient, the marquis, is bonded to the benefactor, the king, through the donated object. In the economy of gift giving, the object that constitutes the gift changes its market value for a different social value, that of establishing a pledge or attachment between donor and recipient. Selling the gift one has received from a person who is of a more elevated status would be tantamount to denying the allegiance the gift has created. Had he sold Chicaba, as he did other slaves in his household, the marquis would have breached the tangible bond that made him part of the king's influence and God's providence.

This stress in the text of the *Vida* may explain its need to create euphemisms for Chicaba's abduction and her life as a slave in Madrid between 1685 and 1703. Thus, the narrative depicts her kidnapping as the acquisition of a treasure by a rightful owner, the king of Spain, since she is associated synecdochically with her golden bangles and jewels and is thereby metaphorized as a gift. The hagiographic assertion that the slave Chicaba was a gift narratively converts her capture into the miraculous act of finding a mystical treasure, an embellishment to the king's court. She would have shared the same status as poets, artists, and saints, who in seventeenth-century Catholic peninsular society opinion were adornments to the king's image of power and majesty. Her future spiritual work becomes the possession of Spaniards through her putative connection to Carlos II or his mother, the Queen Regent. In this light, Chicaba belonged to the entire nation. Despite both the funeral oration and the hagiography representing her transfer to the Marquis of Mancera, this did not invalidate the notion of the Crown owning her.

There is a difference in emphasis between the *Oración fúnebre* of 1749 and the *Vida* of 1752 with respect to representing Chicaba as a gift. On the one hand, the *Oración fúnebre* organizes its narrative around the metaphor of the gifts the Magi brought to the Christ Child; in this figuration Chicaba is a God-given present to her royal owners and Christian Spain. On the other hand, the *Vida* offers a more nuanced interpretation of the topos, where Chicaba becomes the recipient of gifts as well as the donor of favors. The latter treatment shows an evolution in the estimation of Chicaba, who becomes a member of a spiritual community. This transformation in the compiler's imagination is a prerequisite for the construction of a hagiography, the purpose of which is to argue for its subject's affiliation with the communion of saints.

That Chicaba was a gift from either royal person to the marquis is probably a fiction, for the last will and testament signed by Doña Juliana Teresa Portocarrero y Meneses in 1703 makes it very clear that Chicaba was her property (see Appendix 4). Doña Juliana had married the Duke of Arcos in 1663, and upon his death she had inherited a periodic payment of four thousand ducats from endowments until she remarried.[72] Therefore, her second marriage, to the Marquis of Mancera, had to be more economically advantageous than her widowhood. One can infer that she brought Teresa Chicaba, whom she named Teresa Juliana del Espíritu Santo, with her from Andalusia to her new household in Madrid.[73]

The slave Chicaba was not all that Doña Juliana brought into this new union with the elderly Don Antonio. Juliana Portocarrero was independently wealthy. The *encomienda* in Peru she had been granted included an endowment of six thousand ducats, and she exercised sole control over the money from these funds (Hampe Martínez and de la Puente Brunke 98). Upon her death, she left money for an *obra pía* (foundation), which was customary among the wealthy. In her will, Doña Juliana refers to Teresa Juliana del Espíritu Santo as "my slave."[74] If Chicaba had been a gift to the marquis, as the *Oración fúnebre* and the *Vida* both assert, the marchioness would not have been able to dispose of her husband's property so generously by, a few days before dying, bequeathing freedom to Teresa Chicaba.

Both the funeral oration and the hagiography elide the notion of Chicaba's purchase as a common slave by making her a royal gift. While in the *Vida*, written later, Chicaba is given to the marquis by Carlos II himself, who had received her as a present from an unnamed family from Seville, the *Oración fúnebre* says that the Marquis of Mancera received Chicaba from the mother of "the king of the earth," meaning Queen Mother Mariana of Austria.[75] Calling King Carlos II "king of the earth" might have been a subtle allusion to King Solomon's reception of the Queen of Sheba. This biblical association with Ethiopia—not Guinea—is an important second motif in the *Oración fúnebre* alongside the trope of the gifts of the Magi. This earlier biographical text transforms the Middle Passage into the long journey of the Three Wise Men. In fact, gold and the associated metaphor of a treasure appear in the *Oración fúnebre* in a passage *before* Chicaba's kidnapping and enslavement. In this context, Chicaba is a metonym for the riches of Africa: "But there was never a ship loaded with a richer cargo than this one which contains Chicaba, such a rich treasure" (*Oración fúnebre* 7).

Though her role as a spiritual gift, the text transforms Chicaba, the slave girl, into an instrument of salvation for her owners in what becomes a role reversal. From this perspective on her enslavement, the *Vida* represents Chicaba as the master of spiritual matters, while the marquis and the marchioness continue as her masters in all other respects and for all practical purposes. In what constitutes an example of a Hegelian dichotomy, the world of the spirit is presented as an antithesis to the material world as well as its complement. The association between teacher and disciple seems to upset power relations in Teresa's favor; however, the master-slave relationship is not entirely compensatory or equivalent. Teresa purchases heaven for her owners with her prayers and spiritual work. She, therefore, is their slave not only in the material world but also in the spiritual one. She is the perfect slave.

The *Oración fúnebre* and the *Vida* try to stress the merits of this Black woman through the rhetorical conversion of her status as a former slave into an extended metaphor of gold, treasure, and gift, but the metaphor of the gift in the production of Teresa Chicaba's sainthood was at odds with the actual economy of slavery in early modern Spain. A gift, especially one to or from a sovereign, is governed by a different set of rules than those that regulate the ordinary exchange of commodities. For instance, a presentation from a king does not circulate and cannot be exchanged or sold by the recipient. However, Chicaba's status as a slave also made her a commodity, a human being whose sale could produce gold. Thus, the metaphor of the gift Chicaba represented for Catholic Spain is a case of *catachresis*, a misuse of a metaphor, as the text employs it to conceal the stark reality of Chicaba's legal status—a commodity always in jeopardy of further trade until freed or removed from circulation.

While Chicaba's Black body marked her as a target for slavery, gold and jewels should have set her apart and exempted her from the predation of the trade. The tension between her lived reality as an object of abjection as a slave versus her status as a free, precious daughter of a respected man of the Ewe community constitutes the oxymoronic strain under which the narrative will operate into her future until the end of its plot. That is, from the Middle Passage onward, the *Vida* will struggle to insert the irretrievable past, a hazy memory transformed by Chicaba's acculturation, into a future marked by the uncertainty and insecurity of a slave. But religion will be the voucher to restore her exalted position when she becomes a bride of Christ in La Penitencia. The inner logic of the *Vida*'s discourse on slavery makes religion the indirect cause of her bondage; at the same time, religion will allow her to become legally free.

Life in Juliana Portocarrero's household was lived under a quasi-conventual religious regime. The *Vida* indicates as much, and independent evidence suggests that Doña Juliana was a very pious woman, which was in keeping with her high social status. Visits to the enclosure of cloistered nuns were not unusual for a lady of her rank, and for this she even obtained permission from the pope.[76] The example the marchioness set in the household was probably behind the decision to provide the young African slave with a modicum of education in reading and writing. Apparently in seventeenth-century Madrid this was not completely unusual.[77]

The *Vida* states that the marquis and his wife provided Chicaba with an *aya* (governess). This is contrasted with the atmosphere of violence against Chicaba on the part of other servants in the household. Three major incidents exemplify the threat against Chicaba's life and physical well-being during these years. The first one is her near-drowning in the pond at Buen Retiro Park in Madrid (Chapters 10 and 11). The second is the incident with the Turkish girl who attempted to kill her (Chapters 11 and 12), and the third one is her attempted kidnapping by the mysterious character Juan Francisco (Chapters 17 and 18).

As part of the *Vida*'s endeavor to present Teresa Chicaba as a princess, the narrative of her sojourn as a slave of the Manceras contains elements of a Renaissance *educatio principis*, but the recipient of the education has been stripped of social status. Life in the Mancera household becomes an important stage in Chicaba's intellectual and spiritual journey to saintly transformation. The house is a site of profound inconsistencies very much like the chronotopes—narrative features where time and place, era and location, are fused—present in Baltasar Gracián's allegorical Byzantine romance *El criticón* (1651–1657). Drawing on this highly metaphorical genre, the hagiography depicts the Mancera household as a site where the youthful protagonist undergoes a traditional period of learning. There and then she confronts a world of contradictions. For instance, within this pious environment of priests and devout practices there is overt violence, including sexual abuse and threats of abduction, and the devil puts the house under siege.

As Delfis de Calvo explains, Spanish Byzantine romance, especially in its most allegorical form, created chronotopes characterized by a profound "derealization of space and time."[78] Space—the Mancera household—is a real place where things happen in a span of time, the period of Chicaba's enslavement. When the two combine, they provoke a sense of things outside reality. Thus, in the *Vida*, the specific location of this slave's captivity is doubly symbolic: First, it represents the greater reality for Blacks living in Madrid at the end of the seventeenth century. Second, the Mancera household becomes a site of incarceration for Chicaba, who seems unable to leave it except on one occasion, during which she is almost killed. It is a figural repetition of the hold of the ship that transported her in the

Middle Passage. The experience of this confinement overwhelms her in Spain. The house is a kind of jail and insane asylum. Central to this merging of narratives (the education of the prince combining with the jail full of mad people) in Chapter 9 is the character of the *aya*—a warden of sorts—who is put in charge of Chicaba's education.[79] This governess is further textual evidence of Teresa Chicaba's literacy and, therefore, of her ability to pray the Divine Office before she enters the convent of La Penitencia.

The atmosphere at the Mancera household must have been dreadful for Teresa. She seems to have made enemies among the servants. The role of the villain in an exemplary narrative like the *Vida* is often an old maid like the governess, who is a very difficult person and who abuses Teresa Chicaba verbally and physically. The scars from her blows mark Chicaba's body for the rest of her life. The *aya* is an instance of contradiction, for she is both a symbol of Chicaba's elevated status—which the *aya*, as another servant, resents—and the personification of the indignities visited on enslaved people of the time: the infliction of psychological and bodily injury. The representation is another instance of confused categories in the motif of the princess-slave. Though the *Vida* calls this character a governess, the text later indicates that this woman was someone under the authority of the majordomo—not the typical location of a governess in the social hierarchy of an aristocratic house's domestic staff. The representation of the *aya* emphasizes the royal quality of Chicaba by indicating the "appointment" of this woman by the Manceras expressly for Teresa's instruction. But her behavior instead reveals that she was probably only someone in charge of servants and slaves.

The dual condition of princess and slave represented in these chapters of the *Vida* creates instability in the discourse of sainthood. Privileged education and physical violence are combined in almost equal parts. The narrative details the insults and aggression directed at Teresa, and yet the perpetrators act with impunity. Humor becomes the tool to lessen the impact of their behavior against the protagonist. *Aya* and maidservants suffer a metaphorical change in their personalities and appearance when, according to the text, their faces "turn Black" with fury at seeing the special treatment their masters give the Black slave, whom they mockingly call a "feigned *infanta*." However, the violence is real, as exemplified by scars, which write the story of Chicaba's suffering across her body. These physical marks serve to keep fear alive in her memory. They also are a sign of the power of the master over the body and the spirit of the bondsperson. The text of the *Vida* addresses this violence as one more trial, another instance of suffering, sent by God to be accepted, indeed embraced, by the future saint. She could complain to the marquis and his wife as an appropriate recourse for her mistreatment. However, she chooses to suffer in silence. In doing so, she removes the agency from the hands of her masters, who are left without the obligation to intervene and restore justice. Consistent with her Christian charity, Teresa forgives the persecution she suffers in the Mancera household, but her physical scars do not disappear from her body, and she will recount the story of cruelty and abuse to the day she dies. Teresa forgives but cannot forget. That would be impossible.

The brutality against Chicaba in Chapter 10 comes at a critical point in the narrative. The *Vida* is at pains first to conceal this violence as a story of diabolical intervention foiled by a miraculous deliverance and second to rationalize the cruelty, an essential feature of slavery, as the means by which a chosen few emulate Christ's suffering and achieve sainthood. Thus, slavery has a particular value in Teresa Chicaba's case, for through it she is transplanted like a flower into fertile soil (*Oración fúnebre* 1). That is, her virtue can only grow in the Christian ground of Spain.

This is not strictly true for Chicaba because her encounters with the White Lady and her Child begin in Africa. The presence of these Christian visions in her homeland suggests another plot that is truncated by her capture. Not only does she continue to yearn for home, but also home will eventually become a site of familial redemption.

For example, in the same Chapter 10, Chicaba rejects an opportunity for *sankofa* (a return to Africa) when it is mystically prefigured.[80] During a day-trip with fellow servants to Buen Retiro Park, someone pushes her into the pool. All who are present blame the majordomo of the household, only to discover later that the perpetrator had been the devil in disguise. The scene gestures toward an attempt on her life. After her rescue by a celestial being, later identified as the "glorious archangel Saint Raphael," she recalled that "under the waves she was as pleased as she had been in the little meadow back in her homeland," where she first encountered the White Lady with her Divine Child. The memory of Africa in this life-and-death situation puts Madrid and her country in Guinea at opposite ends of the spectrum of the *locus amoenus* topos. In Guinea the scenes near the water were suggestive of a godly presence, while in Madrid, the devil seems to hover all around. Furthermore, her contact with the divinity seems to be related to water. But water is also a source of danger once she leaves Africa.

There are at least two possible interpretations of this portent under the surface of the pond. First, the cost of a happy return to Africa is clearly death by drowning. Second, the vision does not depict her loving family but rather the site of her betrothal to the White Child whose "home" is Europe—specifically Spain, and certainly not Guinea. In the text of the *Vida*, Guinea is a perplexing reality, the "dark" land of paganism and the site where Chicaba first encounters Christ. The moment of *sankofa*—the going back to get what one has left behind—that this incident implies ends with a "rescue" by the angel who is paradoxically the instrument of her enslavement as well as her return to bondage in the marquis's household.

The second story of violence takes place in Chapter 11. The protagonists are Chicaba and another slave of the Manceras, whom the *Vida* simply calls "the Turkish girl."[81] It was the owners' legal duty to instruct their slaves in the Christian religion. This was neglected to a large extent, especially in the case of Muslim slaves. Many owners justified their inaction with the pious excuse that they could not force conversion on Muslims. Somehow the Manceras had not accomplished the Christianization of this Turkish slave by the time Teresa arrived under their roof. The story of the Turkish girl, her beauty, and her sexual transgression is set against Chicaba's sexual purity. The *Vida* maintains that, over an extended period, the devil inspires the Turkish girl to try and kill Chicaba. During this time Chicaba tries to convert her fellow slave but to no avail; it is not until the girl is dying that she accepts Christianity. On her deathbed, the Turkish girl confesses only to Chicaba that she had been seduced by a priest who had promised to help her gain freedom by fleeing with her to northern Africa.

Chicaba's relationship with the young Turkish woman is problematic because it is sexualized. The comparison and competition between the two is obvious throughout this episode. The *Vida* asserts that the unnamed Turk was beautiful, in contrast to Chicaba, who could not be attractive because she was Black. The attractiveness of the (white) Turkish girl was the reason for her seduction by the priest. Thus, beauty is a menace to the concept of *limpieza de sangre*, as it incites illicit sexual intercourse and its logical consequence, the generation of an impure race. Also, location in this story is significant, as the adventure of the Turkish girl takes place in the Mancera household, an aristocratic site where several "bloods" live together. In the case of Chicaba, her Black complexion is deemed a form of ugliness. Spared the attention of white men, Chicaba's body becomes an ally to her quest for liberation on the condition that she accepts the racialized social norm that makes her unattractive. In this discourse, race is understood as a measure of sexual desirability.

The Turkish girl represents the figure of the doppelgänger for Chicaba—her white double and her opposite. She serves the purpose of enhancing the representation of Chicaba's Christian faith, her miraculous powers, and her Blackness—that is, her ugliness. This latter factor is directly connected to her chastity, which the narrative extols oxymoronically in the context of the normative belief that sexual purity is impossible for a Black slave woman; Blackness is a sign of lasciviousness.[82] Chicaba's "natural" ugliness is the correlate of her "natural" Blackness, and it becomes a favor from God. Her ugliness/Blackness spares her from being sexually assaulted. This episode therefore contains an implicit assumption of sexual violence.

The episode is fraught with anxiety. Beauty and the sexual desire it instigates threaten the racial purity of the Mancera household, which represents the entire Spanish Christian community; both are the instruments for the defilement of the blood, race, nation, and religion, for the unnamed priest who seduces the Turkish girl is someone for whom sexual intercourse is forbidden by his religious vow of celibacy. More importantly, the priest's false promises to flee with the Turkish girl to North Africa imply an attempt to abjure his Catholic faith.

This incident in Chapter 11 is the first time Teresa's Black complexion is compared unfavorably with the color of a white woman. However, the equation of whiteness with physical beauty is a category of cultural value throughout this work. Thus, in spite of the protestation in Chapter 1 about the comeliness of Black people in Africa, whiteness is clearly synonymous with beauty—even early in the narrative, when Teresa observed the Child Jesus and His Mother by the fountain. Therefore, by this logic, it is no wonder that a Turkish slave woman must be beautiful even as Teresa is naturally ugly. This African character must have been acutely aware of the differences in the esthetic standards of her environment, especially in the complicated domestic space of the Mancera household.

The violent desire of the beautiful Turkish woman to kill Chicaba seems irrational, for there is no apparent reason for her resentment except that the (white) Turkish girl has fallen victim to an act of seduction and is no longer virginal, a condition that makes her vulnerable to evil. Like so many times in Spanish literature, the opposition between Christianity and Islam is familiar. It enlists the audience's empathy for the Christian—even for this Black woman. As readers-listeners, they have access to the Turkish girl's beauty only through Chicaba, via the incident of her loss of virginity. The Black slave woman is the only one who becomes privy to the origin of the Turkish girl's vengeful rage and her susceptibility to the devil's violent suggestions. Importantly, Chicaba seems to be the only object of her murderous desire.

The relationship between the two is one that excludes the participation of any male church authority, even as a confessor. In fact, the Muslim woman accepts baptism only after she confesses to Chicaba, who in her Blackness and physical repugnance—her lack of femininity—is able to adopt a decidedly masculine role in the conversion. Chicaba performs as a confessor, the vehicle for her fellow slave's Christianization before dying.

Following Mary S. Gossy's contention that Western narrative literature is organized by oedipal desire—where most novels and stories represent the female body as a lack that is only completed or eradicated by male desire—the death of the Turkish girl is necessary for the hagiographic plot to continue.[83] There is a butch/femme relationship between Chicaba and the Turkish girl that excludes male participation. Her saintly rejection of heterosexual profligacy is exemplified later in life, when she will be endowed with the gift of identifying heterosexually impure people by their smell. The sexual tension of the Turkish-girl episode is resolved in typical oedipal fashion, with the death of the beautiful woman and the termination of Chicaba's desire for friendship with and love for her fellow woman captive. Had the Turkish girl converted and remained alive, her relationship with Teresa Chicaba would have constituted a challenge to Chicaba's plans to marry Christ.

Right after the end of the story of the Turkish girl, the *Vida* returns to the motif of slavery and exclusion through another episode in which Islam, slavery, and captivity are central. If the Turkish girl was Chicaba's doppelgänger, her double and opposite, Christ in the figure of the Ecce Homo also becomes her double in Chapter 13 through a significant anecdote of exclusion and identification with the suffering Christ. In this episode, prints of the image of the *Christ of Medinaceli* in Madrid were distributed in the Mancera household, but somehow Teresa did not receive one. Miraculously, one of these prints "hides itself," only to fall into her hands. The story of the *Cristo de Medinaceli* is rife with connotations of enslavement, captivity, and rescue in the midst of the religious confrontation between Muslims and Christians. The Trinitarians had rescued the image in 1682 from Meknes, where it had been taken in triumph after Sultan Mulay Isma'il conquered the Spanish fortress of La Mamora (Mehdia) the year before. The "rescue" of this holy representation of Christ during the last hours of His passion took place during protracted negotiations that ended in the liberation of more than one thousand Moroccans from Spain, who were received in Meknes amid enormous jubilation.[84] That Sor Teresa Chicaba may have had an affinity for the *Cristo de Medinaceli* as a fellow slave or captive is further supported by the establishment of a confraternity dedicated to His patronage in 1710; this group bears the significant title of *Archicofradía de la Real e Ilustre Esclavitud de Nuestro Padre Jesús Nazareno* (Confraternity of the Royal and Illustrious Enslavement of Our Father Jesus the Nazarene). Prints depicting the damage of this icon at the hands of Muslims inspired double reparations from the faithful: physical recompense was made in gold and jewels and spiritual reparation through prayer and mortification for the sacrilege it had endured. Thus, the image becomes a true simulacrum of Christ's passion and, by extension, Chicaba's own captivity. It signifies for her the violence and abuse she suffers at the hands of fellow servants in the Mancera household. This print of the *Christ of Medinaceli*, which she kept throughout her life, becomes an expression of her promised salvation from slavery and her restoration to royal dignity.

The last episode of violence during Chicaba's enslavement comes at the point when her owners have begun to accept Chicaba's desire to enter a convent. Juan Francisco, an alleged former inhabitant of her ancestral land, had also been abducted into slavery. He had then been presented to the king of France, Louis XIV, who had treated him as befitted his rank among his own African people.[85] Juan Francisco arrives in Madrid and is presented in the court of Carlos II, where he hears of Chicaba's existence. Claiming to be her uncle, he visits her and tells her that her parents converted to Christianity before their deaths, and with them most of their kingdom as well. This announcement has an important moral effect on the narrative of the *Vida*. It allows the *Vida* to establish a retrospective Christian genealogy for Teresa, an important element in the canonization process.

Juan Francisco then proposes marriage, to be followed by the couple returning home to reign over the now-Christian kingdom. With the deaths of everyone else in her immediate family, Teresa is no longer just a princess, but the heir apparent and, therefore, a queen. Thus, when she rejects this proposal, her renunciation of her rightful earthly power appears more meritorious than her childhood rejection of royal status in the early chapters of the *Vida*, when enslavement was presented as an act of Divine Providence. Now her choice to remain in Spain is a conscious decision made of her free will.

In this episode with Juan Francisco, the topos of the slave princess appears again with all its narrative threat to Chicaba's religious destiny. Juan Francisco pursues marriage to Chicaba to expand the mercantile alliances of France and Spain in Africa. The *Vida* does not say what kind of commerce he wishes to undertake with France and Spain, but the slave trade should be in the minds of the reader—something the text cannot say without sending the entire narrative into crisis. The hagiography dares not depict Chicaba as queen of a puppet kingdom providing slaves to European nations and their empires—as queen of a barracoon, a warehouse of slaves. This is another silence in the text.

Chicaba rejects the marriage proposal by hiding and through silence. What ensues is an effort by her putative uncle to kidnap her. This violent attempt against her occurs while she is in the company of her "foster" family. The king of Spain was reportedly in favor of the betrothal, and his courtiers collaborate with Juan Francisco's plot. Since Juan Francisco's purpose is to further his commercial relations with slaving powers such as Spain and France, this incident threatens to reinsert Teresa into the Middle Passage, but in reverse. The court wants to send her into another kind of enslavement.

The account of the marriage proposal to Chicaba and her rejection of it mirrors the story of Saint Ephigenia, one of the African saints venerated among Black communities in Portugal and Brazil at the time. Saint Ephigenia was a Nubian princess who converted to Christianity in the first century and was baptized by none other than Saint Matthew, the apostle. She founded a monastery for nuns, and yet she had to resist a marriage proposal from her father's successor to the throne. Saint Matthew preached against this proposed marriage with words that could fit Chicaba's predicament:

> Since marriage is a good thing, we who are present well know that if a servant
> dared to molest the king's spouse, he would deserve not only the king's displeasure,
> but death besides; and this not because he wished to take a wife, but because
> he violated the king's marriage by carrying off his wife. And thou, O king, who
> knowest that Ephigenia is espoused to the eternal King, how canst thou purloin the
> spouse of One mightier than thou, and take her to wife?[86]

The new king tried to burn down Ephigenia's convent, but divine intervention foiled his criminal plans. Her iconography reflects this miracle; she is represented holding a flaming church. Juan Franciso can likewise be accused of attempting to "purloin" Chicaba, since she has pledged her troth to Christ—a king mightier than Juan Francisco—and marriage would threaten her future as a nun.

This incident with Juan Francisco is crucial to the structure of the hagiography because the genre customarily depicts the future bride of Christ as confronted with the choice between religious life and other inducements: involvement in the prevailing secular heteronormative sexual and financial economies. Such an option accentuates how the structure of religious life mirrors and transforms the secular politics of gender with its attendant institutionalization in marriage, as well as how a nun's vow of poverty eschews personal financial benefits. The title of Chapter 17 describes the long-lost uncle's proposition as a "ruse of the devil to stop" Chicaba's vocation, her espousal to Christ. This concern with her betrothal is pivotal to the textual representation of her strategies for negotiating the economy of gender—secular and ecclesiastic—as she moves toward achieving sanctity. For example, the decision to marry is predicated on a return to her homeland, which is the only place appropriate for such a union between Blacks: a place where Chicaba's beauty is evident and where her agency is possible.

However, the representation of Guinea in the *Vida* is vexed. The narrative insists that as a child Chicaba was already promised to the white Christ Child during a series of heavenly visitations at a pastoral spring or fountain located in her father's kingdom. Guinea becomes the primary site of her encounter with Christianity and whiteness, but supposedly prior to any contact with European missionaries. However, while the narrative thus privileges her native land, it at the same time makes clear that her religious destiny requires her leaving home, where, according to her brother's apprehension, she might have been destined to assume her father's stool as ruler. The choice between secular or state leadership (returning home) and religious or heavenly marriage (staying in Spain) is again placed in stark opposition.

Chicaba's preparation to enter the convent is a highly fictionalized part of the *Vida*. The hagiography recounts a story of the slave who tells her owners that God has chosen her. They reluctantly accept parting with this precious jewel, not wishing to be an obstacle to God's intentions. The *Vida* creates dramatic dialogues between the marchioness and Chicaba before the latter's departure for the convent in Salamanca. The marchioness's last will in April 1703 (Appendix 4) indicates very clearly that her slave Teresa Juliana del Espíritu Santo was to enter religious life after her owner's death, as in fact happened. In the first mention of Chicaba, the marchioness specifies a convent in Murcia as her preference:

> Iten, después de los días de mi vida, quiero y es mi voluntad que Theresa Juliana del Espíritu Santo mi esclava quede libre enteramente y la ruego por lo mucho que la he querido se entre religiosa en el convento de Santa Ana, que antiguamente estuvo sujeto a los Padres Dominicos de la ciudad de Murcia y hoy está sujeto al Obispo de dicha ciudad de Murcia. Y para su entrada se le dé de mis bienes todo lo necesario. Y también lo necesario para su profesión.

> [Item. Once the days of my life are finished, I want and it is my wish that Theresa Juliana del Espíritu Santo, my slave, may be entirely free. I also pray to her, on behalf of how much I have loved her, that she enter as a religious the Convent of Saint Anne, formerly under the rule of the Dominican friars, in the city of Murcia, and now subject to the bishop of the aforementioned city of Murcia. And for her admission she may receive all that is necessary from my estate, as well as everything necessary for her profession.]

In the second mention of Chicaba, the marchioness assigns to her a stipend:

> Iten, mando a Theresa Juliana que hoy es mi criada y esclava y la dejo libre, en professando de religiosa, se le dé de mis bienes cincuenta ducados el cada un año para los gastillos y otras cosas que se le pueden ofrecer durante su vida.
>
> [Item. To Theresa Juliana, who is now my servant and slave, and I set free, if she professes as a religious, she will receive from my estate fifty ducats every year for the rest of her life, for her expenses and petty cash.][87]

The choices Chicaba would have had in Madrid once her owner was dead were few. A Black woman slave had a double reason to try to stay a virgin. In addition to the difficult circumstances of motherhood that assailed seventeenth- and eighteenth-century women in Europe—the danger of death during childbirth or afterward—a Black woman had to be concerned about her child not being legally hers to protect—he or she could be sold at any time—and the likelihood the child would be illegitimate. In most respects, a Black woman slave in Spain was the exact opposite of the Virgin Mary, the bride of God the Father and the mother of Jesus, to whom the Ave Maria declares, *Benedicta tu in mulieribus* (literally "You are most blessed among women"). Teresa Chicaba was excluded from the universe of women who aspired to emulate the Blessed Virgin as described in the foregoing verse. The prayer apostrophizes, *Benedictus fructus ventris tui* (blessed is the fruit of thy womb), but a Black enslaved woman's womb was cursed, for it could give birth only to slaves, never to free children. The Latin phrase in the Ave Maria that blesses the womb of Mary had a counterpart in legal Latin: *Fructus sequitur ventrem*—the child follows the condition of the womb it came from. The child of a slave woman is a slave.

For the slave Teresa Chicaba, entering a convent was a means of obtaining legal freedom. As a grandee of Spain, the Marquis of Mancera took as a matter of honor the execution of his wife's will and the payment of Teresa's dowry. In a gift economy, according to Marcel Mauss, there is an obligation to give and an obligation to receive.[88] Mancera's expectation was that any convent would have probably been honored to receive a gift from a former viceroy of Mexico, a member of the Council of State, and a major broker in the recent change of dynasty in Spain that ushered in the Bourbons in 1700. But that was not the case. According to the *Vida*, the nuns of several monasteries, both Dominican and Franciscan, rejected Teresa's candidacy.[89] The economy of the gift exchange was breaking down in early modern Spain. The marquis believed that he would be honoring a convent by allowing a former member of his household to enter it. The convents that rejected the gift Teresa represented were, however, under the pressure of social laws concerned with purity of blood, which did not permit them to accept a Black woman. Like the nuns in Cuzco studied by Kathryn Burns, a convent would lose authority—that is, social worth—if it admitted nonwhites.[90] Nonwhites brought disrespect, and they diminished the prestige of a monastery. This attitude must have shocked Mancera, whose tenure in Mexico had allowed him to experience the racial diversity of nuns' convents throughout New Spain.[91] But the exclamation of the aristocratic nun of Alba de Tormes explains it frankly: "'¡Una negra,' decía, 'en mi convento! No en mis días; no está fundada esta casa para negras'" ["A negress," she said, "in my convent! Not for as long as I live. This house was not founded for negresses"] (Chapter 19).[92]

LIFE IN LA PENITENCIA— CHAPTER 19 THROUGH THE CONCLUSION

This section of the *Vida* opens by relating the last in a series of rejections of Don Diego Gamarra's advocacy on behalf of the Manceras for Teresa's entry into several second order monasteries.[93] Enclosed (cloistered) communities of women (i.e., nuns) that have close canonical relationships with male (first) orders constituted second orders in the hierarchical nomenclature for Roman Catholic religious. The women who joined these communities were not only members of what historian Asunción Lavrín called a "spiritually privileged class," but they "constituted also a socially privileged minority due to the restrictive character of the admissions policy followed by convents."[94] For example, the name by which people know the Dominican second order convent of Santa Maria in Salamanca is a reflection of the nuns' social status. When Juana Rodríguez Maldonado founded the community in 1419, she intended at first to create a home where *dueñas* (pious ladies) could retire or retreat (a kind of *béguinage*).[95] By the end of the century, her palace had become a monastery of Dominican nuns. Like most of these kinds of women's religious communities, they enlarged the original building situated near the friary of their brother religious and the cathedral. Such a premium location placed them close to the religious heart as well as the financial and social center of Salamanca. The townspeople nicknamed the residence the "Convento de las Dueñas" (literally "the convent of the gentlewomen"). This informal designation for the monastery of second order Dominicans persists today and preserves in its title the social position of the women who founded the community and those who inhabited its confines in the seventeenth and eighteenth centuries.

By contrast, the women of the third order Dominicans, who accepted Teresa Chicaba, usually occupied different social locations or lower-class statuses. In Chapter 21, the *Vida* relates an abbreviated history of La Penitencia: "During its first years, it was a house of retirement where those women who had become disillusioned with their *vices* could give them up in greater calm" (italics added). The title of this branch of the Dominican order was the Brothers and Sisters of Penance.[96] The combination of the title, the dedication of the monastery to Saint Mary Magdalene, and the foregoing ambiguous description of the first inhabitants of the community may have given rise to one version of their origins, which states that they were initially a group of reformed prostitutes.[97] Of course, this insinuation serves well the construction of this *vida* because it gestures back to the hagiography of Mary of Egypt, the reformed harlot, without implicating Teresa Chicaba in literal impurity. The biblical figure of Mary Magdalene personified passion and desire. The traditional stories of her life represent a concupiscent or lascivious woman who, when she reformed, became a loving and fervent follower of Christ. Her ardent devotion led her to the foot of His cross and to His sepulcher when even male apostles lacked the courage to do the same.

The "Dominican Order of Penance of Saint Mary Magdalene," as the third order is occasionally called, originally consisted of independent individuals or small communities of devout Catholics in the thirteenth and fourteenth centuries, like the *beguines* and *beghards* in the Low Countries during the same period. They originated as resolute followers of the Ordo de Poenitentia formulated by Francis of Assisi. However, by 1285 they came under the supervision of the Dominicans (friars in the Order of Preachers) when Muñón de Zamora, the seventh master-general of the order, devised a rule by which they should live and a structure for their governance.⁹⁸ The local provincials and the master-generals—members of the first order—had jurisdiction over communities in their region. Like all Dominicans, they followed some form of the Augustinian rule. Ecclesiastical authorities deemed this close scrutiny necessary when the behavior of autonomous third order members and groups drew attention to themselves for their alleged theological errantry and their many internal arguments over transition of leadership. So, many members were organized into convents and monasteries of third order regulars as a method of controlling what some termed excesses in their behavior and of assuring the honorable reputations of the communities. Certainly the pronouncements some members of the order made, based on their own mystical revelations, caused concern in the Church. Also, women's unchaperoned appearances in public may have constituted a form of excessive or unseemly behavior that cast their virtue in doubt. Religious authorities decided that claustration was the remedy for their transgressions—social and religious.⁹⁹

La Penitencia, the cloistered foundation Chicaba joined in Salamanca, was an institute of this third division of Dominicans, which was located on the edge of the city and which probably did not draw many members from the nobility, pulling mostly from the merchant classes. If this monastery had not accepted Teresa Chicaba, her prospects as a free Black woman would have been few and less secure. One option available for Spanish women was to join a *recogimiento*, institutions extant in different parts of the Catholic world for women who wanted to lead a religious life and were not eligible for or did not wish to enter a convent. However, the informality of these communities would have presented Chicaba with two difficulties. First, according to Antonio Rubial's study of some women in Mexico City who founded and inhabited these informal female communities, such arrangements were very unstable, especially when the Inquisition intervened after reports of mysticism and miracles came to its attention. (The Mexican Inquisition launched more than forty processes of this nature in the seventeenth century.)¹⁰⁰ Since Black women were often the focus of inquisitional attention because their race was associated with witchcraft and the demonic, these arrangements would have been very dangerous for Teresa. Second, Madrid and other Spanish cities had similar *recogimientos*, but they were not suitable choices for Chicaba, for as a Black woman, she would most likely have encountered similar or worse obstacles to her acceptance from one of these informal groups of white women—some poor and some not—as from members in established orders of nuns.

Another possibility for a Black woman leaving a private household was for her owners to donate her to a hospital or even a convent as a charitable gift in exchange for Masses and other spiritual services from the recipients. In some cases, the agreements stipulated that the donation was for a term, after which the slaves were to be freed. In other cases, a slave woman would petition the priest who administered the hospital for her freedom after a certain number of years of service. She would implore him and the board of governors, reminding them of the charitable motives for her former owner's donation, and thereby appeal to the very spirit of charity that gave rise to the gift. This was not the case with Chicaba, whose owner Doña Juliana twice mentioned Teresa del Espíritu Santo (Chicaba) in her will, specifying that her slave was being freed to enter a convent.

Among the qualifications for vowed religious life is the freedom to make one's own decisions. This holds true no matter where an order or congregation falls in the hierarchy of religious communities. Perhaps the biography's insistent claim that Chicaba entered La Penitiencia before the death of her benefactor was an attempt to allay any suspicion that the Black aspirant to religious life was a mere *donada* (donation) to a religious order. The text of the will is ambiguous about her status. That is, was she freed so that she could join a convent, or was her entering religious life a condition of her emancipation? But the hagiography and its commissioning seem to attest to her community's acceptance of her legal freedom. Perhaps the hesitance to admit her in any regular status to religious orders rested not only on her color but also on her assumed correlative position as a slave. Thus, an unspoken (but understood by an eighteenth-century audience) subtext to the narrative was that one impediment to her vocation would have been doubt about her right to make a pledge—a lifelong binding promise—under both church and civil law.

Asunción Lavrín asserts that a woman's "deep religious feeling" was "the major motivating factor in choosing monastic life as a manner of living" and that the prioress and chaplain of a religious community examined a candidate "about her vocation and her *free will* to profess" (367–68; emphasis added). The narrative in Chapters 16 through 18 of the *Vida* comprises the proof for the reader of Chicaba's sincerity and authenticity in seeking to live as a monastic. As is traditional in a saint's life, the aspirant faces a series of tests. In Teresa Chicaba's case the first was from her spiritual director, Father Araújo, who wanted to ascertain if "her desire was ardent and constant" (Chapter 16). He attempted to calculate the depth of her devotion to the Eucharist and her willingness to obey his directives to abstain from the consolation the sacrament offered no matter the spiritual pain and hunger the sacrifice caused. Her profound yearning for Communion was a sign of her intense zealousness for union with her Beloved. Her second test required her to seek permission from the marchioness, who tried to dissuade her by appealing to her sense of spiritual responsibility and her need for material security. The mistress contended that her soul improved in Teresa Chicaba's "company." Furthermore, the noblewoman reasoned that her companion was often ill and fragile even in the "ease" and "leisure" of the Mancera household; therefore, she wondered how Chicaba would survive the rigors of monastic life. In addition, the marchioness maintained that she allowed the young woman all the time she desired for contemplation and prayer, so the noblewoman did not understand what was prompting the young slave to leave the security of a position with which she was familiar for the uncertainty of a difficult situation where she might fail (Chapter 16).

In reality, the decision to seek the spiritual and material sanctuary of a religious community was a choice much like that faced by the Caribbean slave woman Pauline Villeneuve, whose mistress left her in a Benedictine convent in France for training in proper comportment. Historian Robert Harms describes her choice to sue in 1716 for entrance to the monastery of the Sisters of Calvary in Nantes as probably one of both "pious conviction" and a determination not to return to slavery.[101] Lavrín maintains that as long as a strong religious feeling coexisted with "social extraction"—that is, status, family, and ethnicity—"and *manners*" (emphasis added), then "economic reasons for seeking the security and shelter of a convent" were not inappropriate motives for pursuing admission to a monastic community (368). The *Vida* does not admit of an alloy of spiritual and practical intentions; however, this is a common concern of present-day readers, who often give more weight to what they believe must have been her "true" desire to exchange her enslavement for the freedom that the convent provided.

For the religious communities of the seventeenth and eighteenth centuries and for the readers who shared their worldview, religious objectives eclipsed the issue of security. But nothing effaced the importance of "purity of blood" as a requirement to profess vows as a nun. This introduction has discussed at length the issues of *limpieza de sangre* as they pertain to genealogy, color/race and, to some extent, "social extraction." Since monasteries required two or more notarized affidavits attesting to the candidate's flawless lineage, one can assume that the story of Chicaba's royal background was an essential element in her assertion of purity of blood. This narrative was no doubt part of what gave her value as a gift and would become a crucial aspect of her posthumous life-story. Though the *Vida* does not explicitly record what Don Diego Gamarra, the marquis's emissary, said or presented to the prioresses of the various second order monasteries he visited, the papers he carried with him surely must have certified Teresa's noble ancestry. But clearly this was not enough to whiten her, as religious orders of that time required (Lavrín 367–68).

There was another essential aspect of her *probanza*, that of her ladylike comportment, that the sisters could not witness in her absence, but which figures subtly in the pivotal episode of her journey to Salamanca.[102] A proper demeanor affirmed the dignity and graciousness of her aristocratic background that the official papers asserted; "blood will out," so to speak. Lavrín maintains that, occasionally in New Spain, convents made some concessions for applicants with "defects of birth," if they were "white, devout, and *properly brought up*" (369; emphasis added.)[103] But it seems that whiteness was absolutely essential for profession as a choir nun in Spain. For instance, Chapter 21 reports that, when Chicaba visited the monastery of Saint Isabel of Alba de Tormes, where the nuns had "blackballed" her, they observed "how kind, courteous, and prudent she was," and they "regretted the error they had committed in not admitting her."[104] Thus, the *Vida* vindicates Chicaba in the name of appropriate decorum and thereby grants her a textual "concession" despite her race. The preceding chapter had implied the possibility of such a "dispensation" when word of La Penitencia's affirmative decision arrived.

If the abduction of Chicaba from her native land, her enslavement, and her incarceration in a "madhouse" are emblematic components of Spanish Byzantine romance, then her pilgrimage to the convent of La Penitencia constituted the next, more felicitous stage in that genre. The religious journey is usually undertaken as a token of thanksgiving for liberation from captivity. This pilgrimage normally ends in a spiritual transformation of the protagonist as she reaches a holy place, which is Rome for Cervantes's protagonists in *Persiles*. In the case of Chicaba, the holy places include Alba de Tormes, where she visits Saint Teresa of Ávila's shrine, and Salamanca, where her pilgrimage ends at La Penitencia and another adventure begins.

The episode about Chicaba's departure and pilgrimage to Salamanca begins as a joyful installment in the *Vida*'s plot, which moves intermittently between accounts of her suffering and moments of consolation. Chapter 21 marks the end of a series of painful setbacks in the course of becoming a bride of Christ. The narrative describes her journey as if it were something between a royal progress and an elaborate bridal procession. With its typical ambivalence toward Teresa's enslavement, the text depicts her as "a member of the Mancera family." Thus, the hagiography represents Chicaba almost as a ward or a foster or adopted Black daughter of the childless couple who, like traditional parents of the betrothed, weep at their loss.[105] This portion of the *Vida* is at least in part a fiction because records show that the marchioness had died in April 1703, months before Chicaba left for the monastery, which she entered in October of that same year. Though in reality the marchioness has already died, she remains a shadowy presence in the accounts of Chicaba's early years with the Dominicans. The sponsorship of this unusual candidate to the convent by the aristocratic couple bolsters the *Vida*'s claims that Teresa expected full acceptance in the community of La Penitencia.[106] The portrayal of the marquis, who, with his customary largesse, provides not only for her comfort on the journey but evidently also sends a retinue of family members to accompany her, is yet another example of this textual device. In addition, the account contends that he provided for a side-trip through Alba de Tormes so that she could venerate the relics of her patron saint Teresa of Ávila and visit with the community at Saint Isabel, which had rejected her so emphatically.

The narrative strategy here is to stress the obvious comparison between Teresa Chicaba's pursuit of spiritual perfection and that of the most famous Spanish woman mystic; thus, it underscores the relationship between the African Dominican's hagiography and the famous autobiography of Teresa of Ávila, *Libro de la vida*, which was a model for most Spanish women's spiritual self-writing. For example, during the account of the visit to Alba, the text of the eighteenth-century *Vida* prompts the habitual reader of saints' lives to remain alert to examples of the similarities between the two Teresas—that is, spiritual exercises, devotion to contemplation, and physical signs of a *burning* love for Christ. These resemblances begin the construction of another kind of lineage for Teresa Chicaba that the text creates in an attempt to avoid the hazard that race presented to establishing nobility.

So when she meets the blind person, a genderless Tiresias, the discourse on color is further problematized. The importance of this encounter is not that the sightless prophet is unaware of her *raza*, but that being attentive to how she appeared to others, "the favored soul" could sense Chicaba's greatness and communicate this silently to others. Situated immediately before the meeting with the nuns at Saint Isabel, discussed above, this parable establishes a backdrop against which to believe the justness and sincerity of the nuns' remorse for rejecting Teresa.

But the sense of equanimity is short-lived, for the narrative returns to the discourse of suffering. This vacillation between relief or solace and the pain of disappointment mirrors the vicissitudes of religious life for which her spiritual director tried to prepare Teresa while she was still in the Mancera household. The story of the bishop's changing the terms of her admittance to La Penitencia is a traditional element in the testing of a saint's mettle for a life modeled on the suffering Jesus. The prelate's authority to withhold the veil and to raise the amount of Chicaba's dowry reveals much about the external structures of monastic governance, the economy of women's spiritual institutes, and the internal organization of communities.

First, the constitutions of the Sisters of Penance place them under the supervision and jurisdiction of the highest-ranking male Dominican superior in their local province and under the presiding bishop of their diocese, who may witness the profession of a nun "into the hands" of her prioress or may preside himself over the vow ceremony.[107] No matter how much autonomy a woman's monastic community has according to its rule and constitutions, it behooves the nuns to keep the appropriate authority in the diocese informed of major changes in their house—whether it is a practical recognition of episcopal responsibilities for running the diocese or out of respect for protocol.

Monsignor Don Francisco Calderón de la Barca had the power to intervene in and amend decisions of the convent's council. His response to learning of Chicaba's application to La Penitencia—increasing the levy for her entrance—was predictable in light of her sponsorship by the Marquis of Mancera. Given that the grandee expected his wealth to help secure a place in a second order monastery for Teresa del Espíritu Santo, it seems reasonable to assume that it might have been a successful inducement in the case of this third order monastery, for he paid the additional incentive to secure Chicaba's acceptance. All this is perfectly spelled out in the *carta de pago* (payment letter) that all parties signed on April 19, 1704 (Appendix 1).[108] In this document, Teresa signs as "de Santo Domingo" as in the act of profession a couple of months later, although she still uses the middle name Juliana, which she will drop in the act of profession (see Appendix 2). The *carta de pago* calls her a *seglar o terzera beata* (secular or tertiary religious), as if insisting that she is not going to be a nun. The document also recognizes that she is wearing a habit of the order, a way to signify that she is somehow a member of the Dominican order. And the dowry she brings to the coffers of La Penitencia is considerable: 10,800 *reales*.

The convent of La Penitencia was not as rich as Las Dueñas, but it was not poor either. The 1749 *Catastro* (land registry and census) of Ensenada indicated that La Penitencia, like other ecclesiastical institutions in the city of Salamanca, possessed a network of rural properties that produced revenues either in money or in kind.[109] Chicaba's annuity of fifty ducats bequeathed to her by the marchioness—what Doña Juliana's last will describes quaintly as *para sus gastillos* (for her petty cash)—was in reality no small quantity to add to the convent's coffers. Even considering that she may not have regularly collected the amount bequeathed her by the marchioness, Sor Teresa probably received her yearly allotment from 1703, when she entered, until 1715, when the marquis died. The *Vida* reports that the remittances dried up after his death (Chapter 32). This means that she would have received monies in excess of 600 ducats (or 6,600 *reales*).[110] This is an appreciable figure, especially when compared to dowries paid by other women of her time. An example is the case of Doña Rosa de Rojas, who entered the novitiate at twenty-six in 1716 with the intention of being a choir nun. Her family gave La Penitencia a *censo* worth 2,436 *reales* as a dowry; however, they could not make the payment in cash. Chicaba entered La Penitencia in 1703, when she too was twenty-six.[111] The amount she paid over the 12 years before the death of her benefactor, combined with her dowry of over 10,800 *reales*, was roughly 7 times that of Doña Rosa's dowry; besides, Teresa Chicaba's annuity and dowry were paid in hard cash. In addition, through her appointment to nurse the "demoniac" María Francisca, the monastery received four thousand *reales* (Chapters 30 and 31). The *Vida* also intimates that she obtained funds from benefactors who visited her in the speak room, which she used to augment the dowry of novices whose funds were less than the tariff set by the convent (Chapter 34).

The monastery accepted Doña Rosa as a choir nun, a member of the highest status in the monastery. Such women were from the privileged classes and could afford the highest dowries. In addition, they had to be literate because they were responsible for governance as the only voting members of the community and for reading and singing the Divine Office, the Prayer of the Church. The long black veils they wore signified their elite position in the order's hierarchy. The second level of sisters, white-veiled or short-veiled nuns (lay sisters in English-speaking convents), paid smaller dowries and had no vote in elections, nor could they hold administrative offices. In some convents, literate lay sisters participated in the Divine Office; illiterate white-veiled nuns and others even lower in the hierarchy simply recited a prescribed group of rote prayers instead. White-veiled nuns did some manual labor, but in convents with servants, most white-veiled nuns supervised those in menial positions. The hagiography suggests that even after she took a short veil, Chicaba performed the most strenuous physical labor in the convent.

Reception of a veil of any color signified a nun's chaste marriage to Christ (Ibsen 3–4;

Burns 32–24, 119–27. So when the bishop decreed that Teresa Chicaba would not receive a veil at all, he was denying her the very privilege the White Child had promised. The hagiography reports that he would allow her to enter only as a *tercera* (tertiary) or a third order "secular"—a person who professes some form of simple vows and wears some sign of belonging to the order, perhaps even a habit.[112] The *Catastro* of Ensenada, begun the year after Sor Teresa died, records the number of residents as twenty-three full-veiled choir sisters and six *monjas de medio velo* (lay sisters or short-veiled nuns). Then it lists a category called *criadas seglares* (secular servants). There is no way of knowing whether, by the time of her death, Sor Teresa wore a *medio velo*, was a third order secular (perhaps covered by the category of *criadas seglares*, which indicated those living outside the monastic enclosure), or held some other status.

The *Vida* reveals the profound liminality of Teresa's position among the nuns. Though the bishop arrived at the monastery with an entourage to witness her admission to La Penitencia, the question of her status among the nuns goes unsettled. And while the narrative maintains that the prelate gave her "the habit from his own hands" and the nuns welcomed her with appropriate ceremony (Chapter 22), the actual meaning of that ceremony remains a cipher. The wearing of a veil is not an issue at this point in the course of her "formation" (training): while postulants received some form of dress to distinguish them as members of the community—uniforms, so to speak—they usually did not wear veils associated with official membership in the order until at least six to twelve months later, after the first profession of vows.

For traditional entrance ceremonies among monastics, the nuns formed two lines in order of seniority and processed (walked solemnly) into the choir with the new postulant at one end of the group. The choir was the chamber where those literate sisters of the upper echelon of the community sang or recited antiphonally the Divine Office, also called the Liturgy of the Hours. The breviary (the prayer book and lectionary for the Office) divided the Psalms to facilitate performance as call and response during the seven periods the nuns gathered each day. Throughout the seventeenth and eighteenth centuries, the weekly psalmody included all 150 Psalms, plus additional prayers and hymns, so a choir nun spent the greater part of her day in the worship space or in her cell, engaged in prayer. Liturgy was her primary "work"; it was the labor for which benefactors donated funds, in the conviction that these prayers ensured the security and prosperity of their city and their lives. The structure of the choir reflected its purpose. Two ranks of stalls facing each other lined the walls, perhaps with a lectern at the front of the chamber. The postulant usually took her place in the middle of the room between these rows of stalls for her reception into the community.

The bishop's pronouncement had cast doubt on Chicaba's opportunity to live a vowed life as a true bride of Christ; therefore, the ritual in which she participated had little canonical force. She clearly had no other earthly authority to whom she could appeal. However, as a member of two societies—as an Ewe among the Spanish—both of which reckoned proper relationships through lineage or ancestry, it was fitting that her spiritual forebears, her ancestors, sanction her admission. So, according to the hagiography, the entire community—living and dead—welcomed Teresa. This was one of two visions—this one celebrating her entrance into the community, the other accrediting her profession—that ceremonially and "virtually" valorized her belonging to the community of La Penitencia.

Her everyday life continued to evidence her marginality. For example, the community assigned her living quarters in the infirmary. Often convents of the era had a designated room or a cluster of cells for those in formation (the novitiate), while their professed members lived in another enclosed area designated for their cells. The infirmary was a liminal space, where physicians or other practitioners from outside could tend the ill without violating the cloister. It was also the section where occasional boarders—for instance, the aforementioned demoniac whom Teresa Chicaba nursed—lodged. The Black woman was keenly aware of her isolation from her "sisters." The hagiography attributes Chicaba's despondency about her exclusion to diabolical interventions: first, the fiend tempted her to remember that she could have returned to Africa and assumed leadership of her people, and then the demon suggested the work the nuns assigned her were the tasks allocated to a slave.

The prioress intervened by feigning illness and joining her in the infirmary. During those few nights with Chicaba, the nun counseled her in the strategy for resisting temptations to "step back from the spiritual road" on which she had embarked (Chapter 23). The advice was for her to show humbler obedience to her superiors; nowhere is there a suggestion that at some future date her sisters would move her to a cell inside. In fact, one suspects that she never inhabits a space in the enclosure. For instance, when she reports that later in life she displeases her Divine Spouse by allowing two priests in her cell, the reader suspects that she lives on the margins of the cloister, and even outside of it, because she would not have dared conduct men through the common living space that was in the private core of the monastery. Therefore, the growing silence of the hagiography about her physical liminality after the episode with María Francisca, the demon-possessed ward, serves to construct a textual cloister around her and works to regularize her position in community through representational sleight of hand or elision.

A clue to the nuns' doubt about her prospects for full incorporation into the community is their negligence in appointing a mistress of novices to supervise Chicaba's formation. Histories of women's convent life during this period stress the importance of formally preparing novices and postulants for their professions. The nun responsible for guiding them made sure that her charges were familiar with the rule and constitutions of the order; she assigned them spiritual readings such as saints' lives and instructed them in the protocols of ceremonies and liturgical customs (Burns 108 and Lavrín 372). For example, the mistress was supposed to teach the intricacies of setting up the breviary for the recitation of the Divine Office. Thus, when Sor Maria Teresa of San Jacinto discovered that they had overlooked preparing Chicaba for her life in community, she offered to instruct the postulant in how to say the Liturgy of the Hours. However, the hagiography explains that Teresa Chicaba already knew how to prepare the breviary according to the readings prescribed by the liturgical calendar and to say the Psalms in the appropriate order. There remained only her tutelage in the special Dominican practices for feast days of the order. This incident reported in Chapter 23 is significant, for it affirms the African woman's literacy and her eligibility for inclusion among the ranks of choir nuns. Further, through describing the kind act of one nun, the text sustains the hopes of both the reader and Chicaba for her ultimate full incorporation in the community of La Penitencia.

Perhaps nowhere in the *Vida* is her ambiguous status more obvious than the accounts of her exclusion from the choir. The text laments that the sisters vacillate about where she could perform communal prayer: "At times, they let her sit in the choir; at times, they send the Black woman outside with the other women" (Chapter 24). Exile to the other side of the grille placed the tertiary among the laity—that is, among those with no canonical ties to the monastery.[113]

The story of the bishop's concession to profess her appeared to be an indication of some movement toward regularizing her position in the monastery. His change of heart seemed so resolute because he shortened her period of probation by four months and placed the white veil on her head himself. The impulse to read the truncated waiting period and the veiling as signs of the prelate's recognition of Teresa's exemplary virtue is thwarted by the following explanation of the significance of the ceremony: though compassion (and Providence, perhaps) inspired him to present her with the veil on that, she remained a tertiary (third order secular), "and her profession amounted only to that occasion" (Chapter 24). In other words, in spite of Teresa making the three vows—obedience, poverty, and chastity—common to all who profess, no matter their status in the Order, and despite the reception of the outward sign of her espousal to Christ, the text leaves her place in the community hierarchy at the time of this ceremony unclear. Sor María Eugenia Maeso, in her modern hagiography of Sor Teresa Chicaba, acknowledges the same point. Maeso is not sure whether the vows Sor Teresa Chicaba made were "private" rather than public. She is of the opinion that Sor Teresa Chicaba was a "secular tertiary with vows that we could call private. What is true is that she always belonged to a category below the other women religious, including the lay ones" (Maeso 75). However, at the end of Chapter 24 of the *Vida*, almost as an afterthought, Paniagua's text reports, "After some time, she renewed her vows in the hands of a [Dominican] friar from the illustrious convent of San Esteban." This ceremony must have formalized her status as a veiled tertiary, as she appears as in her official portrait (Figure 1).[114]

No wonder the chapter focuses on the celestial affirmation of her vows: it acts as a corrective for the pretense—no matter how charitable its intent—of the bishop's ceremony. In this second of the visions authenticating her vocation, the narrative does not identify the members of the celestial choir who witnessed the profession, but it names Saint Dominic as the presider. The next passages rehearse the tribulations she endured prior to mystical ratification, and then the text explains that this recognition by the patriarch of the order strengthened her fervor and determination to fulfill her vows to perfection. In comparison with this mystical experience, the final canonical ratification of her position in the order by her religious brother becomes a textual anticlimax.[115]

From Chapter 25, after her profession, to the end of the *Vida*, the text conforms to the dictates of the hagiographic genre, for it is less predicated on the chronology of events than on a discussion of Teresa Chicaba's spiritual practice, the perfection of her vowed life, and the miracles she performs. At this point, the trajectory of the saint's life has moved from recounting the process of spiritual transformation to describing the relatively static experience of transcendence. However, there is one constant that pervades the transformational and transcendent stages represented in the narratives of those striving for saintliness—that is, suffering.

The *Vida* draws a distinction between distress caused by others and self-inflicted mortification in solidarity with the passion of Christ. But no matter the difference in their etiologies, both forms exemplify the theological tenet of incarnation because, as they address issues of the subject's personhood—bodily and psychically—they reflect and emphasize the humanity of a nun's Divine Spouse. Thus, according to Asunción Lavrín, sacrifice and the suffering it produces are emblematic of the religious life (367)—so much so, that it is a major concern that repeats itself throughout Teresa Chicaba's *Vida*, propelling the narrative forward from one doleful incident to another. In addition, patient endurance of affliction necessitates the exercise of the vows of humility and obedience.

Chapters 25 and 27 recapitulate Chicaba's tribulations before she entered La Penitencia—the cruelty of members of the Mancera household and her rejections by other monasteries. They also recount her "repeated disappointments" immediately after she entered the convent: her exile to the infirmary, the bishop's threat to withhold the veil, and the hostilities of servants toward her soon after she entered the community. Then, before relating the "mortification" that she endured after her profession, the narrator postulates that Teresa's ability to endure patiently and humbly the spite of those whom God used to test her revealed more about her sanctity than all her fasting and lacerating of her flesh (Chapter 25). For instance, Teresa remained serene when a nun exclaimed loudly in Choir that she resented the influence "a negress" had over the newly elected prioress (Chapter 27). The biography maintains that this was but one of many such remarks she would endure in her monastic life, and it concludes with the following observation: "One can only say that her sorrows were accompanied by patience and tolerance" (Chapter 27).

One of the most important examples of Teresa's exercise of the vows of humility and obedience was her accepting without question the assignment to supervise María Francisca, whom the *Vida* identifies as a relative of the patriarch of the Indies (Chapters 30 and 31). Chicaba's ward had suffered the effects of the War of Succession and witnessed the bombarding of Barcelona during her childhood. She never recovered from the experience and was eventually diagnosed as a demoniac. Her parents had approached La Penitencia in despair and asked to board María Francisca in the monastery infirmary. The conventual superiors saw fit to assign the care for this very difficult young woman to their Black sister. One can surmise that the choice of Teresa Chicaba as the nurse of María Francisca was no accident, as she was the former slave of a distant relative of her charge.[116] To subdue the young woman, Chicaba would have to battle the devil. Probably the monastery chapter was familiar with the spiritual literature of Spain and Spanish America, which cited many examples of the relationship between the devil, Blacks, and Africa.[117] In her role as a nursemaid, Chicaba had to take care of this difficult girl, whose behavior was unladylike. For example, María Francisca did not observe proper piety, suffered fits of rage, and chewed copious amounts of tobacco or dipped snuff. Speaking through the possessed girl, the devil complained of being mistreated by the Black woman.[118] Chicaba, in turn, kept the devil at bay through the spiritual use of her own body. At one point, the *Vida* tells us, Chicaba burned the devil with her saliva while combing María Francisca's hair. In this episode, the reader observes a paradoxical combination of Teresa's humble submission to the will of the monastery administration and her ability to negotiate skillfully the religious and cultural strictures defined by her race and gender. Despite the doubts eighteenth-century society harbored about the behavior of Black women, she managed to reproduce in her patient the patriarchal ideal of deportment for a woman of high social status. Furthermore, she exposed the devil that possessed her ward but did not expel it, for this was the purview of male priest-exorcists. She made apparent the boundaries between the evil in the world and the holiness she embodied (Chapter 31).

The discourse of the third monastic vow, chastity, is predicated on eighteenth-century ideologies: politics of gender, sex, and the body. Essential to articulating the logic behind women's religious life is the figurative language associated with marriage: betrothal, dowry, espousal, and bride. These marital metaphors constitute a principal function in structuring the narrative of the *Vida*, which moves from Chicaba's betrothal at the fountain in Africa to her profession in the first section of the hagiography—that is, the plot of transformation—and settles down in a kind of domesticity, in the second transcendent portion of the spiritual biography. To understand the impetus that drives her to pursue her religious calling despite a series of rejections from convents and to insist on receiving a veil, the reader must recall that the text identifies her childhood home in Guinea as the place and time of her betrothal. The theological significance of this contract is that it mandates virginity and humility. Thus, her accepting this proposal explains the need for the narrative's consistent and repetitive assertion of her blamelessness.

This early commitment at the crystalline fountain in Africa and the several temptations to disregard her promise together are a variation of a fort-da gifting ritual, as is the Christ Child's dangling from His hand a shiny ribbon that He proffers to young Chicaba and then retrieves over and over again (Chapter 4).[119] Lewis Hyde, in his work *The Gift*, explores several cross-cultural instances of comparable narratives and ceremonial behavior and describes them as emblematic of "the cardinal property of the gift" (4), observing that "the spirit of the gift is kept alive by its constant donation (xiv)"and that "the gift must always move" (4).[120] In this light, the vignette of the exchange-game metaphorizes the persistent and unremitting call of Christ to his beloved and the steadfastness and constancy of her response.

Further, Hyde, using the writings of Meister Eckhart on the mystical experience, outlines the grammar that organizes the principles of the religious life. In sketching the fourteenth-century writer's argument, Hyde observes that, on the spiritual level, the continuous interchange between human and spirit (God) is energetic and "escalating" (54). An example of this is in the *Vida*'s portrayal of Chicaba's zealous pursuit of union with her Intended through prayer and ritual. Hyde paraphrases Eckhart, who describes the impetus for living a life of solitude and poverty, the vocation Sor Teresa pursued; he maintains that true Christians realize that life itself is a gift, and that those who appreciate the profundity of this endowment cut themselves off from worldly attachments and redirect their lives toward God: "A second gift comes to any soul that has thus emptied itself of the world—a Child is born (or the Word is spoken) in the soul emptied of 'foreign images'" (54). Eckhart explains that the soul devoid of such material "images" is truly *virginal*, in a state beyond bodily purity and abstinence but sometimes signified by it: "That [one] should receive God in [oneself] is good, and by this reception [one] is a virgin. But that God should become fruitful in [a person] is better; for the fruitfulness of a gift is the only gratitude for the gift" (qtd. in Hyde 54). A productive virgin spirit is in this way transformed into a "wife" or spouse of God (Hyde 55). Embedded in this fourteenth-century mystic's theology is the primacy of the Christian belief in the Incarnation, the enfleshment of God through the Virgin Mother Mary in the birth of Christ (truly human and divine). This is the foundational and mysterious rationale for consecrated, religious life, particularly as it is regulated by ideologies of gender. While Eckhart's description of the call-and-response between the deity and the human soul clearly portrays the working of God in men as well as women, the church applies the gendered terminologies of "virgin," "wife," and "mother" differently and more consistently to women (nuns) than to men (monks, friars, or priests). These metaphors are codified in monastic life as the vows pertaining to celibacy that were historically differently envisioned and enforced by church authorities for males than for females (Warren x). This theology becomes literalized as scholars begin to articulate the different roles each religious enacts according to traditional discourses of gender. On the one hand, priests dramatize and enact the Incarnation through consecrating the Eucharist and also can achieve mystical union with Christ, but on the other hand, women's bodies, through their capacity literally to reproduce, represent both an advantage and a hazard in attaining oneness with the Deity. The possibility of defiling the vessel that would mystically hold the Christ produces an anxiety that only chastity can allay.[121]

The *Vida*'s depiction of Sor Teresa's entrance into and membership in a religious community is in terms of the gendered tropes of virgin, wife, mother, and sister. The plot trajectory moves purposefully from the child Chicaba's precocious religious intuitions about the nature of God, an early indication of her extraordinariness, to her childhood vision of the White Lady and Child that augurs her espousal, and to the method of her capture by a "gallant young man"—invisible to all but Chicaba. These are but a few of the early textual indicators that she was especially chosen by the Christian God to pursue a life of religious dedication. Within the world of eighteenth-century Spain, profession in a religious order as a bride of Christ was the customary way a woman expressed this singularity of purpose.

The preservation of her chastity evidenced a woman's single-mindedness in pursuit of a religious life, for virginity was the prerequisite for a woman's acceptance to and profession of vows in a religious order. It was the hallmark of the authenticity of a nun's vocation, and it warranted the value of her faithfulness to her calling. In the words of Elizabeth M. Makowski, "nuns were specially blessed (or burdened) with an obligation to preserve a chastity that took on an almost mythical significance and importance" (quoted in Warren 18). These values required women who aspired to and lived religious vocations to guard not only physical chastity but also their good reputations. That is, nuns and their clerical supervisors were responsible for religious women's—nuns and members of secular orders—public conduct because it reflected on their spiritual and sexual purity. As was the rule for all women marrying above their station—becoming a bride of Christ was the quintessential case in point—a religious order evaluated a candidate spiritually. They appraised her suitability by her good character and trustworthiness expressed as sexual constancy, and they assessed her fiscally by the dowry she could contribute to the monastery coffers (Warren 18). By these measures, Chicaba arrived at the gates of La Penitencia as the perfect candidate, with an annuity from the Marchioness of Mancera in hand and testament to her chastity writ across her Black and therefore uncomely face. As discussed earlier in this introduction, through the episode of the Turkish girl in Chapters 11 and 12, the *Vida* constructs a counterdiscourse to the popular notion that Black women were licentious by asserting that Chicaba's Blackness, equated with ugliness, protected her virtue.

Enclosure was the architectural representation of nuns' inviolate bodies; it signified the guard they kept over their good names, thus ensuring their spiritual value. In fact, the walls around this Dominican community were of particular significance because in the fourteenth century members of the Dominican Order of Penance throughout Catholic Europe came under ecclesiastical scrutiny for irregularities in their religious lives. As a method of controlling their behavior and of assuring the honorable reputations of members of these groups, some were organized into convents and monasteries of third order regulars and cloistered. As noted above, La Penitencia was an institute of third order Dominicans. Whether the monastery in Salamanca was really a foundation of former prostitutes or whether their history represents the intervention of a folk interpretation of all female transgression as sexual, there is no way of ascertaining (Warren 3–30).

But in the light of the unsavory reputation of Black women, where the community situates Teresa's cell is of great importance. It is an insinuation about her chastity, which the hagiography is at pains to obscure. Her location in the liminal space of the infirmary becomes less a categorical discourse of exile as the narrative unfolds to present her as a nurse of the elderly and of the patient María Francisca. In addition, the episode in Chapter 29, when she confesses that she naively invited priests to see her cell, is double-edged. It reports her transgression of the rules of claustration only to affirm her as a true bride of Christ, who is a jealous and watchful spouse, and it confirms her innocence through the portrayal of her childlike ignorance of the implications of her act.

As a consecrated wife and virgin, Teresa emulates Mary and thereby performs motherhood not just by caring for María Francisca but also by supporting novices. During the hagiography's exposition of Chicaba's boundless hope, it reveals that, "through her agency," penurious novices found the dowries that enabled them to profess (Chapter 34). In addition, she offered wise counsel to those who sought her advice in the speak room. Chapter 37 enumerates many instances of her maternal love for her neighbors: She restored health to the sick, even when their illness was so repugnant that no one else would tend them. Those who could not see a way out of distressing circumstances found counsel and direction from her, and her determined pursuit of sinners saved many from perdition.

The gendered metaphors for the positions nuns occupy in the theological imagination are intricately and complexly connected as the reflection on the tenets Eckhart explained centuries earlier. With profession, a woman becomes the bride of Christ, and the incarnational aspect of this mystical union with the Divine extends the marital metaphor to include an association with the motherhood of Mary and a relationship as (foster) sister of Christ. As His sibling, each nun, especially Teresa Chicaba, hopes that her community members will recognize their relation to her through Him.

However, the *Vida* demonstrates how difficult it was to cultivate this rapport with Chicaba's entire community. A poetic lament included at the end of Chapter 35 seems to reflect the effect of all the slights from her sisters at La Penitencia. This poem is both a lover's complaint at being forsaken and a claim of equality to the other members of her religious community. The mention of the biblical figures of Martha and Mary in the piece drives the point home by gesturing to Chicaba's lowly role in the spiritual economy of sisterhood of the monastery. Of the few direct quotations attributed to the protagonist of the hagiography, the poem about Sor Teresa's spiritual jealousy of Christ captures the attention of readers.

As with many hagiographic texts about nuns written by priests, there is always the possibility that the author may have donned the nun's veil in an act of authorial and spiritual transvestism. Close textual analysis, however, indicates that the hagiographer probably did not compose the poem as an act of pure fiction, for both its content and its linguistic peculiarities make it more attributable to Chicaba than to him.[122]

The female poetic voice addresses Jesus by both pleading for his attention and accusing him of abandoning her. This piece is remarkable theologically because it depicts the speaker's relation with Jesus as part of a polygamous communion of female saints, acknowledging that as a mystical bride, she is not the only sister Christ has espoused. The jealous complaint is unusual because the poetic voice recognizes other women as objects of Jesus's affection: "Oh, Jesus, what shall I say? / If you go out with other women, / What shall I do?" The mystical marriage of a nun to Jesus is expressed in exclusively monogamous terms. This is not the case here.

The poem performs an unusual reading of the scripture. It is striking in its use of a traditional interpretation of the story of Martha and Mary (Luke 10:38–42) as a lens on the politics of monastic hierarchical structure. In a traditional exegesis of this passage, each woman is a personification of contrasting forms of religious life—a contemplative or active calling. Teresa's verse gestures toward this traditional representation of both women and applies what they symbolize to their different statuses and work in the hierarchy of community—the division between the prayerful work of choir nuns and the menial labor of others.

Catholic theology has been at pains to explain away the idea of a polygamous Christ, the logical consequence of His mystical marriage to so many nuns.[123] The feeling of jealousy, which the *Vida* rationalizes as a manifestation of Teresa's intense love, might have been a reflection of real circumstances experienced in La Penitencia, where the Black nun was relegated to manual labor, the work of a convent drudge. In this regard, the recrimination might suggest a complaint against a perceived injustice visited on the protagonist by the other sisters—for instance, the grinding toil that occasions rare figural slippages after her profession into the metaphor of slavery. The tension between Martha and Mary in the biblical story might gesture toward this interpretation.

In the Gospel of Luke, Martha complains to Jesus for encouraging Mary to sit at his feet immersed in conversation instead of insisting that both sisters work together to prepare the house for their distinguished Visitor. Jesus's response gives authority to Mary's contemplative attitude—the choice to pay rapt attention to the Guest. In the light of the spiritual hierarchy Christ establishes, the poem demands an explanation from Jesus for placing the household drudge at the bottom of the conventual social order. Chicaba observes, "I have seen it before: / Martha and Mary, / You have loved them. / Oh, Jesus, where shall I find you?" Thus, the poem echoes Martha's plaintive question to Christ, who in detaining Mary from performing her kitchen duties explains that conversation with Him is "the better part" (Luke 10:42).

As a third order secular assigned to menial tasks, Teresa Chicaba's main function in La Penitencia was to work and to care for patients in the infirmary and to perform kitchen tasks. Though some of her service for disabled laity brought income to the community, the production of spiritual benefits through the prayers of a lowly Black nun in comparison to the contemplation of Spanish choir nuns was of lesser importance in her convent's spiritual economy.

This poetic complaint represents the voice of a Black female subject with spiritual aspirations. In the light of these yearnings, the *Vida* intimates that the lament attributed to Chicaba reflects her belief that Jesus loved Martha and Mary equally and that, through her dual call as an active and a contemplative nun, Teresa personified both sisters in the scriptural drama. By representing these verses as Chicaba's, the hagiography argues that as a spouse of Christ, she had the right to pray and meditate like the other nuns. Further, the stanzas express the subversive discourse, arising out of her triply intersecting identities of African, Christian, and woman, that the tenet of an individual, monogamous marriage to Christ by several nuns was absurd and, more importantly, that the social division of labor in her monastery was not just. That is, these lines attributed to the pen of a woman who claimed to be an African "princess" and a freed slave in Europe proclaim the profound disparity between the material conditions in which she tried to be true to her spiritual calling and her sisters' privileged social statuses, which were conducive to their performing spiritual "work." Thus, through a deft metatextual, self-conscious interpretation of Teresa's life embedded in the hagiography, what started as a jealous protest transformed a biblical passage about the difference between two sisters into a theological study of and a pious reflection on the social positions of women religious in the gendered structures—the economies—of the eighteenth-century Spanish Catholic Church.

After the lover's lament in Chapter 35, the discourse of suffering makes way for one of consolation. What follows in the remaining narrative are accounts of spiritual favors and graces bestowed on the transformed or purified soul. This is the essence of the final hagiographic project: proving the worthiness of the would-be-saint with a catalogue of good deeds and profound devotions, as well as the spiritual benefits a virtuous life had earned her. The focus of the last nine chapters of the *Vida*, therefore, is to do more than relate what Teresa did; they have to offer testimony about what God did for and through Teresa as evidence of her sanctity. Prophecy, healing, and miracles supposedly substantiated the claims of her worthiness for ecclesiastical recognition by those who promoted her cause—the Dominican order, the Theatines, and those clerics and laity who had sought her spiritual advice through visits at the grille and in correspondence.

The rules of evidence in the eighteenth century for verifying miracles and the accuracy of prophecy were not as strict as they are in today's Catholic Church. Often simply informing one's spiritual director or another reliable spiritual authority about the content of a vision or the nature of a premonition was sufficient. For example, in Chapter 36, the *Vida* offers a series of incidents that illustrate the miraculous power of Teresa's love for the Eucharist. To moderate the nun's insatiable hunger for the sacrament, Abarrategui, her director, had restricted her access to Communion. "She obeyed with patience and resignation," reports the biography, but she made a special pleading to her Spouse, who influenced the priest to relent and to arise early in the morning to bring her the host. The authority for this unusual occurrence was the director himself. Elsewhere in the same chapter, there is the story of how her intense yearning for the Eucharist enabled her to rise from her sickbed after suffering what must have been a stroke and to walk to the choir for Eucharist without evidencing signs of her paralysis.

The text records numerous examples during her life of her power to predict events, to detect vulnerabilities in the depths of people's souls, to smell the aroma of sin and inspire repentance, to cure infirmities, and to envision holy souls rising out of purgatory to heaven. But at the publishing of the *Vida*, Teresa Chicaba had only three miracles (i.e., cures) to her credit. The last chapter opens by addressing the paucity of extraordinary phenomena to prove her sanctity, her worthiness of recognition. The text cannot explain why grace has not favored her yet. It can only observe that she belongs to the category of venerable departed whom God favors slowly and infrequently. However, the hagiography marvels at the faithfulness of those devoted to her memory that arrive at La Penitencia "to request any rag from her clothing to keep as a relic!" This fidelity of her devotees, then, is what is truly miraculous, as is the effect on the "pious reader" who strives to learn from her example (Chapter 44).

The penultimate chapter records wonders connected with her bodily remains in the immediate aftermath of Teresa's death: the transformation of her skin color and her final acceptance by her community of sisters. As a variation on the slave narrative, the *Vida* is part of the production of Blackness through recounting the vicissitudes of bondage and oppression. This hagiography is in a virtual dialogue with other slave life-stories through its comprehensive exposition of the consequences of having a Black body in eighteenth-century Spain. For example, Chicaba's color is evoked over and over in a series of different contexts: Her Black skin makes her cute while a ten-year-old living in Seville; it makes her ugly and undesirable in the episode of the Turkish girl. Her Blackness causes the envy of other servants in the Mancera household, who see color as a contradiction to the privileged position she sometimes enjoys. It is the main source of rejection by several convents. Yet while on her pilgrimage from Madrid to Salamanca, a blind person perceives her Black skin and prophesizes her future saintliness. The bishop of Salamanca is loath to allow her to enter La Penitencia because her Blackness is a sign of her condition as a former slave. A furious nun disrupts prayer in the choir to decry the influence of a Black with the community hierarchy. Finally, in the episode with María Francisca, even the devil is furious at having to contend with a Black woman who had power over him. But once Chicaba is dead, the narrative tries to perform an act that will erase her Blackness as it describes how Chicaba's skin turns miraculously white.

The first section of this introduction has already discussed at length how the report of Sor Teresa's whitening works within the narrative structure of the hagiography, especially in comparison to Mary of Egypt. But Chicaba's whitening after death still operates within the economy of her Blackness as materiality and body. This body of a former slave, now dead, is narratively and ideologically more useful as a white one, as a relic.[124] Therefore, it might be helpful to revisit the phenomenon of Chicaba's whitening/lightening and to analyze it from another point of view: the traditions of the Church about the bodily remains of saints. The *Vida*'s first exploration of the subject of relics occurs when Chicaba travels through Alba de Tormes on her way to La Penitencia. The putative intention for this excursion was for her to pray before the incorrupt relics of Saint Teresa of Ávila's body: her arm and her "seared heart." The text makes bold to imply a comparison between Chicaba and the famous Spanish mystic: "During the course of her life, our Teresa enjoyed a favor very much like the one experienced by the Holy Mother in her heart" (Chapter 21).

The autobiography of Teresa of Ávila records the spiritual experience of the "transverberation of her heart": A small angel stood at her left side. "He was very beautiful, and his face was so aflame that he seemed to be one of those sublime angels that appear to be all afire." He plunged a large golden fire-tipped dart into her heart several times, and when he withdrew it, she says that he took away "with him the deepest part of [her], and he left [her] all afire with great love of God." The description of the pain of the experience is theologically significant because she assures the reader that this was a transcendent experience in her soul, but the body "shared in it" as well.[125] This famous relic seems to bear material witness to the connection between spirit and flesh that testifies to the incarnational aspect of Teresa of Ávila's spirituality. Guides in Alba de Tormes still point out the wound left in the heart by the heavenly messenger, thus literalizing on and in the body the spiritual experience. This spiritual gift was physically felt.

The point of representing Teresa Chicaba's devotion before these relics was to establish that they were more than a source of inspiration. They were an affirmation of her spirituality, which her *Vida* describes in a variety of fiery terms several times in the text, and a sign of her call to the contemplative life, no matter the obstacles to her fully exercising this vocation. For example, in the descriptions of her deep and abiding love for her Beloved Spouse, early in the hagiography, the narrative recounts how, under the spiritual direction of Father Araújo, "the Holy Spirit fanned the flame of her virtue. The volcano of love that had been lit inside her burned more and more toward her celestial Master. Impelled by this fire, she was determined to brush the world aside and withdraw to the cloister" (Chapter 16). The tropes of flames of love, volcanic eruptions of the heart, and spiritual fire continue to modulate upward until they reach a crescendo in an impassioned, extended passage attributed to her as a direct quotation in Chapter 35:

> So it is very painful when my heart is serene and calm. It becomes burning when my love rises excessively to the point of wishing to fulfill all my duties and obligations. But I am not saying it right because it is not excessive, because it is reasonable. I am burning, I feel I am being seared, I would shout aloud, but I scream inside myself. . . . The pain I feel in my heart is so great that inside I feel as if it is covered in sweat.[126]

The foregoing apostrophe confirms another in a series of comparisons throughout the hagiography between Teresa of Ávila and her namesake Teresa Chicaba. Thus, they share across time a kind of spiritual sisterhood that the African woman had difficulty achieving during her lifetime. For example, a devout eighteenth-century reader would associate the description of the odor of sanctity Chicaba's corpse emits with accounts of the pleasant fragrance of Teresa of Ávila's incorrupt exhumed body. Chicaba's whitening after death, with all of its racial freight, is part of this network of reverential lore about corporeal indications of holiness (Chapter 43). These manifestations prompt meditations on the Resurrection of Christ and on the afterlife that perfected and transformed believers await. In Alba de Tormes, Chicaba reproduced Catholic traditions around relics; and others reproduced the same customs and values when they requested pieces of her habit as sacred talismans.

Finally, the *Vida* laments the small attendance at her interment. There were only a few poor townspeople, some Theatine priests, and her community. In addition, it complains that nothing distinguishes her grave from others in the community cemetery. The text concludes that this was another instance when "human beings mortified her." However, there is another reading of her modest burial rites. Her inclusion in the monastery graveyard constitutes a final full acknowledgement of her membership as a Dominican sister. If the departed welcomed her lovingly on her admission day, then her slipping into their ranks quietly and unobtrusively is appropriately humble and gracious, and as such, it reflects her perfect formation in the monastic life despite the absence of a living mistress.

At last, with the publishing of a long obituary in the Acts of the Chapter of Toro a few months after her death, came the first official public recognition of her relationship as a daughter of Saint Dominic and therefore as a sister of her fellow nuns (Appendix 3).

Today's pilgrims to her grave and exhibit at Las Dueñas and readers of this hagiography know that after the publication of her *Vida*, La Penitencia's nuns were ordered to abandon their monastery before the bombardment of the city during the Napoleonic occupation of 1810. They carried only one cherished item with them, the body of Sor Teresa Chicaba, recording the act officially (Figure 7). Furthermore, the more aristocratic second order monastery of Las Dueñas welcomed both her body and her community of third order sisters. This is a great final testament to her centrality in the communal life of Dominican sisters.

NOTES TO THE INTRODUCTION: SECTION 2

We use a combination of notes and parenthetical citations to credit sources. When we have multiple references to a single work, we use an end note the first time we mention a source and parenthetical citations thereafter.

1. See John W. Blassingame's "Introduction," in *Slave Testimony: Two Centuries of Letters, Speeches, Interviews, and Autobiographies*, for a history of the debate about the authenticity of slave narratives, especially dictated or recorded oral histories (Baton Rouge: Louisiana State University Press, 1977). Joycelyn Moody traces this evolution in a book-length study of African American women's spiritual narratives entitled *Sentimental Confessions: Spiritual Narratives of Nineteenth-Century African American Women* (Athens: University of Georgia Press, 2001). The first of these narratives, a dictated as-told-to spiritual autobiography, is striking because Belinda's childhood abduction while at prayer is similar to the story of Chicaba's in the *Vida*. See Belinda 253–55. See also the discussion of "authenticity" in literary versus oral slave narratives in Lindon Barrett, "African-American Slave Narratives: Literacy, the Body, Authority," *American Literary History* 7.3 (Autumn 1995): 415–42.

   A few who have attended our many presentations on the *Vida* doubt the veracity of the narrative and/or disagree with our assertion that Chicaba might have had a role in the preparation of this biographical narrative. Our argument is less about the "authenticity" of the hagiography than about attributing some small "voice" or agency to the Black slave woman in her own representation. We have wondered if this reluctance to "hear" Chicaba in the text of her own life-story isn't analogous to the skeptical reception such writers as Phillis Wheatley, Harriet Wilson, and Harriet Jacobs received when they published. A discussion of Black authorship doubted is in Henry Louis Gates Jr., *The Trials of Phillis Wheatley*. See also Harryette Mullen, "Runaway Tongue," which we discussed in Section 1.

2. Robin Law describes the Slave Coast geographically as "normally reckoned as running from the mouth of the Volta River east to the Lagos channel, a distance of about 200 miles, although the precise boundaries were a matter of some dispute. It thus comprised, roughly, the western half of the Gulf or Bight of Benin. In terms of modern political geography, it corresponds to the coastal portions of southeastern Ghana, the Republics of Togo and Benin (formerly Dahomey), and the southwestern corner of Nigeria. This area became called the Slave Coast, of course, in reference to its role as a supplier of slaves for the Atlantic slave trade, and in contrast to the Gold Coast (modern Ghana) to the west, which initially (prior to the eighteenth century) exported gold rather than slaves" (*The Slave Coast of West Africa, 1550–1750* [Oxford: Clarendon Press, 1991], 13).

3. Two bulls by Nicholas V legitimized the Portuguese claim to slaves in Africa: *Dum diversas* (1452) and *Romanus Pontifex* (1455). In the discussion of Chapters 7 through 18 there will be further reference to these documents.

4. Portuguese geographers of the seventeenth and eighteenth centuries called the area "Mina Baja" (Lower Mina). It was situated east of the old fort of São Jorge da Mina. If this is information from Chicaba, it is improbable that, during her childhood in Africa, she knew her homeland by this name, but she could have heard it from those who transported her to the island of São Tomé or from the traders who sold her in Spain.

5. Robin Law maintains that the "bulk of the [Slave Coast] population belonged to a single linguistic group. . . . It has been argued, indeed, that the languages of this region are so closely related that they should be regarded as dialects of a single language" (*Slave Coast* 21).

6. Differences in spelling can be explained by the differences in the phonological systems of the Ewe and Spanish languages. The sound /sh/ does not exist in Castilian Spanish, although it is a common occurrence in the southern region of Andalusia, where the sound is spelled "ch." Sor Teresa spent her first Spanish years in that region. The same happens with the spelling of the second element of the word, -ba- or -va-. The Spanish language does not have a phoneme /v/ either, thus the variation in spelling in Paniagua's writing. Curiously, in the *Oración fúnebre* the spelling is consistent: *Chicava*. This is probably the spelling Sor Teresa preferred for her name.

We thank Professor Moses Panford, who confirmed the meaning of *sika* and *va/ba* in Akan, as related respectively to "gold/money" and "child of" in e-mail (January 2, 2006).

7. Chicaba had two other brothers. One of them was called *Ensú*, a Hispanicized spelling of *Nsu*, which in Guin-Mina (a dialect of Ewe) today means "gallant youth." Professor Panford, in his above-mentioned e-mail, speculates about the meaning of the name *Ensu* or *Nsu* as a last name; it means "you did not cry" or "you do not cry" in Fanti, a language in the same group. As to the name of the other brother, *Joachim*, it could be a variant of *Kwaakye* or *Kwakyen*, which were respectively pronounced "Cuaache" and "Cuachin," putting them quite close to the spelling in the *Vida*. Or it could be *Watchi* (discussed below as a calling among some Ewe in Togo); see Nadia Lovell, "Wild Gods: Containing Wombs and Moving Pots," in *Locality and Belonging*, edited by Lovell (London: Routledge, 1998), 53.

8. There is evidence of the use of gold in royal ceremonies among the Asante, who inhabit areas near the Ewe, in the 1702 account of French Capuchin Godefroy Loyer, although those events took place in areas west of the Volta River. See Suzanne Gott, "Golden Emblems of Maternal Benevolence: Transformations of Form and Meaning in Akan Regalia," *African Arts* 36.1 (2003): 69. The role of the smith in the social structure of the former Ghana-Mali Empire and the ethnic communities that remained in its wake is complex. Because gold and copper require lower temperatures to smelt, objects made from these two metals appeared before ironwork. But ironically, copper was more prized for ornamentation by the majority of African societies over gold except in the region from which Chicaba comes (E. W. Herbert, *Red Gold of Africa: Copper in Precolonial History and Culture* [Madison: University of Wisconsin Press, 2003]). Since the development of iron enabled communities to create agricultural implements and weapons, the technology of blacksmithing was valuable to most African societies. Therefore, the majority of the research on smithing focuses on iron workers, who, because of their powers to transform ore, are believed to have supernatural powers—healing and prophetic. Cultural heroes of some West African ethnic groups are depicted as sacred kings and smelters. Of the scant references to goldsmiths in the literature, scholars observe that smiths who work in gold are universally connected with royalty. See, for example, Laye Camara, *The Dark Child* (London: Collins, 1955), 31–40. Chicaba could have been a member of a smith's family, which is transformed into a "royal" family in the *Vida*; or, given her abilities to heal and prophesy, she could have been the daughter of one of these gifted smiths. See the explanation of Ewe polity in this section of the Introduction, and see also the note below about healers among the Ewe (P. M. McNutt, "The African Ironsmith as Marginal Mediator: A Symbolic Analysis," *Journal of Ritual Studies* 3.2 [1991]: 75–98; and W. J. Dewey and Allen Roberts, visiting curators, *Iron, Master of Them All*, catalog [Iowa City: University of Iowa Museum of Art and The Project for Advanced Study of Life and Art in Africa, March 5–July 25, 1993]).

9. Professor André Teko, who is a Guin-Mina speaker from Togo, provided us with this information in a personal communication in February 2005. In his e-mail communication from January 2006, Professor Panford confirmed that the mother's name, *Aba* or *Abar*, exists in Fanti; *Aba* is a name for a woman born on a Thursday, and *Abar* means "whip."

10. Birgit Meyer, "Setting the Scene: Peki Past and Present," in *Translating the Devil: Religion and Modernity among Ewe in Ghana* (Trenton, NJ: Africa World Press, 1999), 1–27; Kathleen O'Brien Wicker, "Abijan Mamiwater: Traveler in Search of a Home/Land," in *Togbi Dawuso Dofe: Mami Water in Ewe Tradition*, edited by Kathleen O'Brien Wicker and Kofi Asare Opoku (Legon, Ghana: Sub-Saharan Publishers, 2007), 1–25.

11. Sandra E. Greene, *Gender, Ethnicity, and Social Change on the Upper Slave Coast: A History of the Anlo-Ewe* (Portsmouth, NH: Heinemann Press, 1995), 27.

12. Chicaba claims to remember her father's face but not his name. As a member of a patrilineal ethnic group that practiced polygyny, the child may not have interacted much with her father. Young children of both genders lived with their mothers. Eventually the boys went to their fathers for instruction in the ways of their people.

13. Text and translation:

> Aqui yace la casta, la pura, la inocente, y mortificada, Paloma en el Alma, si en el cuerpo negra, negra pero hermosa; nacio Reyna, y murio Esclava, pero por Esclava, Reyna. Reina

porque reinó en si propria; y porque reino en si propria, ahora Reyna: buscas donde Passagero? pues imitala en las virtudes, y sabras donde: su cuerpo aquí yace, su alma espero vive en donde por una eternidad Requiescat in pace. Amen. (*Oración fúnebre* 24)

Here lies the chaste, the pure, the innocent and self-sacrificed dove in the soul. Although Black in her body, Black but comely. She was born a queen and died a slave, but because she was a slave, she was a queen. Queen because she had dominion over herself, and because she had dominion over herself, she is a queen now. Where are you looking, wayfarer? Now, imitate her in her virtues and you will know where. Her body lies here, her soul I hope lives where there is an eternity without end. Amen

A shorter version of this epitaph appears in Bernardo Dorado's *Compendio histórico de la ciudad de Salamanca* (Salamanca, 1776), 400.

14. María Eugenia Maeso, OP, *Sor Teresa Chikaba: Princesa, esclava y monja* (Salamanca: Editorial San Esteban, 2004).
15. Sandra E. Greene, "Religion, History, and the Supreme Gods of Africa: A Contribution to the Debate," *Journal of Religion in Africa* 26.2 (1996): 122–38.
16. In *Summa theologica*, Saint Thomas Aquinas writes, on the doctrine of natural or actual grace:

    Our natural knowledge begins from sense. Hence our natural knowledge can go as far as it can be led by sensible things. But our intellect cannot be led by sense so far as to see the essence of God; because sensible creatures are effects of God which do not equal the power of God, their cause. Hence from the knowledge of sensible things the whole power of God cannot be known; nor therefore can His essence be seen. But because they are His effects and depend on their cause, we can be led from them so far as to know of God *whether He exists*, and to know of Him what must necessarily belong to Him, as the first cause of all things, exceeding all things caused by Him. (part 1, question 12, article 12 [emphasis added])

    In the next article, Saint Thomas recognizes that a more perfect knowledge of God only happens through grace—that is, through conversion to Christianity. Our quotations from *Summa theologica* come from *Basic Writings of St. Thomas Aquinas*, edited by Anton C. Pegis (Indianapolis: Hackett, 1997), which is a revision of Laurence Shapcote's early twentieth-century English Dominican translation of St. Thomas.
17. See Greene, "Religion, History, and the Supreme Gods of Africa," on the Supreme Being. Her entire article focuses on this debate.
18. Olabiyi Babalola Yai, "From Vodun to Mawu: Monotheism and History in the Fon Cultural Area," in *L'invention religieuse en Afrique: Histoire et religion en Afrique Noire*, edited by Jean-Pierre Chrétien (Paris: Editions Karthala, 1993), 245; William Bosman, *A New and Accurate Description of the Coast of Guinea, divided into the Gold, the Slave and the Ivory coasts* (London, 1721). Bosman's informant on religious matters concerning the Fida people is a Black man who "in his Youth lived amongst the French, whose language he perfectly understood, and spake, [and] he had amongst them imbibed the Principles of the Christian Religion, and somewhat toward a just Notion of the true God, and how he is to be Worshipped; to whom, and not to his Country Gods, he ascribed the Creation of all Things" (368).
19. Kofi Asare Opoku, "Abijan Mamiwater as a Priest," in Wicker and Opoku, 25–44.
20. The text is paraphrasing a famous passage in "Noche oscura" ["Dark Night of the Soul"] by the Spanish poet and mystic Saint John of the Cross: "Aquesta me guiaba / más cierto que la luz del mediodía / adonde me esperaba / *quien yo bien me sabía* / en parte donde nadie parecía" [This [light] guided me / better than the light at noonday / to the place where *the one I very well knew* / was awaiting / apart from everybody's view]. Juan de la Cruz, *Poesía*, edited by Domingo Ynduráin (Madrid: Cátedra, 1989), 261.
21. Sandra Greene discusses pools, ponds, and streams as sacred sites among the Ewe. It is therefore significant that Chicaba encounters Christ and the Virgin at a small body of water. See "Of Water Spirits," in *Sacred Sites and the Colonial Encounter: A History of Meaning and Memory in Ghana* (Indianapolis: Indiana University Press, 2002), 35–60.

22. It is clear from Greene's description of this deity that it predates the introduction of Mami Water centuries later. However, this may be a spirit with whom Mami Water syncretizes later.
23. Raymond Oke, "Les siècles obscurs du Royaume Aja du Danxomé," in *Peuples du golfe du Bénin: Aja-Éwé*, edited by François de Medeiros (Paris: Centre de recherches africaines, 1984): 53.
24. The son of a Spanish conquistador and an Inca *palla* (lady, in Quechua, member of the Inca royal family) Garcilaso de la Vega (known also as "el Inca") elaborated a narrative of "preparation for Christianity" in his *Comentarios reales* with respect to the belief system in the Sun among the Incas of Peru, who were his maternal royal relatives (*Comentarios reales de los Incas* [Caracas: Biblioteca Ayacucho, 1976], 1:61–76). For further discussion on the issue of how a nonwhite intellectual "translates" and interprets non-Christian religious practices into a Western-style cosmology, see Nicolás Wey-Gómez, "'Nuestro Padre el Sol': Scholastic Cosmology and the Cult of the Sun in Inca Garcilaso's *Comentarios Reales*," *Latin American Literary Review* 26.52 (1998): 11. For Inca Garcilaso's concept of pre-Christian preparedness, see Margarita Zamora, *Language, Authority, and Indigenous History in the "Comentarios reales de los incas"* (Cambridge: Cambridge University Press, 1988), 114. Writing a few decades after the publication of Sor Teresa's *Vida*, Olaudah Equiano is also interested in comparing the Igbo and their native land in Africa with the ancient Jews in Israel. See *The Life of Olaudah Equiano, or Gustavus Vassa, the African* (Mineola, NY: Dover Thrift Editions, 1999), 17–18.
25. The presence of healers from the Lower Mina in different parts of the Atlantic is well documented. One of the best studies is that of the Afro-Brazilian Domingos Álvares, a contemporary of Sor Teresa Chicaba. He used his knowledge of healing acquired in his homeland once he was enslaved and transported to Brazil, where he gained freedom through his practices. The accounts of Álvares's activities are among the earliest testimonies of the practice of Vodun in the Americas. See James H. Sweet, *Domingos Álvares, African Healing, and the Intellectual History of the Atlantic World* (Chapel Hill: University of North Carolina Press, 2011), 123ff.
26. Meyer names and discusses the initiation of Ewe girls at puberty. It is not mentioned at all in a much older source by an amateur anthropologist Alfred Burdon Ellis, *The Ewe-Speaking Peoples of the Slave Coast of West Africa, Their Religion, Manners, Customs, Laws, Languages* (London: Chapman and Hall, 1890). This absence in the early literature might reflect the belief of some nineteenth-century anthropologists that initiations betokened backwardness. Yet there is evidence of initiation rituals in the area where Chicaba lived. Neighboring ethnic groups tend to share what anthropologists term "a cultural zone"—that is, ethnic groups that occupy connecting geographical areas also share some social practices. One such practice is the ritual initiation and seclusion of girls. Among these groups are the Krobo, who are not Ewe-speaking people. This rite is called *dipo*. See Joseph Ajaye, "Dangerous Crossroads: Liminality and Contested Meaning in Krobo (Ghana) *dipo* Girls' Initiation," *Journal of African Cultural Studies* 12.1 (1999): 5–26. See also Louis E. Wilson, *The Krobo People of Ghana: A Political and Social History to 1892* (Athens: Ohio University Center for International Studies, 1991). There seem to be two possible forms of initiation. We have just discussed the first; it takes place at or near puberty. It marks a girl's movement into adulthood and her eligibility for marriage.

However, there is another form of initiation among the Ewe, the Mina and the Fon, groups that share a "cultural zone" with the Krobo. These initiations usher people into groups that are configured around the spiritual abilities or gifts the initiates have in common. The Watchi are a group among the Ewe who initiate people with spiritual gifts; among them is healing. Women are often members of this group. Some of these Watchi constitute a class of Ewe women diviners, *amegasi*. They undergo a long initiation period (between six and twenty years) in enclosure. "Throughout the apprenticeship, the novice is subject to strict rules of obedience, poverty, and chastity" (Klaus Hamberger, "From Village to Bush in Four Watchi Rites," *HAU: Journal of Ethnographic Theory* 4.1 (2003): 138. Any of these initiations could have been what Chicaba remembers from her youth. It is possible that before she was captured, her family had begun to notice her spiritual gifts and prepared her for initiation among the Watchi. It was common for some Watchi to frequent the land beyond the village, the bush, where they communed with spirits. See also Nadia Lovell, "Wild Gods, Containing Wombs and Moving Pots: Emplacement and Transience in Watchi Belonging," in *Locality and Belonging*, edited by Nadia Lovell (London: Routledge, 1998), 53–77, and Nadia Lovell, *Cord of Blood: Possession and the Making of "Voodoo"* (London: Pluto Press, 2003), 1–5, 10–18.

27. After the conquest of São Jorge da Mina by the Dutch in 1637, Portuguese slave traders were allowed to do business in only four ports of the Leeward Coast of Mina: Popo, Ajudá (Ouidah/Whydah), Jaquin, and Apa. See Pierre Verger, *Trade Relations between the Bight of Benin and Bahia from the 17th to the 19th Century* (Ibadan, Nigeria: Ibadan University Press, 1976), 21. Arada is spelled many ways: Allada, Arda, Ardra, Ardres, Hardre, Arada (Verger 9). It is today's Porto-Novo, in the Republic of Benin. Many people from this area were enslaved and transported to Haiti by the end of the seventeenth century and early eighteenth century, where they were known as Rada. In different parts of Latin America they were known as Arará.

28. Mateo de Anguiano, *Misiones Capuchinas en África*, vol. 2: *Misiones al reino de la Zinga, Benín, Arda, Guinea y Sierra Leona*, introduced and annotated by P. Buenaventura de Carrocera (Madrid: Consejo Superior de Investigaciones Científicas, 1957). Father Anguiano gave an account of the ensuing mission to Arada. The king of Arada explained to the missionaries that his embassy to Philip "no fue para mudar de creencia y admitir otra ley que aquella en que vivía y habían vivido sus mayores, sino para que se sirviese de enviarle algunos budonos o sacerdotes cristianos que les conjurasen los nublados, por ser muchos los estragos que hacen en aquella tierra.... Con esta respuesta quedaron los religiosos desahuciados de lograr fruto alguno" (54) [It was not intended to change his belief and accept a law other than that he and his ancestors had lived with. Rather, he asked for some *budonos* or Christian priests who might conjure storms that so devastate those lands.... With this response the priests lost hope of obtaining any fruit in their mission]. As a reward for their efforts, the king of Arada gave the Capuchin missionaries eight boy slaves. When the priests left their mission in Arada for the province of Cumaná in Venezuela, they sold them. Nájera calls them *bodunos*, and Anguiano *budonos* (*Espejo mystico*. Madrid, 1672). See Archivo General de Indias, Audiencia de México 1070, libro 30, fol. 340v, in *Colección de documentos para la historia de la formación social de Hispanoamérica, 1493–1810*, edited by Richard Konetzke (Madrid: CSIC, 1953), 2.2:522–23. For a historical summary and analysis of the embassy of the king of Arada to Spain and the Spanish Capuchin mission sent in response, see Robin Law, "Religion, Trade and Politics on the 'Slave Coast': Roman Catholic Missions in Allada and Whydah in the Seventeenth Century," *Journal of Religion in Africa* 21.1 (1991): 42–77, especially 46–49.

29. The translation of the Spanish *Doctrina christiana* into the Arada language was attributed to Vans (also known as Bans), a representative of King Toxonu of Arada in the court of Philip IV. Vans's arrival in Madrid caused a sensation, with one observer testifying that "es hombre de muy buena disposición y arte, más que de negro" [he is a man of great presence and manners, rather than what one would expect in someone Black] (Jerónimo de Barrionuevo, *Avisos de Jerónimo de Barrionuevo (1654–1658)* [Madrid, 1892], 1:107). In developing his knowledge of the Vodun religious system, he received the invaluable help of his servant Antonio, an African who knew Fon, Portuguese, and Spanish and was probably familiar with Christian theological concepts (Olabiyi 249). See the facsimile of *Doctrina christiana y explicación de sus misterios: En nuestro idioma español y en lengua arda* (Madrid, 1658) in Henri Labouret, *Le royaume d'Arda et son évangélisation au XVIIe siècle* (Paris: Institut d'Ethnologie, 1929).

30. José de Nájera, *Espejo mystico en que el hombre interior se mira practicamente illustrado* (Madrid, 1672), 278.

31. See Sandra E. Greene, "Cultural Zones in the Era of the Slave Trade: Exploring the Yoruba Connection with the Anlo-Ewe," in *Identity in the Shadow of Slavery*, edited by Paul E. Lovejoy (London, Continuum, 2000), 72–86.

32. António Brasio, *Monumenta missionaria Africana* (Lisbon: Agência Geral de Ultramar, 1952–1985). This multivolume collection of documents offers a wealth of information on the religious and political relations between the crown of Portugal and the different kingdoms of the Lower Mina area around the time Chicaba lived there. The Capuchin order, mentioned in the *Vida*, had a very active presence in Portuguese Angola and the surrounding areas. They

also expanded their action to São Tomé and the kingdoms of Arada and Werri (called Oere in Portuguese, Italian, and Latin documents). The Capuchins provided intelligence to the crown of Portugal about the presence of different Europeans in different coastal ports, all engaged in the slave trade (Brasio, vol. 13, doc. 65). The relations of the different West African rulers with the Portuguese were old and continuous. The king of Werri requested priests from São Tomé repeatedly and as late as 1684, the year before Chicaba's capture is recorded in the *Vida*. The Capuchin missions established in Benin must have been important because the bishop of São Tomé left the island to visit them (Brasio, vol. 13, docs. 143, 144, 175, 243).

33. Diplomatic relations between different European courts and the Lower Mina kingdoms intensified around the time of Chicaba's childhood. A portrait of Ambassador Matheo Lopes was produced in France, together with one of the king of Arada (Brasio vol. 13, doc. 114). See Christina Brauner, "To Be the Key for Two Coffers: A West African Embassy to France (1670/1)," IFRA-Nigeria E-Papers Series, no. 30 (October 14, 2013), 1–26; *www.ifra-nigeria.org/IMG/pdf/Key-for-Two-_Coffers.pdf*.

34. The Portuguese governor of Angola preferred to train young Black men as soldiers rather than as priests (Brasio, vol. 13, doc. 220). The response from the Royal Council in Lisbon was to limit the number of ordinations of Black seminarians (Brasio, vol. 13, doc. 223).

35. The definition of *raza* (old spelling *raça*) in the first dictionary of the Spanish Academy, *Diccionario de la lengua castellana* (Madrid, 1737) points to the term's religious associations: "Hablando de los hombres, se toma regularmente en mala parte" [In talking about men, normally it is a bad term]. It also cites the Constitutions of the Military Order of Calatrava:

> Ordenamos e mandamos que ninguna persona, de cualquier calidad y condición que fuere, sea recibida a la dicha Orden, ni se dé el Hábito, si no fuere Hijodalgo, al fuero de España, de partes de padre y madre y de abuelos de entre ambas partes, y de legítimo matrimonio nacido, y que no le toque raza de Judío, Moro, Hereje ni Villano.

> We decree and order that no person, whatsoever his quality or condition, shall be inducted in the aforementioned Order, nor shall he receive the Habit, unless he is of noble origin from both father and mother and grandparents on both sides, according to the laws of Spain, and born from a legal marriage, and he should not be of a race of Jews, Moors, Heretic, or plebeian.

Jews and Muslims in Christian Spain gradually lost their legal and religious autonomy from the late fourteenth century onward, culminating with the establishment of the Spanish Inquisition in 1478, in a movement of increased religious and social uniformity. See also Robert Bartlett, *The Making of Europe: Conquest, Colonization and Cultural Change, 950–1350* (Princeton, NJ: Princeton University Press, 1993), 240–42.

Some questioners who heard and read the lectures and essays we produced in our preparation of this book contended that Chicaba's exclusion from the living spaces of the monastery was "not unique." We maintain that *conversas* and Hispano-Arabs were no longer admitted to convents in the eighteenth century, when Sor Teresa Chicaba was in *La Penitencia*, and we also remind those critics that descendants of Jews and Muslims belonged to the same racially marginal social location as the African Chicaba. In fact, no *vida* or hagiography of a nun in early modern Spain would have discussed openly in its pages the tainted genealogy of its subject, as it would have been scandalous. Thus our contention that race was the motive for her exclusion is still valid, and the text of Chicaba's *Vida* says so repeatedly.

36. Different Spanish moralists in the sixteenth century—Tomás de Mercado, Esteban Fagúndez, and Francisco García—remarked how the Portuguese used childish trinkets to lure their Black victims into captivity. See Jesús M. García Añoveros, *El pensamiento y los argumentos sobre la esclavitud en Europa en el siglo XVI y su aplicación a los indios americanos y a los negros africanos* (Madrid: CSIC, 2000), 179.

37. See an extended theoretical discussion of "voice" in the first part of this introduction. This is another example of competing voices and ideologies in the *Vida*.

38. Marcus Rediker, *The Slave Ship: A Human History* (New York: Penguin, 2007), 14–40.
39. Saidiya Hartman, *Lose Your Mother: A Journey along the Atlantic Slave Route* (New York: Farrar, Straus and Giroux, 2008), 155.
40. The best-known examples of the genre are Lope de Vega's *El peregrino en su patria* (1604) and Miguel de Cervantes's *Los trabajos de Persiles y Sigismunda* (1617). All draw heavily from the Spanish sixteenth-century translation of Heliodorus's *Aithiopikai* and Fernando de Mena's *Historia etiópica de los amores de Teágenes y Cariclea* (1587). The genre took an allegorical turn by the middle of the seventeenth century with works like Baltasar Gracián's *El criticón*. In all these works the concept of *peregrinatio* (travel after an initial traumatic separation from the homeland) is the central motif. See Lope de Vega, *El peregrino en su patria*, edited by Juan Bautista Avalle-Arce (Madrid: Castalia, 1973); Miguel de Cervantes, *Los trabajos de Persiles y Sigismunda* (Madrid: Cátedra, 2004); Heliodoro de Emesa, *Historia etiópica de los amores de Teágenes y Cariclea*, edited by Francisco López Estrada and translated by Fernando de Mena (Madrid: Aldus, 1954); and Baltasar Gracián, *El criticón*, edited by Santos Alonso (Madrid: Cátedra, 2004).
41. The topos of captivity at the hands of pirates and enslavement in a ship is present in Miguel de Cervantes's *Persiles*. Slavery is also present in theatrical versions of Heliodorus's *Ethiopian Story* by Calderón de la Barca in *Los hijos de la fortuna, Teágenes y Cariclea* (1664). The *Ethiopian Story* and its Spanish sequels also record the presence of a white princess who is the daughter of Black (Ethiopian) parents (Javier González Rovira, *La novela bizantina de la Edad de Oro* [Madrid: Gredos, 1996]).
42. Cristina Maria Seuanes Serafim, *As Ilhas de São Tomé no século XVII* (Lisbon: Centro de História de Além-Mar, 2000), 218.
43. Enriqueta Vila Vilar, "Aspectos marítimos del comercio de esclavos con Hispanoamérica en el siglo XVII," *Historia naval* 19 (1987): 113–31.
44. Sowande Mustakeem, "'I Never Have Seen Such a Sickly Ship Before': Diet, Disease, and Mortality in 18th-Century Atlantic Slaving Voyages," *Journal of African American History* 93.4 (2008): 474–96.
45. Locke was referring to white Europeans or white British American colonials. See his *Fundamental Constitutions of Carolina* (London, 1669): "Every Freeman of Carolina shall have absolute power and authority over his negro slaves of what opinion or religion soever." In John Locke, *Political Essays*, edited by Mark Goldie (Cambridge: Cambridge University Press, 1997), 180. See also David Armitage, "John Locke, Carolina, and the *Two Treatises of Government*," *Political Theory* 32.5 (2004): 609.
46. The Marquis of Mancera's behavior exemplified Spanish attitudes toward slavery. He tried to curb the enslavement of indigenous people in Mexico even after they rebelled, which would have been legal grounds for their enslavement. Instead, he granted lands free of taxes to the indigenous of Nuevo León. He also put limits on the traffic in Black slaves to his viceroyalty by foreigners; instead, he favored the involvement of Spanish traffickers. In addition, he issued orders to repress a rebellion of mulattoes whom the Inquisitor reported for communicating with "external enemies." For this, he created a special military company of one hundred men to deal with what he considered a threat. However, the government in Madrid ordered him to use less extraordinary means. Manuel Rivera, *Los gobernantes de México* (Mexico City, 1872), 224, 232, 237.
47. For a modern edition, see Alonso de Sandoval, *Un tratado sobre la esclavitud*, introduced and transcribed by Enriqueta Vila Vilar (Madrid: Alianza Universidad, 1987).
48. Francisco José de Jaca, *Resolución sobre la libertad de los negros y sus originarios, en estado de paganos y después ya cristianos*, edited by Miguel Anxo Pena González (Madrid: Consejo Superior de Investigaciones Cientícas, 2002); Miguel Anxo Pena González, *Francisco José de Jaca: La primera propuesta abolicionista de la esclavitud en el pensamiento hispano* (Salamanca: Publicaciones Universidad Pontificia de Salamanca, 2003). Francisco José de Jaca also condemned the enslavement of the indigenous population in Spanish America, in a letter to the king of Spain warning him that the freedom of his indigenous vassals was not being respected. See

Miguel Anxo Pena González, "Un documento singular de Fray Francisco José de Jaca, acerca de la esclavitud práctica de los indios," *Revista de Indias* 61.223 (2001): 704. Jaca and Moirans spoke and wrote against the enslavement of Blacks earlier than other famous abolitionists in Protestant countries, including the Quakers of Philadelphia in 1688.

49. Georges Scelle, *La traite négrière aux Indes de Castille: Contrats et traités d'assiento* (Paris, 1906), 1:710.

50. The Council of the Indies issued several royal orders aimed at correcting abuses in the treatment of Black slaves. One from 1683 seems to be a direct response to a memorandum sent by Father Francisco José de Jaca to King Carlos II (in Archivo General de Indias, Indiferente General 340, libro 42, fol. 297v). Two other orders (archived as Indiferente General 537, libro 8, fol. 11, and Audiencia de Guadalajara 231, libro 5, fol. 271) are in Konetzke 2.2:754 and 762. The royal orders insist on approaching the offending masters in a confidential manner, without public pronouncements (Archivo General de Indias, Audiencia de Santo Domingo 333 and 376, libro 27, fol. 307, in Konetzke 2.2:40). King Philip V issued a similar decree in 1710 that was a model of good intentions but had no measures to enforce it. It entreated owners not to mistreat their slaves so the latter would not flee. The decree also asks the owners to dress slave women with appropriate decency (Pena González, *Francisco José de Jaca* 372).

51. In his instructions to his successor in Mexico, dated October 22, 1673, and anthologized as "Relación del Marqués de Mancera (Antonio Sebastián de Toledo Salazar)" in *Los virreyes españoles en América durante el Gobierno de la Casa de Austria*, edited by Lewis Hanke and Celso Rodríguez (Madrid: Atlas, 1978), the Marquis of Mancera expressed the views of many. He analyzes the negative effect of leaving the African slave traffic in the hands of foreigners:

> La introducción de negros bozales en las provincias de las Indias corre por asiento a cargo de Domingo Grillo y Ambrosio Lomelín, genoveses, debajo de condiciones tan irregulares, que sólo conocerlas con alguna atención se percibe la gran inopia de esclavos que padecen estos reinos cuando se ajustó el contrato. Llegué de España por fines de julio de 1664 al puerto de Veracruz, donde ya hallé surto un bajel del asiento cuyo capitán era Santiago Daza Villalobos. Mi forzosa detención hasta despachar las dos naos que me condujeron, facilitó a mi curiosidad algunas horas para hacerme capaz de todos sus papeles. Y habiéndolos considerado y ponderado, propuse a mi ánimo desembarazarme con la brevedad posible de aquel huésped poco útil (según mi corta inteligencia) a la religión, estado y tranquilidad de estas provincias. Y mediante consulta y parecer del real acuerdo, a quien conferí mi cuidado, encaminé su expedición acelerada, honestándola con título de aviso para que se hizo a la vela por febrero de 1665 . . . [El asiento beneficia] naciones enemigas de la corona y de la iglesia, a donde no es difícil que lleven noticias que dañen y de donde es fácil que traigan doctrinas y dogmas que escandalicen, que fuera la peor permutación, aun cuando cesase la de los demás géneros prohibidos. (5:23)

> The introduction of Black *bozales* in these provinces of the Indies takes place through the *asiento* run by the Genoese Domingo Grillo and Ambrosio Lomelín. The contract is run in such an irregular manner that once studied with a bit of attention, one can see the reason these kingdoms [Mexico and the rest of Spanish America] have suffered such dearth of slaves since the *asiento* was signed. I arrived from Spain in July 1664 at the port of Veracruz, where I already found a vessel from the *asiento*, the captain of which was Santiago Daza Villalobos. As I had to delay my travel until I sent back to Spain the two ships that had brought me there, those few hours stimulated my curiosity to obtain all the vessel's papers. After having seen them and thought about them, I made up my mind to get rid [of them] in the shortest time possible, according to my little understanding, of an outsider of little use to the religion, the state, and the tranquility of these provinces. And after consulting and obtaining an opinion from the royal advisors, to whom I expressed my worries, I expedited the consultation with celerity, qualifying it as a warning to His Majesty. It was sent by sail around February 1665. . . . [The *asiento* benefits] those nations that are enemies of the Crown and the Church, and it will not be difficult for these ships

to carry news that may harm us, and it will be easy for them to bring doctrines and dogmas that cause scandal. This latter thing would be the worst exchange, even if the traffic in other illegal goods ceased.

As we mentioned in an earlier note, *bozales* was a term for people ignorant of the Spanish language (or any other European language, for that matter). The marquis is discussing slaves who had presumably been imported directly from Africa. *Asiento* refers to the trafficking monopoly granted by the king of Spain.

52. Manuel Lobo Cabrera, "La población esclava de Telde en el siglo XVI," *Hispania: Revista española de historia* 42 (1982): 47–89.
53. Torres Villarroel was not unique as a slave-owning cleric. However, he felt the need to explain in his autobiography that he treated his slaves and other servants with an evangelical sense of equality: "Todos comemos de un mismo guisado y de un mismo pan, nos arropamos de una misma tienda y mi vestido ni en la figura ni en la materia se distinguen de los que yo les doy" [We all eat from the same stew and the same bread, we get our clothes from the same store, and my dress is not different in either form or fabric from the one I give them]. Diego de Torres Villarroel, *Vida, ascendencia, nacimiento, crianza y aventuras*, edited by Guy Mercadier (Madrid: Editorial Castalia, 1972), 151.
54. The seminal study on Spanish slavery during modern times is Antonio Domínguez Ortiz's "La esclavitud en Castilla durante la Edad Moderna," in *Estudios de historia social de España*, edited by Carmelo Viñas y Mey (Madrid: Consejo Superior de Investigaciones Científicas, 1952), 2:367–426, 368.
55. The most comprehensive study of slavery in Spain and Portugal to date is William D. Phillips Jr.'s *Slavery in Medieval and Early Modern Iberia* (Philadelphia: University of Pennsylvania Press, 2014). Black slaves concentrated mainly in southern Spain and Extremadura. For Extremadura, the region south of Salamanca, Rocío Periáñez Gómez is one of the foremost scholars dedicated to the study of slavery in Spain during the early modern period, with a particular emphasis on the region of Extremadura. See her doctoral dissertation, "La esclavitud en Extremadura (siglos XVI–XVIII)" (Universidad de Extremadura, 2008). She has also paid attention to the situation of women slaves in her essay "La mujer esclava en la Extremadura de los tiempos modernos," in *Marginados y minorías sociales en la España moderna y otros estudios sobre Extremadura*, edited by Francisco J. Mateos Ascacibar and Felipe Lorenzana de la Puente (Llerena, Spain: Sociedad de Historia, 2005), 135–45. For the same region, see also S. Aragón Mateos and R. Sánchez Rubio, "La esclavitud en la Alta Extremadura, proceso de auge y decadencia," *Norba, Revista de Historia* 7 (1986): 108, and Fernando Cortés Cortés, *Esclavos en la Extremadura meridional del siglo XVII* (Badajoz, Spain: Excelentísima Diputación Provincial de Badajoz, 1987), 95. The Andalusian region at one point had the largest concentration of Black enslaved people in Spain, both in cities and the rural areas. See Antonio M. González Díaz, *La esclavitud en Ayamonte durante el Antiguo Régimen (siglos XVI, XVII y XVIII)* (Huelva, Spain: Diputación de Huelva, 1996). See also Aurelia Martín Casares and Margarita García Barranco, eds., *La esclavitud negroafricana en la historia de España, siglos XVI y XVII* (Granada, Spain: Comares, 2010). For studies about the Atlantic connection of Sevillian slavery, both in Africa and the Americas, the work of Rafael M. Pérez García and Manuel Fernández Chaves for the sixteenth century is fundamental. See their essay "Las redes de la trata negrera: Mercaderes portugueses y tráfico de esclavos en Sevilla (c. 1560–1580)," in Martín Casares and García Barranco, *La esclavitud negroafricana*, 5–34, and their "Sevilla y la trata negrera atlántica: Envíos de esclavos desde Cabo Verde a la América española (1569–1579)," in *Estudios de historia moderna en honor al profesor Antonio García-Baquero*, edited by León Carlos Álvarez Santaló (Seville: Universidad de Sevilla, 2009), 597–622.
56. Claude Larquié, "Les esclaves de Madrid à l'époque de la décadence (1650–1700)," *Revue Historique* 244 (1970): 41–74.
57. Henry Kamen, "Mediterranean Slavery in Its Last Phase: The Case of Valencia, 1600–1700," *Anuario de Historia Economica y Social* 3 (1970): 211–34.
58. Aurelia Martin Casares, *La esclavitud en la Granada del siglo XVI: Género, raza y religión* (Granada: Editorial Universidad de Granada, 2000), 464–65.

59. Manuel Lobo Cabrera and Ramón Díaz Hernández, "La población esclava de Las Palmas durante el siglo XVII," *Anuario de estudios atlánticos* 30 (1984): 187.
60. The association of Blackness, Africanity, and non-Christianity was the essential definition of slavery as seen in a royal decree from August 9, 1682, which ordered the owners of slaves in the island of Cuba to baptize Blacks. Their religion was the main legitimate reason for their enslavement in a Christian land. "Habiendo Dios nuestro Señor dado tanta felicidad a los negros bozales, que vienen a esta isla entre cristianos, es una de las mayores dichas el gozar el santo bautismo; y porque estamos informados que muchos dueños de esclavos los tienen en su servicio más ha de dos o tres años, y no los han bautizado" [God our Lord having given so much happiness to the ignorant [*bozal*] Blacks who come to this island to live among Christians, their greatest fortune is to enjoy the benefits of holy Baptism. And yet, we have been informed that many slave owners have had them under their service for more than two or three years and they still have not had them baptized]. José Antonio Saco, *Historia de la Esclavitud de la raza Africana en el Nuevo Mundo y en especial en los países américo-hispánicos* (Barcelona, 1879), 286.
61. The *asiento* of 1609 indicates very clearly that only dark-skinned Blacks from certain areas of West Africa (Cape Verde, Mina, Angola, all connected to the Portuguese crown) could be transported to the American colonies as slaves, and there was a total prohibition against importing Muslims, mixed-race Blacks, and those who could speak Spanish or Portuguese already or who were married in Spain or Portugal (which would make them Christian):

    No aya de yr ni vaya ningun mulato ni mestizo, turco, morisco, Berverisco, Jelofes ni esclavos negros ladinos, ni cassados en estos reynos, si no es llevando a sus mugeres e hijos, ni de otra nacion, sino negros atezados de los dichos yslas y Rios de la Corona de Portugal.

    [No one may go there who is a mulatto or mixed-race, Turk, Morisco, from the Barbary Coast, Wolof or Black slaves who can speak our language, nor Blacks who are married in our kingdoms, unless they bring with them their wives and children. And they should not be of any other origin than dark-skinned Blacks from the aforementioned islands and rivers that belong to the crown of Portugal.] (Scelle 813).

62. Notarized record of a sale. Archivo Histórico de Protocolos Notariales de Madrid, protocolo 11.410, fol. 79, February 6, 1677:

    Venta de dos esclavos moros, otorgada por Sebastián Antonio de Toledo y Molina, Marqués de Mancera, a favor de Juan de Artieda, el uno llamado Almanzor amulatado, alto de cuerpo con una señal de herida en el carrillo derecho, pelo pasas, de edad de hasta treinta años. Y otro llamado Jergues, negro atezado, pelo pasas, de buen cuerpo, romo, cuyas señas les sirvan de conocimiento. Por precio y cuantía de ciento y cincuenta ducados de vellón cada uno, que hacen tres mil trescientos reales de vellón.

    Sale of two Moor slaves, by Sebastián Antonio de Toledo y Molina, Marquis of Mancera, in favor of Juan de Artieda. One is called Almanzor, mulatto, tall of body and with a scar in his right cheek, nappy hair, around thirty years of age. The other is called Jergues, dark-skinned Black, nappy hair, fine body, flat nose. These marks shall help to recognize them. For the price of 150 ducats paid in bullion money each one of them, which amount to 3,300 bullion *reales*.

63. Some of the earliest Black religious confraternities, all related to the establishment of slavery in the late Middle Ages and the early modern period, appeared in Barcelona, Valencia, Seville, Jaén, Huelva, Cádiz, Granada, Puerto de Santa María, Medina-Sidonia, and Jerez de la Frontera. Larger cities, like Seville, Cádiz, Madrid, and Granada, had more than one. See Aurelia Martín Casares and Christine Delaigue, "The Evangelization of Freed and Slave Black Africans in Renaissance Spain: Baptism, Marriage, and Ethnic Brotherhoods," *History of Religions* 52.3 (February 2013): 214–35. The best study to date of a Spanish Black confraternity is Isidoro Moreno Navarro's comprehensive historical analysis, *La antigua hermandad de los negros*

64. Richard Gray, "The Papacy and the Atlantic Slave Trade: Lourenço da Silva, the Capuchins and the Decisions of the Holy Office," *Past and Present* 115.1 (1987): 54.
65. Alonso Ramírez de Vargas, *Elogio Panegírico, Festivo aplauso, Iris Político y Diseño triunfal de Eneas verdadero con que la muy Noble y Leal Ciudad de México recibió al Excmo. Señor Don Antonio Sebastián de Toledo y Salazar: Marqués de Mancera* (Mexico City, 1664).
66. Nancy H. Fee speculates that the depiction of Mancera as Perseus defeating Medusa was a reference to his political relationship with Queen Mariana of Austria. Perseus killed Medusa in order to free his mother from a forced marriage, which could be read as a metaphor for Mancera's involvement with intrigues in the court of Carlos II. The description of this triumphal arch appears in an anonymous publication with the title *Diseño de la alegórica fábrica del Arco Triumphal, que la Santa Iglesia Cathedral de Puebla de los Angeles erigió en aplauso del Excellentissimo Señor DON ANTONIO SEBASTIAN DE TOLEDO, Marques de Mancera: Señor de las 5 Villas, y de la del Marmol....* (Puebla, Mexico: Viuda de Ivan de Borja, 1664). Nancy H. Fee, "La Entrada Angelopolitana: Ritual and Myth in the Viceregal Entry in Puebla de Los Angeles," *The Americas* 52. 3 (1996): 303.
67. Elías Trabulse, *El círculo roto* (Mexico City: Fondo de Cultura Económica, 1984), 38–39.
68. Sor Juana Ines de la Cruz (1648–1695) was the illegitimate daughter of Spaniard Pedro Manuel de Asbaje and *criollo* Isabel Ramirez. She spent her early years on the hacienda of her maternal grandfather, where she learned to read and write in Spanish, Latin, and Nahuatl. At sixteen she went to Mexico City, where she became the protégé of and companion to Vicereine Leonor de Carreto, the wife of Antonio Sebastian de Toledo, the Marquis of Mancera. After Sor Juana's death, her great friend the Countess of Paredes, wife of Viceroy Laguna, took possession of her manuscript of poems. When the countess returned to Madrid, she published the poems as *Fama y obras póstumas del Fénix de México, Décima Musa, Poetisa Americana....* (Madrid, 1700). The volume included the first official biography of Sor Juana, by Father Diego Calleja. Calleja reported that the Marquis of Mancera, who cherished the memory of Sor Juana and had taken a major interest in this publication, was an important source of information about Sor Juana's life.

    Mancera had wanted to know the source of Sor Juana's knowledge, so he reportedly subjected her to a tribunal of forty learned men—poets, humanists, theologians, and professors from the University of Mexico—who questioned her on topics concerning science, literature, and religion (Octavio Paz, *Sor Juana Inés de la Cruz o las trampas de la fe* [Mexico City: Fondo de Cultura Económica, 1985], 141; Octavio Paz, *Sor Juana or the Traps of Faith* [Cambridge, MA: Harvard University Press, 1988], 98). This questioning is similar to what Phillis Wheatley underwent when her authorship of poems was questioned by white authorities a century later.
69. Leonor de Carreto was the daughter of the German ambassador in Madrid, and a lady-in-waiting to the Queen Mother (Paz, *Sor Juana Inés* 129). Mancera was later appointed major-domo to the Queen Mother, Mariana de Austria, and he suffered political banishment with her during the tumultuous years after his return from Mexico (188).
70. Mancera's written opinion in the Council of State was that Louis XIV would help the new king preserve the territorial integrity of the Spanish monarchy. However, the French would soon control the entire business of the *asiento de negros* (royal monopoly on the slave trade). See Pere Molas Ribalta, *La Razón de Estado y la sucesión española* (Valencia, Spain: Publicaciones de la Real Sociedad Económica de Amigos del País, 1999. rseap.webs.upv.es/Anales/99_00/A_281_La_razon_y_sucesion.pdf), 287, 288.
71. In his instructions to the next viceroy of Mexico, Mancera referred to Blacks and slavery in several paragraphs, showing fear of their presence in the viceroyalty mixed with expressions of benignity toward newly arrived enslaved Africans. About mulattoes and Creole Blacks he says that they are "naturalmente altivos, audances y amigos de la novedad. Conviene mucho tenerlos en respecto y cuidar de sus andamientos y designios, pero sin mostrar desconfianza, trayendo la mano ligera en la exacción de sus tributos" [They are haughty by nature, audacious

and friends to any new change. It is a matter of caution to keep them in mind and observe vigilance with their comings and goings and their plans, but without showing distrust. One should not exercise the collection of their taxes with too much zeal] ("Instrucción que de orden del Rey dio el Virrey de México, D. Antonio Sebastián de Toledo, Marqués de Mancera a su sucesor," *Instrucciones que los Virreyes de Nueva España dejaron a sus sucesores* [Mexico City, 1873], 104). His opinion of *bozales*, enslaved Blacks newly arrived from Africa, shows a tendency to see them as docile with a disposition to be obedient: "Los negros bozales, conducidos de Guinea, se reducen a una porción muy limitada; y aunque fuese crecida, nunca pusiera en cuidado por su natural dócil y servil" [Black slaves newly brought from Guinea are a small number, and even if there was a large quantity of them, they would never be cause to worry, because of their docile nature and predisposition to serve] (106).

72. Archivo Histórico Nacional, Sección Nobleza, Osuna, Caja 121, document 82, March 1, 1664. In document 84, referring to the same prenuptial agreement with her first husband, the Duke of Arcos, she renounces her paternal and maternal inheritance in exchange for a dowry of seventy thousand ducats and an *encomienda* (grant of lands and indigenous serfs living and working in them) in Peru (Teodoro Hampe Martínez and José de la Puente Brunke, "Mercedes de la Corona sobre Encomiendas del Perú: Un aspecto de la política indiana en el siglo XVII," *Quinto Centenario* 10 [1986]: 91).

73. In 1685, the year that Chicaba arrived in Cadiz according to the *Vida*, this city was not an insignificant slave market. For example, in that year alone, 283 sales were recorded, which included slaves from the Mina region (Arturo Morgado García, "El mercado de esclavos en el Cádiz de la Edad Moderna (1650–1750)," *Tiempos modernos* 18.1 [2009]: 4). The majority of buyers of slaves in Cádiz were women (22). The price paid for a ten-year-old girl was probably around 110–115 pesos, which was the average for the year 1685 (15–17). The name "Del Espíritu Santo" was a common surname assigned to slaves.

74. Testamento de Juliana Teresa Portocarrero, Meneses y Noroña, Marquesa de Mancera, otorgado el 10 de abril de 1703, Archivo Histórico de Protocolos Notariales de Madrid, libro 13.977, fol. 135v.

75. The structure of this gift is a metaphor of the exchanges between the Queen Mother and Mancera. In the 1680s Mancera was appointed Queen Mariana's majordomo and main political advisor. She knew how to reward his loyalty, as he, during his tenure in Mexico, had sent her a rich bejeweled box from Mexico containing one thousand gold coins, which the queen then publicly passed on to her new prime minister, Father Juan Everardo Nithard, to the consternation of the court, which mocked the transaction (Paz, *Sor Juana Inés* 131). See also Gabriel Maura Gamazo, *Carlos II y su corte* (Madrid, 1911), 1:262.

76. Bula de Alejandro VII a la (V) duquesa de Arcos, Juliana Meneses Portocarrero, para que pudiese entrar cuatro veces en cuatro años en los conventos religiosos y menores de San Francisco de Andalucía, con ciertas condiciones [Bull of Alexander VII to the Fifth Duchess of Arcos, Juliana Meneses Portocarrero, allowing her to enter four times in four years in the convents of Saint Francis, both religious and of friars minor, throughout Andalusia, under certain conditions], October 23, 1665, Archivo Histórico Nacional, sección nobleza, Osuna, Caja 135, docs. 63–64.

77. Chicaba was not the only slave woman who knew how to read and write, as corroborated by "Donación otorgada por Francisco González de Cisniega, a favor de Gabriel de la Cruz y Regúlez, de una esclava que sabe leer y escribir" [Donation by Francisco González de Cisniega in favor of Gabriel de la Cruz y Regúlez of a female slave who knows how to read and write], a contemporary document in the Archivo Histórico de Protocolos Notariales de Madrid, protocolo 11.060, fol. 232, April 28, 1701.

78. Emilia J. Deffis de Calvo, *Viajeros, peregrinos y enamorados: La novela española de peregrinaciones del siglo XVII* (Pamplona, Spain: Ediciones Universidad de Navarra, 1999), 127.

79. According to the 2016 edition of the *Diccionario de la Real Academia de la Lengua*, the word *aya* (*ayo* in masculine form) is from the hypothetical Gothic *hagja* (guardian). *Aya* is an old-fashioned term corresponding to a person who took care of the education and well-being of a young aristocrat or royal. In the case of the royal family, this caregiver and tutor was normally

a person of high status, making the office a politically important one. All the old definitions have a decided gender bias in favor of male children and their education. The term *aya* meant something slightly different than *ayo*, as the education of girls was different and for different purposes.

80. See discussion of *sankofa* in Rediker, *Slave Ship*, 301–3.
81. In eighteenth-century Spain, "Turkish" described any person from the lands under the jurisdiction of the Ottoman Empire.
82. See the discussion of the color Black in the section on Mary of Egypt in Section 1.
83. Gossy marks the exceptionality of *Don Quijote* in Western literature because the book does not sacrifice a single female body to its narrative. See Mary S. Gossy, "Aldonza as Butch: Narrative and the Play of Gender in *Don Quijote*," in *Entiendes? Queer Readings, Hispanic Writings*, edited by Emilie L. Bergmann and Paul Julian Smith (Durham, NC: Duke University Press, 1995), 24.
84. Patricia Mercer, "Palace and Jihād in the Early 'Alawī State in Morocco," *Journal of African History* 18.4 (1977): 550.
85. This episode bears a certain resemblance to the case of a West African "prince" called Aniaba, mentioned in note 59 in Section 1, who showed up at the court of Louis XIV in 1687, having been brought to France by two Dominican missionaries. In 1700, news arrived in France of the king of Assinie's death. Louis XIV sent Aniaba back to the Ivory Coast in a warship to take possession of the kingdom and thus ensure French influence in the area and in the slave trade. The story ends with a surprise for the French envoys: they find out that no one in Assinie regards Aniaba as the heir apparent, thereby rejecting him as a former slave (McCloy 16). McCloy cites other cases in France of African Blacks who claimed to be princes. What is interesting in Aniaba's case is that his voyage back to West Africa happens when the Spanish throne is about to pass to Philip of Anjou, Louis XIV's grandson.
86. *The Golden Legend of Jacobus de Voragine*, translated and adapted by William Granger Ryan and Helmut Ripperger (London: Longmans, Green, 1941), 561–66.
87. Testamento de Juliana Teresa Portocarrero Meneses y Noroña, fol. 135v.
88. Marcel Mauss, *The Gift: Forms and Functions of Exchange in Archaic Societies*, translated by Ian Cunnison, with an introduction by E. E. Evans-Pritchard (London: Cohen and West, 1966), 11.
89. It looks as if the Marchioness of Mancera miscalculated in her attempt to send her slave Teresa Chicaba to Murcia. The Dominican convent of Santa Ana in Murcia was an aristocratic religious institution that housed women from the highest ranks in the city, as the rosters of nuns' names indicate. As a second order Dominican convent they were unlikely to accept a Black woman who had been a slave. Furthermore, the convent of Santa Ana de Murcia had had recent conflicts with aristocratic houses from Madrid that did not fulfill their financial obligations toward it. Santa Ana de Murcia, by the time the Manceras approached them, was relying on the local aristocracy for financial support. See María Trinidad López García, "Aproximación al convento de Santa Ana de Murcia de Monjas Dominicas," in *La clausura femenina en España: Actas del Simposium, 1/4-IX-2004* (San Lorenzo del Escorial, Spain: RCU Escorial-María Cristina, Servicio de Publicaciones, 2004), 898–901.
90. Kathryn Burns, *Colonial Habits: Convents and the Spiritual Economy of Cuzco, Peru* (Durham, NC: Duke University Press, 1999), 33.
91. There are documented cases of Black slaves from Guinea in Spanish eighteenth-century convents. Fréderique Morand, "El papel de las monjas en la sociedad española del setecientos," *Cuaderenos de Historia Moderna* 29 (2004), 49n15. In Mexico, the Marquis of Mancera also was firmly opposed to the proliferation of servants, including Black slave women, inside the enclosure of convents. Some of the convents in the main cities of the viceroyalty had up to five or six servants for every nun. He tried to restrict their presence to the areas of the convents outside the canonical enclosure, but he met with strong opposition from the nuns themselves and the Audiencia—the legislative, judicial, and administrative body of the viceroyalty—where some aristocratic nuns had important allies among relatives and friends (Rivera 229–30).

To a lesser measure, Spanish convents were no strangers to the presence of Black women in their midst, but mostly as slaves or in some cases as *donadas*. The instructions in this respect by Archbishop of Seville Pedro de Castro in the early part of the seventeenth century indicate that the nuns' ability to provide these women with religious education left a lot to be desired:

> Las Negras que están sirviendo en Conventos de Monjas, si fueren sujetas al Ordinario; o a cualquier Clérigo seglar, su visitador tomará a su cargo dar orden en lo que se hubiere de hacer. Pero si los Conventos fueren sujetos a Religiosos, se remite a la prudencia y santo zelo de los Prelados, que den orden cómo se asegure la salvación y Baptismo de las Negras que sus Conventos sirvieren.

> Black women who serve in convents of nuns: if the latter are under the jurisdiction of the bishop, or any secular priest who may be their visiting authority, the latter should be put in charge of giving orders as to what should be done. But if the convents are subject to priests belonging to regular orders, it will be up to the prudence and zeal of the Superiors of the convent, who shall give orders as to ensure the salvation and baptism of the Black women serving in their convents.

The instructions were published as *Instrucción para remediar y asegurar cuanto con la divina gracia fuere posible, que ninguno de los Negros que vienen de Guinea, Angola y otras Provincias de aquella costa de África carezca del sagrado Baptismo, por mandado del Ilustrísimo Señor Don Pedro de Castro y Quiñones, Arzobispo de Sevilla* (Seville, 1614). On the issue of the need to baptize Blacks in the territories of the Spanish monarchy on both sides of the ocean, see Berta Ares Queijo, "La cuestión del bautismo de los negros en el siglo XVII: La proyección de un debate americano," in *Mirando las dos orillas: Intercambios mercantiles, sociales y culturales entre Andalucía y América*, edited by Enriqueta Vila Vilar and Jaime J. Lacueva Muñoz (Seville: Fundación Buenas Letras, 2012), 469–85. Alonso de Sandoval's *De instauranda aethiopum salute* (1627 and 1647) was partly inspired by Archbishop de Castro's efforts to baptize and give Christian instruction to Blacks (Ares Queija 478).

92. The translation of the word *negra* presented us with several problems. We decided to translate it differently according to context. Sometimes we use "Black girl," when the term referred to Chicaba in her younger years, and sometimes as "Black woman." We use the old-fashioned English term "negress" only when Chicaba is referred to in overtly racist ways. This is one of those cases. A similar problem appears with the translation of *Negrita*, as in *la Negrita de la Penitencia*, which we have chosen to translate as "the Little Black Woman of La Penitencia," a term that was used to refer to Sor Teresa Chicaba in her time and still is used today in Salamanca.
93. While the names of the other convents remain anonymous in the *Vida*, only one is mentioned by name, Santa Isabel of Alba de Tormes in the province of Salamanca, perhaps intentionally. The Marquis of Mancera's ancestral home was in the village of Mancera, which is now between the provinces of Salamanca and Ávila.
94. Asunción Lavrín, "Values and Meaning of Monastic Life for Nuns in Colonial Mexico," *Catholic Historical Review* 58.3 (October 1972): 367–87. While this article discusses nuns in Mexico during the seventeenth and eighteenth centuries, we have extrapolated from Lavrín's data about a slightly more lax part of the empire than peninsular Spain because Teresa Chicaba would even have had difficulty entering Mexican monasteries during the same period in terms other than as a *donada* or a servant to another nun.
95. A *béguinage* was a house or cluster of cottages that housed Roman Catholic religious communities; the height of their activity was in the thirteenth and fourteenth centuries. These women lived in a loose semi-monastic community without formal vows. *Béguinages* proper were founded and flourished in the Low Countries; however, loosely organized religious communities of women appeared all over Europe.
96. Besides some reference to "Brothers of Penance" in a Catholic Encyclopedia (cited below), we have sought information on the history of the third order from Sister Mary Paul, OP, of Saint Dominic's Monastery, in Linden, Virginia. She found one, the Dominican Sisters of the Holy Rosary in Milwaukee (*dsopr.org*). This community is strictly called an "institute." We had

inquired of Sister Sandra Schneiders, IHM, an authority on Catholic women's religious life, to learn more about enclosed third order nuns. She said that these communities were very rare in the United States (*www.ihmsisters.org*).

97. According to Bernardo Dorado in his history of Salamanca, the convent of Santa María Magdalena, known popularly as La Penitencia (The Penitence), had existed in the parish of San Blas as a house for repentant women, mostly former prostitutes. In 1548 two noblemen, Don Alfonso de Paz y Zúñiga and Don Suero Alfonso de Solís, helped found a Dominican convent for nuns, although they followed the rule of Saint Augustine, according to the documents of foundation (Dorado 396). In Dorado's account of La Penitencia the story of Sor Teresa Chicaba occupies the main part of the section dedicated to this convent (397–400).

98. Most monastic orders are divided into three hierarchical classes: the first order are men; the second order are enclosed nuns; and the third are usually laity who observe aspects of the rule and who take vows to remain constant in their commitment to attain spiritual perfection. However, La Penitencia represents an unusual classification of religious communities, a third order community of cloistered women—technically a tertiary community that was not lay. These *terceras* probably developed from spontaneous associations of women who lived in the style of beguines and who were influenced by the spiritual practices and piety of monastic Catholic religious congregations. These tertiary orders lived in accordance with the rule of their chosen order and practiced penance, continence, and poverty. In 1285, when Muñón de Zamora united disparate groups of such laity, they called themselves the Order of Penance, under a rule entitled the Penance of Saint Dominic, which had developed around Dominican friaries (or convents) that were united under the direction of the Order of Preachers. As two branches of the order of Dominican friars challenged each other's jurisdiction over the third order, the development of communities of penitential brothers and sisters diminished. However, a few of these groups flourished, among them a fraternity in Siena, where the Catholic mystic Saint Catherine of Siena was a member during the mid-fourteenth century. Under the guidance of Raymond of Capua and Thomas Caffarini of Siena, the third order of Saint Dominic received renewed papal approval in 1401. This third order, unlike many others, includes a few cloistered convents of nuns, some active congregations of sisters, and laity organized in congregations. Teresa Chicaba was a member of an enclosed community of nuns; however, her status in that convent was unique.

99. B. Jarrett, F. Heckmann, B. Zimmerman, L. Oliger, O. Jouve, L. Hess, et al., "Third Orders," *The Catholic Encyclopedia*, vol. 14 (New York: Robert Appleton Company, 1912), *www.newadvent.org/cathen/14637b.htm*. See also Ruth P. Liebowitz, "Virgins in the Service of Christ: The Dispute over an Active Apostolate for Women during the Counter-Reformation," in *Women of Spirit: Female Leadership in the Jewish and Christian Traditions*, edited by Rosemary Reuther and Eleanor McLaughlin (New York: Simon and Schuster: 1979), 139–40, where she quotes from M. Henry-Couännier's *Saint Francis de Sales and His Friends* (311), which reported that it was improper for nuns to walk in the street. See also Nancy Bradley Warren's discussion of how important but fragile the reputations of women without men were at least as early as the Middle Ages. Even innocent women were subject to slanderous assessments of their behavior if they failed to comport themselves in keeping with customs of propriety (*Spiritual Economies: Female Monasticism in the Late Middle Ages* [Philadelphia: University of Pennsylvania Press, 2001], 17–20, 25).

100. See Antonio Rubial, "Las santitas del barrio: 'Beatas' laicas y religiosidad cotidiana en la ciudad de México en el siglo XVII," *Anuario de Estudios Americanos* 59.1 (2002): 14.

101. According to Robert Harms, the author of *The Diligent: A Voyage through the Worlds of the Slave Trade* (New York: Basic Books, 2002), "The French did not import African slaves to their own country. After France's own internal system of slavery (a holdover from the Roman Empire) had gradually transformed itself into serfdom, a common law principle developed that any slave setting foot on French soil became free" (xvi). French ships involved in the slave trade left their homeports with goods for barter and headed for Guinea (Africa). They picked up their human cargo and headed to the French Caribbean without ever coming within four thousand miles of France before returning with materials bought in the colonies

of Guadeloupe, Martinique, and St. Domingue. Slavery on these islands was regulated by the *Code noir* passed by King Louis XIV in 1685, which required all slaves to be baptized as Catholic, forbade the practice of any other religion, ordered all Jews out of the colonies, and regulated all the activities of slaves. When traders brought slaves of European origin to France in the sixteenth century, the captives were freed. However, "the handful of Black slaves who arrived in France beginning in the late seventeenth century were usually residents of France's Caribbean colonies who accompanied their masters on visits to France" (xvi). The status of Black slaves became of legal interest in 1714, when Madame Villeneuve, a Caribbean planter, brought her slave Pauline with her to serve as a personal maid during a transatlantic voyage and her stay in the city of Nantes. Anticipating that she would have access to servants where she was to stay in a yearlong visit with acquaintances in Paris, the mistress left Pauline in the care of the Benedictine Sisters of Our Lady of Calvary, who were to instruct her in "piety, discipline, humility, and manners." When the mistress returned, Pauline refused to go with her. The nuns, after consulting their visitor general, the abbot of Gimont, and securing a patron to pay Pauline's dowry, backed the slave's claim for freedom in the presidial court of Nantes. (In prerevolutionary France, presidial courts of justice were established in cities that did not have parliaments that could establish legislation.) Absent any written laws or official decrees asserting the absence of slavery on French soil, the court found in Pauline's favor on a technicality: Madame Villeneuve had neglected to register her slave upon entering the country. "Therefore, she had no claims on Pauline as property. The girl would stay in the convent. In announcing their decision, the judges used the phrase *in favorem libertatis*, referring to the principle in Roman law that ambiguous cases should always be resolved in favor of liberty" (5–10). So Pauline was professed as a choir nun and cantor who sang the Office in Latin, in 1716, twelve years after Chicaba professed vows in her anomalous status in Salamanca.

102. *Probanza* was a series of written documents that proved *limpieza de sangre* and appropriate social background. Although Chicaba was not a descendant of Jews or Muslims, her slave condition and her Blackness made her ineligible for any position of honor.

103. These concessions notwithstanding, the tendency of Mexican monasteries of nuns was to exclude Indian women, even the daughters of *caciques* (indigenous aristocrats). *Mestizas* (mixed race women) and free Black women could be present in these convents only as servants (Lavrín 370).

104. Some monasteries discussed the eligibility of a candidate and then voted by each choir nun dropping either a white ball for acceptance or a black ball for rejection into a box or basket. This pun on Chicaba's skin color, the reason an irate member of the community gave for rejecting the African woman, was too good for the author of the *Vida* to pass up.

105. The Roman concept of family included not only the married couple and their children but also the servants and slaves of a household. This is a familiar discourse even today in the United States, where former mistresses and masters of slaves or some present-day employers of servants describe their power relationships in familial terms. Slaves in Spain and Spanish America usually took their last names after their owners. The "familiar" link of Sor Teresa Chicaba to Juliana Portocarrero is in her first two names, Teresa Juliana, an inversion of Juliana Teresa Portocarrero's name. It is worthy of note that Sor Teresa Chicaba will drop "Juliana" after she enters the convent of La Penitencia, as seen in her signature at the bottom of the act of profession (Appendix 2). The title page of the Vida, however, restores Juliana to her name, linking her back to the Manceras (Figure 5).

106. In its representation of Chicaba's expectation of inclusion in the monastic community, the *Vida* begins a project of occlusion and dissimulation that avoids a forthright definition of her canonical position in the community, which, like the textual Chicaba, the reader is left to wonder about and to try to determine. The bishop and occasionally her fellow nuns vacillate about whether Chicaba can wear the veil or not, and sit in the choir or not. See Chapters 22 and 24. In instances of textual concealment, Chicaba's exclusion throughout the text seems more distressing.

107. In some monasteries, the candidate folds her hands in the upturned palms of the prioress as the former recites her vows.
108. "Carta de pago y obligación para Teresa Juliana de Santo Domingo, criada del Excelentísimo señor marqués de Mancera, que otorga la priora y religiosas de la Penitencia" (Salamanca, April 19, 1704). This letter of payment was preceded by a bishop's permit "Licencia de D. Francisco Calderón de la Barca, obispo de Salamanca, para que la priora de la Penitencia pueda hacer la obligación con Teresa Juliana" (Salamanca, April 18, 1704). These two documents are in the Archivo Histórico Provincial de Salamanca, oficio 7, escribano Juan Antonio de Paz, protocolo 3931, fol. 613–15. The *carta de pago* includes the following statement (emphasis added):

   . . . dezimos que por quanto tenemos tratado y conferido el que Theresa Juliana de Santo Domingo, criada que fue de los excelentisimos señores marques y marquesa de Manzera, aia de entrar y entre en este dicho convento para vivir en el y servir a Dios Nuestro Señor y quitarse de los trafagos del mundo *estando en el de seglar o terzera beata con nuestro abito, como al presente le tiene puesto*, por todos los días de su vida o el tiempo que fuere su boluntad, dandola la razion que a cada una de nosotras y demas relijiosas de este dicho convento se da y asistiendola en sus enfermedades como a nosotras y pagarla las propinas de las relijiosas que ai y de oi en adelante entraren en este dicho convento durante los dias de su vida, asi de abito como de profesion, sin que tenga obligazion la dicha Theresa de asistir a coro ni serbir a dicha comunidad en cosa alguna mas que lo que fuere su boluntad; y para poderlo hazer nos a dado lizienzia el ylustrisimo señor objispo de esta ziudad, como de ella consta, que orijinal aqui se insiere y dice asi
   Aqui la lizienzia.

   We say, after having discussed and conferred, that Theresa Juliana de Santo Domingo, who was a servant of the most excellent Marquis and Marchioness of Mancera, shall and will enter this convent in order to live in it and serve God Our Lord, and stay away from the toils of this world. She *will stay in it as a secular or tertiary beata, with our habit, as she presently is wearing*, for the rest of the days of her life or the time that determines her own will. We will give her the same ration that we and the other women religious of this convent receive, and we will assist her in her illnesses like we do to us. We shall pay her the same allowance the women religious who live here now and those who may enter in this said convent during the days of her life get, both just donning a habit or professed. The above-said Theresa shall be under no obligation to attend choir or serve this above-said community in any other thing than what comes out of her own will. And in order to do this, the most illustrious lord bishop of this city has given us licence, as it is stated in it, and the original is here inserted and it says as follows:
   Licence here.

109. The *Catastro* consisted of forty questions about the real estate, population, number of homes, churches and convents, and economic activity of every city, town, and village in Castile.
110. The ducat is a unit of accounting and not a coin, and it was divided into eleven *reales*. By the time Chicaba entered La Penitencia, the custom was to count in *reales*, although some documents still cited prices in ducats, as was the case of the marchioness's last will.
111. Archivo Histórico Nacional, Madrid, sección Clero, libro 10779. In 1726 another nun, Sor Isabel de San Juan de Dios, gave the convent a dowry in gold and silver valued at 6,600 *reales* (600 ducats). When the economic crisis set in, between 1739 and 1741, the incoming dowries dropped in value, to 2,200–3,300 *reales* (200–300 ducats).
112. According to Ángeles Atienza López, there was great latitude in the definition of *tercera* or *terciaria* as a category of religious life in early modern Spain (148). Some women were also popularly called *beatas*. The tendency was for these women to make some sort of religious profession, don a habit, and even join a form of conventual or cloistered life. Many *beaterios* (communities of *beatas*) would be transformed into third order convents. See Ángeles Atienza López, "De beaterios a conventos: Nuevas perspectivas sobre el mundo de las beatas en la España moderna," *Historia social* 57 (2007): 145–68.

113. Nuns enclosed in a cloistered community are separated from the laity by a grille or grate. In chapel, the priest and laity are on one side of this barrier and the Choir is on the other. The sisters receive Communion through an opening in the grille. This grille should not be mistaken for the one in the speak room, where the sisters likewise receive guests behind a grate.
114. The official document of her profession is kept in the archives of the convent of Las Dueñas, fol. 46v. Sor María Eugenia Maeso kindly declined to offer us a copy of this document because it is now part of the process for Sor Teresa's beatification, so it is unavailable for our consultation. However, Maeso offers a summary of important details: This more formal act of profession was presided over by the prior of the Dominican convent of San Esteban, Father Manuel García, which indicates that somehow the Dominican order recognized her presence in La Penitencia. The document is filed out of chronological order, not in 1704, but after an act of profession dated November 13, 1705, and "la redacción no es como la de las otras actas" [it is not written like the other acts]. Maeso also speculates that the correction of the date in this document might have been done by Sor Teresa Chicaba herself (Maeso 76–77). The *carta de pago* that we partially transcribed above gives Sor Teresa Chicaba the "right"—she is literally free—to leave the convent at any time. However, the document obviously fails to say or even suggest that the nuns will support her financially if she goes.
115. In our conversations with second order Discalced Carmelites at the Baltimore Carmel during Christmas vacation 2011, one nun suggested that the absence of any mention of a vote on Chicaba's profession prior to the prelate's visit to give her the veil probably gestured toward the irregularity of this particular ceremony. This is in contrast to the depiction in the *Vida* of Chicaba's admission into religious life, when the reader hears about the results of community votes. In a seminar with the same community in 2013, the entire assembly affirmed this analysis.
116. The patriarch of the Indies at this time was Don Pedro Portocarrero y Guzmán, a relative of the Marchioness of Mancera, Doña Juliana, whose last name was Portocarrero, Meneses y Noroña. He should not be confused with the more famous Cardinal Portocarrero, the very influential member of the Council of State who steered the dynastic change in 1700 at the death of Carlos II. Don Pedro and the cardinal were cousins, and they changed sides in the issue of the succession at the last moment, like the Marquis of Mancera, who cast the final vote in the Council of State that recommended the French candidate to King Carlos II (Molas Ribalta 288).
117. The "chapter" was the group of nuns in charge of the governance of the monastery.
118. Customarily, the devil is the one who physically attacks nuns, even leaving marks on their bodies: "Arrastrándola por el suelo, con tales golpes que le paraban el cuerpo y carne acardenalado de color de lirio, porque fue cual otra Esposa en los cantares, lirio entre las espinas de aquellas invidias que infernales la atormentaban" [Dragging her across the floor, striking her so hard that it turned her Blackened body and flesh into the color of lilies, because she was like the Spouse of the Song of Songs, a lily among the thorns of that infernal envy that tormented her.] (Francisco Posadas, *Vida de la Venerable Madre Soror Leonor María de Christo, religiosa profesa de velo negro en el Convento de Santa María de los Ángeles de Religiosas dominicas de la ciudad de Jaén* [Jaén, Spain, 1699], quoted in José Luis Sánchez Lora, *Mujeres, conventos y formas de la religiosidad barroca* (Madrid: Fundación Universitaria Española, 1988), 497.
119. Fort-da is the term used by Sigmund Freud ("Beyond the Pleasure Principle," *The Standard Edition of the Complete Psychological Works of Sigmund Freud*, vol. 18 [London: Hogarth Press, 1953], 14–16) to identify repetitive "games" typical of the behavior of toddlers—for example the offering of a gift only to reclaim it. Hide-and-seek may be such a game. This instance in the *Vida* is an example of two children playing a repetitive ritual: the Christ Child who extends the prize again and again, Chicaba who reaches for it over and over.
120. Lewis Hyde, *The Gift: Imagination and the Erotic Life of Property* (New York: Vintage Books, 1983).
121. Nancy Jay, *Throughout Your Generations Forever: Sacrifice, Religion, and Paternity* (Chicago: University of Chicago Press, 1992), 94–128.
122. One linguistic peculiarity is the use of "don te has ido" instead of "dónde te has ido" (where are

you gone), which constitutes a phonetic transcription of the way Sor Teresa Chicaba probably spoke. A second linguistic particularity is the use of the nonstandard "sin tigo" (without you), which is still used in popular speech in parts of Spain and Latin America and reflected in the lyrics of popular songs, like "Ni contigo ni sintigo / tienen mis males remedio. / Contigo porque me matas, / sintigo porque me muero" [Neither with you nor without you / have my ills remedy. / With you because you kill me, / without you because I die]. It is unlikely that a man of formal education like Paniagua would have used these colloquialisms himself.

123. Though orthodox Catholic theology denies a "polygamous" Jesus, the discourse of the multiple brides of Christ is present as late as the eighteenth century—for example, in a traditional carol sung during the convent's Christmas procession in a Carmelite cloister, written by an American nun who lived in the Antwerp Carmel before taking up residence in Port Tobacco, the first foundation in the original thirteen colonies. This original foundation moved and is now located in Baltimore (*www.baltimorecarmel.org/swflindex.html*). A few handwritten copies of the following verses, to be sung in the kitchen, are in the archives of the Baltimore Carmel: "Be pleased, O Holy Virgin / Into this place to come, / Aid those who herein labor / To nourish your Blest Son, / In the person of His *Spouses*, / For has He not declared, / That as directed to Himself / Such actions He'll reward" (untitled booklet of songs, c. 2010, 12; emphasis added). This poem is significant because it does not display the "jealousy" of a sister-wife that is in Chicaba's poem and because it is an example of the kind of conventual verse that was common among the nuns until recently.

124. At the end of the book, in Chapter 43, when he describes Chicaba's change of skin color right before her death, Paniagua cautiously credits the event as possible by citing "modern writers" in a clear reference to Father Benito Jerónimo Feijóo (1676–1764). A leading exponent of the Enlightenment in Spain, Feijóo doubted that Black people could turn their color white ("Del color etiópico" [On the color of Ethiopians], in *Teatro crítico universal: Discursos varios en todo género de materias, para desengaño de errores comunes*, vol. 7, discurso 3, 66–93). On a recent discussion of Sor Teresa Chicaba's miraculous change in skin color after death, see the recent essay by Erin Katherine Rowe, "After Death, Her Face Turned White: Blackness, Whiteness, and Sanctity in the Early Modern Hispanic World." *American Historical Review* 121.3, June 2016: 727–54.

125. Teresa of Avila, *The Book of Her Life*, in *The Collected Works of St. Teresa of Avila*, translated by Kieran Kavanaugh, OCD, and Otilio Rodriguez, OCD (Washington, DC: ICS Publications, 1976), 1:195. "Víale en las manos un dardo de oro largo, y al fin de el hierro me parecía tener un poco de fuego; éste me parecía meter por el corazón algunas veces y que me llegava a las entrañas. Al sacarle, me parecía las llevava consigo, y me dejava toda abrasada en amor grande de Dios" (*Libro de la vida*, chap. 29, para. 13).

126. "So it is very painful": "De manera que es dolor grande cuando tengo el corazon sereno y quieto. Es ardor cuando el afecto sube con exceso a desear el cumplir con las obligaciones que debo; y no digo bien, que no es exceso lo que es razón. Me abraso, me quemo, diera voces, pero las doy dentro de mí. . . . Tan grandes son (dice) los dolores que tengo en el corazón, que por dentro siento se me cubre de sudor."

Figure 1. Official Portrait of Sor Teresa Chicaba, c. 1749, displayed in the Convent of Las Dueñas, Salamanca, c. second half of the eighteenth century. (Monasterio de las Madres Dominicas Dueñas de Salamanca. Sala de la Negrita).

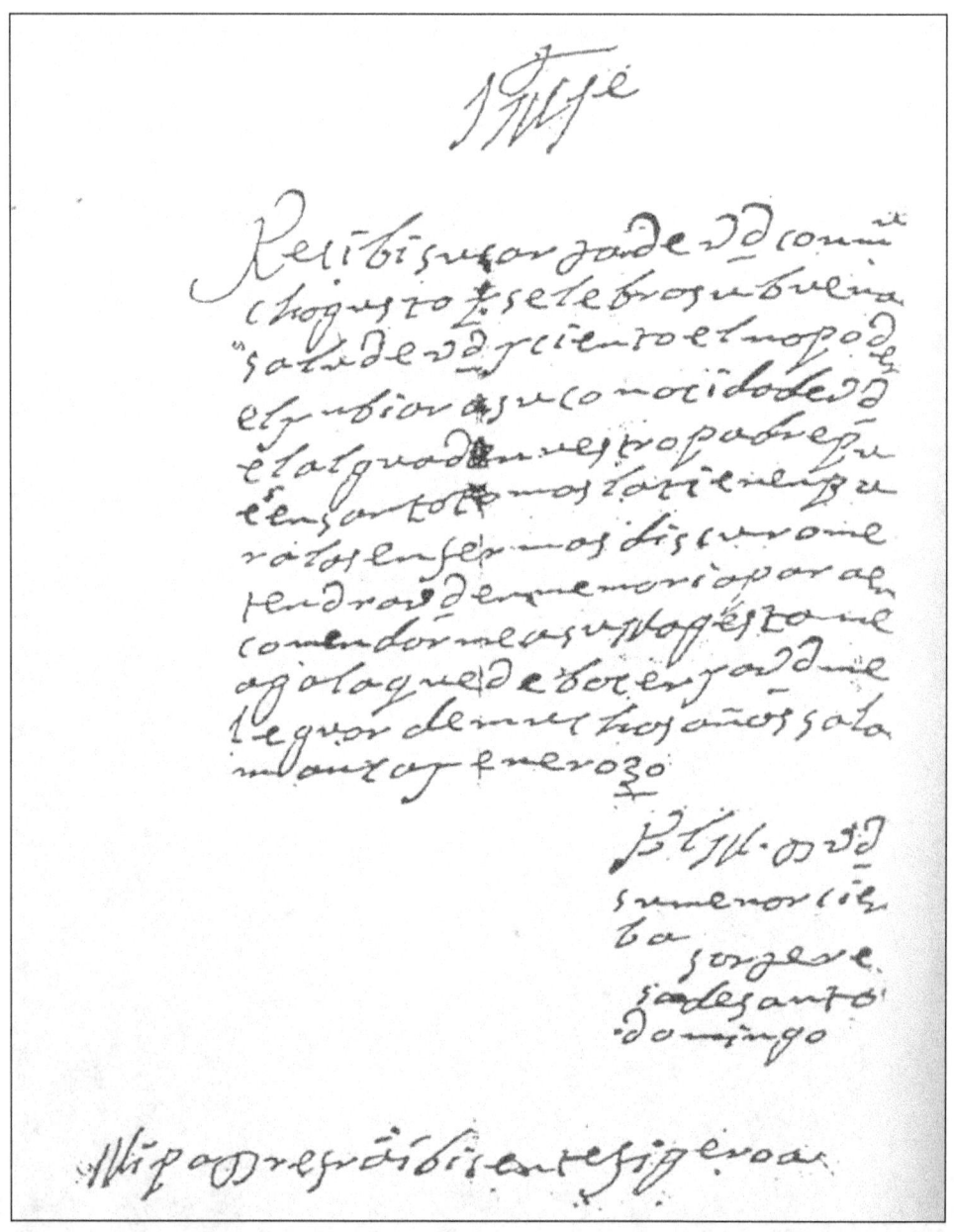

Figure 2. Autograph letter written by Sor Teresa Chicaba to Fr. Vicente Figueroa. It is also signed Sor Teresa de Santo Domingo. (Archivo Histórico de las Madres Dominicas Dueñas de Salamanca. Sección Convento de La Penitencia).

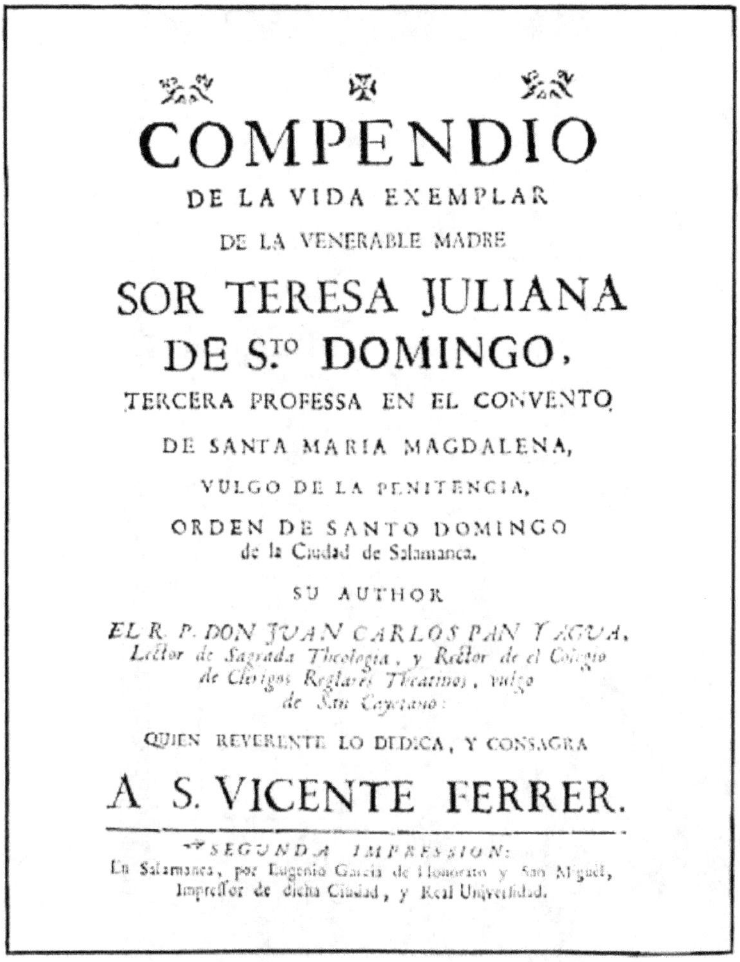

COMPENDIO
DE LA VIDA EXEMPLAR
DE LA VENERABLE MADRE
SOR TERESA JULIANA
DE S.TO DOMINGO,
TERCERA PROFESSA EN EL CONVENTO
DE SANTA MARIA MAGDALENA,
VULGO DE LA PENITENCIA,
ORDEN DE SANTO DOMINGO
de la Ciudad de Salamanca.
SU AUTHOR
EL R. P. DON JUAN CARLOS PAN Y AGUA,
Lector de Sagrada Theologia, y Rector de el Colegio
de Clerigos Reglares Theatinos, vulgo
de San Cayetano:
QUIEN REVERENTE LO DEDICA, Y CONSAGRA
A S. VICENTE FERRER.
SEGUNDA IMPRESSION:
En Salamanca, por Eugenio Garcia de Honorato y San Miguel,
Impressor de dicha Ciudad, y Real Universidad.

Figure 3. Cover of the 1764 edition of the Compendio de la Vida Exemplar de la Venerable Madre Sor Teresa Juliana de Santo Domingo, second edition. Salamanca, 1764. (Archivo Histórico de las Madres Dominicas Dueñas de Salamanca. Sección Convento de La Penitencia).

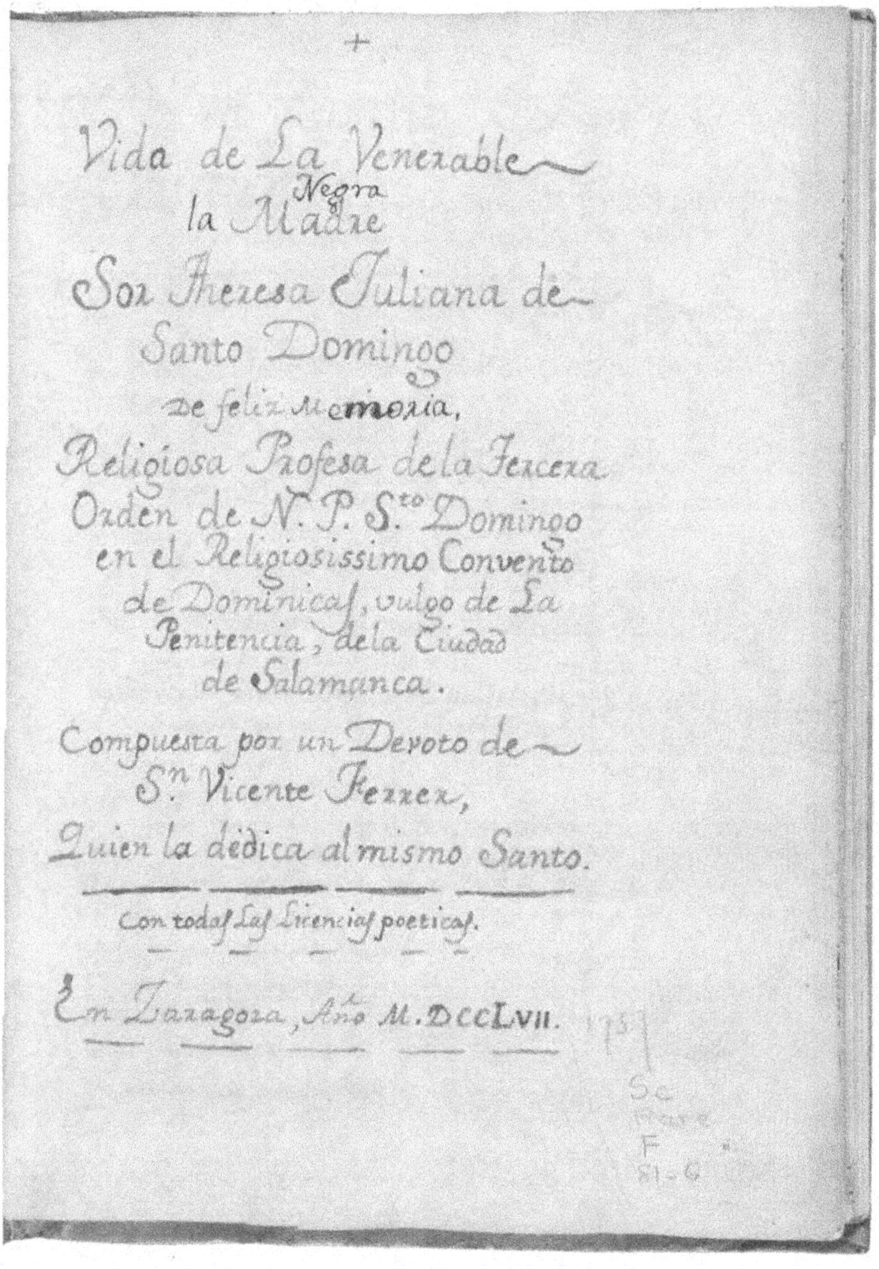

+

Vida de La Venerable
Negra
la Madre
Sor Theresa Juliana de
Santo Domingo
de feliz memoria,
Religiosa Profesa de la Tercera
Orden de N. P. S.to Domingo
en el Religiosissimo Convento
de Dominicas, vulgo de La
Penitencia, de la Ciudad
de Salamanca.

Compuesta por un Devoto de
S.n Vicente Ferrer,
Quien la dèdica al mismo Santo.

Con todas las Licencias poeticas.

En Zaragoza, Año M.DCCLVII.

Figure 5. First page of the manuscript *Vida de la Venerable Negra, la Madre Sor Theresa Juliana de Santo Domingo*, Zaragoza, 1757. Schomburg Center for Research in Black Culture, Manuscripts, Archives and Rare Books Division, New York Public Library, Sc Rare F 81-6. Retrieved from digitalcollections.nypl.org/items/8c985150-e84e-0132-6a54-58d385a7bbd0.

Opposite:
Figure 4. Stained glass window of Sister Teresa Chikaba by artist Silvia Nicholas, St. Dominic Chapel, Providence College, Rhode Island (photo: Patricia Krupinski).

rha de sus penetrantes espinas; con ellas la hallò traspassada su ultima hora; no faltaron preludios de ella, ni à Teresa la cogiò la venida del Esposo desprevenida; dexo la circunstancia de haver faltado en el Rosal una Rosa, que reverente tributaba todos los años para la Fiesta, que Teresa hacia por Agosto à su Padre, y Patriarcha; falta, que por una Religiosa, notada, recelò, y con razon, amenazaba al Convento algun trabajo: omito pues esto, porque solo serà acaso, una prudente piadosa congetura, y Teresa bastantemente claro explicò el fin de su Vida. Muriò pocos dias antes que ella, una Religiosa anciana, llamada la M. S. Agustin, con quien no luciò poco, porque con ella trabajò mucho el amor, y caridad de nuestra Teresa: à poco de enterrada la Difunta, dixo Teresa à unas Religiosas: *En acabando con los Oficios de la Señora San Agustin, empezarán con los mios.* El sucesso acreditò de seguro el vaticinio; pero aun mas claro. El dia quatro de Diciembre, preguntò con grande ansia à una Religiosa; *Si havian yà passado ocho dias de la muerte de la Señora San Agustin?* Señora, la respondiò, hace mañana quince; à que Teresa volviò à preguntar admirada, *quince? pues hemos de menester caminar.* No diga usted esso, Señora, replicò la otra, que me traspassa el alma; entendiòla la frasse sin duda; pero Teresa tan apacible, como mansa, diò en substancia la misma respuesta: *Si, sì, sì, hace quince dias, no tiene remedio, es forzoso el caminar:* y tomò tan presto el camino, que no huvo mas de dos dias de intermedio. Una cruel Perlesìa, con quien havia estado luchando desde fines de Septiembre, fue, quien despues de fortalecida con todos los Santos Sacramentos, la hizo entregar, segun piadosamente creo, en manos de su Criador, el Espiritu, debaxo de la direccion del Rmo. P. Mro. Fray Alonso Rincon, Prior actual del Esclarecido, y Ilustre Convento de San Estevan. Quedò su Cadaver, sin ninguna de aquellas señales horrorosas, comunes à la muerte, y sus palidas sombras. Su Rostro, en medio de su color moreno, tan agraciado, que antes, que miedo, infundia no sè què de amor, y respeto. Muriò en fin Teresa, à rigores de la Perlesìa; pero què sè yo, si fue este accidente, quien la quitò la vida? Poco antes de morir, un dolor fiero le atravesò el pecho; acaso fuè herida de amor de su Celestial Divino Dueño; y como no pareciò este año la Rosa, que todos los demàs la confortaba, no podian sus Hermanas socorrerla con ella; y assi rendida de este deliquio amoroso, partiò de esta vida, à gozar con su Amado, los frutos de su amor en la Patria. Assi lo espero en la Piedad Divina; y ahora ratificando mi protesta, concluire con el Epitaphio para su Lossa.

Cant. 2. v. 5.

AQUI YACE LA CASTA, LA PURA, LA INOCENTE, Y MORTIFICADA; Paloma en el Alma, si en el cuerpo negra; negra, pero hermosa; naciò Reyna, y muriò Esclava; pero por Esclava Reyna; Reyna, porque reynò en si propria; y porque reynò en si propria, ahora Reyna: buscas donde Passagero? pues imitala en las virtudes, y sabràs donde: su cuerpo aqui yace, su alma, espero vive en donde por una eternidad.
REQUIESCAT IN PACE.
Amen.
O. S. C. S. R. E.

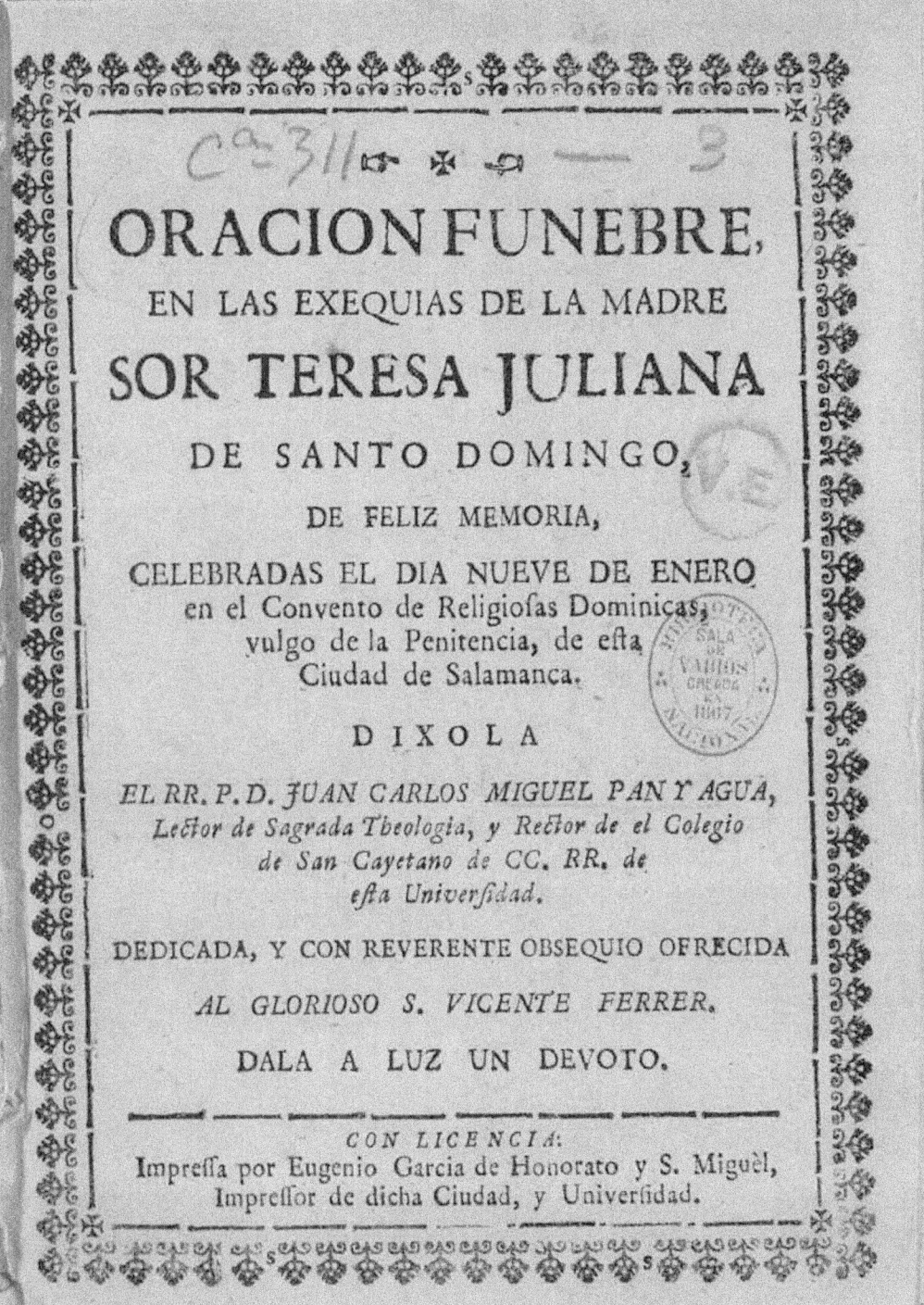

Figure 6. First and last pages of the *Oración fúnebre*, published soon after Sor Teresa Chicaba´s funeral on January 9, 1749. Sor Teresa Chicaba's epitaph is framed on the last page. (Biblioteca Nacional, Madrid).

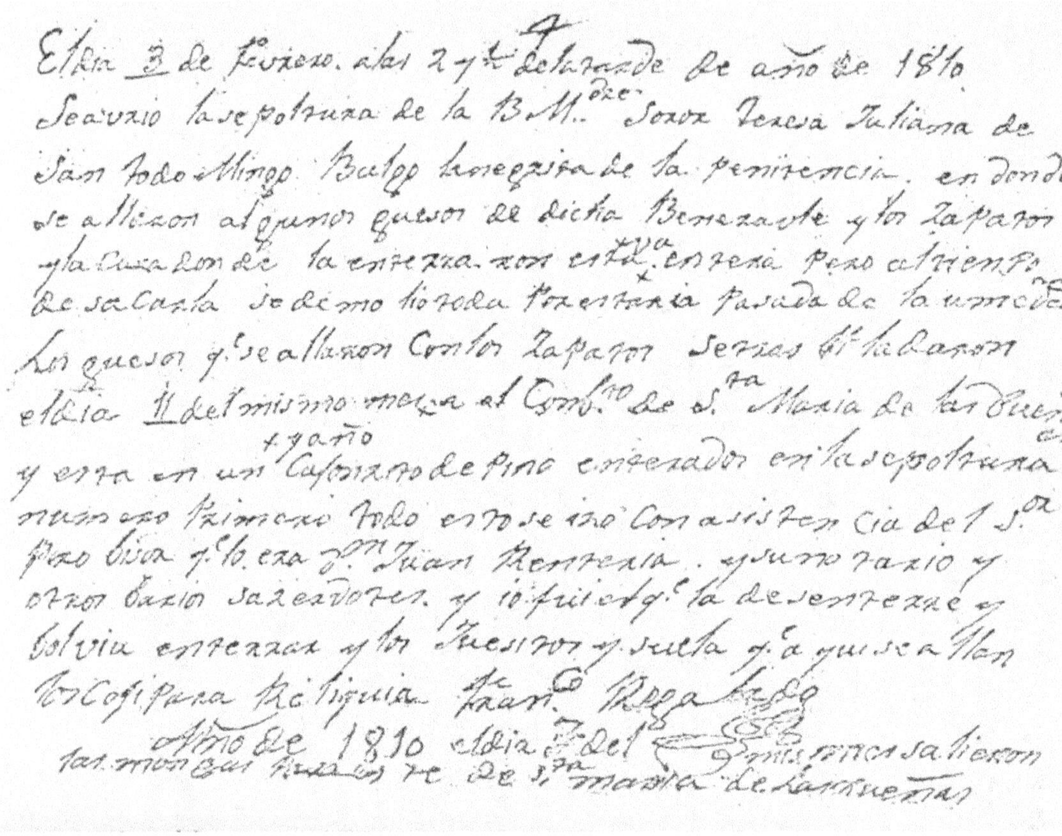

Figure 7. Act of Translation of Sor Teresa Chicaba's body from the convent of La Penitencia to the Convent of Las Dueñas in 1810, during the occupation of Salamanca by the Napoleonic Army. La Penitencia was demolished upon orders from the French military commander. (Archivo Histórico de las Madres Dominicas Dueñas de Salamanca. Sección Convento de La Penitencia).

Translation of the *Vida*

To the most resounding clarion
of the Gospel,
distinguished apostle of Valencia,
illustrious honor of Spain
and exceptional ornament of the Church,
Saint Vincent Ferrer

Soon after I learned that the devotion of an important person from this city was inclined to defray the cost of printing the sermon I preached during the funeral organized by the most observant convent of La Penitencia to honor the immortal memory of Sor Teresa de Santo Domingo, whose life I write, I decided to consecrate it to your name, and so I did. The sermon circulated throughout Spain, and it passed to the Indies. It obtained success in this kingdom of Spain, and in the New World it attained the glory of its inhabitants' appreciation. If it were only due to its merit, that unworthy production of my wit could not have hoped to be so successful. I should attribute it, and indeed I attribute it, to your sweet goodness and powerful intercession. This recognition puts me at your feet a second time. I feel obliged to present to you the little book that contains the life of the same Sor Teresa Juliana, the subject of my *Funeral Oration*. She was the one who made my inexperienced expression tolerable despite my rough style in that work. I pay tribute to you although the shortness of this dedication does not look like proper tribute. I hope, however, that it will be very pleasing to your attention. First, because here I offer a sign of my gratitude, something that is so appreciated by the saints and even by those who are not saints; and, second, because I dedicate to you a life that you already possess with clear title. It is well known that Mother Teresa lived thanks to your support. For these reasons and for others that I wish to omit, I already consider and publicly declare you a staunch sponsor of this little work. In it some will read the deeds of the one who was the admiration of La Penitencia in every sense. Others, especially you, will see my desire to correspond to your many favors and the confidence that my spirit, my wit, and my pen will run from now on under your protection.

Prostrate at your feet and professing this to you,
Don Juan Carlos Miguel Pan y Agua, C.R. Rector.[1]

---

1   The name of the author, spelled "Pan y Agua" (bread and water), has been modernized as Paniagua.

APPROVAL *of the Reverend Fathers Don Cayetano Vergara y Azcárate and Don Gabriel Rodríguez, lecturers in holy theology at their College of the Theatine Regular Clerks of the University of Salamanca.*[2]

Following the order of the Most Reverend Father Don Melchor Arbustante, visitor general of the Regular Clerks in our houses of Spain, who received a special commission from our Most Reverend Father General Don Juan Bautista Mari, we have seen the *Life of the Venerable Mother Sister Teresa Juliana de Santo Domingo*. After reading this with utmost care, we believe that any recommendation is superfluous coming from us, as every line it contains is from a mute yet eloquent tongue that proclaims the most singular praise of its author.[3] Since it is necessary, according to the instruction, to explain our view, we cannot hide the truth though we recoil from praising him because we are so close to the author of this work. For apart from the fact that Saint Gregory Nazianzen praised his own sister without any fear of suspicion,[4] anyone will see that this praise does not come from passionate affection but rather from the sincere truthfulness with which the author writes. This is a virtue that our church father Augustine attributes to good minds.[5] As the Reverend Father Don Juan Carlos Pan y Agua is so well known to be one of these good minds, one must believe that he never says what he does not know; he does not sell as certain what is doubtful, nor what is fabulous as likely. He could well have let his pen run further, discovering other incidents in the life of Mother Teresa, but he understands this to be a most delicate matter, so he

---

2   Since the decree of Urban VIII in 1625, all *vidas* had to be preceded by licenses from the local bishop (called in ecclesiastical Spanish *el Ordinario*, and in Catholic English "the ordinary"), and in the case of members of religious orders, they needed the approval of their own superiors. See Poutrin 253.

3   Symath, Book 3, Epistle 48 [note in the original]. Three possibilities for this citation in the original text of the *Vida* are as follows: (1) "Symath" is a garble of St. Matthew, though there is no Matt. 3:48; (2) "Symath" is short for οι Συμμαθητές (as in, the works τῶν Συμμαθητῶν) the classmates, implying, and this is going out on a limb, the Cappadocian Fathers, who were peers and whose number includes both Sts. Gregory; (3) "Symath" is a collection of works of or about St. Athanasius, perhaps called something along the lines of το Συμαθανάσιον. A stretch, to be sure, but the sentence in question reminds of passages from St. Gregory Nazianzus's "Funeral Oration XXI" about St. Athanasius. Regardless of the nature of the collection (the numbering of which might be completely arbitrary and unique), the possibility of a funeral oration by St. Gregory is tidy considering the adjacent reference to St. Gregory's comments on his sister, which also come from the funeral orations. This last explanation seems the most plausible to us for now. We are grateful to Mr. Gresham for his splendid research in helping us.

4   Nazianz. Ora. 11 in ob *Gorg. sor.* [note in the original]. St Gregory of Nazianzus (also known as St. Gregory Nazianzen), Oration 8, On his sister Gorgonia, para. 11. *www.newadvent.org/fathers/310208.htm*.

5   August. Lib 4 *De Doct. Christ.* [note in the original]. St. Augustine, *De Doctrina Christiana*, book 4. See Augustine, *De doctrina Christiana*, Oxford early Christian texts, edited and translated by R. P. H. Green (Oxford: Clarendon Press, 1995).

describes it all in few words. He is neither tiresome nor annoying. Rather, he entertains and produces enjoyment, in such a way that he attracts us to what is good and diverts us from evil: *Tanta dulcedine captos afficit ille animos*, as Juvenal said.[6] This work does not lack the qualities that the Stoic deems necessary for perfection.[7] We do not say this moved by the affection proper to those who live in the same house as the author. Therefore we are of the view that this book should be printed because it is an incentive to Christian perfection, and it does not contain anything against the privileges of His Majesty, may God preserve him. Given in this College of the Theatine Regular Clerks in Salamanca, October 15, 1751.

Don Cayetano Vergara y Azcárate, CR
Lecturer in Sacred Theology

Don Gabriel Rodríguez, CR
Lecturer in Sacred Theology

PERMISSION FROM THE ORDER

I, Don Melchor Arbustante y Ondeano, visitor general of the Theatine Regular Clerks in Spain, by the present document, and attending what is important to our order, in use of the particular commission that I have for this matter from our Most Reverend Father General, Don Juan Bautista Mari, give permission for the printing of a book entitled *Life of the Venerable Mother Sister Teresa Juliana de Santo Domingo*, composed by the Most Reverend Father Don Juan Carlos Miguel de Pan y Agua, rector of our college in Salamanca, after it was seen and acknowledged by the Reverend Fathers Don Cayetano Vergara and Don Gabriel Rodríguez, both lecturers in sacred theology in the above-mentioned college, to whom I gave this commission, and unless it has anything against our holy faith and good customs, I give the present permission in this house of Saint Elizabeth in Zaragoza on the eleventh day of May, 1751.

Don Melchor de Arbustante y Ondeano
Visitor General of the Theatine
Regular Clerks

Don José Garcés, CR
Secretary

---

6 Juvenal. *Satire* 7, 82–85 [note in the original]: "So charmed are their souls by his sweetness, with such rapture does the multitude listen to him." In *Juvenal and Persius*, with an English translation by G. G. Ramsay, Loeb Classical Library (London: William Heinemann, 1928), 145.

7 Sen. *Sup. Val. Max.* [note in the original]. *Commentarius super Valerium Maximum* by Dionysius de Burgo, bishop (d. 1342). Lucius Annaeus Seneca "The Stoic" is the Roman philosopher Lucius Annaeus Seneca (4 BCE–65 CE).

OPINION

Given at the behest of the provisor by the Reverend Father Master Manuel Bernardo de Ribera, member of the faculty of this University of Salamanca, former professor of philosophy, candidate for the chair of theology in his Order of the Holy Trinity and Redemption of Captives, and regent of studies in the college of the same order in Salamanca.[8]

Ave Maria:

Different pamphlets have appeared in Europe against a modern writer who dared say in a prologue that he was the author of many volumes concerning diverse matters, all of perfect quality. All his critics have demonstrated quite well the rash arrogance of that great man on whom Nature bestowed nothing but hollowness. Although his critics have not read the works of this braggart, they, as people with experience, consider it impossible to write many books of good quality. So one should heed the magnificent adage *ne quid minus, ne quid nimis*.[9] Such abundant genius is seldom found in this world, especially in literary productions.

A medium-size volume—did I say volume?—a booklet of very few pages that comes from the hands of its author with the certainty of elegance and exactness, should in all justice belong in the series of those magnificent revelations that foreigners have started telling us about.[10] For this reason, we especially recommend certain little books in spite of those who count the value of a tome by its thickness. That is why the exceedingly long history of the Amazons is esteemed much less than some little works in which one can hardly see their body because they are all spirit.[11] This is also why I praise the narrative of *Life of the Mother*

---

8 Manuel Bernardo de Ribera also wrote the censure for Paniagua's *Oración fúnebre* in honor of Sor Teresa Chicaba in 1749. It was customary for a professor from the university to add his opinion to a *vida*. Paniagua sought this little essay in order to add prestige to his work. Ribera was professor of philosophy and moral theology at the University of Salamanca. In 1758 he wrote in opposition to the creation of an academy of mathematics at the university. This chair of mathematics was held first by Diego Torres Villarroel, the author of the hagiography of Father Jerónimo Abarrategui, Chicaba's main spiritual director. To give an example of the intellectual climate of the times, Ribera objected to the creation of a new chair in mathematics in part because Torres Villarroel wrote in Spanish rather than in Latin (George M. Addy, "The Reforms of 1771: First Steps in the Salamancan Enlightenment," *Hispanic American Historical Review* 41.3 [August 1961]: 354–55). He was the author of a proposed twelve-volume work in Latin on moral philosophy, *Institutionum Philosophicarum* (Salamanca, 1754–1756), of which only two were printed. Like most ecclesiastics of his formation, he wrote an *Oración fúnebre* published by the same printer who issued Paniagua's *Vida* of Sor Teresa Chicaba. He died in 1765.
9 This sentence seems to be taken, with the order of the terms changed, from the Carthusian monk and spiritual writer John Justus, Landsberg (Joannes Justus Lanspergius) (1489–1543), *Enquiridion militiae christianae*, in *Opera Omnia* (Montreuil-sur-Mer, France, 1890): "Considera in omni re medium, et eam discretionem ubique serva, ut ne quid nimis, ne quid minus." [You must consider the middle point in everything, and observe that wisdom everywhere, so you will do not too much, nor too little" (599).
10 The author of this commentary is being ironic. He is referring to the new fashion of short essay writing originating in France and Great Britain.
11 This might be a reference to the Jesuit Manuel Rodríguez's *El Marañón y Amazonas: Historia de los descubrimientos, entradas, y reduccion de naciones; Trabajos malogrados de algunos conquistadores, y dichosos de otros en las dilatadas montañas, y mayores rios de la America* (Madrid, 1684), which is more than four hundred pages long. In comparison to which the more famous Cristóbal de Acuña's *Nuevo descubrimiento del gran río de las Amazonas* (1641) is a shorter volume of forty-six pages. We are grateful to our colleague Jerome Williams for his help in identifying this reference.

Sister Teresa Juliana de Santo Domingo (known to the people as the Little Black Woman of La Penitencia), written by the Most Reverend Father Master Carlos Paniagua, Rector of the Most Observant College of San Cayetano.[12] The volume is not big, but it could not be written with greater success.

The Most Reverend Father tells the life of Teresa with such sincerity and easy style that those who have not known the Little Black Woman will not read with suspicion, even if they cannot judge the similarity between the textual copy and the original person. He is trustworthy in all he says, and even more praiseworthy for all he leaves unsaid. This is an obvious sign that when he started his work he knew, as it is expected in matters such as this one, that one cannot give credit to every report, nor should one write everything one deems to be true. Saint Thomas has taught us already that even sacred truth must be kept hidden sometimes.[13] How much more care, then, is necessary to treat matters in which error can adopt the disguise of delicate artifice, or where our own inclinations may take different colors to misrepresent the similarity of virtues, as the profane author said? The truth is that in this point we can see indecision among even wise masters. They have suggested rules to discriminate between humble fears and superstitious tales of heroism. Reverend Father Carlos speaks of both with penetration. In those instances in which he may cast his eye on the manifestation of God's sovereign power or the celestial favors He bestowed on Teresa, he offers his critical judgment sparingly and with measure, following, as it seems, the learned advice of Siuri, the great pride of his native Valencia, and singular testimony of the literature written by the Spaniards.[14]

This learned man refers to some revelations received from God by two of His venerable servants to devise a method for using critical rigor devoid of the sweetness from well-ordered devotion in order to temper cases of this nature. He shuns with disdain certain opinions, and is so austere that upon hearing of ecstasies and revelations, dismisses them as gossip and tall tales (if they are not something else). *Medium tenuere beati*, wrote someone with great sense; Siuri and the Most Reverend Paniagua practiced this with notable success.[15]

The erudition of this Father Master is also manifest in this work. An author is not called learned because he may fill all the margins with citations, because this practice, no matter the subject, is either overreaching ambition or pedantry. In the case of history, this is directly in contradiction to the prescriptions handed down to us by those who have mastered the science of writing history.[16] He who writes—but let us not speak here in such general terms—a historian, let us call him, will be creditable if he speaks with good sense and mastery; if he explains at the same time that he understands the meaning of the words and knows, moreover, how to weave information with such artful dissemblance that his studied narrative adornments may seem circumstances that cannot be separated from the event itself. This particular quality for which Father Paniagua is highly regarded is what a

---

12 "The Little Black Woman of La Penitencia" is "La Negrita de La Penitencia" in the Spanish original. See the Introduction, pp. xv, 112n92, for comments on this term and others.
13 Thomas Aquinas, *Summa Theologica*, question 1, article 9, reply to objection 2: "The very hiding of truth in figures is useful for the exercise of thoughtful minds, and as a defense against the ridicule of the unbelievers, according to the words, *Give not that which is holy to dogs* (Matt. 7:6)" (italics in the original).
14 Marcelino Siuri Navarro (1654–1731) was a theologian, university professor, and bishop of Córdoba.
15 *Medium tenuere beati*: "Happy are those who keep a middle way in things."
16 See the Introduction, p. 9, regarding the debate on historical truth and hagiography.

certain critic is reluctant to attribute to the Greeks. Others have celebrated it in Livy, Caesar, Maffei, and other Latin writers.[17] But I do not appreciate it except in Sallust, although sometimes one has to forgive him for his carelessness.[18] Among the French, one should mention Doliers, and among the Spaniards, the intelligent Antonio de Solís.[19] The latter is the model that the author of this book follows, as he sprinkles the pages with well-advised quotations from the ancients. He is superior to him even in the sparse use he makes of them.

The Father Rector's style is not sublime, if we must say. However, that is why it is more appropriate. In order to write history, the most acute masters of eloquence demand the mediocre style. This is the one our Father Master uses. And although at times it seems plain, it will not be deemed as such by the reader who knows the difference between the familiar and the vulgar. That reader realizes that some things lose their spice if they are explained in a high style. Father Paniagua constantly avoids poetic terms. These may look brilliant in any metric piece, but in other kinds of writing, they do a disservice. A very learned and elegant Franciscan author who wrote the lives of the two patriarchs, describing the spiritual joy my father Saint John experienced in the desert, used the following phrasing: *And it seemed to him that he had his domicile among the high mountains and rocks. And he embraced the stones as sisters, and he tenderly complimented the cliffs, as if they were his brethren.*[20] This style of expression would be wonderful in the relation made by Tyndareus's servant, but in the other context it is unbearable.[21] Distancing himself from these risks, he treats everything according to its genre. He follows a certain style in the letters and another in compositions of a different nature and context.

In conclusion, I have read without missing a syllable *The Life* to which the Most Reverend Father Carlos Miguel Paniagua wants to give birth. In it, I have not found a single iota against our Holy Faith, good customs, or royal ordinances. *The Life* is just as the Little Black Woman of La Penitencia lived it. Like hers, it is fitting, perfect, and admirable, the only difference being that Mother Teresa lived with total poverty, and the Most Reverend Paniagua wrote with all the riches of proper style.

This is my opinion, *salvo*, etc.

In the College of the Holy Trinity and Redemption of Captives of Salamanca, February 1st, 1752.

Father Manuel Bernardo de Ribera.

---

17 It is surprising to see the Italian Jesuit Giovanni Pietro Maffei (1533–1603) listed with the ancient Roman historians Livy and Caesar. Maffei wrote a Latin life of Saint Ignatius of Loyola (*Ignatii Loiolae Vita*, 1587) that enjoyed multiple editions, and a history of the Eastern Indies (*Historiarum Indicarum Libri XVI*, 1589) in which the exploits of the Jesuit order appear prominently.

18 Gaius Sallustius Crispus (86 BCE–35 BCE), also known in English as Sallust, was a Roman historian, author of *Catilina's War*, *Jugutha's War*, and the *Histories*. He is considered the first known Roman historian whose works have survived.

19 Antonio de Solís (1610–1686) was the author of *Historia de la conquista de México* (1684).

20 The two patriarchs the author of this opinion is referring to are Saint Dominic and Saint Francis of Assisi. The unidentified author is describing the experience of either Saint John the Baptist, who lived in the desert, or Saint John the Evangelist on the island of Patmos.

21 Tyndareus or Tyndareous was a mythical Greek king and Helen of Troy's father. Medieval writers accepted his historical existence. By the eighteenth century, scholars no longer accepted Greek mythology as historically true. The author of this opinion places the poetic accounts of this myth in opposition to the need to be less lyrical when writing about saints of the Church, whose historical existence is demonstrable.

PERMISSION FOR PUBLICATION BY THE LOCAL BISHOP

We, Licentiate Bernabé de la Torre, attorney before the Royal Councils, canon of this city's Holy Cathedral, and the ecclesiastical judge and vicar general for it and the rest of the bishopric, etc.

We have given orders to read and inspect the book entitled *Life of the Venerable Mother Sister Teresa Juliana de Santo Domingo*, a tertiary who professed in the convent of Santa María Magdalena, popularly known as La Penitencia, located in this city. It was written and published by the Reverend Father Don Juan Carlos Miguel Paniagua, lecturer in sacred theology and rector of the College of Theatine Regular Clerks, popularly known as San Cayetano. The book does not contain anything against our Holy Catholic Faith and morality. As far as we are concerned, we give and grant wide permission and power to any of the owners of printing houses in this city to publish it without incurring in any penalty. Given in Salamanca, on the eighteenth of May of 1751.

Licentiate D. Bernabé de la Torre
Following the mandate of the Lord Ecclesiastical Judge
Bernardo Cayetano López del Hoyo

JUDGMENT OF DR. DON SEBASTIÁN FLORES PAVÓN

Dignitary of the Holy Cathedral Church of Salamanca, a fellow and member of the faculty of this city's university and candidate for the chairs of canon law, former ecclesiastical judge, vicar general, and metropolitan judge for the archbishopric of Zaragoza and its province; also former ecclesiastical judge, vicar general, and governor of the bishopric of Salamanca. At present prosecutor-elect of the tribunal of the Inquisition of Valladolid.[22]

Most Powerful Lord:

Your Highness deigned to ask for my judgment the book entitled *Life of the Venerable Sister Teresa Juliana de Santo Domingo*, a tertiary who professed in the order of this holy patriarch. She lived and died in the most religious and observant convent of religious women of La Penitencia, that belongs to the Order of Saint Dominic in this city. The author is the Most Reverend Father Don Juan Carlos Paniagua, of the Regular Clerk Fathers of Saint Gaetano, lecturer in sacred theology and twice rector of its college in this city. With respectful obedience I undertook the reading of this work. I started with attention, I continued with pleasure, and I finished it full of admiration. I read with attention because this is the duty of every censor. In my case, this becomes a duty in obedience to any order coming from Your Highness. Also, this comes quite naturally in someone who, like me, considers

---

22 Sebastián Flores Pavón was later elected bishop of Cuenca (1771–1777), where he initiated the building of a convent for reformed prostitutes.

one of his major honors to obey the Royal and Supreme Council of Castile. I read with pleasure whenever I see history dealt with in detail and with good judgment, purity of language, and other good properties. This extreme is considered as lacking by some of us in the writers of our time, compared to the older ones. We must deem Moses, Dares, and Pherecydes the first historians, without prejudice of what is said of Crispus Sallust.[23] These latter ones have nothing to envy in terms of the disposition, the eloquence or the truthfulness of their work to modern writers. They do not have to be envied either by the Most Reverend Father Paniagua, who either surpasses or imitates them in this book. In it, the reverend author shows himself to be the elegant and erudite historian and the precise theologian, attentive to detail as well. Without being all these things, it would have been impossible for him to put this book together, because its composition had to be preceded by a mature and detailed examination of different events. In their consideration, one can see what Phaedrus says in a certain passage: *Periculosum est credere, et non credere.*[24] The two extremes of thoughtless acquiescence and overconfident incredulity are equally terrible. These dangers are present as well in matters like those examined by the most reverend author of this book. His Reverence understands me quite well, and the learned penetrate through this issue, because they sense that the life of a subject who is venerable for her good reputation and virtues cannot be written without a lot of hard work. In the composition of this volume, apart from the usual rigorous laws of history, other particular laws, of no less severity, also apply. I can see them suggested in the form of a compendium in another work by the Most Reverend Father, so I will not stop to relate them.[25] Suffice it to say that His Reverence observes them so faithfully and with such care, that one would be at pains to find another person who could have used his pen in a similar endeavor with equal success. In my opinion, it is inappropriate to quote from other texts and authors in short texts like this one, that we call "approvals." For this reason I do not apply to him a passage from the *Author of Several Criticisms*, with the description of the great obstacles faced by historians, and the praise due to those who know how to surmount them successfully. However, I dare not omit a few words from the same author that briefly contain what precisely is more commendable in the most reverend. *Laudatur is qui plus antea meditatus est quam scripsit postea: ac volens multa narrare, pauca prae veritatis amore recensuit.*[26] Finally, I read with admiration, seeing it reduced to such short volume, the miraculous *Life of the Mother Sister Teresa Juliana de Santo Domingo*, the narrative of which I never thought two volumes would be enough. Those of us who have

---

23 By mentioning Moses, Dares, and Pherecydes, this scholar credits them as historians at the same level as Sallust, the well-documented writer of Roman history. The biblical Moses was traditionally considered the author of the first books of the Bible, of which there is not one shred of evidence. Dares the Phrygian, a mythical historian mentioned by Homer in the *Iliad*, is the supposed author of a *History of the Fall of Troy*. Pherecydes of Syros (sixth century BCE) was one of the so-called Seven Sages of Greece. He was considered the first author to write in prose. He still used Greek myths to account for the beginning of the world as an act of creation. Aristotle and Saint Augustine credited him with the idea of the immortality of the soul.

24 "*Periculosum est . . .*": "It is as dangerous to believe as not to believe." Phaedrus's *Fables*, book 3, fable 10 (note in the original).

25 Flores Pavón is referring to Father Paniagua's *Oración fúnebre*.

26 "*Laudatur is qui . . .*": "Those who meditated more than what they wrote later are to be praised, because although they wanted to tell many things, they published little, out of love for the truth." We thank our colleague Tom Hayward from Bates College for his help with the translation of this and other Latin quotations.

lived in Salamanca for some time have already heard of so many and so precious and unique qualities, so many and so different events, so many and so extraordinary marvels about the Little Black Woman of La Penitencia, that they made me believe one would need countless

sheets of paper to tell them. And the same number would be necessary to praise her. But that is the ability shown by the Most Reverend Paniagua, who knows how to adjust a lot in a few words. He treats things with the reflection that should be due to them, preventing those difficulties that at times are the product of the pen's license. The one used by the Most Reverend Father has written nothing in this book against the purity of the Holy Faith, good customs, or the royal privileges of his monarch, God save him. Quite to the contrary, with his good care, culture, and piety, he contributes to Christian teaching; and he makes himself deserve the permission that he has humbly requested from Your Highness.

This is my judgment, *salvo meliori*.[27] Salamanca, August 12, 1751.

Doctor Don Sebastián Flores Pavón

PERMISSION FROM THE ROYAL COUNCIL

Don Ignacio Esteban de Igareda, senior chamber secretary
to the king our lord and of the council government.

I certify that their lordships in the council have granted the license to Father Don Juan Carlos Paniagua, lecturer of sacred theology in the College of San Cayetano in the city of Salamanca for one single time, so he can reprint and sell a book titled *The Compendium of the Exemplary Life of the Venerable Mother Sister Teresa Juliana de Santo Domingo*, who was a professed tertiary nun in the convent of Saint Mary Magdalene, popularly called La Penitencia, of the Order of Saint Dominic, in the above-said city of Salamanca. It must be done in fine paper and good print, and faithful to the copy, which will serve as the original, that contains my signature and rubric at the end. Its reprint should observe the dispositions and provisions of the laws and decrees of these kingdoms. And so it may stand firm, I signed it in Madrid, July 19, 1764.[28]

Don Ignacio de Igareda

NOTICE OF ERRATA

Page 19, line 13, *aca llaban*, read *acallaban*
Page 32, last line, *dioj*, read *dijo*
Page 84, line 23, *pues que dije*, read *pues qué diré*
All these errata have been amended in this reprint.
By this, I affirm that this printed version of *The Life of the Venerable Mother Sister Teresa Juliana de Santo Domingo*, tertiary nun of the convent of La Penitencia, of the Order of

---

27 *Salvo meliori* [*iudicio*], "except if there is better [judgment]," is a Latin formula that means that if a better authority thinks differently, this author will defer to it.
28 This permission indicates that this second edition of 1764 was a reprint of the first edition of 1752. For us it attests to the relative popularity of this *Vida*.

Saint Dominic, is in conformity with what was written by the Reverend Father Juan Carlos Miguel Paniagua, lecturer in sacred theology and rector of the College of San Cayetano of Salamanca

Madrid, February 21, 1752
Licentiate Manuel Licardo de Ribera
Corrector General of His Majesty[29]

VALUATION

Don José Antonio de Yarza, secretary to the king our lord and senior notary of his chamber, as well as of the Government in the Council.

I certify that the lords of the Council have seen this book entitled *The Life of the Venerable Mother Sister Teresa Juliana de Santo Domingo* by the author Father Juan Miguel Paniagua, the rector of the College of San Cayetano, and their lordships have granted a license to print it at the rate of eight *maravedís* per broadsheet.[30] This book seems to contain 19 broadsheets, not including title page and contents; therefore, it amounts to 152 *maravedís*. Their lordships ordered that the book must sell for this price and no more, so the price will be known. And as further assurance, I signed it in Madrid, on the twenty-second day of February of the year seventeen hundred and fifty-two.[31]

Don José Antonio de Yarza

---

29 The corrector general of books for His Majesty was an important official who had to make sure that the manuscript an author submitted to a printer was faithfully copied in print. Since this second edition was a reprint of the first one, the date of the signature by the corrector general is that of 1752.

30 The *maravedí* was an accounting unit in the Spanish monetary system, rather than a real coin. The main coins were the *real* (worth 34 *maravedís*) and the *ducado*, or ducat (375 *maravedís*, the equivalent of 11 *reales* and 1 *maravedí*). The price of 152 *maravedís* set for Paniagua's *Vida* was the equivalent of 38 *cuartos* (1 *cuarto* was a copper coin valued at 4 *maravedís*). Therefore, this book was valued at less than five *reales*. For the sake of comparison, a two-pound loaf of bread cost 11 *cuartos*, or 44 *maravedís*, and a pound of beef was priced at 13 *cuartos*, or 52 *maravedís*. See Vicente Palacio Atard, *La alimentación de Madrid en el siglo XVIII y otros estudios madrileños* (Madrid: Real Academia de la Historia, 1998), 58–59.

31 The valuation of the book corresponds to the first edition of 1752.

IN PRAISE OF THE MOTHER SOR TERESA JULIANA DE SANTO DOMINGO

> DON MANUEL DE LA MOTA SIERRA Y VILLEGAS, VERGER OF THIS HOLY CATHEDRAL CHURCH OF SALAMANCA WROTE THE FOLLOWING SONNET:[32]

Among shadows of blind idolatry
Was born Teresa, but so fortunate
That she banished the dark mist
That her clear reason had in opposition.

The nights she spent in vigil,
    and the days she missed not either,
Contemplating the wondrous machinery
Whereby the least fragrant of plants
Praises God and His wisdom.

With this superior intelligence
She fled the risk and sought the estate
Of the most elevated Penitence[33]

She lived as a teacher in observance,
Her virtue left behind the experience:
Happy model of immortal earnings.

---

32 The *pertiguero* (verger) is a layman who carries the mace or a staff in front of cathedral dignitaries. It is an honorary appointment. Manuel de la Mota Sierra was also the author of a poem dedicated to Saint Isidro, the patron saint of Madrid, that was published in a volume in honor of Our Lady of Atocha, another patron saint of Madrid (*Patrona de Madrid restituida* [Madrid, 1750], 278). This volume, a reprint from an earlier 1609 book, is dedicated also to Saint Vincent Ferrer, like Paniagua's *Vida*. Our Lady of Atocha's devotion is one of the most important ones in the Dominican order, and she is one of the most popular Black Madonnas in Spain.

33 This is a play on words with the name of the convent, *La Penitencia*, which means "penitence" or "penance."

PROLOGUE

One repeats his work with pleasure when he can see the fruit of his sweat doubled. It is sweet relief for all fears that the harvest corresponds with abundance.[1] One of the fruits of intellectual work is to see public recognition for the resulting discourse, one organized with effort of the mind. After I saw how well received were my efforts, it became an expression of my gratitude as well as a way to convey the love I had for Mother Sor Teresa Juliana de Santo Domingo to write the eulogy for the funeral that the Most Respectable convent of La Penitencia consecrated to her sweet memory. All the copies were anxiously sought after and soon were not enough, even if many were printed, to satisfy the devout curiosity in the Old as well as the New World.[2] Therefore, when I saw how well these efforts were received, I decided to duplicate this work, a bit more at length this time. I was not so much flattered by the aura of applause, as to correspond in some way to the one who obliges me to proceed with pleasure for an infinite number of reasons. This is a debt to the love and fondness that this heroic woman professed for my holy family.[3] I am impelled by the respectful gratitude that my sacred religion had from its cradle to the family and habit of the great father Saint Dominic, the same habit that Teresa wore.[4] The Dominican order has many well-sharpened pens, though for matters of more import. Thus, it will be seen better in both families, as it was during the life and in the death of Teresa, that this is done in subordination to the decrees of Divine Providence.[5] Teresa grew in God's arms under the direction of the sons of my Father Saint Gaetano. She produced delicious fruits of virtue nourished by the water of the sons of my father Saint Dominic.[6] I hope that a more delicate pen from the Dominican Family will in time amend and perfect these badly formed words, written by the least worthy of the sons of Providence. The volume is short, as you can see. I am careful to hide a lot, because it is not time yet to tell everything. I am trying to avoid the dangers of writing something with arrogance, or offering a rash opinion. Problems like these are prejudicial to the subject of this book. They make its author appear either overly credulous of the minutest detail, or excessively cautious. I would rather be brief then. In the little I say I am

---

1 The author recalls his prior efforts to publish Chicaba's saintly life in the form of the *Oración fúnebre*.
2 The Prologue insists that the *Oración fúnebre* was read across the Atlantic in Spanish America. This assertion makes the *Vida* one of the earliest African diasporic texts in the Spanish language.
3 Father Paniagua is referring to the order of the Theatines, to which he belonged. Sor Teresa's connection to the Regular Clerks of Saint Gaetano, as they were officially known, is constantly emphasized throughout the *Vida*. See Introduction, p. 3.
4 Paniagua is referring to the order of Saint Dominic, or Dominicans. The convent of La Penitencia belonged to this order, and therefore Chicaba wore its habit. However, as discussed in the Introduction, it is unclear what sort of habit Sor Teresa Chicaba wore, since she was neither a full black-veiled nun nor a lay nun who would have donned a white veil.
5 Paniagua is trying to explain away why he, a Theatine, and not a Dominican priest, was the author of Sor Teresa Chicaba's *Vida*, since she was a member of a Dominican monastic community.
6 The text establishes a genealogy for Sor Teresa's spiritual life. She was first under the direction of the Theatines ("the sons of my Father Saint Gaetano") prior to her profession as a member of the order of Saint Dominic in La Penitencia.

certain to have taken everything from the most authentic sources. These are written declarations made by the Venerable; several consultations made by her in matters spiritual to her spiritual directors; and accounts from several people whose virtue and other circumstances make them believable.[7] But above all, there is the irrefutable testimony of the provincial chapter held in the city of Toro in the year of 1749. In its minutes, quoted throughout this work in several places, the curious reader will be able to satisfy his desire, since those words corroborate everything he may see written here. *Vale.*[8]

PROTESTATION BY THE AUTHOR

In obedience to pontifical decrees, and especially the one by our Lord Urban VIII, when you find in this work the words "venerable," "Blessed," "Saint," or similar ones, referring to a person or persons who have not been declared such by Our Holy Mother the Church, you should receive them as having been said with total acceptance and respect due to the declarations and decisions of the Holy See.[9]

---

7   "The written declarations made by the Venerable" is the first time the text refers to the existence of writings by Sor Teresa, citing them as the main source of information for the *Vida*.

8   *Vale*, Latin for "Stay healthy," was written at the end of letters.

9   In his bull of October 30, 1625, Urban VIII put strict limits on the representation of individuals who had not been either beatified or canonized by Rome, which claimed for itself this exclusive prerogative. The decree also forbade the worship of these persons' tombs and above all the printing of the miracles attributed to them (Michael Ott, "Pope Urban VIII," *The Catholic Encyclopedia*, vol. 15 [New York: Robert Appleton Company, 1912], *www.newadvent.org/cathen/15218b.htm*). All authors of religious *vidas* had to include this protestation at the beginning of their work (Poutrin 242).

IHS

CHAPTER I

Country, parents of this venerable woman, and customs of her land[1]

Authors of the lives and deeds of heroes expend little effort and have less difficulty learning about parents, country, family members, and other relatives of their subjects; however, in the present case, our pen does not flow so easily. The unknown character of her native land and the remoteness of that region make information about her scarce. Had it not been for Mother Teresa herself, who supplied these details, they would have remained completely hidden from us once those who brought her in their ship, the Marquis of Mancera and his wife, all their servants, and the rest of their family died. Otherwise, Teresa's land of origin and parents would have been forgotten. Only the color of her face would be left to trace her back to her native land. She was born in Guinea in 1676 according to the closest estimate. We do not know the day this fortunate creature saw the light of life. We know, however, that she was chosen among thousands by the Powerful Hand and to the praise of Divine Providence.

Guinea is one of the most extensive and vast provinces contained in the huge confines of Africa.[2] It is divided into several kingdoms, each one governing itself independently. La Mina Baja del Oro is among the most important ones. That was where this happy girl was born to a most illustrious family. Her parents were reigning princes. Their scepter ruled all that land in peaceful possession. Time erased her father's name from her memory. She only remembered the shape of his body and the features of his face as if they were a printed image: *My father was*—she says in the account this venerable woman made of her origins—*a man of strong and big body, and with very hairy eyebrows.*[3] Her mother was called Abar and was as important as her father in lineage and nobility. The Venerable Mother had three brothers, all of them older than she. One was called Juachipiter; Ensú was the second; Joachim, the

---

1 Most saints' lives begin with an account of their genealogy and country of origin in order to establish historical legitimacy in the narrative as well as the social rank of the person.
2 In the eighteenth century, the term "Guinea" was used imprecisely for those lands in Western Africa that were associated with the slave trade. "Africa" was a geographic term that described mostly the northern part of the continent, whereas "Ethiopia" referred to the eastern and southern lands.
3 Italics are used only for quotations the reader is to accept as coming directly from Sor Teresa Chicaba's own writings. Otherwise, remarks attributed to conversations between the hagiographer and her, those imagined to have occurred between her and others, or what the hagiographer claims to have learned from pertinent conversations about her are indicated in a variety of ways—not always consistently.

third one.[4] Their birth preceded that of this outstanding woman. When she was born, they called her Chicaba in their language.[5] This princess was born to be a joy to her parents and brothers and a consolation to the entire kingdom. Either because she was a girl or because she was the youngest, all care was lavished on her as though she were a precious jewel.

All the inhabitants of Guinea are of a dark Black color, as we frequently observe of those who come to our countries or read from histories of the greatest authority.[6] Since such is the color with which wise Nature painted all those from that region, parents and brothers and the girl herself could not help but be adorned in the same hue. However dark was their complexion, even darker was their situation. In their blindness, they worshipped the Morning Star.[7] They did not use temples for their worship and sacrifices. Instead, as soon as they saw the star, they came out very early to adore it. What a superfluous vigil that was because, in the very act of seeking out the light, they remained in thicker and denser darkness. During their feast days, the people accompanied the king and queen and all their family. Following the customary ritual of their barbarous ceremonies, they bent their knees in humble recognition and sang praises to the star. These rites lasted until the zeal of the Capuchin missionaries, who entered these lands not long ago, succeeded in planting the

---

4 These names are clues about Sor Teresa Chicaba's place of birth; see the Introduction, pp. 13–14, 57.

5 The name *Chicaba* (or *Chicava*, as it is spelled at times) means "golden child" or "golden gift" in Guin-Mina. The name still occurs in today's Ghana. See the Introduction, p. 57.

6 "Dark Black color" corresponds to "negro atezado" in the original Spanish. The Spanish were aware of several gradations in the color of people from Africa. Darker people were held in lower esteem and associated with slavery. Paniagua tries to explain Chicaba's dark skin color without condemning it as a moral deficiency, whereas some understood race as a category where physical features—specifically skin color—were indicative of moral or mental characteristics. However, Paniagua does draw on recent discussion among "authorities," scientists who attributed Black people's dark skin to natural reasons. Father Jerónimo Feijóo was one such authority ("Del color etiópico"). For this Benedictine friar, the skin color of Blacks was due to climatic reasons and not to their being descendants of Ham, the cursed son of Noah (Genesis 6:25). The problem for him and his colleagues, though, was whether Blacks were descended from Adam, in which case Adam had to be Black. If, conversely, Adam was not Black, Blacks could not be his descendants and were thus not part of the human race. Feijóo compromised on the subject by affirming that the Black color in the skin of "Ethiopians" was only on the surface, and that underneath all humans have the same skin structure. Black skin was provoked by the hot "Ethiopian climate" that would have also influenced the semen of Ethiopians, causing them to transmit their dark skin. With this, Feijóo was trying to explain why Blacks living in colder climates like Spain still had Black children and why their children would not turn white. Feijóo did not reject, however, the commonly held idea among the learned that a Black person could be born from a white woman who had been looking at someone Black—in person or in a painting—during the act of conception. See Rodrigo Zapata Cano, "La teoría de los antojos, el origen de la negrura y la generación en la obra de Benito Feijóo," *Boletín de Antropología* (Universidad de Antioquia) 22.39 (2008): 36. A literary example of this commonly-held belief is present in the play *Virtudes vencen señales*, by Luis Vélez de Guevara (1579–1644), in which a Black prince is born to white parents in the emblematic kingdom of Albania. See the modern critical edition, Luis Vélez de Guevara, *Virtudes vencen señales*, edited by William E. Manson and C. George Peale (Newark, DE: Juan de la Cuesta Hispanic Monographs, 2010).

7 The Morning Star or Lucifer has been interpreted since Saint Jerome (*To Eustochium* 4) as a reference to the devil. Thus, this signifies that Chicaba's people were worshippers of the devil. St. Jerome, edition for *To Eustochium*, *Sancti Eusebii Hieronymi Epistulae*, edited by Isidorus Hilberg, 3 v. (1910–1918; repr., New York: Johnson, 1970).

seeds of the true faith and banished the shadows of idolatry. Mother Teresa heard this news from accounts worthy of credibility even for the most reticent critic. She also received great consolation in knowing that her father and brothers were now members of the Church. I am aware that the Acts of Lypsick speak against the historical truth of those ministers of the gospel's glorious triumph.[8] The authors of those accounts, although erudite, are Protestant after all, so my pen does not need to be unduly concerned with refuting them. Therefore, although I must write about that mission, it is not my intention to present the event of the conversion of those lands as absolutely true and beyond doubt.[9]

---

8   "The Acts of Lypsick" is a reference to *Acta eruditorum*, a German scholarly journal in Latin edited from 1682 to 1782. Famous for publishing the works of important mathematicians and other scientists of the time, it also dwelled on the truthfulness of current historiography, especially ecclesiastical history. *Lypsick*, in the original Spanish, is also the Old English spelling of the German city of Leipzig.

9   Antonio Brasio (*Monumenta Missionaria Africana*, vol. 13, doc. 249, and vol. 14, doc. 61) documents Capuchin missions to Arada and Ouidah in the 1680s. King Philip IV of Spain had sent a mission of Capuchins in 1658 to the kingdom of Arada with the purpose of converting the rulers and establishing a post to better control the slave trade. The missionaries brought with them a catechism in Spanish and Ewe (*Doctrina christiana* [Madrid, 1658]). The Capuchin Father José de Nájera was in charge of producing the book and later of the mission to Arada. He narrates the failure of the mission in his *Espejo mystico* (Madrid, 1672). The Ewe translation of *Doctrina christiana* was perhaps from Vans, Arada's ambassador to Spain. Vans brought with him a servant, Antonio, who was conversant in Fon, Portuguese, and Spanish (Olabiyi 249). See the Introduction, p. 62.

CHAPTER 2

Education of Chicaba, desire to know the true God, and what happened to her in this matter

The moods of the spirit are more diverse than even facial features. If it is rare to find two people who are similar in appearance, it is even less common, or not at all possible, to find two people who resemble each other in inclination or understanding. Chicaba had hardly left infant clothes when she gave clear signs that her genius and leanings were very different, if not totally opposite, to those of the other girls in her country. They had devoted all their attention to childish entertainment. This was in no small part attributable to their parents' carelessness, which allowed them to play until the age of nine to an extent only equal to the sudden privacy with which they then secluded them after they reached this age.[1] The girls of La Mina Baja spent their time in play and games either by permission or by virtue of their youth. Though her age, the example of her playmates, and the illustrious and opulent circumstance of her household invited Chicaba to spend time in licit—because childish—pastimes, this tender girl calmly rejected them. She never took a fancy to a single one of them, showing in this the wisdom of an old woman. When the others sought the diversion of innocent sports, she put her effort only in seeking the Author of her being and of nature. This was the work of natural philosophy, since she was looking for the First Cause of the very things she contemplated in awe.[2] She thought that the best way to find it was to be alone; and with that in mind, she tried all she could. Her tears reached the tender love of her parents, who sent her to the fields, where she found relief in solitude. In a pleasant meadow, among the herbs and flowers, she delivered monologues aloud to herself that, although they exceeded her young age, helped her to discover, little by little, the road along which she came into the knowledge of the Supreme Author. The sight of a small flower might mysteriously captivate her so that she would ask herself: who could have put such beauty there? In the morning, when she arrived at the meadow and saw it watered by the morning dew that the beneficent heavens distilled on it, she would be astonished and in doubt. Who was in charge of watering the fields so often?

She was all doubts and confusion. The girl fought an internal battle, trying unsuccess-

---

1   This is the first mention of the custom of secluding girls at the age of nine (probably at puberty) for at least several months, to maybe as long as a year. When they left seclusion, they were eligible for marriage. Chicaba was captured right before this appointed time, which gives an internal chronology to her life. Thus we can date her birth to around 1676, nine years before her capture. Please see the longer discussion of this custom in the Introduction, pp. 62, 102n26.
2   God is the First Cause, the origin of all things created. The text represents an example of Saint Thomas Aquinas's contention that a human being can prove the existence of God through reason. St. Thomas Aquinas, *Summa Theologica*, First Part, Question 2: The Existence of God, Article Three: Whether God Exists. See *The Summa Theologica of St. Thomas Aquinas*, Second and Revised Edition, 1920. Literally translated by Fathers of the English Dominican Province. In *The Catholic Encyclopedia*, www.newadvent.org/summa/1002.htm.

fully to discover the First Cause she so anxiously sought. At one point she decided to dispel her doubts by asking her father. In her baby talk, she managed to ask who the God was whom she revered. The answer her father gave did not satisfy her. An urge grew in her to do whatever possible to learn the identity of the powerful God who so liberally irrigated the meadow and who so wisely dotted the fields with a profusion of flowers. She thought that her brother might be able to give her a better answer. She asked him the same question that she had posed to her father; he offered her more light, although very dim still. He told her that the God they worshiped and the author of that beautiful variety of things, about which she wondered so much, was the Morning Star. He promised to take her with him to see it, so she could offer the proper veneration. There was no reason why the daughter of a king, although still a child, should remain in ignorance any longer. The child was a bit more at ease with this, and she waited with excitement for the promised day. She thought the hours were centuries, the instants were years, and the minutes were months until she would have the joy of seeing the one she was looking for so anxiously. The day of destiny arrived. The prince kept the promise he had made to his sister and got up very early. Taking the girl with him, he went out with his usual retinue toward a mountain not far from the palace. There the people were already gathered and waited to adore the star according to their custom. As soon as the star appeared on the horizon, the multitude knelt down among shouts, as it was their practice when they were still barbarians.[3] The prince knelt down as well, and pointing toward the star, he told his sister: "There you can see the God you are asking about, who is revered in all this land." Chicaba heard him, but she did not find it right that a small star could be God. With good judgment that exceeded her years and capacity to explain things, she politely asked of her brother who put that star there. Confused, he could not give her an answer. After the superstitious ritual finished, she went back home with her brother.

She entered the palace with more turmoil in her heart than when she had left in hopes of seeing the God for whom she was pining. The prince told his father about his sister's question. Her father, the king, was full of concern and went to calm her. With soft caresses and words coming from the fatherly love that can be transmitted through blood ties, he made her see that her Supreme Author was that star she had seen with her brother in the morning. But the child remained wise in her reflective question. "That star," she ventured haltingly, "stays there like the rest of them. Whoever put it there in the sky had put the rest in the same place. Thus, whoever placed it there and distributed the rest in their positions must be, has to be, more powerful than all of them. Therefore, that one had to be the Supreme Author. That is the one I look for, the one I desire, the one I want you to make me know. That one alone we should adore." Her father listened in amazement to a discourse as strange to him as it was to the rest of his family. Embracing her tenderly, his affectionate muteness made itself understood. He could not find a response to a reasoning that was as pious as it was wise.[4]

---

3   The text operates on the assumption that Chicaba's people ended up converting to Christianity. This is stated in several places, including Chapter 1. As a candidate for sainthood, Chicaba's chances were better if her parents were not pagan, or as it says here, "barbarians." See the Introduction, pp. 59, 79.
4   Chicaba's concerns reflect a theological point in Saint Thomas Aquinas, which asserts that the Divine Lights are present even among pagans. This allows them to seek the true God. See Justin M. Anderson, "Aquinas on the Graceless Unbeliever," *Freiburger Zeitschrift für Philosophie und Theologie* 59.1 (2012): 5–25.

CHAPTER 3

Esteem and praise that Chicaba had among her people. She continues with her desire. God miraculously spares her from the danger in which she had her life.

It is difficult to keep a secret in a palace when one considers the presence of courtiers and servants. The former continuously observe, and the latter spread the rumors of what their masters see. One has to believe then that monarchs live always among monsters full of eyes and lips, as the Satirist used to say.[1] Chicaba's royal chamber was the place where the brief conversation took place in which she gave her father to understand how she thought of a star as too little a thing to be God. The star's light and its dependence on other things for its being made it appear to her as a creature like the rest of them. No sooner had the words come out of her mouth than the girl's discussion with her father passed from one to another. So wise and profound were her words that the astonished courtiers and the rest of the people started to view Chicaba in such high regard that they venerated her as an oracle. People considered themselves fortunate and were filled with joy if they could see her or hear her words, which were more prudent and measured than could be expected from such a young person. In her the restless found calm; the healthy, consolation; and the sick, health. To this end those who could have her visit their homes considered themselves lucky, because they found in her the quickest medicine. There is testimony of the Venerable Mother herself about this point, given at the request and following the orders of her confessors.[2] When they took this young girl to visit the house of someone who had fallen ill, she would put her innocent hands on their head, and with the contact alone they found themselves restored to health. I am determined to stick to the strict laws of writing history without distracting myself with exaggerations, because they go against the nature of this kind of writing and make the truth look suspicious. The statement used by one of her directors to explain this miracle goes as follows: "According to trustworthy depositions, we know that they used to bring her to the sick, and by only laying her hand on their heads, she cured them." Please note anyone here the correspondence between these childhood steps in our girl and those of her darling and beloved Saint Vincent Ferrer.[3] While he performs marvels on his way to school, Chicaba causes miracles almost as soon as she outgrows infant clothing. Her countrymen are stunned by them and ask each other in general amazement who this girl

---

1   "The Satirist" (*El Satírico*) is a reference to the Roman poet Juvenal, author of the *Satires*.
2   According to the *Vida*, the only source of information for these miraculous powers is Sor Teresa Chicaba herself. However, she tells of this only at the request of her confessors, therefore acting in obedience to proper authority.
3   The original calls Saint Vincent Ferrer *amartelado*, which might be translated in the modern idiom as "boyfriend," "sweetheart," or "honey." The language used in the text to refer to her pious devotion to a male saint or to Christ is that of courtly love or romantic relationships. Also, the *Vida* needs to make Chicaba's childhood similar to those of other saints by including the performance of miracles.

is, and where she is going to end up, because the hand of God is visibly on her side. In this manner they celebrated and applauded the very Thing they ignored.[4]

Nevertheless, the girl could not be less aware of this celebrity. All her attention and care were occupied in the anxious search for her God. Her greatest merriment was to be alone in the fields. If she had to stay in the palace, she was all tears and weeping. So much, that in order to stop her crying they would take her out in the morning, and she would spend the entire day in the meadow with more pleasure and happier than in the gilded halls of her house. She would not go back home even to eat, so in order to placate her crying they would bring her daily nourishment out there. Her parents were very worried by what they thought was extravagant behavior. Because she was their little one, they doted on her and let her be, so she would not be upset. This show of love, however, gave them a fright and was almost an occasion for sorrow. She went out one morning like any other with a reduced retinue of female servants. While they enjoyed themselves for a while across the field, they left Chicaba alone. Suddenly she found herself assaulted by a barbarous army that came from an enemy of her nation and her father. They took her prisoner in order to tear her apart. In anguish at seeing from afar the danger in which their lady had fallen, the maids burst into the city shouting. They reached the palace in a confused melee, and with frightened echoes, they gave public news of the peril. The father, as courageous as he was prompt to action, left for the field at once. His vassals came to the call of the voices and valiantly they shattered the barbarous enemies and made them flee. After recovering his most precious treasure, they brought her back to her father in celebration. They congratulated one another for having achieved this victory through a well-taken risk, thereby ensuring through the girl's safety that her miracles would continue giving them solace.[5]

They examined her body carefully because seeing her alive did not assuage their pain, and they could not convince themselves that she was perfectly safe and healthy. But once they were free of their fears and worries, they walked back to the house in festive triumph. The mere sight and presence of the girl restored the jubilation and joy of the entire court, which had been deprived of it by the danger that had menaced her. Learning from their mistake after what had happened, the parents ordered that, to keep her safe, she should not go out to the fields again. This decree caused her more affliction than finding herself among enemy troops, her life awaiting the next stroke of a sword. Chicaba saw that her parents were closing the door to what she was looking for and requesting with so much anguish. She wanted to know the God who painted the meadow with colors and watered the arid soil. Her desire grew more intense, and the tears she shed were many, her grief and affliction were so great at seeing herself deprived of her beloved solitude and dear meadow, that her

---

For example, Saint Vincent Ferrer cured many people in his early years. See Francisco Vidal y Micó, *Historia de la portentosa vida y milagros de San Vicente Ferrer* (Valencia, 1735), 16. See also our other notes on Saint Vincent Ferrer.

4   This is a pre-Christian configuration of Africa. The text implies that the pagans of La Mina Baja were praising God without knowing him by celebrating Chicaba's miracles.

5   This episode of the invading barbarians highlights the notion that her homeland and surrounding areas were not safe places for a future Christian soul, because of their paganism. The *Vida* understands paganism and barbarism, the lack of civilized customs, as synonymous. This paganism/barbarism justifies the enslavement of Africans and their transportation to Christian lands.

parents, torn by their pain, relented in order to give her some relief. They set precise hours as their condition. They also ordered that she should take with her sufficient company, as they were trying to avoid exposing themselves to another distressful moment like the one they had endured. She accepted the conditions with pleasure, and her heart and bosom rejoiced again in her desert solitude, where she kept searching anxiously for the solution to her old questions.[6]

---

6   The desert is used in spiritual literature, especially in contemplative orders, as a metaphor for solitary contemplation or the dryness of unfulfilling prayer. The motif of the desert will be repeated later in the text (Chapters 32 and 41).

CHAPTER 4

She continues with her excursions to the field in order to follow her intent. The Virgin Mary favors her with a singular miracle.

It is not easy for human understanding to fathom Heaven's judgment; God's secrets are incomprehensible. Thus, He arranges things by ways that are extraordinary to our reason. Who would have said that our girl's father, hardly recovered from the past fright of seeing her stolen and her life at risk, would grant permission for her to go out to the fields so soon? This would seem like exposing her to the same, if not greater, peril! But God, who holds human will in His hands, dispersed those melancholy thoughts from his imagination and excited in the girl that restlessness and sadness that found no relief at home. God gently inclined the will of that monarch so that, to the relief of his daughter, he would consent and be pleased to allow her to venture into the fields in pursuit of her consolation.

She started repeating her excursions with pleasure, not so much to give distraction to her physical senses as to try to see if she could find clearer signs of the Magnet of her affection, who, although unknown by her, was revealing so much. Her servants and accompaniment, following the orders her father had given them, never lost sight of her. She began pleasant conversations with them to find out if there was a word that would give answer to what she looked for. If she saw a flower, she would turn to them and ask lovingly: "Who has put this flower in the meadow?" She would arrive at a fountain and the crystalline waters would captivate her. Coming out of her contemplation, she would ask them the same question: "Who put this fountain here?" she said. Nobody could answer in the direction she pointed. With charming impatience, she would reprimand them for their crass ignorance. She assured them that they were wrong in not investigating who decorated the meadow and who made the fountains sparkle and that she would not stop until she found out. Her parents and brothers received punctual reports of everything the girl did and said in the fields. They were all dumbfounded by her wisdom and intelligence, which was so unusual among them. Thus their love for her grew more and more, in the same degree as the girl's desire to dispel her doubt, to which end she spared no effort, travail, or discomfort. She would walk continuously, almost without stopping once the entire day. Her servants were busy keeping her in sight; so as long as they could see her, they would let her walk as far as she wanted.

One day, separating herself from them a good distance, she arrived at a fountain of crystal waters. Completely taken by it, as she was wont to do, she saw what she saw, for she alone knew about it.[1] What she said happened; and she could not keep it from happening. I will say it with the very words of one of her spiritual directors. "In one of these stages along

---

1 The author is echoing a passage from Saint John of the Cross, the Carmelite mystic, which describes the experience of the encounter with the Divine, who is represented by a fountain: "Aquella eterna fonte está ascondida, / que bien sé yo do tiene su manida, / *aunque es de noche*. / Su origen no lo sé, pues no lo tiene, / mas sé que todo origen de ella viene, / *aunque es de noche*" [That eternal fountain is hidden / and I know well where its source is / even though it is dark at night. / I do not know its origin / but I know that everything has its origin in it / even though it is dark at night] ("Cantar del

her way"—he talks about how far Teresa walked to reach the object of her burning desire—"they baptized her as she stood by the fountain, and they gave her the name of Teresa, which later on she was given again, when she was baptized in São Tomé." Her spiritual director says no more. Who administered the sacrament, he does not say, nor does he explain. Any learned person will have no doubt that this happened indeed. An angel must have done it, because at that time there was no one in the entire kingdom yet who could have baptized her.[2] After this incident, Teresa went back more reassured, with more knowledge of who the God was that she was looking for. However, since she was still a child, it does not seem that this knowledge remained so imprinted in her that it could quiet her old desire. She did not stop going about the same business and continued looking for the one whom she still did not know, even if she had Him inside her. This God, so hidden to her, wished to show some clear sign that He was the one she sighed for with loving pain. He appeared to her as a tender child in the arms of his Holy Mother. Teresa, stunned by the sight of such an uncanny vision, remained motionless in sweet contemplation, her eyes fixed on the Lady and her Child, who was as peaceful as He was beautiful. So that Teresa could better understand who He was, He dangled from His hands a ribbon, as resplendent as it was pretty. He touched Teresa's head softly with it, and when she tried to take it, the Child would withdraw His hand with grace so she could not reach it.[3] The Child repeated this action a few more times, with Teresa wishing to grab it; but she could never touch it. This mystical and extraordinary game lasted for a while, after which the Lady and her Son cast their benign eyes on the girl, and disappeared from her sight. In spite of her youth, Teresa was left mixing all sorts of thoughts in her imagination: the beauty of the Lady, the grace and sweetness of her Son, the whiteness of their faces, when all she had ever seen were dark ones.[4] These things became powerful incentives for her prompt and alert understanding, despite her youth. She wanted to find out for good who this God was who was hiding under cover. When the marvel ended, she went back with her people. She did not reveal any part of the vision. A few days later, she gave her brother some information, although vague, to calm his envy.

---

alma que se huelga de conocer a Dios por fe" ["Song of the Soul that Delights in Knowing God by Faith"], in San Juan de la Cruz, *Poesía*, edited by Domingo Ynduráin (Madrid: Cátedra, 1983), 277. Our translation.

The phrase "vio lo que vio, pues ella sola se lo supo" (she saw what she saw, for she alone knew about it) is also echoed almost verbatim in another poem by the Spanish mystic poet, "Noche oscura" (see above).

2   Once again Paniagua accepts as fact that Catholic missionaries established themselves in La Mina Baja del Oro. The presence of the angel at her spiritual baptism will be followed by other angelic apparitions at critical moments of Chicaba's life, such as her abduction into slavery (Chapter 6) and the episode in the Retiro park of Madrid (Chapter 10).

3   See the Introduction, p. 92, for the mystical meaning of this vision of gift giving; see especially the discussion of Christ's enticing Chicaba with a dangling ribbon and its connection to slavery.

4   This is the first instance where the text inserts a racial discourse. Whiteness is proclaimed the color of the divinity, as opposed to the Blackness of Chicaba, who at this point is technically a pagan.

CHAPTER 5

Teresa calms her brother's jealousy. Her father inherits extensive territories and he wants to bring her with him. With tears in her eyes, she obtains permission from him to stay behind. They build a house for her to live in.

Envy is a fiery monster. He spares nobody and tramples everything without concern for age, sex or person. The more elevated an individual in gifts of nature or in virtue and gentle disposition, the more furious its attacks and crueler its shots. Teresa could not have been older than seven or eight years, and her brother could not have been fifteen yet when envy assaulted him with fury. Joachipiter observed the profound love his parents demonstrated toward his sister and the affection shown by the most distinguished courtiers and aristocrats. Everybody praised highly her gracious demeanor. All these things became cruel wrongs to him, wrenching his heart, and fostering in him a deadly jealousy. This passion tends to assault the spirit of sovereigns in what they fear most, which are matters of state.[1] He began to harbor doubts within himself, whether in the future he would hold the scepter, or if his sister's head would bear the crown. Hesitating and confused, he resolved to explain his worries in the following terms:

> I am amazed, sister, by your grace and natural gifts. With them you always enjoy the king's favor and earn Mother's. Those in high positions praise you, and the lowly celebrate you. The entire kingdom acclaims you. What else is there left for you to do but to take the scepter in your hand and crown your head with the diadem? Father will be well disposed in all certainty. Mother's love for you will force her to accept it. The nobility and the lower ones will see in it stability and permanence.

He finished explaining his feelings, and he was not too misguided in his thinking, because the custom of that land makes it possible for any of the royal children to inherit the crown. Adorned with so many unique gifts, the girl's nature seemed to hold great promise for the entire kingdom. But her aims were very different. They were only in accordance with the Omnipotent's goals. The girl listened to her brother's reasons with more attention and care than her years dictated, and she responded with peaceful meekness:

> It is no secret to me, she said, that our parents harbor a great love for me. I see the affectionate demonstrations of the nobles, and I notice the reverent praises of the people.

---

1 *Razones de estado* refers to an anti-Machiavellian political doctrine in seventeenth-century Spain. According to it, the state—when it is ruled by a Christian prince—is the reflection of God's kingdom on earth; therefore, matters of state should be conducted according to God's will. There are no valid *razones de estado* for state officials to commit crimes. Envy in a ruler is an obstacle to performing the duties required by matters of state.

> I do not doubt that, following the dispositions of our laws and customs, the scepter belongs to the one the sovereign designates. Neither my father will exclude you from the crown and entrust its heavy weight on a weak woman, nor would Joachin, who is next to you in age, get it. I would not, in any case, accept the scepter. You should not be worried or upset by such untimely thoughts. You must know that I will not get married in this land to any man but to a White Child that I know.[2]

This was Teresa's answer to her brother's words. He embraced her, either because he was elated by the girl's contempt for the throne and its power, which left the path open to him, or because he was captivated by so much wisdom in such a child. They ended their conversation in one accord and union, although separated by their views.

Her brother ceased to worry, once such a wise and brief statement appeased him. Still, he was unclear and confused by the mention of his sister's intended wedding to a person not even well known to him or her. Teresa was happier to see her brother's frown of envious melancholy disappear. She directed all her attention to her fervent search for the one she loved. Her quest grew more intense because the time was nearing for the completion of the house where she had to live secluded once she reached the appropriate age, following the custom of her land. Those people had the tradition of subjecting all girls to rigorous seclusion once they reached the ninth year of age. No girl was allowed to leave until she married a person appropriate to her status. They have several houses to this effect in the kingdom to keep the girls under strict guard. No girl misses any of the necessities to her person or proper teaching. The powerful go to great pains to build rich houses for their daughters, either together with many others or by themselves. Teresa's father had already begun one for her, as sumptuous as it should be for the beloved daughter of a monarch. It had not been finished because she was not nine years old yet, which was the deadline for seclusion, as has been said.

During this time, death struck down a potentate who lived a long distance from the kingdom where Teresa's father lived. Either by disposition of the deceased, or by right, he was entitled to that dominion. The father readied himself for the journey and the entire royal family with him. His first thought was to bring the girl with him as he took possession of his inheritance. While everyone was happy, she was disgusted to the extreme; her weeping, her sighs, and her whimpering in hopes of avoiding the journey made her father change his mind, much to her relief. He gave orders that Teresa's brothers would go with him and that the girl should stay in the court with her mother. But he decreed that she should not be allowed to leave the house, as an inviolable law. He bid her good-bye. To oblige her to comply faithfully with his orders, he assured her of his love and affection; it was not to upset her that he was leaving without her. In exchange, he only wanted her not to leave the house and palace. He was afraid that in his absence she might run into another danger like the past one. This would expose him and the kingdom to another conflict. Having said this, he left the presence of his dear treasure, never to see her again in his life.

---

2 This is the first mention of marriage to the White Child in the text. It is Chicaba who expresses the idea.

CHAPTER 6

She goes out of the house, and guided by Divine Providence, she arrives at the location where she was apprehended. Events that occurred until she arrived in the harbor of São Tomé

With the confidence and security of knowing that his orders and precepts would be observed to the letter regarding the custody of his daughter, Teresa's father went off with his sons to take possession of his newly aggregated provinces. The mother was equally intent on enforcing and executing the monarch's law, since it was of utmost importance to observe it and thus ensure her daughter's security. A new Argos, she would not allow her out of her sight.[1] But what is human purpose against divine decision? This amorous vigilance and care lasted four days. The same love was the occasion for a lapse, which her mother would lament with inconsolable tears for a long time. Stealing herself from her mother's watch—how she did only God knows—and fooling the vigilance of the guards, Teresa was able to leave her house. Once out, she hurried toward her beloved meadow, hoping to see by the fountain that Lady with the White Child who had so completely taken hold of her affection. Seeing that she could not find the Magnet of her love there, she continued walking far away from her court and house, overtaken as she was by her passion. Unable to figure out the way back and ignorant of what was at the end of such a long walk, she was feeling the heat of the sun. Fatigued after such effort, she sat down under the shade of a tree.[2] Protected by it from the sun's fierce heat, she cleaned the sweat from her face. Finding relief and rest, Teresa, although a child and in such desert solitude, remained unafraid and completely without fear. Doing what was more proper for her years, she took off her wrists beautiful and precious bangles, and started playing with them. She was as calm and serene as she could be in her own house. Let us leave Teresa immersed in her games, because a vessel has suddenly appeared on shore that will take away such a priceless jewel.[3] Instead, let us see what her mother and her family were doing.

As soon as they noticed that she was missing, it was as if cold ice ran inside everybody's veins. Not a single servant found the courage to bring to the mother such deadly worry. She,

---

1 In Greek mythology "Argos" means "watchdog" and probably refers here to a hound of Hades that possessed one hundred eyes, so he could see in all directions.
2 This is another scene taken from mystical literature. The image metaphorizes Teresa as a new Eve, who is rescued from sin under the proverbial Tree of Knowledge, the scene of Adam's temptation. Saint John of the Cross: "Debajo del manzano, / allí conmigo fuiste desposada, /allí te di la mano, / y fuiste reparada, / donde tu madre fuera violada" [Under that apple tree / you were wed to me. / I gave you my hand there / and you were restored / where your mother had been violated] (*Cántico espiritual* [*Spiritual Canticle*], stanza 23 in Juan de la Cruz, p. 254; our translation and modernized Spanish).
3 The kidnapping of Chicaba is in the style of a scene describing enslavement from *Aithiopikai* (*Ethiopian Story*) written by the Greek author Heliodorus (c. 300 CE). There was no contemporary narrative of enslavement that could serve as an acceptable model in Paniagua's time. Accounts of slavery had not circulated widely enough to act as narrative models. See the discussion on the Byzantine romance in the Introduction, p. 66.

at first, did not notice her daughter's absence, thinking that she was playing with the other girls in some room of the house. To think that she had left was completely unimaginable, considering the stern orders she had received. But after some time, she enquired about her daughter. As they were not giving her a straight answer, she became quite concerned and started searching the entire house by herself. She could not find her, and by now very worried, she repeated the question to the servants. Where was her daughter? In their mute silence, for they responded with nothing, they provided more than sufficient answer. They did not know where or how she was faring. They could say only that she was missing. Here came the furor, the anger, and the wrath. At once the mother set off like an enraged lioness with all her people, to search the fields. She quickly went to the meadow, and no valley, hilltop, depth, or mountain was left unexamined. They did not obtain better fruit from their work than increased pain and sorrow. When all were finally tired of searching for her, they returned home. They figured that without a doubt the savages had been more diligent and had secured the capture of the prey who had been rescued before thanks to their spirited effort. However, this time it would not be because they had not been able to chase their presumed adversaries.[4]

How distraught must the mother have been to return home with her own sorrow, which would be increased by what her husband would feel when he came back from his journey? How much anguish—how disconsolate she must have felt at the loss of the absent girl cannot be easily imagined, and likewise all her vassals? The sick cried for their lost health, and the sad for their consolation and all their relief. The father came back from his trip, and as all bad news wears wings, even before he reached his court he received the report that was as ill-fated for him as for the rest of his company. Perhaps only the prince did not feel the same, because seeing the scepter free of hurdles and obstacles is reason enough to lessen even the worst of sad news. Seeing the king's pain and his crying made the queen and the entire court shed more tears, though the ones they had wept since the loss of Teresa had not yet dried up. But the passage of time, which cures everything, lessened their pain and weeping. They were finally able to see with serene eyes the rays of the gospel's light, and be reborn with joy in the waters of baptism, thanks to the favors of the Capuchin Fathers.[5] Their own daughter years later told the truth of this, which she knew from authentic accounts she had received from her land. And bidding farewell to it, I go back in search of Teresa.

We left Teresa resting under a tree, when a Spanish vessel appeared on the shore, and suddenly a gallant young man seized her by an arm and took her with the jewels she was wearing.[6] He led her closer to the seashore, and those on the ship discovered her, but they

---

4   The name *cafre* (kaffir) is used by the author to mark a distinction between civilized Blacks—Chicaba's nation—and barbarous ones, with the latter typically accused of cannibalism. *Cafre* remained a pejorative term used by some Europeans well into the twentieth century.

5   The text gives ample credit to the Capuchin mission to the kingdom of Arada, which took place in the middle of the seventeenth century, twenty years before the events related here. However, the text may be echoing other testimonies of Christian presence on the coast of La Mina Baja from the 1670s, most of which were the result of communication between São Tomé and the kingdom of Arada. See Law, "Religion, Trade and Politics," 44ff.

6   The detail about the jewels Chicaba was wearing when she was kidnapped is very important in the later narrative of her life. They are supposedly indicative of her identity as a person of royal descent. According to the text, they seem to have been instrumental in her presentation to King Carlos II of Spain.

never saw the man who was taking her because he became invisible to their eyes.[7] One of them jumped overboard and took her to the ship. She took to the high seas without tending to any other concern or business. Anguished to see they were taking her away from her land, with tears in her eyes, and with the distress also of seeing herself among strange people, Teresa was on the brink of death. The sadness and grief, as well as the thirst, were suffocating her. She moaned helplessly, and all in the vessel tried everything they could to soothe her. But the tears were caused more from her consuming thirst than from any other pain, although so many feelings tormented her. Yet no one could calm her because they did not know what she wanted. By chance, she saw a glass of water, and thrusting herself toward it in a hurry, she was able finally to quench her thirst.[8] Having restored herself to life, refreshed and more at ease, she was caressed by her captors, and with this, little by little she started to recover from the fright. However, she did not cease in her wish to go back to her land and to the presence of her dear parents. It distressed her not to know how to swim because with this ability and skill she thought that, although a small child, she might liberate herself from such painful slavery.[9] Seeing that she could not accomplish this remedy, she devised the following childish plan, as she told later on: The vessel is sailing further away against the current; if I jump into the water, it will take me to my land, since its currents go in that direction. As she finished her thought, she tried to put it into action. But when she was about to execute it, a Lady appeared to her whose majesty and grandeur clearly indicated that she was the same one Teresa had seen on the happy occasion at the fountain back in her motherland. The Lady dried her tears with peaceful calm, and she also allayed her distress with her caresses. With this she freed her completely of the affection she harbored in her bosom for her motherland, which would occasion the most lamentable drowning.[10]

---

7   This is the second presence of an angelic figure in Chicaba's life. The account in the *Oración fúnebre* (1749) mentions that Chicaba was taken into slavery with a female cousin. This contradicts the depiction in the *Vida* of her being lost in solitude at the time of her abduction.
8   It is likely that the text follows Chicaba's recollection of those moments. There are testimonies of slaves suffering from hallucinations because of dehydration. See the Introduction, p. 66.
9   This is the first time the term "slavery" is used to refer to Chicaba's condition. However, this enslavement is softened because it is filtered through the perspective of a child who exhausts herself in tears. The reader might observe that this representation of her childishness is inconsistent with her depiction as a girl who reasons with her father and brother on theological first causes.
10 See the Introduction, p. 66, for the discussion of ceremonies to make enslaved individuals forget their kin and country of origin.

CHAPTER 7

She arrives at the city of São Tomé.[1]

Navigation from Guinea to the city of São Tomé is rather risky and subject to accidents, but the vessel that carried Teresa overcame all perils and arrived in São Tomé guided by Divine Providence. After all put ashore, their first concern was that Teresa receive the sacrament of baptism. This done, she joined the Catholic fold with the name of Teresa. Who could doubt that the angel who had given her this name beside the fountain would make sure that men would give it to her also? The congruence in both ceremonies is rather convincing. When the ship took on board everything necessary for the voyage, it set sail for Spain. The crew and passengers suffered considerable distress en route, so many and continuous were the storms. They barely escaped becoming victims to the whitecaps. Perhaps hell was envious and foresaw the continuous triumphs Teresa would win against it with her virtue and righteousness. So the devil thought that in order to take away one life, he could easily drown everyone. We are persuaded of this by the persistent shrieks of a band of crows that tormented the ship for a long time. They flew so close to the girl that they threatened to tear her apart with their beaks and talons. It was necessary to take her below deck for safety. But Divine Providence was keeping watch over Teresa and completely foiled hell's scheme. The vessel was delivered through storms and gales and docked safely in the famed city of Seville.[2]

Teresa was close to ten years of age when she arrived. She was sent to lodge in a wealthy home. Her hosts received her with great displays of joy, both because of her youth and her affable and lively temperament. This was also due to her strange skin color as well as the information about her social rank and noble birth given by those who brought her. This was confirmed by the jewels and other precious ornaments she was wearing when she was carried off at the seashore. This generous welcome was well imprinted on her heart, and even in her last years of life she remembered it vividly. She still recounted humorously the splendid meal of welcome they gave her. Teresa's masters allowed her to rest from her voyage in the most comfortable leisure. But she was looking for other toys and recreation than those that were appropriate to her age, preferring seclusion as her only form of entertainment. Her masters interpreted this as melancholy at being away from her home

---

1 The islands of São Tomé had always been a midpoint in the Portuguese slave trade. Ships from Angola, Congo, and Mozambique stopped there on their way to Brazil, but in the seventeenth century its centrality in the slave trade had decreased. After the fall of Elmina Castle to the Dutch in 1637, São Tomé increased in importance for Portugal since the slaving expeditions had no *feitoría* (port base) on the western African coast. In 1673, the Portuguese crown allowed São Tomé to establish commercial relations with the western coast of Africa. This included trade in slaves from the Lower Mina region. As seen in the Introduction, Section 2, there are abundant references in Brasio's *Monumenta Missionaria Africana* to the attempts by the bishop of São Tomé and requests from the rulers of Arada to send missionaries.

2 Chicaba had to arrive first at the port city of Cadiz, since Seville's river port could no longer accommodate big ships by the late seventeenth century.

and native land. Divine Providence saw this was wisdom and prudence—the beginnings of solid virtue—and it was right.

There was a statue of the Holy Virgin with her sovereign Son in her arms in the house where Teresa was staying.[3] Whenever she could steal away from everyone's sight, she would spend time at the feet of this sovereign Queen, spellbound in contemplation. She would confide to Mother and Son all sorts of endearments, which both Majesties accepted graciously as coming from someone without any malice at all. She would take her afternoon snack and hurry to the room to be with the Magnet of her soul. With affectionate simplicity, she invited Mother and Son to partake of the food with her.[4] The divine and omnipotent Master, who lives and abides with the pure and simple of heart, accepted the invitation with pleasure. One afternoon, as was her custom, Teresa went in and invited Mother and Son to eat with her. On that occasion the Christ Child left the comforting arms of the Virgin Mary and assumed His human incarnate form to descend with love and affection to the girl. Teresa spent the happiest and most pleasant afternoon in sweet conversation, talking of loving subjects and sharing the snack with Him. Once they finished, the Child went back to the arms of His Holy Mother. I am perfectly aware that there are examples of this sort of event in the Annals of the Church. But, nevertheless, the rare and special favor granted by the Lord to our Teresa is no less unusual because it had occurred on previous occasions. By accepting her invitation, he honored this poor slave girl, who was also dark-skinned. In contrast, others in their human vanity and presumption would later scorn Teresa because of her complexion and refuse to admit her to their company.

---

3   The text uses the word *hospedarse* (meaning "to lodge" or "to stay") here instead of "to enslave." This gives the impression that Chicaba was always privileged and that enslavement was a transitory stage in her life.

4   Her practice of inviting Christ to eat with her is a child's devotion that can be interpreted in hagiographic terms as a reversal of the Last Supper and Holy Communion. However, this can also be a retention in Chicaba's memory of her ancestral practices, back in Africa, where it was customary for some peoples to share the sacrificial meal among themselves or where the favorite foods of a divinity were distributed among those gathered to worship.

CHAPTER 8

She leaves Seville for Madrid.
They present her to King Carlos II.¹ He in turn
presents her to the Marquis of Mancera.

Once her masters had allowed Teresa to recover from the painful voyage, they decided to travel to the court with the girl. She went to bid farewell to her Spouse—although he had already taken up permanent residence in her soul.² What favors she received during this farewell only her soul knew. Occasionally she related stories to others about celestial visitations and visions, but she only wrote down the one referred to in the previous chapter.³ Encouraged by her Spouse's favors, she began her journey cheerfully, with no other goal or direction than the one her masters wished to give her. They arrived at the Imperial and Royal Court of Madrid still reflecting on the treasure they had found in the girl. They reasoned that she might be a gift worthy enough to present at the feet of Carlos II, who was the reigning king. He received her gladly and listened with particular pleasure to the donors about the circumstances in which she had been found and taken. The adornments and jewels she was wearing were all clear signs that the slave girl was the daughter of some prince or king in that land.⁴

Teresa found herself separated from her first owners; however, this situation was more fortunate for her, because she was now protected by the clemency of no less than the king of Spain. The king heard that the Marquis of Mancera liked foreigners, a natural result of the compassionate love with which he consoled and ministered to the Indians during his tenure as viceroy.⁵ The king presented Teresa to him to be raised and educated in his household. He received her with the greatest demonstrations of pleasure and happiness, both because of who had handed her to him and because she deserved it by her own right. The love and

---

1 We use the name Carlos II for the last Spanish monarch of the Hapsburg dynasty to distinguish him from his English contemporary Charles II, the Stuart king. Anglophone historians seem inconsistent on this point. Some call the Spanish Carlos by his translated name, while others keep the Spanish one.

2 The Spanish for permanent residence is *moraba en su pecho de asiento*. The word *asiento* means a contract between the king and a private person, as in exclusive licenses the king of Spain gave to individual businessmen and companies for the importation of slaves, as in *asientos de esclavos*. In this context, Chicaba's Spouse lives in her soul as its rightful dweller and its master in exclusivity.

3 This comment gives credence to the existence of Sor Teresa's own spiritual writings, as Paniagua notes the scarcity of supernatural events like this one.

4 The summary of the narrative heard by the king of Spain belongs to the typical accounts found in books of chivalry and Byzantine romances. In these stories, the slave girl is not really a slave but a princess. Later in the text, Chapter 17, there is an *anagnorisis* (recognition scene), in which a prince from her native land recognizes her. See the discussion on the Byzantine romance and the *Vida* in the Introduction, Section 2.

5 Mancera would have been used to having people of different ethnicities in his household, since he had been the viceroy of Mexico. He owned Muslim slaves in Madrid. See, for instance, our discussions of the Turkish girl. See Introduction, p. 76.

esteem the marquis and the marchioness showed the girl, as well as the way they treated her, were as if she were a beloved daughter rather than a slave received as a gift.[6] She repaid this love to both of them quite handsomely. The example of Teresa's virtue became an incentive for them to lead a life of rectitude, even in the midst of all the activity, pomp, and circumstance imposed by the variety of high offices and the renown of their blood and house. They became disciples of their own slave, and they obeyed her unconditionally in all points of Christian perfection. Through this means, they were able to lessen their penances [in purgatory] and also gain eternal happiness thanks to Teresa's prayers and supplications. This is corroborated in a response to a letter written by her and dated in Barcelona, August 10, 1743, the original of which is still preserved. Its content is as follows:

> You have taken a long time to communicate to me the holy news about the souls of our saintly marquis and marchioness. This is a source of great pleasure to all in their Catholic family and especially for me. I attended them for a long time in their last illnesses. Both died in my arms. I learned about the marquis's soul on the day he died. They told me that a lay Franciscan brother, famous for his virtue, while his community was reciting the Office of the Dead, turned toward the corpse and asked him in the following or similar words: "Hey, friend, how is it going over there? You were in danger indeed." Those present came to the sensible conclusion that his soul had not been lost.

These are the sentences taken from the letter written by the Most Reverend Father Don Andrés Teruel, a member of the Order of Regular Clerks of Saint Gaetano.[7] He is an individual known for his virtue who served as a page in the marquis's house when Teresa was being raised there. From the letter, it is evident that the souls of this lord and lady had been able to leave that painful prison once their penalties had been lessened thanks to the intercession and prayers of Teresa. In gratitude, they must have paid a visit to her to give her thanks. This was the joyful news that she gave Father Teruel, who had served and attended them so faithfully and with so much love for a very long time. She seems to be somehow late with her news, according to the Father's complaint in his answer. This shows how much interest the marquis put in this jewel presented to him by the royal liberality of his monarch. Teresa took the same care to pay back the love they had shown to her when they received her in their house.

---

6 The narrative reintroduces the term *esclava presentada*, which asserts that Chicaba was a slave presented as a gift. In Paniagua's *Oración fúnebre* for Chicaba she is repeatedly called a gift, and this term takes on allegorical importance. See the discussion of the gift in the Introduction, Section 2.

7 In Chapter 40, Chicaba receives supernatural news of Father Teruel's death. He belonged to the same order, the Theatines, as Chicaba's hagiographer Paniagua and as Father Jerónimo Abarrategui, who was Chicaba's spiritual director and confessor during some of her time in the convent. According to the *Catholic Encyclopedia*, the Theatines had a missionary spirit that led them to have contact with people outside of Europe (Franciscus Ragonesi, "Theatines," *The Catholic Encyclopedia* [New York: Robert Appleton Company, 1912], *www.newadvent.org/cathen/14557a.htm*). This might account for their interest in Chicaba. The Marquis of Mancera left five hundred ducats for the Theatines in his will (Archivo Histórico de Protocolos Notariales de Madrid, libro 13.994, fol. 37ff., February 11, 1715).

CHAPTER 9

Education of Teresa in the house of the marquis. Envy of the other female servants. Ill-treatment suffered at their hands. Ruse by the devil to take her life

Once the marquis and the marchioness understood the lively yet docile spirit of their slave, they made every effort to give her teachers so she could be educated in everything she might learn at that age. Their first preoccupation was to give her more and more instruction in the rudiments of our holy faith. With that purpose, they put her under the direction of a priest who also served as chaplain to Their Excellencies. He was as virtuous as he was full of other perfections. He accepted this new occupation gladly, and after a few lessons he was so delighted by Teresa's progress that his own work had accomplished its goal. It could not have been difficult to teach her matters the Author of Grace Himself had taught her when she was younger. Finding his disciple so well versed in the rudiments of the faith, her director and teacher began to introduce her to a more elevated sort of life. He made her seek a more intimate acquaintance with God through prayer. Teresa embraced this acquaintance with God so earnestly that she never abandoned it, but rather perfected it for the rest of her life. She felt attracted and enticed, as if it were a piece of candy, by the bait of love the divine Master communicated to her during prayer.[1] She spent every moment she could afford alone in the oratory, involved in this peaceful recreation. This was her exercise, her yearning. Here she found complete calm. For the remaining exercises and accomplishments required of a woman, the marquis and his wife appointed a governess to teach her. However, this person was of such dour disposition that more than a teacher, she was a torturer for Teresa. The marquis and his wife showed the girl all the consideration owed to her nobility and blood. This, and the fact that they had received her in their house not as a slave but as a daughter, was the reason Their Excellencies asked her to sit with them at the table. The governess and the other maidservants, seeing their masters show such appreciation for a negress, were fuming.[2] In a short time, there were many Black faces in that household, and while one was Black by nature, the others had turned Black with envy.[3] They called her mockingly "The Queen." Seeing that she sat at the table, they made jokes about a negress being held in such high esteem by her owners. They ridiculed her, calling her a feigned

---

1 The use of candy in the comparison emphasizes the idea of Chicaba's religious experience as childish, as it happened during her visions of the White Lady by the fountain in her homeland. Another moment of childishness was when she shared her snack with the Child Jesus while living in Seville. This comparison to a child also has gender component. Chicaba is childish in her mystical reactions because she is female.
2 As we mentioned earlier, we use the English term "negress" only in those instances when the Spanish word *negra* has a pejorative connotation. For all other cases when the Spanish word *negra* appears, we use the expressions "Black," "Black girl," or "Black woman," as appropriate to Chicaba's age in the text.
3 With a mixture of horror and amusement, the text describes the servants' animosity toward Teresa. The words *humos* (soot) and *rostro* (face) are used in a pun: the fuming of the servants, *humo*, is what turns their faces Black. During theater representations and religious parades, blackface was achieved by the practice of smearing faces with soot.

infanta, though indeed she had been born a true princess.[4] The marquis and his wife saw this as a clear attack, manifest opposition, and envy. To restore some order in the family, they deprived themselves of the consolation of having Teresa at the table during their meals or at their side. Hiding their love for her to a certain extent, from then on, they began to treat her differently. Although they were still affable and gentle, the change would have made a negative impression in someone else, except in Teresa. It did not make a single dent in her spirit that suddenly they treated her like a servant, when not long before she had been held as a daughter. Following the advice of her director about self-knowledge, any place and treatment was appropriate to her. She accepted with no change in her mood the feigned coldness yet calm love of her owners.

The maidservants were happy to have succeeded, or so they thought, in pulling the negress down in the esteem and good opinion in which her owners held her. They congratulated each other repeatedly on their triumph. But since envy can never be satisfied and its rage gains new energy, it grew and increased in the servants with their apparent victory. Not happy after mocking Teresa, they moved from harsh words to deeds. The governess, whose charge was to teach her, took special delight in this. It looks as if the Enemy of the human race, with Heaven's permission, took this woman as an instrument to purify and test Teresa during these early years. What species of ill treatment did this woman not try on her! What number of beatings and cruelties did she not subject Teresa to! And this meek and peaceful lamb did not part her lips or open her mouth. A single word from her—according to what she said during the last years of her life—addressed to the marquis or the marchioness about how badly the governess treated her would have had an immediate effect on the governess.[5] She at least would have lost her position in the marquis's household for the rest of her life.[6] Instead, Teresa suffered and underwent her torments and sorrows in silence. She preferred to endure her sorrows, pains, and torments rather than complain and deprive the governess of her position. The latter attributed the former's silence to stubbornness, stupidity, and lack of intelligence. With this vain belief, she multiplied her penalties and punishments on Teresa. One time, angry after having unleashed her wrath as she was accustomed to in repeated acts of cruelty, she struck Teresa so harshly in a delicate part of her body that even in an older person this would have been enough to kill her. But the omnipotence of God tempered the blow, which otherwise might have taken her life. Still, it was hard enough to make Teresa suffer not just for months and days afterward, but for the rest of her life. She carried the mark left by that blow to her grave.[7] What should Teresa do with such cruel pain, occasioned by so merciless a blow? Say nothing and suffer with patience and in silence, looking for soothing and consolation in the One that the next chapter will relate.

---

4   These scenes were typical in comedies and *entremeses*—one-act skits—during the seventeenth and eighteenth centuries. The Black woman who disputes with others over her noble origin in Africa was a stock character from the early days of Spanish theater. See Baltasar Fra-Molinero's *La imagen de los negros en el teatro del Siglo de Oro* (Madrid: Siglo XXI Editores, 1995).

5   It was common to subject a slave to physical abuse. In this case, Chicaba's acceptance of this maltreatment redounds to her credit on her path to spiritual purification.

6   Servants found it hard to find employment. A woman like the governess could expect no other position of a similar nature anywhere else since her placement was probably obtained through patronage.

7   Scars and other physical marks of abuse become means of inscribing the history of her suffering on her body. Chicaba's body, like the bodies of all slaves, is the surface where continuous acts of physical violence become a text that cannot be erased. This is the case in the instances with the governess. The silence during these incidents is broken at the end of her life.

CHAPTER 10

End of the matter from the previous chapter regarding the devil's ruses to take away her life. Heaven's care in defending her

We left Teresa struggling with the natural feelings caused by the governess's wrath and her cruel blow and with her forbearance and patience. The first induced her to tell the marquis and his wife of her strange hardship. Their prudence would dictate an opportune remedy, either by modifying the governess's terrible temper or by appointing a new teacher—one who would be genuine and not such a cruel torturer as the governess was. This is what human prudence dictated to her, but her sense of forbearance and patience corrected these natural sentiments, and instead she felt encouraged to remain constant in her travails. She was readying herself for a more elevated life, where the most grievous pains, afflictions, and difficulties weave the most precious of garlands. Contented with that resolution, which had been inspired by Heaven, she decided to communicate to no one her pains and torments except to her celestial Divine Spouse. As soon as the governess's wrath gave her some respite, she rushed into the oratory, and with humble resignation, she started to give a detailed account of her travails in front of a holy image of the majesty of Christ. It was an image of the Ecce Homo.[1] Her divine Master, mixing peace with severity, with only one glance, seemed to reprimand her. She was complaining of so little compared to what He had suffered for the love of her, which was infinite. He offered her consolation at the same time for having resolved not to communicate her sorrows to anyone.

But the governess was also led to sorrows by her own impatience. Thanks to her decent employment, which she owed to her masters in spite of having served them so badly, she left the house of the marquis to get married to an individual of her same quality and gifts. She thought herself favored by her good fortune and free of the worries of those who have to be servants. But when she was promising herself a pleasant existence in her own house, she found life with her husband very hard and upsetting. His condition was even more terrible and choleric than his wife's. He was the instrument Heaven used to make her pay in just retribution for what she had made her pupil Teresa suffer. For as long as she lived after she married, her days were a theater of torment and affliction. Heaven decided that she would recognize that so much misfortune was not simply the occurrence of a bad marriage, as happens to many women, but rather a just punishment for her hasty anger. All the children she had were born with the same mark on their bodies that she had stamped with her blow on Teresa's—a punishment appropriate to her perfidy, and just penance for her anger and im-

---

[1] The phrase *Ecce homo* (Here's the man) is attributed to Pontius Pilate in the Vulgate version of the Bible when he presents Jesus to the crowd in Jerusalem. There are popular representations of the scene depicting the scourged Christ on the morning of his crucifixion. Roman soldiers dressed Jesus in a red cape, put a crown of thorns on his head and a cane in his hands, and hailed him mockingly as "King of the Jews" (Matthew 27:27–29). Teresa, like all saints, experiences her life as a symbolic mirror of events in Christ's life. The text implies that she, like Christ, is of royal blood, and for this reason, she is beaten and mocked. See the discussion of this picture in the Introduction, p. 78.

patience.² The Enemy of the human race was quite disappointed at seeing his ruse foiled by Divine Providence. He had been the instigator of the governess's blows and mistreatment, to deprive Teresa of her life. But although he had been foiled, he did not concede defeat. In his malice he understood that Teresa would give him a very bad time as a grown-up since she had already endured her sufferings with constancy at such an innocent age. Therefore, he set new snares and invented new means to achieve his depraved end. His malevolence found a new good occasion, but divine hands defended her in the following episode.

One afternoon the marchioness sent all the maidservants, including her little Black girl, out for a walk, a licit and decent sport. They obeyed the mistress's orders and went to the site of the Buen Retiro.³ Among its variety of beautiful fountains, gardens, and pools, they planned to entertain themselves that afternoon. As the sun was setting, they all approached the big pool and climbed to its corbel. Some were standing on it, and others were sitting, and all were distracted with the soft noise of the waters when they saw a man who looked like the marquis's majordomo by all the external signs. He approached them, and they did not think anything of it, since they saw him as another member of the household. Without a word, he approached Teresa, who was standing on the corbel and did not pay attention to his presence. The false majordomo kicked Teresa into the water. They were all taken by surprise by such an irregular action in an individual they all considered a fellow domestic. They were astonished at noticing Teresa's danger. They were paralyzed since they did not know how to remedy the accident. They remained confused for a long while, which would have been enough for the water to take away Teresa's life, were it not for the divine help she received. She said that under the waves she was as pleased as she had been in the little meadow back in her homeland.⁴ Once her companions recovered from the surprise and confusion, they started to discuss among themselves the remedy, but they could not find any means to help her, so they turned and turned with sorrow and tears. At the same time, Teresa was bathing under the waters, full of pleasure and contentment. A few steps away from there, still inside the Buen Retiro, they found a young man, as gallant as he was well disposed. They informed him of the cause for their tears, and he obliged them by asking

---

2   Christians asserted that the figure of God as a just avenger was common in the Old Testament; this appears frequently in saints' lives. Yet Christians believe humans are not supposed to take revenge into their own hands, but rather to leave it up to God. This miraculous intervention in the form of special "stigmata" is the reverse of the stigmata of Christ's passion some mystics had imprinted on their bodies as a special favor of God's election. Here the governess's sins are marked on her children, the flesh of her flesh. Another interpretation is that Teresa has powers. Vodun religion sometimes interprets these interventions as the result of a petition from the person who is protected by a spirit that avenges victims of bodily harm. Here the narrative may be interpreting something Teresa told her hagiographer; this may be an example of syncretism of African retentions with popular Christian folk beliefs.
3   The Buen Retiro was on the grounds of today's biggest urban park in Madrid. The kings of Spain had used it as a place of retreat and rest in the past. It would not be open to the public until the reign of Carlos III, after Chicaba's death. However, well-connected aristocrats like the Manceras had privileged access to the Buen Retiro grounds.
4   The memory of the homeland in this life-and-death situation puts Madrid and La Mina Baja del Oro at opposite ends of the spectrum of the *locus amoenus* literary topos, a term for "Edenic place of safety." In Africa, the scenes near the water indicated a godly presence, while in Madrid the devil seems to be hovering around.

   The image of water in the text is ambiguous. Chicaba's contact with divinity is frequently related to water. She encounters the White Child and His Mother by a fountain. In Chapter 6, the figure of a young man appears at the moment of her enslavement by the seashore, and again as her rescuer in the pond at Buen Retiro. See the Introduction, p. 76.

them to take him to the site. He recognized the place where Teresa had fallen. Without his doing more than standing by the shore, the water reverently put Teresa into his hands. She appeared as happy, gay, and joyful as if she had never fallen into the water, and her clothes were not wet. He returned Teresa to her fellow servants. They were so busy with their joy at seeing their dear Teresa restored to them that they did not bother to ask who the young man was. The same had happened before with the one they had believed to be the majordomo; in their panic they forgot to find out what had happened to him or where he had gone.

CHAPTER II

The false majordomo's mischief is discovered. Account of who took her out of the water. The devil attempts to take her life away by means of another slave girl.

Once Teresa's companions recovered from the fright of having lost her in front of their very eyes and after that gallant young man restored her to them, they left the Buen Retiro and returned to their master's house. Teresa was as happy as if nothing had happened to her at all. Her companions discussed among themselves the majordomo's cruel action. There was no cause or motive possible for doing something so cruel to a person like Teresa, who was the object of their masters' affection.[1] They hurried back home, impatiently eager to give their masters an account of what had happened. They feared that the news might reach the marquis and the marchioness from a sinister or distorting source that would cause pain to them. They rushed into the house and immediately recounted the incident. They decried the majordomo's crime in loud voices and shrieks. They described how he, ashamed and embarrassed for what he had done, suddenly fled from their sight. Also, they explained how he wanted to hide as much as he could that he was the author of such a dastardly deed. But he did not succeed because they had recognized his face and other signs of his identity—what he was wearing, including his ruff, which was the fashion in those days.[2] They also told how Teresa had spent a long time under the water and how she had emerged through the good offices of a gallant young man.

The marquis and his wife listened in astonishment to the narrative of such an unexpected and strange event. On the one hand, the good judgment of their majordomo, his talents, and his character, and also the love he felt for Teresa because of her virtue, induced them to believe that he could not have done a thing so repugnant to his Christian and noble character.[3] On the other hand, they heard their maidservants' unanimous account of the event. The master and mistress's good judgment attributed it to a conspiracy of the maids against the majordomo—something majordomos of noble houses found themselves exposed to often because of petty domestic complaints. However, they were dissuaded from dismissing the incident when they noticed that Teresa kept silent and did not make accusa-

---

1 We translate *dueños* and *amos* as "masters" in plural, when these words really mean "master and mistress." We privilege the masculine in our translation to reflect the Spanish grammatical usage of the time.
2 The mention of the ruff adds a note of historicity to the narrative. This sartorial detail indicates that the scene took place sixty years in the past. There is an ironic distancing from the old times of the Hapsburg dynasty in comparison to the French fashion of the day in Bourbon mid-eighteenth-century Spain.
3 As appropriate to a grandee of Spain, the Marquis of Mancera's household is a replica of the royal court. The role of the majordomo was one of heightened status among the servants. He was supposed to be a *hidalgo* (a person of dignity), not a lower-class individual. This fact would gain him the respect from his master and deference from the other servants, who saw him as representing the moral authority and voice of the master.

tions like the others, when she was the aggrieved one. Because of her well-known virtue, they were convinced that she would not join the others in supporting a tattletale story, especially in a matter of such import. To dispel the doubt, once the ladies were calmed and quiet, the marquis took it upon himself to make an inquiry about the event. Calling the majordomo into his presence, he asked him how he had spent the afternoon and where he had been. The majordomo responded that during the entire afternoon he had been in his room in the quarters where his office was located. "How so?" the marquis replied. "You have not been in the Buen Retiro? You did not see the ladies and the maids by the big pool, and with them my beloved Teresa?" "Sir," the majordomo said, "I have neither seen the Retiro, nor the pool. I have not seen the ladies or Teresa either. I have not left the house all afternoon. If Your Excellency does not believe me, ask the other members of the household, and you will find out that I have not left the house at all this afternoon." "Enough," said the marquis. "There is a mystery here." After taking depositions from other servants and certifying that the majordomo had not left the house, he explained to the ladies that they were hallucinating. They insisted that their account was true. The personal signs they all noted in the one who kicked Teresa into the water belonged to the house majordomo. After she fell, they had tried to ascertain whether it was he, but he could not be found anywhere in sight.

When despite the majordomo's innocence the maids insisted on their story, the marquis and his wife were completely convinced that all had been a ruse from hell to deprive Teresa of her life. They were eager to identify the person who had rescued her from the water. Curious, they asked Teresa, but she could not give them any answer other than his description. Based on this, the marquis and his wife investigated for a while and showed Teresa a printed image of the glorious archangel Saint Raphael. As soon as she saw it, she said, overjoyed, "This is the one who took me out of the water."[4] Once they pondered the circumstances of the incident, her owners could doubt no longer. What Teresa said was so. From then on, they held her in even greater affection, which is all that the infernal Dragon gained from his cunning trick, one well prepared but badly executed.

In his perfidy he tried once more to kill Teresa by means of a Turkish slave girl, who was dissimilar to Teresa in color—the Turk was as white as she was beautiful—but equal in their common position as servants.[5] Since both were slaves, even if their owners held them in very different esteem, they had become very close friends. The devil, therefore, availed himself of this Turk to kill Teresa. He incited in her so strong an urge to murder Teresa that

---

4   The presence of holy prints is recurrent throughout the text. These prints are more than representations. They also possess the capacity for providing the identity of a saint, an angel, or Christ Himself. These prints also have thaumaturgy powers when Teresa Chicaba uses them, as we will see in a later chapter, when Sor Teresa stops the bombing of Salamanca by displaying a print of Saint Vincent Ferrer in one of the windows of the convent of La Penitencia (Chapter 33).

5   For the first time, Teresa's Black color is compared unfavorably with the complexion of a white woman. The equation of whiteness and physical beauty is a category of cultural value throughout this work. Thus, in spite of the protestation of Chapter 1 about the beauty of Black people in Africa, whiteness is seen as synonymous with beauty, even early in the narrative when Teresa observed the Child Jesus and His Mother by the fountain. Therefore, by this logic a Turkish slave woman will be beautiful while Teresa is naturally ugly. Teresa must have been acutely aware of the differences in standards of beauty around her, especially in the complicated household of the Marquis of Mancera. The Turkish slave girl remains nameless throughout the episode. "Turkish" meant in eighteenth-century Spain any person from the lands under the jurisdiction of the Ottoman Empire. See the Introduction, p. 77.

she felt determined to do it more than once. This blind passion would often overwhelm her, and the Turk would tell Teresa about it. However, the latter was confident of her divine protection. She paid little or no attention to these threats, considering from whom they came. Under the spell of a diabolical suggestion, the Turk was determined to kill Teresa and on more than one night kept a sharp knife under her pillow. When she tried to raise the knife and carry out her perverse intention, she found her furious passion suddenly calmed by the Omnipotent Arm that mitigates everything.[6] From then on the Abyss was always foiled; Teresa was freed; the Turk completely calmed.

---

6   This constitutes a biblical parallel with the passage of the sacrifice of Isaac (Genesis 22:1–19).

CHAPTER 12

Persuaded by Teresa, the Turkish girl converts.
She receives baptism. Teresa falls seriously ill.
God restores her heath with a miracle.

Once the Turkish girl was free from the infernal suggestion to kill Teresa that had disturbed her for so long, the ties of love and attachment grew stronger between them. The shared condition and common lot as slaves, together with their awareness of being so far away from their homelands, imprinted a common affection on their souls. Teresa pitied her friend for still being so close to the false law of Mohammed that it would not open her heart the slightest bit to the evangelical law.[1] Teresa used every opportunity she could find in their conversations to introduce the topic with skill and ability. But she only found disappointment, as the Turk persisted in her attachment to perverse dogmas and false beliefs. Such are the feigned flattery and promise of pleasures that religion instills in those who follow it. Teresa knew very well that the heroic deed of converting her was dependent solely on the effect of grace, but she did not cease in her fervent attempts to convince the Turkish girl of her error. The Turkish girl listened graciously to the well-reasoned arguments Teresa put forward; although they sweetly encroached on the Turk's powers of understanding, her will still refused to surrender to the soft yoke of the gospel.

Instead, the Turkish girl surrendered more easily to the ugly pleasure of a certain individual of supposed high character, who found himself prisoner to and smitten by the Turkish girl's beauty.[2] Forgetting the obligations of the position the Supreme Majesty had put him in, he cast aside all decency in order to follow his desire.[3] With promises and cant flattery, and also with the hope of fleeing with her back to her native country, he induced the Turkish girl to commit sin.[4] Once he had satisfied his pleasure, then like the most indecent of men, his desire waned instantly, and he was moved to the other extreme of hatred.

---

1 The presence of Muslim slaves in the household of the Marquis of Mancera is well attested to in documents describing the sale of two "Moorish" dark-skinned male slaves, one called Almanzor and the other Jergues (Archivo Histórico de Protocolos Notariales de Madrid, protocolo 11.410, fol. 79, year 1677).

2 We have translated the Spanish *elevado carácter* as "supposed high character" to heighten the irony of the description of the priest, who is an individual devoid of morality. The narrative supplies an excuse for the Spaniard by asserting that the beauty of the Turkish girl was nearly irresistible.

3 The text uses euphemistic language to indicate that the man who seduced the Turkish girl was a priest. The seduction of young women by priests, called "solicitation," was a serious crime. If the priest seduced a young girl under the guise of spiritual direction, he could be subject to the penalties of the Inquisition.

4 The promises were as outrageous as they were criminal. For a Christian, especially for a priest, to escape to a Muslim country was considered apostasy, a crime under the jurisdiction of the Spanish Inquisition. It was not uncommon for Spaniards to flee to North Africa—*Berbería*—and become Muslims, the so-called *renegados*. The Turkish slave girl had false hopes that this man would help her and become a *renegado*, a member of that exiled class of people who had exchanged religion and allegiance south of the Mediterranean.

When he obtained what he wanted, the Turkish girl found herself grievously deceived, and she never again saw the individual who had been the cause of her shame. The Turkish girl howled inside herself, but she never communicated her sorrows to anyone, because sorrows of this kind should never even reach one's lips. If previously she had refused to brush aside her false sect and surrender to the yoke of our holy faith, after this event she lived in a state of agitation caused by her dishonor and insult. She could only think of revenge. Teresa saw that her companion was sad—as was appropriate to such a plight. She asked insistently for the cause of her friend's sadness, concerned as she was for her health and her soul. But from the Turk came nothing but silence. As she did not denounce the author of her dishonor and thus avenge her affront on him, her sadness and melancholy led her to contract a mortal illness.

The marquis and his wife were attentive to the Turkish girl's physical health and the cure of her soul. For the first task, they entrusted all kinds of care and attention to physicians. For the second, they requested the presence in their household of individuals with the best credentials and reputation in the city. But as the physicians learned the mortal nature of her illness, the others discovered how little they could hope for the conversion of her soul, which was so addicted to the laws of her Mahomedan godlessness.[5] To every persuasive word spoken by learned individuals, all full of fervor and eloquence, she gave the same answer: "Allah no want me be Christian." They insisted with more efficient methods, but she did not change her response. Grace had reserved Teresa as the instrument of this victory. Following orders given by the marquis and his wife, Teresa went into the room to speak to the girl once the physicians had advised that she did not have much longer to live. Teresa approached the bed and spoke to her with that affability and sweetness that were so much a part of her. The sick girl, more at ease, answered: She could not become a Christian because she had a secret that she would not reveal to anyone. And that was the obstacle. "You will not tell it even to me?" replied Teresa. The Turkish girl answered back: "Yes, to you, I will tell. Get closer. I don't want them to hear." Teresa drew closer, and the sick girl gave her a brief account of everything that had happened to her, and concluded by saying: "From what I have learned about your Law, and according to what you, Teresa, have explained to me, I know that there is an order to forgive with all of one's heart those who have caused us injury. I will not forgive in any way this affront, or the one who caused it to me. See now if I can become a Christian!" This was the Turk's explanation, and in the short space of human discourse, she seemed to close all doors to her own remedy. Two words only Teresa said softly in her ear, and she laid down her wrath and anger against the author of her dishonor—Oh, the power of grace! The Turkish girl said loudly: "Me forgive, for God's sake, and die Christian."[6] It was done as she wished. Since Teresa had been working to explain to her the mysteries of the faith, she was baptized at once. Everybody approved and all rejoiced, especially the marquis and his wife. They could not stop wondering about the secrets of grace. It had rejected the most appropriate ways from so many spiritual and

---

5   We use the pejorative English term "Mohammedan," as it was customary in both English and Spanish texts of the time. The sickness of body and soul is presented in complementary fields: that is, the Turkish girl's body is condemned to death because of the state of her unrepentant and unconverted soul.
6   The use of broken Spanish by the Turkish girl singles her out as a non-acculturated individual, in contrast with the standard Spanish Teresa uses on every occasion. In fact, the Turkish slave girl speaks like Muslim characters in Spanish seventeenth-century theater.

learned men, and it had used Teresa to convert the Turk.[7] The latter, a few hours after being baptized, sent her soul flying directly to heaven.

Teresa took great consolation with the happy state of her friend, and the marquis, his wife, and the rest of the family were amazed at the depth of grace they were discovering in Teresa. Everybody's love for her was growing more and more when suddenly a fatal accident almost deprived them of the soothing consolation they found in her. Teresa was attacked by a high fever, accompanied by a stomach disease so severe that she could not keep down anything she ate. The marquis and his wife cared for her with great love. The physicians, eager to please them with the cure of such a precious treasure, used all their art and industry. But her stomach, stubborn in its disease, continued to throw up all food. The perverse humor was so rebellious to the medicines that it prevented Teresa from improving. She stayed in danger until Heaven came to her rescue with a miraculous event. One afternoon a religious man of well-known virtue came to visit her. He was a son of the Seraphic Francis.[8] Having been informed of Teresa's illness, he decided to ascertain her wishes and asked her if she wanted anything. Some fresh plums, said the patient; that is what I will eat with the least revulsion. The other maidservants laughed at a fancy so out of season, since they were in the worst of winter. But Heaven soon turned their laugh into amazement. The holy friar gave a light touch to his sleeve, and from it dropped the plums desired by the patient. They were as luscious and fresh as if they had just been picked from the branches during their appropriate season. Coming back to themselves from the amazement occasioned by the unexpected surprise, they all rushed to pick as many as they could. But the holy man contained their impulse with wit and humor, saying: Calm, ladies, calm. This fruit is for the patient. Let's give her one, and with it she can be cured from her malady. They did as he said. They gave one plum to the patient, and it was such efficient medicine that instantly her stomach was restored and she found herself as if she had never suffered any illness. She did not experience such a violent episode again.

---

7   The conversion of the Turkish girl has theological implications. Since it is grace that causes her conversion, the Turkish girl listens to the voice of a Black slave woman, powerless in the world, with more attention than she does to priests and other learned ecclesiastics.
8   The phrase "He was a son of the Seraphic Francis" means that Teresa's visitor was a Franciscan friar.

CHAPTER 13

Virtuous exercises in which she employed herself and the devotion with which she practiced them

Teresa had to reciprocate for and repay the repeated great favors with her virtues.¹ These clearly miraculous events and marvels were the work of the Almighty, who wanted to preserve her life free from those natural diseases that might be expected in someone who lived in a climate so distant from the one where she had been born.² The venerable priest from the previous chapter was put in charge of Teresa by the marquis and his wife, since he was their chaplain. He instructed her in the rudiments of spiritual life. Taught by him how to converse intimately with God through prayer, Teresa became so fond of the practice that she spent all her free time in this devout exercise. She hid from the sight of ladies and fellow maidservants, and she spent many hours in the solitude of the oratory with her celestial divine Master. If they were looking for her and they could not find where she was, they knew immediately that she would be in the oratory without fail. That was her home, where she could assure that her spirit would thrive.

Eager to pay back the great love the marchioness professed her, she wanted to make her mistress a participant in these spiritual matters. With the God-given eloquence of royalty, she made her mistress take to prayer so fervently that the marchioness at one point stopped receiving visits in order to spend entire afternoons with Teresa in prayer and spiritual exercises.³ Teresa continued in her fervor. She did not pay any mind to those things that the world

---

1   *Pagar* (to pay back) was an important ideological concept in the language of slavery, as it meant religious redemption through slavery. The slave has to pay back for the benefit of Christian salvation with work and with the exercise of virtue. Here virtue is obedience to the owner as well as to Catholic orthodoxy.

2   The author attributes Teresa's illness to the difference in climate between her native Africa and Spain. Medical science in the eighteenth century strongly believed that many illnesses were the product of particular climates, and changing from one to another would make the individual, normally a white European, subject to them. The occasions are few when the same argument is applied to the climatic needs of Black slaves in the Americas. In fact, the importation of Africans to the Americas was justified on the basis of similarity of climates between the two continents. Teresa's illness comes to justify this theory because she has been placed in the wrong climate, signifying that Spain was not a natural place for Black slaves.

3   Her spiritual ascendancy over the Marchioness of Mancera is explained through Chicaba's being of royal descent. In this, the text subscribes to the notion that all kings were put there by God, whether Christian or not. The devotional practices of the marchioness indicate a trend in Catholic spirituality among the upper classes. Married women of the aristocracy were advised to conduct their lives in a manner similar to that of someone in the convent. Many wealthy women, in fact, spent their widowhood in monasteries. An important example from the seventeenth century is that of the Infanta Isabel Clara Eugenia, ruler of the Netherlands who, after becoming a widow, adopted a nun's habit while still ruling the Spanish possession. See Cordula Van Wyhe, "Court and Convent: The Infanta Isabella and Her Franciscan Confessor Andrés De Soto," *Sixteenth Century Journal* 35.2 (2004): 421. Many Counter-Reformation convents were founded by widows, who sought a place of retreat in them. See Ángela Atienza López, "De beaterios a conventos. Nuevas perspectivas sobre el mundo de las beatas en la España moderna," *Historia Social* 57 (2007): 157. In some cases, older married couples chose to live monastic lives in separate convents. See Josefina Muriel, "Los conventos de monjas en la

appreciates and esteems. She was meek and peaceful with everyone, more humble than anyone else, and she chose to be the least of them, their inferior and slave. She was eager to become more and more one with God by means of Holy Communion. Through repeated requests and supplications, she obtained this favor from her director with more frequency.[4] At the same time that her love increased, she was becoming a more ardent Catholic, for which sake she had given up her own name so happily. So, whenever the ambassador of one of those princes, on whom the infelicity of heretical shadows had darkened the light of truth, visited the marquis or the marchioness, Teresa would come out screaming that they not deal with such people. She became so agitated by the fire of faith, which burned inside her, that things got to a point where the marquis and his wife ordered to have Teresa locked up whenever they received those visits again.[5] Such was the animosity she felt toward these night birds, who lacked the strong eyesight to see the rays cast by the Holy Eucharist. They avoided looking at it.[6] Instead, they covered their eyes with the hem of their capes, which was to deny with impiety the very real and physical presence of the majesty of Christ in the August Sacrament, which forever should be venerated.

In the sacrament, Teresa found the most glorious light. Christ tenderly unveiled for her the path she had to follow to be more intimate with her Master, which was the exercise of virtue those who wanted this kind of joy must practice. The progress was so quick, and the steps she gave on this path were so gigantic that her director became suspicious of his own advice, and made her communicate her spiritual concerns with several individuals. Many of them together might see what he suspected he could not see by himself. They might be able to discover if there was deceit there or not.[7] They put her through repeated tests, they

---

sociedad virreinal," *Artes De México* 198 (1979): 7–23. *Acta Capituli Provincialis Provinciae Hispaniae Ordinis Praedicatorum Celebrati in Conventu Sancti Indephonsi Regali Taurensi, Die 27. Aprilis, anni Domini 1749.* Sub R.A.P.N. Fr. Eugenio de Basualdo. Magistro Concionatore Regio. Priore Conventus S^ti Thomae Matritensis, Vicario Generali & Provinciali electo eiusdem Provinciae. Madrid, 149.

4   Access to Communion was not as frequent in the seventeenth and eighteenth centuries as it became later. The practice of daily Communion, for instance, was actively discouraged. In the case of women, their spiritual directors had strict control over their access to the sacrament of the Eucharist, sometimes denying it in order to create a sense of humility. It was not until in the twentieth century that the practice of frequent Communion was encouraged, by Pope Pius X (1903–1914). See Chapter 16 for limits imposed on Chicaba by her director.

5   The anti-Protestantism of Teresa is a reaction to her owner's political position, which was connected to the slave trade. The Marquis of Mancera, as a member of the Council of State, had frequent dealings with ambassadors from Holland and England, two Protestant countries heavily involved in the trafficking. Earlier in his life, during his father's viceroyalty, Mancera had led the naval defenses of Peru against the Dutch. As viceroy of New Spain, Mancera also led efforts to organize the defense of the coasts against English privateers. In his final report to the Crown as viceroy of Mexico in 1673, he expresses his opposition to the policy of the *asiento*, the royal monopoly of the slave trade granted to foreigners (Hanke and Rodriguez 5:23). When Chicaba arrived in Spain, in 1685, the *asiento* had passed to a Dutch man, Balthazar Coymans, who to no one's surprise was a Protestant living in Madrid and Seville. See María Cristina Navarrete, *Génesis y desarrollo de la esclavitud en Colombia: Siglos XVI y XVII* (Cali, Colombia: Universidad del Valle Programa Ed., 2005), 55.

6   The text refers to Protestants as "night birds" (*aves nocturnas*), a metaphor for bats. Twice in this hagiography, situations associated with the demonic or with evil are connected to bats or dark birds. Given their association with slavery, this text might also be an indictment of the slave trade.

7   The spiritual director is afraid that Teresa may be the victim of an illusion, a false sense of the divine, through no fault of her own. Being a woman and being Black made her doubly suspect of indulging in this kind of religious practice, which was not acceptable to the Church.

examined her continuously, and they only found new ways to praise the hand of God, who gives His favors so freely, the way He wants, and to those mortals He wants. They encouraged Teresa and comforted her director, assuring both of them that it was indeed God's spirit and His narrow perfect way. The priest who directed Teresa was perfect himself, and yet he had misgivings and fear. This was a clear sign that God was granting many favors to his darling, but their account has been kept from us, because of Teresa's humility and modesty. However, the marvel that follows could not be hidden in silence.

A lay brother in the Order of the Holy Trinity of the illustrious Discalced Family, a man of a most exemplary life, rescued in Barbary an image of Christ, our Eternal Good. The image had been dragged there by the impious, who are perpetually hungry for gold.[8] He rescued this sovereign effigy in the year 1682. He came to Madrid, and he took it out in a procession, surrounded by general applause. The entire city attended; and in the devotion of their hearts, the image found some satisfaction for the indecorous treatment suffered at the hands of the perfidious Moors. In order to promote and increase even more the affection of the faithful and the devotion to that image, several prints were made in which the entire event was represented. The image itself had experienced some of the torments that our Redeemer had suffered in his most Sacred Body.[9] The prints were distributed throughout the court. The Marquis of Mancera, as a person of high distinction, was offered a copy for every member of his household.[10] Only Teresa was left without the gift, perhaps because the one who distributed them was a bit careless, or because Heaven wanted to give it to her by itself, as the prodigy would demonstrate. Not having such a precious possession saddened Teresa, and the only consolation for her pain, thanks to her humility, was to see herself as unworthy of owning it. She suffered in silence, but she remained restless. One day she was in a big room with other companions, when suddenly the top of a big freight trunk full of clothes opened. All were startled. Teresa, who was not afraid of anything in this world, went to see what had happened. She found what she was sighing for. She found that because the

---

8   The Order of the Holy Trinity, or Trinitarians, had as their mission to rescue Christians who had been captured by North African Muslims and taken to Algiers, on the Barbary Coast. Many people left money in their wills for the ransom of Christian captives, on whose behalf the Trinitarians negotiated. The Marchioness of Mancera donated funds for this purpose. This was also done by less affluent people. For example, a slave, Catalina de la Cruz, left one *real* for this purpose ("Testamento de la esclava Catalina de la Cruz," Archivo Histórico de Protocolos Notariales de Madrid, protocolo 8.635, fol. 494, December 6, 1663).

9   This is the statue *Cristo de Medinaceli*, a popular subject of devotion in Spain. The image was transported from Mahdia (Mazarrón) in Morocco to Madrid after the Spanish lost the town to Moroccan troops in 1681. Therefore, these events took place well before Sor Teresa Chicaba arrived in Spain. The text in the *Vida* may be referring to the erection in Madrid of a new chapel in 1689 on a plot of land ceded by the Duke of Medinaceli, a member of the Council of State (as was the Marquis of Mancera). Prints depicting its damage in the hands of Muslims inspired double reparation: physical restoration of gold and jewels, and the spiritual reparation for the sacrilege it endured. The image becomes a true simulacrum of Christ's passion, but with some changes. The *berberiscos* (inhabitants of Algiers) are in the role of the perpetrators of Christ's torture and crucifixion. Thus, the author, consistent with the popular image, represents them as the national and religious enemies of Christian Spain. See the discussion of this image in the Introduction, p. 78.

10 "Household": The original says *familia*, to be understood in the Roman sense of "members of a household," which included servants and slaves. *Familia* comes from *fama* (fame), alluding to those who are known by the name of the master. In this anecdote the text presents the true status of Chicaba in the Mancera household and her exclusion from favors.

lock had burst open, a quite large print was showing from one of the sides of the trunk. She took it in her hands, and she saw that it was Jesus the Nazarene. She slipped it away; and, reflecting upon it to herself, she realized that no one could have put it there, because the coffer did not belong to anybody in particular who might be able to lift it. It was one of those trunks that rarely were open. She recognized that it was a gift from her celestial Master, as a reward for her humble suffering. The print is still preserved in the convent of La Penitencia, under the care of someone who keeps it in the esteem it deserves.

CHAPTER 14

Furious persecution launched by infernal cunning against Teresa's director

The common Enemy of humankind was embarrassed and ashamed to see how the Highest One foiled with tender and secret providence his malevolent ruses to take Teresa's life away. After he had tested his powers to make her renounce her path and spiritual call with no other fruit than his own confusion, he was determined to spend the remainder of his guile seeing if he could destroy everything in one stroke. He sneaked in a new strategy, this time more dangerous because it affected Teresa more fully. What were the means? They were the most extraordinary that his perverse and obstinate mind could have imagined. He aimed his shots against the director, so he could take the two of them away in one blow. Once he had the director and teacher defeated and at his feet, he fancied it would be easy to overcome Teresa. Because the house servants always made Teresa's cross a heavier one to bear, he used them to achieve and put his ruse into action.

These house servants saw and noticed the exemplary and ordered life Teresa led under the direction of the venerable priest.[1] They observed that both maintained composure and devotion. Secular business found them withdrawn and distant, even in household matters that appeared necessary. Their moments of prayer were many and Teresa took Holy Communion frequently.[2] The evidence of such virtuous life made teacher and disciple advance, without pursuing it, in the good graces of the marquis and his wife. Envious of the favors and esteem they all saw that they missed in themselves, the house servants started to conspire against the director with an animus and determination that were truly diabolical. They stubbornly demanded that the priest should give them a detailed and extensive account of Teresa's life. Who could believe this request in a family as Christian and Catholic as that of the Marquis of Mancera and his wife! As befits Catholic heroes, they always prided themselves as having a most virtuous household! Who could have thought that this nonsense could even cross the mind of a Catholic person? How could a confessor give an account of the intimate matters that go on in the soul of someone under his direction and rule?[3] And such a Christian mouth proposed this petition! What else can it be but the devil's cunning, a request made through his malice, so one and the others might fall into the fatal abyss?

The venerable priest listened to the proposition not without scandal, but he followed his duty and refused to answer so impertinent a question. His refusal to yield and answer

---

1 The text in Spanish uses the word *ajustada*, which means "right," "moderate," or "well ordered." This implies that Teresa did not show an inclination toward sexual or any other kind of license.
2 Teresa takes Communion in front of the other servants. She needed permission from her director to do so. This is a public display of her virtue and his favoritism. Through spiritual practices, Teresa created a different hierarchy in the household, which otherwise placed her at the bottom of its social ranks.
3 This request was not only sinful but also criminal, because it constituted sacrilege. The seal of secrecy, which governs the confession theoretically, does not distinguish between classes—masters and slaves. However, the marquis and his wife could exert pressure on the priest to tell them about Teresa's intimate matters. He was their chaplain and their employee.

became a point of honor for the curious servants, and they let him know in public. There was no excess, distress, or domestic problem customary in the houses of the great that they did not attribute to him. He was well aware of the assaults and ploys of his adversaries, but he remained constant in his determination and purpose. He paid no attention to them. Every time there was some disturbance or some problem, they would ask questions. To each enquiry, he always answered with his silence. Some days the persecution was so unbearable and excessive that it was reflected in the venerable director's face. Teresa noticed it. As a faithful disciple desiring to alleviate her teacher's distress, she would enquire with worry the reason for his sorrow. She asked what was wrong, but although she repeated the question many times, she could not extract the slightest word from him.[4] Here finally the Enemy had Teresa concerned about her director's sorrow and had him distressed by the repeated attacks and insistence of silly questioners. However, Teresa offered her dedication and the director his patience, and together they freed themselves from the infernal cunning.

The impertinent inquirers saw how little they advanced with their words, intrigues, and gossip in overrunning the fortitude and constancy of the minister. Instead of distancing him from the esteem of his masters, they saw how it kept increasing. So they took the cruel decision to pass from words into actions. They waited for the pale shadows of the night to accomplish their plan. Using a false pretext, they took the venerable priest to a room in the most remote area of the house. Once there, they closed the door with violence. They asked him: "Tell us all about the kind of life that negress leads and of the false pretense of the two of you, your stories, and the schemes you use to keep the marquis and his wife deceived. You two are the only ones who enjoy their confidence, and they do not pay attention to the rest of their family. If you do not tell us, you will lose your life, and without it, the negress will not be able to use you as the author of her high tales, with which you have put the entire house in disarray." They spoke to him full of fury, and they tried to break his determination by putting a firearm to his chest. But the venerable priest was neither defeated by their threats nor frightened by the proximity of the gun. With peaceful meekness, he made them understand that their question was of such a nature that he could not give them an answer, even if he lost a thousand lives. The only life he had he would sacrifice to God with pleasure in order to keep the secret and reserve due to his religious orders and his position.[5] "Kill him!" replied one who was more furious at seeing such courage and spirit undaunted by such great risk. Another one, a bit more peaceful or maybe less blinded by his wrath, quieted the rest, once he realized how ugly the case would be if they took the life of a minister of God, or maybe because he feared his own fate, if they executed the priest.[6] He explained to them the danger they risked if they put into effect their intentions. They listened and reflected a bit on it, which was not a small thing, and they suspended their diabolical impulses. But they all agreed that they should punish the refusal to answer that they called stubbornness and perversity. Grabbing the venerable priest among them all, they tossed him up and down in a blanket until they felt they had punished him enough for the pretended fault, thus releasing their wrath and anger.

---

4 The silent suffering of the spiritual director functions in the text as a virtuous example of the indignities of slavery that Teresa Chicaba also underwent in silence.
5 The scene promotes the example of a heroic priest, but it reveals also the atmosphere of violence present in the Mancera household, where several slaves lived.
6 Killing a priest was a very serious crime, a sacrilege, which was punished with the death penalty. It would have brought dishonor to the Mancera household.

CHAPTER 15

Teresa's director leaves the house of the marquis. Under the order of Divine Providence, he hands her over to the Sons of our Great Father Saint Gaetano.[1]

The ill-doers were pleased and haughty after their daring act. Forgetting themselves and their Christian birth, they had laid hands on the virtuous priest. But the latter was even happier, because he had endured insults and harassment while remaining resolute in defending the obligations of his position and dignity. Only the Abyss was foiled and shamed once again. All the schemes its malice had devised had been frustrated, though they might have been powerful enough to destroy a life so virtuous and a direction so perfect; both made the devil restless and provoked his agitation and sorrow. So no sooner had the ministers of impiety finished their cruel prank on the priest, than they opened the room where they had locked him and kicked him out of the house. The priest gave due thanks to God that He had liberated him from so manifest a danger to his life and had given him the fortitude and courage to stand firm in his obligations without surrendering to the frenzied threats they made against him.

Nobody in the house of the marquis heard the fracas. The remoteness and seclusion of the room, the precautions taken by the authors of the scene, and the suffering and patience with which the venerable priest behaved shrouded this event in oblivion. It would have never come to light had Teresa not uncovered it. She was concerned, as I have said, to see her director with melancholy and sadness written across his face. However, after the attack, his face no longer expressed any worry. So after repeated requests, she forced him to reveal the cause of such a sudden change. He condescended to her request, telling all that had happened. Teresa listened, not without amazement. And while her patience sealed her lips about her own sorrows, afflictions, and anguish, when she saw the priestly dignity abused and offended in the person of her director and father, she became a lioness in the defense of God's honor in His ministers and priests. She told her confessor that she would not stop until she told her masters, so they would punish those mad people and avoid future insolence of this kind. The director tried to calm her as much as he could with tenderness and words of prudence. "I"—said Teresa—"do not mind the pain I feel about how they have treated you. I agree that you should forgive this affront out of your Christianity and virtue. But is it right to leave unpunished the injury committed against my celestial and divine Spouse by offending one of his ministers? Certainly not. You must forgive me, but I will tell the marquis and his wife of this serious act of disrespect, so they will punish, as they must, your aggressors for the insult done to my God in the person of Your Worship."[2]

Thus, Teresa explained the zeal that burned in her heart to defend God's honor by taking care of the good name and glory of His ministers. Since he realized that he was not going to

---

1   This is the first mention in the text of the early relation Sor Teresa had with the Theatines.
2   Chicaba is speaking here in the first person and addressing her director in a tone used by royalty or people accustomed to rule others.

convince her and that she was bent on her resolution of tell her masters what had happened, the confessor had to resort to his authority and expressly command her not to tell anyone about the incident. Teresa bowed to the voice of obedience. She closed her lips and offered her sorrow as a sacrifice to God in compensation for the injury that had been committed against Him through His minister. She obeyed the precept so faithfully that she complied with it beyond death itself. Only many years after her director, the marquis, and his wife had passed away into a better life did she relate the incident. The venerable priest remained in the house of the marquis only for a short while after these events. When he received a new assignment and position of more importance outside Madrid, he was forced to leave the court.[3] One of the great travails Heaven sent Teresa throughout her life was how short a time her directors were with her.[4] As soon as she settled with one, a new position, or death, would take him away from her sight. And since this sorrow would last for the rest of her life, Heaven wished her to embrace this cross early. She asked her director, since his absence was going to be unavoidable, to find someone else to be in charge of her soul. He accepted the request with pleasure and left her under the charge and care of Father Ignacio Araújo, of the Regular Clerks of Saint Gaetano. From that point onward, Teresa never was without a director from that saintly family.[5] She kept this allegiance even after she professed and gave obedience to the sacred Order of Preachers, under the command of the highly respected prior of the convent of San Esteban, as I shall say later.[6] The most important director, and the one who brought out more facets to her virtue, was the Venerable Father Don Jerónimo Abarrategui y Figueroa. Known for his virtue, Teresa's growth was entrusted to his spiritual teachings by all those who directed the aforementioned convent.

---

3   It is noteworthy that the text omits the name of the director and the details of his departure from the Mancera household.
4   One could speculate that in some cases, her position as a slave woman, and later as a *tercera*, was the motivation behind the frequent change of directors. This observation appears again in Chapter 27.
5   Father Jerónimo Abarrategui becomes Chicaba's future spiritual director. Through him and other directors who belonged to the Theatines, the *Vida* establishes a genealogy of her directors, those in charge of her spiritual life. Thus the *Vida* becomes a Theatine document that supports the members of the order in their attempts to canonize one of their own.
6   The text is referring to her profession as a member of the secular tertiaries in the Dominican convent of La Penitencia.

CHAPTER 16

Teresa's desire for religious life. Difficulties that slowed her entrance

Once Teresa's first director left the household of the marquis and his wife, she surrendered her obedience to Father Araújo, who recognized in her fertile ground that could yield abundant fruit. The evangelical seed multiplied with his counsel. He convinced her of the need for more contemplation and withdrawal from all worldly affairs—even those that appear necessary and obligatory in a grandee's household.[1] He had her spend more time in intimate exchange with God through prayer. He unfurled the sails of her fervor and love with repeated access to Holy Communion. The Holy Spirit fanned the flame of her virtue. The volcano of love that had been lit inside her burned more and more toward her celestial Master. Impelled by this fire, she was determined to brush the world aside and withdraw to the cloister. She reasoned correctly that in seclusion she would find peace and satisfaction in the desire to give herself up wholly to God. She would then celebrate her mystical nuptials with that White Child to whom she had made a vow so long ago.

Teresa informed her director of her decision. Wisely and prudently, he wished to take some time before coming to a resolution so that he could explore and see if her desire was ardent and constant, because it could have been one of those infertile fires that blind with their brightness and daze by their false light. I do not know why philosophy calls these manifestations "Saint Elmo's fire."[2] It would be more proper to name them *false flames*, a name that is more appropriate. This is the case with those unhappy creatures that spend miserable lives in religious seclusion or even outside in the world for not having examined whether it was the Holy Spirit who moved them to choose their vocation or just a flame coming from their own desire. One must discern one's calling over considerable time. In the case of Teresa, this time produced the desired effect and proved that her desire was coming from God. She remained constant in the midst of repeated and rigorous tests put to her by her director. The one that was most conducive to the life she wanted to choose consisted of completely breaking her own will. Whenever Teresa eagerly proposed a particular spiritual exercise, her director would most surely reject it. When suffused with love, she would seek both relief and fuel for her fire in Holy Communion; her director would skillfully deny the Holy Bread to her and then find Teresa eager for the sacrifice.[3] Once he certified by these and other repeated tests that her vocation came from God, Teresa's confessor decided to give her the permission she sought. He told Teresa, and she, full of happiness and joy,

---

1. The text repeats almost verbatim what Teresa had done under the previous director. Like other saints of lowly extraction (such as Saint Isidro and Saint Martin de Porres), their prayer seems to be at odds with their servile duties. It represents a clash of authorities, one on earth and one in heaven. This sets the scene for the poem on Chapter 35.
2. In the original Spanish, "Saint Elmo's fire" appears as *fuegos fatuos*, a translation of the Latin *ignis fatuus*; it is also known in Spanish as *El fuego de san Telmo* and in English as "will-o'-the-wisp." It refers to the ghostly lights sometimes seen at night or twilight—often over bogs. It looks like a flickering lamp and is sometimes said to recede if approached. Much folklore surrounds this phenomenon.
3. As noted in earlier chapters, denial of Communion was a typical test given by confessors and spiritual

congratulated herself repeatedly for her good fortune. He directed her to present her case to the marchioness, who had to give her consent and permission.[4] For without it, Teresa, for many reasons, could not achieve her goal.[5]

Teresa waited for the appropriate occasion to comply with her director's command. When it presented itself, she told the marchioness of her desire, the particular favors God had bestowed on her, and finally, the vocation He had given her. Not to answer God's calling would be ungrateful. The marchioness listened carefully and with peaceful meekness answered her:

> Daughter, God forbid that I be a party to obstructing the vocation God has given you. But you must realize that the sort of religious life you wish to undertake is full of rigors and hardships, more than you can either fathom or endure. You can hardly stand on your feet in my house, amidst ease and leisure, because of the difference you find in this climate, so contrary to yours.[6] How are you going to withstand the sufferings of the religious life you are seeking? In my house, by being conscientious and virtuous, do you not have the same means that lead to the goals of a religious life? Who puts barriers to your retreat? Do you not live continuously in the oratory, doing your spiritual exercises? Do you have any other obligation than to take care of your soul? Do you not go to church often enough and with the appropriate decency whenever your director commands you to? If all this is true, then why do you want to leave my house, Teresa, and start a life that you may not be able to continue? Do you want to leave me alone when, as you can see, my soul improves in your company? Although Heaven may deprive me of you, I would accept it with resignation and be happy to make the sacrifice; but what really gives me pause, my daughter, are my doubts. Is this God's calling or just a sudden impulse, which therefore may not be firm and permanent? Please consult your director once again. Put it in God's hands, and I will make others do the same. May His Majesty give us light as to whether your intention is to His greater honor and glory.[7]

---

directors to nuns and women in general. The sacrifice would increase the desire for the sacrament. Again, courtly love themes form the controlling metaphor for this relationship of mystical union. This practice of withholding the Eucharist is an example of the trope of the deferral of consummation.

4 The text indirectly acknowledges that the real authority lay with the Marchioness of Mancera, as Teresa's legal owner. This passage encodes three reasons for seeking this permission. First, the marquis and the marchioness were surrogate parents, whose permission Chicaba needed; second, Chicaba asserts that she is a free agent in pressing for her religious vocation; third, Chicaba is a slave and must be emancipated before entering a convent. See the Introduction, p. 80.

5 There were basically four possible impediments to her profession as a nun: she was the marchioness's slave, she was Black, her allegedly noble birth might be in doubt, and the marchioness would have to provide the money for Chicaba to enter a convent.

6 This is the second mention of difference in climate to explain why Teresa's health was not good. The text uses the racialized discourse of the world's climates that was fashionable at the time in order to explain why a Black nun might not be eligible for cloistered life. What that difference would be remains unexplained, but it was deemed sufficient. As late as the end of the 1950s or the beginning of the 1960s, when racial integration was clearly becoming a reality, some priests in the United States still maintained that Black women were psychologically unsuited for religious life. A few separate congregations for Black women were founded in the United States in the nineteenth century. Most other congregations either excluded Black candidates or segregated their housing in convents until the early 1960s.

7 The marchioness's "to His greater honor and glory" is a rephrasing of the Jesuit motto *Ad maiorem Dei gloriam*, "To the greater glory of God."

CHAPTER 17

Teresa continues with the impulse for her vocation. Ruse from the devil to stop it

Teresa listened carefully to the sound reasons her mistress offered. Since Teresa always held her in the esteem due a person of her station, her mistress's words echoed in her soul. But a strong vocation, one divinely driven, was knocking at the door of her heart. No human argument could subdue her desire. Once again, she told her director about the matter, and he realized that such a delicate flower was better transplanted to a religious cloister than left exposed to the winds of the world. Therefore, he made her go back to her mistress and make the same plea. Teresa acted as she was told; with the most expressive words that grace provided her, she spoke to the marchioness in such a fashion that she made her mistress realize that Teresa's vocation was genuine, and that it was God who spoke through her. In her, He wanted to fulfill His most holy will. Her Excellency took under her charge to speak to the marquis. It was more difficult to obtain his permission. He was less willing than the marchioness to let go of the affection he had for the Black slave. Teresa and the marchioness had reasons to fear that he would not grant her desire so easily. But the human heart is in God's hands. The marchioness had little difficulty in getting his permission, and even the marquis became the advocate of Teresa's cause.

Mistress and servant both offered thanks to God with great demonstrations of love because their intent was being accomplished. The marquis was considerate and favorable to the idea, but the infernal Enemy was enraged to see that the Black woman was about to hit right into the white of the target.[1] He devised a means that would have frustrated all their intentions, and the marquis and his wife would not have been able to stop it. It was the case that a French vessel went to Guinea, arriving in La Mina Baja del Oro, Teresa's homeland.[2] An uncle of hers was among the slaves they captured. The French sailed back and having received information from the other slaves about this individual—his high birth, wealth, nobility, and authority—they thought he would be a worthy present to His Majesty Louis XIV, who ruled France at the time.[3] Notified about this slave, and about his person and his qualities, with true regal spirit the king treated him as was appropriate to his high birth and blood. All expenses were charged to the public treasury. He remained in that court for some

---

1 *La negra estaba tan próxima a acertar en el blanco de su dicha*: A play on words for the bull's eye of a target, which during these times was white and not black.
2 The involvement of the French in the slave trade increased during the third part of the seventeenth century. French vessels trafficked with the kingdom of Arada as early as 1670. When they visited the kingdom, they noticed the presence of Christians there. The king of Arada had been educated by the Portuguese in São Tomé and was familiar with Christian customs, although he had chosen not to become a Christian himself (Law, "Religion, Trade and Politics," 44ff.).
3 Diplomatic relations between Arada and France started with Matheo Lopes, who had been an ambassador of the king of Arada to the court of Louis XIV in 1670. The king of Arada requested the presence of Christian missionaries for his existing Christian community. Matheo Lopes had been a translator for the French traders who had visited the kingdom. The French sent two Capuchin friars to the area in 1671 and later between 1681 and 1684 (Law, "Religion, Trade and Politics," 49–52).

time. Never to miss an opportunity to increase their commerce, the French thought that the best way to further their interest would be to restore the prisoner to his own court, so that once installed there, he would protect their commercial ships. Under his shelter, they could navigate safely to that large kingdom.[4] Just as they devised it, they put the plan into action. On his way back to his kingdom, he wanted to travel through Spain. He came with letters of introduction for the king and his cabinet from France. He was received and lodged by order of His Majesty with the splendor that befitted such a guest and such a host.[5] Mancera was one of the grandees King Carlos II held in highest esteem. So once Juan Francisco (this was the Black man's name) paid his respects to His Catholic Majesty, he went to visit the Marquis of Mancera. He was informed that the marquis had a Black woman in his family. Juan Francisco wanted to see her and ask about her homeland. He knew from the answer that, in front of him, he had the very one whose absence had filled his and her parents' eyes with copious tears.[6] Ecstatic with joy at having found his niece, after so much time and in a place so distant and remote from their people, he revealed to her who he was. He told her of the joyous conversion of her parents and most of their vassals, and also that her father, mother, and brothers, reborn in the baptismal waters, had already passed away.[7] Since there was no closer heir than she, the scepter and rule belonged to her by right.

Teresa was confused, although she felt encouraged by so much strange news.[8] She had not heard anything from her homeland since she left it. She gave her uncle a brief account of her voyage, the dangers she had encountered, and the miracles Heaven had worked to deliver her. She now was happy and content. The marquis and his wife loved her very much. She was thankful for their welcome and goodwill toward her. But above all, she told him about the privileges given her from God's hands. With this, she finished the conversation, and the first visit ended. The visit had not made a big impression on her soul. She was only interested in following the fervent impulses of her vocation. Hell, however, could not stand Teresa's constant foiling of its ruses. She was securing her fortune in Religion. The devil tried to obstruct with all its might the accomplishment of her desire. He planted in her uncle thoughts that were even more dangerous because they were disguised under the cloak of

---

4 This is an example of a silence in the text. Refusing to talk directly about slavery saved the intellectual class from having to call into question accepted ideologies of race. The *Vida* is euphemistic here. By commerce, it is referring to the slave trade. The utterance of this word would send the entire narrative into a crisis, as the text would imply that Chicaba's people were providers of slaves themselves, and Chicaba was a queen of a slave-trading kingdom. The balance that the hagiographic genre must maintain is a delicate one that asserts Chicaba's royal origins and downplays slavery.

5 The king of Spain is not to be outdone by Louis XIV. Exchanges of hospitality to strangers of noble blood, even if unknown and in exile, are indications of chivalrous behavior.

6 The scene of recognition is part of the genre of the Byzantine romance that had been a staple in seventeenth-century literature. See the Introduction, p. 74.

7 The story of her parents' conversion and with them the rest of the kingdom to Christianity has a moral effect on the reader of the time. The future saint's parents die as Christian, and the text thereby establishes a Christian genealogy for Sor Teresa. See the Introduction, pp. 62, 74.

8 As in much of the narrative tradition of slaves in the United States, the motif of the return to Africa—*sankofa*—is present here as well. This is a repetition of the temptation to return that is in the scene of the pond at the Retiro Park in Chapter 10. The encouragement of news from home gestures toward the idea that a memory of home is still alive with Chicaba. Without this memory, we cannot account for the vivid recollections in the opening chapters. For the concept of *sankofa* (the return to Africa) and memory of Africa, see the Introduction, p. 76.

God's service. The uncle planned to take his niece with him. He presented his intention to several courtiers. Taking Teresa with him would be a great service to Christendom. Being the king's daughter, she had all the right to claim the crown. If he married her, scepter and rule would pass to their issue without leaving the family. Acting politically, the courtiers heard the Black man. They liked his reasons and informed Carlos II. This Catholic prince remanded the matter to Teresa for her to resolve. They told the marquis and his wife what was happening. They in turn acted in the same way and gave her freedom to choose whatever she liked.

These conversations reached Teresa's ears, and her worries and anguish cannot be described sufficiently. She pleaded with her sweet Spouse to undo this intrigue that the Infernal Malice had created to upset her. The devil would not live or rest until he saw Teresa totally destroyed. Her uncle the king came to tell her of his intent. He tried with as many arguments as he could muster to incline her to his opinion. He presented her with the opportunity for increasing the Catholic faith among her vassals and in the entire kingdom. But Teresa remained firm and constant. She told him with absolute clarity that she would not follow him. He could go back to his homeland with her blessing, for since God and Nature had put the crown on his head, his greatness and majesty would be sufficient to care for the propagation of the Christian faith without any need of her presence. The king was sad and disconsolate when he saw the firmness Teresa showed in turning down the chance to follow him. But thinking that in the end she would relent, he did not give up hope for his enterprise. He repeated the visits and conversation without obtaining more fruit than the sheer disillusionment of seeing that he could not turn her strong mind around. Once he saw that sweet and tender means produced nothing, the uncle resorted to violent and rough ones. With the private help of courtiers, he tried to take his niece by force at the time of his departure. The very ones who would help him escape were covering his back, for in case they received orders to look for him, they would perform a comedy rather than a real search. Everything was arranged so that they all thought it would be impossible to fail. The uncle and a sizable retinue went to the marquis's house to bid farewell to His Excellency and to his niece. Early in the visit he asked for his Teresa. The marquis and his wife gave orders to call her, but she was not unaware of the malicious plan the visit involved. She hid in such a way that no servant, either male or female, was able to find her anywhere in the whole house. Juan Francisco realized that the hour marked for his departure was approaching; so, against his will, he had to go without seeing his niece, or accomplishing the goal of his well-laid plan.[9]

---

9 Juan Francisco, the uncle, represents a false African prince, a figure circulating in European courts during the seventeenth and eighteenth centuries. His coming from the French court echoes other examples present in the literature of the time, such as the case of Aniaba (McCloy 16–18), which we described in the Introduction, pp. 46n59, 111n85. The Spanish dynastic change was influenced by the French, In a household like Mancera's, which was so well connected with the affairs of France at the time of Spanish dynastic change, when French influence was becoming very present, hearing of these African princes would not have been uncommon.

CHAPTER 18

*The marquis and his wife give orders to have
Teresa's wishes fulfilled. A spiritual person tells her
in which convent she is going to be a nun.*

We left Teresa hiding and concealing herself to foil her uncle and his companions' attempt to kidnap her. As soon as he left the marquis's house, she came out of seclusion from the room. She was happy and joyful at having thus triumphed over herself through the work of grace by renouncing the advantages of power and the scepter.[1] Her appearance calmed the apprehensions she had caused to her owners. Not having been able to find her had confused them. When they saw her, they realized with satisfaction how much love and affection this new Christian showed for the tender yoke of the gospel because she generously despised everything in order to remain under it.[2] In truth this was one of the devil's most dangerous ruses, the most cunning of his tricks planned and tried against Teresa's virtue and perfection. As a child she had experienced veneration and acclaim by her people. She had been uprooted from that prominent station, and had fallen to the lowly one of a slave. When she had the opportunity to go back and re
cover easily scepter, homeland, power, and crown, she renounced and rejected everything with a generous and resolute spirit. What else could it be but the effect of divine grace?

Impelled by that grace, Teresa's desire to become a nun grew in her bosom. The marquis and his wife put all their effort and care into this affair. Teresa had no particular religious order in mind. That there were no nuns in Spain like there were in other places from the religious institute to which Father Ignacio belonged contributed in no small part to her indecision.[3] As Teresa's spiritual director, he would have coveted this precious treasure for his family if there were any monastery for her to enter. She thought all were appropriate to serve her Master. So her owner gave orders to make insistent requests at different convents, all within Madrid. But none was successful.[4] When everything seemed completely arranged,

---

1 The figure of the uncle, Juan Francisco, serves several functions in the text. His marriage proposal comes after Chicaba has made clear her intentions to enter a convent. Marriage prospects were the most important obstacle for a woman to fulfill her religious vocation, and these episodes are present in many *vidas*. The protagonist has to reject a tempting marriage proposal. The other function the text presents in this adventure is the rejection of political and social uplift. Marriage would have restored Chicaba to her royal status back in her homeland, which she rejects.
2 The term "new Christian" as applied to Chicaba has overtones in the discourse of *limpieza de sangre* (purity of blood) that still prevailed in Spain. Old Christians were eligible for social privilege, whereas "new Christians"—converted from Judaism, Islam, and other religions—and their descendants faced serious social barriers.
3 Father Don Ignacio is Father Ignacio Araújo, another Theatine. As her spiritual director, he is trying to place Teresa in a convent, although without success. The Theatines did not have a women's branch or "second order" like the Dominicans, Franciscans, or Augustinians.
4 No convent in Madrid would accept her, even though her patron was the marquis of Mancera. The requirement for *limpieza de sangre* and racial prejudice were so strong that the practice of exclusion overruled even the entreaties of someone as powerful as a former viceroy of Mexico and a member of one of the king's councils.

all difficulties settled, and her entry in the cloister imminent, an unexpected, even minimal mishap, the slightest obstacle, came to undo everything. This pained Teresa inconsolably. Judging herself unworthy of so much joy, she humbled herself in conformity to the Sovereign Will. Impelled and encouraged by the love that the Spirit kept stirring, her desire grew. She pleaded with her celestial Spouse constantly in her prayers. She mortified her innocent flesh with new torments, cilices, and punishments to keep Heaven favorable.[5] Between the anguish of her desire and the humble disappointment of not obtaining what she wanted, she lived in a continuous state of anxiety.

Never in her virtuous life had Teresa worried about whether Nature had clothed her face in white or Black.[6] But this time it served her as an occasion for martyrdom because it delayed her loving wishes so much. In all the convents of Madrid where they discussed her entry, attempts proved fruitless just because she was Black.[7] The gold offered by the marquis and his wife with a liberal and generous hand for this purpose could not compensate for her natural defect.[8] In the end she could not obtain the consolation of wearing a religious habit in Madrid. Her soul was left with this sorrow, and although she accepted it, she entered the darkest of nights in the midst of the worst tribulations. The marquis and his wife tried to soothe her with wise excuses, but she found her greatest consolation in her spiritual father. He encouraged her with tender and sweet words and urged her not to slacken one bit in the practice of her spiritual exercises. He said to her that all the previous difficulties would be overcome with the help of divine grace. God was wont to test those souls that truly seek their Master so that they do so free from other concerns. She should accept this with resignation, and she would see her wish fulfilled to her entire satisfaction and consolation. Heaven did not overlook her plight but helped her in her anguish. So when her sorrows were at their worst, a spiritual person of renowned virtue went to see her. After uttering words of consolation for her sorrow, he told her as he bid farewell: "In the end, Teresa, you will be a nun in the Order of Saint Dominic in the city of Salamanca, in the convent they call La Penitencia." I do not believe that Teresa had ever heard of that city or that convent, but the result gave credit to the pronouncement.

---

5 In the original Spanish, *cilicios* is a kind of rough garment used to mortify the flesh. In modern times it is a barbed metal piece that is applied around the upper arm or leg. The use of this form of mortification had to be supervised by a spiritual director.
6 This is an example of the racial discourse in the text. Sor Teresa's Blackness is defined as an accident of nature and not constitutive of the human character. The author will slip into considering her color a defect, first social in nature and then moral. This passage depicts a naive Teresa who is unaware that her skin color is related to her enslavement and who must believe that her virtue will be the primary criterion for her entrance in the convent and that her race will not be an obstacle.
7 Blackness is now a sign of martyrdom and suffering. The use of the word *martirio* by the author is a synecdoche for torture or torment. Martyrs suffered bodily torment for their faith. Teresa is another martyr for the faith because of her skin color. Teresa suffers insults because of the color of her body, like Christ suffering insults at being clad in a red cape and crowned with thorns.
8 The marquis and his wife offer money as Chicaba's dowry to these convents, but the text reports that racial discrimination was stronger than the assurance of their patronage. Blackness is now a defect that cannot be expunged with gold. Money could not serve as the social equalizer it usually was, so it was inadequate to clean the social disability of Teresa's skin color.

CHAPTER 19

The efforts to let Teresa become a nun continue, but no place will admit her.

When all their efforts to get permission for Teresa to don a religious habit in Madrid were thwarted, the marquis and his wife decided to look for a place where it could be arranged. Things were almost settled in many places, but it would not happen in any of them.[1] Divine Providence reserved this joy for the convent of La Penitencia.[2] Alba de Tormes was one of the towns where Teresa's agents set their course.[3] Nevertheless, the accident of her being Black ended their intention, almost as soon as it was revealed. The Marquis of Mancera and his wife had given orders to Don Diego Gamarra to request Teresa's admission.[4] This gentleman had been a longtime acquaintance and in continuous communication with the Fathers of Saint Gaetano.[5] He was a very special benefactor to the order, so much that he instructed his children to continue this special relationship in perpetuity. He had received from these Fathers long accounts of Teresa's virtue, good character, and vocation since they were put in charge of her spiritual direction.[6] Eager to see Teresa cross the gates of the Franciscan convent of Saint Isabel in the town of Alba, he took it upon himself to request this in earnest. But since the divine will had decided that Teresa would not be a nun there, he saw his hopes completely dashed. In view of so many delays, it looked as if there was a contest for her love between the Seraphic Francis and the Cherubic Dominic as to which of the two would take such a shining star to their own religious heaven.[7] In the end, Dominic won, as events would prove later. Don Diego went to the convent of Saint Isabel and presented to the nuns the request he had from the marquis, testifying to the good character

---

1 From the will of the marchioness, it is clear that they had approached the Dominican convent of Santa Ana in Murcia as the original intended destination for Teresa, but clearly she did not enter there. Most of the nuns in Santa Ana came from the local aristocracy. Their standing afforded them connections that gave them considerable financial and social autonomy, to the point of being able to turn down a request from a grandee of Spain, if this ever took place. See the Introduction, p. 80.

2 The name of the convent was Santa María Magdalena de La Penitencia, a third order Dominican convent of nuns. For a discussion on the meaning of "third order" convents, see the Introduction, p. 82. Chicaba's acceptance to a third order community seems to hold out a promise that she may eventually achieve inclusion in that monastery.

3 Alba de Tormes, in the province of Salamanca, is the town where Saint Teresa of Ávila died and is buried. The hagiography portrays Teresa Chicaba's life as modeled on her namesake, Teresa of Ávila. See the Introduction, p. 86.

4 Once again, the *Vida* re-creates the fiction that the marchioness was still alive when Teresa entered the convent, when in fact she had died earlier that same year, in April 1703.

5 The Theatines were founded by Saint Gaetano (San Cayetano in Spanish). See the Introduction, pp. 2–3 for the relation of the Theatines to the production of this *Vida*.

6 Her confessor at the time was Father Ignacio de Araújo, a Theatine. See Chapter 18.

7 The Seraphic Francis is Saint Francis of Assisi, founder of the Franciscan Order, and the Cherubic Dominic is Saint Dominic of Guzmán, founder of the Dominicans. The history of third order Dominicans shares both saints as founders: First, Francis took over the supervision of laymen and laywomen (*beghards* and *beguines*), and then those who conformed to rules of religious life were taken under the supervision of the Dominicans.

and nobility of the candidate, and her heroic virtue, which had been proven by spiritual men after repeated tests. He also asked them to consider how good this would be for their monastery and house because, beside the material generosity of the marquis, which should not be disdained, they were gaining the good graces of such an illustrious individual, one of the principal figures in the court. In addition to the marquis's supplication he presented them with the authoritative letter of recommendation from the Duke of Alba he was bringing to the nuns in favor of the novice.[8] In sum, he explained to them at length all the good reasons that should have led to the desired goal, speaking as a true representative of the marquis. Don Diego retired from their presence and went home, where he impatiently waited for the outcome.[9] It did not go as he thought. The nuns conferred with one another on the matter. Most of them had realized how convenient it would be for the convent to have such a special gem, more for her virtue and righteous life than for any other benefits. They were almost resolved to admit her. A lady belonging to the highest nobility in Spain heard the news of what was going on. She had renounced her high birth and lived as a poor nun in the same convent. She had given up everything, yet she could not give up her own pride and barred Teresa's admission. Her vain pretext was that the postulant was Black: "A negress," she said, "in my convent! Not for as long as I live. This house was not founded for negresses. So, ladies, stop the talking, because I will make every effort possible to stop this from happening." And since she was a lady of such high standing and superior nobility, all the others had to be silent and agree. Teresa was excluded for being Black.[10] The same person who barred her admission later lamented her mistake. A few years after this event, she received news of the heroic virtue that shone from Teresa. The lady was remorseful that her vain pride had made her reject Teresa for being Black. She envied the nuns in La Penitencia for their fortune and good sense, as she explained repeatedly to the Venerable Father Jerónimo during the long time that he directed Teresa spiritually.[11]

Don Diego promptly went back to receive the answer, and he was dumbfounded when they told him that they could not admit her. They explained the cause—how it all resulted from the illustrious lady's opposition. Don Diego prudently acquiesced to Sovereign Providence's incomprehensible judgment. He thought that the proposal that had been so

---

8   The House of Alba was originally from Alba de Tormes. They were at the time, and still are today, the aristocratic family with the most titles of nobility and land holdings in Spain.
9   Paniagua uses the word *gradas* (steps), a juridical term, as if he were pleading a case in front of a court of the nuns who will make the final decision about Teresa. Nuns usually had the ultimate say in who could enter their community.
10 Many convents had exclusionary clauses for admission, including proof of *limpieza de sangre*. For example, in Salamanca the Dominican convent of Las Dueñas, another monastic community of upper-class women, had this rule (Concha Torres Sánchez, *La clausura femenina en la Salamanca del siglo XVII: Dominicas y Carmelitas descalzas* [Salamanca: Ediciones Universidad de Salamanca, 1991], 65). Las Dueñas was a second order Dominican convent, while La Penitencia *was* a third order community. Class difference marked to a large extent who could aspire to each convent. In Las Dueñas at least 44 percent of the nuns declared to be of noble origin (Torres Sánchez 71). The Carmelites did not have such restrictions, following Saint Teresa of Ávila's reform. However, in the aforementioned monastery of Alba de Tormes, like in others, not all the nuns had the right to vote on matters of admission. Those who could vote were members of the "chapter," which consisted of choir nuns in permanent vows and with certain seniority. It was customary in many convents to use white and black balls to indicate votes for or against. In matters of admission, one single black ball would suffice to defeat a candidacy
11 The Theatine Father Jerónimo Abarrategui, Sor Teresa Chicaba's most influential spiritual director, was already mentioned in Chapter 14.

frustrated would have benefited that house and monastery greatly. What he had thought to accomplish so easily had come to nothing through the mere accident of the color of a face. He told the marquis what had happened, and the news made Teresa more disturbed and apprehensive. Looking for a solution, she took refuge in prayer to calm the anguish of her loving heart. The Acts of the Provincial Chapter of the Dominican Friars of Toro of 1749, speaking of this notable woman, say the following words: "Our most glorious Father gave her consolation, assuring her that her wishes would be fulfilled."[12] They were fulfilled, through means and ways that could not have been more unexpected by her and her benefactors.

---

12 Sor Teresa's obituary was recorded in the proceedings of a meeting of Dominican friars from all over Spain held in the city of Toro in 1749 (see Appendix 3). They described her death, extolled her virtues, and proclaimed her African royal origin. This mention was rather extraordinary for a nun of La Penitencia; her obituary was longer than that of most friars (Maeso 143). The acts of this meeting, written in Latin, mention Chicaba's place of birth in Ethiopia, avoiding the name of Guinea, always associated with slavery. It is a deliberate use of Latin to avoid the mention of Guinea. See the discussion of the name of Guinea/Ethiopia in the Introduction, pp. 17, 56.

CHAPTER 20

Teresa's admission to the convent of La Penitencia is finally arranged. Brief review of the convent's origin and virtuous persons who lived there

After his request was rejected, Don Diego Gamarra, as I said, informed the marquis, who in turn told him to do everything in his power to secure entrance anywhere else. In view of this, he came to this city [Salamanca]. This gentleman had a very close friend in Mother Jesus, whose virtue shone at the time in the convent of La Penitencia. She was an example of virtue and righteous life, and they venerated and held her in their esteem as one of the souls most favored by Heaven. Don Diego went to visit her quite casually, and in the course of their conversation, he told her of his mission and problem. He related to her what had happened in Alba with the nuns of Saint Isabel. Mother Jesus listened carefully to him; moved, as enlightened spirits tend to be when confronting arduous enterprises, she removed all his difficulties. She renewed the gentleman's expectation of obtaining his request, to give the marquis and his wife satisfaction, as well as relief to Teresa's sorrow. She simply proposed her own convent, if Don Diego deemed it appropriate for his plans.

Don Diego accepted the offer with pleasure, at the same time admiring how Heaven had taken care of things. His problem was solved so easily, after he had thought that a favorable outcome would cost him considerable trouble. They agreed that the community should hear the proposal. Mother Jesus would send him a message with the result. The nuns had little say in admitting Teresa, because the Supreme King had destined this as the place to deposit His treasure. The nuns were there only to open the door for her to come in. Mother Jesus communicated the community's resolution to Don Diego, and he responded by going to thank them in person.[1]

From then onward, there were no difficulties whatsoever in the negotiations and arrangements because the marquis and his wife's generosity provided the means splendidly and liberally as befitted their nobility. Don Diego informed the marquis and his wife that he had already settled the admission. They told Teresa, who considered all her anguish and travails worth the fulfillment of her intent. The news spread through the household. Among many who came to congratulate her, there was the spiritual person who had foretold her admission to religious life. He added: *Didn't I tell you? If you had believed me, wouldn't you have spared yourself many bad moments?* Quite pleased, Teresa responded with amiability: *It is not that I did not give credit to Your Worship's words. It is that I completely forgot what you told me then.*[2] This is something worthy of notice, because among the different situations

---

[1] There is a contradiction in the narrative. Here the nuns seem to be following the dictates of the Holy Spirit. However, the next chapter shows evidence of negotiations about Chicaba's status in La Penitencia.

[2] Note that in Spanish the "spiritual person" addresses Teresa in the second person singular (*tú*), a form of address reserved for intimacy or with those who are social inferiors at the time. Teresa responds in the third person singular, addressing this person with the honorific for a social superior. This conversation is printed in italics in the original *Vida*, signaling these as words of Chicaba herself.

this notable woman experienced in the course of her life, whether it was travails or moments of consolation, in almost all of them she received an announcement from heaven. This happened always in the most special and unusual cases, and it was done by means of either her internal light or an external communication from a spiritual person living an exemplary life. But it always happened in such a way that as soon as she had been informed and warned, she did not remember such a notice until the event had taken place in front of her eyes. Then she remembered that it had indeed been foretold ahead of time. So in the present case, she had never recalled the forecast and announcement made to her by that spiritual person until the nuns of La Penitencia admitted her, and she saw it fulfilled in her.[3] And since we have found already a safe place and abode where this chaste dove is going to build her nest, it will not be out of the question to give a brief account of this monastery's origins.

During its first years, it was a house of retirement where those women who had become disillusioned with their vices could give them up in greater calm.[4] It served this purpose for many years. In it, the repenting women spent their lives in withdrawal, without more order, profession, or rule than their life of retreat. Some years passed in this situation, until in 1548 two men of the most qualified nobility, Don Alonso de Paz and Don Suero de Solís, donated a great part of their rents to this house. They took advice and received permission from Don Pedro de Castro, who at the time occupied the Episcopal See, to transform it into a monastery under the patronage of Saint Mary Magdalene.[5] It will not be easy to find out what religious rule the primitive nuns professed, because the book of professions of that monastery starts only during the century before ours.[6] So for 1548 we have no specific account of what religious rule those nuns professed. The only sure thing is that at the time these two gentlemen converted this house into a monastery, Gil González Dávila refers to its foundation and gives it the title of "convent of the Augustinian nuns."[7] The truth is that from the last century on, their external habit has been the Dominican one. Their life has consisted of observing the rule of the third order of Saint Dominic very closely and with rigor.

This convent has had nuns of notable and exemplary life who shone with heroic virtue. Many of them have passed away into the other life with the fame of sainthood. Such was

---

3   Paniagua is using theological prudence here. For Teresa Chicaba to claim the power of prophecy would have been an act of arrogance at best, and at worst a proposition bordering on heresy.

4   Formerly the convents in this order sometimes sheltered women of "low character"; some may have been prostitutes. These convents still exist in the Dominican order (see Rumer Godden's *Five for Sorrow, Ten for Joy* [Chicago: Loyola Classics, 2007]). The veneration and patronage of Mary Magdalene, whom popular religious legend contends was a prostitute, is significant in the convent of La Penitencia. Some believed that Mary Magdalene was the sister of Lazarus and Martha, and so she is the one chosen to receive "the better part" of the relationship with Christ—prayer and contemplation.

5   Don Pedro de Castro Lemos was bishop of Salamanca between 1545 and 1553. He was probably following a movement to transform beguine houses into convents, under the authority and control of local bishops. By Chicaba's time, the monastery had obviously changed its mission from being a refuge for fallen women—a term Paniagua uses quite loosely, because it was probably a house of beguines or religious women who associated freely in community—into that of a convent of enclosed nuns, following a general movement in Spain after the Council of Trent (Atienza Alonso 148).

6   Paniagua refers to her as a *tercera*, as if she were a vowed layperson attached to La Penitencia in Salamanca. His description would make her a tertiary of the Tertiary Order of Penance. His inability to define clearly her status among Dominicans accentuates her liminality among her sisters. See the Introduction, p. 88.

7   Gil González Dávila, *Historia de las antigüedades de la ciudad de Salamanca* (Salamanca, 1606), 489.

Mother Sor Antonia of Saint Francis, who was the prioress when the protagonist of this *Compendium* was granted admittance.[8] She observed the rule with extreme zeal. Sor Ana of Jesus also shone in all sorts of virtues, so much that the space of the monastery was not enough to hold it, and her fame spread among the people outside the cloister. Sor Teresa of the Conception was also a woman of notable sanctity. For fourteen consecutive years she did not go to bed once because she wanted to be ready to do her tasks and vigils. In order to test her even more and pass her virtue through the crucible, His divine hand kept her crippled for many years until He took her. Sor María Teresa of Saint Jacinto shone in her zeal for God's worship and her love for saintly poverty. With her zeal, she acquired many things for the vestry and adornments for the altars and the church. Her love of poverty was such that she would not consent to wear new clothes but instead mended for herself what the others rejected. She was prioress for ten years, during which she did not lack for travails, both external to the monastery as well as internal. Purified by all of them, she flew directly to her eternal rest. This monastery has had other souls that pleased God. The ones I have referred to are enough for a short work such as this one. This was the origin and beginning of this house of religion, the theater where Teresa also exercised so many virtues and enjoyed so many and so singular favors, as I will mention to the end of this *Compendium*.

---

8   This is confirmed by the *carta de pago* (letter of payment) signed by Sor Teresa Chicaba on April 19, 1704. See the Introduction, p. 87. See also Appendix 1.

CHAPTER 21

Teresa's journey to Salamanca. Incidents that happened while she traveled

With loving and impatient eagerness Teresa wanted to see herself already in religious habit. Days seemed centuries before the attainment of her desire. The marquis deeply regretted that he had to release his dear Black and be separated from her. The marchioness, who had been closer to and could better understand the depths of Teresa's virtue, considered the prospect of not seeing her anymore an intolerable martyrdom.[1] She realized that in the Black woman she did not have a slave who served her, but rather a spiritual teacher who had taught her. She went back over the moments, the entire afternoons and evenings, that both of them had spent together in the tender exercise of prayer. Seeing the fruits her own soul had gained in her company, she felt Teresa's absence as a cruel pain. The rest of the family realized that the center of calm and peace in domestic disputes was leaving. Because Teresa had acquired influence with and the good opinion of the marquis and his wife, she could soften her owners' fits of rage and keep peace in the household. All in the family cried at seeing themselves separated from her. Only Teresa, happy and pleased to have found the harbor she had long wished for, tried to ease everyone's feelings with her smile.

Everything necessary was arranged for the journey. The munificence of the marquis and his wife provided for Teresa's comfort everything these noble people considered adequate for her pleasure and assistance. Teresa left with the blessing of these parents that God had given her in the absence of her natural ones.[2] Their tender and affectionate tears were the silent indication that the separation was forever. Teresa left Madrid at the end of October of the year 1703 with a retinue and company fitting such a sojourner and those who sent her.[3] They had a good journey. During it Teresa acted with her usual composure and sense of modesty, which was not an obstacle for her companions to indulge in honest and licit entertainment. Not being haughty at all, she never upset anyone in her entire life. Because of her devotion and affection for them, Teresa received from the marquis and his wife the favor of making the trip through Alba.[4] There, she was eager to venerate the relics of her patron saint and

---

1 Once again in the *Vida*, the author presents the Marchioness of Mancera as still alive when Teresa left for Salamanca, in November 1703. The marchioness had died in April of that year. Her fictive presence at this point in the narrative reinforces the theme of the owner of a slave as a loving parent. Emancipation thus becomes a form of painful separation.
2 The adoptive parents' image in this sentence serves to hide that, as slave owners, the marquis and his wife are indirectly responsible for Teresa's orphanage, which is euphemistically described as the "absence" of her biological father and mother.
3 Chicaba seems to have entered the convent in November 1703. Her profession did not take place until eight months later, on June 29, 1704, as the document of her profession indicates (Appendix 2). The *carta de pago* for her dowry, was signed in April 1704 (Appendix 1). See the Introduction, p. 115n108.
4 As pointed out in the Introduction, p. 85, the town where Saint Teresa of Ávila died, Alba de Tormes, is symbolically important in Chicaba's journey to the convent in Salamanca, for the *Vida* often asserts its connection to Carmelite spirituality through frequent allusions to the writings of Saint Teresa and Saint John of the Cross. Saint Teresa of Ávila was also her namesake, an important fact in Catholic devotion, as the text explains.

protector, the Seraphic Doctor Saint Teresa of Ávila, whose name Heaven had given her in her homeland at the foot of that glorious fountain.⁵ This name was confirmed later when she received holy baptism in the city of São Tomé.⁶

When Teresa arrived in Alba, she went to adore and venerate devoutly that arm whose fingers touched the soft harp of divine contemplation as if they were the feathers and wings of her heart—fingers with which Saint Teresa has made the resonances of mystical theology more harmonious in the Church.⁷ She venerated that seared heart, which even behind glass still breathes like a volcano, to the point that it is necessary to open little windows in the glass so it can breathe and heat may have a way out. What her soul felt and experienced during this visit, Teresa kept to herself.⁸ One has to believe that she undoubtedly experienced a great deal. Saint Teresa, who has always favored her devotees, would not have made an exception of this dear one. She had taken Teresa under her tutelage and patronage a long time before. During the course of her life, our Teresa enjoyed a favor very much like the one experienced by the Holy Mother in her heart. It would not be difficult to believe then that in some way the Seraphic Doctor would favor Teresa at the beginning of her spiritual career because later Heaven made her participate in pleasures similar to those the Seraphic Doctor enjoyed.⁹ In this same town, Heaven showed another favored soul the jewels of perfection that Teresa would attain in her career. They informed this person of the condition, virtue, and circumstances surrounding the Black woman. Illuminated by the Sovereign Light, this person foretold the progress that Teresa would make in her religious life. This person could see with the eyes of the soul what the corporal ones that were deprived of material sight could not.¹⁰ This person gave an account of Teresa's face, person, and physical figure, as if seeing her body. The blind person brought her close and caressed her with particular joy. Speaking little, these acts made it clear that this person saw a great deal in the Black woman.

---

5   Saint Teresa of Ávila was officially declared a doctor of the Church—her writings were recognized as important teaching in religious matters, especially in mystical ones—by Pope Paul VI on September 27, 1970. That the text calls her a doctor in the eighteenth century attests to her importance in Spanish devotion. The occasion serves also to remind the reader that Sor Teresa Chicaba became a Christian in her homeland by miraculous means.

6   This journey to the convent becomes a pilgrimage that reverses her middle passage as a slave—that is, it represents a different journey home. The name of Saint Teresa is linked to Chicaba's mystical and baptismal naming in her homeland and in São Tomé. This is the fulfillment of the promised made at the fountain near her native home. The irony resides in the fact that the Marquis of Mancera helped Chicaba find a place in La Penitencia thanks to his connections with Salamanca. The village of Mancera, his ancestral home, is in that province.

7   This is one of the most baroque examples of the *Vida*'s rhetorical style. As Teresa venerates the uncorrupted arm of the saint, the author ponders how Saint Teresa's fingers played the divine music of contemplation more like the feathers of a dove's wings than as human fingers. The text is praising Saint Teresa for having helped regulate the theology and spirituality of mysticism that so many times set the church authorities in crisis. The Catholic hierarchy viewed mystical manifestations with some suspicion, especially among laypeople and even more especially among women. Saint Teresa provided a sort of practical guide for souls to follow on their way to mystical perfection, in works like *The Interior Castle*, and *The Way of Perfection*, and especially in her autobiography, *The Book of Her Life*. See the Introduction, pp. 8, 42n30.

8   *Ella sola se lo supo* ("She alone knew it") paraphrases again the words of Saint John of the Cross in his poem "Dark Night." See the Introduction, p. 101n20.

9   The word used by the author is *consuelos*, which in the language of courtly love means pleasurable acts or words that give consolation to an otherwise pining lover. The term is used even now to denote the occasional sense of fulfillment one experiences in prayer.

10 The paradoxical figure of the blind person who sees what is hidden from those with physical vision

While in Alba, Teresa also visited the nuns of Saint Isabel, who as I have already said had refused to admit her. They saw how kind, courteous, and prudent she was, and they heard much about her virtues and decent life from what the accompanying members of the family professed, as the marquis and his wife had charged them to do. The nuns truly regretted the error they had committed in not admitting her, and they would have accepted her as a great favor then if Teresa stayed with them, had she been even Blacker.[11] Teresa completed her obligations in Alba, both pious and political, of visiting the Holy Mother and the other people in the town who showed considerable interest in the news of a Black woman and came to visit her. After this she continued her journey to this city of Salamanca. She was already anxious to arrive and see herself a happy spouse of her beloved White Child, the one and only white center in the target of her affection.[12] She arrived in this city at the beginning of the month of October.[13] When she thought that there would be no further obstacles to her aims, hell dealt its last effort to frustrate her goals, as the next chapter will tell.

---

is common in literature. This blind person can see the spiritual future of Teresa. Like in many other hagiographic and heroic accounts, a blind person can "see" the moral character of the hero or heroine inscribed in the future saint's soul.

11 The text insists that the reason for the refusal by the nuns in Santa Isabel was Teresa's Black skin. Her physical appearance before them and the fame of virtue that accompanied her is in contrast with their color prejudice. This sentence seems to indicate God had deprived these nuns of the latter because of their prejudice.

12 The text plays with the word *blanco*, in *blanco Niño* (the White Child Jesus) and *blanco* as the center of a target (see Chapter 17). The racialization of the Child Jesus and of the Virgin Mary is obvious and intentional in the text. It would be unthinkable to depict Jesus in any way other than as a white European. This racialization of God further legitimates Teresa's enslavement because she is Black; she comes to white Europe, the cradle of Christendom, the land of white Jesus.

13 There is a contradiction in these dates. A few paragraphs earlier we read that Teresa left Madrid at the end of October 1703. Here, we learn that she arrived in Salamanca at the beginning of October. We know for a fact that she was in Salamanca in April 1704, when she signed the *carta de pago* (Appendix 1).

CHAPTER 22

Teresa meets more embarrassing obstacles to her admission procedure. They are overcome easily. She takes the habit, not without an intervention from heaven.

An experienced pilot is no stranger to dangers because he knows he is always exposed to difficulties. He is more afraid of the risk he may encounter in the harbor, where he thinks he is safe. In the harbor of religious life—calm and quiet—Teresa believed that all the difficulties and tempests she had weathered before her arrival had been overcome and put behind her. At that point, the Infernal Abyss tried to make a ruckus at the mouth of the very harbor of her peace. At the time Teresa arrived in Salamanca, the bishop of this Holy Church was Monsignor Don Francisco Calderón de la Barca, an individual of qualities deserving of a higher episcopal see than Salamanca.[1] The convent of La Penitencia, like many others, was subject to his jurisdiction.[2] In accordance with their duty, the nuns informed him of Teresa's impending entrance in order to obtain his permission and agreement. This prelate looked with some repugnance on this business for reasons only he knew.[3] After many discussions and the intercession of reputable men, the best concession that he would grant was that Teresa would enter the convent not as a full nun, but as a tertiary. Later on she might be able to become fully professed. She also had to pay more dowry than the others.[4] This matter

---

1 A nephew of the famous playwright Pedro Calderón de la Barca, Francisco Calderón de la Barca was bishop of Salamanca between 1693 and 1712. During his tenure, he founded the Theatine College of San Cayetano, where Paniagua was the rector. This connects the bishop with the Theatines and Sor Teresa Chicaba's entire canonization project.

2 Following the decrees of the Council of Trent (1545–1563), a female monastery had to answer both to the bishop—*el ordinario*—and the general of the order. The bishop therefore had the final say in the admission of a nun to a religious community.

3 "Repugnance": in the Spanish original, *repugnancia*. Absent any other explanation, Bishop Calderón was loath to admit a Black woman to one of the convents in his diocese.

4 These negotiations took a decidedly material tone, as the reader will see. They decided to induct her as a *seglar o terzera beata*, as the *carta de pago* stipulates (see note in Chapter 20). This document also confirms that her dowry was higher than usual. The Marquis of Mancera paid 10,800 reales, when the normal fee for a future black-veiled nun (a choir nun) was between 4,000 and 6,000 reales, and Chicaba was not even entering as a nun. As discussed in the Introduction, Section 2, Sor Teresa Chicaba's status was ambiguous. Her treatment in part might be because there were considerably fewer women of African descent in Spanish monasteries or convents than in religious communities in Spanish America. Elsewhere, the text calls her a *tercera*, which may refer to a layperson that has taken vows in a secular congregation of the order. There were often two kinds of nuns in the monastic orders of Spain and America: Choir nuns (*monjas de velo negro*) who wore long black veils after taking vows, and lay sisters (*monjas legas, de medio velo*), who normally donned veils of a shorter length or of another color. There is always a distinction between their habit and that of the choir nuns, sometimes very slight and sometimes strongly marked. Black-veiled nuns take their permanent vows; their most important duties are liturgical. They also performed administrative duties; therefore, they had the rights that pertained to running of their communities, including the right to vote in chapter. Lay nuns took solemn vows as members of the community, but they did not usually participate in the recitation of the Divine Office, though they recited certain prayers in the vernacular. In some orders, lay sisters

was finally settled because the marquis and his wife came to the rescue with their wealth and largesse.⁵

They told Teresa, so she might know the kind of life she was embarking on. Since her humility did not have room for vain points of honor, she agreed with everything proposed to her in order to follow her Spouse. This humble resignation was perhaps the reason that when the prelate himself gave her the white veil, she found in this external garment a form of acknowledgment of her as chaste spouse of His Supreme Majesty.⁶ The dawn of the ninth day of November of the above-said year finally came for Teresa, once all the difficulties for her admission to the convent were settled to the satisfaction of all parties involved.⁷ The bishop himself dressed her and gave her the habit from his own hands.⁸ Divine Providence knows how to soften and change human hearts. Full of affability and love, the bishop attended the pious function with all his family. After he gave Teresa her habit, she finally had all her desires satisfied. The nuns received her with all the appropriate festive demonstrations of happiness. One could read in their faces the interior joy they all felt at the good fortune that was entering their house that day. The community at the time was presided over by Mother Antonia of Saint Francis. She was a woman of exemplary virtue. It was the depth of that virtue that helped her discover how much Teresa would improve in her spiritual life. She immediately developed a very special esteem and a singular affection for Teresa.

Once the ceremony came to an end, the bishop left. He was astonished at the piety

---

were as strictly enclosed as the choir nuns. Sometimes the difference reflected the social status of the women before they joined the community. Lay sisters usually were responsible for menial labor in the convent or monastery. The editors of this hagiography have looked at the Ensenada census (1749), which enumerates the inhabitants of La Penitencia as six short-veiled nuns and twenty-three full-veiled ones. The census also mentions the category of *criadas seglares* (secular servants). The extant picture of Sor Teresa shows her with a short white veil; Paniagua, who interviews his subject in her old age, does not depict her leaving the enclosure, but neither does he identify her as a lay sister. We believe that the representation of Chicaba's liminal status is a product of the tension between her conviction that making her vows in the hands of Saint Dominic himself bestows on her the status of a fully professed nun in the order and her lived status as a third order secular. She might have conveyed this conviction to her amanuensis.

5 This is probably information Sor Teresa Chicaba furnished to Paniagua. Since the *Vida* states that she entered the convent in November 1703 and the *carta de pago* is not signed until April 19, 1704, there are reasons to believe that the higher fee was a matter of negotiation, which probably took time.

6 The text depicts the incident of the white veil not to emphasize Teresa's low status in the convent, but as a symbolic proclamation of her chastity. However, this white veil is an image that the text itself occasionally contests. This contestation is an example of the *Vida*'s ambiguity about the veil. This contributes to the text's obfuscation of Chicaba's status. This concealment makes the story of her marginalization more painful for the audience to read.

7 There is considerable fumbling with the dates here. November 9, 1703, was probably the date Teresa Chicaba physically entered La Penitencia. However, another document states that she was finally admitted on June 29, 1704. This official document has the date amended; it states that she "professed" from the hands of the bishop "or his representative," and it bears Chicaba's signature as "Sor Teresa de Santo Domingo." As noted above, this document is out of place within La Penitencia's book of professions, as it is inserted after another item with the date of November 13, 1705 (Maeso 76).

8 The act of profession (Appendix 2) states that it was either the bishop or his representative, a common priest who acted as his *visitador* (inspector). The text mentions the habit, without specifying what kind of habit. Tertiaries donned different sorts of habits that signaled their religious life, but this did not mean that they had professed officially as nuns (Atienza Alonso 146). Furthermore, there is no mention here of what kind of veil—white or black—Teresa would wear.

shown by Teresa when he gave her the habit. All present, including his family, were no less impressed with the Black woman's devotion. She had achieved her desired admission and gained her happiness. Thus ended this felicitous ceremony. We already have Teresa in the harbor to which she had directed her sail for so long. We saw how happily and full of joy the nuns received her at the door. But another community, invisible to those present but noticeable to the Black woman, received her with pleasure at the door of the rule.[9] As she entered the convent, Teresa noticed two choirs of nuns at each side. They were four altogether. She looked at them carefully. At the beginning, she could not believe her eyes. She thought that maybe her eyes were confused, and they were doubling things. The four lines processed toward the choir. Paying closer attention, Teresa noticed now that two of them were more conspicuous than the others. Her soul was not disturbed. On the contrary, she looked in perfect calm and peace at each of their faces and expressions, and she felt an indescribable joy. She saw them behave with the modesty and composure that was appropriate to the ritual they were enacting and the life they led. But in these two rows every detail stood out much more than in the others. She saw the affability without affectation, an external composure devoid of the least atom of hypocrisy, and the bliss in their faces, which was markedly different from the rest because they were already in possession of the happiness that can never disappear. The others had their joy mixed with many other things that could serve as obstacles to true happiness. The two extra lines of nuns that Teresa saw were those who had led virtuous lives in the convent and had found eternal rest in the Lord. These nuns, following a special command from God, came to receive her in visible form and shape at the door, and they accompanied her to the sacred ceremony of investiture. We owe this information to Teresa herself.[10] Indeed, she told those still alive about the faces and particular features of those nuns who had already died before she had even entered the convent. Taking this incident into account, we have enough evidence to venerate her and not to question heaven's secrets.

---

9   In the original, *la puerta reglar* (the cloister door) physically separated the external world from the space inhabited by those admitted to the full observance of the rule of the Dominican order. In the mystical ceremony that Teresa experiences with the celestial members of her order, the nuns in heaven receive her in their choir, though she had been denied a place as a choir nun in her earthly community.

10 The text reports directly from Teresa herself that two ceremonies took place at the same time, one in heaven, and one on earth. Teresa claims to be privileged to witness them both. The two ceremonies are markedly different. On earth she is given the last and most humble place, while in the celestial ceremony she is placed among the full black-veil nuns. However, in Chapter 24 there will be a second mystical ceremony.

CHAPTER 23

Teresa begins her novitiate. Cruel temptation suffered during it, which she overcomes with the help of divine grace

Happily considering herself already a nun, Teresa began her spiritual course with the fervor and force her strong vocation promised.[1] God was going to guide this soul through a unique path, and so her initial steps were also special. The practice of humility had to be the foundation of that building, as is necessary with all nuns. However, the process in her case would be very different. It is common in every monastery to put a novice under the authority and direction of a mistress.[2] By the supervision of a mistress of novices, the community ensures the education of its young women. In them, as if on soft wax, the mistress's example and teaching impress the virtues and everything pertaining to religious life and customs. According to the rule, this is the norm for all novices, and the convent of La Penitencia still practices it with anyone they admit. Although this was the custom in this most religious of houses, it was not practiced with Teresa. She did not have a teacher to direct her. Nobody in particular was appointed to educate her. This happened either because it was not done with the tertiaries, or because God alone wanted to be her teacher, her compass and guide.[3] He would teach and guide her softly and gently in the secrecy of her heart. What most probably happened in this case was that during the debates that preceded Teresa's entrance, they compromised on an agreement to admit her only as a tertiary, and not as a full nun; therefore, the community considered itself exempt from the obligation to treat her as a novice and the necessity of appointing a teacher to direct her in the customs of religious life.[4] For this reason she did not participate with the community in any act. The nuns went to Choir, and Teresa knelt on the other side of the grille, or in the anteroom of the choir, in all humility and patience, and in an attitude of submission. When they went to the refectory, Teresa

---

1 The word in Spanish is *religiosa* (woman religious), which is an ambiguous word meaning anyone with any status within a religious community. It can also mean anybody who is of a religious disposition.
2 In English, the role of the teacher of novices in a monastery is still called "novice mistress or mistress of novices," which is etymologically closer to the Spanish *maestra*. In this chapter, we will use the terms "mistress" and "teacher" wherever they are appropriate.
3 This narrative is at a loss as to what to call Chicaba in the convent; she is referred to as *tercera* in Spanish. This means that Chicaba's status was that of a lay tertiary in the convent, and not that of a *donada*, as was the lot of many Black women in Spanish and Spanish American convents. See the Introduction, pp. 88, 115n112. for a discussion of the term *tercera* and its ambiguity as applied to Chicaba.
4 The practice of discrimination between the two types of nuns was marked by the rule of the order. Lay nuns did not receive the same training as choir nuns. Also, if Teresa was never expected to be a "nun" in the fullest sense of the word, then they probably did not make any provision to afford her the normal formation as a nun. As mentioned before, there were two Dominican women's monasteries in Salamanca: a second order community, Las Dueñas, which drew from the upper and middle classes, and La Penitencia, which was poorer and drew from women of slightly lower classes. This text was written at a point in history when this enclosed third order was living a life close to or exactly like second orders and adopted their strict hierarchical structure.

could not go in. They would not allow her to have a bed in the dormitory. The little sleep she had took place in the infirmary.[5]

But if Teresa did not attend to these community acts because they did not let her, she was the first one to perform acts of humility. She was the first among them to pick up the broom to sweep. She helped the cooks in the kitchen. She washed all the dishes spotless and completely clean.[6] She showed great affection and solicitude to all the nuns, because of the love she had for them in her heart. In spite of not having a teacher, and without the obligations proper to a "novice in the strict sense"—as it was then said—she led a more righteous life than others who were considered perfect. If she regretted anything, it was seeing herself deprived of the company of such righteous souls more often than she wished. One of them, impelled by her own sense of charity, saw Teresa's docile and virtuous nature, and took charge of her education. She was Sor María Teresa of San Jacinto, who acted as both mother and teacher for Teresa. She taught her to say the Divine Office. Teresa was already quite advanced in this since she had learned it in the house of the marquis, and she prayed it every day without fail, if she was not ill. The teacher only had to instruct her in the way of praying according to the Dominican ritual.[7] She taught her everything she knew and could, so her life would be perfect. The fervent disciple applied herself so much that it would not be an exaggeration to say that she overtook her teacher in perfection, something the latter discovered over the course of time.

With this arrangement, God's hand corrected the deficiency in spiritual teaching Teresa would have otherwise had, because of the shortsighted manner in which humans make decisions. The devil noticed the endurance and patience Teresa showed during this episode and how her soul, inspired by the Holy Spirit and Mother Saint Jacinto's direction, improved in virtue. He did what he could to make her abandon the course she had begun. He sent such a strong temptation to her that she might well have shipwrecked if her celestial Spouse had not come to her aid. The devil fanned the flames of her imagination and her heart by reminding her of all the unpleasantness she had suffered since her admission,

---

5 Chicaba's segregation in the infirmary accentuates her liminal status in the community. Often in enclosed religious communities, the infirmary is a liminal space, both inside and outside. Since doctors and priests can minister to nuns in this space, it is both a part of the cloister and part of the secular world.

6 This is the first time the author suggests the nature of her menial work. Chicaba was not unfamiliar with it, but, from the previous chapters that narrate her life as a slave, we only knew of her spiritual activities. In the convent, however, where she is legally a free woman and her spiritual life was supposed to thrive, she is made to work in activities reserved for servants, who were not expected to have access to the same levels of spirituality as the upper-class nuns. This is another instance of the reversal of roles in the story of the royal slave that permeates the narrative of her life.

7 This passage indicates that Chicaba learned to read in the Mancera household and that she knew Latin, in some form, before entering the monastery. One should not forget, however, that many nuns sang the Office in Latin but did not necessarily know the meaning of the words they said. They only knew how to pronounce the words. The Benedictine nun Pauline Villeneuve had received a similar education (see Introduction, pp. 84, 113n101). The mistress of novices only had to teach Chicaba the particular liturgical practices of her religious order, the Dominicans. The Divine Office is a complicated book that one has to learn how to use for the prayers that occur throughout every day. It is composed of volumes divided according to the liturgical seasons, then by weeks of the church year, and then by days, with exceptions for holidays and special feast days.

which was caused by trying to emulate the nuns who did not allow her to attend liturgy with them; who treated her like a slave; who prevented her from sleeping in the room with the rest of them or going to the refectory and the choir.[8] And if they did this to her while the marquis and his wife were still alive, out of whose respect they should have treated her differently, what would they do after their deaths?[9] The devil told her: The opposition you experienced in all those places before being admitted is a clear sign that your vocation was not divinely inspired, but only a fancy of your mind. What about the prophecies concerning your religious life? Just lies invented by the Enemy, who sought your damnation and ruin by these means. Would it not have been much better to accept the invitation made by your uncle and go with him to your homeland? There, with your authority and nobility, and with the rule of your scepter you could have finished the work of spreading the Catholic faith all over your dominions.[10] This would have been your service to the Christian religion. You would have had an easier life, more calm and secure. You would have served God and have been served by your subjects instead of being here in a strange land, despised by people who, perhaps in your land, would not have even been admitted to service in your house. You have strayed. You have lost your way.

The infernal cunning tried to disturb and agitate Teresa's heart. The torment was so fierce, and she struggled so deeply within herself, that the prioress ended up noticing it, either because a superior light enlightened her (which would not have been strange given her virtue) or because she saw how forlorn Teresa was. Looking after Teresa's well-being and peace, the prioress acted with prudent dissemblance and let the nuns believe that she was a bit sick. It would be necessary to move her bed to the infirmary, the room where Teresa slept. It was done as she had ordered. Sick for reasons of charity, the prioress waited until night and its silence to see if in the midst of its mute shadows Teresa would explain her troubles. She spent the entire night without uttering a word on the matter. The prioress noticed only that the novice had not slept at all, and this had already been happening for several nights. Perhaps Teresa's imagination tormented her more during those hours, when it was stimulated by such cruel temptation. The nights passed one after another, and in the silence of one of them, the prioress asked her why she could not sleep. What was keeping her awake? The prioress had observed that the same thing had occurred during previous nights. Teresa prudently answered that she felt a little ill and that this slight indisposition kept her from getting some rest and calm. The wise prioress briefly reviewed with her the main temptations with which the common Enemy tends to subject the inexperienced on the path of perfection. She instructed her also in how to resist his infernal cunning because, with it, he tries to make the soul step back from the spiritual road already taken.

---

8   Catholics today usually employ the term Liturgy of the Hours. "Liturgy" is a Greek word that means "divine office" or "divine service." Today, *liturgy* can refer to the Mass or the Divine Office.

9   The hagiographic narrative keeps the marchioness alive for months, if not years, after she had died. She died before Chicaba entered the convent. Her death was, in fact, the event that enabled Chicaba's emancipation. See last will and testament (Archivo Histórico de Protocolos Notariales de Madrid, libro 13.977, fol. 135ff., April 10, 1703). See Appendix 4.

10 All of this is appropriate to the genre of hagiography. They are examples of the temptations of a saint. The hagiography first establishes the saint's royal or aristocratic origins only to show how she or he rejects those origins and accepts a humble destiny. This echoes the temptations of Christ during his forty days in the desert (Matthew 4:1–11).

Teresa's soul and heart were highly impressed by these wise words from the prioress. Although she had not even given a thought to turning back from the road she had started, she had found herself in a sea of anguish and sorrows with so many misapprehensions. But having heard the sweet and tender words from the prioress, she became completely calm, putting away the specters of her fantasy that had upset and disquieted her under the influence of the Adversary. She recovered her joy, and she followed her devout practices with more fervor and force. She recovered her sleep, although it was short, and with it her rest. She finally recovered completely. The prioress saw that Teresa was well and that she rested despite the brief time she gave her body repose. She stayed in Teresa's company for a few more nights until she assured herself that Teresa's rest was permanent. Finally, she left her alone and ordered her bed be sent back to the dormitory. She recovered from the malady that her ardent charity had caused in sympathy with Teresa.

CHAPTER 24

Teresa's visible and invisible profession

Readers in Chapter 22 learned how Bishop Don Francisco Calderón de la Barca was almost resolved not to give permission for Teresa to enter the convent, and they also read that in the end, through the good offices and insistence of reputable persons, he softened his determination to some extent so that Teresa could take the habit. Surely they will admire how tenderly Divine Providence turns around and changes human hearts, because it has power to do so! May the readers peruse the following lines and compare them with what they have already learned, and they will find clear and patent proof of what I say. Teresa's soul was calm and quiet, once the waters of opposition raised by the Abyss trying to drown her had receded. Her life then passed amidst the exercise and practice of virtue. June of 1704 came, and it had been eight months since her admission into religious seclusion.[1] According to the rule of the order, she still had four months before she could confirm the promise of her vows and ensure her stay in the convent. The bishop, more benign now than he had been difficult before, condescended and decided that she would make her vows that same month of June, granting the permission, as he was allowed, even before the marquis and his wife requested it with humility.

Once Teresa was certain that the day of her joy was approaching and that her soul was finally going to celebrate mystical nuptials with the White Child, she readied herself for the ceremony that she had been anticipating for so long. She displayed acts of profound humility and ardent charity, together with the other virtues. The 29th day of June arrived, which is consecrated to the feast of the Princes of the Apostles.[2] This was the day destined for her royal marriage.[3] The bishop went to the church of La Penitencia with his retinue and family. It was in his hands that this victim offered herself in sacrifice with the vows of poverty, chastity, and obedience.[4] Moved by a celestial impulse, no doubt, the bishop gave her and imposed from his own hand the white veil, although she was just a tertiary, and her profession amounted only to that.[5] When he granted his permission to admit her, one of

---

1 The document of her profession indicates June 29, 1704, as the date of her vows, four months before the rule stipulated. The issue of the white veil is further developed. The text is very precise in dating her profession here. This is the moment when she formally becomes the bride of Christ. However, this document appears out of synch in the book of professions of La Penitencia, as though it had been added more than a year later, as mentioned in a note on Chapter 22.

2 On June 29, the Catholic Church celebrates the feast of Saints Peter and Paul. As the two most important apostles, they are called "the two princes."

3 The marriage is royal in a double sense. The bridegroom, Christ, as King, makes it royal. But Teresa, the bride, was also of royal descent, and in fact, queen apparent after the death of her parents and brothers.

4 These are the three canonical vows that all religious persons take in a solemn ceremony. In monastic communities, women are said to profess their vows "in the hands of the prioress or abbess." The novice places her hands in the upturned palms of the superior.

5 Tertiaries, as lesser in importance and social prestige, did not deserve the attention of the bishop himself to attend the ceremonies of their solemn vows. The solemn profession of secular tertiaries (laypeople attached to monasteries but living in the secular world) seldom required the presence of the

his conditions was that she would not wear any veil.⁶ But God's right hand changes human hearts, and after all the favors He had bestowed on Teresa, He did not want her to be, on the day of her profession, without this external token, which distinguishes those He selects as His chaste spouses.⁷ Teresa received her consecration from the hands of her prelate. Through the three vows, which she would honor so scrupulously all her life, this solemn ceremony came to an end. But another one, even more magnificent, followed. It was hidden from everybody's eyes, and open only to Teresa's.

She had retreated into her inner self a few hours after her profession and gave humble thanks to her celestial Spouse for the gift she had obtained.⁸ Then she experienced a sweet suspension and took leave of all the human senses that might have disturbed her imagination and her powers.⁹ She saw a choir of heavenly dwellers who filled the room where she had retired with joy and merriment. Teresa did not know any of them, but she observed everyone peacefully and carefully. There was one among them who surpassed the rest. His position and the splendor of his glory showed that he presided over that honorable choir. He looked at Teresa with tender and peaceful eyes and took a seat on a majestic chair with Teresa at his feet.¹⁰ Teresa blushed in confusion at being favored by such a celestial prince, because she could not find in herself the slightest reason for such favor, or why she might deserve such merit.¹¹ At a slight gesture from the one presiding, all the things necessary to perform a profession appeared.¹² The sovereign company started saying the prayers. With great joy and consolation of spirit, she knelt down and began to do what they asked her. She repeated her vows and received the veil. The solemn ritual ended when her great father and patriarch Saint Dominic gave her his blessing, for it was he who presided over this religious

---

bishop. But the bishop's intervention here evidences how unusual it was for a Black woman to enter a convent in Spain. This makes the task of identifying Sor Teresa's status even more difficult. Clearly the importance of the bishop's attendance is to show how miraculously his prejudice had disappeared.

6   The details of Teresa's admission become clearer and show the terrible discrimination she suffered. Not to be allowed even to wear the white veil of the lay sisters speaks to the liminality of her station. The veil was the distinctive sign of a nun. Women inside a convent without a religious veil were servants and slaves.

7   The narrative is trying to resignify the white veil from a sign of second-class citizenship into a sign of pure spouse. The text uses the word *externa divisa* to qualify the white veil. The language is reminiscent of courtly love literature. The *divisa* (device) was a piece of paper, or a garment, that signified the love for a lady. The wearing of this device or garment signifies a woman's chastity; the insistence on the part of the text of her worthiness to wear the veil makes clear that she has the requirements to be a bride of Christ—that is, she is undefiled. Thus, the white veil is the outer sign of the intact hymen, which is a bodily mark of a spiritual virtue, one that is made public through the sign of the veil.

8   The mystical profession takes place in two acts. The second and most important one comes when Sor Teresa has retreated away from the outer reality.

9   The word "suspension" indicates a trance state, and it signifies that she is involved in a mystical experience and is dissociated from her body.

10 This vision of the celestial choir is made according to common iconography of saints in heaven. They sit on rich chairs, and the humans having the vision are situated below, usually on stairs leading to the throne. Light and gold are signs of the sanctity of the individuals in the vision.

11 A proof of Teresa's humility repeats the words of the Virgin Mary to the angel during the Annunciation, which are included in the prayer of the Magnificat (Luke 1:38). In conventual liturgy, the act of profession of a nun is compared to the Annunciation of the Virgin, the nun being a virgin who is going to be the spouse of God.

12 The veil she receives from Saint Dominic confirms the legitimacy of her religious profession and questions the legitimacy of the bishop's command that she not wear it.

ceremony.[13] The saint himself told her who he was before disappearing with the rest of the retinue.

We can only speculate but cannot reduce to a few scribblings of a pen what Teresa possibly felt in her soul during such a sacred ritual.[14] What fervor and strength she received from it to fulfill and practice her vows! How many acts of humility she performed and how profoundly, after seeing herself so favored by heaven—particularly when she tried to overcome the vain arrogance of human creatures! Some accept her at one point and exclude her at another. At times, they let her sit in the choir; at times, they send the Black woman outside with the other women.[15] At one point, they make her profess as a tertiary without any veil, and then they give her the white veil because the prelate says so. And then, the supreme prelate of the entire order, our Lord Saint Dominic, favors this dear daughter by receiving her vows in his own hands, and thus marks her as a chaste spouse of the Immaculate Lamb by giving her the veil. This was the profession that was invisible to mortal eyes. However, the angels, saints, and all the blessed saw it perfectly. The account of this favor and miracle is contained in the testimony of Teresa's confessors, which I have seen.[16] It is also in the Acts of the Provincial Chapter of the Order of Saint Dominic that took place in Toro in the year of 1749, which I have read with pleasure.[17] After some time, Teresa renewed her profession in the hands of a friar from the illustrious convent of San Esteban.[18] Impelled by the love that burned in her heart, this soul yearned to offer herself at all hours as a tender victim before His Supreme Majesty.

---

13 Saint Dominic had competed with Saint Francis for her profession, probably because the third order of Saint Dominic is an offshoot of the Franciscan third orders. One of the convents that had rejected her, Santa Isabel in Alba de Tormes, was Franciscan.
14 The mystical experience is one that by definition is considered *ineffable*, impossible to describe with human words.
15 In the Spanish original, "with the other women" appears as "*con las otras*." The text is referring to the lay sisters, secular tertiaries, and servants of La Penitencia, who did not profess full vows and were excluded from the choir.
16 All these are written documents that the author attests to have had in front of him but which no longer exist.
17 The minutes of the Dominican order's assembly of 1749, in Latin, gives a summary of Chicaba's life. Her inclusion among the members of the order who had died the year before is a testament to her reputation. See Appendix 3 for a full translation into English.
18 Since the vows were not perpetual, they were renewed every two years, according to canon law.

CHAPTER 25

A list of Teresa's virtues: first, her humility

I have already used my pen to give some examples of the heroic virtues with which this notable woman, helped by grace, adorned her soul. However, I could not give a long account because I was not fortunate enough to recover or to have access to many of the papers and annotations many of Teresa's directors wrote about her virtue. I have availed myself of a few fragments for this short exposition. Although I am pained by their scarcity, their truthfulness and authenticity and the care with which they were collected give me the confidence to tell something about her virtues, gifts, and divine favors. Teresa finally saw herself in the quiet and calm harbor that she had so much sought. She took up the tasks of her new status, and she tried to discharge them earnestly. Nature had made her queen and free. Chance made her a slave, unless Providence did it. Finding herself better in her particular situation as a slave than in her natural state of freedom, she generously renounced her liberty when it was in her hand to attain it.[1] She preferred to live happy in slavery—that state to which divine grace had brought her—although she could never have been freer.[2] Teresa behaved as a humble slave in all her actions and always acted as such in the house of the marquis. She was everybody's servant and the first to assist all of them in their illnesses.[3] She was always ready to help them in the lowliest tasks of the house. When some of the servants went to do what had been assigned them, they found their tasks already done with diligence and care by the Black woman. On more than a few occasions, the marchioness reprimanded her for getting involved in what Her Excellency believed was beneath Teresa and did not correspond to the high degree of esteem and fondness with which her mistress treated her. Teresa, however, used these occasions quite prudently. Since the marchioness had put herself under her spiritual teaching, Teresa let her mistress understand with a tender expression on her face that humility and lowliness of spirit were the safest way to improve on the path of virtue.

Sometimes the presence of other people did not allow Teresa to teach the marchioness with spiritual examples how important humility was. When she was surprised in the middle of some humble task, she responded with grace and gaiety that she was doing it for sport.[4]

---

1   These lines represent the main argument in the *Vida*'s case for Chicaba's sainthood. She is of royal descent, and she renounces her restored privileges once she is offered marriage and a return to her homeland in the Mina Baja del Oro. In this way, her enslavement is only a temporary test from God, and not a permanent condition. Accepting slavery and a lowly life in the convent will be proof of her heroic virtue. See the Introduction, p. 31.

2   The justification of slavery in Catholic teaching during the seventeenth and eighteenth centuries is that it can serve the soul of the African slave as an opportunity for redemption and salvation. See the Introduction, p. 59.

3   This is another reference to Chicaba's healing powers. In Africa her people were cured by her visit to their houses (Chapter 3). Now, however, there is no reference to healing powers but only that she cared for the sick, which was a job left normally for servants and slaves, as in the case of enslaved women employed by public hospitals in Madrid. See the Introduction, p. 70.

4   The chapter is an exposition of the virtue of humility as practiced by Chicaba. The practice of humility, necessary in a nun, becomes the cloak under which Teresa's true activities in the house of the marquis

Indeed, it would not be contrary to the truth to say that her soul found the greatest amusement in the exercise of virtue. The appreciation with which the marquis and his wife treated her was indescribable torment. This was especially true when Their Excellencies sat her with them at the table. Her humility could take revenge only in the mockery ladies made of her by calling her "the Queen" in jest. She tolerated the true expression of esteem shown to her by the marquis and his wife in order to enjoy the ridicule she suffered as a moment of profound humility.[5] The cruel persecution that the rest of the family raised against her when they saw how devoted she seemed to her spiritual life, all the things that this or that woman did to her, she considered as too kind in comparison to the treatment and words she thought she really deserved. She did not think too much of the torments and punishment the governess inflicted on her while she was a child, and the mockery and envy of the ladies when she was grown up. Her knowledge of humility made her think this way. In the midst of her desire to embrace a religious life and the rejections she suffered in so many places she applied for admission, she did not waver at all. She thought herself unworthy of such happiness, and she suffered and passed through these terrible blows with humble resignation.

Inside the religious cloister, her humility grew in quality and in proportion to the new life she had embraced. Many of the nuns who still live there could tell at length how humbly and respectfully she served all in common and each one in particular. She was the first one in the religious practice of every humble exercise. Since she entered the convent with no other obligation than to serve God, to accomplish this better, she served Him by serving each of the nuns.[6] She attended the services in the choir as if she had entered the convent with only this goal in mind. She served those who did not have access to the choir as if this were her only duty in life.[7] Every day she would carry the coal they needed in the kitchen. She washed the dishes of all of the nuns, an activity she continued for many years. Only after many years and illnesses and other physical frailties—especially a cruel tooth infection—did her confessors command her to abstain from these tasks. They thought, quite prudently, that these duties were damaging her health.[8]

Teresa obeyed with humility. However, in order for her to continue practicing this virtue, they granted her permission to wash the dishes every day of an old nun Teresa had always cared for. She also did the dishes for a woman who was either feeble, vain, simply crazy, or all these things together. As I said in the beginning, all this served as a way for her to exercise her humility. During the course of her life, we did not see anything but profound humility in her. She had total self-knowledge, and thinking nothing of herself,

---

are discussed, and disguised, as voluntary acts of menial work. The text suggests that by exempting her from physical work the Marchioness of Mancera acknowledged Chicaba's condition as a royal slave. However, Teresa helped the servants in their tasks out of her own will and in order to exercise humility. This anecdote emphasizes that Chicaba did menial work out of her own will, not as a condition of her lowly status. The text establishes the paradox that Chicaba freely accepted slavery.

5 This was told in Chapter 9. It is significant that the text repeats it here, at the beginning of her life in the convent.
6 Although the document of her profession does not indicate what her functions would be in the convent, it was understood that her duties would be those of a servant. The *carta de pago* (Appendix 1) indicates that she was free to leave the convent any time she wished. See the Introduction, Section 2.
7 This is the first mention that she is not the only nun who does not wear a black veil in that convent. She becomes the servant of the servants.
8 The importance of the confessor and spiritual director cannot be sufficiently stressed. In this case, the text claims that their orders were enough to change an entire system of work and tasks in the rule of convent life.

she believed she was unworthy of everything. For this reason, there was no worse torture for her than the visitations of serious and learned individuals, either noble or plebeian—people of all classes—who after seeing her proclaimed the good opinion they had of her virtue and sanctity. Since she could not find anything good in herself, these expressions caused her indescribable anxiety. Not a few trusted her good judgment to resolve the questions and doubts they put to her. Teresa, in her humility, never communicated a decision in matters of importance unless she was doing it in obedience to her confessors. She used their authority in giving answers to those who consulted her. With the passing of years, she grew in self-knowledge. Shortly before she departed from this world she wrote to a religious man of notable virtue who lived in the Benedictine Monastery of San Pedro de Cardeña.[9] He was well experienced in spiritual matters, from what we can understand from his letters. Her words were the following: *May you be happy*, she says on the occasion of the Feast of the Nativity of God, *with the Child being born, and please speak to him not to be angry with me, because I keep him upset with my faults*. Thus, this humble soul, already close to her seventieth year, expressed herself. She believes that she had upset the Child God with her faults, which were only slight as long as she lived. Her confessors' testimony says so. But the lives of the righteous are always like this. The humbler they are, the farther they are from any guilt.

---

9   This friar is identified as Father Félix Álvarez de Córdoba (Maeso 78). In his research for the cause of beatification of Sor Teresa, Father Lázaro Sastre Varas, OP, found that Father Félix was employed in the Mancera household during the time Teresa lived there (Maeso 79). Father Félix is cited again in Chapters 30, 40, and 41.

CHAPTER 26

Teresa's mortification and acts of penitence

Once Teresa had acknowledged that she was nothing, her soul was able to continue erecting the edifice of her virtues, which was firm, secure, and stable since it was built on the foundation of humility. In acts of self-mortification and penance, she was as extreme as her life was innocent and free of guilt. Her abstinence was singular to the extreme that one can say it started when she was born. Even before she came to a more perfect knowledge of God, she took pleasure in fasting so as to find this God who was hidden from her. As I said already, all her nourishment consisted only of some bread cakes made under the embers of a fire and a few pieces of fruit native to her land while she lived there.[1] Her greatest pleasure was to ask and inquire about her God in that beloved meadow. And while it is natural for a child to have something in their hands to snack on all the time, Teresa came back every night with very little food in her body but as happy and joyful as if she had spent the entire day eating sweets and appetizing tidbits appropriate to her age and sex. Then, while in the marquis's household, she prudently adjusted to her director's orders, and because the presence of so many witnesses prevented her from fasting as much as she wanted, her soul added obedience to the list of her merits.

The monastery was the place where her fasting and other mortifications shone with greater splendor. Her pure desire for mortification made it more difficult to surrender her will to the dictates of her directors rather than to the practice of penitential exercises.

She took fasting to extremes.[2] All the forty-six years she lived in the convent, she kept a vigil diet, unless obedience made her do the opposite when it was necessary.[3] Even during the illness from which she died, she called loudly for her Friday meal, insisting that she would not recover until she was granted this permission.[4] To the list of prolonged fasts already prescribed by the rule of her order, her zeal added almost the rest of the year.[5] On

---

1   This is a possible reference to a form of ashcakes, bread baked on the hearth, that she would eat. Abstinence from meat and frugality were connected to the practice of poverty.
2   The practice of abstinence from food is a form of mortification that has been amply studied by Caroline Walker Bynum. For a medieval woman, refusal of food, giving away the family's food to the poor, or eating bad food was a public/private form of gaining control over her body, as food production was part of a woman's sphere in a world in which a woman could not easily renounce other things, like marriage, sexual activity with her husband, or family ties. See Caroline Walker Bynum, *Holy Feast and Holy Fast: The Religious Significance of Food to Medieval Women* (Berkeley: University of California Press, 1987), 191–94.
3   Vigils are days of fast and abstinence from meat products. Observant people eat no meat and only one full meal on that day. Her confessors forced her to break this habit, and she obeyed.
4   The Friday meal, before the reform effected by the Second Vatican Council (1963–1965), was one when Catholics substituted fish or legumes and vegetables cooked without meat-based broths for meat products. In many religious houses the Friday meal also included fasting—that is, reducing the food intake to one single main meal.
5   This refers to what is called "the fast of the order," a practice in conventual life that goes from the Feast of the Exaltation of the Holy Cross on September 14 to Easter.

the eve of all the feasts dedicated to the majesty of Christ or His Holy Mother, she believed a bread and water fast indispensable. But her devotion and affection for other saints added many other vigil eves, such as those of her glorious father and patriarch Saint Dominic, Saint Vincent Ferrer her beloved, and Saint Thomas Aquinas, for whom she developed a special devotion after the Lord showed her the great glory he enjoys in heaven; also the glorious father and patriarch Saint Gaetano, for whom she always showed special affection.[6] She intensified her already many and rigorous fasts with so small an amount of food that it almost seemed as if she was not eating enough to live. Her greatest morsel was an egg, while hastily made soup was her more regular and ordinary meal. If she had at times a little fish, it was with so little spice that the best appetite would have rejected it as too rotten to eat.[7]

What can I say of the bed she used to give some rest to her tired body! Rather than a bed, one might reasonable call it a rack of torture. It was just a mattress made of river stones, barely covered with a few straws, yet it looked very soft to those who were not in on the secret.[8] For her head, as a pillow, she used a hard wooden log, which she covered with a blanket to make believe it was otherwise. For a few hours every night Teresa found in this bed not the needed rest but agonizing torment. She firmly maintained this practice for many years, until she was forced to obey and change. She used disciplinary scourges and various devices to lacerate her flesh—rigorous and cruel cilices, graters, and little chains and pieces of tin stuck in her body—whenever her confessors allowed her.[9] To crown all this, she had a wooden cross the size of a third of a yard in which she had nailed seventy-two sharp steel barbs.[10] She used to embrace it to her chest with such eagerness to do penance that her directors always had trouble restraining her. Every day of her life, as long as she was able and not impeded by some illness, she disciplined herself harshly at least once. For this practice, she had collected the most painful instruments, some with steely nails that pierced her virginal body, and another made of an iron rod divided into three branches. With the latter, she imitated the instrument used by her father and patriarch Saint Dominic. She never wore linen for as long as she was in the monastery. Instead her undershirt was made of coarse and thick serge.[11] In the matter of penitential mortification, she observed to the letter what her order's constitutions and rule prescribed. But acting like a cruel torturer of her own body,

---

6 Again, here is a mention of Saint Gaetano, the patron saint and founder of the Theatines—Father Paniagua's order—next to three Dominican saints, who were a logical choice of devotion for someone belonging to the Dominican order.
7 Fresh fish was a rarity in places like Salamanca, especially saltwater fish. To preserve it necessitated a heavy use of condiments to kill the odor of spoilage or putrefaction. Teresa eats her fish in a way that its bad smell would make it unappetizing.
8 This is a biblical reference to Jacob (Genesis 28:11), who slept using a stone as his pillow in the place of the future Bethel.
9 For the word *cilicies*, see note in Chapter 18.
10 The Spanish says *una tercia*, which is a third (279 mm) of a *vara*, a measure roughly equivalent to the English yard. Crosses of this size can be observed in Spanish portraits of nuns and monks of the time. One of the most famous is Diego Velázquez's portrait of Mother Jerónima de la Fuente (1620).
11 The practice of wearing coarse material under the outer garments was another form of penance. Many rich and noble ladies were encouraged to wear coarse cloth (a hair shirt) under their finery as a form of penitential mortification. The description of these physical exercises and practices of self-torment are another way to signify her body as the central place where the drama of the saint takes place. Teresa, as a Black slave, is aware of the radical importance of her body as a source of labor and wealth to others.

she added whatever her fervor for God inspired and what her confessors allowed her to do within the limits of prudence.

How acceptable her acts of mortification were in God's eyes was confirmed by an incident. Heaven used it to convince thoroughly one of her confessors that she should persevere. Teresa's fasting was as rigorous as it was continuous. She ignored all calls for moderation and for liberal interpretation of the rules that allow dispensations and acknowledge human frailty.[12] For that reason, she generally did not have the small breakfast or *parva* that custom introduced even in the most austere and observant of religious houses.[13] Her director had tried to make her drink a little chocolate in the mornings.[14] He was able to persuade her how important it was for the maintenance of her health and that it would enable her to tolerate the myriad burdens she constantly undertook in the practice of her charity. Teresa humbly excused herself as much as she could, explaining to her confessor that she really did not need such a remedy. The confessor believed that what Teresa was requesting constituted an act of resistance, which emanated from her spirit of mortification.[15] After considering seriously that indeed she needed the dispensation, he expressly commanded her to drink chocolate the very next morning. She surrendered at once to the confessor's voice and precept. She drank it the next day, but as soon as the chocolate descended into her stomach, she suffered such violent nausea that it seemed as if she had taken the most deadly poison. Everyone started to fear she was going to die. Full of compassion, the nuns rushed toward

---

She is also aware that others always assume that she is not chaste; that is, that she is spiritually and physically defiled. By suffering these self-inflicting torments, she was proclaiming her equality, if not superiority, to the other nuns in La Penitencia.

12 Confessors use *epichoeia* (*epiqueya* in the original Spanish), meaning "measure" or "good sense," to prescribe the different forms of penitence.

13 *Parva*, in Latin, means "little" or "small," thus its use as a term for a small breakfast or small meal.

14 Chocolate was a luxury but still very much a part of monastic culture. Its consumption had been the source of controversy, as theologians discussed whether chocolate was a foodstuff or only a drink, in which case it could be consumed without breaking the fast before Communion (Beth Marie Forrest and April I. Najjaj, "Is Sipping Sin Breaking Fast? The Catholic Chocolate Controversy and the Changing World of Early Modern Spain," *Food and Foodways* 15 [2007]: 32). Chocolate was drunk in Spain and Spanish America using special cup holders called *mancerinas* after the Marquis of Mancera, during his tenure as Viceroy of New Spain, and not after his father, who had been Viceroy of Peru, as the Spanish *Diccionario de la Real Academia de la Lengua* says. The Marquis of Mancera, a viceroy of New Spain, was famous in Madrid for his frugality, which included the drinking of chocolate during the day instead of taking full meals, as stated by foreign diplomats (see, for example, Duc de Saint Simon, *Mémoires*, vol. 3, chapter 7 rouvroy.medusis.com/tomes.html). On the relation of the word *mancerina* to the Marquis of Mancera's father, see Sophie Coe, and Michael D. Coe. "Estampas del chocolate en Europa," *Artes De México* 105 (2011): 56.

15 By refusing to take chocolate Chicaba was establishing her agency, which the priest rightly interpreted as an act of resistance. She was practicing fasting to a heroic extent. Her refusal to "take" chocolate—a product related to indulgence of the body and luxury—in spite of her frailty was a way to exert control over her physical body, which had been the object of her enslavement before entering the convent, and once in the convent, was the vehicle of her menial work. It was also, and more importantly perhaps, her way to establish equality with the other nuns in the exercise of the virtue of humility. In European societies, women had been the ones in control of food preparation, while men were in control of most economic resources (Bynum 1988: 191). As someone who worked in the kitchen, Chicaba would have to prepare her own chocolate. By refusing to do it, she was subverting the social economy of her community, indirectly forcing others to prepare it for her, to serve her this luxury item, as she had had to do for the others who were socially above her. And she did all this in the name of humility.

her, and after administering her a few quick remedies, they were able to make Teresa throw up the chocolate.[16] Once she recovered a little from this travail, she said in good humor: *I already knew it but, out of obedience, it is not important to die.* In view of this incident, her confessor realized that it was not God's will that this soul should have limitations on the rigors she practiced. God's grace was giving comfort, encouragement, and strength to this soul to endure such extreme acts of mortification.

---

16 That her body does not tolerate chocolate shows that it is under the command of her spiritual wishes.

CHAPTER 27

Persecutions endured by Teresa, and how much mortification human creatures caused her

Self-mortification neither anneals virtue nor tests patience as much as what God sends with His own hand. In the first instance, one can suspect that asceticism may be mixed with false pride. In the second case, there is no room for such suspicion or fear. This is why I decided to write about how much the sovereign hand mortified Teresa by means of His children, aside from the mortification and penance with which she disciplined and punished herself, following her confessors' directions. In this way, Teresa's life of suffering may shine more brilliantly. I have already detailed extensively the afflictions she endured in the house of the marquis. It would be abusing the reader's patience to tell them again. I am limiting myself to the account of her sufferings in the cloister, and in general I will only mention what is necessary to be faithful to the title of this chapter. I will leave out many particular events, because it is not convenient to publish them now. I take that whoever reads here about Teresa's sufferings will not think ill of the persons who were the instrument of her trials. A righteous person may suffer one thousand tribulations, and perhaps no one of those who caused them has incurred mortal sin.[1]

She experienced repeated disappointments and uneasiness from the moment she crossed the threshold of the convent. Whether it was the bishop frowning at her and threatening to withhold the veil, or the different expressions on the faces of the domestic servants, all increased her suffering. She endured this tempest and anguish, uncertain whether she was going to stay or not, depending on whether they settled or rejected the contract for her to remain.[2] Once she professed, when this hurricane seemed to calm, the wind of her tribulations blew even more vehemently, for she was uncertain as to whether she was in the choir with the others or not, since she was not admitted as a nun but only a tertiary.[3] Teresa

---

1 This statement is central to the reasoning in the text's view of the indignities Teresa suffered in the convent. The other nuns were instruments of God when they caused Teresa's sufferings. They were the instruments God used to test her virtue, so their actions did not constitute sinning. Racism, the practice of slavery, and other forms of social oppression do not seem to be part of individual responsibility, according to the text of the *Vida*. The treatment of her suffering at others' hands is markedly different from the way other saints' lives attribute agency and moral responsibility. The punishers of Roman martyrs and of medieval holy women were never considered innocent. They end up having to answer for their actions in front of God. Here, the nuns of *La Penitencia* are not held responsible. This "irresponsibility" for their violent acts marks them as white. Their whiteness makes them innocent from the violence they inflict on this Black person, thus creating a moment of tension in the text. Chicaba's Blackness unsettles their lives, as Toni Morrison expresses it in her analysis of the formation of white American literature as obsessively "innocent" of the presence of a Black population in the country. See Toni Morrison, *Playing in the Dark: Whiteness and the Literary Imagination* (New York: Vintage Books, 1992), 44–45. We wish to thank Professor Charles I. Nero for alerting us to Morrison's discussion of the concept of innocence in white American texts.
2 This contract is the *carta de pago* (letter of payment) referred to earlier. See Appendix 1.
3 Here the text makes a clear distinction between a nun and a tertiary. Not being a nun, Chicaba had no right to pray in the choir.

suffered all this with humble conformity, with courage and constancy, as if someone else was experiencing these insults. She would go with patience and meekness to the anteroom of the choir, where she followed the liturgy, and thus she was able to follow the Divine Office.[4] Even if she was despised, humiliated, and denigrated by the others, she was honored and favored by God. These were trials that would have wounded any soul other than Teresa's. With patience and resignation she allowed herself to be molded by divine will. She took all these tribulations with a smiling face. Neither her face, actions, nor words betrayed the slightest impatience with those who caused her tribulations. Once she had overcome the temptation of seeing herself relegated to the infirmary and separated from where the rest slept, it seems as if with the help of divine grace all the rage was extinguished in her soul.[5] So whatever her fellow creatures did to mortify her, it looked as if someone else was suffering, and not Teresa. This is what happened to her on one occasion. In someone else other than Teresa it would have awakened the most dormant wrath. They chose as prioress of the convent a nun whom Teresa held in particular affection because this nun observed the constitutions and rule very strictly. This was the kind of nun Teresa always preferred. Because she was such a good religious woman, the election was very much to Teresa's liking. One nun did not think the election went so well and was upset that they had not chosen the one who in her opinion was the best. In the place and occasion that was least appropriate, such as in the choir, when Teresa was at a short distance from her, this nun blurted out in the shrillest of tones: *It is a tough thing that we must be ruled by a negress, and because the prioress is totally under her influence, we must live subject to her will.*[6] Not cutting the velocity of her wrath, she blew off steam with some expressions that perhaps were not conceived in a rancorous heart but sounded very harsh.[7] Teresa heard all this and her face was suffused with extraordinary joy. She remained motionless in her seat, offering these rude words as the most grateful sacrifice to her Owner. Teresa would hear more than a few words of this kind in the course of her life, but she acted like a rational stone that was going to be placed in the triumphant Jerusalem, and like such a stone, she let herself be carved by God with the instrument of His children.

What she felt more intensely and tempered her patience was the frequent change of directors. Her anguish put her on the brink of death, and her suffering was indescribable when one of her directors left or died. For this very reason and in order to test her constancy,

---

4   This is another reference to the contradiction between her ability to use the Divine Office (that is, to follow the readings of the Breviary) and her exclusion from the choir. Lay sisters who could not read the Office were not part of the choir. Yet we know from Chapter 23 that Chicaba had used the Breviary since her slave days in the house of the Marchioness of Mancera.

5   In most convents, nuns did not sleep in cells, but in a common dormitory. If they slept in cells, these rooms were clustered inside of the enclosure with no direct egress into the outside space. Chicaba, however, was relegated to sleeping in the infirmary, a liminal space outside the cloistered area of the building, with a door toward the inside of the cloister and one to the outside, from which a physician could have access to a sick nun.

6   The outburst of this nun in the choir indicates that Teresa had developed good relations among the choir nuns, to the point of being influential. Teresa was gaining power, and this fact subverted the social order within the convent. The idea of a Black person who is even seen as having influence on the prioress was something this angry nun and others probably were not ready to tolerate.

7   The expression of racism is justified or excused in the text once again. The nun's fault was in the tone and the place where these words were said, but not in their content. That Teresa might have influence on the new prioress may have been for the author a matter of legitimate concern. Her claim to power is, after all, illegitimate because she is Black.

God gave her this cup of bitterness to drink with regular frequency. She had ten or twelve different directors in a short time period. During the last years of her life, she was almost resolved not to take one regularly in order to avoid the seas of sorrow that their leaving caused her. But she rectified this not yet fully formed decision once she realized that a director was most necessary. In spite of all the feasts that she continually celebrated, she was assailed by grief and many bad moments. There was almost no single occasion when she did not experience some particular sorrow. The saints wanted to season their gifts to her by creating opportunities for Teresa to increase her merits.[8] However, this is not a sufficient reason to allow the pen to reveal how much her fellow creatures mortified her soul. One can only say that her sorrows were accompanied by patience and tolerance.

---

8   Teresa honored many saints on their feast days. In response, the saints sent her more troubles, which the text interprets as gifts for her to increase her sanctity. The saints in heaven were acting on God's behalf. This statement furthers the original argument at the beginning of the chapter, which sees the actions of the other nuns against her as occasions of divine intervention to try her humility and patience.

CHAPTER 28

Teresa's prayer and the infernal ruses to stop her celestial comfort she received from prayer

Teresa would not have been able to suffer with resignation so many sorrows as I have related (and those I have been silent about are many more), if it had not been that she sought the help of supernatural power through prayer. She had undertaken this exercise and resorted to this sovereign Armory since she was a young girl. She became so fond of this practice that her life was a continuous prayer. How many nights with no other dream but to seek the gentlest of balms in her prayers! During the day, when she could free herself from the necessary duties and works of charity, in which she was busy, she spent every hour in prayer. When she was older, her directors ordered her to bed. She spent only three hours resting in the bed that would be better called a rack of torture. After the three hours, she stood up and left for the choir to spend all the time she could afford there. Infuriated by all this praying, the Abyss tried all he knew how and could to obstruct her fervent zeal by distracting her from her pious exercise. If she prayed in her cell, he did all he could to disturb her by appearing in the figure of a greyhound or any other visible form.[1] If she was in the choir, he used all sorts of banging and noises to frighten her. Teresa remained constant, for she knew that it was all a ruse of the Enemy to take her away from such a useful exercise. So she persevered with more constancy and enthusiasm. But, in his stubbornness, the treacherous Adversary did not concede defeat. He assaulted Teresa with new machinations, furiously trying to take her life and thus spare himself from all the problems the Black woman was creating for him. She said it herself, when she told one of her directors who belonged to the Order of Saint Gaetano about the following event: *While I was in prayer I saw*, she says, *a waterwheel. There was an ox tied to it, moving it and making gestures. The ox was trying to attack me. In the midst of this tribulation, I invoked the assistance of the Queen of Angels and everything disappeared.*[2] Thus ends the story of this event, and from it one can see quite clearly how much the Abyss worked to separate Teresa from the useful practice of prayer and how strongly she held her ground, with the help of divine grace.

Heaven rewarded in this life the constancy shown by Teresa. After the horror that she must have felt at seeing the infernal ox and the waterwheel, a series of gentle celestial favors and visits followed. She related personally how on many occasions when she was in the

---

1 The devil is described in many medieval treatises as "the Dog." In Gonzalo de Berceo's *Milagros de Nuestra Señora* the devil appears in this animal form to a drunken monk. He also threatens Saint Dominic in the same author's *Vida de Santo Domingo de Silos*. See Alan Deyermond, "Berceo, el diablo y los animales," in *Homenaje al Instituto de Filología y Literaturas Hispánicas "Dr. Amado Alonso" en su cincuentenario, 1923–1973* (Buenos Aires: Fibacera, 1975), 82–90. Also in *Obras completas de Gonzalo de Berceo*, vol. 4, edited by Brian Dutton (London: Támesis, 1978). In the case of Teresa Chicaba the figure of the devil as a dog is undoubtedly symbolic. Blacks were frequently called *perros* (dogs) as a form of insult.
2 This negative image is a reversal of Saint Teresa of Ávila's image of the waterwheel in her autobiography (*Libro de la vida* ch. 11, para. 7, pg. 187). Together with the dog, the lion, the ox, and the bull are frequent animal figures for the devil. See Psalm 22.

choir, or her cell, during her continuous meditation, the following would happen: *I do not remember how many times I feel an angel, and this I feel within me, without seeing it with the eyes of my body. I am convinced it was my guardian angel, because my spirit became very happy.* Divine Providence was prompt to favor His beloved spouse in order to soften the worries sent to her by hell, as I have said, and will say even more extensively. He sent courtiers from heaven to comfort her not just in her cell, or the choir, but even in the very corridors of the convent, because Teresa continuously prayed. She always kept God present and felt united to her Master (as far as this is possible) through prayer.³ The cell, the choir, or even the corridors were good enough for it. Let her tell it, because her words are better than mine are: *Father, I also want to tell Your Reverence that I am certain that my Father Saint Dominic passed in a hurry through the corridor near the confession boxes on his way to the choir. I was passing by there and I smelled a saint. Afterward, they brought our Father* [Saint Gaetano], *and also those of our Father Saint Dominic and my Father Saint Francis. It has been many days since both patriarchs have been praying together with their hands extended, and both looked at me. I wanted them to pray for me too. I will have seen our Father Saint Dominic some three or four times, but I had forgotten what he said to me. It was to the effect that both should be one. I think he told me so. It's been many days already.* These were Teresa's words.⁴

Heaven cheered this fervent soul with this manner of celestial favors, thus soothing her sorrows with them. He encouraged her fervor and perseverance so that she would stay awake and pray without pausing, and in that way she would aspire always to execute what is most perfect and most gratifying to His divine eyes. No wonder Teresa spent so little time asleep, wishing to dedicate herself fervently to prayer! With it, she enjoyed many celestial pleasures. It is a pity then that our laziness, carelessness, and lukewarm disposition do not seem to be ready to receive these pleasures, even though they are available from God's hands; and He is ready to distribute and communicate them to all according to the disposition of each of us as He did with this blessed and fortunate soul, who was perfectly ready. Years, months, and days pass, and instead of getting ready for the useful practice of prayer, our soul becomes cooler and lazier. This was not the case with Teresa. Through her practice of virtue and her continuous prayer, she ended up deserving frequently the sight and visit of heaven's courtiers.⁵ And as it has been said, if she confessed with them, she must have also enjoyed the presence of her celestial and loving Spouse more than once. She was able to enjoy seeing Him, as well as His most holy Mother, as the next chapter will tell.

---

3   This is a paraphrase of Saint Teresa of Ávila's insistence on praying constantly, even in the kitchen: "Entended que si es en la cocina, entre los pucheros anda el Señor ayudándoos en lo interior y exterior" [You should understand that if it [prayer] takes place in the kitchen, the Lord is among the pots and pans helping you in interior as well as in exterior matters] (*Libro de las fundaciones*, ch. 8, para. 5).
4   In this quotation, Teresa's words indicate her desire for the Dominican and Franciscan orders to join into one. The presence of Saint Gaetano is another indication in the text of the involvement of the Theatines in her beatification process.
5   They are the angels and saints who surround God as King of Heaven.

CHAPTER 29

Teresa's rigorous exercises. Continuation of the account of the divine comfort she received

Teresa's entire life was without a doubt a continuous spiritual exercise. Stirred by love of God and her neighbor, she paid no attention at all to rest. However, she had reserved ten special days in the year when she ignored all external agitation. She used this time with very particular care and study to be alone with her celestial and divine Spouse.[1] On those days, her life belonged more to heaven than to earth. She refused all contact with the human race.[2] So she shut herself in her cell with such rigorous seclusion that she would not go out except to attend Choir or to wash all the nuns' dishes, while they still allowed her to do it. When her age no longer permitted this kind of work, she would do the dishes of an old nun she cared for like a humble slave.[3] She also washed another one's dishes; I will refer to this matter in the next chapter because Teresa had to suffer a lot from her. Teresa had given orders to the doorkeepers that she should not be called by anyone who sought her at all hours of the day looking for comfort and spiritual relief. This included spiritual persons and people who confided in her.[4] We can glean the kind of life she led from this complete retreat and separation from contact with the rest of the human race. Who can tell the harshness of her penance? Who will give an account of her fervent prayers? Who can say what spiritual consolations her soul felt? She alone knew of it, depriving us of that information. However, I cannot be silent about all of her experiences because obedience to her confessors forced her to describe one or another of them. So I will tell about them in her own words.[5]

---

1   Many choir nuns spent a period of each year in retreat; however, it was unlikely that tertiaries or even lay sisters had these spiritual obligations or were extended these contemplative privileges. This description of Chicaba's retreat is an assertion of her special position in La Penitencia and corroborates her self-image as someone who has made solemn profession. She claims to have devised her own calendar of spiritual practice. However, on the days she set aside, she was not exempt from having to do menial work.

2   Paniagua uses the term *criaturas*, which has strong biblical connotations, as "beings created by God." In the same sense, the first editor of Saint John of the Cross's *Cántico espiritual* (*Spiritual Canticle*) introduces the stanza "mil gracias derramando" as "respuesta de las criaturas," the answer of all creation to the question posed to them by the soul in search of her Beloved. "Respuesta de las criaturas." San Juan de la Cruz, *Obra completa*, vol. 1. Ed. Luce López-Baralt and Eulogio Pacho (Madrid: Alianza Editorial, 1996), 60.

3   By the reasoning of the time, virtue in this Black woman is tantamount to behaving like a slave. Slavery thus fits the natural state of a Black woman.

4   This is an instance of *pentimento*, in which Chicaba's voice shines from the background of the text that is superimposed over her voice. This kind of request is typical of choir nuns. That Teresa makes this request is a statement of her seeing herself as an equal to the other nuns. This statement comes right after the text comments that she worked for the other nuns like a slave.

5   "So I will tell about them in her own words" appears in the original Spanish as "Cuyas cláusulas iré siguiendo para referirlos" [literally "I will follow her words to represent them"]. The problem of Teresa's words is mediation. In the absence of independent written evidence, we do not know if the text is quoting her verbatim or paraphrasing her. It was also a common rhetorical practice to put words in the subject's mouth, saying what she should have said in this circumstance.

One day last week, she says, while in prayer, I saw sort of in my mind His Majesty, all beautiful and peaceful, giving His blessing. I asked Him to bless me too. I am sure He gave her His blessing, since even when she was a child He had bestowed upon her blessings of grace. She herself tells that this event occurred about the time when some missionaries full of fervor came to our town, who produced a lot of fruit with their zeal.

Teresa could not be without the comfort of the Blessed Virgin Mary. For this Lady after all was the first one who, back in her land, had awakened her attentions and dedication, and showed her the Blessed Child who was to be her future heavenly Spouse. While at sea, our Lady was the one who had soothed Teresa and dried her tears. Once, she was taken into a spiritual rapture and saw a festive procession in heaven. The Virgin Mary was presiding over it. She tells about it, and asks her director the following question: *Why, she says, do the blessed from my order process on feast days when they are in heaven already? And I think that I saw my Lady, the most Blessed Virgin, among them too.* These are words that speak in their natural sense to one single vision. Nevertheless, without doing violence to their sense, they refer to repeated occasions when Teresa enjoyed the delicious spectacle of those solemnities. Teresa spent her spiritual exercises with the encouragement of these heavenly pleasures. Once, because of her humble, timid, and lowly nature, she found no reason in herself to deserve so much favor. So she started to wonder if these were fantasies or illusions planted by the diabolical cunning to deceive her. To that effect, she tried with considerable force to dismiss them. The Blessed Virgin came to chide her mildly. These are her words after receiving a particular favor from heaven: *But one day, she says, in which I dismissed the favor as a ridiculous ruse, the Holy Virgin told me, "Have faith," and I was embarrassed, and I felt I did not know what was happening to me.*

Embarrassed: Teresa says that is how she felt after the Blessed Virgin tenderly scolded her. Her heavenly Spouse reproved her on another occasion for something that almost did not deserve to be called a fault. But it left her with tears welling up in her eyes. She herself describes a certain occasion when some friars came to say Mass: *I was not aware I was doing something wrong when I invited them to see my cell.*[6] *Your Reverence must not think I am telling a lie. His Majesty became so angry that I received a scolding from the Lord that made me cry. I was so ashamed inside myself that I felt reluctant to approach Communion, and I was covered with sweat. Certainly my intention was not bad, and I did not want to upset His Majesty, and I did not know what to do during that time. I begged the Virgin Mary to intercede, and I told her about the fault I had incurred without meaning it. After that, it seems that my heart felt some consolation.*[7] She had to feel good, because even the most obdurate of souls feels the tender effects of Christ's calm, peace, and relief, after He is placated through the intercession of His Mother. After all, how should a soul feel when she pleased His Supreme Majesty so much? The tender corrective the Virgin Mary gave Teresa echoes the one her sovereign Spouse gave her too, although the occasions were different. I have already talked about the rigorous ex-

---

6   Her cell clearly was outside the cloistered area of the convent. But the text is asserting that no man, not even a priest, would dare cross that threshold unless he had special permission from the bishop.

7   As her husband, Christ is jealous of the presence of other men in Teresa's cell, even if they are worthy priests. She is treated like a foolish bride, and the Virgin, like a mother-in-law, helps her make amends. The discourse of the spouse of Christ is informed by all the sexual and social restrictions invoked for married women of the time. They were not free to receive men in their houses without the knowledge of their husbands. See the Introduction, p. 29.

ercises during which she refrained from daily contact and communication with the nuns. So God told her that if she shunned even those she loved most and had raised since they were girls, should not she avoid outsiders, and even less allow them and ask them to come and see her cell?[8] Inside her cell and alone, Teresa thoroughly enjoyed the favors and pleasures of her loving Spouse. And perhaps she even heard from His lips that she was wrong in making a simple mistake. In her cell, Teresa had a paper print on which the ink was discolored and disfigured over time so much that what it represented or who it portrayed Teresa could no longer make out. For that reason, the print could very well be called the Image of Doubt.[9] Sometimes Teresa thought that the print represented her glorious father and patriarch Saint Dominic. On other occasions, she believed it was the Angelic Doctor.[10] In the midst of this confusion, her heavenly and divine Husband said to her: It is Nicholas of Tolentino.[11] *And it is true,* Teresa concludes, *and I was mistaken, thinking that it was my Father Saint Dominic sometimes or Saint Thomas Aquinas at other times.* These and many other favors Teresa received throughout her life. She obtained them especially during those ten days I have described, which she designated for her exercises.

---

8   Almost in passing, the text tells of one of the tasks she had been given over the years. It is apparent that La Penitencia housed young girls who were educated there, and she was in charge of their care. Later on, in the next chapter, there is an extensive account of one who was an extremely difficult case.

9   The facetious anecdote is set against the backdrop of the times this *Vida* was written. The eighteenth century was a period of fundamental doubts, though not of the kind discussed in this hagiography. What the print symbolizes here, however, is significant. Time has erased the face of the saint the print is representing. All sorts of saints may fit the description. All saints are one.

10 Saint Thomas Aquinas, one of the most important Dominican saints, was proclaimed a doctor of the Church in 1567 by Pope Pius V.

11 The thirteenth-century Italian Saint Nicholas of Tolentino is represented in iconography with two children inside a barrel at his feet, to signify one of his most famous miracles—that of saving people from drowning and shipwreck. This miracle may have resonated with Chicaba's own experience of near-drowning in childhood on the slave ship, after she was captured (Chapter 6), and also the incident of Buen Retiro Park, when she was pushed into the pond by the devil in the form of the majordomo (Chapter 10).

CHAPTER 30

*Hell devises a devilish ruse to upset Teresa,
but only with divine permission.*[1]

All the favors Teresa enjoyed, and as much as she grew in virtue because of them, were as many cruel tortures for the Abyss. The devil was enraged that her humility allowed her to enjoy part of the happiness he had lost out of his arrogance. So he invented new tricks and machinations that would disturb her peace and make her fall from the high state of perfection she had reached thanks to divine grace. He did not want to entrust the enterprise to any mortal creature. He had learned from the victories Teresa had won whenever he had tried to unsettle her through others' actions. Teresa had always turned a profit from what he had thought would be her sure loss. He tried to secure victory by engaging the battle directly himself. To this end his malice used a creature whose body he entered by divine permission.[2] I will tell the event just as I have heard and learned about it from a person who knows, since he is one of the patient's relatives.

Don José Calvo was a well-known person in our town. More than for his high office, he was renowned for his generous nature. His compassion remedied all the needs that reached his ears. To this day, the poor still proclaim it, and the religious communities say aloud that he found solutions to their wants and afflictions. He had a daughter, named María Francisca. While Nature endowed her with singular privileges, she on her part perfected them through her art, ability, and industry. She charmed all who knew her, and she had earned her parents' devotion. As a child, she lived in Madrid, in the house of the patriarch of the Indies, who was her relative.[3] After the death of our lord King Charles II, revolutionary changes befell the monarchy on the issue of its succession. This tempest shipwrecked quite a few of the most distinguished families that walked the path of fatality when they thought they were treading ways of happiness. The patriarch was no small victim of that misfortune, and he had to flee in haste toward Barcelona.[4] In the midst of his sudden flight, he was very

---

1 The devil cannot act independently from God. In a way, he becomes a divine instrument to test the soul. See Henry Ansgar Kelly, *Satan: A Biography* (New York: Cambridge University Press, 2006), 311.
2 *Endemoniados* (the possessed) are people whose bodies have been invaded by the devil. They are not creatures who are cast out of the Christian fold or are considered sinful. In fact, their possession by the devil is considered temporary, and it cannot happen without God's permission. It is not supposed to ruin the soul of the possessed, because that would be contrary to the principle of free will. A person possessed by the devil is not in command of his or her reasoning capacities and thus is not acting sinfully. See Patrick Toner, "Exorcism," *The Catholic Encyclopedia*, vol. 5 (New York: Robert Appleton Company, 1909). *www.newadvent.org/cathen/05709a.htm*. Also William Kent, "Demoniacs," *The Catholic Encyclopedia*, vol. 4 (New York: Robert Appleton Company, 1908). *www.newadvent.org/cathen/04711a.htm*.
3 The patriarch of the Indies was at the time Pedro Portocarrero y Guzmán (1691–1705). He was the author of a political treatise, *Teatro Monárquico de España* (Madrid, 1700). He should not be confused with his very influential relative, Cardinal Luis Fernando Portocarrero, who favored the candidacy of Archduke Karl to the Spanish throne against the French candidate, future king Philip V. At the end, like so many, the Marquis of Mancera included, the cardinal changed sides.
4 María Francisca and her family members probably belonged to the party of Archduke Karl in the War

careful to bring María Francisca with him. He arrived in Barcelona, and the child stayed in his house away from all strife until her parents claimed her back. She returned with them. Although she was very young, only ten, almost everyone liked her and held her in great esteem. This general esteem provoked the envy of some malevolent soul. It was motivated either by a particular animosity against her parents and family, or just because they coveted the honor for themselves. They were eager to upset the admiration María Francisca received. This person put to work the imprudent idea of casting a spell on this girl, and within it was the most infernal of hosts. As soon as this person thought of it, they put it into practice. They gave her an apple, which Heaven mysteriously allowed to contain all the illnesses and maladies that exist. All this vengeful evil was totally alien to a reasonable heart. And the worst part is that the mind of this person was so obstinate and stubborn, that many years after having caused the damage—we are talking of the year 1743—they still had not released her from the spell, even if they could have. I mean "release" as the learned say, who distinguish between hypothesis and its possibility.[5] All this evidence is testified to in a letter that I have in my possession, written to Teresa by Father Félix de Córdoba, a Benedictine monk, about whom I have already written. On this issue, he responded to Teresa with the following formal words: "If she lives under an evil spell it is a hard case, and there is little or no remedy for it. But it is even worse that after so long, the perpetrator still lives without wishing to undo the evil he has caused." Since the damage was caused up to this year we are speaking about, which was 1743, between twenty-one and twenty-two years had passed. The person who had done it persisted still in the obstinacy of their evil, just like the first day.

As soon as María Francisca tasted the apple, she felt the effect of what the envious hand intended for her. Her senses and powers were disturbed in such a way that her own parents could not recognize her. She would be still and peaceful at times, but her quiet did not last long, because the Old Troublemaker would not allow her to stay still. She showed in her choleric and fervid gestures that the Infernal Host dwelt inside her. If she spoke four coordinated words, in a few more she interrupted the flow of her discourse, and all could see that someone was putting obstacles to the free exercise of her mental capacity. One could no longer expect to find any devotion left in her. While she had been devout before, as a result of her sex or her Christian upbringing, the Enemy did not leave a single trace in

---

of Spanish Succession (1701–1714). Different branches of the Portocarrero family took different sides in this conflict, which engaged all the main European powers. Cardinal Portocarrero, the former prime minister of Carlos II, and Luis Antonio Portocarrero, Count of Palma del Rio and head of the branch of the family to which the late Marchioness of Mancera was related, both changed their affiliations when Philip V arrived in Spain. See Juan Antonio Zamora Caro, "Luis Antonio Portocarrero: El conde 'desafecto' (1710–1723)," *Ámbitos: Revista de estudios de ciencias sociales y humanidades* 29 (2013): 81–90.

In 1700, Carlos II proclaimed Philip of Anjou, grandson of Louis XIV of France, as his heir. Philip reigned under the name of Philip V. Karl, the archduke of Austria, contested this proclamation and invaded Spain. The city of Barcelona was the last stronghold of the Austrian party in this war. The city suffered two sieges, one in 1706 and the one in 1714 that marked the end of the conflict, when Archduke Karl had already abandoned his interest in Spain. He had become the new emperor of Austria. María Francisca may have lived through the second siege of Barcelona. She was twenty-three in 1729, when her father placed her in La Penitencia. There is a contract between the convent of La Penitencia and Don José Calvo de Tragacete that stipulates the conditions under which his daughter would live there (Archivo Histórico Nacional de Madrid, sección clero, legajo 5903). See Maeso 81–84.

5   Many were firm believers in the power of the evil eye. The Spanish Inquisition persecuted *hechiceros* (spellcasters). These beliefs were amply contested by the Spanish writers of the Enlightenment. Feijóo attacked them as superstitious (see his *Teatro crítico universal*, discurso 5:116).

her of what she had been before.⁶ The only things that reigned in her heart now were lack of piety, lack of devotion, conceit, and madness.⁷ Her parents were filled with anguish at seeing their daughter in such pain and travail. Their pleasure, their riches, and their joys were all drowned by her condition. They tried with her all the remedies, both divine and human, they could find. They called devout and spiritual experts. In particular, they sought the help of a good Discalced Carmelite friar who lived a saintly life in our city in the College of Saint Elijah. He had gained fame for his singular virtue. He did everything prescribed by our Holy Mother the Church to bring relief to lunatics.⁸ But, because of Heaven's specific wish, he was unable to bring her any comfort. Not only that, but also the devil with his cunning tried to cloak the tyrannical hold it had over her soul. When they saw that conjures and exorcisms did nothing to make her react, her parents decided to take her to several holy shrines where other unlucky souls had found remedy to similar troubles. The exemplary Carmelite went along with her to some of these places, but they were unsuccessful in all of them. God had decided that this young girl would be the one who would braid no small part of our venerable woman's garland.⁹

---

6   Lack of devotion was a sign of mental instability in a woman of the upper class. Queen Juana I of Castile showed similar symptoms—lack of religious devotion— which were reported to her mother, Queen Isabella the Catholic. See Manuel Fernández Álvarez, *Juana la Loca, la cautiva de Tordesillas* (Madrid: SLU Espasa Libros, 2000), 85.
7   The language used here is gendered. The words that mark her transformation after the devil has taken possession of her body are *falta de piedad* (lack of piety), *indevoción* (lack of devotion), *fatuidad* (fatuousness or conceit), and *locura* (craziness). The first two are accusations of inappropriate behavior for women of the upper classes, who were supposed to be devout and pious. The last two refer to social attitudes that are contrary to modesty and humility; both are expected of well-mannered women. The devil, then, makes María Francisca do unladylike things.
8   The word used in Spanish is *energúmenos*, which means "devil-possessed" or "berserk."
9   We translate *corona* as "garland" because saints, like Roman battle heroes, receive a crown of grass, or of laurel, upon their victory. Traditional iconography presents saints' heads surrounded by a crown or halo of light. The crown of the saints is made of good works. The possessed María Francisca would provide many occasions for Teresa to shine in virtue and patience, and ultimately to perform miracles.

CHAPTER 31

María Francisca's parents put her in the convent of La Penitencia under Teresa's care. Account of what this decision produced in Teresa's spirit

María Francisca's parents were frustrated in all their attempts to give her some relief. At a loss to deal with her at home because of her restlessness and the disturbances the infernal hosts visited upon the whole family and household, they decided to put her in La Penitencia. They hoped that the companionship of the Black woman, whose virtue was already well known and renowned, would tame the fury of this indomitable beast. They reached an agreement with the community. Both parties wrote down the necessary contract.[1] María Francisca's parents wanted to be successful and spoke to Teresa on the subject. She listened to them attentively and with pleasure; yet, at the same time, she excused herself from acquiescing to their wishes, for well-founded reasons and motives. When the parents saw their hopes dashed again by Teresa's rejection, they went to someone who could order her to do it out of obedience. Her director imposed this responsibility and at the very echo of his words, Teresa complied willingly. She transformed the sufferings that awaited her into a sacrificial offering to gratify her Spouse. Therefore, the patient was admitted and put in her care. The cunning Enemy thought that this was the most effective means to agitate and disturb Teresa and make her lose some of her merit. Yet he only helped her to increase it. By adding more ornaments to her virtue and obedience, he allowed her to earn more credit in the Eternal Homeland. The aforesaid director wrote to her in his letter the following words: *The Almighty*, he says, *will reward this blessed obedience, liberally.*

As soon as María Francisca entered the company of the Venerable Mother, the latter became her humble slave in everything.[2] She became her personal servant. She put her food on the table; she cleaned her and mended her clothes. She took care of everything pertaining to her service, as if that had been her only assignment and the only reason she had entered the religious cloisters. The devil was furious at such demonstrations of humility. He wailed and shouted through the patient, asking them to take away from her that negress who was her slave.[3]

---

1 The presence of María Francisca Calvo in La Penitencia is well documented. Her father, José Calvo de Tragacete signed a contract with the convent of La Penitencia that established the conditions of his daughter's stay on January 29, 1723 (Archivo Histórico Nacional de Madrid, Sección Clero, legajo 5903, quoted in Maeso 83). Therefore, María Francisca was under Chicaba's care for at least twenty years.
2 The rhetoric of humility in Christian devotional texts calls for a sense of enslavement to God's will. According to Saint Paul (Romans 6:20–23), a Christian is a servant of God, or His "ransomed slave." See Orlando Patterson, *Freedom in the Making of Western Culture* (New York: Basic Books, 1991), 341. The use of the terms "slave" and "slavery" has a dual significance in Teresa's case. On the one hand, she had been a legal slave before entering the convent, and, on the other, she is asked to perform duties that corresponded to those of a slave or lowly servant. Her African origin plays a part in this double slavery. As a former pagan, her enslavement was justified as a form of Christian ransom that continued even after her legal emancipation.
3 The devil insults Teresa with reminders of her former social status as a slave.

When Sor Teresa combed her hair, she used to put a bit of her saliva in her head, and at that point María Francisca started whistling and gesturing like a furious serpent, bursting in a pitiful voice and shouting that the negress was burning and tormenting her.[4] Her saliva was on more than one occasion a remedy to the illnesses that affected quite a few nuns. Teresa did not pay attention to any of this and continued to perform her humble tasks with her. The cowardly Spirit became so afraid of her that he was restrained and contained in the presence of the Mother. When he was more furious and arrogant, it looked as if he wanted to blow the convent up, reducing its womenfolk to pieces. But the very presence of Teresa made his fury go away. In the midst of his fits, he said some times that if it were not for the fear he had for Mother Teresa, he would have already made the nuns drown. Teresa subdued him with her meekness in such a way that she forced him to let the patient do her Christian obligations. I have already said that since María Francisca was struck with her travail, they had been unable to make her hear Mass or even pray a Hail Mary at least. Teresa forced him to let the girl not only to hear Mass and pray the Rosary every day, but also to fast every Friday of the year, the eve of feast days, and three days during Lent. The biggest struggle Teresa had with her for the first few years was to stamp out the fatal vice she had of taking every day four or five boxes of snuff. The Enemy had instilled such passion in her that she would eat it in large quantities like the most gratifying of foods.[5] There are still witnesses to this true event left in the convent, but the Mother reduced her to a state that, even if her passion was great, what she took from then onward was little and in moderation, and this only whenever Teresa gave it to her. How many noises and bangs the devil created in the convent to frighten the nuns at least a little! The courage of this cruel monster is so weak that when he cannot do anything else, he is satisfied with frightening people. But even this did not last long, because under the Mother's rule, he had to stop entertaining himself by frightening the nuns.

He saw that he had advanced little on his malevolent path and that he could not shake up the Black woman. All this was despite everything he threw at her and had placed in her way so many times. So he became a bit more calm and peaceful inside that poor girl, yet he put on her lips words that would torment any strong heart, not just Teresa's, because her words touched on matters of importance. She started saying that the Black woman was starving her to death—that what she gave her to eat was little or nothing. That she had a more than average income (which was true indeed), and that the negress did whatever she wanted with her and did not attend to even half of her needs. She sowed this gossip throughout the convent. Those who were aware of Teresa's virtue and who knew her were aware that these things were the products of the Father of Lies, and as such, they dismissed them. Those who

---

4   The act of wetting the hair with saliva before combing indicates the kind of intimate care Teresa provided for María Francisca. Her physical proximity has the effect of making the devil squirm inside the body of the possessed girl. Teresa's saliva burns the devil. Traditionally saliva has been associated in many cultures and religious systems with the spirit and divinity. Jesus performs miraculous cures by applying his spit (Mark 7:33, 8:23; John 9:6). See José Antonio Artés Hernández, "El uso de la 'saliva' en el Nuevo Testamento (MC 7,32–37, 8,22b–26 y JN 9,1–12): Antecedentes grecolatinos," *Myrtia: Revista de filología clásica* 21 (2006): 155–82. Saliva has a significant role in healing rituals in African Vodun (Suzanne Preston Blier, *African Vodun: Art, Psychology, and Power* [Chicago: University of Chicago Press, 1995] 18, 74–80, 77).

5   It looks as if María Francisca had an addiction to chewing tobacco or perhaps snuff.

were less knowledgeable, believed the words that seemed so simple and clear, took pity, and lamented the fate of the poor thing. They started rumors about the Black woman, which was another test of Teresa's patience. She was not unaware of this ruse from the devil either, but she remained silent and suffered all that they felt like saying in order to gain more merit. The Enemy's insolence became so bold that when María Francisca's relatives came to visit her at the grille,[6] she spent all the time pleading with them to be taken from under the power of that Black woman who treated her like a negress: she did not give her enough food, and she did not know what she did with her income.[7] Her complaints did not impress her relatives as much as they did some of the nuns. Her family knew and had evidence that after Teresa had spent almost all the money in grooming, cleaning, feeding, and dressing María Francisca, and that she employed all that was left in asking for Masses to be said for the patient so that His Divine Majesty would be placated and might free her from suffering. Teresa's achievement was not small because after receiving illumination by a superior and divine light, she said that María Francisca would be healed from her malady. However, they should be prepared because as soon as she was well, her life would not last long. With this, she was freed from so much of the noise, gossip, and words the Enemy had sowed around. Teresa had defeated him with her virtue and her patience. She never let María Francisca out of her sight all the time she was in her charge. She observed the advice given to her by one of her directors, who spoke in the following manner: *The enemies will do whatever is allowed them, but we must hope in the Lord and suffer with patience.* These were words that Teresa engraved in her heart and helped her gain much from the devil's treachery.

---

6 The grille or grate physically separates the members of a convent from their external visitors in the "*locutorios*" or "speak rooms." This is a boundary to the enclosure. In this instance, the *Vida* insinuates that Chicaba meets her company behind the grille. This is yet another site in the text that makes her place in the monastery ambiguous, for here she and her demoniac charge meet guests in an enclosed space.

7 In the Spanish original, "the power of that Black woman who treated her like a negress" is stated as "las [*sic*] sacasen del poder de aquella negra, pues la trataba a ella como a tal." The devil proclaims that Chicaba has inverted the social order of whites and Blacks, and furthermore, that a Black woman has power over him (226).

CHAPTER 32

The perfection with which Teresa observed the three religious vows

We have seen Teresa subject herself to penance. We have observed her mortified by human creatures and persecuted by the Abyss. We will see in time how she was tested by God's own hand through dryness and abandonment.[1] What remains to be seen then is how she complied with the three vows she made when she wed her celestial Spouse.[2] We will end with the three theological virtues in which this distinguished woman excelled. She loved her vow of poverty to such a great extent that having the opportunity to have a lot she chose nothing. Soon after she professed, the marquis and his wife passed away into a better life.[3] The marchioness wanted to demonstrate her love and affection for Teresa beyond her own earthly life. She made provision in her will to give Teresa enough to cover all the daily expenses by designating farmlands to generate the necessary income.[4] During the first years the money was paid on time, especially as long as the old servants and trustees were alive, in particular Don Andrés Bárcena y Velasco, who loved Teresa and held her in his affection like a daughter.[5] But after his death, what she received was little and always late. Nevertheless Teresa was not upset because she did not care for earthly goods and riches. Twice in her generosity, she had rejected many rich estates before coming to the convent.[6] All the

---

1 This is the most important test in the path of the mystic. It is the experience of the *noche oscura del alma* (the dark night of the soul) Saint John of the Cross described in his commentaries to the famous poem of the same title as a negation of the self, a *contemplación purgativa*, or cleansing act of contemplation (*Obra completa*, 427–28). Saint Teresa of Ávila uses the words *sequedad* (dryness) and *desamparo* (abandonment) to refer to the effect created in the mystic's soul by the perception that God is not responding to prayer. These terms come from Saint Teresa of Ávila's mystic vocabulary. She refers to the eighteen years she spent in a state of agitation or *sequedad* (dryness) (*Libro de la vida*, chap. 4, para. 9, 120). She also calls this state *desierto* (desert) (*Libro de la vida*, chap. 20, para. 10, 278). The heart seems to dry up for lack of contact with God, who is the water of life in this extended metaphor, and only the practice of the three theological virtues (faith, hope, and charity) can sustain the soul through that desert. Yet St. Teresa recognizes that through this feeling God is proving his friendship, something the learned men of her time cannot understand (*Libro de la vida*, chap. 25, para. 17, p. 339).
2 It is important to note again that there is no factual evidence that Chicaba pronounced the three canonical vows (poverty, chastity, and obedience) in any official way.
3 As mentioned several times before, this statement does not correspond to the historical facts. Doña Juliana Teresa Portocarrero, the Marchioness of Mancera, died in April 1703, and Don Antonio Sebastían de Toledo, the marquis, died in 1715, twelve years after Teresa entered La Penitencia.
4 The marchioness left Teresa a pension of fifty ducats per year, but there was no mention in her will of any lands to be entailed for this purpose. She also left instructions for Teresa's dowry, to be paid upon entering the Dominican convent of Santa Ana in Murcia, which likely never accepted Chicaba. See our note in Chapter 19 and the discussion of the marchioness's last will in the Introduction, pp. 80–81.
5 Andrés Bárcena y Velasco was the Marquis of Mancera's administrator (Maeso 101). A foundation under the name of Doña Juliana Teresa Portocarrero, Marchioness of Mancera, was indeed created. Its existence was declared extinct in 2007 by a resolution of the Autonomous Government of Madrid.
6 "Twice in her generosity" refers to Chicaba's rejection of marriage to Juan Francisco, which would have included returning to her homeland as queen, and to her earlier rejection of her position as possible heir apparent to her father.

appointments of her cell breathed and spoke of great poverty. Her jewels were the stones she slept on. Instead of paintings, she had prayer cards on the walls, and these were so old and tatty that sometimes she could not even recognize them, as we have already said in the case of Saint Nicholas of Tolentino.[7]

Her habit was poor but clean because she was very particular on this point. Seldom, if ever, did she wear new clothes, because she was happy with whatever the others discarded. She did not have any money of her own. It is true that her few expenses did not necessitate much. She lived very detached from everything that smacked of earthly interest. If anyone ever sent her something of any value—and this happened frequently because of her good reputation among the people—she would spend it immediately for devotions to Saint Vincent (who was the love of her life) or to help with some pressing need in the community or outside of it. For this, she had received a wide license. She did not keep anything for herself. She kept nothing. Once, it seems, she reserved for her own use a small sum, and her celestial and divine Spouse ordered her to get rid of it. But let her tell the incident: *Father*, she says, *after having taken Communion I felt that They asked me about a little money I had put aside for eggs and clean clothes: why are you keeping the money? Give it away.* Her celestial Spouse wanted her soul to be so openhanded that He asked her to give away and dispose of as inappropriate any little sum of money she had either wanted to use for her own needs or more likely kept for the possessed girl she was taking care of. His emphatic question explains it: *what is the money for?* Those who pride themselves for being chaste spouses of His Supreme Majesty should learn and feel ashamed at these words from God. There are many who enjoy the fortune of a religious profession, but there are only few who conform to their vow of poverty. For many, poverty only means having everything supplied that they need for their comfort. This is a point where the carelessness of some religious persons in the practice of poverty surprises me less than the little importance they give to the matter. While Teresa was a dedicated lover of poverty, after this incident she loved it even more eagerly. She lived and died in imitation of her Spouse: in total poverty.

Chastity is the vow through which our human heart becomes one with its Owner by rejecting all carnal affection. It is a virtue so sublime and excellent that by itself it elevates man by enabling him to participate in the qualities and prerogatives proper of the angels.[8] Even more, this virtue is the means by which man can exceed the angel because the latter, by his nature, is incapable of feeling impure sensations from carnal stimuli. However, the human heart is subject to that hardship, but one that if overcome with the help of grace, gives man the laurel and victory that the angel cannot obtain because he does not have to struggle with it. Teresa credited herself not as a weak woman but rather as an angel in flesh, so it seems. This was without doubt the result of divine grace. In any case, it was a special privilege. I have seen in many papers and letters how this venerable woman consulted with her confessors about problems and difficulties, but I cannot find one where she complains to have felt in herself these cruel impulses. I am persuaded that God exempted her from these kinds of temptations, thereby making her similar to the angelic spirits as much as possible. Teresa loved this virtue as much as she loved her God. She could not have been faithful to her Spouse had she not loved chastity and purity, which are the very essence of

---

7 For Saint Nicholas of Tolentino and his connection to saving people from drowning, see Chapter 29.
8 We translate *hombre* as "man" when referring to the entire human race, to be consistent with the text and its time.

this Lord. I am making a pious conjecture that is supported and proven by a singular privilege that, though granted to Saint Philip Neri, is still rare and uncommon: Teresa was able to recognize through her sense of smell those who were either free of or touched by the vice of impurity.[9] This is what the acts and records of the Provincial Chapter of the Dominican Fathers say: *She was endowed with the gift of prophecy. She penetrated the intimate corners of people's hearts. She could recognize the dishonest by their stench.* I will provide irrefutable testimony about the first and second issues in time. The last item demonstrates how much this notable woman loved her chastity and virginal purity when Heaven rewarded her with such singular prerogative.

Her profound sense of obedience further adorned the two virtues of poverty and chastity. She excelled in its practice. Her constant attention to anything that came from her directors' lips proves this. At the slightest command, Teresa performed with resignation and pleasure what they told her to do. There was no worse torment for Teresa during her last years than having to come down to the grille, either to satisfy the curiosity of an infinite number of people who wanted to see her or to give consolation and relief to many who found in her responses a happy outcome to their questions. She was humble, so she did not deem herself of any use. Aware of her reticence many who sought her aid asked her director to command her to see them. Then Teresa would come down without fail if her director told her to do it. Even the ten-day retreat that I have already referred to, when she did her spiritual exercises, would not start unless her director prescribed it. In that way, she would do it as an act of obedience, and it had more merit. She was the first in the observance of the order's constitutions and laws. Blindly obedient, she was never tardy. No matter how busy she was with different affairs, she would drop everything the moment she heard the ringing of the bell, her superior's voice, or that of the director who governed her. This way she complied exactly with her three vows. As someone who took care to advance in the practice of these three virtues, how much progress would she not achieve in the theological ones? We will start alluding to them.[10]

---

9   Saint Philip Neri (1515–1595) was the founder of the Oratorio, a congregation of priests and laypeople. In Antonio Gallonio's *Life of Saint Philip Neri* (San Francisco: Ignatius Press, 2006), one of his friends testified under oath that the saint had told him that in the last thirty years of his life "he had been quite without any urge of the flesh" (46).
10 The three theological virtues are faith, hope, and charity. As we shall see in the next few chapters, they structure the standard Catholic hagiography.

CHAPTER 33

Teresa's faith and remarkable religious practices

Faith enters us through the ear. The voice of the teacher opens the door to the one who listens, so faith can enter the soul. As true as this maxim is, Teresa's faith was most remarkable, since the First One who taught her was the very one who descended from heaven to plant it in all of our hearts. He called her toward him in that mysterious vision at the fountain back in her homeland. He gave her the first signs that stayed imprinted on her soul and were sufficient to make her seek through faith that one she still did not know entirely.[1] She received the holy baptism in the city of São Tomé, as I have said. Once faith had been infused in her soul together with the other two theological virtues, the three grew deep roots inside her. She was still a young girl and only recently instructed in the faith, and yet she acted with zeal to preserve its purity when she cried aloud at the house of the marquis that he should not have dealings with Protestants.[2] Through the power of her strong faith, God's presence in her became constant. Faith cannot remain hidden. It has to manifest itself in fervent deeds. Teresa's was so great that it irrupted in her actions. What else were the eagerness, pleading, petitions, and tears with which Teresa called at the doors of Divine Clemency to have faith spread throughout the world, but especially in her land and her kingdom? This was a living faith, and she longed for its extension throughout the entire roundness of the earth.

With the encouragement of this faith, she venerated its deepest mysteries. Such is the ineffable mystery of the Holy Trinity, for whose observance, apart from the daily exercise, she had dedicated an entire day within the week. From this mystery, which is clearly the most exalted of all, came the ineffable one of the most Holy Sacrament. All her life Teresa had the tenderest affection for the Eucharist. She had such special faith that she contemplated continuously her Master in the holy host; thus, she had almost no difficulty in believing in the real presence of her Master in that sovereign Sacrament.[3] To faith belongs the virtue of religion through which the angels, saints, and other heavenly courtiers are venerated, after God has received His due worship. Teresa's great care in this is seen in her own life. In order to worship every one of them with particular affection, she had all the days of the week dedicated in the following fashion: Sundays were dedicated to the mystery of the most

---

1 The mystical experience is the framework used by the author to explain Teresa's miraculous coming into the Christian faith. She seeks knowledge, although she does not know what she is looking for. Hers is the situation of the Queen of Sheba, a Black queen, in Calderón de la Barca's *La sibila de Oriente*. See a fuller explanation of the importance of the Queen of Sheba in the Introduction, p. 26.
2 For Chicaba's enmity to Protestantism, see Chapter 19.
3 The painting preserved in the convent of Las Dueñas of Salamanca portrays Teresa adoring the Eucharist. Teresa had a strong belief in and devotion to the mystery of Christ's physical presence in this sacrament. Through this dedication, she was in constant contact with God, as the text at the bottom of the painting attests.

Blessed Trinity. Mondays, to the relief of the suffering of the dead because it is an act of faith to believe in purgatory when there have been perverse people who denied its existence. Tuesdays were for the holy angels. Wednesdays were for the apostles and the rest of the heavenly courtiers. Thursdays were for our divine and sacramented Master. Fridays for the passion of our Lord, and Saturdays were dedicated to the veneration of Mary the Blessed Virgin. She served this sovereign Queen with all her heart and all her powers. She venerated her as a Lady and loved her as an affectionate mother, according to what she says herself in the following words: *Lord, I love the Holy Virgin with all my heart.* If she loved this Lady with all her heart, what affection and faith would she put in her veneration? The Mother of Purest Love responded to the affection her dear daughter showed her by comforting Teresa with her celestial presence, as I have said.

Her faith and zeal offered particular acts of worship and veneration to the saints. However, the apostle from Valencia drew her five senses to him like a magnet.[4] All the years she lived, she organized a solemn feast to her patriarch Saint Dominic. However, there was no feast that did not cost her unease and trouble. But she knocked down every obstacle because it was more painful to her not to hold the feast to her Father and patriarch than giving in. The number of disappointments she suffered in this world were countless, but that was not an obstacle to the celebration of the feast every year. In the case of her beloved Saint Vincent, her faith and devotion were clearly great. Nothing seemed enough to offer the saint: she chose the best music; she adorned and cleaned his altar with the utmost care for his feast day. She had to have the most eloquent and skillful preacher, whenever she could find him. She would not use one of those who are their own audience, breaking the rules of oratory and disgracing the sacred chair they hold. Nor would she have one of those with vain ideas, but a preacher well instructed in the precepts of rhetoric and also knowledgeable of the Divine Scripture and the most elegant church fathers. He had to be one who recognized the duty to speak from the pulpit like an apostle. Saint Vincent rewarded Teresa very well for her care and love. Even if Teresa's directors were always among the wisest and most virtuous, Saint Vincent came down several times to impart lessons like a loving teacher to his passionate disciple in matters of perfection and spirituality without entrusting her instruction to anyone else. The humble walls of her cell know this well although they remain silent. But if Teresa and the walls were silent then, because it was for the best, I think that it is now time to tell it in public, once Teresa's spirit is free from the ties of her mortal body and for the honor and glory of God. A sentence in the letter I have already mentioned has convinced me of it. It has enlightened me on this point, and it will shed light on the rest of the actions of this outstanding woman: *Some things*, she says, *I know, but I know to keep them quiet, because God wants it this way now.* If God wanted this at that time, the time has passed. The past is the past, so it is necessary to publicize it now for the honor and glory of God. Let us give to His honor all that we have said about the tender affection with which Teresa venerated Saint Vincent, and the plain language and familiarity she used with him when she expressed her own needs and those of others. How many sick people regained their health through her intercession! How many found a happy resolution to their particular needs—and in some

---

4 The text is referring again to Saint Vincent Ferrer because he preached for the forced conversion of the Jewish community of that city in the early years of the fifteenth century. See our earlier mention of this activity in the Introduction, p. 40n13.

cases very desperate ones! It would take too long to list them and it is idle to count their number since they were evident to all those who knew and talked to her. During public calamities, such as drought, Teresa would place a print of the saint on her window, so he would have to look at the heavens and thus she would obtain rain through his intercession. Thus, her faith obtained the appropriate remedy and consolation. There was no occasion in which Teresa put her patron saint on the window that she did not obtain abundant rain. In the last conflict this city found itself surrounded by enemy squadrons who tried to take it by assault. They threatened to commit the ultimate atrocity on the entire population.[5] Teresa put her saint in the window to spare her convent from the bombs the enemy frequently lobbed. She had such success that she not only preserved her monastery from any damage, but she also brought peace and quiet to the entire city in just a few minutes.[6] The saint thus rewarded quite visibly the love and veneration she professed to him.

---

5   The text is referring to the siege of Salamanca during the War of Spanish Succession (1701–1714). The Portuguese army took Salamanca in 1706. "Ultimate atrocity" (*último estrago*) refers to the threat to sack the city and the warning that civilian lives would not be spared.
6   Her intercession also stops the bombs of the enemy. Once again, her spiritual life has physical benefits for those around her. It was typical among Catholics to put sacred images on display as talismans of spiritual and physical protection during times of war and other catastrophes.

CHAPTER 34

Hope in Teresa, confirmed with miracles and marvels

Hope is a firm anchor with which the vessel of our soul finds security among the tempestuous waves of this life. Teresa practiced this virtue with excellence even in her childhood. What else was that solicitous inquiring about God when she was a tender child, if not a firm hope to find Him? Was not the search for the White Child to be her Spouse an unwavering hope to find Him? He allowed her to find Him in the salutary waters of baptism. Once in Madrid, Teresa revived her hopes of celebrating the nuptials she was striving to consummate in her homeland.[1] Through the three vows, she hoped to obtain and gain possession of eternal life. That is why in spite of all the rejections, deep in her soul she always harbored the hope of accomplishing what she desired, even as she saw all the doors close to her. Once inside the religious cloisters hope gave her wings. She always hoped to find God's right hand ready to shelter her through His divine goodness. Confident, she subjected herself to the profound pain of having to serve and care for the lunatic girl. She never doubted that, with her Spouse's protection, she would defeat and keep in check all of hell. Her hope always gave her strength because everything she tried was for the greater honor and glory of God.

For that reason, she attempted and achieved extraordinary deeds—undoubtedly things that exceeded the limits of her powers. She was a poor woman with a very small allowance for her upkeep, and this was subject to the discretion of others; yet she took upon herself, as a matter of honor, such great expenses that even the rich and affluent were not able to afford them.[2] Such were the expenses she incurred on the above-mentioned holy days. The gifts she gave to her Saint Vincent were many and very costly. She did not hesitate at their huge cost because she found that her hope was insurance enough for her income.[3]

How many Sisters are now happily nuns who when they entered did not have any other dowry other than what they obtained through the agency of Teresa? And when they were admitted did Teresa find a more secure way than putting her hope in Divine Providence? Some were discouraged when at the end of their novitiate year they found themselves without the money for the dowry and other necessary expenses. The novices were very upset and

---

1   Africa, or Guinea, is invoked through the term *patria* (homeland), a term that really means the land of the father or fatherland. Since her mystical baptism, we are reminded again, took place in Africa, at the fountain, her *patria* or fatherland is thus made sacred and not a heathen land. With this mystical baptism came her mystical marriage to the White Child, Jesus. This reinforces the concept of her African place of birth as a site visited by God, and not a land of pagans that had to be extracted from there to be saved by Christianity through slavery. This narrative is reinforced by the statement that her official baptism was in São Tomé, once enslaved. Therefore, she arrived in Spain already a Christian.
2   The word used here is *alimentos*, which means the money given by the marchioness to her in her will for her maintenance. The passage alludes to her practice of spending that allowance on the celebration of saints' festivals. These funds would go to pay for Masses and other ceremonies.
3   The text is referring to donations in money Sor Teresa Chicaba received from individuals in exchange for her prayers. It may also be referring to the money left to her by the Marchioness of Mancera in her will, which seems to have dried up after the death in 1715 of the marquis.

decried their misfortune at having to return to the whirlwind of the world for lack of means. But Teresa was firm and constant and with a smiling face bade one to stop crying and dry her tears. She calmed another one with the aid of Divine Providence. She told them all: "Put your hope in God because He will not allow your wishes to be undone." With these tender words, they found themselves with a dowry from places and at times they least expected.

This is what happened to a nun who, after the year as a novice, found herself as short of money as she was rich and full of desire to find safety in the harbor of religious life through the three vows. She was very upset because neither she nor the others knew who could get them out of this predicament. Their only remedy remained to hope that the passage of time would play to her advantage. Originally Teresa had covered all the expenses to admit the novice. Trusting Divine Providence and putting all her hope in God, Teresa proceeded with all the necessary preparations for the ceremony of religious profession. She went to kill the hens for the next day's feast and said with good humor: "It is already the eve of your profession, and you are still dawdling?" The nun answered: "And what are we gaining by killing the hens if the ceremony will not take place tomorrow because I lack the principal thing? Where is it going to come from?" To which Teresa said again: "Madam, you go and kill the hens because tomorrow the novice will profess without fail." The nun had a hard time believing this. But her lack of faith worked to prove how much God was pleased with Teresa's hope. The next morning without fail, a person like many others who sought Teresa came to visit her. Generous and pious, this person gave the convent all that was necessary for the novice's dowry. In this way and through miracles, Divine Omnipotence showed how much He liked the hope of His beloved spouse. Apart from the marvels that she experienced, Teresa worked tirelessly in the realm of the natural, doing things that seemed to exceed her weak powers. Her hope in God was firm; thus, she expected a good outcome in every endeavor with His protection.

She struggled and worked even more than her strength allowed because experience had taught her that when her weak constitution failed her, her efforts would be secure with the help of grace. She worked hardest on the days before the feasts of Saint Dominic and Saint Vincent. There were no other times when she would do so much work. If her love gave her wings, hope increased her physical powers. And if Teresa was too tired of working or completely devoid of strength and could not complete her tasks, Heaven soon came to relieve her and to help her rest. This is what happened on the following occasion.

On one of those holy days, Teresa tired herself to a greater extent than she used to. Whether the work was too much or her advanced age did not give her the vitality to endure the exertion, she had to go inside herself and ask her Spouse for help, as He was the master of her secrets. In brief and deeply felt words she told him of her fatigue, pleading with Him to send someone who could come and finish her duties. The miracle showed that her supplication had pleased Heaven, because a short while later she heard a nun come downstairs. Teresa saw her and asked where she was going. The nun responded: "Madam, to the choir. They have called me, so it must be the time." "Oh, no, my daughter," Teresa told her, "it's not time for Choir. It's one in the morning." "But madam, if they have called me . . . ," she replied again, to which Teresa said: "No, my daughter, it's not that. It's our Father Saint Dominic who has called you to help me finish this work, so let's go for it." The nun helped her, not without admiring what she had heard Teresa say, but she was particularly happy to have been the one God had used as His instrument to give Teresa some respite.[4] Out of the trust and hope in which she lived, the Lord came in this benign way to help Teresa. My pen could have collected many other marvels to prove how much this virtue shone in Teresa's soul. The ones I have just told are sufficient. Apart from their being original and authentic, those who saw and experienced them are still alive. These incidents will give the reader a brief idea to what high degree this happy and fortunate soul possessed the virtue of hope.

---

4 This is another textual instance when the true nature of Chicaba's menial work in the convent is emphasized. She was clearly overworked and only miracles helped her. This prepares us for the tone of the poem in Chapter 35.

CHAPTER 35

Teresa's ardent charity

This virtue, as queen of all others, deserves the most eminent place. As such, it was so highly placed in Teresa's soul that the pen will have abundant material to write what is left of the account of her admirable life. Charity is an act of divine love. It rules all the movements of the will toward God; and, once in God, it directs them as the Supreme Good worthy of love. It is a flame that purifies every earthly aspect of the self and leaves a rational creature a clean and perfect image of the Supreme Majesty. The flame that enlivened Teresa's soul proclaims how much this virtue made her shine like a jewel. What pen could report all the extremes of her love? Not mine, because I know that if she was not the only one who practiced so much charity in our time, she was one among those God set apart for their excellence. Teresa loved so much that we can believe everything I have told so far and recognize the degree of perfection achieved by her soul, and how much charity she harbored in it. As a soul that had been forgotten by many at the beginning, that later was respected by an infinite number despite her discomfort with that attention—a soul that was despised by not a few—she loved God with all her heart and affection. Love took her out of her homeland, and love was what gave her courage in the house of her owners to endure her suffering. Love gave perfection to her soul in the religious cloisters.[1]

She followed the divine oracle and commandment of love to the letter. What had been commanded of all of us for a long time, God Himself taught to Teresa by means of a singular event. Her soul was eager to keep divine grace in itself and in the souls of all rational creatures. With that end she promptly asked her celestial Divine Spouse the means to achieve this. The following response was handed down to her: *I felt*, she says, *inside my heart that everyone should love Him very much*. And Teresa loved Him a lot indeed with all her heart, powers, and senses, and that is why she advanced so much in charity. *I do not know*, the venerable one goes on, *what it is to love God, or how to please Him; but it seems to me that He would like for an attentive heart to be truthful in everything. The heart should be attached only to those things that pertain to His Glory, casting away from itself all worldly things from everything created. The heart should look at the Creator alone, as the Lord is the only thing the heart can call its own. Soul, life, and heart must spare nothing for His Majesty. I am well aware that I know this, but it needs yet to be done.* That is how it seemed to you, Teresa, but you did not stop a moment from doing what you felt and knew. If you think that you did not do enough, what then was all that eagerness of *I love you, I love you, I love you* that on occasion burst from your chest, shaken uncontrollably by that very love? People heard it. If you did not know how to love, why were you so jealous when your Spouse was absent?

Good love has a certain element of jealousy that is a faithful proclaimer of how active this volcano is, as it also serves as a harbinger of the most intense affection.[2] In Chapter

---

1 Slavery is defined here as an act of charity. Being kidnapped, we have seen, was an act of God to which she submitted as a loving creature. In this way the agency of the slavers is erased, as they become mere instruments in God's design.
2 Following the rhetoric of courtly love, with the term *fino amor* so often used by Spanish and other

29, we saw the Divine Lover a bit jealous of our venerable one when the majesty of Christ reprimanded her for that slight lapse of admitting to her cell the priests who had said Mass at the convent.[3] This was a clear sign that He loved her because He was very jealous. Teresa's love for her Master wanted to take credit for its elevated nature, by also being a little jealous. After one of her Master's absences, this jealousy made her exclaim spontaneously the following verses.[4] The lack of artifice in them could well have been the ploy of a lover, wishing to act without restraint:[5]

> Oh, Jesus, where are you gone?
> I cannot stand a moment
> Without seeing you.
> Oh, Jesus of my soul,
> Where are you gone?
> It seems you are not coming back
> And you are lost.
> Oh, Jesus, what shall I say?
> If you go out with other women,
> What shall I do?
> I will wail, I will cry
> Till I see God,
> And if not, if not,
> I will die of love.
> And I say,
> Because I am so lonely,
> That you have not come.
> And if you are with someone else,
> I have seen it before:
> Martha and Mary,
> You have loved them.
> Oh, Jesus, where shall I find you?
> I feel giddy[6]

European mystics of the fifteenth and sixteenth centuries, jealousy shows the intensity of the passion felt by the lover, but it also tests the beloved's resolve.

3   The constitutions of cloistered orders prohibited direct contact between men and women. Only extern sisters and laypersons were allowed to talk alone with visiting priests without the barrier of the iron grille between them. This anecdote attests to Chicaba's liminal position within the community, as she did not live in the same quarters as the rest of the nuns. It is important to note that her cell was situated outside the cloistered area, and not officially part of the cloister. However, she takes Christ's jealous rebuke as proof that He considers her as much a spouse as the fully cloistered nuns and holds her to the standards demanded of them. This anecdote reads as an attempt by Chicaba to include her cell as an extension of the cloister.

4   In Catholic mystical language, the perception of the absence of God from the soul is referred to in different ways, such as a night of the soul or as traveling through the desert. See Chapter 32, note 1.

5   "Lack of artifice" is a phrase the text uses to reinforce the idea of sincerity of feeling, especially that of a Black woman.

6   The original Spanish says "*tan tonta me tiene*," using the word *tonta* with the meaning of loss of physical and emotional equilibrium, a kind of dizziness akin to being inebriated by love. Saint Teresa used the word *tonta* (dizzy, silly) to refer to the feeling of confusion as she was passing from what she called the third degree of prayer, prior to total contemplation or *quietud* (stillness). Saint Teresa mentioned the example of Martha and Mary that the poem refers to: "Esto, aunque parece todo uno, es diferente de

When I have you.
Good-bye, good-bye, love,
Good-bye, Lord,
Good-bye, heart,
No more, no more,
No more.[7]

These verses are evidence that love makes the lover intolerant. Teresa's love complains impatiently about her Spouse's tardiness and that another soul detains Him. On the other hand they express how well Teresa did the office of love when she laments: *I am well aware that I know this, but it needs yet to be done.*

The impulse of divine love burning in this happy soul's breast was so fierce that the weight of her body could not contain the agility of her spirit. Her spirit lifted her up in rapture more than once, raising her off the ground.[8] People saw her in this state only a few times, because she hid herself and kept it as secret as she could. Once, however, they were able to see her without her noticing them. Impelled by her love, she was completely transported in her celestial divine Master, her face resplendent, her cell bathed in light, enjoying in solitude supreme pleasures. She stitched this fine love to her breast and heart so securely that she felt deeply what His Supreme Majesty allowed no other pen but hers to

---

la oración de quietud que dije, en parte porque allí está el alma que no se querría bullir ni menear, gozando en aquel ocio santo de María; en esta oración puede ser también Marta (ansí que está casi obrando juntamente en vida activa y contemplativa)" [This form of prayer, although it looks one and the same thing, is different from the prayer of stillness that I referred to. In part, because in that sort of prayer the soul stays as if it did not want to budge or even move, as it is enjoying Mary's holy leisure. In this other form of prayer one can also be Martha, so one is involved in both active and contemplative life] (*Libro de la vida*, chap. 17, para. 4, p. 245). A similar expression for the effects of the mystical experience: "Los días que durava esto andava como embovada" [During the days it lasted, I was out of sorts] (*Libro de la vida*, chap. 29, para. 14, p. 385)

7   We have transcribed the text in Spanish respecting the original spelling and punctuation in this case.

Aih Jesvs, don te has ido,
que un instante no puedo
verme sin tigo.
Aih Jesus de mi alma,
donde te has ido,
que parece no vienes,
y te has perdido.
Aih Jesus, què dirè yo?
si os vais con otras,
què harè yo:
Clamarè, llorarè
hasta vèr à Dios,
y si no, y si no,
morir de amor.
Y yà lo digo,
pues estoy tan sola,
que no has venido.

Y si estàs con otra,
Yà yo lo he visto;
a Marìa, y Marta
las has querido.
Aih Jesvs! Dónde te ha-
llarè yo
pues tan tonta me tiene,
cuando te tengo:
A Dios, à Dios, amor,
à Dios, Señor
à Dios corazon,
no mas, no mas,
no mas.

8   In the Catholic tradition, levitation is God's gift to those who have renounced earthly attachments that encumber the spirit. Thus, when the body loses importance in a mystic's life, the spirit takes over and the physical laws governing a material body are temporarily suspended.

tell.⁹ No one but her could express even the slightest trace of what she felt: *In this pain*—she speaks of an extraordinary pain that she felt in her heart—*I come to understand that the Lord is inside my heart always. Therefore, if I get upset, or I am not in conformity with Him, this pain goes away. So it is very painful when my heart is serene and calm. It becomes burning when my love rises excessively to the point of wishing to fulfill all my duties and obligations. But I am not saying it right because it is not excessive, because it is reasonable. I am burning, I feel I am being seared, I would shout aloud, but I scream inside myself.* And you shouted out too, oh fortunate soul, because you could not contain yourself. Is this the same person who knew love but did not practice it? Is this the same one who did not ignore the acts, but did not put them into execution? Oh my God, how tender you are with those who seek and love You. Let Teresa finish the explanation of the event: *The pain I feel in my heart is so great*, she says, *that inside I feel as if it is covered in sweat. I do not know how to explain myself except in this manner. His Majesty will help Your Reverence understand everything I would like to say but cannot in this short explanation.* So her pen wrote, but here is also where mine recoils from the fear of being seared by so much fire and flame, though I would be happier.¹⁰ Those who are learned may reflect on this marvel, that although church history records similar cases, hers is nonetheless magnificent. God performs these works to teach us.

---

9   The text claims to quote directly from Chicaba's writings. The same scene of a sweet pain in the heart occurs in Saint Teresa of Ávila's famous description of the angel that pierces her heart with a golden dart (*Libro de la vida*, chap. 29, para. 13, p. 384).

10 The word "pen" is again used as a quotation mark to close Teresa's own words, as if to separate them from the narrator's discourse.

CHAPTER 36

Teresa's tender love for the majesty of Christ in the Eucharist. Miracles the sovereign Master made through her

The love Teresa had for the supreme and divine majesty of God necessarily focused and concentrated in a singular and pure love for the majesty of Christ, who is all good. There are many reasons to love Him as both man and God because although the Divine Word is still God after becoming man, it seems as if He absorbed all our love when He deigned to partake of our nature.[1] Teresa's love was so pure that when she contemplated the life of our Redeemer she never erased Him from her memory. This contemplation always revived her living flame of love.[2] It gave her those loving emotions that, as she says, perhaps became fear and made her consult her director in the following terms: *Sir, I have a fear. I love our Lady the Holy Virgin with all my heart, but it seems that I love her Most Holy Son even more. I would not like the Holy Virgin to have complaints against me because I owe her a lot. I am saying this so Your Reverence can tell me what you think of it.* Thus, she explained her love and through this we can see the unalloyed affection she had for her sovereign Redeemer.[3] Teresa showed all her tenderness for a print she had of Christ carrying the cross. When she saw Him with such a heavy burden on His shoulders, her love for Him made her own cross seem very light.

Teresa excelled in her love and affection for the majesty of Christ in the Most Holy Sacrament.[4] Her soul found complete rest in this mystery of love. She never failed to visit her Beloved during the exposition of the sacrament. On Holy Thursday and Good Friday, she did not leave His presence one moment.[5] Her love for this Heavenly Bread went beyond this life because she insisted with affectionate eagerness to have her body buried in a place where she could at least be in view of the Tabernacle. So even after her body was dead and

---

1 "The Divine Word is still God after becoming man" is a biblical paraphrase: "And the Word became flesh, and dwelt among us" (John 1:14). For Catholics the mystery of the Incarnation is the belief that Christ is both divine and human and that at the moment of conception (which took place at the Annunciation) "the Word became Flesh." Nuns believed that their vocation—that is, their "calling"—was a spiritual reflection of the Virgin Mary's Annunciation. Thus, their virginal bodies were important in the spiritual economy for a number of reasons: First, they understood themselves as called to be spouses of Christ; and, second, that their bodies were empty and pure vessels like Mary's so that they paradoxically participated in the mystery of the Incarnation of their Beloved. The Incarnation comes to full fruition at the Nativity celebrated on Christmas. See the note in Chapter 24 in relation to Teresa's mystical ceremony of profession. By maintaining her virginity, Chicaba was proclaiming her right as a Black woman to partake in the mystery of the Incarnation of Christ. By proclaiming herself a Black bride of Christ, she also proclaimed herself a Black mother of Christ.

2 This is a reference to the Saint John of the Cross poem *Llama de amor viva* (*Living Flame of Love*) (*Poesía*, 263).

3 Since Petrarch, love and affection have been defined in terms of gold, jewels, diamonds, and the like. The word *firmeza* in seventeenth-century Spanish meant both loyalty in love (firmness) and a diamond, which was considered the firmest of stones.

4 For a discussion of her portrait with the sacrament, see our note in Chapter 33.

5 The phrase refers to the liturgical practice in the Catholic Church of displaying the Eucharistic host—the consecrated wafer—in churches for the adoration of the faithful. People stay overnight in church because the host should not be left unattended, as it represents a king appearing in public.

buried, all would know that her sacramental Master was the magnet of her love. From that love came a celestial hunger to eat at that Sacred Table all hours of the day. Her directors restrained this eagerness in order to test and train her. But her Master satisfied this hunger with repeated miracles. The Venerable Father Jerónimo commanded his daughter not to receive Holy Communion until he allowed her to do so.[6] Teresa obeyed with patience and resignation. She explained the director's command to her Spouse, expressing and at the same time sacrificing in front of Him all the affection of her burning heart. This loving Master, pleased with Teresa's resignation, took to His heart her love and pure desire. He hinted to the Venerable Father to lift so harsh a command on Teresa. Heaven only knows the means and the manner in which it was done. The effect was that this faithful servant of God obeyed his Lord's voice and went to the church of La Penitencia early in the morning. He called his beloved daughter and told her to take Communion that very morning, leaving her soul happy and joyful, satisfied and content with the celestial Meal. With these sovereign favors such a fine Spouse repaid Teresa's deep love and veneration for the divine host.

Why wonder that Teresa's love for the most Holy Sacrament was so heroic, when her Spouse was so generous and open with her? I do not know who of the two was more consumed by desire, Teresa to receive Him in her heart or this loving Master to enter hers. We saw proof of the first instance in Teresa's eagerness to receive the sacrament of Communion frequently. The second instance can be seen in the following event. One day Teresa was in front of the small opening in the grille ready to receive Communion, and the priest had the host in his hand.[7] Her hidden Master's love made Him so impatient that He slipped from the priest's hands into Teresa's mouth. The short time that it would take Him to reach her lips seemed too long a delay for Him who desired to be united and together with a soul that He loved and who pleased Him so much. The priest was astonished at what he saw. It would have astonished the most spiritual seraph when he saw so much favor and mercy coming from the Supreme Majesty. Thus, the Spouse repaid even in this life the love and affection Teresa professed for Him. This flame, this fire or volcano burning in her heart, lightened the burdens occasioned by illness, feebleness, and the passage of years, giving her strength to abandon her bed and seek relief and consolation in the Eucharist. This was certified by eyewitnesses who dwelled in the convent, who noticed and admired it during the last days of her life. The miracle is told verbatim as follows.

The fatal accident that would cost her life in the end left Teresa so weakened that she could not move any limb at all on the side where the paralysis affected her most. She spent some days in her cell like that, suffering more from the absence of her celestial Master in the Sacrament than from the accident itself. One of those mornings she called a nun who helped her and asked for help getting dressed. The nun was astonished at such a strange request and responded that there was no point in getting dressed when she could not even stand on her feet. "Your Worship, please bring my clothes," Teresa said, "and we will see if I can or cannot." The nun brought her clothes to her more in an effort to please her than

---

6   This is again Father Jerónimo Abarrategui, her spiritual director, and founder of the Theatine house in Salamanca. He resided there under Bishop Francisco Calderón de la Barca, the prelate who initially opposed Chicaba's admission to La Penitencia.

7   This is an instance when Chicaba seems to be behind the grille and in the enclosed part of the monastery chapel, for the priest passes the host through an opening in the grate to the nuns in enclosure. The priest does not go inside to say Mass. This is another ambiguity about her position as represented in the *Vida*.

because she imagined what would happen next. She started to help Teresa into them quite slowly. As she got dressed she noticed new strength and vigor on that side. Once she finished getting dressed she told them to go to the choir because the priest was on his way to give Communion. However, there was no priest in the church, neither did they expect one, and the one who came even less. The nuns were dumbfounded at the news that Mother Teresa was all dressed and all came to see such a new and strange thing. The prioress was most worried because at every step Teresa took she felt a pang in her soul, fearing the nun would fall due to her feebleness. Any fall would have been fatal in someone so old, and the prioress did not trust the strength and robust condition divine grace had invested in her. She was all directions, orders, and plans to see how the patient could go down to the choir without risk. When Teresa saw her so troubled and worried she said in good humor: "Ladies, please give our Lady Prioress some cherry water, because she looks very frightened." She kept repeating "cherry water for the Lady Prioress" as she descended the stairs, which were steep and difficult. She did not require help, although most of them were around her. The fright seemed to have had a contagious effect in all.

She arrived in the choir, and the priest was already in the church. He gave her Communion, thus satisfying her desire. Once her soul received the pleasure of her Beloved's presence, she went back upstairs with the same agility she had come down. The nuns guided Teresa's steps toward her cell, and she told them no, that they should go toward the infirmary. She got there and lost her vigor and strength like before, just as the cruel paralysis had left her at the beginning. All the nuns of the monastery were eyewitnesses to this miraculous case. The priest himself was a witness too. He wondered about what had happened when he realized that he had left his house without special reason. He then had directed his steps toward that convent without any special need to do so. But Teresa's fine Lover was particularly careful in this, because He wanted to communicate with her in the Holy Eucharist.

CHAPTER 37

Teresa's charity toward her neighbors. Ardent zeal for the good of all

Here it is necessary to muzzle my pen with caution. If I wanted to tell at length the different miraculous cases in which Teresa manifested her ardent charity toward her neighbor, perhaps I might defame someone.[1] Apart from being against divine law, against my own intention, and against the goal of this history, defamation would also upset Teresa very much. While on earth, she cared a lot for the good name of all Christians. In Glory (where piety makes us believe she is now) she will not have lost that noble inclination. Therefore, I will say briefly something about all the things Teresa did for her neighbor. Her charity for everyone was so profound that because she was Black, she became the slave to all.[2] Those who were afflicted found consolation in her. The ones in need found help; the sick found health, although her humility made her hide her good deeds. She attributed to her dear Saint Vincent any miracle of that nature. Anyone coming to her for counsel would find it without fail. Those who looked for it found direction, and that is why so many people seeking Teresa in their distress and finding in her a shelter made her unspeakably tired. Whenever she saw someone in her monastery who was distressed and sad, she did not rest or stop until she took care of the sorrow and left the other person happy and comforted. As for religious needs, which are regular and frequent in a convent as poor as this one, she found solutions for all whenever she could. With the sick her charity and virtue shone most. She used her charity in attending on them, serving and curing them. She cared for them with extreme cleanliness in all that she thought necessary for their health and comfort.

For a long time she attended a lay patient who lived in the convent. This woman had sores that repelled anyone who looked at them, either because of their number or the fetid smell issuing from them.[3] The assistants could not tolerate the vile odor. Although their charity for the sick woman was great, all or most of them stayed away and cared for her only at the prescribed times. But Teresa's ardent charity undertook her care. She cured her with her own hands, by cleaning and grooming her. She found in the open sores of the patient a good occasion to mortify her appetite, which she offered as a pleasant holocaust to her Spouse. Overcoming her natural repugnance and encouraged by love, she licked the sores

---

1   The word in Spanish is *deshonor* (to cause dishonor). In the culture of the time, to have one's name associated with weakness or a state of need might cause dishonor. It was risky to name directly anyone who might still be living or whose relatives were still alive in this hagiography.
2   *Propiamente como negra*: since she was "properly a Black," then she acted as one, becoming the slave of all. Here the text equates Teresa's Black skin color to her natural social role in the time. The text maintains that she "honored" her race by becoming the best slave possible to as many people as she encountered.
3   As in the case of María Francisca, it seems that the convent of La Penitencia admitted different laywomen who suffered from different health problems, and Sor Teresa Chicaba was the one in charge of caring for them.

while she cured her. Her lips were a sponge into which she sucked the filth of the matter. Charity gave her strength to do such a heroic action. Teresa also assisted another nun, who was suffering from a cancerous ulcer, the entire time of her illness until her death. She cured and washed her with her own hands. She would not let anyone else deal with the bandages that she had to take away. She also cared and assisted an old nun called Lady Saint Augustine. Her virtuous and religious life made Teresa love her a great deal. She cared for her especially during her last years, when because of her advanced age she was disabled to the point of needing help to eat. To tell everything Teresa did throughout her life would be a never-ending story. Suffice it to say that there was no patient in the convent Teresa did not assist with compassion, comforting and cheering her. There were even some whom she healed instantly just with her saliva. Still today, many attest to this experience. It is not strange that the saliva that burned and tormented the forces of hell—as the Enemy himself explained through the mouth of the demoniac—would comfort the sick and restore them to health.[4]

But the ardent love of Teresa's soul did not stop solely at bodily ailments. She moved on to far more dangerous maladies, which we do not make much of because we do not see them. However, their victims deserve much more pity. I am talking about those people who live stubbornly enmeshed in their vices and are mortally ill in their souls. Whenever Teresa learned that someone was in a bad way—through information received from above, and in this she was very well versed—it is unbelievable the amount of effort she made to get the person out of it. She cried out with tender eagerness for God to awaken those souls from their culpable lethargy. She would punish her virginal body with unspeakable torments to force her celestial Spouse to give these souls special and efficient help, and to temper and abate His righteous anger. She would send messages to that soul with tact and discretion. Her messages were as noncommittal and the words as equivocal to the person carrying them as they were clear and open to the individual to whom they were directed. Some other times she asked them to come see her at the grille.[5] Once she was alone with them, she would reveal to them their own consciences with holy shrewdness. She rebuked them for their sins with such effective words that could soften a rock and overcome the most stubborn obstinacy. Those who listened to her prudently were able to come out of the slough of their faults. Those who were deaf to her tender words increased the obstacles to their own healing by their very compulsive sinning. A particular instance of this happened to her. She knew of a person who had made religious profession but who led a most unobservant life. Zealous for the well-being of that soul, Teresa sent repeated messages to that person. Her skill and art kept the messenger ignorant of the goal, yet they touched the delinquent to the quick of the soul. The person did not pay attention and went on with their affairs and pleasures in the same way. When the Venerable Mother saw how little progress she had made with messages, she sent them notice to come see her at the grille. The person responded affirmatively. After some time, when Teresa saw that the person would not show up, she sent a second and a third message. This person gave a polite answer to all, but not the response the Mother was

---

4   The power of her saliva against the devil had been demonstrated in the episode of María Francisca (Chapter 31). She had been healing people in Africa before being enslaved in Spain (Chapter 3).
5   This grille is different from the one separating the choir from the rest of the chapel. This is the grille in the speak room that separates nuns from outside visitors.

looking for, which was to amend their way of life.[6] The person did not fulfill the promise to visit her and continued living without any noticeable change in their ways. But, oh just vengeance from on High! A short time after, this person died suddenly as an example to others and to the horror of those who had been aware of this person's perversities. Teresa's love did not benefit the living only. It extended with vigor also to the dead. All her penances she could afford to apply to them, and there were many, she reserved to speed them to their eternal rest. Not a single day passed that she did not say the nightly Office of the Dead.[7] The number of prayers she said aloud was countless. She earmarked part of her meager funds for support to have Masses said for them. Her soul was hardly satisfied with all the things she did, and still she mentioned in all her prayers the blessed souls in purgatory. When a well-known nun or religious man died, she would write to her spiritual correspondents so they could take under their charge to commend that soul to God.[8] I could copy here several sentences from her letters to prove this matter, but I will omit them because the most authentic letter of all on this issue was her burning charity. Through prayers and Masses for the dead, she helped a large number of souls leave purgatory. Its dwellers knew well how effective Teresa's pleas and supplications were in alleviating their suffering. Many of these souls came to visit her with divine permission. She says it herself in her letter: *Sir, in relation to what we spoke about in the confessional about the dead, I say again that it was a multitude of them of all social ranks. And I saw more: some had wings, and all had diverse garments. Their faces were many, and among these, I could only distinguish some from my house.*[9] From these words—what they explain and what they leave to be understood—one can infer the intense commerce between those in purgatory and this Venerable Mother. One understands that she spoke of the dead in the confessional, and indeed she did because she told the Venerable Father Don Jerónimo several times when he was her director. She had repeatedly seen the souls coming out of their penance and going to heaven all suffused in glory. She told him, and she wrote it too. But the paper was misplaced by the Venerable Father out of some secret command from Heaven. He sent it to the observant convent of Augustinian Mothers, the Recoletas, inside a bundle containing some amices.[10] A daughter of confession he had in that convent had to mend them. When the Venerable Father realized his mistake, taking

---

6   In the Spanish text, the gender of the person being referred to has been left unspecified.
7   "Nightly Office of the Dead": in the original Spanish, "el nocturno de difuntos." This is another indirect reference to Chicaba's literacy, as it implies that she could read the Latin of the Office of the Hours. The Office of the Dead of the Catholic Church includes the nocturnes, which are three series of three psalms and three readings sung at Matins (the early hours of the day, before dawn). See Fernand Cabrol, "Office of the Dead," *The Catholic Encyclopedia*, vol. 11 (New York: Robert Appleton Company, 1911). www.newadvent.org/cathen/11220a.htm.
8   There is evidence of this correspondence in the convent of Las Dueñas in the form of her letter to Father Vicente Figueroa. See Figure 2.
9   The Afro-Peruvian Úrsula de Jesús wrote or dictated a series of visions of purgatory in the middle of the seventeenth century in which she gave notice of different people she and her community knew who were still in purgatory. See the Introduction, p. 12. The different clothing may refer to different social classes on earth or new rank in heaven. In heaven rank is not supposed to follow the laws of the earth.
10 The amice is a piece of white cloth that must be made of either flax or hemp. The priest places it around his neck and over his shoulders under the alb and the chasuble. Amices were often (and still are) laundered and mended by nuns in convents as a special favor. See Herbert Thurston, "Amice," *The Catholic Encyclopedia*, vol. 1 (New York: Robert Appleton Company, 1907). www.newadvent.org/cathen/01428c.htm.

one paper for another, he hurried to the aforementioned convent. He called his daughter of confession and asked for the paper. The nun had already read it, and she refused to give it to him. The Venerable Father, rather than explaining his reasons, simply told her: "Congratulations, don't give it to me, but burn it at once, because I order it." She obeyed with resignation and burned the paper, but it remained impressed in her memory so we could all know of the ardent charity Teresa had for the dead and how important to them her charity was.

CHAPTER 38

*Heaven endows her with prophetic light,
proven by certain miracles.*

The gift of prophecy, as one of those graces *gratis datas* (given graciously)[1] is not an infallible proof of sanctity, because it can be found in those who are not saintly, but it nevertheless has to make us elevate the opinion of an individual who is adorned with such distinction. I do not need to say more to the learned. Those who are not, and they are not destined to learning either, do not need to know more. Teresa was gifted with this prerogative, and she knew ahead of time about the death in Coria of her venerable director, Father Jerónimo, whose *Life* has been given to the press by Doctor Diego de Torres Villarroel, a faculty member of the University of Salamanca, where he holds the chair of mathematics.[2] His death occurred in the year 1749. In that *Life*, chapter 14 states at length that at the moment when that portentous man's soul left the mortal prison of the body, it came in triumph and glory to bid farewell to Teresa, because for a long time he had been giving her instruction on how to please and serve God better while her pilgrimage lasted in this world.[3] Giving her his loving blessing, he left her with it and told her things that were happening in Coria that would have been impossible to know in Salamanca in any other way.[4]

Thus Teresa knew through an interior light what happened to other people. She penetrated the most intimate rooms of many consciences and hearts. A righteous and virtuous priest experienced this. His name was Don Juan Díaz. He was saying Mass one day and Teresa was in attendance. In the middle of the Sacrifice a sort of fright assaulted his conscience. He concluded the Mass with great difficulty. As soon as he disrobed in the vestry, the Venerable Mother was already by the turnstile. She explained to him in tender words what had happened to him. She reassured him that the species of his fright was not true, and it certainly was not. He could rest and live in peace and calm. These words had the effect of dispelling his scruple, producing in his soul the most stable and firm peace.[5] On

---

1 Our translation.
2 As mentioned in the Introduction, p. 3, Torres Villarroel's hagiography of this Theatine priest was part of a program of canonization that included the production of Chicaba's hagiography. Chicaba's story appears in Torres Villarroel's *Vida* of Father Jerónimo Abarrategui, 107–9. The use of the present tense indicates that Paniagua and Torres Villarroel were good friends, as shown by this collaboration.
3 Chicaba saw a white bird surrounded by light on the site where Father Abarrategui used to hear confessions. Then she heard the voice of Father Abarrategui and saw him "rodeado de luces clarísimas de un color más subido que el oro que se aprecia en el mundo (frase con que explicó la Venerable Negra la visión)" [surrounded by a very clear light, of a color brighter than any gold the world values (a phrase the Venerable Black Woman used to explain the vision)]. Torres Villarroel, *Vida*, 107–9.
4 Coria is a city south of Salamanca, where Father Abarrategui died. The miraculous vision is given credence because the distance between the two cities would have made it impossible for anyone to cover it in one day.
5 "Scruples" is the term the Church uses to explain a psychological disorder affecting religious people, who feel a profound sense of guilt and a sense of sin about trivial things, and this results in erratic behavior (Joseph Delany, "Scruple," *The Catholic Encyclopedia*, vol. 13 [New York: Robert Appleton Company, 1912]. Retrieved from New Advent, *www.newadvent.org/cathen/13640a.htm*).

a different occasion, the Venerable Mother was in the choir with another nun next to her. The latter looked very distressed by some thoughts that had taken away all her calm and interior peace. She fought for a long time with virile and courageous spirit.[6] Illuminated by a superior light, Teresa saw the affliction of this soul and told her: "Why don't you tell your confessor what is happening to you and you will be at peace?" The nun was astounded at seeing her interior so revealed. Recovering from the fright, she took her advice and told her confessor her concern, after which she was free from that sorrow. Teresa kept the interiors present, because the Divine Light manifested to her the inside of people's consciences.

The conscience of a novice was very perturbed, because she feared her lack of health to tolerate the hardships of religious life would deprive her of taking the habit. This was not something the other nuns ignored, since she looked so ill. Teresa noticed and, eager to comfort the novice, she asked her with sweet words. But although the words from the Mother were soft and gentle, they did not dispel the fear and sorrow of the novice—not until Teresa told her, after seeing it with divine and superior light, that she would see herself professing and healthy enough to continue her religious life. Teresa's prediction came to be. The novice professed, and she is still healthy, following for years now the hardships practiced in her religious order. That same nun asked her to commend a brother of hers to God who was about to leave for Madrid on some business, so His Majesty would give him a safe and successful journey. Teresa heard her calmly and responded with a smile: "I will not have to ask God to give him a good journey, because your brother will not go to Madrid." "How come, Mother, if he is waiting only for my word to take with him, and the journey is already arranged?" "Your brother will not go to Madrid," Teresa responded. And that was the case, because the journey was canceled for no special reason. The nun was amazed at the prescience of Teresa, illuminated as she was by divine light. Teresa used it also to bring peace to the bitter dissensions of a married couple. The occasion was a filthy animal that had swallowed a leather pouch full of coins. Teresa discovered who the thief was and brought them back to their old concord. The anecdote was funny, but one that has been omitted, because the witnesses in the matter carelessly forgot to depose it as they should have, even if it would have been only out of gratitude. Because of this, the event cannot be certified as is necessary in these matters.[7]

It would be a never-ending story to refer to all the things Teresa discovered with the

---

6 In Spanish Renaissance and Baroque literature, "virile spirit" is a term used frequently to refer to the courage exhibited by some women on special occasions. Women, like children, were not supposed to have the temperament or proper state of mind to endure difficulties. Their nature was considered weak. Saint Teresa of Ávila recommends that her nuns act with a virile spirit despite their feminine nature: "Es muy de mujeres y no querría yo, hijas mías, lo fueseis en nada, ni lo parecieseis, sino varones fuertes: que si ellas hacen lo que es en sí, el Señor las hará tan varoniles que espanten a los hombres. ¡Y qué fácil es a Su Majestad, pues nos hizo de nonada!" [It is very much like being like women, and I would not want you to be like them in anything, nor even seem to be like them; but like virile men. If women do what is necessary, the Lord will make them so manly that they will put fear in men. How easy it is for His Majesty to do this, for He made us from almost nothing] (*Camino de perfección*, chap. 7, para. 8. In Santa Teresa de Jesús, *Obras completas: Estudio preliminar y notas explicativas por Luis Santullano* [Madrid: Aguilar, 1970], 308).

7 This commentary leads one to think that some sort of process to collect evidence for her beatification was initiated at the time. However, nothing has been found in the archives of the diocese of Salamanca. For processes of beatification and canonization, there needs to be eyewitnesses to or direct beneficiaries of the incident. In this case the only evidence is hearsay, which necessitates further investigation by the Church.

prophetic light with which Heaven adorned her. Among the people of Salamanca, it could be said that when they were drowning in suffering or full of doubts, there was a saying to signify their safety. As in the Scriptures, where "Eamus ad videntem" was said,[8] the people of Salamanca would say, "Let us go to the Black woman of La Penitencia, because she knows what is going to happen." I will discuss, however, the following event, because it happened to someone who was a passionate devotee of hers, and he left this world not long ago.

His name was Francisco Hernández. Aware of Teresa's virtue he professed a profound respect for her all his life. He had a journey ahead of him to a fair. The cargo had already been loaded, the men had been called, and everything was ready to be on the way. He went to see the Mother and receive her blessing and permission, as was his custom. He went to the grille and told her that he came to say farewell. Teresa asked him when he was leaving. "Right now, Madam," Francisco answered. "Everything is ready." The Mother replied, "Your Worship must not leave town until tomorrow at such and such hour." Francisco rejected the advice, because that left him little time at the fair, and if he delayed his departure, he risked losing business. But the Mother was adamant that he should not leave his home until the hour she had told him. Since the traveler had experienced many times that Teresa's words were not to be cast to the wind, he stopped his servants and suspended the trip until the next day. He left after the hour marked by the Mother. On his way he met a poor man who had been robbed by bandits of all he had. They had hurt him badly and left him with his hands tied. Francisco calculated and he realized that had he not suspended his journey until the hour Teresa had told him, he would have experienced and suffered that disgrace without fail. Giving due thanks to God for having delivered him from such mishap, he was further confirmed in his credit and esteem for Teresa's virtue and life. Paying attention to these events and many others similar to the ones that appear referred in the Acts of the Provincial Chapter that we have already mentioned, those grave and learned capitulars had no doubts in having Teresa given, without any limitation, the following praise: "She was endowed with the gift of prophecy."[9]

---

8 "Venite, et eamus ad videntem": "Come, and let us go to the seer," I Samuel 9:9.
9 "She was endowed": "Prophetiae dono fuit illustrata," *Acta Capituli Provincialis Provinciae Hispaniae Ordinis Praedicatorum* (*Acts of Toro*), 31.

CHAPTER 39

*Many who are sick recover their health through Teresa.
Others are saved from imminent dangers.*

It should not be surprising that the grace of God frequently performed miracles through Teresa on behalf of her neighbors. This happened not only when her virtue had grown to perfection but also during the first years of her life. When she was still a young girl in her homeland, she was already making miracles, as God dispensed health and happiness to the sick and ailing through her. I have said before that back in her kingdom they took her from house to house where she laid her hands on the heads of the sick and that they found remedy to their illnesses. However, the girl did not know what was happening, nor did those who recovered their health recognize the means by which they were healed. Teresa was at that time as far from vainglory in her soul as her countrymen were blind to their need to thank God almighty, who had used that weak instrument to restore them to health.[1] Once she entered the religious cloisters, with her virtue already tempered, our Venerable Mother obtained from Heaven dispensations of grace through her pleas and supplications. Every time she brokered someone's health through her powerful prayers, when they returned to show their gratitude, she avoided all vainglory and responded humbly: "Go to Saint Vincent with that, he is a great saint. I tell you, keep him pleased if you want to have success." In her humility, she gave the saint all the glory for what God and Saint Vincent himself did through her intercession.

She displayed such prudence and self-effacement on this matter that although many recovered their health through the extraordinary miracles her prayers brought about, she was able to put a veil in front of most people's eyes so they would not value or even pay particular attention to these miracles. With her customary words of thanks to God and Saint Vincent—"don't come to me with that"—she managed to hide the miracles in forgetfulness and silence. But no matter how much her prudent self-effacement tried, she was not able to conceal all of them. One person or another had to give evidence as to how the favors were obtained through her insistent supplications. I omit here the number of occasions she cured the nuns from their ailments with her saliva, and instead I will tell of some other miracles. There was a nun who suffered the unspeakable torment of an acute pain caused by colic. She could not find relief or rest at all. Teresa saw her suffer in her pain. Her heart took pity at seeing the patient hurting so much, and she told her that if she wanted to be well again

---

1 This commentary on Chicaba's miraculous healing powers as coming from God has the effect of dispelling the idea that her homeland was in the power of the devil, as was believed by many about non-Christian areas of the world. This included the Americas prior to the Spanish conquest. See María José Rodilla León, "Bestiarios del Nuevo Mundo: Maravillas de Dios o engendros del Demonio," *Rilce: Revista de filología hispánica* 23.1 (2007): 201. This was especially the case with Guinea. As noted in Chapter 34, note 1, the text establishes a strategy by which the presence of God through Chicaba's miracles—performed even before she was officially a Christian—develops the notion that her land and her people were ready for the spread of the Gospel.

and find relief for her cruel pain she had to go to bed and stay still there. The nun thought that the proposed remedy was impertinent. She had gotten up because in bed the suffering increased. However, since she had enough experience of Teresa's virtue, she resolved to do what she had been told. She withdrew more out of a sense of obedience than the conviction that she would get some rest. But this remedy alone took her pain away so completely that she found herself well and healthy afterward, when she could not find rest there before. It was an easy cure, albeit a strange one, and reserved to Teresa's virtue. The echo of her voice alone was capable of frightening the humor that had been tormenting the nun so much. Ashamed and confused, the humor left the nun's body, never to return and give her another bad moment.[2]

Many and frequent were the bad moments Doctor Don Francisco Vélez gave his wife, Doña Josefa Herrero, and his entire family. The cause was a perverse illness that had him in the throes of death for several days. When the crisis appeared, she became anxious for her husband's health and sent Don Juan Manuel Vélez, the patient's brother, to the convent of La Penitencia to tell Teresa of her grief, and to ask her to pray in earnest for the patient's health. Teresa heard the request and gave the brother a glass with some water from the glorious father and patriarch Saint Dominic. She had cured quite a few with this medicine. When she gave it to him she asked him to tell Doña Josefa that as they gave the water to the patient, they should do it with faith and hope in God and Saint Vincent, because through it the sick man would recover his health. She added, "It will be very, very close, but he will not die of this." Don Juan arrived with the water and they gave it to the patient. His wife waited, certain in her hope that he would recover his health, but the symptoms became more serious, to the point that the patient was close to dying. The friends and all present did nothing else but start preparations for his burial. They thought it would occur naturally without fail the next day. The following day came, and they all believed the patient had passed away the night before. This was helped by the echo of the school bells that were tolling for the death of another graduate who had died the previous night. However, they discovered with their own eyes how erroneous their thinking was. From that day on, the patient started to get better, though very slowly, and he eventually recovered his health completely. A critic may scrutinize this case as to whether Nature could have performed one of its own miracles, or if the cure was the marvelous effect of medicine. And although I cannot reject this criticism as due and wise circumspection, in this case I cannot refrain from seeing proof of the prophetic spirit of our Teresa. She had forecast the future, when she declared these words: "It will be very, very close, but he will not die of this." Don Juan Manuel Vélez is a truthful witness of these words, because she told them to him.

In order to demonstrate the point of this chapter more clearly, I will conclude with the following case. Since Teresa enjoyed a very good opinion in the entire city and her fame and virtue were so well known, everybody considered it a great fortune to be acquainted with her. Low and high, commoners and nobles sought her eagerly. The noble houses sent their small children to her many afternoons. They may have hoped that Teresa would cast

---

2 People of this era believed that the human body was composed of four humors or tempers, the alteration of which caused illnesses or "distempers." In Spain this was still the orthodox medical explanation for illnesses. But the humors, like the devil, seem to obey the dictates of God when it comes to virtuous people.

a fortunate glance their way. They also may have hoped that their affection and devotion toward Mother Teresa, imprinted since their childhood, would continue in them once they grew up. The Countesses of Villagonzalo and Ablitas took particular care to do this.[3] These two ladies would send their children to visit Teresa on many holy days. The Venerable Mother enjoyed spending some time with them, contemplating how deeply grace dwelt in their souls.[4] One of those afternoons, one of the children of the Countess of Ablitas, called Don Joaquín, was kidding around in typical fashion for his age. He stepped on a staircase and fell, tumbling down without stopping. Teresa heard the noise and, predicting the tragedy, raised her voice and said: "Joaquín, hold still!" At that sound, the child stopped rolling down the staircase that was so very steep. The maids who had brought him to the convent rushed to him in terror. They were with Teresa in the parlor, not paying attention to the child; therefore, they expected to find the child badly hurt. But the One who stopped him in the middle of the stairs also took care that no harm came to him. They lifted him and found him safe and sound, without the slightest mark of having fallen. Obviously Teresa emulated Saint Vincent in a saintly manner. She imitated him whenever she could. Both of them shouted a "hold still, halt!" that revoked the fatal risk of people who had fallen. Saint Vincent arrested the fall of someone in the construction of a building with only his voice. Teresa did likewise with the child that fell down, stopping him in the middle of the stairs. Both marvels were performed by Heaven to give credit to these two elevated spirits.[5]

---

3   The name of these aristocratic women speaks of the reputation of Chicaba among women with a certain interest in learning at the time. One of these two women, Ana María Masones de Lima, Countess of Ablitas, would be an active participant with other women in the literary circles of Madrid, among them the Academia del Buen Gusto (Emilio Palacios Fernández, *La mujer y las letras en la España del siglo XVIII* [Alicante: Biblioteca Virtual Miguel de Cervantes, 2008], *www.cervantesvirtual.com/nd/ ark:/59851/bmcsf389*). The Countess of Villagonzalo's name was Josefa Boil y de Cernecio. The title of Count of Villagonzalo had been recently created by Philip V. This family was from Salamanca.
4   Children are naturally in a state of divine grace, because they have not reached the age of reason when they can discern good from evil; therefore they are not capable of sinning.
5   "Two elevated spirits" is a possible reference to a recent miracle attributed to Saint Vincent Ferrer in 1735 (Vidal y Micó 11). This would make Chicaba follow the steps of her favorite saint and perform miracles at the same time.

CHAPTER 40

Teresa's illness. Prophecy she gave of her own death

More than advanced in years, and they were many, Teresa was advanced in the seasoned fruits of virtue. It seems just that Heaven should call her to a reward corresponding to her travails. How eagerly her soul looked forward to this joy! How many tears did she shed over her exile from her Homeland. We have complete evidence of Teresa's longing from the letters Father Félix de Córdoba wrote in answer to hers, which we have cited several times before: "I say in truth"—this spiritual man wrote to her—"that I also want to leave this exile and pass on to the beloved Homeland to rest."[1] So if he too wanted to rest, to leave this life, it is a clear sign that Teresa had written to him indicating her strong desire to die. It is reasonable that the righteous find themselves in this world as if they were in exile. They lament that they cannot leave and fly to their Homeland, which is the Empyrean.[2] Since Teresa was so righteous, as we have seen in this brief sketch of her life, she had to have a strong desire to conclude her painful pilgrimage and ascend to her Homeland to rest. She had a revelation of her happy end and, encouraged by it, she developed the strength to finish her course on earth. One of her former directors finished his own course happily. He had been a servant and page of the Marquis of Mancera during the time Teresa lived in that house. His name was Father Don Andrés Teruel, of the Regular Priests of Saint Gaetano.[3] His death was so sudden that they learned about it in Madrid before they had heard of his illness in Salamanca. The Father Rector of the College of San Cayetano went to give Teresa the news early in the morning on a Tuesday, so she would commend his soul to God. The Venerable Mother, however, already knew of it. Before he even started speaking—looking as he did, a bit out of sorts and saddened—she asked him what was the cause of his sorrow. Before he could give her an answer, the Mother told him: "So, you are out of sorts because God has finished off Father Teruel's life like a morsel? This tells us that we must live prepared, because He will do the same with us tomorrow."[4] The Father Rector was astonished at hearing these words from her because the Mother could not have been informed of Father Teruel's illness and much less his death by any living being. When he went to tell her for the first time,

---

1 This Benedictine friar is mentioned in Chapter 25. He and Chicaba had maintained an epistolary relation. Their friendship went back to the days when they both lived in the Mancera household.
2 "The Empyrean" is a name for heaven that appears in Dante's *Paradiso*, cantos 30 to 33. It is the realm of light where God is surrounded by the saints.
3 Father Teruel had been introduced in Chapter 13. This is another instance of the spiritual genealogy the text creates between Sor Teresa and the Theatine order going back to the Mancera household. Paniagua maintains that Teresa kept up correspondence with former members of the Mancera staff throughout her life. Salamanca was a logical destination for former employees of the Manceras' who chose a religious life. As mentioned before, the Marquis of Mancera had extensive land holdings in the area. The Mancera namesake corresponds to two small municipalities, Mancera de Arriba and Mancera de Abajo, located next to each other between today's provinces of Salamanca and Ávila.
4 This is the first time in the text that death is presented through a metaphor in which God eats people: in Spanish, *se ha merendado*.

he found her already informed. The forewarning of the morsel became true that same year, when God made one out of her, as she had explained in her mysterious statement.

The month of September of the year 1748 came, and nothing new had happened to Teresa's health other than feeling "sort of old," as she would explain. She had been tormented for years by an acute pain in one of her knees. The pain was so intense that at times she could not move. They gave her a sort of wooden prie-dieu to rest on, something she had rejected until then.[5] The pain increased, but Teresa did not cease or slow down in her pious exercises because of this. Instead, she developed a new fervor in her prayers, which she always did on her knees, thereby increasing her torments and pains. I am convinced that this continuous exercise was the cause of the pain and torment, for she was accustomed to being on her knees not only in the choir during prayers but also at the grille, where she looked for a dark corner and knelt whenever priests visited. She feigned sitting down but kept her regular position. The darkness of the speak-room made this constant kneeling unknown to others. Those priests who knew of this artifice commanded her to sit down, which she did at once, because she always had such respect and obedience for all priests. A tumor developed in one of her knees from this constant kneeling, which mortified her flesh and made her patience meritorious. At the end of September of the above-mentioned year, she arose very early in the morning on the feast of Saint Michael.[6] She was eager to give a small breakfast to a nun who was sick. She took the chocolate maker, which she used for these acts of charity, and when she stood up to make the chocolate, a cruel paralysis overtook her and made her lose consciousness.[7] The nuns who lived next to her were frightened at hearing the noise her body made when she fell and came quickly to her assistance. They were beside themselves when they saw such an unforeseen accident, but they were filled with admiration for the tender and loving providence of God toward Teresa, because they found that her head had fallen between the wall and an old chest that probably served to keep Saint Vincent's decorations.[8] Her position was dangerous because between the wall and the chest it looked as if she had hurt her head, yet they found her totally free from injury.

Having recovered a bit from their fright, as occasioned by the sudden accident, they raised Teresa from the floor. She came back to her senses slowly and, with the strength of her burning charity, which this perverse accident could not weaken or diminish, repeated with trembling lips the following badly expressed words: "Chocolate for Saint John" (that was the sick nun's name), "Chocolate for Saint John, who is sick." They calmed her down, telling her that it would be done, and took her clothes off, laying her on her poor bed. They called the doctors, who considered Teresa's advanced age and the perverse and treacher-

---

5 This signifies Teresa's humility. The prie-dieu, the kneeler that women of a certain class had in church, also indicated their social status by the richness of its wood carvings, as did their proximity to the altar, which was according to social class.
6 The feast of the Archangel Saint Michael is on September 29 in the Catholic calendar.
7 The text has Sor Teresa Chicaba caring for the sick again until she can no longer move, even if the *Vida* presents this as a voluntary act of charity. It is noteworthy that the stroke that would eventually cause her death occurred while she was preparing chocolate for a sick nun. Sor Teresa Chicaba had an aversion to consuming chocolate herself. For the consumption of chocolate in women's convents throughout Spain and Spanish America, see our note in Chapter 26.
8 In the convent of Las Dueñas in Salamanca, they still keep a chest, which was probably this one that was saved when the convent of La Penitencia was demolished during the Napoleonic occupation of Salamanca in 1810.

ous nature of the malady. They were very pessimistic about her health and her life. They said that the Holy Viaticum should be administered to her.[9] For Teresa this was the most special remedy. Despite the negative prognosis of the physicians, the last and fatal stroke was delayed for a few months. The entire city was shaken by Teresa's illness because she was famous and venerated everywhere. Those who considered how much Teresa benefited the city started to lament the terrible loss that awaited Salamanca.[10] We can see here that the death of the righteous is one of the punishments God uses to show his wrath to the people.

---

9   When someone suffered a life-threatening accident, it was customary to ask for the sacrament of the Eucharist to be administered as an emergency measure. The priest carrying the Eucharist from the church would be accompanied by an acolyte ringing a bell. People who heard the bell would make way respectfully.

10 The word "benefited" used by the author is *servía*, which expresses how useful Teresa was for Salamanca, and how well Teresa served this community with her free gift of miracle working. The verb *servir* still carries today the sense of work done by someone of an inferior social status. Recently, writer Félix de Azúa, a member of the Spanish Academy of the Language, got himself in a controversy when he criticized Mayor of Barcelona Ada Colau: "Una ciudad civilizada y europea como Barcelona tiene como alcaldesa a Colau, una cosa de risa. Una mujer que debería estar sirviendo en un puesto de pescado" [A civilized and European city like Barcelona has Colau as mayor. Makes you laugh. A woman who should be serving in a fishmonger stand] (Luis Calvo, "Félix de Azúa," *Tiempo* [January 4, 2016], *www.tiempodehoy.com/entrevistas/felix-de-azua*)

CHAPTER 41

Teresa's patience during her illness.
he suffers spiritual dryness.

Teresa looked forward eagerly to her death, so when she saw it approaching, she could not help but look at it with a good spirit. The physicians recommended that she receive the Last Sacraments.[1] Teresa heard the orders they gave, and she resigned herself to them without fear, as would be expected from her perfect life. She made her confession, and her confessor got final confirmation of the purity and innocence of her soul. He found that she had never committed a mortal sin in her entire life. She surrendered to the presence of the Divine Sacrament in her heart. Once this pious and tender religious ritual ended, Teresa's health started to improve greatly, although one side of her body remained completely disabled. Thus Teresa spent her days in complete acceptance of divine will. She gave the nuns the most extraordinary examples of humility and patience. The latter put all their effort into lavishly caring for her, since they had an investment in Teresa's life. Because she could not manage for herself, they groomed her with compassion and affection and fed her with their own hands. The saintly woman was shocked to see herself pampered, as the physicians had ordered, and to receive gifts from her followers. She would say with humor and grace: "Ladies, Your Graces are wrong. If you want to see me well, let me eat my porridges and my soups, because so much pampering kills me."[2]

Teresa was thus perfecting her crown. Her illness and the medicines needed to cure it had disabled and mistreated her body. But how can one tell what her spirit went through and suffered? God's hand tried her by sending her terrible spiritual dryness and a sense of being abandoned.[3] She had experienced these feelings several times before, but especially

---

1 The last sacraments may include the Viaticum—Communion—and the administration of extreme unction (also called the Anointing of the Sick). "Extreme unction," the ritual traditionally performed on the dying, is an anointing of the external organs that represent the five senses, which prepares the person to leave this world and enter the other in a state of purity. Today it is applied to the sick as much as to the dying. This extended use of this sacrament is particularly popular among African Catholic communities.

2 In the Spanish original, "my porridges and my soups" appears as *mis gazpachos y mis sopas*. This indicates that Teresa favored humble food, *gazpacho* being a poor man's meal in the eighteenth century, consisting mainly of day-old bread in water, with olive oil and garlic and other vegetables.

3 The soul, as spiritual bride, feels the absence of the Spouse as a form of dryness or abandonment. The spirit is moved exclusively by faith and love, without sensing that it is being *corresponded* to by God, who does not give any signs to the soul in these trying moments. Saint John of the Cross describes the process of *sequedad interior* (interior drought) in his explanation of the *Cántico espiritual*:

> Y por eso, temiendo el alma mucho carecer, aun por un momento, de tan preciosa
>   presencia, hablando con la sequedad y con el espíritu de su Esposo, dice esta canción:
> Détente, cierzo muerto,
> ven, austro, que recuerdas los amores,
> aspira por mi huerto,
> y corran sus olores,
> y pacerá el Amado entre las flores.

in this last illness. The above-mentioned Acts testify about it: "When she arrived," they say, "to the end of her life and after having withstood many travails with patience, she suffered anguish in her soul, which she had already known before by divine revelation."[4] These are the sentences written to confirm the terrible interior dryness she had to suffer. These moments were so many that only He who gave her this chalice to taste and she herself knew how bitter it was, who had to drink of it.[5] She could not find rest or calm in anything. Everything was darkness and torment. Her sweet and tender Spouse seemed far away. Also by divine disposition, one of her directors and confessors was absent following orders from his superiors, while the rest were somehow tardy and lazy in providing relief and consolation to Teresa, without knowing why. They professed considerable affection for Teresa; therefore, the only cause for their withdrawal from her was that God willed and ordered it to be that way. In this way He could test and purify His beloved bride one last time. Amidst this terrible tempest, some consolation and divine light shone in her soul through the miracle that allowed her to rise from her bed and go down to receive Communion by herself. This miracle gave her afflicted spirit considerable nourishment, and she repeated it some other times, after they installed her bed in the infirmary.

She remained there for the rest of her life, and after that consolation received by her soul at the sight of her sacramental Master passed, the interior dryness came back more strongly and fiercely. Teresa looked for relief, and she could not find anything but affliction and torment. The struggle was cruel and fierce, yet her fortitude and constancy were greater. She told of her distress to her old correspondent, the Benedictine friar, so he might commend her to God.[6] The latter responded a few weeks before Teresa died with words of encouragement: "It is good for all of us to have a little bundle of myrrh to offer to the Lord, so it may be good for our souls. In this conformity I have asked God to give Mother Teresa strength to suffer for His love."[7] Divine Mercy answered such a prudent request. Teresa received the courage and strength to carry such a heavy cross. Because it was so heavy, Heaven

---

> And because of this, as the soul is in great fear of not having, even for a moment, such precious presence, speaking to the dryness and to the spirit of her Spouse, says this song:
> Stop, cold wind that kills.
> Come, south wind that wakes up love,
> Blow through my orchard
> And let their scents run,
> And the Beloved shall graze among the flowers.

The Spanish excerpt above is from Juan de la Cruz, *Obra completa*, vol. 2 (Madrid: Alianza Editiorial, 1996), 109–10. See also Chapter 32, note 1.

4   "When she arrived": "Denique ad extremum vitae deveniens, magna cum patientia toleratis doloribus, animique dessolationibus, quas iam dudum, revelante Domino, noverat," *Acta Capituli Provincialis Provinciae Hispaniae Ordinis Praedicatorum* (*Acts of Toro*), 31.
5   This is a Christological moment. She has to taste the bitter chalice before death like Christ in the Garden of Olives, when he pleads not to drink the bitter chalice (Mark 14:35).
6   The Benedictine friar is Father Félix de Córdoba, introduced in Chapter 25. She knew him from her days in the Mancera household.
7   Myrrh was considered a medicine used to soothe bodily ailments. It was one of the three gifts that the Magi offered the Child Jesus (Matthew 2:11), and it symbolized His humanity and the physical sufferings He would have to endure. The image of myrrh is central in the *Oración fúnebre* that Paniagua wrote in honor of Sor Teresa in 1749. In it Paniagua draws from the tradition that associated myrrh with the Black Magus. See the Introduction, p. 27.

had already given her warning of it on previous occasions. Now with the presence of her divine Master, Teresa was able to progress with less spiritual dryness. They said Mass in the infirmary, and when she did not have Communion, a privilege she enjoyed frequently, at least the sight of her Master comforted her soul, and thus her interior afflictions and sorrows received some ease.

CHAPTER 42

Teresa tells the nuns that her death is approaching.
She surrenders her spirit but not without miracles from Heaven.

Despite being besieged by inner sorrows, surrounded by afflictions and anguish, but helped by grace, Teresa was finishing the weaving of her own crown.[1] By the end of the month of November of the year 1748, Mother Josefa of Saint Augustine died. Prompted by her ardent charity, Teresa had served this nun as if she were her humble slave. She aided Mother Josefa greatly with her prayers in the hour of her death. Teresa managed to learn about her imminent passing, despite the efforts of the other nuns to hide from her the rites of the Viaticum, and extreme unction. They did not want to upset her, or so they thought. But things happened so contrary to their plan that even if Teresa pretended not to know, she had heard everything. Her pleas and prayers helped the dying nun, as Teresa herself later said. Once Mother Saint Augustine died and her burial ceremonies were finished, Teresa said: "As soon as you finish with the services for Mother Saint Augustine, you will start with mine." Those who heard her at the time did not make much of it. Either Heaven did not allow them to pay much attention to her words or the illness did not look particularly dangerous, since she appeared to be getting better. The month of December came, and it was a proper December for the convent because its rigors withered the beautiful flower that was its jewel and beauty. Teresa asked if the services for Mother Saint Augustine had been completed. They told her they were, and that they had been finished a few days before. "Yes," Teresa replied, engulfed in joy: "We must move on. There is no other way, we need to move on the path."

With so many signs, Teresa proclaimed that her death was nearing. On the fourth of December, she requested to have Mass said in the infirmary for her and to receive Holy Communion. It was done as she had requested. By the fervor and spirit with which she welcomed her Spouse, she gave clear signs that this would be her last time to receive Him in this way. It is not an exaggeration to say that her eyes were resplendent and clear. They looked as if they were about to come out of their orbits, and through them as though her heart wanted to leave and join her Master faster than the priest could put the host between her lips. After having received Communion, she stayed in an inner and sweet suspension with her divine Master. Once her spirit became calm and serene, all the afflictions and dryness that had tormented her soul were banished, and she spent the rest of the day without anything special or new occurring. But the next day, the treacherous illness assaulted this most important life. She recovered from it, and the physicians ordered to have the Holy

---

1 The image of the weaving of the crown makes reference to the crown of grass that the winners of a battle received in Roman times. The crown of thorns that the Roman soldiers put on Jesus's head was meant to be a parody of that triumph as well as a form of torture (Matthew 27:29, Mark 15:17, and John 19:2, 5). In early modern Spain and Spanish America the heads of dead nuns were frequently adorned with crowns of flowers to signify their final spiritual triumph. See Alma Montero Alarcón, *Monjas coronadas: Profesión y muerte en Hispanoamérica virreinal* (Mexico City: CONACULTA, 2008).

Viaticum called for her. Teresa received it with the most expressive and tender eagerness as a farewell. The sixth of December arrived, and after dusk Teresa felt quite unwell, although inside she was so robust that, in her face, one could perceive the interior joy that enlivened her and offered consolation. A nun noticed and saw it. When she encouraged Teresa to have some broth, Teresa responded: "I can't have any more." Casting her eyes away from the mug or cup in which it was being offered, she fixed her eyes on the opposite wall. With a sweet smile and joyful face, she stared for a while as if she were seeing something very much to her pleasure.

At eleven in the evening of the above-mentioned day, her illness made its last sign of wanting to snuff the vital flame of her life. The nuns were frightened, because the physicians had declared earlier in the evening that she was in no particular danger that night. The nuns sent word everywhere to have someone come and administer the last rites, which she had not received. Some tried to give courage to the patient, and others tried to liven her up. Some cried and sighed. Another nun, raising her voice, asked her what seemed to be hurting her. Teresa, without uttering a word, signaled that it was her chest. During her illness, she had repeatedly said: "I felt a very sharp pain there." Maybe the sweat, which had suffused her heart in the violence of love, as she herself said, now was melting that heart in her chest under the influence of that same love.[2] The priest arrived to administer the holy oil. Near midnight, as the day of the eve of the Immaculate Conception of Mary approached, Teresa surrendered her soul to the hands of her Creator. That triumphant and glorious spirit abandoned the ties of the body. "She died," the Acts conclude, "having lived seventy-two years without the blemish of a mortal sin."[3] In view of this praise, it would be disrespectful of me to add any more.

---

2   See Chapter 35 for another reference to the sweating of the heart.
3   "She died": "E vivis discessit cum vixisset septuaginta duobus annis, nullo infecta peccato laethali," *Acta Capituli Provincialis Provinciae Hispaniae Ordinis Praedicatorum* (*Acts of Toro*) 31.

CHAPTER 43

Some notable incidents that occurred at Teresa's death and burial

The righteous attain possession of the eternal good they desired and awaited so long in this world by means of their death. Heaven itself is full of joy and mirth after the new dweller has obtained this supreme good. Thus paradise often makes its jubilation known to those inhabiting the sublunary realm through repeated miracles and signs.[1] These portents show its elation at the same time that they incite and encourage humans to follow the steps of the righteous in hope of the same reward. When Chrysostom speaks of the triumph of the saints, he claims we can be what they are if we do what they practiced.[2] People observed signs at the time Teresa passed away and after her death. Her life was so righteous that Heaven indeed celebrated her departure from earth. The color of her face, Black by nature, became white before she expired. It even stayed like that for quite a while after her death.[3] Not all the people who attended the burial noticed this transformation. Some of the nuns saw it clearly, and so did the surgeon who attended her in her illness. He is still talking about it in amazement today. I relate this event without qualifying it because I am aware of what some modern writers have said about the cause of color mutation in corpses.[4]

At the time Teresa was dying, a nun saw her humble bed transformed into a kind of heaven that was encircled by brilliant stars. She was astounded to see such a marvel. As she testified, if she had appreciated the Venerable Mother in life, she esteemed her more when she came to understand that mysterious vision. She learned that everything this woman had done in the course of her life had been performed with the rightful intention of giving greater honor and glory to God. All her deeds now shone in the presence of God like stars in the sky. This is what she saw, this is how others explained it to her when she described the event, and this is how she testified under the vow of obedience. The hour when Teresa died is equally significant. When she passed away, it was a few minutes before midnight on

---

1   Those inhabiting the sublunary realm are the people on earth. The text subscribes to the ancient idea that heaven is located in the sky, above the planets.
2   This is a reference to Saint John Chrysostom's concept of *theosis*, in which saints partake of God's essence—that is, they become like God. Thus, the imitation of the example of saints makes the Christian become more divine. See John Chrysostom, *The Cult of the Saints* (Yonkers, NY: St. Vladimir's Seminary Press, 2006), 99.
3   The miracle of Black saints turning white before or after death was a commonplace in Spanish seventeenth-century theater. It reflected a long tradition in hagiographic texts, as did the case of Saint Mary of Egypt, whose darkened body after years in the desert turned white in death. See the Introduction, pp. 15, 97, for more discussion of this tradition in medieval literature and in Spanish seventeenth-century theater.
4   Paniagua may be referring to Father Benito Jerónimo Feijóo and his essay "Del color etiópico." Against the pious tradition of the Black saint's change of color, the text has to interpose the possibility of a natural cause, as expressed by Father Feijóo, who subscribed to the theory of hot climates as the origin of Black skin while simultaneously insisting on the inner whiteness of all human beings in order to prove that all human beings are descended from Adam and Eve. See our earlier notes on Feijóo.

the day before the eve of the Immaculate Conception of the Virgin Mary, as I have already said. Following the method of the Congregation of the Holy Rosary, Teresa had chosen this hour to make a special gift to this great Queen. Adorned with fruits, laden with virtues and triumphs, the Virgin Mary chose this very hour to present Teresa to her Son.

At the time Teresa passed away, it seems that she went to notify and say good-bye to her intimate and loving devotee Francisco Hernández. He was already in bed at that hour, completely ignorant of what was happening in La Penitencia. He heard knocking at the door and his name being called. He did not pay attention, thinking it was his imagination or a dream. The call came a second time, and for a second time he decided to ignore it. A third time they called more insistently and he heard with clarity what they said to him: "Hernández, get out of bed." He did it quickly and opened the window at once. He asked who was calling him, but the caller was already gone. He returned to bed, but he could not get back to sleep for the rest of the night. The next morning, when the news of the death of La Negrita had spread through the city, he realized what had happened, when he checked the hour; it was the same time when they had knocked on his door.[5] He did not have any doubt that it was his devoted and beloved Teresa who had stopped by his house to say good-bye. He could only blame his laziness for not having left his bed as soon as he was called the first time; otherwise he might have enjoyed her sight and presence. Or maybe the knocks and the calling of his name were how Teresa told him to rise and start on the path she had just finished, because he survived the Mother by only ten more months. The learned know whereof I speak in this particular case.

Teresa's corpse did not present those horrible signs that the face of death puts on others. Her affable and quaint face, even clearer now than when she was alive, was a sign that hers had not been death, but rather rest and peaceful sleep. More than a few nuns stated that they had sensed a celestial fragrance that exceeded in quality all the aromatic compositions compounded in this world. This is how her body remained. But who is going to interpret the Lord's judgment! Who was going to believe that in the very city where Teresa died and was held as a saint, venerated and applauded so much by high and low, noble and plebeian, learned and rustic, the entire population would not abandon everything to attend her burial? Who would not believe that the church of La Penitencia, which is small and limited in space, would have been too small for the crowds in attendance? In fact, it was more than ample, and it was almost totally empty. The burial was arranged for December seventh, at ten in the morning. The sons of the great father and patriarch Saint Gaetano, for whom the Venerable Mother had developed a particular affection, and who reciprocated her love, and four or five poor folks from the neighborhood, were the only ones aside from her community who were in attendance in the interment of her virginal body. But indeed men were not needed when there were thousands of angels present at her burial. They buried her in the place reserved for the nuns because they now considered it an insult to separate her from their company in her death. Yet more than once during her life the older ones who had already died had belittled Teresa because she was Black. They put her in the community burial plot then and buried her without making any special distinction. I say

---

5   We use "La Negrita" intentionally, reflecting the original Spanish. The term appears in Torres Villarroel's *Vida del Padre Jerónimo Abarrategui*. As discussed earlier, the diminutive applied to Black people is intended to soften the terms *negro* and *negra*, which are considered insulting and demeaning.

this as evidence that, even after her death, human beings mortified her. All her humble desire, wishes, and supplications while she lived were to have her body buried in the sight and presence of her sacramental Master.[6] However, objections were raised that I wish not to examine now and her wish was not granted. Thus, she lies and rests in the cloister until Divine Providence disposes differently.[7]

---

6   As noted in Chapter 36, Chicaba's devotion to the Holy Sacrament is represented in her official portrait by her kneeling down in adoration of the Eucharist. See Figure 1.
7   Indeed, Chicaba's body now lies in a different convent, Las Dueñas, which was at the time the more important of the two communities of Dominican nuns in Salamanca. She was transferred there in 1810, when La Penitencia was demolished during the Napoleonic occupation of Salamanca (see Figure

LAST CHAPTER

Miracles experienced through the intercession of the Venerable Mother after her death

Although the gift of miracles (like the gift of sanctity) is *gratis data* [freely given], theologians are well aware of the distinction between miracles made to prove the sanctity of someone and those performed to testify about doctrine. The Church has powerful reasons and prudent motives to expect that miracles will justify the causes of venerable individuals. There are some among the latter whom God has not given such a privilege. Others have received this benefit from His Majesty, but infrequently and slowly. Our Teresa belongs to the second group. From her death until now, we can count only three miracles. One happened to Doña Isabel Navarro, the daughter of Don Francisco Navarro and Doña Micaela del Olmo.[1] This young lady suffered a terrible discharge from the eyes. Physicians performed on her as many attempts and remedies as their art had taught them. But the only fruit they collected was disappointment. The illness was incurable because it was diagnosed as "amaurosis," the effect of which is a serene expression that hides a profound disturbance in the eyesight.[2] The family was feeling very sad when a neighbor came to them. She had come into possession of a bead from the Venerable Mother's rosary. She persuaded them to have faith in the relic and to apply it to the girl, who was already totally blind. She told them that there was a chance that God might restore the girl's sight through the intercession of Mother Teresa. They took the advice, applied the bead to her eyes, and left it tied around her collar. They went to bed full of confidence that the Mother would grant their daughter what they so much desired. Their faith was not misplaced. The blind girl woke up at midnight and saw the light they had left in the room. She called her little sister, who slept next to her. She asked her if there was light in the room. She repeated again, was there light in the room. The other one responded: "Yes." "So, can you see now?" To which the one with the sickness said, "Of course I can see. There is this and that," giving her a detailed account of the things in the room. Since they were children, they did not pay special attention to the miracle. But the parents did the following morning. When they went to see their blind daughter, they found she could see. This was the reward for the faith they had in Teresa's intercession. It

---

5). Chicaba is buried in the cloister, in sight of all visitors. Her tomb has become a place of veneration. The nuns of the convent of Las Dueñas have opened a small museum on the second floor of the Renaissance cloister that houses the community.

1 Miracles that happen to people of social relevance have a better chance at being accepted as true. Physicians are involved, and the social prominence of the beneficiaries ensured some degree of support for the cause of the would-be saint.

2 Amaurosis is a condition of the retina that provokes sudden but temporary blindness. The text seems to refer also to the condition known in Spanish at the time as *gota serena*, a retinopathy that obscures the field of vision and eventually blinds the person. When light is applied to the eye the iris does not react, thus the adjective of *serena* ("serene" or "undisturbed").

has been three years since the miracle took place. The girl's eyesight is still well and clear and has not given her the slightest problem.

Another woman went to the convent of La Penitencia to give thanks. She said that through the intercession of Mother Teresa the Lord had restored her eyesight, of which she had been deprived for years. Through the means of a small piece of the Mother's veil, God gave consolation to another suffering woman. She suffered from very hard labor when giving birth. She had not been able to deliver one single child who had not been taken out in pieces through the use of forceps and other instruments. Teresa died. The woman was pregnant at that time, and having learned from her past difficulties, she obtained the intercession of the Mother. She requested one of her relics, and it proved effective. She was able to obtain part of the veil we have referred to.[3] The feared hour arrived; and with the first pains, she applied it to her belly. After that she did not feel any other pains because she gave birth immediately without suffering to a robust and healthy baby. After that she never needed forceps or any other instruments. Quite a few people confess to having received miraculous benefits through the intercession of this venerable woman. Many have obtained relief from their maladies through simple contact with some of the remnants of her poor clothes.[4] Her clothes were all given away, since her devotees requested them eagerly. Those who obtained the smallest piece of any rag she had been in contact with during her illness considered themselves lucky and happy. I can certify all three miracles. But I will not cease to admire how unfathomable is God's wisdom. Few people, almost nobody, attended Teresa's burial! All came, however, to request any rag from her clothing to keep as a relic! These are the secrets of the Highest One, and they infinitely transcend the capacity of human understanding.

This is, pious reader, a brief sketch, a single expression of the extraordinary life of this happy Black woman.[5] You will see in it the mysterious effects of a vocation made powerful by grace.[6] With it Divine Mercy took her out of the Black and idolatrous shadows. You will notice a faithful example in this virtuous life. You will find what to admire and what to imitate. You will admire God's liberal hand; the many favors He did for this happy creature by Himself, through His angels and saints. You will find what to imitate in her heroic virtues

---

3 We have discussed the white veil of Teresa before. It was a matter of contention throughout the text. Even when she was allowed to wear it, the veil was the outer sign that she did not belong to the community as a full nun (i.e., a choir nun). There were also times when she was not allowed even to wear it. For example, the bishop had denied her the use of the white veil. After her death it became miraculous. In her official portrait she appears with a white veil (Figure 1).

4 The things that the saintly person used in life are considered to have a special power to invoke his or her intercession. The Catholic Church considers them "secondary relics." They are important only after "primary relics," which are parts of saints' bodies or the instruments of Christ's Passion (such as thorns or splinters of the Holy Cross). People believe that it is the very objects (e.g., clothing, rosary beads, or any personal effects) that possess the power to perform the miracle. Church doctrine is more nuanced, since relics are instruments for the faithful to reflect on the life of the holy person whose intercession they seek through prayer. As mentioned in the Introduction, p. 5, after Chicaba's death the nuns of La Penitencia preserved one of her shoes and a clay drinking cup, which are now on display at the museum dedicated to her in the convent of Las Dueñas.

5 *Feliz negra* (happy Black woman): the oxymoron was clear to the eighteenth-century reader. *Negro* (*negra*, feminine) was an adjective that denoted unlucky occurrence: *negra suerte* (bad luck), *tener la negra* (to have bad luck), and so on.

6 Efficient grace is the gift God gives to every human being to recognize His existence as an aspect of natural law.

and her righteous way of life. I have written this compendium using the ost authentic papers.⁷ They are Teresa's reports to her directors, and the narrative of her parents' country and land she wrote with her own hand a few months before she died.⁸ I have also seen the responses sent to Teresa from several spiritual individuals. What I say is very little because what Teresa kept hidden was a lot. Let it all yield honor and glory to God and credit to His powerful arm.

OSCSRE⁹

---

7   The author refers to Chicaba's autograph papers and her correspondence to assert the historicity of this hagiography. See Introduction, p. 4.
8   This statement attests to Chicaba's active role in the production of this *Vida*. The account she supposedly wrote refers to the years of her life in Africa, before her enslavement—the period of life for which she was the only source of information, most of which is collected in the first six chapters of this work.
9   OSCSRE is the Latin acronym for *omnia submitto correctione Sanctae Romanae Ecclesiae* [I submit all this to the correction of the Holy Roman Church]; Paniagua is thus pledging humble allegiance to the orthodoxy of the Catholic Church.

Appendixes

APPENDIX I

Carta de Pago (**Letter of Payment**)

Excerpt of the letter of payment [*carta de pago*] signed by the nuns of the Convent of La Penitencia of Salamanca, the representative of the Marquis of Mancera, and Teresa Juliana de Santo Domingo (Sor Teresa Chicaba). Through this document, the convent admits Sor Teresa Chicaba as a secular or tertiary [*tercera*] after a payment of 10,800 *reales*. Sor Teresa Chicaba accepts the conditions, one of which stipulates she is not a nun. She renounces the money paid for her acceptance. This document was signed most probably around the time the *Vida* speaks of Sor Teresa's receiving the habit from the bishop (Chapter 22). Note Sor Teresa Juliana de Santo Domingo's signature (Archivo Histórico Provincial de Salamanca, Oficio 7, escribano Juan Antonio de Paz, Sección de Protocolos Notariales. 19 April 1704. Protocolo 3931, fols. 613r–615v). Emphasis added.

Translation [613r]
We say that after having discussed and conferred [about the situation] Theresa Juliana de Santo Domingo, who was a servant of the most excellent marquis and marchioness of Mancera, shall and will enter this convent in order to live in it and serve God Our Lord, and stay away from the toils of this world. She will remain in the convent **as a secular or tertiary *beata*, with our habit, that she is presently wearing,** for the rest of the days of her life or the time that her own will determines. We will give her the same provisions as we and the other women religious of this convent receive, and we will assist her in her illnesses like we do with us. We shall pay her during the days of her life the same gratuities as the women religious who live here now receive, and those who may enter in this said convent in the future, both those who simply wear a habit and those who profess. The above said Theresa shall be under no obligation to attend choir or serve this above-said community in any other thing than what her own will should say. And in order to do this, the most illustrious lord bishop of this city has given us license, as stated in it, and the original is here inserted and says as follows. . . .

Y debajo de ello dezimos que por quanto tenemos tratado y conferido el que Theresa Juliana de Santo Domingo criada que fue delos Excelentisimos Señores Marques y Marquesa de Manzera aia deentrar y entre eneste dicho conuento para bibirenel y servir aDios Nuestro Señor y quitarse delos trafagos del mundo estando **enel deseglar oterzera beata** con nuestro abito como al presente le tiene puesto portodoslosdias desubida oel tiempo que fuere su boluntad dandola la Razion queacada una denosotras ydemas Relijiosas deeste dicho conuento seda yasistiendola ensus enfermedades como-

This page contains a photographic reproduction of a handwritten manuscript document in Spanish colonial script. The text is largely illegible due to the quality of the reproduction and the cursive handwriting style. Only fragments can be discerned, including what appears to be references to "Convento," "doña Theresa Juliana," dates, and signatures at the bottom of the page.

anosotras y pagarlalas propinas de las relijiosas queai y deoi enadelante entraren en este dicho conuento durantelos dias de subida, asi de abito como de profesion sinquetenga obligazion la dicha Theresa de asistir acoroniserbiradicha comunidad en cosaalguna mas deloquefuere su boluntad y parapoderlohazer nos a dado lizienzia el Ylustrisimo señor Obispo deesta ziudad como deella consta que orijinal aqui seinsiere y dizeasi. . . .

Translation [614r]
[margin: acceptance] And I, the said Theresa Juliana de Santo Domingo, who has been and am present to what has been said and declared in this contract, accept it in everything as it appears herein. **And in conformity with it I require myself to stand and accept everything contained in it and that I shall not ask at any time from this convent or any of the nuns in it the said ten thousand eight hundred *reales de vellón* or part of it, because I leave and give them to the said convent so that they will give me provisions as if I were a nun of this said convent** and assist me in my illnesses as with the said nuns in it. And with respect to the rest contained and declared in this contract I shall not move against it or even part of it at any time. And if I were to do it, my motion shall not be valid nor heard and admitted in court or outside it. . . .

[margen: azetazion] E Yola dicha Theresa Juliana de santo domingo questado Yestoi presente alo dicho Y declarado en esta scriptura la azeto en todo como enella se contiene **Y conforme aella meobligo aestar ypasar portodoloaqui contenido ya quenopedire enningun tiempo aeste dicho Conuento ni Relijiosas del losdichos diez mil yochozientos Reales deuellon ni partedeellos por quelos dejo Y doi a dicho Conuento con tal quemeandedar La Razion comosi fuera Relijiosa destedicho Conuento** y asistirme en misenfermedades como a las dichas Relijiosas del Y todo lo demas contenido Y declarado enesta escriptura contra todo lo qual niparte de ello no yre ni bendre entiempo alguno Y silo yziere quenomebalganisea oida ni admitida en juizio ni fuera del. . . .

APPENDIX 2

Act of Profession

"Act of profession" or document attesting to Sor Teresa Juliana de Santo Domingo's admission into the Convent of La Penitencia of Salamanca. Note that the signature of Sor Teresa de Santo Domingo drops the name of Juliana that tied her to her mistress. Significantly, there are no signatures from the prioress or any other nun of La Penitencia unlike in the *carta de pago*, or letter of payment. This document probably corresponds to the events of Sor Teresa Chicaba's profession described in Chapter 24 of the *Vida*. There is an addendum at the end of this document in the form of a short obituary (Archivo Histórico del Monasterio de las Madres Dominicas Dueñas de Salamanca. Sección Convento de la Penitencia).

In the city of Salamanca [*blotted and written over*] 29 June 1704, in the convent of Santa María Magdalena de La Penitencia, of the Order of our Father St. Dominic, Sister Teresa de Santo Domingo, tertiary of the above-said order, made her profession at the hands of the Most Illustrious Lord Don Francisco Calderón de la Barca, Bishop of the City, and Prelate of the Convent. The Most Excellent Lord Marquis of Mancera paid the dowry, tips, and alms [*on the right margin:* paid dowry and tips], as it is written in a deed signed before Don Juan Antonio de Paz, Royal Notary Public in this city. It is the obligation of the aforesaid Convent to maintain the aforesaid person in the same manner as it does the other religious women in the Convent. And it was signed by the Bishop or in his name by Don Diego de Mora y Varona, priest in the Parish of St. Blas of this city, and inspector for the Bishopric. Witnesses to this act were Don Miguel del Pozo, secretary to the Bishop, Don Phelipe del Campillo, and Don Manuel Pernea, servants to the Bishop. In Salamanca, as above.

Sor Teresa de Santo Domingo [*autograph signature*]
[*illegible initials as signature*]
Don Diego de Mora y Varona [*autograph signature*]
[*illegible initials as signature*]

[*Left margin*] gave dowry and

This lady was the legitimate daughter of the king of the Lower Gold Mine and his wife, called Abar. In her land they called Mother Teresa Chicaba. Divine Providence took her out of her land through a marvelous intervention. Protected by divine grace she led in this convent a life as exemplary as it was observant of the rule.

She passed away on December 6, 1748, with the same virtue and usual fortitude she had lived with. Her virtues are epilogued in the funeral oration pronounced on January

En la Ziu.ᵈ de Salamᵃⁿᶜᵃ ~~~~~~~ de Mil Setezienₜₒˢ y
quatro estando en el Conbᵗᵒ de Stᵃ Maria Magdalena de la
pᵉⁿⁱᵗᵉⁿᶜⁱᵃ del Orden de Ntro Pᵉ Stᵒ Domingo Sorᵉ
Teresa de Stᵒ Domingo terzera de dha Orden hizo
Su profesion en Manos del Illmᵒ Señor Dⁿ Franᶜᵒ
Calderon de la Barca Obispo desta Ziuᵈ y Prelado
de dho Combᵗᵒ abiendo pagado el Exmᵒ Señor Mar
-ques de Manzera la dote propinas y alimentos
Como Consta desᵃ Escritura otorgada Ante Juan
Antᵒ de Paz escrivano Real y del numero
desta Ziuᵈ quedando con la obligacion dho
Combᵗᵒ de Alimentar a la Sobreᵈʰᵃ Segun

dió dote
7 pₛᵒˢ
pₒᵣ día

y Como a cada una de las Relixiosas de dho
Combᵗᵒ y para que Conste lo firmo dho Illmᵒ Señor
Opor ᵈ.ᴹ el Sᵉⁿᵒʳ Dⁿ Diego de Mora y Varo
na Veneficiado de la Parroquial del Señor
San Blas y visitador de dho Obispado si
endo testigos Dⁿ Miguel del Pozo Secretario
de dho Illmᵒ Sᵃ y Dⁿ Phelipe del Campillo
y Dⁿ Manuel Perera familiares de dha Illᵃ
Salamᵃⁿᶜᵃ Vt supra =   Sorᵉ Teresa de Stᵒ
                           domingo

Jdo Dⁿ Diego de Mora
              Varona

fue essa Sᵒʳᵃ hija lexitiᵐᵃ de el Reí de la Mina de la de el oro, y de su Muger lla-
ma-da Abar, llamada en su tierra a la Mᵈ Theresa, lu Chi-
caba. Salio la Divina Providenzia a costa de Maravillas de su tierra, y provista de la Divina grazia, hizo
en este convento una Vida tan exemplar como ajustada
fallezio el dia 6 de Diziembre del año de 1748 con la
misma Virtud y Comun edificazion que havia vivido.
Sus Virtudes estan espresados en la Oracion funebre

de
1749

que se dijo el dia 9 de Enero en las exequias, y exercᵃˢ
devotos se hizieron a su memoria en la Yglesia de
este Convento.

9, 1749, during the obsequies paid by her devotees in honor of her memory in the church of this convent.

[*Left margin*] + 1749

En la ziud. de Salamca. a [*tachado*] 29 de junio de mil setecientos y quatro estando en el Convento de Santa Maria Magdalena de la Penitencia del Orden de Ntro. Padre Sto. Domingo Soror Teresa de Sto. Domingo tercera de dha Orden hizo su profesión en manos del Illmo. Señor Dn Franco. Calderón dela Barca Obispo desta ziud. y Prelado de dho Conbto abiendo pagado el Exo. Sr. Marqués de Manzera la dote propinas y alimentos como costa des Critura otorgada ante Juan Antto. de Paz escrivano Real y del numero desta Ziud. quedando conla obligación dho Conbto. de alimentar a la sobredha según y como acada una delas relixiosas de dho Conbto. y para que coste lo firmo dho Illmo Señor opor Su Illa el Lizdo. Dn Diego de Mora y Varona Veneficiado de la Parroquial del Señor San Blas y visitador de dho Obispado siendo testigos Dn. Miguel del Pozo Secretario de dho Illmo. Sr y Dn Phelipe del Campillo y Don Manuel Pernea familiares de su Illa.
    Salamca. ud supra. Soror Theresa de Santo Domingo.
    Ldo D Diego de Mora Varona.
    [*illegible*]
    [*illegible*]

[*Margen izquierdo*] dio dote y propinas.

Fue esta Sra. hija lexitima del Rei dela Mina Baja de el Oro y de su Muger llamada Abar. Llamavan en su tierra a la Md. Theresa, la Chicaba. Sacola la Divina Providenzia a costa de maravillas de su tierra y protegida de la Divina gracia hizo en este Convento vna vida tan exemplar como ajustada. Fallecio el dia 6 de Diziembre de el a;o de 1748 con la misma virtud y comun edificacion que havia vivido. Sus virtudes estan epilogadas en la oracion fúnebre que se dijo el dia 9 de enero en las exequias q. a expensas de devotos se hicieron a su memoria en la Yglesia de este Convento.

[*Margen izquierdo*] + de 1749

ACTA
CAPITULI PROVINCIALIS
PROVINCIÆ HISPANIÆ
ORDINIS PRÆDICATORUM,
CELEBRATI IN CONVENTU
SANCTI ILDEPHONSI
REGALI TAURENSI,
Die 27. Aprilis, anni Domini 1749.

SUB R. A. P. N.

FR. EUGENIO DE BASUALDO,
MAGISTRO CONCIONATORE REGIO,

PRIORE CONVENTUS S^{ti} THOMÆ MATRITENSIS,
Vicario Generali, & Provinciali electo ejusdem
Provinciæ.

MATRITI: Ex Typographia Gabrielis Ramirez. Anno 1749.

APPENDIX 3

Obituary of Sor Teresa Chicaba contained in the Acts of the Chapter of Toro

The Acts of the Chapter of Toro contain the acts (i.e., minutes) of an assembly held in the city of Toro in 1749. It was attended by Dominican friars from all over Spain; this group is referred to within the translation of the *Vida* as "the Provincial Chapter of the Dominican Friars of Toro" and other variations of that name. Sor Teresa Chicaba's death is recorded, and she is eulogized in a manner reserved for venerable friars and nuns (Archivo Histórico de las Madres Dominicas Dueñas de Salamanca. Sección Convento de La Penitencia).

Translation of the obituary in honor of Sor Teresa Juliana de Santo Domingo, published in the Acts of the Chapter of the Province of Spain of the Dominican Order, Toro, 1749, pages 29 to 31.

> Sor Teresa Juliana de Santo Domingo died in the convent of La Penitencia, a monastery not subject to our Order's jurisdiction. She was a singular example of Divine Providence because though born the daughter of an idolater king in the Lower Mina in Ethiopia, she converted to our faith, together with her entire family and kingdom. Also, when she reached the age of reason she began to search for the Ultimate Cause. Learned people in her country instructed her that the morning star was their god; so she asked them to show it to her. When she saw the morning star for the first time and was told to prostrate herself and venerate it, she asked: "Tell me please, who put it there for us to worship?" And she never bent her knee before the star.
>
> Later on she frequently went to her father to ask him questions. She felt sorry to find him so ignorant about a thing of such importance. So she proposed to him: "My dear father, I will look in the fields and in the wilderness to find out who it is; and I shall not rest until I get an answer." From that day and for the following five years, this was her only thought. She did nothing else. During this time the Blessed Virgin, Mother of God, appeared to her on a white cloud several times. She was carrying the Child Jesus on her lap. [Teresa] ardently wished to take from the Child's hand a golden band that he dangled above her head, but she was fooled at this game every time she tried. This increased her thirst for Him even more, and so she continued searching until this thirst led her to a fountain, where she finally drank from the waters of baptism. She took the name Teresa. The Lord sustained her with His milk during these pleasant practices.
>
> One day, as she was sitting under the shade of a tree, a most beautiful youth approached her. She showed no fear as he took her by the hand and brought her towards the seashore. Yet, noticing that she was being captured, she cried for a long time, for she was losing her father. But as soon as she started feeling this way, Our Blessed Virgin herself ceased her crying by giving her a profound sense of joy, and from then onwards she was always cheerful. While she was transported to Spain, she was attacked by many crows that threatened to tear her body apart with their beaks.

Presented to the Catholic King to be a servant in his household, he passed her on as a gift to the most Excellent Count and Countess of Mancera. They received her as if they were her parents and entrusted her education to a pious priest. This priest, along with other very learned teachers he chose, examined her about her desire to enter the state of perfection.

The devil persecuted her in cruel ways, such as illnesses as well as all kinds of distress in the form of the demeaning tasks assigned only to the vilest of slaves. All these tested her will, but she overcame everything with constant prayer. Heaven often consoled her with signs of a better life in the future. She grew in all virtues, especially patience and humility.

A sort of heavenly competition arose between our two most holy fathers Francis and Dominic as to which Order would win her. After many places rejected her, she was called to our Order, and our Father Dominic insured her status in the monastery. While living in the world, she punished her body with cilices, self-flagellation, vigils, and other austere penances; and she redoubled them once she entered the monastery.

In the forty-six years she lived in the convent, she abstained from eating meat; and she added the rest of the year to the long periods of fasting observed by the Order. On many vigils, besides the main ones dedicated to our Lord and the Blessed Virgin, she was content with only bread and water. She slept on a hard cot and only for short periods, because she dedicated the remainder of the night to prayer, which she continued for the whole day. She took communion frequently.

At the time she entered the convent, the sisters, who now sleep in the Lord, stood in respect and received her with joy. When she made her profession in the hands of our Father Dominic, many saints were present at the ceremony, among them our Angelic Doctor; she was astonished as she admired his glory. It is not easy to tell how many gifts she received from her favorite Saint Vincent Ferrer.

She received the gift of prophesy. She penetrated the secrets of the heart and could feel those who were stained by the sins of the flesh through their stench. She knew beforehand of the death of many, and she saw many souls go to heaven as well.

She reached the end of her life having suffered with patience the pains and desolation of the spirit, which the Lord had told her would happen. She left the world of the living at the age of seventy-two, not stained even once by mortal sin. For this reason, we piously believe that she flew to heaven.

APPENDIX 4

Last Will and Testament of Juliana Teresa Portocarrero, Marchioness of Mancera

Last Will and Testament of Doña Juliana Teresa Portocarrero Meneses y Noroña, Marchioness of Mancera, granting freedom to her slave Teresa Juliana del Espíritu Santo, and describing plans for her to enter a convent, establishing funds for her dowry together with an annuity of 50 ducats. Teresa is mentioned twice in the document, in separate items from the rest of the female servants in the household (Archivo Histórico de Protocolos Notariales, Madrid. 10 April 1703. Libro 13.977, fol. 135v).

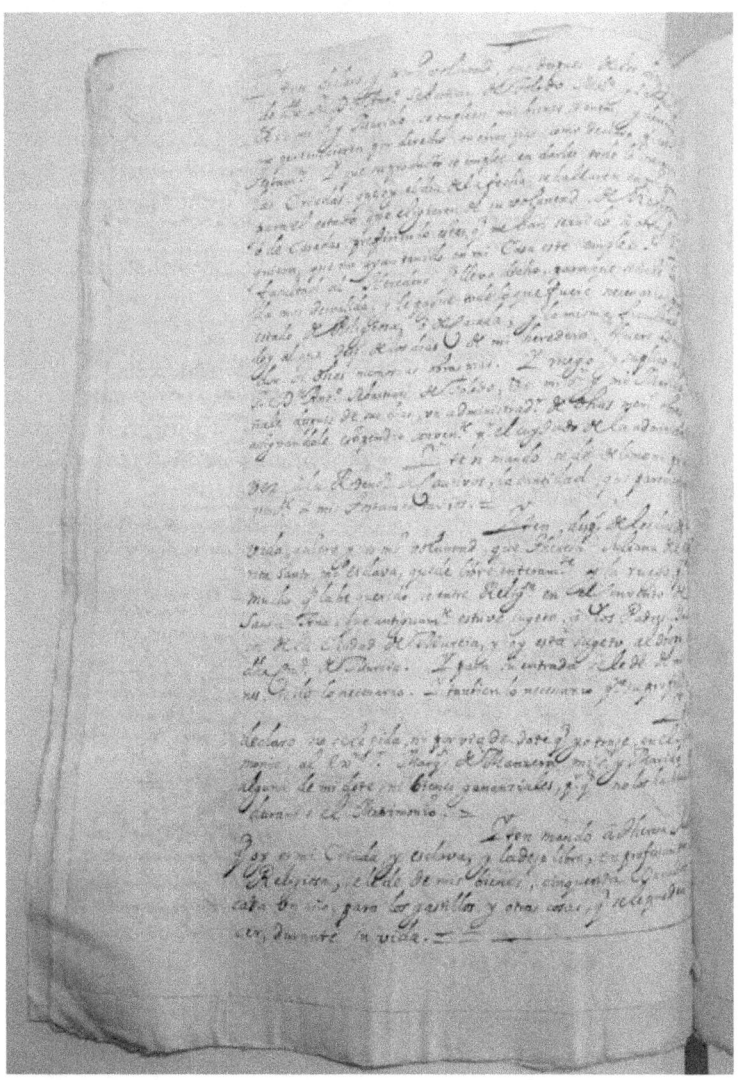

First mention, indicating the preference for a convent in Murcia (Teresa did not go there).

Item. Once the days of my life are finished, I want and it is my wish that Theresa Juliana del Espíritu Santo, my slave, may be entirely free. I also pray to her, as a sign of how much I have loved her, that she enter as a religious the Convent of St. Anne, formerly under the rule of the Dominican friars, in the city of Murcia, and now subject to the bishop of the aforementioned city of Murcia. And for her admission she may receive all that is necessary from my estate, as well as everything necessary for her profession.

Iten, despues delos dias de mi vida, quiero y es mi voluntad, que Theresa Juliana del Spiritu Santo mi esclava, quede libre enteramente y la ruego por lo mucho que la he querido se entre Religiosa en el Convento de Santa Ana que antiguamente estuvo sugeto a los Padres Dominicos dela Ciudad de Murcia, y oy esta sugeto al Obispo de dicha Ciudad de Murcia. Y para su entrada se le de de mis bienes todo lo necesario. Y tanbien lo necessario para su profession.

Second mention, with the assignment of the 50 ducats of rent per year:

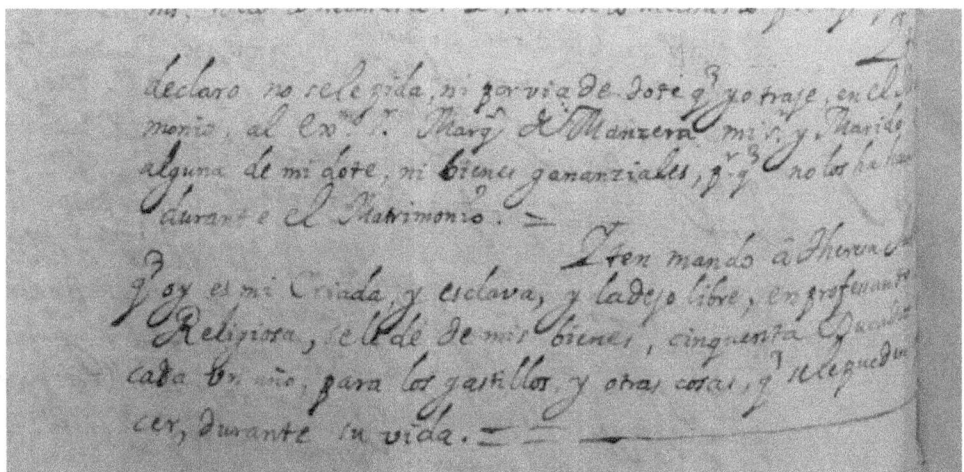

Item. To Theresa Juliana, who is now my servant and slave, and I set free, if she professes as a religious, she will receive from my estate fifty ducats every year for the rest of her life, for her expenses and other things that may come up to her.

Iten mando a Theresa Juliana que oy es mi criada y esclava, y la dejo libre, en professando de Religiosa, sele de de mis bienes, cinquenta Ducados cada un año, para los gastillos y otras cosas, que se le puedan ofrecer, durante su vida.

Bibliography

Acta Eruditorum Lipsicusium (Acts of Leipzig). Leipzig, 1682–1731.
Acta Capituli Provincialis Provinciae Hispaniae Ordinis Praedicatorum (Acts of Toro). Celebrati in Conventu Sancti Indephonsi Regali Taurensi, Die 27. Aprilis, anni Domini 1749. Sub R.A.P.N. Fr. Eugenio de Basualdo. Magistro Concionatore Regio. Priore Conventus Sti. Thomae Matritensis, Vicario Generali & Provinciali electo eiusdem Provinciae. Madrid, 1749.
Addy, George M. "The Reforms of 1771: First Steps in the Salamancan Enlightenment." *The Hispanic American Historical Review* 41.3 (1961): 339–66.
Adjaye, Joseph K. "Dangerous Crossroads: Liminality and Contested Meaning in Krobo (Ghana) Dipo Girls' Initiation." *Journal of African Cultural Studies* 12.1 (1999): 5–26.
Akyeampong, Emmanuel Kwaku. *Between the Sea & the Lagoon: An Eco-social History of the Anlo of Southeastern Ghana, c. 1850 to Recent Times*. Athens, OH: Ohio UP, 2001.
Althusser, Louis. "Ideogoly and Ideological State Apparatuses (Notes towards an Investigation)." *Lenin and Philosophy and Other Essays*. 1968. Trans. Ben Brewster. New York: Monthly Review, 1971. 127–86.
Alvar, Manuel. *La vida de Santa María Egipciaca; estudios, vocabulario, edición de los textos*. 2 vols. Madrid: Consejo Superior de Investigaciones Científicas, 1970.
Anderson, Justin M. "Aquinas on The Graceless Unbeliever." *Freiburger Zeitschrift für Philosophie Und Theologie* 59.1 (2012): 5–25.
Andrews, William L. *To Tell a Free Story: The First Century of Afro-American Autobiography, 1769–1865*. Urbana: U of Illinois P, 1986.
———, et al. *Sisters of the Spirit: Three Black Women's Autobiographies of the Nineteenth Century*. Bloomington: Indiana UP, 1986.
Anguiano, Mateo de. *Misiones capuchinas en África*. Unpublished ms (Ms18.178). Biblioteca Nacional. Madrid, 1648. Madrid: Consejo Superior de Investigaciones Científicas, 1950.
Anne of St. Bartholomew (Ana de san Bartolomé). *Autobiography and Other Writings*. Ed. and trans. Darcy Donahue. Chicago: U of Chicago P, 2008.
Aquinas, Thomas. *Basic Writings of St Thomas Aquinas*. Ed. Anton C. Pegis. Indianapolis: Hackett, 1997.
———. "*Summa Theologica*, First Part, Question 2: The Existence of God, Article 3: Whether God Exists." *The New Catholic Encyclopedia*. 2008. <www.newadvent.org/summa/1002.htm.>.
Aragón Mateos, Santiago, and R. Sánchez Rubio. "La esclavitud en la Alta Extremadura, proceso de auge y decadencia." *Norba: Revista de Historia* 7 (1986): 93–109.
Ares Queijo, Berta. "La cuestión del bautismo de los negros en el siglo XVII: La proyección de un debate americano." *Mirando las dos orillas: Intercambios mercantiles, sociales y culturales entre Andalucía y América*. Ed. Enriqueta Vila Vilar and Jaime J. Lacueva Muñoz. Seville: Fundación Buenas Letras, 2012. 469–85.
Armitage, David. "John Locke, Carolina, and the Two Treatises of Government." *Political Theory* 32.5 (2004): 602–27.
Artés Hernández, José Antonio. "El uso de la 'saliva' en el Nuevo Testamento (MC 7,32–37, 8,22b–26 y JN 9,1–12): Antecedentes grecolatinos." *Myrtia: Revista de filología clásica* 21 (2006): 155–82.
Atienza López, Ángela. "De beaterios a conventos: Nuevas perspectivas sobre el mundo de las beatas en la España Moderna." *Historia Social* 57 (2007): 145–68.

Augustine of Hippo (Saint). *De doctrina Christiana*. Ed. and trans. R. P. H. Green. Oxford, New York: Clarendon P, 1995.
Barrett, Lindon. "African-American Slave Narratives: Literacy, the Body, Authority." *American Literary History* 7.3 (1995): 415–42.
Barrionuevo, Jerónimo de. *Avisos de D. Jerónimo de Barrionuevo (1654–1658). Precede una noticia de la vida y escritos del autor*. Colección de escritores castellanos. 4 vols. Madrid, 1892
Barthes, Roland. *Image-Music-Text*. Ed. and trans. Stephen Heath. London: Fontana, 1977.
Barthes, Roland. *S/Z: An Essay*. 1970. Trans. Richard Miller. New York: Hill and Wang, 1974.
Bartlett, Robert. *The Making of Europe: Conquest, Colonization, and Cultural Change, 950–1350*. Princeton: Princeton UP, 1993.
Bauer, Raymond A., and Alice H. Bauer. "Day to Day Resistance to Slavery." *The Journal of Negro History* 27.4 (1942): 388–419.
Begg, Ean C. M. *The Cult of the Black Virgin*. London: Arkana, 1985.
Belinda. "Petition of an African Slave, to the Legislature of Massachusetts." *American Women Writers to 1800*. Ed. Sharon M. Harris. New York: Oxford UP, 1996. 253–54.
Belsey, Catherine. *Critical Practice*. London: Methuen, 1980.
Benegassi y Luxán, Joseph Joachín. *Vida del portentoso negro San Benito de Palermo: descripta en seis cantos joco-serios del reducissimo metro de seguidillas con los argumentos en octavas*. Madrid, 1750.
Berceo, Gonzalo de. *Obras completas de Gonzalo de Berceo*. 5 vols. Ed. Brian Dutton. London: Támesis, 1978.
Bhabha, Homi K. *The Location of Culture*. London: Routledge, 1994.
Bilinkoff, Jodi. *Related Lives: Confessors and Their Female Penitents, 1450–1750*. Ithaca: Cornell UP, 2005.
Blassingame, John W. *Slave Testimony: Two Centuries of Letters, Speeches, Interviews, and Autobiographies*. Baton Rouge: Louisiana State UP, 1977.
Blier, Suzanne Preston. *African Vodun: Art, Psychology, and Power*. Chicago: U of Chicago P, 1995.
Bosman, Willem. *A New and Accurate Description of the Coast of Guinea, Divided into the Gold, the Slave, and the Ivory Coasts. . . . Illustrated with Several Cuts. Written Originally in Dutch by William Bosman*. 2nd ed. London, 1721.
Boulukos, George E. "Olaudah Equiano and the Eighteenth-Century Debate on Africa." *Eighteenth-Century Studies* 40.2 (2007): 241–55.
Brakke, David. "Ethiopian Demons: Male Sexuality, the Black-Skinned Other, and the Monastic Self." *Journal of the History of Sexuality* 10.3/4 (2001): 501–35.
Brásio, António, et al. *Monumenta missionaria africana. Africa ocidental*. 13 vol. Lisboa: Agência Geral do Ultramar Divisão de Publicações e Biblioteca, 1952–85.
Brauner, Christina. "To Be the Key for Two Coffers: A West African Embassy to France (1670/1)." *IFRA-Nigeria E-Papers Series*. 2013. <www.ifra-nigeria.org/publications/e-papers/ifra-e-papers/63-brauner-christina-2013-to-be-the-key-for-two-coffers-a-west-african-embassy-to-france-1670-1>.
Brooks, Peter. *Reading for the Plot: Design and Intention in Narrative*. New York: A.A. Knopf, 1984.
Burns, Kathryn. *Colonial Habits: Convents and the Spiritual Economy of Cuzco, Peru*. Durham, NC: Duke UP, 1999.
Bynum, Caroline Walker. Foreword. Mooney ix–xii.
Bynum, Caroline Walker. *Holy Feast and Holy Fast the Religious Significance of Food to Medieval Women*. U of California P, 1988.
Cabrol, Fernand. "Office of the Dead." *The Catholic Encyclopedia*. Vol. 11. New York: Robert Appleton, 1911. <www.newadvent.org/cathen/11220a.htm>.
Calderón de la Barca, Pedro. *El árbol de mejor fruto*. Pamplona-Kassel: U de Navarra-Reichenberger, 2009.
———. *Comedia famosa. La Sibyla de Oriente y Gran Reina de Sabá*. <www.cervantesvirtual.com/obra/comedia-famosa-la-sibila-del-oriente-y-gran-reyna-de-saba/>.

———. *Los hijos de la fortuna, Teágenes y Clariclea*. <www.cervantesvirtual.com/nd/ark:/59851/bmctjod7>.
Calvo, Luis. "Félix de Azúa." *Tiempo de Hoy* 1 Apr, 2016. <www.tiempodehoy.com/entrevistas/felix-de-azua>.
Camara, Laye. *The Dark Child*. Trans. James Kirkup. London: Collins, 1955.
Castro y Quiñones, Pedro. *Instrucción para remediar y asegurar cuanto con la divina gracia fuere posible, que ninguno de los Negros que vienen de Guinea, Angola y otras Provincias de aquella costa de África carezca del sagrado Baptismo*. Seville, 1614.
Catastro de Ensenada: magna averiguación fiscal para alivio de los vasallos y mejor conocimiento de los reinos, 1749–1756. Madrid: Ministerio de Hacienda, Secretaría de Estado de Hacienda, Dirección General del Catastro, 2002.
Catherine of Siena. *The Dialogue*. Trans. Suzanne Noffke, OP. New York: Paulist P, 1980.
Certeau, Michel de. *The Mystic Fable*. Chicago: U of Chicago P, 1992.
Cervantes Saavedra, Miguel de. *Los trabajos de Persiles y Sigismunda*. Ed. Carlos Romero Muñoz. Madrid: Cátedra, 1997.
Coe, Sophie, and Michael D. Coe. "Estampas del chocolate en Europa." *Artes de México* 105 (2011): 52–61.
Contreras, Fray Pedro de. *Sermon funebre en las honras de la Venerable Magdalena de la Cruz, negra de nacion*. Sevilla, 1735.
Cortés Cortés, Fernando. *Esclavos en la Extremadura meridional del siglo XVII*. Colección Historia. Badajoz: Excelentísima Diputación Provincial de Badajoz, 1987.
Cortina Iceta, Luis. *El siglo XVIII en la pre-ilustración salmantina: Vida y pensamiento de Luis de Losada, 1681–1748*. Madrid: Consejo Superior de Investigaciones Científicas, 1981.
Craddock, Jerry R. "Apuntes para el estudio de la leyenda de santa María Egipcíaca en España." *Homenaje a Rodríguez Moñino*. Ed. J. Homer Herriott et al. Vol. 1 Madrid: Castalia, 1966. 99–110.
Crenshaw, Kimberlé. "Mapping the Margins: Intersectionality, Identity Politics, and Violence against Women of Color." *Stanford Law Review* 43.6 (1991): 1241–99.
Cruz, Anne J. and Rosilie Hernández. *Women's Literacy in Early Modern Spain and the New World*. Farmham, UK: Ashley Publishing, 2011.
Culler, Jonathan D. *Structuralist Poetics: Structuralism, Linguistics, and the Study of Literature*. Ithaca: Cornell UP, 1975.
———. *The Pursuit of Signs: Semiotics, Literature, Deconstruction*. Ithaca: Cornell UP, 1981.
Dash, J. Michael. "Writing the Body: Edouard Glissant's Poetics of Re-membering." *World Literature Today* 63.4 (1989): 609–12.
Davis, Charles T. "The Slave Narrative: First Major Art Form in an Emerging Black Tradition (1979)." *Black is the Color of the Cosmos: Essays on Afro-American Literature and Culture, 1942–1981*. Ed. Henry Louis Gates, Jr. Washington DC: Howard UP, 1989. 83–120.
Deffis de Calvo, Emilia I. *Viajeros, peregrinos y enamorados: la novela española de peregrinación del siglo XVII*. Pamplona: Ediciones U de Navarra, 1999.
Delahaye, Hippolyte. "Hagiography." *The Catholic Encyclopedia*. Vol. 7. New York: Robert Appleton, 1910. <www.newadvent.org/cathen/07106b.htm>.
Delany, Joseph. "Scruple." *The Catholic Encyclopedia*. Vol. 13. New York: Robert Appleton, 1912. <www.newadvent.org/cathen/13640a.htm>.
De Lauretis, Teresa. "Sexual Indifference and Lesbian Representation." *Performing Feminisms: Feminist Critical Theory and Theater*. Ed. Sue-Ellen Case. Baltimore: Johns Hopkins UP, 1990. 17–39.
Dewey, William J. "Iron, Master of Them All." Exhibit at the Museum of the U of Iowa. Curated by William J. Dewey, and Allen F. Roberts. Project for Advanced Study of Art and Life in Africa. Iowa City: U of Iowa, 1993.

Deyermond, Alan. "Berceo, el diablo y los animales." *Homenaje al Instituto de Filología y Literaturas Hispánicas "Dr. Amado Alonso" en su cincuentenario, 1923–1973.* Buenos Aires: Instituto de Filología y Literaturas Hispánicas Dr. Amado Alonso, 1975. 82–90.

Diseño de la alegorica fabrica del Arco Triumphal, que la Santa Iglesia Cathedral de Puebla de los Angeles erigio en aplauso del Excellentissimo Señor DON ANTONIO SEBASTIAN DE TOLEDO, Marques de Mancera: Señor de las 5 Villas, y de la del Marmol. Puebla, Mexico, 1664.

Domínguez Ortiz, Antonio. "La esclavitud en Castilla durante la Edad Moderna." *Estudios de historia social de España.* Ed. Carmelo Viñas y Mey. Vol. 2. Madrid: Consejo Superior de Investigaciones Científicas, 1952. 367–426.

———. *Los judeoconversos en España y América.* Madrid: ISTMO, 1971.

Dorado, Bernardo. *Compendio historico de la ciudad de Salamanca.* Salamanca, 1776.

Elaw, Zilpha. "Memoirs of the Life, Religious Experience, Ministerial Travels, and Labors." Andrews 76–82.

Ellis, A. B. *The Ewe-Speaking Peoples of the Slave Coast of West Africa Their Religion, Manners, Customs, Laws, Languages, &C.* London, 1890.

Equiano, Olaudah. *The Interesting Narrative of the Life of Olaudah Equiano or Gustavus Vassa, the African. Written by Himself.* London, 1789.

Equiano, Oladudah. *The Life of Olaudah Equiano, or Gustavus Vassa.* Mineaola, NY: Dover, 1999.

Farwell, Marilyn R. *Heterosexual Plots and Lesbian Narratives.* The Cutting Edge: Lesbian Life and Literature. New York: New York UP, 1996.

Fee, Nancy H. "La Entrada Angelopolitana: Ritual and Myth in the Viceregal Entry in Puebla de Los Angeles." *The Americas* 52.3 (1996): 283–320.

Feijóo y Montenegro, Benito Jerónimo. "Uso de la magia." *Teatro crítico universal.* Madrid, 1728. <www.filosofia.org/bjf/bjft205.htm>.

———. "Color etiópico." *Feijóo y el debate internacional sobre las razas y la historia de las naciones.* Ed. Paola Martínez Pestana. Murcia: Biblioteca Saavedra Fajardo de pensamiento político hispánico, 2009. 27–39.

Fernández Álvarez, Manuel. *Juana la Loca, la cautiva de Tordesillas.* 2nd ed. Madrid: Espasa Calpe, 2000.

Ferrús Antón, Beatriz. "Sor Teresa Juliana de Santo Domingo, Chicaba o escribir en la piel de otro." *Cuadernos dieciochescos* 9 (2008): 181–92.

Fisch, Audrey, ed. *The Cambridge Companion to the African American Slave Narrative.* Cambridge: CUP, 2007.

———. Introduction. Fisch 1–10.

Foote, Julia A. J. "A Brand Plucked from the Fire." Houchins 1–124.

Forrest, Beth Marie, and April I. Najjaj. "Is Sipping Sin Breaking Fast? The Catholic Chocolate Controversy and the Changing World of Early Modern Spain." *Food and Foodways* 15 (2007): 31–52.

Foster, Frances Smith, ed. *Love and Marriage in Early African America.* Lebanon, NH: Northeastern UP, 2008.

Fra Molinero, Baltasar. *La imagen de los negros en el teatro del siglo de oro.* Madrid: Siglo Veintiuno Editores, 1995.

Freud, Sigmund. "Beyond the Pleasure Principle." *The Standard Edition of the Complete Psychological Works of Sigmund Freud.* Vol. 18. Ed. James Strachey. London: Hogarth P, 1955. 3–64.

Fulton, DoVeanna S. *Speaking Power: Black Feminist Orality in Women's Narratives of Slavery.* Albany: SUNY P, 2006.

Galduf Blasco, Vicente, OP. *Vida de san Vicente Ferrer.* Barcelona: Juan Flors Editor, 1961.

Gallonio, Antonio. *The Life of Saint Philip Neri.* Trans. Jerome Bertram. San Francisco: Ignatius, 2005.

García Añoveros, Jesús Manuel. *El pensamiento y los argumentos sobre la esclavitud en Europa en el siglo XVI y su aplicación a los indios americanos y a los negros africanos.* Madrid: Consejo Superior de Investigaciones Científicas, 2000.

Gates, Henry Louis, Jr. *The Classic Slave Narratives.* New York: Signet, 2002.

———. *The Trials of Phillis Wheatley: America's First Black Poet and Her Encounters with the Founding Fathers.* New York: Basic Civitas Books, 2003.

Germeten, Nicole von. "Juan Roque's Donation of a House to the Zape Confraternity, Mexico City, 1623." McKnight and Garofalo 83–103.

———. *Black Blood Brothers: Confraternities and Social Mobility for Afro-Mexicans.* Gainesville, FL: UP of Florida, 2006.

Gilbert, Françoise. "Las varias formas de saber y su transmisión en el auto de Calderón *El árbol del mejor fruto* (1677)." *Actes du colloque La transmission du savoir licite ou illicites au Siècle d'or (19–21 mai 2008), Hommage à André Gallego.* Ed. L. González with T. Rodríguez. Toulouse: CNRS-U de Toulouse-Le Mirail, 2011. 267–90.

Gilroy, Paul. *The Black Atlantic: Modernity and Double Consciousness.* London: Verso, 1996.

Girón-Negrón, Luis M. "'Your Dove-Eyes among Your Hairlocks': Language and Authority in Fray Luis de León's *Respuesta que Desde su Prisión da a sus Émulos.*" *Renaissance Quarterly* 54.4 (2001): 1197–250.

Godden, Rumer. *Five for Sorrow, Ten for Joy.* New York: Viking, 1979.

Goldenberg, David. *The Curse of Ham: Race and Slavery in Early Judaism, Christianity, and Islam.* Princeton: Princeton UP, 2003.

Gómez de la Parra, José, and Manuel Ramos Medina. *Fundación y primero siglo: crónica del primer convento de carmelitas descalzas en Puebla, 1604–1704.* México City: U Iberoamericana, 1992.

González Rovira, Javier. *La novela bizantina de la Edad de Oro.* Madrid: Gredos, 1996.

González Dávila, Gil. *Historia de las antigvedades de la civdad de Salamanca.* Salamanca, 1606.

González Díaz, Antonio Manuel. *La esclavitud en Ayamonte durante el Antiguo Régimen.* Huelva: Diputación Provincial de Huelva, 1997.

Gossy, Mary S. "Aldonza as Butch: Narrative and the Play of Gender in *Don Quijote.*" *Entiendes? Queer Readings, Hispanic Writing.* Eds. Emilie L. Bergmann and Paul Julian Smith. Durham, NC: Duke UP, 1995. 17–28.

Gott, Suzanne. "Golden Emblems of Maternal Benevolence: Transformations of Form and Meaning in Akan Regalia." *African Arts* 36.1 (2004): 66–81, 93–96.

Gould, Philip. "The Rise, Development, and Circulation of the Slave Narrative." Fisch 11–27.

Gracián, Baltasar. *El criticón.* Madrid: Cátedra, 2004.

Gray, Richard. "The Papacy and the Atlantic Slave Trade: Lourenço Da Silva, the Capuchins and the Decisions of the Holy Office." *Past & Present* 115 (1987): 101–15.

Greene, Sandra E. *Gender, Ethnicity, and Social Change on the Upper Slave Coast: A History of the Anlo-Ewe.* Portsmouth, NH: Heinemann, 1996.

———. "Religion, History and the Supreme Gods of Africa: A Contribution to the Debate." *Journal of Religion in Africa* 26.2 (1996): 122–38.

———. "Cultural Zones in the Era of the Slave Trade: Exploring the Yoruba Connection with the Anlo-Ewe." *Identity in the Shadow of Slavery.* Ed. Paul E. Lovejoy. New York: Continuum, 2000. 72–86.

———. "Of Water Spirits." *Sacred Sites and the Colonial Encounter: A History of Meaning and Memory in Ghana.* Ed. Sandra E. Greene. Indianapolis: Indiana UP, 2002. 35–60.

Greer, Allan. "Colonial Saints: Gender, Race, and Hagiography in New France." *The William and Mary Quarterly* 57.2 (2000): 323–48.

Hamberger, Klaus. "From Village to Bush in Four Watchi Rites: A Transformational Analysis of Ritual Space and Perspective." *HAU: Journal of Ethnographic Theory* 4.1 (2014): 129–53.

Hampe Martínez, Teodoro, and José de la Puente Brunke. "Mercedes de la Corona sobre Encomiendas del Perú: Un aspecto de la política indiana en el siglo XVII." *Quinto Centenario* 10 (1986): 85–108.

Hanke, Lewis, and Celso Rodriguez. *Los virreyes españoles en América durante el gobierno de la Casa de Austria.* Biblioteca de Autores Españoles. Madrid: Atlas, 1976.

Harms, Robert W. *The Diligent: A Voyage through the Worlds of the Slave Trade*. New York: Basic Books, 2002.
Hartman, Saidiya V. *Lose Your Mother: A Journey Along the Atlantic Slave Route*. New York: Farrar, Straus & Giroux, 2008.
Heffernan, Thomas J. *Sacred Biography: Saints and Their Biographers in the Middle Ages*. New York: Oxford UP, 1988.
Heliodorus, Fernando de Mena, and Francisco López Estrada. *Historia etiópica de los amores de Teágenes y Cariclea*. Real Academia Española Biblioteca selecta de clásicos españoles ser. 2. Madrid: Aldus, 1954.
Henry-Couannier, M. *Saint Francis de Sales and His Friends*. New York: Alba House, 1964.
Herbert, E. W. *Red Gold of Africa: Copper in Precolonial History and Culture*. Madison: U of Wisconsin P, 2003.
Hinks, Peter P. *To Awaken My Afflicted Brethren: David Walker and the Problem of Antebellum Slave Resistance*. University Park, PA: Pennsylvania State UP, 1997.
The Holy Bible. Revised Standard Version. Catholic ed. Camden, NJ: Thomas Nelson, 1966.
Houchins, Sue E. "Introduction." *Spiritual Narratives*. New York: Oxford UP, 1988.
Ibsen, Kristine. *Women's Spiritual Autobiography in Colonial Spanish America*. Gainesville: UP of Florida, 1999.
Jaca, Francisco José, and Miguel Anxo Pena González. *Resolución sobre la libertad de los negros y sus originarios, en estado de paganos y después ya cristianos: la primera condena de la esclavitud en el pensamiento hispano*. Madrid: Consejo Superior de Investigaciones Científicas, 2002.
Jacobs, Harriet A. *Incidents in the Life of a Slave Girl: Written by Herself*. Ed. Jean Fagan Yellin. Cambridge, MA: Harvard UP, 1987.
Jacobus, William Granger Ryan, and Helmut Ripperger. *The Golden Legend of Jacobus de Voragine*. 2 vols. London: Longmans, Green, 1941.
Jarrett, B, F., et al. "Third Orders." *The Catholic Encyclopedia*. Vol. 14. New York: Robert Appleton, 1912. <www.newadvent.org/cathen/14637b.htm>.
Jay, Nancy B. *Throughout Your Generations Forever: Sacrifice, Religion, and Paternity*. Chicago: U of Chicago P, 1992.
Jenson, Deborah. *Beyond the Slave Narrative: Politics, Sex, and Manuscripts in the Haitian Revolution*. Liverpool: Liverpool UP, 2011.
Jerome (Saint). *Sancti Eusebii Hieronymi Epistulae*. 1910–18. New York: Johnson, 1970.
John Chrysostom (Saint). *The Cult of the Saints. Select Homilies and Letters*. Ed. and trans. Wendy Mayer. Yonkers, NY: St. Vladimir's Seminary P, 2006.
John of the Cross (Saint, see Juan de la Cruz, San).
Johnson, Phyllis, and Brigitte Cazelles. *Le Vain Siècle Guerpir: A Literary Approach to Sainthood through Old French Hagiography of the Twelfth Century*. Chapel Hill: U of North Carolina P, 1979.
Juan de la Cruz (San, known in English as St. John of the Cross). *Obra completa*. Ed. Luce López-Baralt and Eulogio Pacho. Madrid: Alianza Editorial, 1996.
———. *Poesías*. Ed. Domingo Ynduráin. Madrid: Cátedra, 1983.
Juana Inés de la Cruz. *Fama y obras posthumas del Fenix de Mexico, Décima Musa, Poetisa Americana, Sor Jvana Inés de la Crvz religiosa professa en el convento de san Geronino de la Imperial Civdad de Mexico*. Madrid, 1700.
Juvenal. "Satire 7." *Juvenal and Persius*. Ed. and trans. G. G. Ramsay. The Loeb Classical Library. London: William Heinemann, 1928.
Kamen, Henry. "Mediterranean Slavery in Its Last Phase: The Case of Valencia, 1600–1700." *Anuario de Historia Económica y Social* 3 (1970): 211–34.
Kammer, Michael P., and Charles W. Mulligan. *Writing Handbook*. Chicago: Loyola UP, 1958.
Kelly, Henry Angsar. *Satan: A Biography*. New York: Cambridge UP, 2006.
Kent, William "Demoniacs." *The Catholic Encyclopedia*. Vol. 4. New York: Robert Appleton, 1908. <www.newadvent.org/cathen/04711a.htm>.

Knorr, Heather. "The Struggle between Reason and Will in the *Vida de Santa Maria Egipcíaca*." Thesis. U of North North Carolina at Chapel Hill, 2006.

Konetzke, Richard. *Colección de documentos para la historia de la formación social de Hispanoamérica, 1493–1810*. 5 vol. Madrid: Consejo Superior de Investigaciones Científicas, 1953.

Labouret, Henri, and Paul Rivet. *Le royaume d'Arda et son évangélisation au XVII. siècle*. Travaux et mémoires de l'Institut d'ethnologie, VII. Paris: Institut d'ethnologie, 1929.

Landers, Jane. "Cimarrón Ethnicity and Cultural Adaptation in the Spanish Domains of the Circum-Caribbean, 1503–1763." *Identity in the Shadow of Slavery*. 30–54.

Landsberg, John Justus (Joannes Justus Lanspergius). "Enquiridion militiae christianae." *Opera Omnia*. Vol. 4. Montreuil-sur-Mer, 1890. 505–601.

Lanser, Susan Sniader. *Fictions of Authority: Women Writers and Narrative Voice*. Ithaca: Cornell UP, 1992.

Larquié, Claude. "Les esclaves de Madrid à l'époque de la décadence (1650–1700)." *Revue historique* 244 (1970): 41–74.

Lavrin, Asunción. "Values and Meaning of Monastic Life for Nuns in Colonial Mexico." *Catholic Historical Review* 58.3 (1972): 367–87.

Law, Robin. "Religion, Trade and Politics on the 'Slave Coast': Roman Catholic Missions in Allada and Whydah in the Seventeenth Century." *Journal of Religion in Africa* 21.1 (1991): 42–77.

———. *The Slave Coast of West Africa, 1550–1750: The Impact of the Atlantic Slave Trade on an African Society*. Oxford Studies in African Affairs xii. Oxford: Clarendon P, 1991.

Lee, Jarena. "Religious Experience and Journal." Houchins 1–97.

León, Fray Luis de. *Obras completas castellanas*. Ed. Padre Felix García. 2nd ed. Madrid: Editorial Católica, 1951.

Lerner, Gerda. *The Creation of Feminist Consciousness: From the Middle Ages to Eighteen-Seventy*. New York: Oxford UP, 1993.

Liebowitz, Ruth P. "Virgins in the Service of Christ: The Dispute over an Active Apostolate for Women during the Counter-Reformation." *Women of Spirit: Female Leadership in the Jewish and Christian Traditions*. Eds. Rosemary Reuther and Eleanor McLaughlin. New York: Simon and Schuster, 1979. 131–52.

Lobo Cabrera, Manuel. "La población esclava de Telde en el siglo XVI." *Hispania: Revista española de historia* 42 (1982): 47–90.

———. "La población esclava de Las Palmas durante el siglo XVI." *Anuario de Estudios Atlánticos* 30 (1984): 157–316.

Locke, John. *Locke: Political Essays*. Ed. Mark Goldie. New York: Cambrdige UP, 1997.

López García, María Trinidad. "Aproximación al convento de Santa Ana de Murcia, de monjas dominicas." *La clausura femenina en España: actas del simposium*. Ed. Francisco Javier Campos and Fernández de Sevilla. Vol. 2. El Escorial: Real Centro Universitario Escorial-María Cristina, 2004. 891–918.

Lovell, Nadia. "Wild Gods: Containing Wombs and Moving Pots." *Locality and Belonging*. Ed. Nadia Lovell. London: Routlege, 1998. 53–77.

Maeso, María Eugenia. *Sor Teresa Chikaba: Princesa, esclava y monja*. Salamanca: Editorial San Esteban, 2004.

Maffei, Giovanni Pietro. *De vita et moribus Ignatii Loiolae*. Rome, 1585.

———. *Io. Petri Maffeii Bergomatis e Societate Iesu Historiarum Indicarum libri XVI: selectarum item ex India epistolarum eodem interprete libri IIII: accessit Ignatij Loiolae vita postremo recognita: et in opera singula copiosus index*. Venice, 1589.

Magennis, Hugh, ed. *The Old English Life of St Mary of Egypt: An Edition of the Old English Text with Modern English Parallel-Text Translation*. Trans. Magennis. Exeter: U of Exeter P, 2002.

Maier, John R. "Sainthood, Heroism, and Sexuality in the *Estoria de Santa Maria Egipçiaca*." *Revista Canadiense de Estudios Hispánicos* 8.3 (1984): 424–35.

Maraqten, Mohammed. Rev. of *Queen of Sheba: Treasures from Ancient Yemen*, by St. John Simpson. *Journal of the Royal Asiatic Society* 15.1 (2005): 102–04.

Mariblanca, Rosario. *Historia del Buen Retiro*. Madrid: La Librería, 2008.
Martín Casares, Aurelia. *La esclavitud en la Granada del siglo XVI: género, raza y religión*. Granada: U de Granada, 2000.
———, and Margarita García Barranco. *La esclavitud negroafricana en la historia de España, siglos XVI y XVII*. Granada: Comares, 2010.
———, and Christine Delaigue. "The Evangelization of Freed and Slave Black Africans in Renaissance Spain: Baptism, Marriage, and Ethnic Brotherhoods." *History of Religions* 52.3 (2013): 214–35.
Maura Gamazo, Gabriel. *Carlos II y su corte*. Madrid: F. Beltrán, 1911.
Mauss, Marcel. *The Gift: Forms and Functions of Exchange in Archaic Societies*. London: Cohen and West, 1966.
McCloy, Shelby Thomas. *The Negro in France*. Lexington: U of Kentucky P, 1961.
McKenzie, John L. "Sheba." *Dictionary of the Bible*. By John L. McKenzie. New York: MacMillan, 1965. 796–97.
McKnight, Kathryn Joy, and Leo Garofalo. *Afro-Latino Voices: Narratives from the Early Modern Ibero-Atlantic World, 1550–1812*. Indianapolis: Hackett, 2009.
McNutt, Paula M. "The African Ironsmith as Marginal Mediator: A Symbolic Analysis." *Journal of Ritual Studies* 3.2 (1991): 75–98.
Mena García, Carmen. "Religión, etnia y sociedad: Cofradías de negros en el Panamá colonial." *Anuario de Estudios Americanos* 57.1 (2000): 137–69.
Mercer, Patricia. "Palace and Jihad in the Early 'Alawi State in Morocco." *The Journal of African History* 18.4 (1977): 531–53.
Meyer, Birgit. *Translating the Devil: Religion and Modernity among Ewe in Ghana*. Trenton, NJ: Africa World P, 1999.
Molas Ribalta, Pere. "La Razón de Estado y la sucesión española." *La Razón de Estado y la sucesión española*. Eds. Rafael Rus Rufino, et al. Valencia: Publicaciones de la Real Sociedad Económica de Amigos del País, 1999. 283–90.
Montero Alarcón, Alma. *Monjas coronadas: Profesión y muerte en Hispanoamérica virreinal*. Mexico City: CONACULTA, 2008.
Moody, Joycelyn. *Sentimental Confessions: Spiritual Narratives of Nineteenth-Century African American Women*. Athens: U of Georgia P, 2001.
Mooney, Catherine M. "Voice, Gender, and the Portrayal of Sanctity." Mooney 1–15.
———, ed. *Gendered Voices: Medieval Saints and Their Interpreters*. Philadelphia: U Pennsylvania P, 1999.
Moreno Navarro, Isidoro. *La antigua Hermandad de los Negros de Sevilla: etnicidad, poder y sociedad en 600 años de historia*. Sevilla: U de Sevilla, 1997.
Morgado García, Arturo. "El mercado de esclavos en el Cádiz de la Edad Moderna (1650–1750)." *Tiempos modernos* 18.1 (2009): 1–25.
Morgan, Philip D. *Slave Counterpoint: Black Culture in the Eighteenth-Century Chesapeake and Lowcountry*. Chapel Hill: U of North Carolina P, 1998.
Morrison, Toni. *Playing in the Dark: Whiteness and the Literary Imagination*. New York: Vintage, 1992.
———. *A Mercy*. New York: Knopf, 2008.
Mota Sierra, Manuel de la. "Quintilla sobre el mismo asunto de la devoción de san Isidro." *Patrona de Madrid restituida, poema heroico a la antiquísima y milagrosa imagen de Nuestra Señora de Atocha, de Alonso Jerónimo de Salas Barbadillo*. Madrid, 1750. 282–84.
Mott, Luiz. *Rosa Egipcíaca: Uma santa africana no Brasil*. Rio de Janeiro: Editora Bertrand Brasil, 1993.
Mullen, Harryette. "Runaway Tongue: Resistant Orality in *Uncle Tom's Cabin, Our Nig, Incidents in the Live of a Slave Girl*, and *Beloved*." *The Culture of Sentiment: Race, Gender, and Sentimentality in 19th Century America*. Ed. Shirley Samuels. New York: Oxford UP, 1992. 244–64.

Muriel, Josefina. "Los conventos de monjas en la sociedad virreinal." *Artes de México* 198 (1979): 7–23.
Mustakeem, Sowande. "'I Never Have Seen Such a Sickly Ship Before': Diet, Disease, and Mortality in 18th-Century Atlantic Slaving Voyages." *Journal of African American History* 93.4 (2004): 474–96.
Myers, Kathleen Ann. "El discurso religioso en la fundación del Convento de la Soledad: La Crónica de la Madre María de San José (1656–1719)." *Mujer y cultura en la colonia hispanoamericana*. Ed. Mabel Moraña. Pittsburgh: U of Pittsburgh P, 1996. 123–38.
———. *Neither Saints nor Sinners: Writing the Lives of Women in Spanish America*. Oxford: Oxford UP, 2003.
Nájera, José de. *Espejo mystico en que el hombre interior se mira practicamente illustrado*. Madrid, 1672.
Navarrete, María Cristina. *Génesis y desarrollo de la esclavitud en Colombia. Siglos XVI y XVII*. Cali, Colombia: U del Valle, 2005.
Nazianzus, Gregory of. "Oration 8, On his sister Gorgonia." *Nicene and Post-Nicene Fathers*. Trans. Charles Gordon Browne and James Edward Swallow. Eds. Philip Schaff and Henry Wace. Vol. 7. 2nd series. Rev. and ed. for New Advent by Kevin Knight. Buffalo, NY: Christian Literature Publishing, 1894.
Oke, Raymond. "Les siècles obscurs du royaume Aja du Danxome." *Actes du Colloque International sur les Civilisations Aja-Ewe*. Cotonou: U Nationale du Bénin, 1977. 52–84.
Opoku, Kofi Asare. "Abijan Mamiwater as a Priest." Wicker and Opoku 25–44.
Ott, Michael. "Pope Urban VIII." *The Catholic Encyclopedia*. Vol. 15. New York: Robert Appleton, 1912. <www.newadvent.org/cathen/15218b.htm>.
Painter, Nell Irvin. "Soul Murder and Slavery: Toward a Fully Loaded Cost Accounting." *U.S. History as Women's History: New Feminist Essays*. Eds. Linda K. Kerber, Alice Kessler-Harris, and Kathryn Kish Sklar. Chapel Hill: U of North Carolina P, 1995. 125–46.
Palacio Atard, Vicente. *La alimentación de Madrid en el siglo XVIII y otros estudios madrileños*. Madrid: Real Academia de la Historia, 1998.
Palacios Fernández, Emilio. *La mujer y las letras en la España del siglo XVIII*. Alicante: Biblioteca Virtual Cervantes, 2008. <www.cervantesvirtual.com/obra-visor/la-mujer-y-las-letras-en-la-espana-del-siglo-xviii--0/html/01ee5680-82b2-11df-acc7-002185ce6064_75.html#I_8_>.
Paniagua, Juan Carlos Miguel de. *Oracion funebre en las exequias de la Madre Sor Teresa Juliana de Santo Domingo, de feliz memoria, celebradas en el dia nueve de enero en el Convento de Religiosas Dominicas, vulgo de la Penitencia*. Salamanca, 1749.
———. *Compendio de la Vida Exemplar de la Venerable Madre Sor Teresa Juliana de Sto. Domingo, Tercera profesa en el convento de Santa Maria Magdalena, vulgo de la Penitencia, Orden de Santo Domingo de la ciudad de Salamanca. Su autor el R. Don Juan Carlos Pan y Agua*. Salamanca, 1752.
———. *Compendio de la Vida Exemplar de la Venerable Madre Sor Teresa Juliana de Sto. Domingo, tercera professa en el convento de Santa María Magdalena, vulgo de la Penitencia, Orden de Santo Domingo de la ciudad de Salamanca*. 2nd ed. Salamanca, 1764.
———. *Compendio de la Vida Ejemplar de la Venerable Madre Sor Teresa Juliana de Sto. Domingo, Tercera profesa en el convento de Santa María Magdalena, vulgo de la Penitencia, Orden de Santo Domingo de la ciudad de Salamanca. 1752*. Salamanca: Imprenta Calatrava, 1999.
Patterson, Orlando. *Freedom in the Making of Western Culture*. New York: Basic Books, 1991.
Paz, Octavio. *Sor Juana Inés de la Cruz, o las trampas de la fe*. México City: Fondo de Cultura Económica, 1985.
———. *Sor Juana, or, The Traps of Faith*. 1985. Trans. Margaret Bayers Peden. Cambridge, MA: Harvard UP, 1988.
Pena González, Miguel Anxo. "Un documento singular de Fray Francisco José de Jaca, acerca de la esclavitud práctica de los indios." *Revista de Indias* 61.223 (2001): 701–13.

———. *Francisco José de Jaca: La primera propuesta abolicionista de la esclavitud en el pensamiento hispano*. Salamanca: U Pontificia de Salamanca, 2003.

Pepin, Ronald E., et al. *Saint Mary of Egypt: Three Medieval Lives in Verse*. Kalamazoo, MI: Cistercian Publications, 2005.

Pérez García, Rafael, and Manuel Fernández Chaves. "Sevilla y la trata negrera atlántica: envíos de esclavos desde Cabo Verde a la América española (1569–1579)." *Estudios de historia moderna en honor al profesor Antonio García-Baquero*. Ed. León Carlos Álvarez Santaló. Seville: U de Sevilla, 2009. 597–622.

———. "Las redes de la trata negrera: mercaderes portugueses y tráfico de esclavos en Sevilla (c.1560–1580)." Martin Casares 5–34.

Pérez, Joseph. *Los judíos en España*. Madrid: Marcial Pons Historia, 2005.

Pérez de Montalbán, Juan. *La comedia famosa de la gitana de Memphis, Santa Maria Egypciaca*. Madrid, 1756. U de Sevilla. Fondo Antiguo. Fondos digitalizados. <fondosdigitales.us.es/fondos/libros/6346/2/la-gitana-de-menfis-santa-maria-egypciaca-comedia-famosa-del-doct-d-juan-perez-de-montalvan/>.

Periáñez Gómez, Rocío. "La mujer esclava en la Extremadura de los tiempos modernos." *Marginados y minorías sociales en la España moderna y otros estudios sobre Extremadura*. Eds. Felipe Lorenzana de la Puente and Francisco J. Mateos Ascacíbar. Llerena, Spain: Sociedad Extremeña de Historia, 2006. 135–45.

———. "La esclavitud en Extremadura (siglos XVI–XVIII)." Diss. U de Extremadura, 2008.

Phillips, William D. *Slavery in Medieval and Early Modern Iberia*. Philadelphia: U of Pennsylvania P, 2014.

Pierce, Yolanda. "Redeeming Bondage: The Captivity Narrative and the Spiritual Autobiography in the African American Slave Narrative Tradition." Fisch 83–98.

Portilla, Anselmo de la, ed. *Instrucciones que los vireyes de Nueva España dejaron á sus sucesores. Añádense algunas que los mismos trajeron de la corte y otros documentos semejantes á las instrucciones*. Mexico City, 1873.

Portocarrero y Guzmán, Pedro. *Teatro Monarquico de España*. Ed. Carmen Sanz Ayanz.
Madrid: Boletín Oficial del Estado, 1998.

Posadas, Francisco. *Vida de la Venerable Madre Soror Leonor Maria de Christo, religiosa professa de velo negro en el Convento de Santa Maria de los Angeles de Religiosas dominicas de la ciudad de Jaen*. Jaén, Spain, 1699.

Poutrin, Isabelle. *Le voile et la plume: autobiographie et sainteté féminine dans l'Espagne moderne*. Madrid: Casa de Velázquez, 1995.

Radner, Joan N. and Susan S. Lanser. "Strategies of Coding in Women's Cultures." *Feminist Messages: Coding in Women's Folk Culture*. Ed. Joan Newton Radner. Urbana: U of Illinois P, 1993. 1–29.

Ragonesi, Franciscus. "Theatines." *The Catholic Encyclopedia*. Vol. 14. New York: Robert Appleton, 1912. <www.newadvent.org/cathen/14557a.htm>.

Ramírez de Vargas, Alonso. *Elogio panegirico, festivo aplavso, iris politico, y diseño trivnfal de Eneas verdadero. Con qve la muy noble, y leal ciudad de Mexico recibio al ex mo. señor d. Antonio Sebastian de Toledo, y Salazar: marques de Manzera*. Mexico City, 1664.

Ratunil, Pearl Suson. "Medieval Blackness: Blackness and Medieval Hagiography." Thesis. U of Illinois at Chicago, 2008.

Real Academia Española de la Lengua. *Diccionario de la lengua castellana*. Madrid, 1737.

———. *Diccionario de la Real Academia de la Lengua*. Madrid: Espasa-Calpe, 1992.

Rediker, Marcus. *The Slave Ship: A Human History*. New York: Viking, 2007.

———. "The Poetics of History from Below." *Perspectives on History: A Newsmagazine of the American Historical Association* 48.6 (2010): 36–38.

Reid-Pharr, Robert. "The Slave Narrative in Early Black American Literature." Fisch 137–49.

Ribera, Manuel Bernardo de. *Institutionum Philosophicarum*. Salamanca, 1754–56.

Rivera Cambas, Manuel. *Los gobernantes de México. Galería de biografías y retratos de los vireyes, emperadores, presidentes y otros gobernantes que ha tenido México, desde don Hernando Cortes hasta el c. Benito Juarez*. 2 vols. Mexico City, 1872.

Rodilla León, María José. "Bestiarios del Nuevo Mundo: Maravillas de Dios o engendros del Demonio." *'Cálamo currente': Homenaje a Juan Bautista Avalle-Arce*. Ed. Miguel Zugasti. Spec. issue of *RILCE, Revista de filología hispánica* 23.1 (2007): 195–205.

Ramírez de Vargas, Alonso. *Elogio panegirico, festivo aplavso, iris politico, y diseño trivnfal de Eneas verdadero. Con qve la muy noble, y leal ciudad de Mexico recibio al ex mo. señor d. Antonio Sebastian de Toledo, y Salazar: marques de Manzera*. Mexico City, 1664.

Rowe, Erin Kathleen. "After Death Her Face Turned White: Blackness, Whiteness, and Sanctity in the Early Modern Hispanic World." *American Historical Review* 121.3 (2016): 727–54.

Rubial García, Antonio. "Las santitas del barrio. "Beatas" laicas y religiosidad cotidiana en la ciudad de México en el siglo XVII." *Anuario de Estudios Americanos* 59.1 (2002): 13–37.

Russell-Wood, A. J. R. "Black and Mulatto Brotherhoods in Colonial Brazil: A Study in Collective Behavior." *The Hispanic American Historical Review* 54.4 (1974): 567–602.

Saco, José Antonio. *Historia de la esclavitud de la raza africana en el Nuevo Mundo y en especial en los paises américo-hispanos*. Barcelona, 1879.

Saint Simon, Duc de (Louis de Rouvroy Saint-Simon). *Mémoires*. Paris, 1829. <rouvroy.medusis.com/tomes.html>.

Sallust (Gaius Sallustius Crispus). *Catiline's Conspiracy. The Jugurthine War. Histories*. Oxford World's Classics. New York: Oxford UP, 2010.

Sánchez Lora, José Luis. *Mujeres, conventos y formas de la religiosidad barroca*. Madrid: Fundación Universitaria Española, 1988.

Sánchez-Prieto Borja, Pedro, Rocío Díaz Moreno, and Elena Trujillo Belso. "Santa María Egipcíaca." *Edición de textos alfonsíes. Real Academia Española: Banco de datos (CORDE). Corpus diacrónico del español*. 7 Mar. 2006. <www.rae.es>.

Sancho de Sopranis, Hipólito. *Las cofradías de Morenos en Cádiz*. Madrid: Instituto de Estudios Africanos, 1958.

Sandoval, Alonso de. *Un tratado sobre la esclavitud (De instauranda aethiopum salute, 1647)*. Ed. and trans. Enriqueta Vila Vilar. Madrid: Alianza U, 1987.

Santa Teresa, Silverio de. *Procesos de beatificación y canonización de Santa Teresa de Jesús*. Burgos: Monte Carmelo, 1934–35.

Saraiva, Antonio José. "Le père Antonio Vieira S. J. et la question de l'esclavage des Noirs au XVIIe siècle." *Annales. Économies, Sociétés, Civilisations* 22.6 (1967): 1289–309.

Scelle, Georges. *La traite négrière aux Indes de Castile, contrats et traités d'assiento; étude de droit public et d'histoire diplomatique puisée aux sources originales et accompagnée de plusierus documents inédits*. Paris: L. Larose and L. Tenin, 1906.

Scheil, Andrew P. "Bodies and Boundaries in the Old English Life of St. Mary of Egypt." *Neophilologus* 84.1 (2000): 137–56.

Schiller, Ben. "Selling Themselves: Slavery, Survival, and the Path of Least Resistance." *49th Parallel* 23 (2009): 1–23.

Scott, Joan W. "Gender: A Useful Category of Historical Analysis." *The American Historical Review* 91.5 (1986): 1053–75.

Serís, Homero. "Nueva genealogía de santa Teresa (Artículo-reseña)." *Nueva Revista de Filología Hispánica* 10 (1956): 365–84.

Seuanes Serafim, Cristina M. *As Ilhas de São Tomé no século XVII* Lisbon: Centro de História de Além-Mar, 2000.

Shackford, Martha Hale. "The Magi in Florence: An Aspect of the Renaissance." *Studies in Philology* 20.4 (1923): 377–87.

Sicroff, Albert A. *Los estatutos de limpieza de sangre: controversias entre los siglos XV y XVII*. Newark, DE: Juan de la Cuesta, 2010.

Slade, Carole. *St. Teresa of Avila: Author of a Heroic Life*. Berkeley: U of California P, 1995.

Smith, E. Valerie. "The Sisterhood of Nossa Senhora Do Rosario: African-Brazilian Cultural Adaptations to Antebellum Restrictions," *Afro-Hispanic Review* 42:1/2 (2002): 121–33.

Smith, Valerie. *Self-Discovery and Authority in Afro-American Narrative*. Cambridge, MA: Harvard UP, 1987.

———. *Not Just Race, Not Just Gender: Black Feminist Readings*. New York: Routledge, 1998.

Smoller, Laura Ackerman. *The Saint and the Chopped-up Baby: The Cult of Vincent Ferrer in Medieval and Early Modern Europe*. Ithaca: Cornell UP, 2014.

Soler y las Balsas, Luis. *Vida de la Venerable Negra, la Madre Sor Theresa Juliana de Santo Domingo de feliz memoria, Religiosa Profesa de la Tercera Orden de N. P. Sto. Domingo en el Religiosissimo Convento de Dominicas, vulgo de la Penitencia, de la Ciudad de Salamanca. Compuesta por un Devoto de Sn. Vicente Ferrer, Quien la dedica al mismo Santo. Con todas las licencias poeticas necesarias*. Unpublished ms. New York Public Library Schomburg Collection. Zaragoza, 1757.

Solís, Antonio de. *Historia de la conquista de Mexico*. Madrid, 1684.

Spivak, Gayatri Chakravorty. "Can the Subaltern Speak?" *Marxism and the Interpretation of Culture*. Eds. Lawrence Grossberg and Cary Nelson. Urbana: U of Illinois P, 1988. 271–313.

Stevenson, Jane. "The Holy Sinner: The Life of Mary of Egypt." *The Legend of Mary of Egypt in Medieval Insular Hagiography*. Eds. Erich Poppe and Bianca Ross. Dublin: Four Courts P, 1996. 19–50.

Stewart, Maria W. "Productions." Houchins 1–84.

Sweet, James H. *Domingos Alvares, African Healing, and the Intellectual History of the Atlantic World*. Chapel Hill: U of North Carolina P, 2011.

Teresa de Jesús (Santa, see also Teresa of Ávila, Saint). *Obras completas*. Ed. Luis Santullano. 10th ed. Madrid: Aguilar, 1966.

———. *Libro de la vida*. 1562–65. Ed. Otger Steggink. Madrid: Castalia, 1986.

Teresa of Ávila (Saint, see also Teresa de Jesús, Santa). *The Collected Works of St. Teresa of Ávila*. Ed. and trans. Kieran Kavanaugh and Otilio Rodríguez. 2nd ed. Washington, DC: ICS Publications, 1987.

Thérèse de Lisieux. *The Autobiography of St. Therese of Lisieux: The Story of a Soul*. 1895–97. Trans. John Beevers. New York: Image Books/Doubleday, 1989.

Thornton, John Kelly. *The Kongolese Saint Anthony: Dona Beatriz Kimpa Vita and the Antonian movement, 1684–1706*. Cambridge: Cambridge UP, 1998.

Thurston, Herbert. "Amice." *The Catholic Encyclopedia*. Vol. 1. New York: Robert Appleton, 1907. www.newadvent.org/cathen/01428c.htm.

Toner, Patrick. "Exorcism." *The Catholic Encyclopedia*. Vol. 5. New York: Robert Appleton Company, 1909. <www.newadvent.org/cathen/05709a.htm>.

Torres Sánchez, Concha. *La clausura femenina en la Salamanca del siglo XVII: Dominicas y Carmelitas descalzas*. Salamanca: Ediciones U de Salamanca, 1991.

Torres Villarroel, Diego de. *Vida exemplar y virtudes heroicas de el venerable Padre Don Geronymo Abarrategui y Figueroa, Clerigo Reglar Theatino de San Cayetano y fundador de el colegio de Salamanca de San Cayetano y S. Andrès Avelino de la misma religion*. Salamanca, 1749.

———. *Vida, ascendencia, nacimiento, crianza y aventuras*. Madrid: Editorial Castalia, 1972.

Trabulse, Elías. *El círculo roto: estudios históricos sobre la ciencia en México*. México City: Fondo de Cultura Económica, 1984.

Van Deusen, Nancy E. *The Souls of Purgatory: The Spiritual Diary of a Seventeenth-Century Afro-Peruvian Mystic, Ursula de Jesús*. U of New Mexico P, 2004.

Van Wyhe, Cordula. "Court and Convent: The Infanta Isabella and Her Franciscan Confessor Andrés de Soto." *The Sixteenth Century Journal* 35.2 (2004): 411–45.

Vauchez, André. *Sainthood in the Later Middle Ages*. Cambridge: Cambridge UP, 1997.

Vega, Garcilaso de la. *Comentarios reales de los incas*. 2 vols. Caracas: Biblioteca Ayacucho, 1976.

Vega, Lope de. *El peregrino en su patria*. Ed. Juan Baustista Avalle-Arce. Madrid: Editorial Castalia, 1973.

Velasco, Salvador. *San Martín de Porres*. 9th ed. Madrid: EDIBESA, 1992.

Vélez de Guevara, Luis. *Virtudes vencen señales*. Ed. José María Ruano de la Haza. Newark, DE: Juan de la Cuesta, 2010.

Venkatachalam, Meera. "Between the Devil and the Cross: Religion, Slavery, and the Making of the Anlo-Ewe." *Journal of African History* 53.1 (2012): 45–64.

Verger, Pierre. *Trade Relations between the Bight of Benin and Bahia from the 17th to 19th Century*. Ibadan: Ibadan UP, 1976.

Vidal y Micó, Francisco. *Historia de la portentosa vida y milagros de San Vicente Ferrer*. Valencia, 1735.

Vila Vilar, Enriqueta. "Aspectos marítimos del comercio de esclavos con Hispanoamérica en el siglo XVII." *Historia naval* 19 (1987): 113–31.

Vitz, Evelyn Birge. "*La Vie de Saint Alexis*: Narrative Analysis and the Quest for the Sacred Subject." *PMLA* 93.3 (1978): 396–408.

Warren, Nancy Bradley. *Spiritual Economies: Female Monasticism in Later Medieval England*. The Middle Ages series. Philadelphia: U of Pennsylvania P, 2001.

Watson, Paul. "The Queen of Sheba in Christian Tradition." *Solomon and Sheba*. Ed. James B. Pritchard. London: Phaidon, 1974. 115–45.

Wey-Gómez, Nicolás. "'Nuestro Padre El Sol': Scholastic Cosmology and the Cult of the Sun in Inca Garcilaso's 'Comentarios reales.'" *Latin American Literary Review* 26.52 (1998): 9–26.

Wicker, Kathleen O'Brien. "Abijan Mamiwater: Traveler in Search of a Home/Land." Wicker and Opoku 1–25.

Wicker, Kathleen O'Brien, and Kofi Asare Opoku, eds. *Togbi Dawuso Dofe: Mami Water in Ewe Tradition*. Legon, Ghana: Sub-Saharan Publishers, 2007.

Wilson, Louis Edward. *The Krobo People of Ghana, to 1892: A Political and Social History*. Athens, OH: Ohio U Center for International Studies, 1991.

Yai, Olabiyi Babaloa. "From Vodun to Mawu: Monotheism and History in the Fon Cultural Area." *L'invention religieuse en Afrique: Histoire et religion en Afrique Noire*. Ed. Jean-Pierre Chrétien. Paris: Éditions Karthala, 1993. 241–65.

Zamora Caro, Juan Antonio. "Luis Antonio Portocarrero: El conde 'desafecto' (1710–1723)." *Ámbitos: Revista de estudios de ciencias sociales y humanidades* 29 (2013): 81–90.

Zamora, Margarita. *Language, Authority, and Indigenous History in the Comentarios Reales De Los Incas*. Cambridge: Cambridge UP, 1988.

Zapata Cano, Rodrigo. "La teoría de los antojos, el origen de la negrura y la generación en la obra de Benito Feijóo." *Boletín de Antropología, Universidad de Antioquia* 22.39 (2008): 33–51.

Index

Page numbers in italic refer to images.

Abarrategui, Jerónimo de, 2–3, 6, 12, 96, 130, 142, 159, 178, 187, 240, 244, 246, 261. *See also* spiritual directors
abjection, 13, 74
Ablitas, Countess of, 251
Acts of Lypsick, 143
Acts of the Chapter of Toro, 3, 6, 98, 140, 143, 188, 204, 228, 248, 256, *274*
Africa, xi, 13–14, 17, 19, 20, 23, 42–43n33, 51n95, 56, 59, 62, 64, 67, 69, 73, 76–77, 79, 89, 91–92, 99n2, 102n24, 107n52, 141, 142, 147, 156, 157, 161, 163, 166, 171, 205, 232, 243, 265
  as homeland, 4, 17, 23, 57, 58–59, 61, 63, 66, 67, 76, 80, 99n4, 102n25, 147, 155, 160, 163, 181, 182, 183, 184, 193, 200, 205, 223, 226, 229, 232, 249, 252, 255
  as idyllic meadow, 64, 76, 144, 147, 149, 153, 154, 163, 208
  memory of, 57, 74–76, 141, 157, 163, 182 (see also *sankofa*)
  North, 17, 70, 76, 77, 168, 173
  West, 1, 14, 26, 38n4, 45n52, 56, 61–62, 67, 99n2, 100n8, 102n26, 104n32, 108n61, 111n85, 156
African American, x, xi, xvi, 7, 18–20, 25, 32, 55, 56
  women, xii, 20, 23, 36
African and Africans, v, ix, xv, 1, 3, 7, 10–14, 21, 23, 26, 33, 57, 59, 60, 61, 63–65, 67, 68, 74, 77–79, 86, 95, 163, 171, 183, 188, 195, 205, 223, 224, 232
  as barbarians, 59–60, 66, 142, 145, 147, 190
  as civilized, 17, 58–60, 147, 154, 254
  descent, xi, 15, 23, 24
  diaspora, xv, xvi, 2, 15–16, 18, 23, 24, 37, 66, 139
  savagery of, 17, 59, 154
  woman, xii, 2, 13, 15, 17, 18, 35, 55, 89, 98
Africanity, 23, 30
agency, 11, 20, 25, 27, 33–35, 37, 71, 75, 80, 94, 99n1, 180, 210, 212, 232, 235
Agokoli, 57
Akan, xi, 57, 58, 60, 99n6, 100n8
Akwamu, 58, 67

Akyeampong, Emmanuel Kwaku, 38–39n5
Alba de Tormes, 42n30, 81, 85, 86, 97, 98, 112n93, 186, 187, 192, 193, 194, 204
Alexandria, 10
Allada. *See* Arada
Allah, 169
Allen, Reverend Richard, 21
Almadén, 69
Althusser, Louis, 28, 52n103
Amazons, 130
amice, 244
Ana de San Bartolomé, 7, 43n34
Ana of Jesus, 191
Andalusia, 69, 72, 99n6, 107n55, 110n76
  Andalusian accent of Chicaba, 4, 41n19
angel, 14, 21, 22, 40n13, 45n52, 62, 65, 76, 97, 150, 155, 156, 166, 203, 204, 216, 227, 229, 230, 238, 261, 264
  as a gallant young man, 65, 93, 154, 165
Angola, 63, 64, 67, 103n32, 104n34, 108n61, 111–12n91, 156
Aniaba, 46n59, 111n55, 183
Anlo, 38–39n5, 61
Antonia of Saint Francis, Sor, 191
Arada, 62, 63, 64, 67, 103nn27–28, 104nn32–33, 143, 154, 156, 181
Araújo, Father Ignacio, 84, 97, 178, 179, 184, 186. *See also* spiritual directors
Arbustante, Melchor, 128, 129
archives, 5, 8, 12, 32, 52n107, 55, 69, 116n13, 117n123, 247
Arda. *See* Arada
asiento, 38–39n5, 106–7n51, 108n61, 109n70, 158, 172. *See also* slave trade
Atocha, 48n68, 137. *See also* Blacks and Blackness: Madonna
Augustine, Saint, 113n97, 128, 134, 258
Augustinian rule, 42n30, 83, 190
author and authorship, x, xv, 1, 8, 9, 11, 12, 14, 16, 20, 23–25, 27, 28, 29, 32, 33, 35, 43n37, 46n60, 50n90, 56, 68, 69, 94, 99n1, 109n68, 114n104, 127, 128, 129, 130, 131, 132, 133, 134,

295

author and authorship, *continued*
  135, 136, 137, 139, 145, 146, 149, 153, 154, 165, 169, 171, 173, 176, 179, 185, 192, 193, 199, 204, 206, 213, 215, 220, 229, 254, 265
  as amanuensis, 24, 41n18, 55, 196
  authorial acts, 2, 11, 94
  Black authorship, 42n31, 99n1
  as compiler, 12, 45n51, 55, 61, 72
  single author, 13
authority, 12, 15, 21, 22, 45n52, 63, 67, 68, 75, 81, 86, 88, 95, 96, 105n45, 142, 146, 178, 180, 181, 190, 198, 200, 207
autobiography, 1, 5, 6, 7, 11–12, 16, 20, 24, 29, 36, 41n26, 49n77, 56
  Catholic and Protestant autobiography, 21–22, 50n87
  as spiritual autobiography, 8, 19, 23, 55, 99n1
autograph letter, 4–5, 41nn18–19, 56, *120. See also* literacy of Chicaba; writing
Azúa, Félix de, 254

Baltimore Carmel, 43n37, 116n115, 117n123
baptism of Blacks and slaves, 1, 14, 17, 18, 22, 47n65, 62, 69, 77, 79, 108n60, 111–12n91, 113–14n101, 150, 154, 156, 168, 169, 170, 193, 229, 232
Barbary Coast, 108n61, 173. *See also* Africa: North
Barcelona, 91, 108n63, 159, 220, 221, 254
Bárcena y Velasco, Father Andrés, 226
Barthes, Roland, 12, 13
beata, 87, 115n112, 171, 195. *See also* secular; tertiary (*tercera*)
beatification, 1, 2, 3, 5–6, 12, 43n34, 116n114, 207, 216, 247. *See also* canonization; sainthood and sanctity
beauty, 14–15, 48n67, 76–78, 80, 97, 100–101n13, 144, 150, 153, 163, 166, 168, 218, 258
  Black but comely, 17
  Chicaba's ugliness (*see* skin color)
  as menace, 76
beghards/beguines, 82, 186
béguinage, 82, 112n95
Belinda, 19–20, 99n1
Belsey, Catherine, 28
Benedictines and Benedictine Order, 84, 113–14n101, 207, 221, 252, 256
Benin, 38n5, 57, 99n2, 103n27, 104n32
  Bight of, 61, 99n2
Bible, 10, 17, 22, 23, 25, 27, 36, 44n41, 49n77, 51n95, 53n122, 64, 73, 82, 94, 134, 230, 248
  Genesis, 51n95, 65, 142, 167, 209
  1 Samuel, 248
  1 Kings, 26
  2 Chronicles, 26
  Song of Songs, 17, 116n118
  Psalms, 88, 89, 244
  Gospels, 19, 21, 22, 27, 40n13, 95, 127, 143, 154, 249

  Matthew, 79, 258n1
  Mark, 224n4, 256, 258n1
  Luke, 6, 27, 64, 94–95, 203
  John, 224n4, 239, 258n1
  Thessalonians, 14
  Vulgate translation, 162
biography, xii, 2, 4–9, 11, 13, 17, 24, 25, 26, 32, 49n79, 55, 56, 59, 73, 83, 91, 92, 96, 99n1, 109n68
Blacks and Blackness, v, ix, x, xi, xii, xvi, 7, 9, 12–24, 26, 29, 35, 36, 55, 61, 63, 64, 66, 68–71, 73, 75–77, 79, 81, 83–85, 87, 89, 91, 93, 95–97, 123, 137, 142, 160, 161, 163, 166, 170, 171, 172, 180, 181, 182, 183, 185, 186, 187, 192, 193, 194, 195, 196, 197, 198, 203, 204, 205, 206, 209, 212, 213, 215, 217, 223, 224, 225, 229, 236, 239, 242, 246, 248, 256, 260, 261, 264
  Atlantic, 16, 23, 48n71
  body (*see* body)
  Catholic confraternities (*cofradías*), 16, 18, 45n52, 47n65, 48n70, 78, 108n63
  Catholics, xi, xii, xvi, 15, 18, 47n65, 52n106
  clergy, 63–64
  as ethnicity, 2, 14, 23, 38n5, 48n70, 50n89, 57, 60, 69–70, 84, 100n8, 102n26
  Madonna, v, 48n68, 137
  people, 15, 19, 20, 23, 70, 77, 117n124, 142, 166, 261
  skin (*see* skin color)
  slave, 13, 68, 70, 75, 77, 99n1, 170, 171, 181, 209 (*see also* slavery)
  woman, 7, 12, 15, 19–22, 24, 29, 36, 53n122, 55, 63, 70, 71, 73, 77, 81, 83, 89, 91, 93, 97, 111n89, 112n92, 160, 161, 180, 181, 182, 192, 193–95, 197, 198, 203–5, 215, 217, 223–25, 236, 239, 248
Blake (Delaney), 23
blindness, 13, 60, 86, 97, 142, 193–94, 263
bodunos/budonos, 63, 103n28
body, 4, 5, 14–16, 21–22, 32–33, 35–36, 53n121, 61, 64, 68, 73, 75, 77, 78, 91, 92, 93, 96, 97, 98, 108n62, 111n83, 116n118, 126, 130, 141, 147, 161, 162, 163, 169, 173, 185, 193, 201, 203, 208, 209, 210, 211, 216, 220, 222, 224, 230, 237, 239, 243, 246, 250, 253, 255, 259, 260, 261, 262, 264
  bodily remains, 4, 96, 97 (*see also* sainthood and sanctity: relics)
  saliva, 91, 224, 243, 249
  scars, 36, 75, 108n62
bondage. *See* slavery
Book of Her Life. See Libro de la Vida; Teresa of Ávila, Saint
Bosman, William, 61, 101n18
bozal, 42n33, 106–7n51, 108n60, 109–10n71
Brakke, David, 14

Brandenburg, 63
Brazil, 7, 43n35, 45n52, 68, 70, 79, 102n25, 156
breviary. *See* Divine Office
Bride of Christ, 14, 17, 27–31, 64–65, 74, 79, 80, 81, 88, 91, 93–95, 97, 117n123, 158, 183, 194, 196, 202n1, 202n3, 203, 204, 216, 218, 219, 232, 233, 235, 236, 240, 255n3, 256
  betrothal, 17, 31, 62, 79, 80, 91, 92
  betrothal to the White Child, 14, 65, 76
  as Black bride, 48n67, 239n1
  in chaste marriage, 87
Burns, Kathryn, 81, 88
Bynum, Caroline Walker, 6, 8, 9, 24, 208, 210
Byzantine romance, 53n112, 66–67, 74, 85, 153, 158, 182

Cacheu, 67
Cádiz, 13, 47n65, 67, 108n63, 110n73, 156
Caesar, Julius, 132
Calderón de la Barca, Francisco (bishop of Salamanca), 2, 11, 22, 86, 88, 90, 91, 97, 114n106, 115n108, 195–97, 202, 212, 240, 264
Calderón de la Barca, Pedro, 51n98, 105n41, 195, 229
Calvo, José, 220, 221, 223
Canary Islands, 67, 69
canonization, 3, 5, 6, 8, 12–13, 17, 26, 62, 79, 140, 195, 246, 247. *See also* sainthood and sanctity
canon law, 29, 133, 204
Cape Verde, 42n33, 67, 108n61
captivity, 11, 13, 17, 19, 20, 24, 26, 29, 31, 34, 36, 48n71, 50n89, 62, 64, 66–68, 72, 74, 76, 78, 85, 93, 104n36, 105n41, 113n101, 144, 154, 155, 173. *See also* slavery
Capuchin missionaries, 62–64, 68, 70, 100n8, 103n28, 103n32, 143, 154, 181
Carlos II of Spain, 68, 71, 72, 73, 78, 79, 106n50, 109n66, 116n116, 154, 158, 163, 182, 183, 220, 221
Carmelites and Carmelite Order, 7, 41n20, 42n30, 43n34, 43n37, 45n47, 116n115, 117n123, 149, 192, 222
carta de pago (letter of payment), 87, 115n108, 116n114, 191, 192, 194, 195, 196, 206, 212, *268–69*
Castro, Archbishop Pedro de, 111–12n91, 190
Catherine of Siena, Saint, 7, 43n36, 113n98
Catholic Church, 14, 15, 38n2, 43n36, 96, 202, 239, 244, 264, 265
Catholic religion and Catholicism, 2, 6, 9, 11, 14, 15, 17–18, 24, 27, 38n2, 41n21, 49n81, 50n91, 60, 61, 63, 64, 65, 71, 72, 73, 77, 82, 83, 93, 95, 96, 98, 113–14n101, 128, 133, 140, 144, 150, 156, 159, 171, 175, 183, 192, 193, 200, 202, 205, 210, 220, 222, 228, 236, 237, 239, 244, 246, 253, 264, 265
  Catholic audience, 5, 7–8, 60
  Catholics and slavery, 68–69 (*see also* slavery)
  Catholic theology, 27, 95, 117n123
  Catholic women, 6, 9, 12, 21, 112–13n96

celibacy, 31, 77, 92
Cervantes, Miguel de, 85, 105n40, 251
charity, 2, 75, 83, 199, 200, 201, 202, 210, 226, 228, 235, 242, 243, 244, 245, 253, 258. *See also* virtue
Charles II of Spain. *See* Carlos II of Spain
chastity, 9, 14, 15, 35, 40n17, 62, 66, 77, 87, 90, 91, 93, 100–101n13, 102n26, 190, 196, 202, 203, 204, 210, 226, 227, 228. *See also* vows
Chicaba, 1–5, 7, 8, 10–19, 22, 23, 24, 25, 26–37, 55–62, 64–68, 70–98, 130, 139, 142, 144, 145, 146, 147, 150, 152, 153, 154, 155, 156, 157, 158, 159, 160, 161, 163, 171, 172, 173, 177, 178, 180, 182, 184, 185, 186, 188, 189, 190, 192, 193, 195, 196, 198, 199, 200, 204, 205, 206, 210, 212, 213, 217, 219, 226, 229, 234, 236, 238, 239, 240, 244, 246, 249, 251, 252, 262, 264, 265
  anguish in, 17, 34, 36, 66, 147, 154, 177, 183, 185, 188, 189, 201, 212, 213, 222, 256, 258
  attempt to kill, 74–77, 161, 166–68, 209, 233
  as child and childhood of, 1, 2, 8, 13–14, 20, 24, 26, 29, 36, 57, 60–66, 79, 80, 92–94, 99n4, 99n6, 142, 144, 145, 150, 152, 153, 155, 157, 160, 163, 179, 184, 194, 202, 206, 207, 208, 218, 220, 221, 232, 251, 264
  danger in her life, 12, 35, 66–67, 70, 81, 83, 146, 147, 152, 159, 163, 170, 176, 177, 259
  as Mother Sister Teresa, 38n1, 38n3, 39n11, 128, 129, 130, 133, 134, 135, 136
  as princess, 26, 35, 59, 61, 68, 74, 75, 79, 95, 105n41, 142, 158, 161
  as princess-slave, 5, 59, 75
  as Sor Teresa de Santo Domingo, 1, 22, 120, 127, 196
  as Sor Teresa Juliana de Santo Domingo, 1, 5, 39n6, 115n108, 121, 133, 139
  spelling of the name, 5, 39n6, 57, 59, 99n6, 123, 142
  as Teresa del Espíritu Santo, 50n90, 83, 86
  as Teresa Juliana del Espíritu Santo, 39n6, 72, 73, 80
  See also Bride of Christ
choir and choir nuns, 23, 27, 32, 36, 37, 43n34, 43n37, 85, 87–91, 95–97, 113–14n101, 114n104, 114n106, 115n108, 116n113, 187, 195, 196, 197, 198, 200, 203, 204, 206, 212, 213, 215, 216, 217, 233, 241, 243, 247, 253, 264. *See also* liminal space and liminality; nuns
Christ, 14–20, 22–23, 26–27, 29–31, 34, 36, 64, 65, 72, 75, 76, 78–80, 82, 86–87, 92–95, 128, 130, 132, 134, 136, 142, 146, 148, 150, 152, 154, 157, 162, 163, 164, 166, 170, 172, 173, 174, 176, 178, 180, 182, 188, 190, 194, 196, 200, 202, 204, 206, 209, 210, 214, 216, 218, 222, 224, 228, 229, 230, 234, 236, 238, 239, 240, 244, 248, 250, 254, 256, 262, 264
  as Child, 26, 72, 80, 92, 157, 194, 207
  as polygamous, 94–95

Christ, *continued*
  as Spouse, 29, 36, 89, 90, 94, 96, 158, 177, 185, 196, 199, 203, 217, 218, 223, 226, 227, 232, 233, 237, 240, 242, 243, 256, 258
  as White Child, 14, 31, 64, 65, 76, 88, 152, 153, 163, 179, 194, 202, 232
  Christianity and Christian, 6, 9, 10, 11, 17, 18, 19, 20, 21, 22, 23, 24, 26, 29, 34, 38–39n5, 48n68, 49m74, 49n81, 50n89, 51n98, 56, 60–64, 70, 72, 75–80, 92–93, 101n16, 102n24, 103n28, 108n60, 111–12n91, 129, 135, 145, 147, 151, 154, 159, 163, 165, 168, 169, 171, 173, 175, 177, 181, 182, 184, 193, 200, 220, 221, 223, 224, 229, 232, 249
Christina of Markyate, 21
Chrysostom, John, Saint, 260
cilices (*cilicios*), 185, 209
climate, 71, 130, 142, 171, 180
cloister and cloistered nuns, 4, 29, 31, 32, 46n55, 74, 82–83, 89, 93, 97, 113n98, 115n112, 116n113, 117n123, 179, 180, 181, 185, 191, 197, 199, 206, 212, 213, 218, 236, 262
color. *See* Blacks and Blackness; race; skin color
Communion, 3, 7, 14, 43n35, 51n98, 84, 92, 96, 116n113, 157, 172, 175, 210, 218, 227, 229, 239–41, 254–58, 262
  denying of, 179–80, 240
  See also sacraments
confessor, 1, 2, 6–9, 12, 34, 46n53, 50n90, 62, 77, 78, 146, 159, 175, 177, 178, 179, 186, 204, 206, 207, 208, 209, 210, 212, 211, 217, 227, 247, 255, 256. *See also* spiritual directors
contemplation and contemplative orders, 6, 10, 21, 27, 65, 86, 95, 97, 148, 149, 150, 157, 179, 190, 193, 217, 236, 237, 239
convent, 1–6, 11–16, 26, 27, 29, 30–32, 37, 38n1, 40–41n17, 41n20, 42n30, 43n35, 43n37, 46n54, 48n67, 50n90, 52n107, 59, 71, 75, 78, 79, 80–87, 89–91, 95, 104n35, 111n89, 111n91, 113n97, 113–14n101, 114n103, 115n109, 115n112, 116n114, 117n123, 119, 126, 127, 133, 135, 137, 139, 159, 166, 171, 174, 178, 180, 184–87, 189, 190, 192, 193, 195–200, 202, 203–6, 208, 210, 212, 213, 216, 218, 221, 223, 224, 225, 226, 229, 231, 233, 234, 236, 240–45, 250, 251, 253, 258, 262, 263, 264
  admission to, 11, 32, 43n37, 62, 80, 82, 84, 86, 88, 93, 98, 116n115, 179, 185–87, 189, 195–99, 202, 203, 206, 240
  menial work in, 10–11, 27, 36, 45n47, 95
  rejection by, 2, 11, 13, 81, 82, 86, 91, 92, 114n104, 189, 191, 204, 206, 212, 232
  as shelter, 84, 151, 153, 192, 195, 197, 205, 233
conversion, 10, 14, 17, 19, 20, 21, 26, 40n13, 49n77, 57, 61–63, 72, 76, 78, 101n16, 143, 168, 169, 170, 182, 230

converso/conversa, 43n40. *See also limpieza de sangre* (purity of blood)
Córdoba, Father Félix de, 221, 252, 256
Coria, 246
correspondence, 7, 96, 146, 244, 252, 265
Council of Trent, 1, 6, 8, 38n2, 66, 190, 195
Counter-Reformation, 5, 7, 21, 51n98, 66, 113n99, 171
Crenshaw, Kimberlé, 44n42
Cristo de Medinaceli (statue), 78, 173
criticón, El (Gracián), 74, 105n40
Cuba, 23, 68, 108n60
Cuzco, 81

Dares, 134
Davis, Cyprian, 47n65
death, 2, 3, 5–7, 12, 14–15, 21, 31, 67, 70–73, 76, 78–80, 83, 87–88, 96, 97, 98, 117n124, 139, 152, 155, 159, 163, 169, 176, 178, 188, 200, 202, 213, 220, 224, 226, 232, 243, 246, 250, 252, 253, 254, 255, 256, 258, 260, 261, 263, 264
  burial plot, 261
  by drowning, 76
  epitaph of Chicaba, 40n14, 59, 100–101n13, 125
  obituary of Chicaba, 4, 39n10, 98, 188, 275
Deborah, 22
Deffis de Calvo, Emilia, 74
De instauranda aethiopum salute, 68, 111–12n91
Delaney, Martin, 23
Denmark, 63
desert, 9–11, 14, 45n45, 65, 132, 148, 153, 200, 226, 236, 260. *See also* solitude
devil, 8, 14–15, 34–35, 60, 74–77, 80, 89, 91, 97, 116n118, 142, 156, 160, 161, 162, 163, 165, 166, 167, 168, 175–77, 181, 182, 183, 184, 199, 200, 215, 218–25, 243, 249, 250
  as animal, 215
  as Black, 47n62
  sending night birds, 172
  possessed by, 87, 89, 91, 225, 243
Díaz, Juan, 246
dipo, 102n26. *See also* enclosure
Divine Office, 4, 7, 36, 42n32, 87–89, 195, 199, 200, 203, 213. *See also* literacy of Chicaba
Doctrina Christiana, 128
Doliers, 132
Dominic (Domingo) of Guzmán, Saint, 22, 46n56, 90, 132, 136, 139, 186, 190, 196, 203, 204, 209, 215, 216, 219, 230, 233, 250
Dominicans and Dominican Order, 2–5, 11, 15, 22, 30, 31, 38, 39n10, 40n13, 41n20, 46n54, 46n56, 48n68, 52n106, 59, 80, 81, 82, 83, 86, 87, 89, 93, 96, 98, 111n89, 112n96, 113n98, 116n114, 137, 139, 144, 178, 184, 186, 187, 188, 190, 197, 198, 199, 204, 209, 216, 219, 226, 228, 262

as Order of Penance, 82, 86, 93, 112n96, 113n97, 190
as Order of Preachers, 82, 113n97, 178
donada/donado, 12, 46n54, 52n106, 84, 112, 198
Don Quijote (Cervantes), 111n83
doppelganger, 77–78
Douglass, Frederick, 36
dowry, 2, 29, 32, 37, 81, 86–87, 91, 93, 94, 110n72, 113–14n101, 115n111, 185, 192, 195, 226, 232, 233
gastillos (annuity), 81, 87, 279
Dueñas, convent of Las, 3, 4–5, 59, 82, 87, 98, 119, 126, 187, 198, 229, 244, 253, 262, 263

Ecce Homo, 16, 78, 162
Eckhart, Meister, 92, 94
education, 7, 20, 35–36, 42n31, 73, 110n79, 111–12n91, 137, 160, 162, 175, 176, 192, 198, 199, 229, 230
as *educatio principis*, 74–75
Elaw, Zilpha, 21, 22, 23
Elijah, Saint, 222
Elmina, 38n4, 57, 156
enclosure, 6, 29–32, 41n21, 52n107, 74, 88, 89, 102n26, 111n91, 113n98, 116n113, 190, 196, 198, 213, 225, 240. *See also* convent
England, 20, 50n89, 63, 69, 172
English, 50n89, 55, 101n116, 112n92, 128, 129, 132, 143, 144, 158, 160, 169, 172, 179, 198, 204, 209
Enlightenment, 9, 14, 117n124, 130, 221
Ensenada census (*Catastro de Ensenada*), 87–88, 115n109, 196
enslavement and enslaved, 3, 10, 11, 16, 17, 18, 19, 26, 32, 35, 36, 45n52, 48n71, 49n74, 51n95, 53n115, 57, 59, 62, 64–66, 68–70, 72–76, 78–79, 81, 84–85, 102n25, 103n27, 107n55, 108n60, 109n71, 147, 153, 155, 157, 163, 185, 194, 205, 210, 223, 232, 265
as abduction, 1, 29, 65, 66, 67, 72, 78, 85, 99n1, 150, 155
of Indians, 68, 105n46, 105n48
See also slavery
Ephigenia, Saint, 47n65, 79
Equiano, Olaudah, 49n77, 62, 102n24
Eritrea, 17
Espejo mystico (Nájera), 62, 71, 103n28, 143
Esther, 22
Ethiopia, 17, 47n62, 73, 141, 188
Ethiopian Story (Heliodorus), 66, 105n41, 153
Eucharist. *See* Communion
Europe, 7, 13, 14, 17–19, 22–24, 28, 32, 55, 56, 58–65, 67, 68, 76, 79–81, 93, 95, 112n95, 113–14n101, 130, 154, 159, 171, 183, 194, 210, 221, 236, 254
Eve, 153, 260
evidence, 1, 4, 5, 8, 9, 13, 17, 18, 31, 40–41n17, 51n92, 57, 74, 75, 88, 96, 100n8, 102n26, 134, 175, 189, 197, 217, 221, 225, 226, 237, 244, 247, 249, 252, 262
evil, 8, 34, 35, 59, 77, 91, 129, 172, 251
evil eye, 221
Ewe, 1, 13, 27, 38n5, 57–63, 74, 88, 99n6, 100nn7–8, 101n21, 102n26, 143
exclusion, 10–11, 29, 52n107, 70, 78, 81, 89, 94, 104n35, 114n103, 114n106, 173, 184, 187, 213
Extremadura, 48n68, 69, 107n55

family of Chicaba, 13, 38–39n5, 58, 70, 79, 86, 100n8, 102n26, 141–53, 161, 176, 223
Abar (Chicaba's mother), 40n16, 57, 69, 100n9, 141
brothers, 14, 57, 80, 100n7, 141–45, 150–52, 155, 173, 202n3, 247, 250
ceremony of forgetting, 66
conversion to Christianity of, 78, 175
father, 14, 57, 58, 59, 64, 79, 80, 100n12, 141, 143, 145, 146, 147, 149, 152, 155, 182, 209, 221, 226
female cousin, 68, 155
Juan Francisco, pretended uncle, 71, 74, 78–80, 181–84, 200, 226
Nsu (Ensú; Chicaba's brother), 100n7, 141
parents, 8, 13–14, 19, 29, 60, 62, 64, 65, 70, 71, 78, 85, 91, 141, 142, 144, 145, 147, 148, 149, 151, 155, 182, 202, 220, 221, 222, 223, 263, 265
fasting, 91, 208, 209, 210, 221, 224
Figueroa, Father Vicente, 4
flesh, 18, 91, 116n118, 163, 185, 209, 227, 228, 239, 253. *See also* incarnation
Flores Pavón, Sebastián, 46n60, 133, 134n25
Fon, 61, 63, 101n18, 102n26, 103n29, 143
food and eating, 208, 209
bizcocho, 67
bread cakes, 208
chocolate, 210, 211, 253
fish and shrimp, 61
hunger, 84, 96, 240
mis gazpachos y mis sopas, 255
morsel, 252
parva, 210
salt cod, 67
sardines, 67
snack shared with the Child Jesus, 157, 160, 208
See also fasting
Foote, Julia, 21, 22
forgiveness, 75, 132, 169, 177
Foster, Frances Smith, 50n89
France, 23, 43n34, 46n59, 63, 78, 79, 84, 104n33, 111n85, 113n101, 130, 181, 182, 183, 221
Francis, Saint, 82, 132, 170, 186, 193, 196, 204, 216
Franciscans and Franciscan Order, 21, 110n76, 132, 159, 170, 171, 184, 186, 204, 216

freedom, 2, 10, 11, 19, 20, 23–24, 31, 32, 43n35, 45n52, 48n71, 49n74, 56, 70, 71, 76, 81, 83, 84, 95, 102n25, 105n48, 113–14n101, 183, 205, 223
   the convent as liberation, 32, 67, 77–78, 85
   emancipation, 16, 19, 31, 32, 35, 36, 50n89, 84, 180, 192, 200, 223
   as natural state, 205
free will, 20, 79, 84, 220
Frías de Albornoz, 68
Fuente, Jerónima de la, 209
Funeral Oration. See *Oración fúnebre*

Gaetano, Saint, 133, 139, 159, 177, 178, 186, 209, 215, 216, 252, 261
Gamarra, Diego, 82, 85, 186, 187, 189
Gates, Henry Louis, Jr., 48n71
gender, 9, 13, 15, 24, 28–30, 32, 44n42, 52n102, 53n122, 55, 80, 86, 91, 92, 110–11n79, 160, 244
   and Black female subjectivity, 13, 15–16, 95
   gendered and racial readings, 25, 27
   intersectionality of gender and race, 24, 30, 32, 44n42, 95
   male, 7, 8, 20, 22, 24–25, 35, 42n31, 53n115, 59, 61, 70, 77, 78, 82, 86, 91–94, 110n79, 146, 168, 183
genealogy, 21, 55, 62, 85, 104n35, 141, 178, 252
Ghana, 38nn4–5, 57, 61, 99n2, 100n8, 102n26, 142
gift, 2, 12, 21, 26–27, 34, 51n98, 52n106, 71–73, 78, 81–83, 110n75, 116n119, 150, 151, 158, 159, 162, 173, 174, 203, 205, 214, 232, 237, 248, 254, 255, 256, 261, 263, 264
   fort-da, ritual, 92, 116n119
   of Magi, 26–27, 73
   of prophecy, 22, 228, 246, 248
   trinkets, 65, 104n36
Gilroy, Paul, 23, 48n71
God, 7, 8, 10, 11, 14, 19–22, 26, 36, 49n81, 59, 60, 61, 63, 71, 72, 75, 77, 80, 81, 91–93, 96, 101n16, 101n18, 129, 131, 135, 137, 139, 144–47, 149, 150, 151, 153, 160, 161, 163, 168, 169, 171, 172, 173, 176–83, 185, 191, 192, 194, 197–200, 203, 205, 206, 207, 208, 210–14, 216, 217, 219, 220, 222, 223, 226, 227, 229, 230, 232–40, 243, 244–50, 252–56, 260, 263, 264, 265
   as Divine Providence, 40n16, 66, 79, 139, 141, 153, 156, 157, 163, 177, 186, 196, 202, 216, 232, 233, 262
   as Holy Spirit, 43n35, 97, 179, 189, 199
   as Holy Trinity, 22, 132, 229
   as Master, 27, 65, 70, 73, 75, 97, 130, 131, 132, 157, 158, 160, 162, 165, 171, 172, 173, 174, 179, 184, 185, 216, 229, 230, 233, 236, 237, 240, 256, 257, 258, 262
   See also Christ; Jesus

gold, 2, 13, 14, 22, 26, 27, 38n4, 57, 65, 68, 71–73, 78, 97, 100n8, 142, 173, 185, 203, 238, 239, 246
   Chicaba as a golden child, 26, 57, 99n6, 142
   goldsmithing, 57, 100n8
   gold bangles (*manillas*), 2, 13, 65, 72
González Dávila, Gil, 190
Gossy, Mary, 78, 111n83
Granada, 69, 108n63
Great Popo, 67
Greene, Sandra E., 61, 102n22
Greer, Allan, 24
Gronniosaw, James, 19
Guadalupe, 48n68
Guinea, 4, 17, 40n15, 55, 56, 57, 58, 59, 60, 62, 64, 65, 70, 73, 76, 80, 92, 109–10n71, 111n91, 113n101, 141, 142, 156, 181, 188, 232, 249. *See also* Africa

habit (of the order), 3, 42n30, 87–88, 98, 115n108, 139, 171, 185, 186, 192, 195, 196, 197, 202, 208, 227, 247. *See also* veil
Hagar, 65
hagiography, 1–18, 24, 25, 28–32, 34, 36–38, 42n27, 44n44, 46n53, 47n62, 50n87, 50n89, 50n91, 52n106, 55, 56, 59–62, 64, 69, 72–74, 79–80, 82, 84–91, 93–98, 99n1, 104n35, 130, 131, 172, 182, 186, 196, 200, 219, 228, 242, 246, 265
   as fiction, 9, 13, 61, 71, 72, 80, 85, 186
Ham, 19, 26, 51n95, 142
Hammon, Jupiter, 19
Harms, Robert, 84, 113n101
Hartford, Connecticut, 20
Hartman, Saidiya, 66
Havana, 68
Hayward, Tom, 134
health and healing powers, 2, 14, 21–22, 62, 70, 84, 89, 94, 100n8, 102n25, 146, 154, 169, 180, 205–6, 210, 230, 242–43, 247, 249–50, 253–55, 263. *See also* illness
heaven, 22, 43n39, 61, 73, 96, 144, 149, 161, 162, 170, 173, 178, 179, 180, 182, 185, 186, 189, 193, 195, 197, 203, 204, 209, 210, 214–18, 221, 222, 228, 229, 231, 233, 240, 244, 246, 248, 249, 251, 252, 257, 258, 260
hell, 156, 166, 167, 175, 177, 182, 194–95, 202, 215–16, 220, 226, 232, 243. *See also* devil
Hernández, Francisco, 248, 261
Herrero, Josefa, 250
history and historicity, 5, 6, 9, 11, 24, 34, 37, 46n60, 47n65, 56, 84, 132, 134, 158, 165, 265
holiness, 3, 7–9, 14–15, 21, 34, 56, 91. *See also* sainthood and sanctity
Holland. *See* Netherlands
humility, 8, 16, 18, 29, 34, 36, 43n37, 90, 91, 92, 113–14n101, 172, 173, 196, 198, 199, 202, 203,

204, 205, 206, 207, 208, 210, 214, 220, 222, 223, 242, 249, 253, 255. *See also* virtue

iconography, 43n39, 79, 203, 219, 222
   portraits of Chicaba, 3–5, 12–13, 51n98, 90, *119*, 209, 229, 239
ideology, 11–15, 18, 25, 27–31, 34, 47n65, 52n103, 91, 104n37, 182
illness, 1, 6, 21, 42n30, 64, 84, 89, 94, 146, 155, 159, 161, 168–71, 199, 200, 201, 205, 206, 208, 209, 212, 221, 224, 225, 230, 240, 243, 247, 249, 250, 252, 254, 255, 256, 258, 259, 260, 264. *See also* health and healing powers
Inca Garcilaso, 62, 102n24
incarnation, 31, 90, 92, 94, 97, 157, 239
Indians, 50n91, 68, 71, 114n103, 158
Indies. *See* Spanish America
innocence, 18, 35, 60, 94, 100–101n13, 144, 146, 163, 166, 185, 208, 212, 255
Inquisition, 8, 12, 43n35, 45n52, 46n56, 64, 83, 104n35, 105n46, 133, 168
Interior Castle, The (Teresa of Ávila), 8, 42n30, 193. *See also* Teresa of Ávila, Saint
intertextuality, 10–15, 45n48
Isidro, Saint, 137, 179
Islam and Muslims, 42n30, 43n40, 51n95, 64, 69–70, 76–78, 104n35, 108n61, 114n102, 169, 173, 184
   Muslim slaves, 69, 70, 76, 158, 168
   See also Turkish slave girl
Israel, 10, 22, 26, 102n24

Jaca, Francisco José de, 68–70, 105n48
Jackson, Rebecca Cox, 7
Jacobs, Harriet A., 32, 42n31, 99n1
jealousy, 23, 36, 94, 95, 117n123, 151, 218, 235, 236
Jenson, Deborah, 48n71
Jerusalem, 10, 11, 22, 162, 213
Jesuit Order, 64, 68, 130, 132, 180
Jesus, 17, 20, 23, 62, 77, 81, 94–95, 117n123, 160, 162, 166, 189, 194, 224, 232, 236, 237, 256, 258
   as Jesus the Nazarene, 78, 174
   See also Christ
jewel and treasure, Chicaba as, 13, 26–27, 57, 65, 68, 72–73, 78, 147, 152–54, 156, 158, 159, 170, 173, 184, 187, 189, 193, 227, 235, 239, 258
manillas (bracelets), 2
   See also gold
Jews and anti-Judaism, 22, 40n13, 43n40, 44n41, 64, 102n24, 104n35, 113n99, 113–14n101, 114n102, 162, 230
John of the Cross, Saint, 61, 149n1, 153n2, 192n4, 193n8, 217n2, 239n2, 255n3
Jordan River, 9
joy, 132, 142, 145–47, 154, 156, 164, 172, 179, 182, 185, 186, 193, 196, 197, 201–3, 213, 252, 258–60

Juana Esperanza de San Alberto, 48n67
Juana Inés de la Cruz, 71, 109n68
Juliana Teresa Portocarrero y Meneses. *See* Mancera, Marchioness of
Julian of Norwich, 21, 49n81
Juvenal, 129, 146

Karl, Archduke of Austria, 71, 220
Keta Lagoon, 38–39n5
kidnapping, 64–67, 72–74, 153, 154, 235
Kongo, 63
Krepi, 57

Lady Saint Augustine, 243
Lanser, Susan, 25, 28
La Penitencia. *See* Penitencia, Convento de Santa María Magdalena de la
Las Dueñas. *See* Dueñas, convent of Las
last will of the Marchioness of Mancera, 2, 27, 39n6, 70, 72, 80, 87, 115n110, 200, 226, *277*, *278*, *279*
   annuity (*gastillos*), 2, 81, 87, 93
   bequeathing freedom, 73
Latin, 21, 81, 104n33, 109n68, 113–14n101, 130, 132, 134, 135, 140, 143, 179, 188, 199, 204, 210, 244, 265
Latin America, 18, 68, 103n27, 116–17n122. *See also* Spanish America
Lavrín, Asunción, 82, 84, 85, 89, 90, 112n94, 114n103
Law, Robin, 99n2, 99n5
Lazarus, 27, 190
Lee, Jarena, 21
León, Luis de, 8, 44n41
Lerner, Gerda, 53n122
Libro de la Vida, 8, 42n30, 47n62, 117n125, 193, 215, 226, 237, 238. *See also* Teresa of Ávila, Saint
Life of Mary of Egypt, 44n44
Lima, 12, 46n54, 52n106, 251
liminal space and liminality, 29, 37, 52n107, 59, 88–89, 93, 190, 196, 199, 203, 213, 236
   burial and, 98, 250, 258, 260, 261, 264
   cell as, 29, 30, 31, 32, 45n47, 52n106, 89, 93, 216, 218, 219, 236
   infirmary as, 10, 29, 30, 52n106, 88, 89, 91, 93, 95, 199, 200, 213, 256, 257, 258
   kitchen as a, 10–11, 45n47, 52n106, 95, 117n125, 199, 206, 210, 216
   speak room and grille as, 13, 46n55, 87, 89, 94, 96, 116n113, 119, 225, 228, 236, 240, 243, 253
limpieza de sangre (purity of blood), 8, 13, 17, 43n40, 52n107, 76, 81, 84–85, 114n102, 184, 187. *See also* nobility
Lisbon, 43n35, 63. *See also* Portugal
literacy of Chicaba, 4, 7, 8, 31, 35–36, 42n31, 43n37, 48n71, 56, 75, 87–89, 244. *See also* education; writing

Little Black Woman. See *Negrita, La*
Liturgy of the Hours. See Divine Office
Livy, 132
Llama de amor viva, 239. See also John of the Cross, Saint
Locke, John, 68, 105n45
locus amoenus, 76, 163
locutorio. See liminal space and liminality: speak room and grille as
love, 20, 23, 29, 31, 43n35, 49n81, 71, 78, 86, 94–98, 134, 139, 144, 145, 147, 149, 151–53, 157–59, 161, 162, 165, 168, 170–72, 179, 181, 184–86, 191, 196, 199, 203, 204, 217, 226, 227, 230, 231, 233, 235–40, 242–44, 255, 256, 259, 261
    carnal, 35, 227
    courtly, 146, 180, 193, 203, 235
    as fire, 86, 97–98, 150, 172, 179, 193, 208, 224, 235, 237–40, 244, 253, 259
    as pain, 150
Low Countries. See Netherlands
Lucifer, 60, 142. See also devil

Madrid, 2–4, 14, 39n8, 48n68, 69, 70, 71, 72, 74, 76, 78, 81, 83, 97, 108n63, 137, 150, 158, 163, 172, 173, 178, 184, 185, 186, 192, 194, 205, 210, 232, 251, 252
    Buen Retiro Park in, 14, 34, 74, 76, 150, 163, 165–66, 182, 219
Maeso, Sor María Eugenia, 5, 38n1, 59, 90, 116n114
Maffei, Giovanni Pietro, 132
Magdalena de la Cruz, 42n33
Magi, 26, 51n98, 72, 256
Maier, John, 10
Maldonado, Juana Rodríguez, 82
Mama Bate (Mami Water), 61, 102n22
Mamora, La (Mahdia), 78
Mancera, Marchioness of, Juliana Teresa Portocarrero y Meneses, 2–4, 39n6, 41n19, 50n90, 71–74, 80–81, 83, 87, 93, 110n76, 111n89, 114n105, 116n116, 159, 161, 163, 165, 171, 173, 180–81, 186, 192, 205, 206, 213, 221, 226, 232. See also last will of the Marchioness of Mancera
Mancera, Marquis of, Antonio Sebastián de Toledo, 2, 3, 7, 13, 35–37, 39n8, 67, 70–76, 81–86, 106n51, 108n62, 109n, 115n108, 116n116, 141, 158–59, 165–68, 172–76, 178, 182–84, 186, 193, 195, 199, 207, 210, 220, 226
    as Perseus, 71
    as viceroy of Mexico, 48n68, 71, 81, 105n46, 109n71, 111n91, 158, 172, 184, 210
Mancera de Abajo and Mancera de Arriba, 252
Mancera household, 2, 7, 16–18, 21–22, 26, 27, 29, 34–37, 52n108, 53n118, 69–78, 81, 83, 84, 86, 91, 97, 114n105, 144, 158, 160, 161, 163, 165, 166, 168, 173, 175, 176, 178, 179, 183, 189, 190, 192, 199, 207, 208, 218, 223, 224, 236, 237, 239, 252, 256
    Manceras as family to Chicaba, 85–86, 110n79, 114n105, 159, 170, 175–76, 182–83, 192, 206
    suffering and violence at the, 2, 35, 36, 74–75, 160–63, 206
Margery Kempe, 21
Mari, Juan Bautista, 128, 129
María Francisca, 14, 87, 89, 91, 94, 97, 220, 221, 222, 223, 224, 225, 242, 243
Mariana of Austria, Queen of Spain, 71, 73, 109n66, 109n69
Marrant, John, 19
marriage, 18, 20, 31, 32, 72, 79, 91, 94, 102n26, 104n35, 109n66, 144, 152, 184, 202, 205, 208, 226, 232
    to Christ, 62, 80
    monogamous, 58, 94, 95
    polygamous marriage to Christ, 94–95
    polygynous marriages, 27
    See also Bride of Christ; Christ: as Spouse
Martha and Mary, 10, 16, 23, 25, 36, 94–95, 190, 236, 237
Martin de Porres, Saint, 12, 46n54, 52n106, 179
martyrdom, 6, 20, 185, 192
Mary Magdalen, Saint, 4, 23, 82, 135, 190
Mary of Egypt, Saint, 9–11, 14–15, 20, 44n44, 45n52, 46n61, 82, 97, 260
Mary Paul, Sister, 112n96
Mass, 1, 63, 71, 83, 200, 218, 224, 225, 232, 236, 240, 244, 246, 257, 258
Massachusetts General Court, 20
Mauss, Marcel, 81
Mawu, 61
Medinaceli, 52n107, 78, 173
meditations, 20
Mehdia, 78
Meknes, 78
Mendouça, Lourenço, 70
Mercado, Tomás de, 68, 104n36
metanoia, 9, 20
Mexico, 48n68, 71, 81, 83, 105n46, 106n51, 109n68, 109n71, 110n75, 111n91, 112n94, 158, 172, 184
Michael, Saint, 253
Middle Passage, 1, 66, 68, 73–75, 79. See also enslavement and enslaved
Mina Baja del Oro, La, 1, 17, 38n4, 38n5, 40n16, 57–62, 64, 67, 99n4, 102n25, 103n27, 104n33, 108n61, 110n73, 141–42, 144, 147, 150, 154, 156, 163, 181, 205
miracles, 2, 4, 6, 9, 14, 15, 21, 40n13, 46n60, 62, 79, 83, 90, 96, 140, 146, 147, 149, 168, 182, 204, 219, 222, 232, 233, 234, 239, 240, 242, 246, 249, 250, 251, 254, 256, 258, 260, 263, 264
    change of color, 117n124 (*see also* skin color)
    interpretation, 66
    levitation, 237
    power, 77, 96, 146

INDEX   303

missions and missionaries, 5, 7, 56, 62, 63, 103n28, 104n33, 111n85, 143, 150, 154, 156, 173, 181, 189, 218
money, 42n30, 50n90, 70–73, 108n62, 110n72, 115n110, 136, 159, 173, 180, 185, 195, 225–27, 232, 233
    annuity of Chicaba (*gastillos*), 81, 87, 277, 279
Montserrat, 48n68
Moody, Joycelyn, 19, 21, 99n1
Mooney, Catherine M., 24, 25, 27, 45n51
Morning Star, 26, 60, 61, 142, 145
Moses, 134
Mother Jesus, 189
Mother Saint Augustine, 258
Mullen, Harryette, 25, 36, 53n115
Murcia, 80, 111n89, 186, 226
Myers, Kathlyn A., 6
myrrh, 26, 27, 256. *See also* gift
mystical experience and mysticism, 2, 7, 8, 12, 17, 21, 26, 31, 45n45, 49n81, 53n122, 61, 62, 72, 83, 90, 92, 94, 95, 113n98, 150, 153, 160, 179, 180, 193, 197, 202, 203, 204, 229, 232, 236, 237, 239
    dryness, 148, 226, 255, 256
    ecstasy, 22, 43n36, 46n60, 131
    noche oscura (dark night), 226
    sweating, 98, 139, 153, 218, 238, 259
    tonta, 236, 237
    visions, 3, 6, 10, 21, 30, 31, 61, 76, 90, 93, 96, 150, 158, 160, 193, 203, 218, 229, 244, 246, 260, 263

Nájera, Father José de, 62, 63, 71, 103n28, 143
Nantes, 84, 113–14n101
Napoleonic wars, 4, 98, 126, 253, 262
narrative. *See* slave narrative
nativity, 207, 239
Navarro, Isabel, and family, 263
negra, 3, 39n11, 42n33, 81, 100n13, 111–12n91, 160, 181, 225, 242, 246, 261, 264
negress, 37, 81, 91, 112n92, 160, 161, 176, 187, 213, 223, 224, 225
Negrita, La, 112n92, 119, 130–31, 132, 135, 261
Netherlands, 43n34, 63, 68–69, 82, 112n95, 171, 172
New World. *See* Latin America; Spanish America
Nicholas of Tolentino, Saint, 219, 227
Nigeria, 38n5, 57, 99n2
Noah, 19, 26, 51n95, 142
nobility, 13, 17, 35, 46n56, 59, 60, 83, 85, 86, 104n35, 141, 160, 161, 181, 187, 189, 190, 200. *See also* genealogy
Notsie, 57
nuns, 1, 2, 4, 6, 7, 11, 13–14, 16, 18, 21, 22, 23, 25, 29, 31–33, 36, 37, 40n17, 41n21, 42n30, 43n34, 43n37, 45n47, 56, 59, 79, 80, 81, 83, 85–96, 111n89, 112n94, 112–13n96, 113n98, 113–14n101, 114n104, 116n113, 116n115, 117n123, 180, 184, 186, 187, 189, 190, 194, 195, 196, 197, 198, 199, 200, 206, 209, 210, 212, 213, 214, 217, 219, 224, 225, 232, 236, 239, 240, 241, 243, 244, 247, 249, 253, 255, 258, 259, 260, 261, 262, 264
    Chicaba as Black nun, ix, x, 13, 61, 95, 180
    lay sisters, 43n37, 87, 88, 195, 203, 204, 217
    novitiate, 36–37, 87, 89, 94, 187, 198, 199, 200, 202, 232–33, 247
    racial diversity of nuns, 81
    See also choir and choir nuns; enclosure; veil

obedience, 6, 11, 16, 71, 89, 90, 91, 133, 140, 146, 171, 178, 179, 202, 207, 208, 211, 217, 223, 226, 228, 250, 253, 260. *See also* vows
Office of the Dead, 159, 244
Oporto, 70
Oración fúnebre, 1, 2, 3, 5, 15–17, 25, 26, 27, 39n10, 40n16, 42n33, 57, 59, 68, 71–73, 76, 99n6, 100–101n13, *125*, 128, 130, 134, 139, 155, 159, 256
orality and oral tradition, 2, 6, 18, 25, 28, 36, 48n71, 50n89, 53n115, 55–58, 99n1
oratory, 21, 160, 162, 171, 180, 230
orthodoxy, 7, 12, 18, 27, 30, 47n64, 71, 117n123, 171, 265
Otaduy, Lorenzo, 8
Ottoman Empire, 69, 166
oxymoron, 74, 77, 264

paganism, 11–20, 51n98, 56–60, 64, 67, 76, 145, 147, 150, 223, 232
pain, 34, 84–86, 97, 98, 147, 148, 153, 154, 155, 158, 159, 161, 165, 173, 177, 192, 196, 209, 222, 230, 232, 238, 249, 250, 252, 253, 259. *See also* suffering
Painter, Nell Irvin, 34, 37, 53n116
Panford, Moses, 99–100nn6–7, 100n9
Paniagua, Father Juan Carlos Miguel de, 1–3, 5–9, 11–13, 15, 16, 19, 25, 26, 27, 29, 35, 40n13, 46n60, 50n90, 55, 56, 67, 90, 99n6, 116–17n122, 127, 130, 131–32, 133, 134, 135, 136, 137, 139, 142, 150, 153, 158, 159, 187, 190, 195, 196, 209, 217, 246, 252, 256, 260, 265
    as Pan y Agua, 38n1, 127, 128, 129
Paris, 43n34, 113–14n101
patience, 18, 91, 96, 161–63, 176, 177, 198, 199, 212–14, 222, 225, 240, 253, 255, 256
Paul III, 68
Peki, 57
Penitencia, Convento de Santa María Magdalena de la, 2, 4, 10–12, 15, 26, 29, 30, 32, 36, 37, 41n19, 41n21, 50n90, 52n107, 56, 71, 74–75, 82, 83, 85–89, 91, 93–98, 104n35, 112n92, 113nn97–98, 114n105, 115n108, 116n114, 131–33, 135, 137, 139, 166, 174, 178, 185–87, 189, 190, 193, 195, 196, 198, 202, 204, 210, 212, 217, 219, 221, 223, 226, 240, 242, 248, 250, 253, 261, 262, 263, 264

Pentecost, 22
perfection, 7, 86, 90, 129, 193, 199, 200, 226, 230, 235, 249
   Chicaba as candidate, 93
   Chicaba as slave, 73
Persiles (Cervantes), 85, 105n40
Peru, 62, 72, 102n24, 110n72, 172, 210
Phaedrus, 134
Philip IV of Spain, 103n29, 143
Philip V of Spain, 71, 106n50, 220, 221, 251
Philip Neri, Saint, 228
Phoebe, 23
piety, 2, 7, 18–20, 58, 66, 71, 74, 76, 82, 84, 95, 96, 113n98, 113–14n101, 135, 145, 146, 194, 196, 197, 215, 222, 228, 233, 242, 253, 255, 260, 264
pleasure, 41n18, 133, 139, 147–49, 157–59, 163, 168, 176, 178, 189, 192, 197, 204, 208, 222, 223, 228, 241, 259
poem, Chicaba's, 3, 10, 23, 25, 27, 28, 31, 36, 94–95, 117n123, 137, 150, 179, 193, 226, 234, 236, 239
Pontius Pilate, 162
Pope, the, 21, 140, 172, 193, 219
Portocarrero, Cardinal Fernando, 221n4
Portocarrero, Pedro, 116n116, 220n3
Portugal, 43n40, 45n52, 63, 79, 99n3, 103n27, 104n32, 107n55, 108n61, 156
poverty, 80, 90, 92, 113n98, 132, 191, 202, 208, 226, 227, 228. *See also* vows
prayer, 2, 8, 15, 20, 27, 35, 39n6, 43n34, 45n47, 59–61, 73, 81, 84, 87–89, 92, 95, 97, 148, 159, 160, 171, 175, 179, 185, 188, 190, 192, 193, 195, 199, 203, 215–18, 226, 227, 232, 236, 237, 244, 249, 253, 258, 264
priest, 1–3, 7, 12, 13, 17, 18, 22, 25, 29, 35, 61–64, 71, 74, 76, 77, 83, 89, 92, 94, 96, 98, 139, 160, 168, 170, 171, 173, 175, 176, 177, 178, 180, 196, 199, 210, 218, 228, 236, 240, 241, 244, 246, 252–54, 258, 259. *See also* spiritual directors
Prince, Mary, 48n71
Productions (Stewart), 20
profession (act of), 2, 4–5, 22, 31–32, 40n17, 50n90, 52n107, 80, 85–88, 90–91, 93–95, 114n105, 115n112, 116nn114–15, 139, 178, 180, 190, 192, 196, 202, 203, 204, 206, 217, 227, 233, 239, 243, 271, 272
prophecy and prophetic spirit, 21, 34, 86, 96, 97, 100n8, 190, 246, 248, 250
prostitution, 15, 45n52, 82, 93, 113n97, 133. *See also* Mary of Egypt, Saint
Protestants and Protestantism, 7, 9, 11, 18–20, 22, 24, 68, 69, 143, 172, 229
purgatory, 46n54, 96, 159, 230, 244
purity of blood. *See limpieza de sangre* (purity of blood)

race, 2, 9, 13, 14, 18, 19, 28, 29, 30, 44n42, 45n52, 48n71, 52n102, 52n107, 53n115, 57, 64, 69, 77, 83, 85, 86, 91, 104n35, 108n61, 114n103, 142, 182, 185, 217, 227, 242
   heresy and race, 45n52, 104n35, 172, 190
   raza, 64, 86, 104n35
   See also Blacks and Blackness; skin color
Radner, Joan Newton, 25, 53n115
Raphael, Saint, 76, 166. *See also* angel
readers, 6–7, 9–14, 16–18, 28, 29, 32, 34–35, 42n31, 51n92, 52n108, 56, 58–62, 64, 79, 84, 86, 89, 91–92, 94, 96, 97–98, 114n106, 116n115, 132, 140, 141, 155, 182, 193, 195, 202, 212, 234, 264
   disloyal, 16, 25, 33, 47n64
   as interpreters, 11, 13, 31, 36, 37, 56, 65, 67, 74, 87, 89, 94, 98, 128, 133, 213, 244
Rediker, Marcus, 37
religion, 14, 18, 20, 22, 25, 27, 63, 74, 76, 77, 79, 80, 84, 91, 95, 101n18, 105n45, 106n53, 108n60, 109n68, 113–14n101, 139, 154, 163, 168, 181, 182, 191, 200, 209, 229
reparations, 34, 78
resistance, 16, 18, 25, 27, 30–37, 47n64, 50n90, 53n115, 55, 210
return to Africa, 14, 17, 23, 76, 79–80, 89, 182n8. *See also sankofa*
Ribera, Manuel Fernando de, 130, 132
Rio de Janeiro, 45n52
Rivera, Bernardo de, 14
Rodríguez, Gabriel, 128, 129
Rojas, Rosa de, 87
Rome, 43n36, 68, 70, 85, 140
Rosa Maria Egipcíaca da Vera Cruz, 7, 43n35, 45n52
Royal, Colonel Isaac, 20
royalty, 13, 17, 26, 35, 59, 65, 71–73, 75, 78–79, 85, 100n8, 102n24, 110n79, 146, 151, 152, 154, 158–59, 162, 165, 171, 177, 182, 184, 188, 199, 200, 202, 205, 206
   crown, 13, 67, 151, 152, 162, 183, 184, 209, 222, 255, 258
   royal origins, 13, 17, 35, 182
   scepter, 13, 141, 151, 152, 154, 182, 183, 184, 200

sacraments, 84, 96, 150, 156, 172, 180, 229, 239, 240, 254, 255. *See also* baptism of Blacks and slaves; Communion
sacrifice, 27, 60, 84, 90, 167, 178, 179, 180, 202, 213. *See also* suffering
sacrilege, 78, 173, 175, 176
sainthood and sanctity, 3–10, 12–18, 20–22, 24–26, 34–35, 59–62, 64, 70, 72–73, 75, 79, 85–86, 89, 90, 91, 94, 96–98, 140, 145, 190, 191, 203, 205, 206, 207, 209, 214, 246, 263
   appropriate and saintly behavior, 5, 8, 33, 52n108, 85, 92, 116n119, 147, 180, 205, 217, 222, 246

odor of sanctity, 98
relics, 5, 96–97, 263–64
socially constructed, 6 (*see* canonization)
veneration of Chicaba as saintly, 5, 86, 197, 254, 261, 262
Salamanca, 1–5, 11, 13, 15, 26, 40n13, 41n19, 46n56, 59, 80, 82, 83, 85, 87, 93, 97, 107n55, 112n92, 113n97, 113–14n101, 130, 166, 185, 187, 189, 190, 192, 193, 194, 195, 198, 209, 229, 231, 240, 246, 247, 248, 251, 252, 253, 254, 262
salvation, 17, 19, 20, 22, 49n81, 64, 65, 67, 73, 111–12n91, 171, 205
San Cayetano, College of, 3, 39n9, 131, 133, 135, 136, 186, 195, 252
Sandoval, Alonso de, 68
San Esteban, convent of, 90, 116n114, 178, 204
San Jacinto, Sor María Teresa de, 89, 199
San Juan Bautista (ship), 67
sankofa, 76, 111n80, 182n8. *See also* Africa: memory of
San Pedro de Cardeña, monastery of, 207
Santa Ana, convent of, 80, 111n89, 186, 226
Santa Clara, convent of, 12
Santa Isabel, convent of, 85, 86, 112n93, 186, 189, 194, 204
Santa María Egipcíaca. *See* Mary of Egypt, Saint
Santa María Magdalena. *See* Penitencia, Convento de Santa María Magdalena de la
Santiago (ship), 67
São Tomé, 1, 63, 67, 99n4, 104n32, 153, 154, 156, 181, 193, 229, 232
Satan, 21, 220. *See* devil
Scott, Joan W., 28, 52n102
seclusion, 29, 32, 62, 102n26, 144, 152, 156, 177, 179, 184, 202, 217
Second Vatican Council, 208
secular, 2, 19–20, 23, 29, 31, 52n107, 87–88, 90, 93, 95, 115n108, 178, 195, 196, 199, 202, 204
servants and servitude, 16, 19, 26, 29, 34, 36, 46n54, 52n106, 53n118, 58, 61, 74–76, 78–79, 81, 87–88, 91, 97, 107n53, 111n91, 112n92, 113–14n101, 114nn104–5, 143, 149, 153, 154, 160, 161, 162, 164, 165, 166, 173, 175, 176, 181, 183, 196, 199, 203, 204, 205, 206, 212, 223, 226, 240, 248, 252
and Mayor Ada Colau of Barcelona, 254
Seville, 67, 68, 73, 96, 108n63, 111–12n91, 156, 158, 160, 172
sexuality, 9, 15, 24, 28, 30, 35, 44n42, 52n102, 74, 76, 77, 78, 80, 93, 175, 208, 218, 221
sexual violence, 35, 74, 77
Shakers, 7
Sheba, Queen of, 17, 26, 51n98, 73, 229
sickness. *See* health and healing powers; illness
silence and silencing, 22, 26, 28, 52n102, 54n124, 75, 79, 154, 161, 165, 169, 173, 176, 182, 187, 192, 200, 215, 217, 225, 230, 249

sin, 9, 10, 15, 19, 21, 70, 94, 153, 163, 210, 237, 243, 246
sincerity, 84, 86, 131, 236
Sisters of Calvary, 84
Siuri, Marcelino, 131
skin color, 2, 11, 13–15, 18, 22, 28, 35, 44n44, 51n95, 56, 63–64, 77, 84, 85, 87, 96–97, 108n61, 114n104, 141, 142, 150, 156, 157, 160, 166, 168, 185, 188, 194, 195, 242, 246, 260
Chicaba's, 141, 188, 260
color mutation, 117n124, 260
Ethiopians and, 14, 17, 26, 117n124, 142, 260
physical beauty, 35, 77, 166
as physical mark of paganism, 57
pigmentation and the devil, 14
and ugliness, 15, 77, 93, 97, 166, 168, 176
whitening of, 85, 97, 98
See also Blacks and Blackness; whites and whiteness
Slade, Carole, 8, 43n39
Slave Coast, 38n4, 57, 60, 67, 99n2, 103n28
slave narrative, 1, 2, 6–16, 18, 19, 25, 26, 27, 28, 30–32, 34–37, 48n71, 49n77, 50n87, 50n89, 55–57, 59, 61–62, 66, 68, 72, 74, 75, 77–80, 84–86, 88, 90, 91, 92, 94, 96, 97, 99n1, 153, 182, 192, 198, 199, 200, 203, 232, 265
and African American spiritual narratives, 18–21, 50n87
ambiguity in, 25, 27, 28, 29, 32, 65, 82, 84, 89, 196, 198, 240
as-told-to, 19, 48n71, 56, 99n1
and captivity narratives, 19, 24
coding, 25, 33, 37, 52n105
competing narratives, 65
crisis, 7
as genre, 5, 6, 8, 9, 11, 15, 17, 18, 19, 21, 24, 25, 31, 34, 48n71, 50n89, 56, 58, 66, 67, 74, 80, 85, 132, 182, 200
liberation, 32
loyal narrative, 36, 50n91
strategy, 66, 86
technique, 28, 30
Western narrative literature, 78
slave ownership, 17, 20, 34, 35, 45n52, 53n115, 65, 67–73, 75, 76, 78, 78, 80, 81, 83, 106n50, 108n60, 114n105, 131, 132, 133, 146, 156, 157, 158, 160, 162, 165, 166, 171, 172, 175, 176, 177, 178, 180, 184, 192, 235
slavery, 1, 10–11, 13, 17, 18, 20, 28–29, 31, 34, 36, 48n71, 51n95, 53n116, 55–57, 64–76, 78, 96, 105n46, 108n60, 109n71, 113n101, 113–14n101, 142, 150, 153, 155, 157–58, 165, 171, 172, 176, 182, 188, 205, 206, 212, 223, 232, 242
abolition of, 50n89, 68, 70
as donation, 27, 70, 72, 83–84, 88, 173, 190
as exile, 68, 91, 94, 168, 182, 252

slavery, *continued*
   as former status, 7, 22, 45n52, 73, 91, 97
   economy of, 73
   happy state of, 205
   legality of, 65, 68
   metaphor of, 95
   as pilgrimage/journey, 10–11, 13–14, 19, 26, 32, 67, 73–74, 85–86, 97, 113–14n101, 152, 154, 156, 158, 192–94, 246–48, 252
   as sin, 23
   in Spain, 68, 107nn54–55
   violence of, 21, 29, 34, 36, 53n116, 67, 74–79, 161, 170, 176, 183, 210, 212, 218, 259
   whites absolved from blame of, 18
   See also captivity; enslavement and enslaved
slave ships, 37, 64, 66–67, 156, 182, 219
slave trade, 1, 11, 23, 29, 38n5, 56, 58, 62, 65–69, 79, 99n2, 103n27, 104n32, 109n70, 111n85, 113n101, 141, 143, 156, 172, 181, 182, 235
   abolition of, 50n89
   legitimacy of, 57
Smith, Valerie, 44n42
Soler y las Balsas, Luis, 3, 39n11
Solís, Suero Alfonso de, 113n97
solitude, 8, 45n45, 61, 65, 92, 144, 147, 155, 171, 237
Solomon, King, 26, 51n98, 73
Spain, 1–7, 10, 11, 13–18, 23, 26, 28, 34, 56, 58, 62, 63, 67, 68, 69, 70, 71, 72, 73, 75, 76, 78, 79, 80, 81, 85, 91, 96, 127, 128, 129, 137, 142, 143, 151, 154, 156, 163, 165, 171, 172, 173, 182, 184, 186, 187, 188, 190, 195, 203, 210, 221, 232, 243, 250, 253, 258
   as a slave society, 68
Spanish America, 3, 6, 7, 16, 38–39n5, 40n13, 46n53, 68–69, 91, 106n51, 127, 132, 139, 195, 198, 210, 220, 253, 258. *See also* Latin America
Spanish Inquisition. *See* Inquisition
spiritual directors, 1, 2, 3, 6–7, 12, 46n53, 84, 86, 96–97, 130, 140, 146, 149, 150, 159, 160, 161, 168, 172, 173, 176–79, 184–87, 206, 208–10, 213–15, 218, 223, 225, 228, 239, 240, 244, 246, 256
spiritual economy, 27, 94, 95, 239
spiritual life and spirituality, 1, 2, 7, 12, 18, 24, 38, 62, 65, 97, 139, 171, 178, 192, 193, 196, 199, 206, 230, 231
   exercises, 22, 86, 180, 185, 218, 228
   transformation, 10, 85, 90
Spivak, Gayatri C., 54n124
Stephen, Saint, 6
Stewart, Maria, 20–23
submission, 11, 20, 36, 37, 91, 198
suffering, 10, 17, 18, 20, 21, 34, 59, 75, 78, 85, 86, 90, 96, 155, 161, 174, 176, 177, 185, 210, 212, 213, 225, 230, 235, 240, 243, 244, 248, 250, 264

   discourse of, 86, 96
   insults, 75, 169, 177, 185, 213, 215, 223, 261
   isolation, 29, 62, 89
   as mortification, 18, 34, 65, 91, 185, 208, 209, 210–13, 242
   torments, 160–62, 173, 185, 206, 210, 243, 253
   See also slavery: violence of
synecdoche, 26, 72, 185

teacher. *See* education
Teko, Andre, 100n9
temptation, 17, 153, 182, 198, 199, 200, 213
Teresa of Ávila, Saint, xvi, 7, 8, 21, 41n26, 42n30, 43n34, 43n36, 43n39, 45n47, 47n62, 49n81, 50n85, 85, 86, 97, 98, 117n125, 186, 187, 192, 193, 215, 216, 226, 236, 238, 247
Teresa of the Conception, 191
tertiary (*tercera*), 4, 38n1, 56, 87–90, 113n98, 115n108, 133, 135, 190, 195, 198, 202, 204, 212. *See also beata*; veil: white
Teruel, Father Andrés, 159, 252
Theatines and Theatine Order, Order of Regular Clerics, 1–3, 12, 39n8, 96, 98, 128, 129, 133, 139, 159, 177, 178, 184, 186, 187, 195, 209, 216, 240, 246, 252
theology, 6–8, 11–13, 17, 20, 24, 27, 34, 43n35, 43n37, 65, 92, 103n29, 117n123, 128, 129, 130, 133, 135, 136, 193
theosis, 260
Theresa, Saint. *See* Teresa of Ávila, Saint
third order, 11, 15, 31, 39n11, 41n21, 52n107, 82–83, 87–88, 93, 95, 112n96, 113n98, 115n112, 186, 187, 190, 198, 204
Thomas Aquinas, Saint, 60, 101n16, 131, 144, 145, 209, 219
Tiresias, 86
tobacco, 91, 224
Togo, 14, 38nn4–5, 57, 60, 99n2, 100n7, 100n9
Toro. *See* Acts of the Chapter of Toro
Torre, Bernabé de la, 133
Torres Villarroel, Diego de, 3, 69, 107n53, 130, 246, 261
trabajos de Persiles y Sigismunda, Los (Cervantes), 85, 105n40
translation, 5, 18, 24, 55, 58, 60, 61, 63, 102n24, 112n92, 134n96, 146, 150, 153, 165, 168, 179, 181, 204, 222, 227, 246
Trinitarians, Order of the Holy Trinity, 78, 130, 173
tro/trowu, 61
Turkish slave girl, 15, 16, 21, 29, 34–35, 52n108, 76, 77, 78, 93, 97, 111n81, 158, 166–70
Tyndareus, 132

uncle. *See* family of Chicaba: Juan Francisco, pretended uncle
United States, 47n65, 112–13n96, 114n105, 180, 182

INDEX

Urban VIII, 68, 128, 140
Úrsula de Jesús, 12, 46n54, 244

Valencia, 69, 70, 108n63, 127, 131, 147, 230
Valladolid, 133
Vauchez, André, 5
veil, 22, 43n34, 86–88, 90, 91, 92, 94, 114n106, 116n115, 196, 203, 204, 212, 249, 264
    black veil, 43n34, 87, 195, 206
    Chicaba as a veiled tertiary, 90
    medio velo, 88, 195
    white, 2, 23, 43n34, 87, 90, 139, 196, 202–4, 264
    See also habit (of the order)
Velázquez, Diego de Silva, 209
Vélez, Francisco and Juan Manuel, 250
Vergara, Cayetano, 128, 129
Verger, Pierre, 67
vida, 1–5, 7–19, 23–25, 27–38, 50n90, 55, 56, 57–68, 71–76, 78-98, 128, 130, 135, 136, 137, 139, 140, 146, 147, 155, 158, 173, 178, 182, 186, 189, 192, 193, 196, 205, 212, 215, 219, 225, 240, 246, 253, 261, 265. *See also* autobiography; biography
Vida de la Venerable Negra, 3, 39n11, *123*
Villagonzalo, Countess of, 251
Villeneuve, Pauline, 84, 113–14n101, 199
Vincent Ferrer, Saint, 3, 38n1, 39n11, 40n13, 127, 137, 146, 147, 166, 209, 230, 232, 233, 249, 250, 251, 253
virginity, 16–17, 30–31, 77, 81, 92–94, 209, 228, 239, 243, 261
Virgin Mary, 10, 48n68, 61, 81, 66, 81, 92, 101n21, 149, 157, 194, 203, 218, 230, 239, 261
    as White Lady, 14, 61–66, 76, 93, 160
virtue, 6, 16, 20–21, 24–25, 29–30, 35–36, 62, 76, 83, 90, 93, 97, 128, 131, 134, 137, 139, 140, 144, 151, 156, 157, 159, 165, 166, 170, 171, 172, 175, 177, 178, 179, 184–94, 196, 198, 199, 200, 202, 203, 205–8, 210, 212, 216, 217, 220, 222–25, 227, 228, 229, 232, 234, 235, 242, 248, 249, 250, 252, 261, 264
visions. *See* mystical experience and mysticism
Vitz, Evelyn, 10
vocation, 17, 21–22, 35–36, 65, 80, 84, 90, 92–93, 95, 160, 179, 180–82, 186, 198, 200, 206, 239, 261, 264
    doubts about, 8, 21–22, 30, 34, 36, 42n31, 68, 83, 84–85, 88–89, 180, 202, 219
    opposition to Chicaba's, 22, 63, 187, 200, 202
voduwo, 61
voice, 2, 11, 21, 24–30, 32, 34, 37, 42n27, 50n90, 52n105, 53n115, 55, 65, 94–95, 99n1, 147, 165, 170, 178, 210, 224, 228, 229, 240, 246, 251, 259
    as *pentimento*, 217
Volta River, 19, 38n5, 58, 61, 67, 99n2, 100n8
vows, 2, 4, 22, 31, 40n17, 52n106, 83–84, 86, 88, 90–93, 112n95, 113n98, 113–14n101, 115n107, 187, 195, 196, 202, 203, 204, 226. *See also* profession (act of)

Walker, David, 20, 23
War of Spanish Succession, 91, 220–21, 231
Watchi, 14, 57, 100n7, 102n26
water and water deity, 14, 22, 61, 65–67, 76, 101n21, 102n22, 149, 155, 163–66, 215, 226
    dehydration during the Middle Passage, 67, 155
    drowning, 14, 66, 155, 219, 227, 248
    fountain, 22, 61, 62, 65, 77, 80, 91, 92, 149, 150, 153, 155–56, 160, 163, 166, 193, 229, 232
    under the waters, 163, 165
whites and whiteness, 14–16, 19, 32, 53n115, 63–64, 68, 76–77, 80, 83, 85, 105n41, 105n45, 117n124, 142, 150, 166, 171, 181, 194, 212, 225
    White Child (*see under* Christ)
    White Lady (*see under* Virgin Mary)
    whitening/lightening of Chicaba at death, 14–15, 97–98, 260
    See also skin color
Whydah, 63, 103n27
Wilson, Harriet, 99n1
witchcraft, 45n52, 64, 83
work, 2, 23, 27, 36–37, 87, 88, 95, 196, 199, 206, 209–10, 217, 234
    Chicaba's spiritual, 2, 72–73
writing, 3–12, 15, 18, 20–24, 27, 28, 35–37, 42n31, 43n37, 45n51, 46n60, 48n71, 50nn89–90, 55, 61, 64, 68, 70, 74, 75, 92, 99n6, 116n114, 127, 130, 131, 132, 134, 139, 143, 146, 204, 212, 217, 219, 221, 235, 244, 252, 254, 256, 264
    Chicaba's, 14, 161, 217, 238, 244
    coded, 10, 25, 33, 34, 37
    as collaboration, 12, 13, 67, 246
    signature of Chicaba, 4–5, 114n105, 135, 136, 196
    documents, 7, 40n17, 70, 204
    See also literacy of Chicaba

Yai, Olabiyi, 61, 103n29, 143
Yarza, José Antonio de, 136
Yoruba, 38, 57, 62

Zape, 48n70
Zaragoza, 3, 39n11
Zosimas, 14, 15, 45–46n52

www.ingramcontent.com/pod-product-compliance
Lightning Source LLC
Chambersburg PA
CBHW081759300426
44116CB00014B/2170